# 730 Rapid Recipes For Busy Cooks

WHEN it comes to fast food full of "from scratch" flavor, you can depend on this seventh edition of the cookbook based on the recipes from *Quick Cooking* magazine.

This *2005 Quick Cooking Annual Recipes* cookbook conveniently gathers every fuss-free recipe published in *Quick Cooking* during 2004—that's 730 recipes in all—and combines them in one reader-friendly collection. This recipe-packed volume is filled with hundreds of mouth-watering photos so you can see what many of the dishes look like before you prepare them.

Here's what else you'll find inside:

**Chapters That Meet Your Needs.** With 21 chapters that correspond to popular features in *Quick Cooking* magazine, it's a snap to find a recipe that matches your family's taste and timetable. (See page 3 for a complete list of chapters.)

For example, when you have a mere 10 minutes to spare in the kitchen, rely on Teriyaki Chicken Sandwiches, Sweet and Sour Pork Chops, Beef Onion Soup, Fruit-Topped Frozen Yogurt or any of the 19 other timeless recipes in the "10 Minutes to the Table" chapter.

Or when your family is eyeing the table and you're eyeing the clock, see the "30 Minutes to Mealtime" chapter for 15 complete meals that go from start to finish in less than half an hour.

**Mix and Match 30-Minute Meals.** Our food editors listed more entrees and other dishes you can fix in a half hour or less. Just group any of these recipes you like to create a 30-minute menu. (This time-saving tool appears on page 4.)

**Award-Winning Recipes.** You'll get all the palate-pleasing, quick-to-prepare foods that earned top honors in the six national recipe contests we held last year: Slow Cooker Sensations, Fuss-Free Company Fare, Pizza Pleasers, Fast 5-Ingredient Favorites, Bread Machine Marvels and 30-Minute Appetizers.

**Easy-to-Use Indexes.** To make all 730 recipes easy to find, we've listed them in two indexes. (See page 332.) The general index lists every recipe by category and/or major food ingredient. The alphabetical listing is great for folks who are looking for a specific family favorite. In both indexes, you'll find a bold red checkmark (✓) in front of all recipes that use less fat, sugar or salt and include Nutritional Analysis and Diabetic Exchanges.

Every rapid recipe and helpful hint in this *2005 Quick Cooking Annual Recipes* cookbook was specifically selected with the busy cook in mind. You're sure to enjoy this timeless treasury for years to come...and you'll be able to treat your loved ones to comforting, wholesome home cooking without spending all of your precious time in the kitchen.

## *2005 Quick Cooking Annual Recipes*

**Editor:** Michelle Bretl
**Art Director:** Lori Arndt
**Senior Editor/Books:** Heidi Reuter Lloyd
**Food Editor:** Janaan Cunningham
**Associate Editors:** Julie Schnittka, Deb Mulvey, Faithann Stoner
**Graphic Art Associates:** Ellen Lloyd, Catherine Fletcher
**Editorial Assistant:** Barb Czysz
**Cover Photography:** Dan Roberts, Rob Hagen
**Senior Food Photography Artist:** Stephanie Marchese
**Food Photography Artist:** Julie Ferron
**Senior Vice President, Editor in Chief:** Catherine Cassidy
**President:** Barbara Newton
**Chairman and Founder:** Roy Reiman

*Taste of Home* Books

5400 S. 60th St., Greendale WI 53129

International Standard Book Number:
0-89821-422-X
International Standard Serial Number:
1522-6603


Printed in U.S.A.

**PICTURED ON THE COVER:** Honey Wheat Breadsticks (p. 168), Chocolate Peanut Butter Cake (p. 17) and Festive Spaghetti 'n' Meatballs (p. 90).

To order additional copies of this book or any other Reiman Publications books, write: *Taste of Home* Books, P.O. Box 908, Greendale WI 53129; call toll-free 1-800/344-2560 to order with a credit card or visit our Web site at **www.reimanpub.com**.

## *Taste of Home's* QUICK COOKING

# Contents

# Mix and Match 30-Minute Meals

PLANNING weeknight dinners for your family is a snap with the *2005 Quick Cooking Annual Recipes* book. And you can start right now by simply glancing at the helpful guide on these two pages.

Here's how to use it: Our food editors selected various recipes from this book that can be fixed in only a half hour or less. Begin by choosing an "Effortless Entree" listed on this page, whether it's a beef, poultry, pork, seafood or meatless main dish.

Next, pair that entree with one or more of the "Easy Accompaniments"—side dishes, salads, breads and desserts—on the opposite page. Customizing a swift family supper has never been easier!

For even more complete meals that can be prepared in just a half hour or less, turn to the "30 Minutes to Mealtime" chapter (p. 20).

## Effortless Entrees

### Beef



### Chicken & Turkey

### Pork & Sausage

### Seafood

### Meatless

## Easy Accompaniments

# Chapter 1

# The Busiest Cooks in the Country

BUSY COOKS often start their days early in the morning and keep going well into the evening. Between work, events at school and other activities, you probably pack as much as possible into each day.

It's no wonder that you think there's little time to prepare a wholesome, hearty dinner for your hungry family. But this chapter pleasantly proves that speedy yet memorable meals are within reach.

Here, six other rushed cooks from across the country share their own rapid recipes, time-saving tips and menu-planning pointers, all of which are guaranteed to put you on the meal-making fast track in no time.

**FAMILY FARE.** Clockwise from top: Cocoa Cake Brownies, Pasta Vegetable Salad and Lemon Herb Chicken (all recipes on p. 15).

# Easy Meal Plan Makes for Fast Flavorful Fare

Lifetouch

EFFICIENCY is the word of the day at Kimberly Lund's Park City, Kansas home. The full-time teacher, wife and mother of three is a consummate planner, whether she's fine-tuning her lesson plans, creating weekly dinner menus or putting together recipe albums that showcase her scrapbook skills.

"I teach prekindergarten and kindergarten students with autism," writes Kimberly, who's been married to Dan for 13 years. "I love the challenge of it and can't imagine doing anything else.

"I'm highly organized in both my personal and professional life," she adds. "Because I don't have to stress over the next lesson I'm going to teach or the next meal I'm going to cook, I can be more patient with my students and with our children, Brady, Mykiah and Chesney."

On hectic weeknights, Kimberly relies on time-saving tactics to ease into dinnertime. "By the time the kids and I get home from school, everyone is hungry. So I give them a small snack while I'm cooking supper so that I don't feel rushed," she explains.

"I'm also a big believer in convenience foods," she says. "I'm not going to get an award for always making real mashed potatoes, but I will cherish the extra time I have with our children because I used a box of instant potatoes."

Dan's work schedule plays a role in the family's menu choices. "He's a route manager for a frozen-food home-delivery service," Kimberly says.

"He usually works late one or two days a week. On those days, it's important that the dinner I fix is easy for him to reheat later that evening and remains flavorful," she explains.

To make weekdays fuss-free, Kimberly plans menus and shops for groceries on weekends.

"When we get back from shopping, Dan browns ground beef, shreds cheese and does other prep work," she says. "He then divides everything into meal-sized portions and puts them into the freezer.

"That way, when I get home from work on a weeknight, I can put a meal together quickly," she notes.

Her Bacon Swiss Meat Loaf is a tasty main dish that fits into busy-day menus perfectly.

"It's quick because I already have packages of cooked bacon and shredded cheese in my freezer. I just defrost them and add them to the ground beef mixture," she explains.

For a comforting accompaniment, Kimberly serves Colby Hash Browns. "We love potato dishes, and this is one of our favorites," she notes.

It's easy to assemble because it calls for frozen hash browns, so there's no peeling or slicing potatoes. "When I take it to potlucks, I always return with an empty dish," she says.

For dessert, Kimberly uses convenience items to fix her Crunchy Chocolate Pudding Squares.

"This is the best dessert ever!" she assures. "The secret is the rich crunchy crust made with chopped pecans. It's so simple to make, but tastes wonderful."

## Bacon Swiss Meat Loaf

**1 egg**
**1/4 cup evaporated milk**
**1-1/2 cups (6 ounces) shredded Swiss cheese, *divided***
**1 cup crumbled cooked bacon (about 12 bacon strips), *divided***
**1/2 cup soft bread crumbs**
**1/2 teaspoon garlic powder**
**1/2 teaspoon onion powder**
**1-1/2 pounds ground beef**

In a large bowl, combine egg, milk, 1 cup Swiss cheese, 3/4 cup bacon, bread crumbs, garlic powder and onion powder. Crumble beef over mixture and mix well. Shape into a loaf in a greased 11-in. x 7-in. x 2-in. baking dish.

Bake, uncovered, at 350° for 1 hour or until meat is no longer pink and a meat thermometer reads 160°. Drain. Sprinkle with remaining cheese and bacon. Bake 3-5 minutes longer or until cheese is melted. Let stand for 10 minutes before slicing. **Yield:** 6 servings.

## Kimberly's Reliance on Appliances

- During the winter, I try to plan one slow cooker meal a week. It may be as simple as a roast and vegetables, but there is nothing better than driving home from work knowing that dinner is already cooked.
- I use the microwave almost daily to defrost frozen meats. Although I plan meals a week at a time, I like being able to decide what I'm cooking after I get home at night. Without the microwave, I would have to follow my menu plans more strictly.
- We love our tabletop electric grill. My husband often brings home meat from his work. I love being able to put chicken or beef on the grill and concentrate on the side dishes while the main dish is cooking.

*—Kimberly Lund*

## Colby Hash Browns

**1 cup milk**
**1/2 cup beef broth**
**2 tablespoons butter, melted, *divided***
**1 teaspoon salt**
**1/4 teaspoon pepper**
**Dash garlic powder**
**1 package (30 ounces) frozen country-style shredded hash brown potatoes**
**2 cups (8 ounces) shredded Colby cheese**

In a large bowl, combine the milk, broth, 1 tablespoon butter, salt, pepper and garlic powder. Stir in hash browns. Heat remaining butter in a large nonstick skillet. Add hash brown mixture. Cook and stir over medium heat until the potatoes are heated through. Stir in cheese.

Transfer to a greased shallow 2-qt. baking dish. Bake, uncovered, at 350° for 40-45 minutes or until the potatoes are tender. **Yield:** 6 servings.

## Crunchy Chocolate Pudding Squares

**2 cups self-rising flour**
**1-1/2 cups finely chopped pecans**
**2/3 cup packed brown sugar**
**1 cup butter, melted**
**1 package (8 ounces) cream cheese, softened**
**1 cup confectioners' sugar**
**1 carton (8 ounces) frozen whipped topping, thawed, *divided***
**3 cups cold milk**
**1 package (5.9 ounces) instant chocolate pudding mix**
**Colored sprinkles, optional**

In a bowl, combine the flour, pecans and brown sugar. Stir in butter. Press into an ungreased 13-in. x 9-in. x 2-in. baking dish. Bake at 375° for 15-20 minutes or until lightly browned. Cool on a wire rack.

In a mixing bowl, beat the cream cheese and confectioners' sugar until smooth. Fold in 1 cup whipped topping. Spread over the crust. In another bowl, whisk the milk and pudding mix for 2 minutes. Spoon over the cream cheese layer. Refrigerate for 15 minutes or until set. Spread with the remaining whipped topping. Chill until set. Garnish with sprinkles if desired. Cut into squares. **Yield:** 12-15 servings.

**Editor's Note:** As a substitute for *each* cup of self-rising flour, place 1-1/2 teaspoons baking powder and 1/2 teaspoon salt in a measuring cup. Add all-purpose flour to measure 1 cup.

# Special Dinner Starts With Basic Baking

DINNERTIME is family time for Michele Field of Sykesville, Maryland. "Since we all have busy schedules, it lets us share our day with one another," she writes.

"My husband, James, works as a heating sales representative, but he makes every effort to be home regularly for dinner," says Michele.

"Our daughters, Sierra and Savannah, are home-schooled, but they also have dance, piano, tae kwon do and riding lessons," she explains.

"I love learning about home-schooling techniques, so I always research concepts and share them with other parents," Michele adds. "I'm also developing a course about teaching health- and fitness-related subjects to teenagers.

"Planning field trips for home-schoolers is something else I enjoy," she continues. "And as a home-school reviewer, I help six families meet the state's education requirements."

Her free time is often spent crafting, hiking, sketching or painting with her daughters. "And, of course, I love to cook...an interest our whole family shares.

"Everyone helps at dinnertime," says Michele. "We work together, even if it means that someone simply sets the table or pours the beverages."

Planning is key as Michele balances active agendas with meal preparation. "A bread machine is practically a requirement in our home," she writes. "I create several batches of our favorite bread mix at once, so I can easily bake a fresh loaf anytime.

"I measure out the recipe's dry ingredients into resealable bags. When I want to bake a loaf, I pour the contents from one bag into the bread machine," explains Michele. "I add the liquid and yeast, then push a button for warm bread for dinner."

Michele uses her basic bread mix often, sometimes adding spices that complement her main course. Such is the case with the golden rolls and savory shrimp entree shared here.

"I mix seafood seasoning and cheese into the dry ingredients and use the dough setting on my bread machine," she says of Seasoned Parmesan Rolls.

Michele bakes them in the oven while Barbecue Shrimp over Pasta cooks on the stovetop. "This dish is done in just minutes," she promises. "Diced bacon and barbecue sauce really give it a fun kick."

To round out the meal, Michele prepares White Chocolate Mousse Cups. Eye-appealing individual chocolate bowls are filled with smooth homemade mousse, then garnished with warm raspberry jam.

"The cups can be prepared early in the day and refrigerated until you're ready to fill them," she notes. "So they're great for entertaining, too."

## Seasoned Parmesan Rolls

✓ Uses less fat, sugar or salt. Includes Nutritional Analysis and Diabetic Exchanges.

**1-1/2 cups warm milk (70° to 80°)**
**2 tablespoons butter, softened**
**1 tablespoon sugar**
**1/2 cup grated Parmesan cheese**
**1 tablespoon dried minced onion**
**2 teaspoons seafood seasoning**
**4 cups bread flour**
**4 teaspoons active dry yeast**

In bread machine pan, place all ingredients in order suggested by manufacturer. Select dough setting (check dough after 5 minutes of mixing; add 1 to 2 tablespoons of water or flour if needed).

When cycle is completed, turn dough onto a lightly floured surface. Divide into 24 portions; shape each into a ball. Place 3 in. apart on greased baking sheets. Cover and let rise in a warm place until doubled, about 30 minutes. Bake at 350° for 15-20 minutes or until lightly browned. Remove to wire racks. **Yield:** 2 dozen.

**Nutritional Analysis:** One roll (prepared with fat-free milk) equals 105 calories, 2 g fat (1 g saturated fat), 4 mg cholesterol, 33 mg sodium, 18 g carbohydrate, 1 g fiber, 4 g protein. **Diabetic Exchanges:** 1 starch, 1/2 fat.

**Editor's Note:** If your bread machine has a time-delay feature, we recommend you do not use it for this recipe.

## Leftovers Cut Kitchen Time

I often plan for future dinners as I'm surveying leftovers from our current meal.

I reserve one freezer-proof storage container for what I call "convertible dinners". These are leftovers I can convert into a completely different meal on another day. For example, leftover grilled chicken might become diced chicken and pesto over pasta.

The second container is for extra food that reheats well for our weekday lunches. Small amounts of vegetables or sauce go into the last container, which I freeze until I'm ready to simmer a pot of homemade soup. *—Michele Field*

## Barbecue Shrimp over Pasta

**1 package (1 pound) linguine**
**12 bacon strips, diced**
**1 medium onion, chopped**
**1-1/4 pounds uncooked large shrimp, peeled and deveined**
**1-1/4 cups barbecue sauce**
**1/3 cup grated Parmesan cheese**

Cook linguine according to package directions. Meanwhile, in a large skillet, cook bacon over medium heat until crisp. Remove with a slotted spoon to paper towels; drain, reserving 1 tablespoon drippings. Saute onion in the drippings until tender. Add shrimp; cook and stir until no longer pink.

Return bacon to the skillet. Add barbecue sauce; cook and stir over medium heat until heated through. Drain linguine; top with shrimp mixture. Sprinkle with Parmesan cheese. **Yield:** 6 servings.

## White Chocolate Mousse Cups

**6 squares (1 ounce *each*) semisweet chocolate, chopped**
**1 tablespoon shortening**
**1-1/2 cups heavy whipping cream, *divided***
**6 squares (1 ounce *each*) white baking chocolate, chopped**
**1/3 cup confectioners' sugar**
**2 teaspoons vanilla extract**
**2 tablespoons seedless raspberry jam**
**Fresh raspberries and mint, optional**

In a microwave, melt semisweet chocolate and shortening. Brush evenly on the inside of six paper or foil muffin cup liners. Chill until set, about 25 minutes. Add a second coat of chocolate if necessary; chill until set. Carefully peel the liners off of the chocolate cups and discard.

For mousse, combine 1/2 cup cream and white chocolate in a saucepan; cook and stir over low heat until chocolate is melted. Cool to room temperature.

In a mixing bowl, beat remaining cream until it begins to thicken. Add confectioners' sugar and vanilla; beat until stiff peaks form. Fold into cooled chocolate mixture. Spoon into chocolate cups. Refrigerate until chilled.

In a microwave, warm raspberry jam. Transfer to a resealable plastic bag. Cut a small hole in a corner of bag; drizzle onto dessert plates. Place mousse cups on plates. Garnish with raspberries and mint if desired. **Yield:** 6 servings.

# Family Dining Comes Out of Fun Pastimes

YOU DON'T NEED to have a green thumb to be a good cook, but if you're like Denise Loewenthal, having one makes cooking even more fun.

"I enjoy reading, gardening and cooking," relates the wife and mother of three boys from Hinckley, Ohio. "We have a big garden in the summer. There is so much pride when you grow your own produce.

"Plus, there's nothing like being able to just walk outside and pick the vegetables, fruits or herbs you need to make a meal. It's awesome!"

Denise's husband, Howard, is a mechanical engineer for a home medical equipment company. Their boys—Brandon, Ashton and Nathan—are busy with sports, music lessons and various clubs at school.

When Denise is not attending one of their activities, you might find her lending a hand in their small community near Cleveland.

"I belong to the Hinckley Women's Club and the Brunswick Preschool PTA," she says. "I also volunteer at our children's schools and help out at the hunger center occasionally."

Denise enjoys experimenting in the kitchen, trying a few new recipes each week. "It's easy to cook for Howard, because he eats anything!" she says with a laugh. "But the boys are a different story. All three are somewhat picky eaters."

Fortunately, Denise is familiar with choosy palates. "I'm the oldest of three girls and started cooking when I was in sixth grade," she recalls. "I learned to cook from my mother, who made traditional meat-and-potatoes meals because her kids were picky eaters, too!

"Mom still likes to cook for a crowd," Denise notes. "I am the same way. Howard and I entertain quite often and enjoy cooking together when we can.

"For our family, I fix a sit-down dinner at the same time every night so everyone can plan around it," she adds.

"The most important consideration when planning menus is finding a variety of foods that are nutritious, economical, tasty and quick."

To find recipes that meet these criteria, Denise relies on just one cookbook—a binder of recipes she compiled. "It's one of the best projects I ever did for myself," she says.

"I glued copies of recipes from newspapers, magazines, cookbooks and pamphlets onto paper, then sorted them by category, such as salads, soups, main dishes, etc.

"Next, I put them in plastic sheet protectors and filed them in a binder with dividers for each category. When trying new recipes, I use my own rating system by writing next to the recipe whether it is 'very good', 'good', 'okay', etc. I may even add little notes like 'quick' or 'time-consuming'.

"This way, I don't have to dig through drawers of recipes or page through 10 cookbooks to find a particular recipe."

The rapid recipes for the following menu are among the favorites included in Denise's cookbook.

"I came up with Pork Teriyaki when I had leftover cooked pork that I wanted to use up," she explains. "The whole family enjoys this entree. It's easy even if you don't have leftover meat, because the pork cooks so quickly. Or you can use chicken instead," she suggests.

To complement the main dish, Denise prepares Soup Carrot Coins. "I have always loved the carrots in my mom's chicken soup, so I tried to imitate the flavor in this side dish," she relates.

To cap off the meal, Denise bakes Banana Snack Cake. "It doesn't need any frosting—just a dusting of powdered sugar," she notes. "Guests are always amazed that I made this treat from scratch."

## Pork Teriyaki

**1 envelope teriyaki sauce mix**
**1/2 cup water**
**1/2 cup all-purpose flour**

## Denise's Frugal Freezer Tips

- Besides the freezer with our refrigerator, we have a big freezer in the basement. To keep track of what we have on hand, I keep a running list for each freezer. The lists include the foods in each freezer and which shelf each is on. Knowing exactly what's available simplifies my meal planning.
- To save time and money, we often rely on leftovers during the week. I cook a large cut of meat on the weekend, when I may have more time, then freeze the leftovers to make a completely different meal another day.
- We have strawberries, blueberries, apples, pumpkins, green beans, tomatoes, zucchini, parsley and oregano in the freezer. Some came from our garden or fruit trees and some I froze when the items were in season. *—Denise Loewenthal*

1 pork tenderloin (1 pound), cut into 1/2-inch slices
2 tablespoons vegetable oil
Hot cooked rice

In a small bowl, combine teriyaki sauce mix and water until dissolved; set aside. Place flour in a large resealable plastic bag; add pork and shake to coat.

In a large skillet, brown pork in oil until juices run clear. Add teriyaki sauce. Bring to a boil; cook and stir for 1-2 minutes or until slightly thickened. Serve with rice. **Yield:** 3-4 servings.

**Editor's Note:** This recipe was tested with Kikkoman teriyaki sauce mix.

## Soup Carrot Coins

✓ Uses less fat, sugar or salt. Includes Nutritional Analysis and Diabetic Exchanges.

**1 can (14-1/2 ounces) chicken broth**
**3-1/2 cups sliced fresh carrots**
**1 small onion, chopped**
**1/2 teaspoon dried celery flakes**
**1/2 teaspoon dried parsley flakes**
**1 bay leaf**
**Dash pepper**

In a saucepan, bring broth to a boil. Add the remaining ingredients; return to a boil. Reduce heat; cover and simmer for 5-7 minutes or until carrots are tender. Drain; discard bay leaf. **Yield:** 4 servings.

**Nutritional Analysis:** One serving (3/4 cup) equals 59 calories, trace fat (trace saturated fat), 0 cholesterol, 446 mg sodium, 13 g carbohydrate, 4 g fiber, 2 g protein. **Diabetic Exchange:** 2 vegetable.

## Banana Snack Cake

**1-2/3 cups all-purpose flour**
**1 teaspoon baking soda**
**1 cup packed brown sugar**
**1/2 cup water**
**1/3 cup mashed ripe banana (about 1 small)**
**1/3 cup vegetable oil**
**1/2 teaspoon vanilla extract**
**Confectioners' sugar**

In a large bowl, combine flour and baking soda. In another bowl, whisk the brown sugar, water, banana, oil and vanilla. Stir into dry ingredients just until moistened. Transfer to a greased 8-in. square baking dish. Bake at 350° for 30-35 minutes or until a toothpick inserted near the center comes out clean. Cool on a wire rack. Dust with confectioners' sugar. Cut into squares. **Yield:** 9 servings.

**Editor's Note:** This recipe does not use eggs.

# Streamlining Leads to Super Sit-Down Supper

SOMEONE is always on the go at the Turner home in Upland, Indiana. "Not only are my husband, Stewart, and I busy with our home business, but our three daughters' activities keep us on the run as well," Helen says.

Daughter Patti and her husband, Jonathan Steflik, are students at Brigham Young University in Utah while Hannah and Afton keep things lively at the family's rural home.

"They participate in everything from church groups and piano lessons to soccer teams and cheerleading practice," notes Helen. "To stay involved in their lives, I volunteer for as many school-related groups and committees as I can, including a parent-teacher organization," she continues.

"I am also the librarian for our church, and I'm a substitute teacher for a daily gospel class that high school students attend weekday mornings. This is so fulfilling for me, because it's inspiring to work with teenagers who want to make a difference."

In addition to this bustling schedule, Helen also holds a full-time job. "Stewart and I run a forestry consulting business from our house," she explains.

"As vice president and treasurer, I handle the mountains of paperwork required of small corporations. I also perform some fieldwork with Stewart and update the company Web site."

Helen admits that owning a business offers the chance to create her own work schedule. "But it also means that I sometimes need to work 16-hour shifts, depending on the season and the workload," she says.

"When I started working from home, I thought I'd have more time to cook. Between running our business and attending the children's activities, however, I rarely have more than an hour to get dinner ready."

But that doesn't stop Helen from fixing nightly meals. "I love coming together as a family at the end of the day and talking over a homemade supper," she notes. "I wish we could all sit down for breakfast as well, but we have very different morning schedules, so that rarely happens."

To streamline dinner prep, Helen looks for dishes that freeze well. "My motto is, 'Make a lot so you don't have to make it again for a while.'

"I often prepare enough food for two meals," she points out. "I serve one meal and freeze the other for a night when I don't have much time.

"I also cook extra chicken, ground beef, sausage and ham, then freeze them for future meals," she relates. "In addition, I use packaged frozen items, like chopped onions and diced peppers, to save prep time."

When she gets a moment to herself, Helen likes exercising, reading and crafting. "I sew, crochet and knit," she adds. "I also love to experiment by making foods that are both easy and tasty."

That's true of the three dishes Helen shares here. Her mouth-watering menu begins with tender Lemon Herb Chicken. Prepared on the stovetop, the effortless entree requires only five kitchen staples.

"I adapted this main course from a fish recipe," writes Helen. "Since I always keep boneless chicken breasts in the freezer, we enjoy this meal regularly."

She couples the tender poultry with colorful Pasta Vegetable Salad. "It only takes minutes to cook the tricolor pasta, but to really beat the clock, chop the vegetables ahead of time," she suggests.

"I sometimes give the salad southwestern flair by adding black beans, frozen corn and salsa. Then I top it off with a tomato-based dressing that I've spiced up with taco seasoning."

Cocoa Cake Brownies round out this trio of tastes. "These fudgy brownies are delicious," Helen says of the fast from-scratch sweets. "People say that the moist treats have a texture somewhere between chewy and cake-like brownies.

"We like to break them into pieces and create a trifle with chocolate pudding, toffee chips and whipped topping," she adds.

"I love to eat, but the real joy for me always comes from the process of preparing something for my family. I believe that the kitchen truly is the heart of the home...and I like 'baking' someone happy!"

## Making More of Kitchen Time

- I can't cook in a messy kitchen, so I clean as I go along. I wash bowls and utensils when I finish with them and put away ingredients after they're used. I found this keeps the kitchen relatively clean and organized while I'm making dinner.
- A little conversation always makes cooking more fun. Invite a friend over for a visit while you're baking or ask your spouse to help you prepare dinner. You'll be surprised at how many new cooking and time-saving ideas you get.
- When you're in the mood to cook, cook a lot. I can work in the kitchen all day if I'm in that frame of mind and if I have the time. If it's that sort of a day for me, I prepare several meals at once. These dinners keep me from having to cook when I'm tired or overbooked. *—Helen Turner*

## Lemon Herb Chicken

✓ Uses less fat, sugar or salt. Includes Nutritional Analysis and Diabetic Exchanges.

**4 boneless skinless chicken breast halves (4 ounces *each*)**
**1/4 cup chicken broth**
**3/4 teaspoon lemon-pepper seasoning**
**1/2 to 1 teaspoon dried thyme**
**1/4 teaspoon garlic powder**

Flatten chicken to 3/8-in. thickness; place in a skillet. Add broth; bring to a boil over medium heat. Reduce heat; cover and simmer for 5 minutes. Turn chicken; sprinkle with seasonings. Cook 3-5 minutes longer or until juices run clear. **Yield:** 4 servings.

**Nutritional Analysis:** One serving equals 129 calories, 2 g fat (trace saturated fat), 66 mg cholesterol, 218 mg sodium, trace carbohydrate, trace fiber, 26 g protein. **Diabetic Exchange:** 3 lean meat.

## Pasta Vegetable Salad

**1-1/2 cups uncooked tricolor spiral pasta**
**1/2 cup fresh broccoli florets**
**1/2 cup cauliflowerets**
**1/2 cup chopped cucumber**
**1/2 cup chopped celery**
**1/3 cup sliced carrot**
**1/4 cup chopped tomato**
**1/4 to 1/3 cup ranch salad dressing**

Cook pasta according to package directions; drain and rinse with cold water. Place in a large bowl; add vegetables. Drizzle with salad dressing; toss to coat. Cover and refrigerate for 1-2 hours. **Yield:** 4 servings.

## Cocoa Cake Brownies

**1 cup butter, melted**
**1 cup sugar**
**4 eggs**
**2 teaspoons vanilla extract**
**1 cup all-purpose flour**
**7 tablespoons baking cocoa**
**1 teaspoon baking powder**
**1/2 teaspoon salt**

In a bowl, combine the butter and sugar. Add eggs, one at a time, stirring well after each addition. Stir in vanilla. Combine the flour, cocoa, baking powder and salt. Gradually add to butter mixture; stir until moistened.

Transfer to a greased 13-in. x 9-in. x 2-in. baking pan. Bake at 350° for 20-25 minutes or until a toothpick inserted near the center comes out clean. Cool on a wire rack. **Yield:** about 2-1/2 dozen.

# She Counts on Shortcuts for Home Cooking

IF YOU VISIT Patricia Eckard, you're likely to find her in one of two spots, the kitchen or the garden.

"My family had a big garden when I was a child," she writes from Singers Glen, Virginia. Gardening certainly grew on Patricia, who now plants her own vegetables. "I juice the tomatoes and can our green beans," she adds.

Even though she'd like to spend more time gardening, reading and working on counted cross-stitch crafts, Patricia and her husband, Jim, find it hard to come by free time.

In addition to their full-time jobs—Patricia is an office coordinator at a university and Jim sells industrial supplies—the couple keeps busy with sons Joshua and Micah.

"Both of the boys play soccer," Patricia explains. "Joshua is on the track team and Micah is in Boy Scouts. During any given week, I attend four to six of their activities.

"Jim also takes evening classes at a seminary, and both he and I volunteer with a weekly church group," she says.

"I take these obligations into consideration when making my weekly meal plan. Luckily, I learned a lot about cooking from my mother."

Homemade food was the norm during Patricia's childhood. "I grew up in a Mennonite home where everyone was skilled in the kitchen," she recalls.

"Mom let me help out with the cooking as much as I wanted. She gave me money so I could purchase the groceries I needed to make meals myself.

"She also made lots of casseroles without using recipes, and she happily taught me to do the same, explaining what ingredients go well together.

"I still rely on casseroles today," Patricia adds. "They come together easily, and I often double the amounts so we can enjoy one dish for dinner and keep a second in the freezer.

"I sometimes use packaged mixes to prepare my casseroles even faster, and I keep cooked turkey in the freezer to mix into whatever casserole I'm creating," she notes. "I also find that casserole leftovers are perfect for rushed evenings because they heat up well in the microwave."

Using leftovers plays a big part in Patricia's meal plan. "I make large dinners on Saturday so we can enjoy the extras a day or two later," she says.

The busy mom certainly knows how to cut corners in the kitchen, but the one thing that Patricia never skimps on is flavor. For example, one of her most requested recipes is a quick and comforting casserole—Taco Crescent Bake.

"A friend shared the recipe with me, and I've prepared it monthly ever since," she writes. "The crust is made from refrigerated crescent roll dough. While the ground beef is browning, I simply press the dough into a baking dish.

"Whether I use crescent dough or mix things up by using refrigerated corn bread twists instead, guests always comment on the tasty crust as well as the zesty filling and crunchy topping."

A perfect complement to the easy entree is Confetti Bean Salad. "People often ask for this recipe," she says. "They love the tangy and sweet flavors in the salad dressing." And when she's really in a pinch, Patricia speeds things up with canned vegetables.

When it comes to completing a meal, the busy mom likes to bake Chocolate Peanut Butter Cake. "The original recipe was a from-scratch cake, but I use a boxed mix to save time," she explains. "I hope you enjoy the rich dessert as much as we do."

## Taco Crescent Bake

**1 tube (8 ounces) refrigerated crescent rolls**
**2 cups crushed corn chips, *divided***
**1-1/2 pounds ground beef**

## Menu-Planning Pointers

- Before I even begin making out my weekly dinner plan, I flip through supermarket flyers and my newspaper's coupon section to see what items have the best sales. I then incorporate these items into my plan by using recipes that call for them.
- When choosing a weekly menu, I try to use recipes that require some of the same ingredients. For instance, if a dish calls for shredded cheese but doesn't use an entire package, I'll plan on serving another meal later in the week that gives me the opportunity to use up the cheese. Nothing goes to waste, and I don't have to purchase as many groceries.
- My sons are not big vegetable-eaters, but they do like fresh corn. Planting our own corn not only saves a little money, but it also gets the kids excited to eat something that they helped grow. When the corn is ready, however, there is a lot of it, so I'm sure to keep the volume of our produce in mind when choosing menus. *—Patricia Eckard*

**1 can (15 ounces) tomato sauce**
**1 envelope taco seasoning**
**1 cup (8 ounces) sour cream**
**1 cup (4 ounces) shredded cheddar cheese**

Unroll crescent dough into a rectangle; press onto the bottom and 1 in. up the sides of a greased 13-in. x 9-in. x 2-in. baking dish. Seal seams and perforations. Sprinkle with 1 cup of chips; set aside.

In a large skillet, cook beef over medium heat until no longer pink; drain. Stir in tomato sauce and taco seasoning; bring to a boil. Reduce heat; simmer, uncovered, for 5 minutes. Spoon over chips. Top with sour cream, cheese and remaining chips. Bake, uncovered, at 350° for 25-30 minutes or until crust is lightly browned. **Yield:** 8 servings.

## Confetti Bean Salad

**1-3/4 cups frozen French-style green beans**
**1-3/4 cups frozen peas**
**1-1/2 cups frozen white *or* shoepeg corn**
**1 package (10 ounces) frozen lima beans**
**1 medium red onion, chopped**
**2 celery ribs, chopped**
**1/2 cup chopped sweet red pepper**
**1 jar (2 ounces) sliced pimientos, drained**
**1 cup sugar**
**3/4 cup cider vinegar**

In a large bowl, combine the first eight ingredients. In a small saucepan, bring the sugar and vinegar to a boil; boil for 3 minutes. Pour over vegetables. Cover and refrigerate until serving. Serve with a slotted spoon. **Yield:** 8 servings.

## Chocolate Peanut Butter Cake

**1 package (18-1/4 ounces) devil's food cake**
**1 cup creamy peanut butter**
**1 tablespoon vegetable oil**
**1 can (16 ounces) chocolate frosting**

Prepare and bake cake according to package directions, using a greased 13-in. x 9-in. x 2-in. baking pan. In a small mixing bowl, combine peanut butter and oil until smooth; spread over warm cake. Cool completely on a wire rack.

Place frosting in a microwave-safe bowl. Microwave on high for 25-30 seconds or until pourable. Carefully pour and spread over peanut butter layer. Let stand until set. **Yield:** 12-15 servings.

# Swift Fare Is Fancy Enough For Company

PREPARING and serving fantastic dishes is a snap for Bernadette Bennett. In fact, it's nothing for her to plan a meal that feeds 200 people or more!

"I work as a food and beverage director for a hotel chain," she explains from Waco, Texas. "I'm responsible for the menus at various events, where I feed anywhere from 10 to a crowd of a few hundred people."

Working with food isn't merely a 9-to-5 interest for Bernadette. "I love to cook at home, too," she notes. "I'm even pursuing a degree in culinary arts because I enjoy coming up with new recipes and trying unique foods. When I make my weekly grocery list, for example, I always include the ingredients for at least one new dish."

Bernadette credits her grandmothers with her interest in cooking. "They were both great cooks," she writes. "One was from Italy and the other from Texas, so I learned to appreciate both Italian and southwestern foods.

"Their skills influenced me in many ways, but the most meaningful thing they taught me is the importance of making good meals for your family...no matter how big or how small your family is."

Even though Bernadette lives alone, she rarely sits at the table by herself. "I have someone over for dinner at least four nights a week," she says. "I usually count on my dad to stop by for supper, and I often invite cousins and friends for dinner as well."

Finding the time to cook, however, can be somewhat of a challenge for Bernadette. "Depending on the events that the hotel is hosting, I work anywhere from 40 to 80 hours per week," she notes. "In addition, I'm often scheduled for split shifts. I start the day by getting food ready for an event, go home and then return at night to see the event through.

"I also volunteer with an animal rights group, and I like to reserve time for exercising, playing softball and gardening. So even though I'm likely to have dinner guests on weeknights, the menus have to come together quickly," she explains.

To help her serve family and friends in a flash, Bernadette cooks up a storm on Sundays. "I prepare several meals at one time," she says. "I make items that keep well in the freezer, so I can heat them up after work and before my dad or anyone else arrives for dinner.

"I also mix seasoning blends that I know I'll use during the week. I combine the spices and herbs in storage bags," says Bernadette. "Then I label the bags with the names of the dishes that they go with."

With the meal she shares here, Bernadette demonstrates her flair for fast weeknight fare that is special enough for company. Her enticing entree, for instance, comes together in a mere 30 minutes, yet guests assume that she fussed.

"I wanted to try something new with beef, so I created this recipe," says Bernadette. "Now, I prepare Family Flank Steak a few times a month. The sauce adds wonderful flavor, and it is versatile enough to go with just about any meat.

"Because I like steak with potatoes, I came up with Honey-Mustard Potato Slices," she notes. Any meat-and-potato lover will request these sensational spuds. Simply seasoned with salad dressing, the slices bake to a golden brown in less than an hour.

For a second stress-free side dish, consider Bernadette's Basil Buttered Beans. "I grow green beans and basil and thought I'd try combining the two," she says. "The results were yummy, particularly since the beans remain crisp and fresh tasting.

"This is a comforting meal, whether you're entertaining or need a satisfying supper in a pinch. I hope that you're able to fit it into your dinner plan."

## Family Flank Steak

✓ Uses less fat, sugar or salt. Includes Nutritional Analysis and Diabetic Exchanges.

**1 beef flank steak (1 pound)**
**1 tablespoon canola oil**
**1/4 cup red wine *or* beef broth**
**1 tablespoon Worcestershire sauce**
**1 teaspoon minced fresh basil *or* 1/2 teaspoon dried basil**

## Notebook Eliminates Guesswork

To make sure guests leave my house satisfied, I keep track of their food preferences. In a notebook, I list the names of friends and family I usually cook for. Next to their names, I specify the foods they like and don't like, their allergies and so forth.

Now, when I have dinner guests, I refer to the notebook so I can prepare a meal everyone enjoys. If I have a large party, the notebook guarantees a buffet with an assortment of foods to please all palates.

The notebook also comes in handy when I want to bake treats for gifts. With a quick look, I'm reminded of who prefers brownies, who is allergic to nuts and so on. *—Bernadette Bennett*

**MUSHROOM WINE SAUCE:**
- 1 cup sliced fresh mushrooms
- 3/4 cup beef broth
- 1/4 cup red wine *or* additional beef broth
- 1/4 cup chopped green onions
- 1 teaspoon butter
- 1 teaspoon pepper
- 2 teaspoons cornstarch
- 1 tablespoon cold water

In a large skillet, brown the steak in oil. Stir in the wine or broth, the Worcestershire sauce and the basil. Bring to a boil. Reduce heat; simmer, uncovered, for 2-4 minutes on each side or until the meat reaches desired doneness (for rare, a meat thermometer should read 140°; medium, 160°; well-done, 170°). Remove the steak and keep warm.

To the skillet, add mushrooms, broth, wine or additional broth, onions, butter and pepper. Bring to a boil. Reduce heat; simmer, uncovered, for 5 minutes or until mushrooms are tender.

Combine cornstarch and water until smooth; stir into sauce. Bring to a boil; cook and stir for 1 minute or until thickened. Thinly slice steak across the grain; serve with sauce. **Yield:** 4 servings.

**Nutritional Analysis:** One serving (3 ounces cooked meat with 1/4 cup sauce, prepared with reduced-sodium beef broth) equals 265 calories, 13 g fat (5 g saturated fat), 49 mg cholesterol, 139 mg sodium, 4 g carbohydrate, 1 g fiber, 26 g protein. **Diabetic Exchanges:** 3 lean meat, 1 vegetable, 2 fat.

## Basil Buttered Beans

✓ Uses less fat, sugar or salt. Includes Nutritional Analysis and Diabetic Exchanges.

- 4 cups water
- 1 teaspoon chicken bouillon granules
- 1-1/2 pounds fresh green beans, trimmed
- 1 to 2 tablespoons butter, melted
- 3/4 teaspoon dried basil

In a large saucepan, bring water and bouillon to a boil. Add the beans. Cook for 3-4 minutes or until crisp-tender; drain. Stir in butter and basil. **Yield:** 4 servings.

**Nutritional Analysis:** One 1/2-cup serving (prepared with 1 tablespoon butter) equals 79 calories, 3 g fat (2 g saturated fat), 8 mg cholesterol, 317 mg sodium, 11 g carbohydrate, 6 g fiber, 2 g protein. **Diabetic Exchanges:** 2 vegetable, 1/2 fat.

## Honey-Mustard Potato Slices

- 2 pounds potatoes, peeled and thinly sliced (about 4 cups)
- 1/2 cup honey mustard salad dressing
- 1/2 teaspoon seasoned salt
- 1/2 teaspoon pepper

In a large bowl, combine all ingredients. Transfer to a greased 15-in. x 10-in. x 1-in. baking pan. Bake, uncovered, at 350° for 50-55 minutes or until tender. Stir before serving. **Yield:** 4 servings.

# Chapter 2

# 30 Minutes to Mealtime

DURING the busy-day rush, wouldn't it be wonderful to have an appealing assortment of menus and entrees that you can put together in just half an hour?

When your hectic schedule doesn't allow you to spend even one hour in the kitchen, rely on these 15 complete meals—plus additional main dishes—that get to the table in only 30 minutes or less.

Each and every fast-to-fix favorite comes from the recipe file of a fellow busy cook. So your family is sure to enjoy each of these quick creations.

**SPEEDY SUPPER.** Citrus Shortcake, Great Garden Veggies and Grilled Pepper Steaks (all recipes on p. 29)

# Hearty Supper Has Weeknight Ease

ON BUSY weeknights, you don't have time to spend hours in the kitchen cooking up a satisfying meal. And with this must-try menu of reader recipes compiled by our home economists, you don't have to!

You'll find that all three dishes rely on common convenience items such as orange juice, spreadable fruit and refrigerated dough, so you can get a homemade dinner on the table in half an hour or less.

For the entree, Bernadette Bennett contributes her mouth-watering Orange Basil Chops. The no-fuss pork chops and simple sauce come together easily on the stovetop in one skillet, so cleanup is a breeze.

"With its hints of orange, garlic and basil, it's a tasty main dish that impresses company yet is ready in no time," she writes from her home in Waco, Texas.

The tangy side dish is a snap to stir up, too. Pineapple-Glazed Carrots have a unique honey-pineapple coating that's sure to have diners asking for the secret.

The rapid recipe is an ideal accompaniment to most any entree. "Even kids like these carrots," says Leonora Wilkie of Bellbrook, Ohio.

Alma De Fazio rounds out the sensational supper with appealing Spiral Cheese Slices. The Erie, Pennsylvania baker jazzes up refrigerated crescent roll dough by using cheddar cheese, green onions and garlic powder to create the delightful spirals.

"I serve them as appetizers, too," she says. "They're very easy to make—and very delicious." Bake a batch for your family tonight.

## Orange Basil Chops

**1 cup orange juice**
**1/4 cup Dijon mustard**
**2 tablespoons minced fresh basil *or* 2 teaspoons dried basil**
**1/2 teaspoon garlic salt**
**1/2 teaspoon pepper**
**4 bone-in pork loin chops (1/2 inch thick)**
**2 tablespoons butter**
**1 tablespoon cornstarch**
**2 tablespoons cold water**

In a bowl, combine the first five ingredients; set aside. In a large skillet, brown pork chops in butter. Add orange juice mixture. Bring to a boil. Reduce heat; cover and simmer for 6-8 minutes or until meat juices run clear. Remove pork to a serving platter and keep warm. Combine cornstarch and cold water until smooth; stir into skillet. Bring to a boil; cook and stir for 2 minutes or until thickened. Serve with pork chops. **Yield:** 4 servings.

## Pineapple-Glazed Carrots

**3 cups baby carrots *or* medium carrots, quartered**
**1/2 cup pineapple spreadable fruit**
**2 tablespoons honey**
**2 tablespoons butter**

Place carrots and a small amount of water in a saucepan. Bring to a boil. Reduce heat; cover and simmer for 10-15 minutes or until crisp-tender. Drain. Set aside and keep warm. In another saucepan, bring the fruit, honey and butter to a boil. Drizzle over carrots; toss to coat. **Yield:** 4 servings.

## Spiral Cheese Slices

**1 tube (8 ounces) refrigerated crescent rolls**
**1/4 cup chopped green onions**
**1/8 teaspoon garlic powder**
**1/4 cup shredded cheddar cheese**

Remove crescent dough from tube; do not unroll. Cut into eight slices; place cut side down on an ungreased baking sheet. Top with green onions. Sprinkle with garlic powder and cheese; lightly press cheese into slices. Bake at 375° for 14-16 minutes or until golden brown. Serve warm. **Yield:** 8 servings.

### Orange Juice Options

When a recipe calls for orange juice, you may use freshly squeezed juice, the kind you prepare from concentrate or the purchased refrigerated variety. Many busy cooks choose store-bought refrigerated juice because it cuts down on prep work.

Use undiluted concentrate if your recipe specifically calls for orange juice concentrate.

# Serve Satisfying Meal in a Snap

IT IS RARE to find Kelly Olson at her Moab, Utah home. The busy reader is always on the go...literally!

"I love to go hiking, biking, swimming and camping," she writes. "My husband, Ross, and I are also long-distance runners. We like running on the dirt trails that line the cliffs of the canyons or in the La Sal Mountains near our home.

"Moab is a tourist town, thriving on mountain biking, river rafting and hiking," Kelly explains. "Our weather is almost always beautiful, so Ross and I try to spend our free time outdoors."

Ross works for the state of Utah, and Kelly is a part-time server at a restaurant. "We're both ordained ministers and host Bible studies in our home," Kelly adds.

"I'm also involved in a women's support group, I'm a board member of a crisis center and I volunteer with a highway cleanup program."

When Kelly's not on the run, you'll likely find her in the kitchen. "I love to cook and bake, but rarely use a recipe," she says. "I enjoy creating my own dishes to suit our tastes."

For the menu she shares here, Kelly suggests starting with Pork 'n' Bean Soup. "I like to make this comforting soup at least once a month," she notes.

"It simmers on its own while you prepare the rest of the meal. Try adding cooked elbow noodles or cubed chicken," she suggests.

Because she and Ross like to eat healthy, Kelly serves a salad with this meal. "Whenever I make the soup, I toss together Ranch Spinach Salad," she writes. "It relies on packaged greens and a handful of other ingredients, so it comes together in no time."

Topping off the swift supper are Ice Cream Tortilla Cups. The cinnamon-sugar cups set up easily in muffin tins and bake to a crispy perfection.

"The favorite part of my restaurant job is making desserts for customers," she says. "I love to serve them a fancy presentation.

"I based this dessert on something I made in my high school Spanish class," Kelly recalls. The tasty treats look impressive, but call for just a few items.

## Pork 'n' Bean Soup

**2 cans (11 ounces *each*) pork and beans**
**1 can (15-1/2 ounces) great northern beans, rinsed and drained**
**1 package (16 ounces) frozen corn, thawed**
**4 cups chicken broth**
**3 pickled jalapeno peppers, seeded and chopped**
**1 teaspoon garlic salt**

In a large saucepan, combine the beans, corn, broth, peppers and garlic salt. Bring to a boil. Reduce heat; simmer, uncovered, for 20 minutes or until heated through. **Yield:** 6 servings.

**Editor's Note:** When cutting or seeding hot peppers, use rubber or plastic gloves to protect your hands. Avoid touching your face.

## Ranch Spinach Salad

**1 package (6 ounces) baby spinach**
**1 small sweet red pepper, julienned**
**1/2 cup shredded pepper Jack cheese**
**1 can (2-1/4 ounces) ripe chopped olives, drained**
**1 green onion, finely chopped**
**1/3 to 1/2 cup ranch salad dressing**

In a large salad bowl, combine the spinach, red pepper, cheese, olives and onion. Add dressing; toss to coat. **Yield:** 6 servings.

## Ice Cream Tortilla Cups

**1/4 cup butter, melted**
**6 flour tortillas (7 inches)**
**6 tablespoons sugar**
**1/2 teaspoon ground cinnamon**
**Strawberry ice cream *or* flavor of your choice**

Brush butter on one side of each tortilla. Combine the sugar and cinnamon; sprinkle evenly over tortillas. Press each tortilla sugar side up into a greased muffin cup.

Bake at 400° for 6-8 minutes. Cool for 5 minutes. Gently separate edges. Place a scoop of ice cream in each tortilla. **Yield:** 6 servings.

# Fresh-Tasting Fare's Fast to Fix

FRESH flavors are the hallmark of meals at Gloria Warczak's dinner table in Cedarburg, Wisconsin.

"I enjoy all phases of cooking, including gardening, canning and freezing vegetables, drying herbs and baking yeast breads," she says.

And the retired secretary-bookkeeper has had plenty of practice perfecting these skills. She and husband Pat have been married for 44 years, have raised three sons and have two grandchildren.

"Pat is project manager for a steel company," she writes. "As soon as he gets home, we like to take off and do things we did not have time for when our boys were growing up.

"I also have many other interests, including reading mysteries, writing poetry and playing piano."

But these hobbies don't keep Gloria out of the kitchen. "I try to cook at least two large meals each week. I serve enough for dinner, then store extras for later in the week," she explains.

Gloria shares one of her quick menus here. "The original recipe for Microwaved Cod came from my grandmother, who baked it in the oven," she recalls.

Today, the fish, which has a pleasant lemon-and-herb flavor, cooks quickly in the microwave. "My family has always raved about it," she adds.

Gloria takes advantage of her garden bounty to prepare Sauteed Summer Squash. "We like squash best when it still has a little crunch, which results in a shorter cooking time," she notes.

To round out the meal, Gloria tosses together a refreshing fruit-and-vegetable medley.

"Pineapple Cucumber Salad is my own creation," she says. "I first prepared it for an Easter dinner. It was an instant hit with Pat, who loves pineapple."

## Microwaved Cod

**1-1/2 pounds cod *or* haddock fillets**
**1/2 cup white wine *or* chicken broth**
**2 tablespoons lemon juice**
**1 tablespoon grated lemon peel**
**1 tablespoon minced chives**
**1 tablespoon minced fresh parsley**
**1/2 teaspoon dried tarragon**
**Pepper to taste**

Place the fillets in an ungreased 11-in. x 7-in. x 2-in. microwave-safe dish. Cover and cook on high for 6 minutes; drain. Add the wine or broth, lemon juice, lemon peel, chives, parsley, tarragon and pepper. Cover and cook 4-5 minutes longer or until fish flakes easily with a fork. Let stand for 5 minutes before serving. **Yield:** 6 servings.

**Editor's Note:** This recipe was tested in a 1,100-watt microwave.

## Sauteed Summer Squash

**2 small zucchini, julienned**
**2 small yellow summer squash, julienned**
**1 small sweet red pepper, julienned**
**1 small onion, julienned**
**2 tablespoons vegetable oil**
**1-1/2 teaspoons seasoned salt**
**1/2 teaspoon pepper**

In a large skillet, saute the zucchini, summer squash, red pepper and onion in oil for 8 minutes or until crisp-tender. Sprinkle with seasoned salt and pepper. **Yield:** 6 servings.

## Pineapple Cucumber Salad

**1 can (8 ounces) pineapple chunks**
**2 medium cucumbers, halved and thinly sliced**
**1 cup seedless grapes**
**2 teaspoons snipped chives**
**2/3 cup mayonnaise**
**1/3 cup sugar**
**1 teaspoon prepared mustard**
**1/4 teaspoon celery seed**
**1/4 teaspoon prepared horseradish**

Drain pineapple, reserving 1 tablespoon juice (discard remaining juice or save for another use). In a bowl, combine the pineapple, cucumbers, grapes and chives. In another bowl, combine the mayonnaise, sugar, mustard, celery seed, horseradish and reserved pineapple juice. Pour over pineapple mixture; gently stir to coat. Serve with a slotted spoon. **Yield:** 6 servings.

# Casual Menu Cuts Prep Time

WITH this time-saving trio of dishes from readers, you can have an appealing informal meal ready in less than a half hour—even on a hectic weeknight.

Start off by assembling Refried Bean Pizza from Gail Eltgroth. The Austin, Texas cook uses a tube of corn bread twists to create the crust for this south-of-the-border specialty.

"This recipe combines our love of pizza and Mexican food," she notes. "I basically adapted a layered dip recipe and re-created it in pizza form. It has become a favorite for any busy day...and it's meatless, too.

"To serve, I use a pizza cutter to slice the pizza into wedges first, then I add tomatoes, green onions and sometimes shredded lettuce. Otherwise, it's difficult to cut through without knocking off all of the toppings," Gail explains.

"Besides salsa or picante sauce, you can also garnish with sour cream and guacamole," she suggests.

For an easy side dish, try Pecan Tossed Salad sent in by Bonnie Gluhanich, Muskegon, Michigan.

The simple salad relies on packaged salad greens that get flavor and crunch from toasted nuts. Preparation of the tasty vinaigrette is streamlined by using a packet of Italian salad dressing mix.

For dessert, stir up a speedy batch of White Chocolate Cereal Bars. "A friend gave me this recipe that's a different take on traditional crisp rice treats," says Anne Powers of Munford, Alabama.

"My husband loves them," she adds. "They're so quick to make. When you are watching TV, you can prepare them during a commercial and you won't miss much of your program."

## Refried Bean Pizza

**1 tube (11-1/2 ounces) refrigerated corn bread twists**
**1 can (16 ounces) refried beans**
**1 can (4 ounces) chopped green chilies**
**2 cups (8 ounces) shredded Colby-Monterey Jack cheese *or* Mexican cheese blend**
**1 can (2-1/4 ounces) sliced ripe olives, drained**
**Chopped tomatoes, salsa and sliced green onions, optional**

Unroll the bread twists and press onto a greased 12-in. pizza pan. Bake at 375° for 11-13 minutes or until lightly browned. Combine refried beans and chilies; spread over crust to within 1/2 in. of edge. Top with cheese and olives. Bake 5-8 minutes longer or until cheese is melted. Cut into wedges. Serve with tomatoes, salsa and green onions if desired. **Yield:** 6 servings.

## Pecan Tossed Salad

**1/2 cup olive oil**
**1/4 cup balsamic vinegar**
**2 tablespoons water**
**1 envelope Italian salad dressing mix**
**1 package (10 ounces) ready-to-serve salad greens**
**1/3 cup pecan halves, toasted**
**1/4 cup shredded Parmesan cheese**

In a jar with a tight-fitting lid, combine the oil, vinegar, water and salad dressing mix; shake well. In a large salad bowl, combine greens, pecans and Parmesan cheese. Just before serving, drizzle with the dressing and toss to coat. **Yield:** 6 servings.

## White Chocolate Cereal Bars

**4 cups miniature marshmallows**
**8 ounces white candy coating, broken into pieces**
**1/4 cup butter, cubed**
**6 cups crisp rice cereal**

In a microwave-safe bowl, combine the marshmallows, candy coating and butter. Microwave, uncovered, on high for 2 minutes or until melted, stirring every minute. Add cereal; stir to coat. Transfer to a greased 13-in. x 9-in. x 2-in. pan and gently press mixture evenly into pan. Cut into squares. **Yield:** about 3 dozen.

**Editor's Note:** This recipe was tested in a 1,100-watt microwave.

# Favorites Get Easy Updates

TIME-CRUNCHED COOKS can always use complete meal ideas that are not only a snap to assemble, but also sure to please everyone at the dinner table.

The reader recipes included here are taste-tempting twists on much-loved mainstays, so they'll likely have your family asking for seconds.

All of the ingredients are commonly found at your local grocery store. Best of all, you can whip up the entire meal in half an hour or less.

To hurry preparation along, start with fuss-free Seasoned French Fries from Sharon Crider of Stoughton, Wisconsin. The simple spuds come together easily with frozen crinkle-cut fries and just a few other ingredients. They're perfect with a sandwich, hamburger or hot dog.

While the fries are baking, heat up the griddle for Nita Crosby's Bacon-Tomato Grilled Cheese. This robust revision of an all-American lunch classic gets heartiness from bacon and extra flavor from onion, sour cream and oregano.

Toasted to a golden brown, the sandwich is always a hit at Nita's home in St. George, Utah.

To complete this menu of fast-paced fare, Anne Powers of Munford, Alabama shares Marshmallow Fudge Topping. She suggests serving the warm chocolate sauce over ice cream or sliced pound cake.

"This thick sauce is so yummy," she promises. "It takes just a few minutes to prepare on the stovetop, so it's great for a quick dessert or late-night snack."

## Seasoned French Fries

**5 cups frozen crinkle-cut french fries**
**1 teaspoon onion salt**
**1/4 teaspoon paprika**
**1/3 cup grated Parmesan cheese**

Arrange french fries in a greased 15-in. x 10-in. x 1-in. baking pan. Sprinkle with onion salt and paprika; stir to coat. Bake at 450° for 15-20 minutes or until lightly browned. Sprinkle with Parmesan cheese; stir to coat. **Yield:** 4 servings.

## Bacon-Tomato Grilled Cheese

**8 slices sourdough bread**
**4 slices mozzarella cheese**
**2 large tomatoes, thinly sliced**
**8 bacon strips, cooked**
**4 tablespoons sour cream**
**4 tablespoons finely chopped onion**
**1/4 teaspoon dried oregano**
**4 slices cheddar cheese**
**2 tablespoons butter, softened**

For each sandwich, top one slice of bread with one slice of mozzarella cheese, a fourth of the tomato slices, two bacon strips, 1 tablespoon sour cream, 1 tablespoon onion, a pinch of oregano, one slice of cheddar cheese and another slice of bread. Spread outside of sandwiches with butter.

On a hot griddle over medium heat, grill sandwiches for 3-4 minutes on each side or until lightly toasted. **Yield:** 4 servings.

## Marshmallow Fudge Topping

**1 cup packed brown sugar**
**1/4 cup baking cocoa**
**1/2 cup milk**
**1 cup miniature marshmallows**
**1 tablespoon butter**
**1 teaspoon vanilla extract**
**Ice cream**

In a saucepan, combine brown sugar, cocoa and milk until smooth. Bring to a boil; cook and stir for 4-5 minutes or until sugar is dissolved. Remove from heat; stir in marshmallows, butter and vanilla until marshmallows are melted. Serve warm over ice cream. **Yield:** 1-1/2 cups.

### Makin' Bacon

- I like to cook extra bacon and store the excess in the freezer to reheat in the microwave on busy mornings or to use in recipes. This really saves on time. *—Tara Calbeck, Eaton, Ohio*
- When it's warm out, I cook bacon in an aluminum pie pan on our outdoor grill. It keeps the odor of bacon out of the house. *—Sharon Shapiro, Middlebury, Connecticut*

# Quick Chicken Dinner Delights

IF YOU visit the quaint country town of Greenbriar, Pennsylvania, you're likely to find Nicole Harris happily cooking away in her kitchen, fixing meals for her husband, Jason, and their daughter, Tama.

While Jason is at work making deliveries for a local beverage distributor, Nicole is a full-time homemaker.

"Being a stay-at-home mom gives me the chance to spend time with Tama and enjoy my favorite hobby—cooking," she writes. "I prepare sit-down dinners for the three of us most weeknights."

One of those suppers is the palate-pleasing meal she shares here, which features flavorful Rosemary Lime Chicken.

"I experimented with herbs and seasonings quite a bit before creating the final version of this entree," she explains. "The tartness of the lime juice really complements the rosemary. Everyone loves it."

It's fast to fix for family dinners during the week, yet it's nice enough to serve weekend company. "I turn to the recipe often because I like to fix meals on the stovetop," she adds. "In the summer, I sometimes make the chicken on the grill with equally tasty results."

While the chicken is cooking, Nicole tosses together her Zesty Garden Salad. A jar of pickled pepper rings and a can of sliced ripe olives put a tasty and convenient spin on traditional salad fixings.

"This salad is frequently on the menu, because there is so little chopping involved and it goes with almost any main dish," Nicole says.

Mandarin Berry Cooler rounds out the tangy trio of recipes. "I like to use my blender and food processor regularly, so this smoothie is popular at our house," Nicole writes.

The frosty beverage relies on fresh strawberries and a banana in addition to canned fruits. "These smoothies are not only quick and refreshing, but they can be adjusted to include whatever fruit you prefer," she suggests.

"We enjoy this meal often because it's quick, simple and tastes so good."

## Rosemary Lime Chicken

✓ Uses less fat, sugar or salt. Includes Nutritional Analysis and Diabetic Exchanges.

**4 boneless skinless chicken breast halves (5 ounces *each*)**
**2 tablespoons canola oil**
**1/2 cup white wine *or* chicken broth**
**1/4 cup lime juice**
**2 tablespoons minced fresh rosemary *or* 2 teaspoons dried rosemary, crushed**
**1/2 teaspoon salt**
**1/4 teaspoon pepper**

Flatten chicken to 1/2-in. thickness. In a large skillet, brown chicken in oil over medium-high heat. Add the remaining ingredients. Cook, uncovered, for 5-7 minutes or until chicken juices run clear. **Yield:** 4 servings.

**Nutritional Analysis:** One serving equals 244 calories, 9 g fat (1 g saturated fat), 82 mg cholesterol, 389 mg sodium, 2 g carbohydrate, trace fiber, 33 g protein. **Diabetic Exchanges:** 4 lean meat, 1/2 fat.

## Zesty Garden Salad

**4 cups torn romaine**
**1 can (2-1/4 ounces) sliced ripe olives, drained**
**1/2 cup chopped tomato**
**1/2 cup shredded cheddar cheese**
**1/4 cup pickled pepper rings**
**1/2 cup Italian salad dressing**

In a large salad bowl, toss the romaine, olives, tomato, cheese and pepper rings. Just before serving, drizzle with dressing and toss to coat. **Yield:** 4 servings.

## Mandarin Berry Cooler

**1 can (11 ounces) mandarin oranges, drained**
**1 can (8 ounces) crushed pineapple, drained**
**1 cup sliced fresh strawberries**
**1 medium ripe banana, cut into chunks**
**6 ice cubes**
**3/4 cup milk**

In a blender, combine oranges, pineapple, strawberries and banana; cover and process until blended. Add ice and milk; cover and process until smooth. Serve immediately in chilled glasses. **Yield:** 4 servings.

# Fast Fare Looks Like You Fussed

WHEN he's not busy working at the local Wal-Mart, you might find Ron Gardner fishing or doing yard work at his Grand Haven, Michigan home.

Chances are, however, he's canning garden-fresh produce or happily preparing dinner for his wife, Susan.

"I've been cooking for 30 years," says Ron. "I love making up recipes and have created approximately 250 of them."

When Ron comes up with a new dish, he thinks of a variety of ways to make it, so it seems different each time.

"I write these options at the bottom of the recipe card," he explains. "When I copy the card for friends, they have these variations to help them fix a dish that best suits their tastes."

Ron offers plenty of options in the 30-minute menu he shares here. When preparing the meal, he starts by fixing the creamy dessert.

"I make the Pineapple Pudding Pie first so it can chill in the refrigerator before dinner," he relates. Ron sometimes makes the pie crust from scratch but recommends using a convenient store-bought crust when time is short.

While the pie chills, Ron assembles the eye-appealing entree, Breaded Pork Roll-Ups. Pretty swirls of ham and a golden coating make the delightful main course perfect for company.

"If you like, add a few tablespoons of grated Parmesan cheese to the dry bread crumbs to give the coating even more flavor," he suggests.

With the chops cooking, Ron moves on to the tasty Raisin Coleslaw. "Using purchased shredded cabbage cuts prep time for this salad," he says.

"And if you don't care for raisins, chop up some dried apricots instead."

## Pineapple Pudding Pie

**1-1/2 cups cold milk**
**1 package (3.4 ounces) instant vanilla pudding mix**
**1 can (8 ounces) crushed pineapple, well drained**
**1 graham cracker crust (9 inches)**
**1-1/2 cups whipped topping**
**1/2 cup flaked coconut, toasted**

In a bowl, whisk milk and pudding mix for 2 minutes. Let stand for 2 minutes or until soft-set. Fold in pineapple. Pour into crust. Spread with whipped topping. Sprinkle with coconut. Cover and refrigerate until serving. **Yield:** 6-8 servings.

## Breaded Pork Roll-Ups

**1 egg**
**1/3 cup milk**
**1-1/4 cups dry bread crumbs**
**1 teaspoon seasoned salt**
**4 boneless pork loin chops (1/4 inch thick)**
**4 thin slices deli ham**
**2 tablespoons vegetable oil, *divided***

In a shallow bowl, lightly beat egg and milk. In another shallow bowl, combine bread crumbs and seasoned salt. Flatten pork chops to 1/8-in. thickness; place a ham slice on each. Fold sides and ends over ham and roll up; secure each with a toothpick. Dip roll-ups in egg mixture, then coat with crumb mixture.

In a large skillet over medium-high heat, brown roll-ups in 1 tablespoon oil for 2 minutes on each side. Add remaining oil. Cook 10-12 minutes longer or until meat juices run clear, turning occasionally. Discard toothpicks before serving. **Yield:** 4 servings.

## Raisin Coleslaw

**1/2 cup mayonnaise**
**1-1/2 teaspoons honey**
**3/4 teaspoon sugar**
**3/4 teaspoon prepared mustard**
**1/8 teaspoon celery salt**
**2 cups shredded cabbage**
**1 cup grated carrots**
**1/2 cup golden raisins**

In a small bowl, combine mayonnaise, honey, sugar, mustard and celery salt. In a serving bowl, toss cabbage, carrots and raisins. Add mayonnaise mixture; stir to coat. Cover and refrigerate until serving. **Yield:** 4 servings.

# Seasoned Steaks Star in Supper

SITTING DOWN to a delicious steak dinner doesn't have to mean spending a lot of time preparing it. The reader recipes shared here not only make a complete meal, but all three can be fixed and on the table within 30 minutes.

Begin by seasoning the Grilled Peppered Steaks sent in by Stephanie Moon. You'll need only five ingredients for these juicy full-flavored steaks that cook up quickly on the grill.

"I once wanted a peppered steak for supper, so I tossed some spices together and came up with this recipe," writes the Nampa, Idaho reader. "My family thoroughly enjoyed it, especially my husband."

Great Garden Veggies from Chris Schmidt are a colorful accompaniment to the peppery entree. Chris jazzes up zucchini, yellow squash and tomato with cheese and seasonings in her Clarksville, Tennessee kitchen.

The no-fuss skillet side dish is perfect for using summer's bounty. Plus, the veggies are great alongside grilled chicken, fish and most other warm-weather fare.

When it comes to dessert, it doesn't get much simpler than Citrus Shortcake. The classic dinner conclusion gets an update when fresh berries meet the convenience of prepared whipped topping, individual sponge cakes and other packaged items.

"It's fast and delicious when time is short," explains Eileen Warren of Windsor, Ontario. "I like to mix the whipped topping with the lemon yogurt early in the day, then store it in the refrigerator until we're ready for dessert.

"I sometimes use scones instead of shortcakes," she notes. "And I like to replace the sliced strawberries with raspberries for a fun change of pace."

Halve the recipe to serve two people, or double it for larger get-togethers.

## Grilled Peppered Steaks

**1-1/2 to 2 teaspoons coarsely ground pepper**
**1 teaspoon onion salt**
**1 teaspoon garlic salt**
**1/4 teaspoon paprika, optional**
**4 New York strip steaks (about 8 ounces *each*)**

In a small bowl, combine the pepper, onion salt, garlic salt and paprika if desired. Rub onto both sides of steaks. Grill, covered, over medium heat for 8-10 minutes on each side or until meat reaches desired doneness (for rare, a meat thermometer should read 140°; medium, 160°; well-done, 170°). **Yield:** 4 servings.

## Great Garden Veggies

✓ Uses less fat, sugar or salt. Includes Nutritional Analysis and Diabetic Exchanges.

**1 medium zucchini, cut into 1/4-inch slices**
**1 medium yellow summer squash, cut into 1/4-inch slices**
**1/4 cup sliced onion**
**1 tablespoon butter**
**1 medium tomato, cut into wedges**
**1/4 teaspoon salt**
**1/4 teaspoon garlic salt**
**1/4 teaspoon dried basil**
**1/4 teaspoon pepper**
**2 tablespoons grated Parmesan cheese**

In a skillet, saute the zucchini, yellow squash and onion in butter until crisp-tender. Add the tomato, salt, garlic salt, basil and pepper. Cook 2-3 minutes longer. Sprinkle with Parmesan cheese. **Yield:** 4 servings.

**Nutritional Analysis:** One serving (3/4 cup) equals 67 calories, 4 g fat (2 g saturated fat), 10 mg cholesterol, 340 mg sodium, 7 g carbohydrate, 2 g fiber, 3 g protein. **Diabetic Exchanges:** 1 vegetable, 1 fat.

## Citrus Shortcake

**1 cup (8 ounces) lemon yogurt**
**1 cup whipped topping**
**4 individual round sponge cakes**
**1/4 cup orange juice**
**2-2/3 cups sliced fresh strawberries**

In a small bowl, combine yogurt and whipped topping. Place sponge cakes on dessert plates; drizzle with orange juice. Spread with half of the yogurt mixture. Top with strawberries and remaining yogurt mixture. **Yield:** 4 servings.

# Morning Meal Starts Day Swiftly

KICKING OFF the weekend with a delicious breakfast doesn't require waking up at sunrise to prepare it. With these easy eye-openers from our home economists, you'll have no trouble surprising family members with a hearty morning meal.

Simply start by mixing up a batch of Cranberry Bran Muffins. Dressing up a boxed mix gives these golden bites down-home flair with only a fraction of the work that's needed for homemade varieties.

And since the muffins call for the same oven temperature as the baked Sweet 'n' Spicy Bacon, prepare this unique side dish next.

Chili powder, cayenne and curry add an unexpected flavor twist to the taste-tempting bacon. With a touch of cinnamon and maple syrup, the well-seasoned strips complement just about any breakfast entree...including the must-try main course here.

Guaranteed to impress, sensational Strawberry Cream Crepes come together easily on the stovetop—without any hard-to-find ingredients.

## Cranberry Bran Muffins

✓ Uses less fat, sugar or salt. Includes Nutritional Analysis and Diabetic Exchanges.

**1 package (8.1 ounces) apple cinnamon muffin mix**
**1/2 cup All-Bran, crushed**
**1/2 cup dried cranberries**
**1/2 cup milk**

In a large bowl, combine the muffin mix, bran and cranberries. Stir in milk just until moistened. Fill greased or paper-lined muffin cups three-fourths full.

Bake at 450° for 15-20 minutes or until a toothpick comes out clean. Cool for 5 minutes before removing from pan to a wire rack. Serve warm. **Yield:** 6 muffins.

**Nutritional Analysis:** One muffin (prepared with fat-free milk) equals 205 calories, 4 g fat (1 g saturated fat), 1 mg cholesterol, 568 mg sodium, 41 g carbohydrate, 2 g fiber, 4 g protein. **Diabetic Exchanges:** 1-1/2 starch, 1 fruit, 1/2 fat.

## Sweet 'n' Spicy Bacon

**1 teaspoon chili powder**
**1/8 teaspoon cayenne pepper**
**1/8 teaspoon curry powder**
**1/8 teaspoon ground cinnamon**
**8 bacon strips**
**3 tablespoons maple syrup**

Combine the seasonings; sprinkle over both sides of bacon. Place on a rack in an ungreased 15-in. x 10-in. x 1-in. baking pan. Bake at 450° for 10 minutes.

Drizzle with 1 tablespoon syrup. Turn bacon and drizzle with remaining syrup. Bake for 6-10 minutes longer or until browned. Remove to paper towels. Serve warm. **Yield:** 4 servings.

## Strawberry Cream Crepes

**1/2 cup biscuit/baking mix**
**1 egg**
**1/2 cup milk**
**1/4 teaspoon vanilla extract**
**Softened butter**
**2 packages (3 ounces *each*) cream cheese, softened**
**1/4 cup sour cream**
**2 tablespoons sugar**
**1/4 teaspoon ground cinnamon**
**1 package (10 ounces) frozen sweetened sliced strawberries, thawed and drained**
**1/2 cup strawberry glaze**

For crepes, in a bowl, whisk biscuit mix, egg, milk and vanilla. Grease an 8-in. nonstick skillet with a small amount of softened butter; pour 2 tablespoons batter into center of skillet.

Lift and tilt pan to coat bottom evenly. Cook until top appears dry; turn and cook 15-20 seconds longer. Remove to a wire rack. Repeat with remaining batter, adding butter to skillet as needed.

In a small mixing bowl, beat cream cheese, sour cream, sugar and cinnamon until smooth. Spoon 2 rounded tablespoonfuls down the center of each crepe; roll up.

In a microwave-safe bowl, combine strawberries and glaze. Cover and microwave on high for 1-2 minutes or until heated through. Serve over crepes. **Yield:** 4 servings.

# Ham Dinner Is Fixed in a Dash

ENJOYING her golden years experimenting in the kitchen suits Ernestine Beoughter just fine. "I'm always in the kitchen coming up with different dishes," she writes from the town of Lawrenceville, a small farming community in southeastern Illinois.

"I lived on a farm as a child, and we always had fresh produce to eat," she notes. That may be why whipping up fantastic fare is a hobby of Ernestine's...and it's a pastime that her husband of 55 years, Hershel, doesn't mind one bit. "Hershel may be retired, but that hasn't slowed down his appetite," Ernestine says with a smile.

The couple has two grown daughters and four grandkids. "I love attending my grandchildren's extracurricular activities," she adds. "I also like gardening, crafting and helping with fund-raising events."

Always looking for ways to beat the clock, Ernestine had no problem coming up with a 30-minute menu to share with other readers. She begins by preparing a frosty favorite.

"Ice Cream Cookie Dessert takes only a few moments to put together," she promises. "Guests always ask for seconds, and my grandchildren have even requested it for their birthday cakes."

With the dessert chilling, Ernestine turns to her speedy Glazed Ham Steaks. "I created this one night, and we've enjoyed it ever since," she says. "Ham steaks cook up fast and offer lots of flavor."

Not only do the ham and its tangy pineapple sauce come together in a pinch, but the entire recipe can easily be halved for two-person households or doubled for larger groups.

While the ham is baking, Ernestine prepares Flavorful Green Beans. "Green beans are a quick-cooking vegetable to begin with," she explains, "but using the microwave moves things along even faster.

"I rely on canned green beans when time is really tight," notes Ernestine, "and I sometimes add extra bacon to give the dish even more flavor."

## Ice Cream Cookie Dessert

**1 package (15 ounces) cream-filled chocolate sandwich cookie crumbs**
**1/3 cup butter, melted**
**1 quart vanilla ice cream, softened**
**1 carton (8 ounces) frozen whipped topping, thawed**
**Chopped pecans and chocolate syrup**

In a bowl, combine cookie crumbs and butter. Press half into an 8-in. square dish. Spread with ice cream. Press remaining crumb mixture into ice cream. Spread with whipped topping; sprinkle with pecans. Serve immediately or freeze until serving. Serve with chocolate syrup. **Yield:** 9 servings.

## Glazed Ham Steaks

**1 can (8 ounces) sliced pineapple**
**2 boneless fully cooked ham steaks (about 2 pounds)**
**1/4 cup packed brown sugar**
**1/2 teaspoon Dijon mustard**
**4 maraschino cherries**

Drain pineapple, reserving 1 tablespoon juice; set pineapple aside (discard remaining juice or save for another use). Cut each ham steak in half; place on an ungreased baking pan.

In a small bowl, combine brown sugar, mustard and reserved juice. Spread over ham. Top with pineapple and cherries. Bake, uncovered, at 350° for 20-25 minutes or until heated through. **Yield:** 4 servings.

## Flavorful Green Beans

**1 package (16 ounces) frozen cut green beans**
**1/4 cup chopped green pepper**
**1 tablespoon real bacon bits**
**1/2 teaspoon dried minced onion**
**1/4 teaspoon salt**
**1/4 teaspoon pepper**

In a 1-qt. microwave-safe bowl, combine all ingredients. Cover and cook on high for 4-5 minutes or until beans are crisp-tender, stirring once. **Yield:** 4 servings.

**Editor's Note:** This recipe was tested in a 1,100-watt microwave.

# Warm Up With Lively Luncheon

ON A SATURDAY afternoon or weekday off, why not gather your family around for a satisfying home-style lunch? It's easy with the following recipes created by our Test Kitchen staff. The complete feast comes together in just 30 minutes.

Simply start by preparing the recipe for tasty Chili Corn Bread Wedges. With a little help from a boxed mix and a can of green chilies, you'll have no trouble baking a batch of the sweet moist triangles.

Those golden bites are perfect alongside sensational Chicken Tortilla Soup. Loaded with tender chicken, Mexican tomatoes and seasonings, this comfort food will bring southwestern flair to your table.

Strudel Pudding Dessert makes a yummy no-bake finale that's guaranteed to get rave reviews. In the fast four-ingredient treat, frozen toaster pastries form a delightful crust while whipped topping and chocolate pudding create a luscious mousse-like layer.

So go ahead...tempt your family at lunchtime or anytime with a memorable can't-miss meal.

## Chili Corn Bread Wedges

**1 package (8-1/2 ounces) corn bread/muffin mix**
**1 egg**
**1/3 cup milk**
**1 can (4 ounces) chopped green chilies**
**2 tablespoons sugar**
**3/4 cup frozen corn, thawed**

Place corn bread mix in a large bowl. Combine the egg, milk, chilies and sugar; stir into mix just until moistened. Fold in corn. Pour into a greased 9-in. round baking pan. Bake at 400° for 20-25 minutes or until a toothpick inserted near the center comes out clean. Cool on a wire rack for 5 minutes. Cut into wedges; serve warm. **Yield:** 6-8 servings.

## Chicken Tortilla Soup

✓ Uses less fat, sugar or salt. Includes Nutritional Analysis and Diabetic Exchanges.

**1 cup chopped onion**
**1 teaspoon minced garlic**
**3 cups chicken broth**
**1 can (14-1/2 ounces) Mexican diced tomatoes**
**1/2 teaspoon chili powder**
**1/4 teaspoon ground cumin**
**1-1/2 pounds boneless skinless chicken breasts, cubed**
**2 tablespoons cornstarch**
**1/4 cup cold water**
**1/4 cup shredded Mexican cheese blend**
**1 tablespoon minced fresh cilantro**
**Tortilla chips, optional**

In a large saucepan, combine the first six ingredients; bring to a boil. Add the chicken. Reduce the heat; cover and simmer for 4-6 minutes or until the chicken is no longer pink. Combine the cornstarch and water until smooth; gradually stir into soup.

Bring to a boil; cook and stir for 1 minute or until thickened. Top servings with cheese and cilantro. Serve with tortilla chips if desired. **Yield:** 6 servings.

**Nutritional Analysis:** One 1-cup serving (prepared with reduced-sodium chicken broth and reduced-fat cheese; calculated without tortilla chips) equals 183 calories, 3 g fat (1 g saturated fat), 67 mg cholesterol, 752 mg sodium, 9 g carbohydrate, 1 g fiber, 30 g protein. **Diabetic Exchanges:** 3 lean meat, 2 vegetable.

## Strudel Pudding Dessert

**4 frozen strawberry-filled strudel pastries**
**2 cups cold milk**
**1 package (5.9 ounces) instant chocolate pudding mix**
**1 carton (8 ounces) frozen whipped topping, thawed, *divided***

Toast pastries according to package directions; cool for 5 minutes. Meanwhile, in a bowl, whisk milk and pudding mix for 2 minutes. Let stand for 2 minutes or until soft-set; fold in 2 cups whipped topping.

Place pastries in an ungreased 8-in. square dish. Spread with pudding. Cover; refrigerate for at least 20 minutes. Cut into squares; dollop with remaining whipped topping. **Yield:** 9 servings.

# Feast Features Super Sandwich

FORGET fast food restaurants when lunchtime rolls around...or when you need a quick, casual meal for an afternoon get-together. Simply turn to the snappy spread featured here.

Keeping busy cooks in mind, our home economists came up with this mouth-watering menu you can assemble in only a half hour. It's perfect to enjoy while watching a midday football game, after coming in from outdoor activities or any time you want to surprise folks with fantastic fare.

Heated in the oven, Warm Layered Sandwich gives hungry diners eight different kinds of classic sandwich staples. Pile the hearty loaf high with meats, cheeses and veggies for a satisfying main course.

To continue the no-fuss feast, toss together Pepperoni Floret Salad. It mixes crunchy vegetables and tops them with convenient bottled dressing. Whenever time's short, you're sure to appreciate this appealing menu addition.

Dessert's a cinch with yummy Chocolate-Oat Toffee Bars. They feature sweet ingredients folks crave... but no one will guess how fast the scrumptious from-scratch sensations are to create.

## Warm Layered Sandwich

**1 unsliced round loaf (1 pound) Italian bread**
**2 tablespoons honey mustard**
**1/4 pound thinly sliced deli turkey**
**1/4 pound thinly sliced hard salami**
**1/4 pound sliced mozzarella cheese**
**2 thin slices red onion, separated into rings**
**1/4 pound thinly sliced deli ham**
**1/4 pound sliced Monterey Jack cheese**
**1 medium plum tomato, sliced**
**3 romaine leaves, torn**

Cut bread in half. Carefully hollow out bottom and top of loaf, leaving a 3/4-in. shell (discard removed bread or save for another use). Spread mustard on cut sides of bread.

On the bread bottom, layer the turkey, salami, mozzarella cheese, onion, ham, Monterey Jack cheese and tomato. Replace top. Wrap in heavy-duty foil; place on a baking sheet. Bake at 450° for 12-15 minutes or until heated through. Place romaine over tomato. Cut into wedges. **Yield:** 6 servings.

## Pepperoni Floret Salad

**2 cups fresh cauliflowerets**
**2 cups fresh broccoli florets**
**1 can (6 ounces) pitted ripe olives, drained**
**1/2 cup sliced pepperoni**
**1/4 cup pickled pepper rings**
**1/2 cup Italian salad dressing**

In a large bowl, combine the cauliflower, broccoli, olives, pepperoni and pepper rings. Add the dressing; toss to coat. Refrigerate leftovers. **Yield:** 6 servings.

## Chocolate-Oat Toffee Bars

**6 tablespoons butter**
**1 cup all-purpose flour**
**1 cup quick-cooking oats**
**1/3 cup packed brown sugar**
**3 tablespoons corn syrup**
**1 cup (6 ounces) semisweet chocolate chips**
**1/3 cup English toffee bits *or* almond brickle chips**
**1/3 cup chopped pecans**

In a large microwave-safe bowl, melt butter; stir in the flour, oats, brown sugar and corn syrup. Press into a greased 9-in. square baking pan.

Bake at 450° for 8-12 minutes or until golden brown. Place on a wire rack. Sprinkle with chocolate chips. Let stand for 5 minutes; spread chocolate over crust. Sprinkle with toffee bits and pecans. Refrigerate until chocolate is set. **Yield:** 15 servings.

# In-a-Hurry Pizza Is Sure to Please

WITH ERRANDS to run, school events to attend and other activities to do, the last thing busy moms want to worry about is what to make for dinner. That's why our home economists created the recipes found in this family-friendly menu.

Not only is the meal loaded with fantastic flavor, but it comes together in only 30 minutes. It even includes dessert!

Start by preparing the tooth-tingling Peanut Butter Candies. No one will believe you created the chocolate-covered bites in time for dinner. Or, whip some up to include on your cookie tray when entertaining.

With the candies chilling, you can begin the main course...Artichoke Chicken Pizza. Give it a try, and you'll see how easily convenience foods can transform your kitchen into an aromatic pizzeria.

Marinated artichoke hearts help give that rich entree a flavorful twist, breaking up ordinary weeknight fare. And if time's tight, save a few minutes by using a package of cooked and cubed chicken.

As the pizza finishes in the oven, toss together the refreshing Greek Romaine Salad. Topped with crumbled feta cheese, the speedy salad features cucumber, red pepper and a lemony homemade dressing.

## Peanut Butter Candies

**1 package (3 ounces) cream cheese, softened**
**1/4 cup chunky peanut butter**
**1/2 cup confectioners' sugar**
**1/2 cup graham cracker crumbs**
**1/4 cup semisweet chocolate chips**
**1 teaspoon shortening**

In a small mixing bowl, beat the cream cheese, peanut butter and confectioners' sugar until blended. Beat in cracker crumbs. Shape into 1-1/2-in. balls. Place on a waxed paper-lined baking sheet.

In a microwave, melt chocolate chips and shortening; stir until smooth. Carefully spoon a small amount of chocolate mixture over each candy. Refrigerate for at least 15 minutes. **Yield:** about 1 dozen.

## Artichoke Chicken Pizza

**1 sheet frozen puff pastry, thawed**
**1 pound boneless skinless chicken breasts, cubed**
**1 medium onion, halved and thinly sliced**
**2 tablespoons olive oil**
**2 cans (14-1/2 ounces *each*) diced tomatoes, well drained**
**2 jars (6-1/2 ounces *each*) marinated artichoke hearts, drained and coarsely chopped**
**1 can (2-1/4 ounces) sliced ripe olives, drained**
**3/4 teaspoon dried oregano**
**3/4 cup prepared Alfredo sauce**
**3/4 cup shredded Monterey Jack cheese**

On a lightly floured surface, roll out pastry into a 15-in. x 10-in. rectangle. Transfer to an ungreased 15-in. x 10-in. x 1-in. baking pan. Prick pastry thoroughly with a fork. Bake at 400° for 11-13 minutes or until lightly browned.

Meanwhile, in a large skillet, saute chicken and onion in oil until chicken juices run clear. Stir in the tomatoes, artichokes, olives and oregano. Remove from the heat.

Spread Alfredo sauce over crust. With a slotted spoon, spoon chicken mixture over sauce; sprinkle with the cheese. Bake for 5 minutes or until cheese is melted. **Yield:** 6-8 servings.

## Greek Romaine Salad

**4 cups torn romaine**
**1 medium sweet red pepper, julienned**
**1 cup chopped cucumber**
**1/4 cup olive oil**
**1 tablespoon lemon juice**
**1 teaspoon sugar**
**1/4 teaspoon garlic salt**
**1/4 teaspoon pepper**
**1 package (4 ounces) crumbled feta cheese**

In a large salad bowl, combine the romaine, red pepper and cucumber. In a jar with a tight-fitting lid, combine the oil, lemon juice, sugar, garlic salt and pepper; shake well. Drizzle over salad. Sprinkle with feta cheese; toss gently. **Yield:** 6-8 servings.

# Special Burgers Speed Up Supper

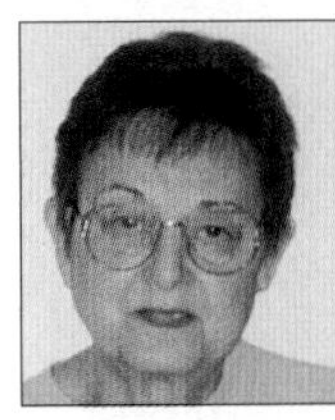

COOKING for two is a daily affair for Agnes Golian...one that she thoroughly enjoys. A retired nurse, Agnes shares a house with her sister, Helen, in Garfield Heights, Ohio. "I cook every day for my sister and me, and I bake at least once a week," says Agnes.

"Even though I'm retired, I have no trouble keeping busy. I enjoy arts and crafts, crossword puzzles and long walks," she notes. "Cooking and baking, however, are the real joys of my life."

Agnes credits her upbringing with her interest in cooking. "My grandparents owned a huge farm," she recalls. "Fresh produce was plentiful, and my grandmother was such a good cook!"

A number of culinary lessons must have been passed on to Agnes because she is rather talented in the kitchen, too.

"I try to prepare meals from scratch even when I don't have much time," explains Agnes. Such is the case with the 30-minute meal she shares here.

"When I fix this dinner, I begin with the dessert," Agnes adds. Perfect for entertaining, dainty Cream Cheese Delights are light as air yet easy to make.

"While the cookies are baking, I whip up the side dish," Agnes says of colorful Peachy Carrots. "This dish requires only three simple ingredients."

After setting the carrots in the microwave, Agnes has plenty of time to mix up juicy German-Style Hamburgers. "I read about these burgers nearly 40 years ago," she recalls. "I've made them once a month since then because they're so delicious."

## Cream Cheese Delights

**1/2 cup butter-flavored shortening**
**1 package (3 ounces) cream cheese, softened**
**1/2 cup sugar**
**1 egg yolk**
**1 teaspoon vanilla extract**
**1 cup all-purpose flour**
**1 teaspoon salt**
**Halved maraschino *or* candied cherries**

In a small mixing bowl, cream shortening, cream cheese and sugar. Beat in egg yolk and vanilla. Combine flour and salt; gradually add to the creamed mixture.

Drop by teaspoonfuls 2 in. apart onto greased baking sheets. Top each with a cherry half. Bake at 350° for 12-15 minutes or until lightly browned. Cool for 1 minute before removing to wire racks. **Yield:** 2 dozen.

## Peachy Carrots

✓ Uses less fat, sugar or salt. Includes Nutritional Analysis and Diabetic Exchanges.

**3 cups fresh baby carrots**
**1/3 cup peach preserves**
**2 teaspoons butter**

Place the carrots in a shallow microwave-safe dish. Cover and microwave on high for 10-12 minutes or until crisp-tender; drain. Add preserves and butter; cover and microwave for 30-60 seconds or until melted. Stir to coat. **Yield:** 4 servings.

**Nutritional Analysis:** One 3/4-cup serving (prepared with reduced-sugar preserves) equals 110 calories, 2 g fat (1 g saturated fat), 5 mg cholesterol, 64 mg sodium, 22 g carbohydrate, 2 g fiber, 1 g protein. **Diabetic Exchanges:** 1 starch, 1/2 fruit.

**Editor's Note:** This recipe was tested in a 1,100-watt microwave.

## German-Style Hamburgers

**1/2 cup frozen shredded hash brown potatoes, thawed**
**1/2 cup chopped onion**
**2 tablespoons Worcestershire sauce**
**1/2 teaspoon salt**
**1 pound ground beef**
**4 hamburger buns, split**
**Lettuce leaves and tomato slices**

In a bowl, combine potatoes, onion, Worcestershire sauce and salt. Crumble beef over mixture and mix well. Shape into four patties, about 1/2 in. thick. In a skillet, cook patties over medium-high heat for 10-12 minutes or until no longer pink, turning once. Serve on buns with lettuce and tomato. **Yield:** 4 servings.

# Festive Fare Is Fit For Guests

YOU don't have to wait for a special day to arrive in order to light candles, set the table with good china and enjoy a dazzling dinner with your family. With the mouth-watering meal offered here, you can celebrate the Christmas season over good food whenever you wish...and without much work on your part.

In a mere half hour, you can prepare and serve all of the reader recipes that follow. And even though this traditional supper is simple enough for weeknights, it can lend an impressive flair to Saturday dinner parties and other get-togethers as well.

No matter when you serve the memorable menu, everyone is sure to be delighted as you pass around a basket of oven-fresh Eggnog Biscuits.

"I was making biscuits during the holiday season one year and substituted eggnog for milk," explains Angie Jones from West Point, Utah. "These yummy bites were the outcome."

When the biscuits are in the oven, you can start the succulent Lemony Brussels Sprouts. "A tangy lemon glaze and toasted almonds make this quick vegetable dish popular at my dinner table with both family and company," writes Trisha Kruse.

"The recipe even pleases those who don't care for brussels sprouts," she notes from Boise, Idaho.

With the vegetables in the microwave, you can assemble the easy entree. Tender Cranberry Turkey is made entirely on the stovetop and ready in minutes.

"My husband and I love these special slices," says Sharen Clark of Sunnyside, Washington. "And they don't result in a lot of leftover turkey."

## Eggnog Biscuits

**1 cup plus 1 tablespoon biscuit/baking mix**
**1/3 cup eggnog**
**1/4 to 1/2 teaspoon ground nutmeg**

In a small bowl, combine biscuit mix and eggnog just until moistened. Turn onto a lightly floured surface; knead 8-10 times. Pat or roll out to 1/2-in. thickness; cut with a floured 2-1/2-in. biscuit cutter. Place 2 in. apart on a greased baking sheet. Sprinkle with nutmeg. Bake at 450° for 8-10 minutes or until lightly browned. Serve warm. **Yield:** 6-8 biscuits.

**Editor's Note:** This recipe was tested with commercially prepared eggnog.

## Lemony Brussels Sprouts

✓ Uses less fat, sugar or salt. Includes Nutritional Analysis and Diabetic Exchanges.

**1 pound fresh brussels sprouts, trimmed and halved**
**2 tablespoons water**
**2 tablespoons butter, melted**
**2 tablespoons lemon juice**
**2 teaspoons grated lemon peel**
**1/4 teaspoon salt**
**1/4 teaspoon lemon-pepper seasoning**
**1/4 cup sliced almonds, toasted**

Place the brussels sprouts in a microwave-safe dish; add water. Cover and cook on high for 7-9 minutes or until tender, stirring twice; drain. Stir in the butter, lemon juice, lemon peel, salt and lemon-pepper. Sprinkle with almonds. **Yield:** 4 servings.

**Nutritional Analysis:** One 3/4-cup serving (prepared with reduced-fat margarine) equals 113 calories, 6 g fat (1 g saturated fat), 0 cholesterol, 263 mg sodium, 12 g carbohydrate, 5 g fiber, 5 g protein. **Diabetic Exchanges:** 2 vegetable, 1 fat.

**Editor's Note:** This recipe was tested in a 1,100-watt microwave.

## Cranberry Turkey

**1 pound turkey breast slices**
**1 tablespoon vegetable oil**
**1 cup whole-berry cranberry sauce**
**2 tablespoons orange marmalade**
**1-1/2 teaspoons Dijon mustard**

In a large skillet, cook turkey in oil over medium-high heat for 3-4 minutes on each side or until juices run clear. Remove and keep warm. Combine the cranberry sauce, marmalade and mustard; add to skillet. Cook and stir until heated through. Serve with turkey. **Yield:** 4 servings.

# Entrees Please In A Half Hour

PREPARING a tasty main dish for your family meals or weekend get-togethers doesn't have to take any longer than 30 minutes...as all of the following reader recipes prove.

Each one requires just half an hour—or less—to make from start to finish. So enjoy the convenience of appetizing entrees that you can fix fast.

## Spring Lamb Supper

*Whenever I prepare brown rice, I fix a big batch so I'll have leftovers to make this quick dish on a busy weeknight. Tender chunks of lamb are tossed with summer squash, tomatoes and mushrooms for a hearty meal.* —*Michelle Armistead Marlboro, New Jersey*

**1 pound boneless lamb, cut into cubes**
**2 teaspoons olive oil**
**2 cups thinly sliced yellow summer squash**
**1/2 pound fresh mushrooms, sliced**
**2 medium tomatoes, seeded and chopped**
**1/2 cup sliced green onions**
**3 cups cooked brown rice**
**1 teaspoon salt**
**1/2 teaspoon garlic powder**
**1/2 teaspoon pepper**
**1/2 teaspoon dried rosemary, crushed**

In a large skillet, saute lamb in oil until no longer pink; remove from the skillet with a slotted spoon. In the same skillet, stir-fry squash, mushrooms, tomatoes and onions for 2-3 minutes or until tender. Return lamb to the pan. Stir in the rice and seasonings; cook and stir until heated through. **Yield:** 4 servings.

## Chicken 'n' Noodle Skillet

*I am a mom of three grown boys. Back when they were in school and I needed to put a meal on the table in a hurry, I could always count on this easy recipe. Served with a simple green salad and milk, it always filled them up.* —*Eileen Hagist Bancroft, Iowa*

**2 packages (4.3 ounces *each*) quick-cooking chicken flavor noodles and sauce mix**
**1-1/2 cups cubed cooked chicken**
**1 can (4 ounces) mushroom stems and pieces, drained**
**1 tube (12 ounces) refrigerated buttermilk biscuits**

In a large skillet, prepare the noodles and sauce mix according to package directions. Stir in chicken and mushrooms; cook over medium heat until heated through. Meanwhile, bake the biscuits according to package directions. Transfer the noodle mixture to a serving bowl; top with biscuits. **Yield:** 5 servings.

## Philly Cheese Steak Pizza

*(Pictured below)*

*I cover a crescent roll crust with deli beef, mozzarella cheese and sauteed veggies. The quick combination offers the terrific taste of the traditional sandwich in a fun new way.* —*Maria Regakis, Somerville, Massachusetts*

**1 tube (8 ounces) refrigerated crescent rolls**
**1 medium green pepper, chopped**
**1 medium onion, chopped**
**1/4 teaspoon beef bouillon granules**
**2 tablespoons olive oil**
**1/2 pound thinly sliced deli roast beef**
**1 tablespoon prepared Italian salad dressing**
**1-1/2 cups (6 ounces) shredded mozzarella cheese**

Unroll crescent roll dough and place in an ungreased 13-in. x 9-in. x 2-in. baking pan. Press onto the bottom and 1/2 in. up the sides to form a crust; seal perforations. Bake at 375° for 7-10 minutes or until lightly browned.

Meanwhile, in a large skillet, saute the green pepper, onion and bouillon in oil until vegetables are tender; set aside. Arrange beef over crust. Brush with the salad dressing and sprinkle with mozzarella cheese. Bake 4-5 minutes longer or until the cheese is melted. Top with green pepper mixture. Cut into squares. **Yield:** 6 servings.

Philly Cheese Steak Pizza

## Mandarin Orange Chicken

*(Pictured below)*

*Jazz up meals with this mouth-watering recipe. Simply treat juicy chicken breasts to a tangy sauce, featuring plenty of citrus flavor.* —*Clara Coulston*
*Washington Court House, Ohio*

✓ Uses less fat, sugar or salt. Includes Nutritional Analysis and Diabetic Exchanges.

**4 boneless skinless chicken breast halves (4 ounces *each*)**
**2 tablespoons all-purpose flour**
**1/4 teaspoon salt**
**1/4 teaspoon pepper**
**1 tablespoon canola oil**
**1/2 cup orange juice**
**1/4 cup orange marmalade**
**2 tablespoons honey mustard**
**1/4 teaspoon dried rosemary, crushed**
**1 can (11 ounces) mandarin oranges, drained**
**1 teaspoon grated orange peel**
**Hot cooked rice, optional**

Flatten chicken to 1/4-in. thickness. In a shallow dish, combine the flour, salt and pepper; coat chicken. In a large skillet, brown chicken in oil on both sides.

Combine orange juice, marmalade, mustard and rosemary; pour over chicken. Bring to a boil; cook for 5-8 minutes or until chicken juices run clear and sauce is thickened. Stir in oranges and orange peel. Serve over rice if desired. **Yield:** 4 servings.

**Nutritional Analysis:** One serving (prepared with reduced-sugar marmalade; calculated without rice) equals 254 calories, 6 g fat (1 g saturated fat), 66 mg cholesterol, 240 mg sodium, 21 g carbohydrate, 1 g fiber, 27 g protein. **Diabetic Exchanges:** 3 lean meat, 1-1/2 fruit.

Mandarin Orange Chicken

## Veggie Pork Saute

*When time is of the essence, try this swift meal-in-one. I serve a lightly sauced combination of pork, mushrooms, zucchini and tomato over a bed of cooked rice.*
—*Audra LeGay, Grand Junction, Colorado*

**5 tablespoons all-purpose flour, *divided***
**1 teaspoon Italian seasoning**
**1/2 teaspoon salt**
**1/4 teaspoon pepper**
**1 pound boneless pork, cubed**
**5 tablespoons butter, *divided***
**1 tablespoon olive oil**
**1 medium onion, halved and sliced**
**2 celery ribs, sliced**
**1/2 cup sliced fresh mushrooms**
**1 medium zucchini, halved and sliced**
**1 medium tomato, diced**
**1-1/2 cups chicken broth**
**1 tablespoon balsamic vinegar**
**Hot cooked rice**

In a large resealable plastic bag, combine 3 tablespoons flour, Italian seasoning, salt and pepper. Add pork; seal bag and shake to coat. In a large skillet over medium-high heat, brown pork in 3 tablespoons butter and oil; remove and keep warm.

In same skillet, saute onion, celery and mushrooms in remaining butter for 5 minutes. Add pork and zucchini; saute until meat juices run clear and vegetables are tender.

Stir in the tomato. Place the remaining flour in a small bowl; stir in the broth and vinegar until smooth. Add to skillet. Bring to a boil; cook and stir for 2 minutes or until thickened. Serve with rice. **Yield:** 4 servings.

## Creamy Ham Macaroni

*I jazz up macaroni with plenty of hearty ham, cheddar cheese and a jar of sliced mushrooms to make this family-pleasing fare. If you like, sprinkle each serving with chopped cashews for added flavor and a bit of crunch.*
—*Beulah Johnston, Fort Myers, Florida*

**2 cups uncooked elbow macaroni**
**1 can (10-3/4 ounces) condensed cream of mushroom soup, undiluted**
**2/3 cup milk**
**2 cups (8 ounces) shredded cheddar cheese**
**2 cups cubed fully cooked ham**
**1 jar (4-1/2 ounces) sliced mushrooms, drained**
**1 jar (2 ounces) diced pimientos, drained**

Cook macaroni according to package directions. Meanwhile, in a large saucepan, whisk soup and milk; stir in cheese. Cook and stir over medium heat until cheese is

Cantaloupe Chicken Salad

melted. Drain macaroni; add to pan. Stir in ham, mushrooms and pimientos; heat through. **Yield:** 4 servings.

## Onion Steak Sandwiches

*My husband, Harold, and I like to have these delicious steak sandwiches for dinner as a change of pace.*
*—Sharon Crider, Lebanon, Missouri*

**1 can (8 ounces) tomato sauce**
**1 teaspoon dried oregano**
**1/2 teaspoon dried minced onion**
**1/2 teaspoon Worcestershire sauce**
**1/4 teaspoon salt**
**1/8 teaspoon garlic salt**
**1/8 teaspoon pepper**
**1 medium onion, halved and thinly sliced**
**3 tablespoons butter**
**1-1/2 pounds beef round steak, cut into thin strips**
**1 tablespoon olive oil**
**6 Italian rolls, split**

In a small saucepan, combine the first seven ingredients. Bring to a boil. Reduce the heat; cover and simmer for 10 minutes.

Meanwhile, in a large skillet, saute onion in butter until tender; add the steak. Cook and stir until meat reaches desired doneness; drain. Stir in the tomato sauce mixture. Brush oil over cut side of rolls; fill with steak mixture. **Yield:** 6 servings.

## Cantaloupe Chicken Salad

*(Pictured above)*

*When I want a refreshing meal, I fix this simple chicken salad with sweet cantaloupe. For a different presentation, arrange the melon like flower petals on a lettuce-lined plate, then mound the salad in the center.*
*—Shirley Leister, West Chester, Pennsylvania*

**1-1/2 cups diced cooked chicken**
**2 celery ribs, sliced**
**1/3 cup mayonnaise**
**2 tablespoons diced pimientos**
**1 tablespoon finely chopped onion**
**1/2 teaspoon salt**
**1/8 teaspoon pepper**
**1 small cantaloupe**
**Lettuce leaves**
**3 tablespoons lemon juice**

In a bowl, combine the first seven ingredients; stir well. Cut cantaloupe in half; discard seeds. Cut into 1-in.-wide wedges; peel. Place cantaloupe on four lettuce-lined plates; sprinkle with lemon juice. Serve chicken salad alongside melon. **Yield:** 4 servings.

Orange Pork Stir-Fry

## Orange Pork Stir-Fry

*(Pictured above)*

*Orange juice and grated orange peel lend a citrusy touch to this colorful pork-and-vegetable medley. It gets even more flavor from teriyaki sauce, mustard and garlic.*
*—Kathleen Romaniuk, Chomedey, Quebec*

✓ Uses less fat, sugar or salt. Includes Nutritional Analysis and Diabetic Exchanges.

**2 teaspoons cornstarch**
**1/3 cup orange juice**
**1/3 cup teriyaki sauce**
**1 tablespoon Dijon mustard**
**2 teaspoons minced fresh gingerroot**
**1 teaspoon minced garlic**
**1/2 to 1 teaspoon grated orange peel**
**1 pound pork tenderloin, cut into 2-inch strips**
**1 tablespoon canola oil**
**1 package (16 ounces) frozen Japanese-style stir-fry vegetables**
**Hot cooked rice**

In a small bowl, combine cornstarch and orange juice until smooth. Stir in the teriyaki sauce, mustard, ginger, garlic and orange peel; set aside.

In a large skillet or wok, stir-fry pork in oil until no longer pink; remove and keep warm. Add vegetables to the pan; cook and stir for 2-3 minutes or until tender. Stir orange juice mixture; add to pan. Bring to a boil; cook and stir for 1 minute or until thickened. Stir in pork. Serve with rice. **Yield:** 4 servings.

**Nutritional Analysis:** One 3/4-cup serving (prepared with reduced-sodium teriyaki sauce; calculated without rice) equals 271 calories, 12 g fat (4 g saturated fat), 84 mg cholesterol, 780 mg sodium, 14 g carbohydrate, 2 g fiber, 26 g protein. **Diabetic Exchanges:** 3 lean meat, 1 vegetable, 1 fat, 1/2 fruit.

## Spinach Cheese Tortellini

*I whip up this creamy pasta dish for potlucks. It's a hit at every gathering. I serve it from the slow cooker to keep it warm.* *—Jamie Staggs, Greenbrier, Arkansas*

**1 package (19 ounces) frozen cheese tortellini**
**1/2 pound sliced fresh mushrooms**
**1/2 cup butter**
**1 package (10 ounces) frozen chopped spinach, thawed and squeezed dry**
**1 large tomato, diced**
**1 package (8 ounces) cream cheese, cubed**
**3/4 cup milk**
**3 tablespoons grated Parmesan cheese**
**1 teaspoon garlic salt**
**1 teaspoon Italian seasoning**
**1/2 teaspoon pepper**

Cook tortellini according to package directions. Meanwhile, in a large skillet, saute mushrooms in butter until tender. Add the spinach and tomato; cook and stir for 3 minutes. Stir in the remaining ingredients.

Bring to a boil over medium heat. Reduce the heat; simmer, uncovered, for 15 minutes or until the cheese is melted, stirring occasionally. Drain tortellini; add to skillet. Cook 2-3 minutes longer or until bubbly. **Yield:** 8 servings.

## Au Gratin Turkey Skillet

*This is a tasty treatment for leftover turkey. The creamy comfort food comes together in a snap with a package of au gratin potatoes, some seasonings and a handful of kitchen staples.* *—Ann Wood, Pleasant Hill, Oregon*

**2-1/2 cups water**
**1 package (4.9 ounces) au gratin potatoes**
**1/2 cup chopped onion**

1/2 cup milk
2 tablespoons butter
1/2 teaspoon poultry seasoning
1/4 teaspoon dried rosemary, crushed
2 cups cubed cooked turkey
2 cups frozen peas, thawed

In a large skillet, combine the water, potatoes with contents of sauce mix, onion, milk, butter, poultry seasoning and rosemary. Bring to a boil. Reduce heat; cover and simmer for 15 minutes or until potatoes are tender. Gently stir in turkey and peas; heat through. **Yield:** 4 servings.

## Maple-Apple Pork Slices

*I tried a dish similar to this one while I was on a ski trip. I searched far and wide for the recipe. Once I found it, I turned it into this easy dinner. —Cathy Schmid Pittsburgh, Pennsylvania*

**1 pound pork tenderloin, cut into 1/4-inch slices**
**1/4 cup seasoned bread crumbs**
**2 tablespoons olive oil**
**2 medium tart apples, peeled and sliced**
**1/2 cup apple juice *or* cider**
**1/4 cup maple syrup**
**1 tablespoon prepared mustard**
**1/4 teaspoon salt**
**1/4 teaspoon pepper**

Coat pork slices with bread crumbs. In a large skillet, cook pork in oil over medium-high heat for 2 minutes on each side.

Add the apples and juice; cover and cook for 10 minutes or until the apples are tender. Combine the syrup, mustard, salt and pepper; pour over the pork mixture. Cook, uncovered, for 2 minutes or until heated through. **Yield:** 4 servings.

## Country Skillet

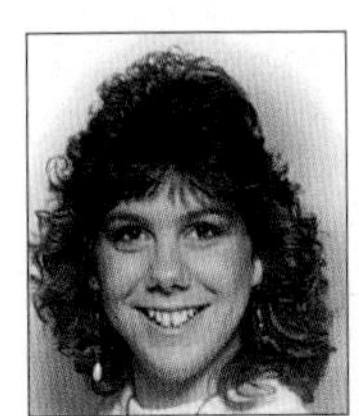

*Whenever I need a fast and flavorful meal-in-one, I turn to this filling combination of kielbasa, rice and veggies sprinkled with Parmesan cheese. It's a hearty dish that's nice for cool weather but tastes great any time of the year. —Terri Adrian Lake City, Florida*

**1 pound fully cooked kielbasa *or* Polish sausage, cut into 1/2-inch slices**
**1/2 cup chopped onion**
**1 tablespoon vegetable oil**
**1-1/2 cups water**
**1 can (10-3/4 ounces) condensed cream of celery soup, undiluted**
**1/2 teaspoon dried basil**
**1/4 teaspoon dried thyme**
**1/4 teaspoon pepper**
**1 package (10 ounces) frozen cut broccoli, thawed**
**1 jar (4-1/2 ounces) sliced mushrooms, drained**
**1 cup uncooked instant rice**
**1/4 cup grated Parmesan cheese**

In a large skillet, cook sausage and onion in oil until onion is tender; drain. Combine the water, soup, basil, thyme and pepper; add to skillet.

Stir in the broccoli and mushrooms. Bring to a boil. Stir in the rice. Cover and remove from the heat. Let stand for 5-7 minutes or until rice is tender. Sprinkle with Parmesan cheese. **Yield:** 4-6 servings.

## Basil Caesar Salmon

*(Pictured below)*

*Since I love both salmon and Caesar salad, I created this "de-lish fish" dish that combines both of those flavors. It's hard to believe it takes so little effort to prepare such a showy entree...and it tastes as good as it looks. —Laurie LaClair, North Richland Hills, Texas*

**4 salmon fillets (8 ounces *each*)**
**1/4 cup creamy Caesar salad dressing**
**Pepper to taste**
**1 cup Caesar salad croutons, crushed**
**1/2 cup grated Parmesan cheese**
**2 teaspoons dried basil**
**2 tablespoons olive oil**

Place salmon in a greased 15-in. x 10-in. x 1-in. baking pan. Spoon salad dressing over fillets; sprinkle with pepper. Combine croutons, Parmesan cheese and basil; sprinkle over fillets and gently press into dressing. Drizzle with oil. Bake, uncovered, at 350° for 15-20 minutes or until fish flakes easily with a fork. **Yield:** 4 servings.

Basil Caesar Salmon

## Spanish Rice

*As a wife and mother on a busy farm, I like family-pleasing recipes that are simple. This is a favorite of ours that came from Liz Cazer, a member of the local 4-H club that I lead. —Mary Anderson, De Valls Bluff, Arkansas*

**1/2 cup chopped onion**
**1/2 cup chopped sweet red pepper**
**2 tablespoons butter**
**1 can (14-1/2 ounces) diced tomatoes, drained**
**1 cup water**
**1 cup uncooked instant rice**
**1/2 to 3/4 teaspoon garlic salt**
**Dash cayenne pepper**
**1/2 cup shredded mozzarella cheese**

In a large saucepan, saute onion and red pepper in butter until tender. Add the tomatoes, water, rice, garlic salt and cayenne. Bring to a boil. Reduce heat; cover and simmer for 5-10 minutes or until liquid is absorbed. Sprinkle with cheese. **Yield:** 4 servings.

## Chili Cheese Turnovers

*(Pictured below)*

*Serve these stuffed pockets with a creamy dipping sauce. They can make a great supper, grab-and-go lunch...even a late-night snack. Using tubes of refrigerated dough keeps the preparation quick. —Margaret Wilson, Hemet, California*

Chili Cheese Turnovers

**2 tubes (10 ounces *each*) refrigerated pizza crust**
**2 cups (8 ounces) shredded Mexican cheese blend**
**1 can (15 ounces) chili without beans**
**1 can (15 ounces) ranch-style beans *or* chili beans, drained**
**1 can (10 ounces) diced tomatoes and green chilies, drained**
**1 cup (8 ounces) sour cream**

On a lightly floured surface, press pizza dough into two 12-in. squares. Cut each into four 6-in. squares. In a bowl, combine the cheese, chili and beans. Spoon 1/2 cup in the center of each square. Fold dough diagonally over filling; press edges to seal.

Place in two greased 15-in. x 10-in. x 1-in. baking pans. Bake at 425° for 13-18 minutes or until golden brown. Cool for 5 minutes. Meanwhile, in a small bowl, combine tomatoes and sour cream. Serve with turnovers. **Yield:** 8 servings.

## Microwaved Italian Eggplant

*If you're trying to cut back on meat, you'll appreciate this main dish. The microwave makes it fast to fix these crumb-topped eggplant slices. —Joan Donahue, Bensalem, Pennsylvania*

**2 small eggplant, peeled**
**1/4 cup dried bread crumbs**
**1/2 teaspoon dried oregano**
**1 tablespoon mayonnaise**
**1 cup spaghetti sauce**
**1 cup (4 ounces) shredded mozzarella cheese**
**2 tablespoons grated Parmesan cheese**

Cut eggplant into 3/4-in. slices. In a small bowl, combine the bread crumbs and oregano. Brush one side of each eggplant slice with mayonnaise. Dip mayonnaise side into crumb mixture, then place crumb side up in a shallow 2-qt. microwave-safe dish. Cover and microwave on high for 8-10 minutes or until tender. Drizzle with spaghetti sauce and sprinkle with cheeses. Cook, uncovered, for 2-3 minutes longer or until cheese is melted. **Yield:** 4 servings.

**Editor's Note:** This recipe was tested in an 850-watt microwave.

## Picante Pork Skillet

*I found this recipe around 10 years ago and added the picante sauce, vegetables and crunchy water chestnuts for extra flair. I've also used apricot preserves and orange marmalade in place of the peach preserves. —Margaret Morton, Eau Claire, Michigan*

✓ Uses less fat, sugar or salt. Includes Nutritional Analysis and Diabetic Exchanges.

**1 pound boneless pork, cut into 3/4-inch cubes**

2 tablespoons taco seasoning
1 tablespoon vegetable *or* canola oil
1 medium onion, chopped
1 medium green pepper, chopped
2 celery ribs, chopped
1 jar (8 ounces) salsa
1 cup picante sauce *or* additional salsa
1 can (8 ounces) water chestnuts, drained and finely chopped
1/3 cup peach preserves
Hot cooked rice

In a large resealable plastic bag, combine the pork and taco seasoning. Seal and shake to coat. In a large skillet or wok, stir-fry the pork in oil for 3 minutes.

Add the onion, green pepper and celery; stir-fry until vegetables are tender. Add the salsa, picante sauce, water chestnuts and preserves. Cook until heated through. Serve with rice. **Yield:** 4 servings.

**Nutritional Analysis:** One 1-cup serving (prepared with pork tenderloin and 16 ounces salsa; calculated without picante sauce and rice) equals 327 calories, 8 g fat (2 g saturated fat), 74 mg cholesterol, 987 mg sodium, 39 g carbohydrate, 6 g fiber, 26 g protein. **Diabetic Exchanges:** 3 lean meat, 2 vegetable, 1 starch, 1 fruit.

Corn Bread Hamburger Pie

## Corn Bread Hamburger Pie

(Pictured at right)

*This one-dish skillet supper is a big hit with children. We've added green beans and other vegetables to it, and it always turns out. To speed up preparation, use frozen chopped green pepper and onion.* —Carol Ellis, Quartzsite, Arizona

1 pound ground beef
1 medium onion, chopped
1 medium green pepper, chopped
1 can (10-3/4 ounces) condensed tomato soup, undiluted
1/4 cup salsa
2 tablespoons ketchup
1 tablespoon steak sauce, optional
1 package (8-1/2 ounces) corn bread/muffin mix
Minced fresh parsley, optional

In a 10-in. ovenproof skillet, cook the beef, onion and green pepper over medium heat until meat is no longer pink; drain. Stir in the soup, salsa, ketchup and steak sauce if desired. Prepare corn bread batter according to package directions; let stand for 2 minutes. Spoon over beef mixture. Bake at 400° for 15 minutes or until lightly browned. Sprinkle with parsley if desired. **Yield:** 4-6 servings.

## Noodle Skillet

*Looking for a mild main dish to satisfy picky palates? Try this beefy stovetop supper. It's a very quick dish. We love noodles, so it's one of our favorites.* —Katie Kuepfer, Milverton, Ontario

5 cups uncooked egg noodles
3/4 pound ground beef
1 medium onion, chopped
1-1/4 cups water
1 can (6 ounces) tomato paste
2 teaspoons chili powder
1 garlic clove, minced
3/4 teaspoon salt
1/4 teaspoon pepper

Cook noodles according to package directions. Meanwhile, in a large skillet, cook beef and onion over medium heat until meat is no longer pink; drain.

Stir in the water, tomato paste, chili powder, garlic, salt and pepper. Bring to a boil. Reduce heat; simmer, uncovered, for 5 minutes. Drain noodles; stir into skillet. **Yield:** 4 servings.

### Mincing Fresh Garlic

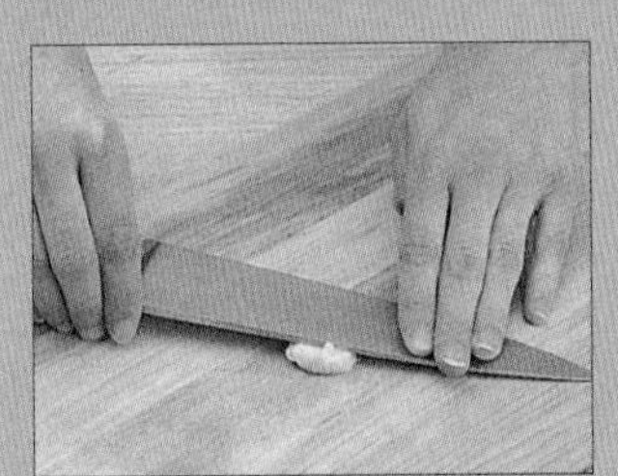

WHEN a recipe calls for fresh garlic, you can purchase it in a jar. But creating your own from fresh cloves takes mere moments.

To peel a fresh garlic clove, crush it using the blade of a chef's knife as shown in the photo above. Then peel away the skin.

Mince the peeled clove using the same knife, cutting pieces that are about 1/8 inch or smaller in size.

# Chapter 3

# Thinking Up a Theme

LIKE TO HOST parties for family and friends? It's easy to turn ordinary get-togethers into extraordinary ones.

By creating five simple menus featuring different themes, the home economists in the *Quick Cooking* Test Kitchen have done the planning for you so your special event will be fun, festive and fuss-free.

From delicious fishermen's fare and a special storybook spread to nature-inspired nibbles, a funny April Fool's Day feast and munchies to light up movie night, you can easily create long-remembered occasions for your relatives and friends with just a short time spent in the kitchen.

**NURTURED NIBBLES.** Clockwise from top left: Garden Snake Sandwiches, Carrot-Shaped Cheese Spread, Flowering Peach Puffs and Dragonfly Snacks (all recipes on p. 53).

# Anglers Will Take the Bait for Fun Feast

PLANNING a special supper or birthday party for the fishermen in your family? Whet their appetites with this string of delicious dishes that they'll go for hook, line and sinker.

This mouth-watering menu from our Test Kitchen is quick and easy to prepare. And the net result will lure guests to your table in no time.

To start off, share the bounty of the deep by serving flaky fish fillets that get a spicy twist from a handful of seasonings.

You'll reel in compliments with the summery salad served in a metal pail lined with a plastic bag. And corn muffins sporting "hooked" snack crackers will get more than a nibble.

For the finale, dish out a delectable chocolate dessert that reflects your guests' preferred pastime.

They are sure to declare the entire meal a trophy-sized treat...and that's no fish story!

## Angler's Delight

*Cayenne pepper, taco seasoning and cumin give this fried fish a colorful coating and fantastic southwestern flavor. The slightly crispy fillets are accented by a splash of lime. Use haddock, cod or any firm fish you prefer.*

**6 frozen haddock *or* cod fillets (6 ounces *each*), thawed**
**1/2 cup lime juice**
**1/2 cup all-purpose flour**
**2 tablespoons taco seasoning**
**1/2 teaspoon ground cumin**
**1/4 teaspoon cayenne pepper**
**3 tablespoons vegetable *or* canola oil**

In a large resealable plastic bag, combine fish and lime juice; seal bag and turn to coat. Let stand for 15 minutes. In a shallow dish, combine the flour, taco seasoning, cumin and cayenne. Drain fillets; coat with flour mixture.

In a large skillet, cook fillets in oil over medium-high heat for 6-8 minutes on each side or until fish flakes easily with a fork. **Yield:** 6 servings.

## Bait and Tackle Salad

*Rising to the aquatic occasion, this fresh vegetable medley mixes tomato "bobbers" with chopped zucchini, yellow squash, cilantro and a sweet tangy vinaigrette.*

**2 cups grape *or* cherry tomatoes**
**2 small zucchini, coarsely chopped**
**2 small yellow summer squash, coarsely chopped**
**2 tablespoons minced fresh cilantro**
**5 tablespoons white wine vinegar**
**3 tablespoons sugar**
**1 teaspoon Dijon mustard**
**1/4 teaspoon salt**
**1/8 teaspoon pepper**
**2 tablespoons olive oil**

In a large bowl, combine tomatoes, zucchini, yellow squash and cilantro. In a blender, combine vinegar, sugar, mustard, salt and pepper. While processing, gradually add oil. Drizzle over vegetables; toss to coat. Cover and refrigerate for at least 20 minutes. **Yield:** 6 servings.

## Cane Pole Corn Muffins

*Guests will grin when they cast a glance at these fast-to-fix corn muffins. Pretzel-stick cane poles dangle fish-shaped snack crackers that are tied with pieces of chive.*

**1 package (8-1/2 ounces) corn bread/muffin mix**
**1/2 cup shredded cheddar cheese**
**1 jalapeno pepper, seeded and chopped**
**1 tablespoon minced chives**
**6 pieces fresh chives**
**6 pretzel sticks**
**3/4 cup miniature fish-shaped crackers**
**1/3 cup spreadable chive and onion cream cheese**

Prepare corn bread batter according to package directions for muffins; stir in the cheddar cheese, jalapeno and minced chives. Fill greased muffin cups three-fourths full. Bake at 400° for 14-16 minutes or until golden brown. Cool for 5 minutes before removing from pan to a wire rack to cool completely.

For fishing poles, tie one end of a piece of chive to each pretzel stick and the other end to a fish cracker. Spread muffin tops with cream cheese. Insert a fishing pole into each muffin. Place on a serving platter. Sprinkle remaining fish crackers on platter. **Yield:** 6 muffins.

**Editor's Note:** When cutting or seeding hot peppers, use rubber or plastic gloves to protect your hands. Avoid touching your face.

## Gone Fishing Mocha Pie

*Before long, this creamy dessert featuring every angler's favorite phrase will be "gone" itself! A chocolate crumb crust holds rich mocha filling that's delightfully decorated.*

**1 package (3 ounces) cream cheese, softened**
**1/3 cup hot fudge ice cream topping**
**1 chocolate crumb crust (9 inches)**
**2 packages (2.8 ounces *each*) mocha mousse mix**
**1-1/2 cups whipped topping, *divided***
**1 piece black shoestring licorice (about 8 inches)**
**1 gummy worm**

In a small mixing bowl, beat cream cheese and hot fudge topping; drop by tablespoonfuls over crust and carefully spread. Prepare mousse mix according to package directions; fold in 1 cup whipped topping. Spread over cream cheese mixture. Chill for 20 minutes.

Place remaining whipped topping in a resealable plastic bag; cut a small hole in a corner of bag. Pipe "Gone Fishing" on pie. Insert a medium star pastry tip into bag; pipe topping around edges of pie. Position licorice on pie in the shape of a fishhook; add gummy worm. **Yield:** 6-8 servings.

# April Fool's Fare Is Deceptively Delicious

DO YOU HAVE a practical joker in your household? On April 1 of each year, does your prankster put salt in the sugar bowl?

Then turn the tables tastefully with a memorable menu that will make April Fool's Day fun for all.

Our Test Kitchen came up with these tricky treats that will tickle your family's taste buds as well as their funny bones.

Start off by serving the luscious-looking layer cake. Once they bite into a savory slice, they'll know this is no ordinary meal.

And striving to sip the make-ahead beverages will confirm your gang's suspicions that the joke, however tasty, is on them.

Tiny taco salads finish the fun feast. These tempting cups are sweetly stacked with sundae fixin's rather than spicy southwestern ingredients.

## Layer Cake Meat Loaf

*If the kids are always asking to eat dessert first, here's your chance. The moist "cake" layers are really full-flavored meat loaves that are decoratively "frosted" with instant mashed potatoes. Ketchup and mustard "icing" helps complete the look.*

**2 eggs, beaten**
**1 can (5-1/2 ounces) spicy tomato juice**
**1/2 cup seasoned bread crumbs**
**1/2 cup quick-cooking oats**
**1 medium onion, chopped**
**1 medium green pepper, chopped**
**1 teaspoon chili powder**
**1/2 teaspoon salt**
**1/2 teaspoon pepper**
**2 pounds ground beef**
**MASHED POTATOES:**
**4-2/3 cups water**
**1 cup plus 2 tablespoons milk**
**7 tablespoons butter, cubed**
**1-3/4 teaspoons salt**
**4-2/3 cups mashed potato flakes**
**Ketchup and mustard**

In a large bowl, combine the first nine ingredients. Crumble beef over mixture and mix well. Pat into two ungreased 9-in. square baking pans. Bake at 350° for 15-20 minutes or until meat is no longer pink and a meat thermometer reads 160°; drain. Let stand for 10 minutes.

Meanwhile, in a large saucepan, bring the water, milk, butter and salt to a boil. Stir in potato flakes. Remove from the heat. Invert one meat loaf onto a serving platter; invert the second loaf onto a cutting board. Spread 1-1/2 cups mashed potatoes over loaf on the platter. Carefully slide second loaf onto the potatoes.

Spread 3-1/2 cups mashed potatoes over top and sides. Spoon remaining mashed potatoes into a pastry bag with open star tip #195. Pipe a shell border around bottom and top edges.

Place ketchup and mustard in resealable plastic bags; cut a small hole in a corner of each bag. Pipe ketchup and mustard on cake. **Yield:** 8-10 servings.

## Tricky Taco Cups

*Fools of all ages will fall in love with these sneaky sweets that look like taco salads. Waffle bowls full of ice cream are topped with tinted coconut "lettuce" and "cheese", maraschino cherry "tomatoes" and black licorice "olives".*

**1 cup ground pecans**
**1 pint chocolate *or* vanilla ice cream**
**1-3/4 teaspoons water, *divided***
**6 drops green food coloring**
**1-3/4 cups flaked coconut, *divided***
**4 drops yellow food coloring**
**6 waffle ice cream bowls**
**6 tablespoons whipped topping**
**3 pieces black rope licorice, cut into 1/4-inch slices**
**9 maraschino cherries, patted dry, halved**

Place pecans in a shallow bowl. Drop small scoops of ice cream into pecans; roll to coat. Place on a baking sheet; freeze until firm. In a large resealable plastic bag, combine 1-1/2 teaspoons water and green food coloring; add 1-1/2 cups coconut. Seal bag and shake to tint. In a small resealable plastic bag, combine yellow food coloring and remaining water; add remaining coconut. Seal bag and shake to tint.

Place coated ice cream balls in waffle bowls. Sprinkle with green coconut. Dollop with whipped topping. Sprinkle with the yellow coconut and licorice; top with the cherries. Serve immediately. **Yield:** 6 servings.

## April Fool's Berry Sodas

*These berry "beverages" look inviting to sip, but they're actually gelatin that's tricky to suck through a straw. So keep some spoons handy!*

**2 packages (3 ounces *each*) strawberry gelatin**
**3/4 cup sliced fresh strawberries**
**3/4 cup fresh raspberries**
**3/4 cup fresh blueberries**
**6 drinking straws**

Prepare gelatin according to package directions. Refrigerate until partially set, about 2 hours. Stir in berries. Pour into six tall drink or soda glasses. Insert a straw into each glass. Refrigerate until set. **Yield:** 6 servings.

### Pasta Prank

According to the Museum of Hoaxes, the top April Fool's Day hoax of all time was the "Swiss Spaghetti Harvest" segment of the BBC news show *Panorama*. In 1957, the respected news show announced that, thanks to a mild winter and virtual elimination of the dreaded spaghetti weevil, Swiss farmers were enjoying a bumper spaghetti crop.

The announcement included footage of peasants pulling strands of spaghetti down from trees. Huge numbers of viewers were fooled, and many called to ask how they could grow spaghetti trees.

# Storybook Supper Is Sure to Get Smiles

HUMPTY DUMPTY would fall head over heels for these nifty nursery-rhyme nibbles. Our Test Kitchen staff created this Mother Goose menu that's just perfect for celebrating a youngster's birthday or other special day.

Best of all, each item comes together like magic and takes no more than a half hour to prepare.

Start with a time-saving "tea" that's easier than boiling water. Let it chill in the refrigerator while you whip up the rest of the meal.

Juicy cheeseburgers will satisfy the hungry Jacks and Jills in your household. And they'll get a twinkle in their eye when they reach for the tasty homemade tortilla chips served alongside.

For dessert, sassy spiders go together easily with store-bought snack cakes, canned frosting and candy. Prepare them early in the day...or let your guests assemble them at the party for a fun activity.

## I'm a Little Teapot Tea

*There's no need to get steamed up over this sweet spot of "tea". The cool colorful punch stirs up in a wink with lemonade and strawberry drink mixes while club soda provides plenty of fizz.*

**4 cups cold water**
**1/2 cup sugar**
**1/2 cup sweetened lemonade drink mix**
**1 envelope unsweetened strawberry soft drink mix**
**1 tablespoon lime juice**
**1 liter club soda, chilled**

In a large pitcher, combine the first five ingredients until dissolved. Just before serving, stir in soda. **Yield:** about 2 quarts.

## Jack 'n' Jill Burgers

*Whether or not family members spent the day fetching pails of water, they're sure to fall for these speedy sandwiches. Topped with Monterey Jack cheese and your favorite fixings, the thick broiled burgers are moist and full of flavor.*

**1 medium onion, finely chopped**
**1/2 cup finely crushed seasoned salad croutons**
**1/4 cup dill pickle relish**
**2 tablespoons ketchup**
**1-1/2 pounds ground beef**
**6 slices Monterey Jack cheese**
**6 hamburger buns, split**
**6 lettuce leaves**
**6 slices tomato**

In a large bowl, combine the first four ingredients. Crumble beef over the mixture and mix well. Shape into six 1/2-in.-thick patties; place on an ungreased broiler pan. Broil 4 in. from the heat for 7-9 minutes on each side or until no longer pink. Top each with a cheese slice. Broil 1-2 minutes longer or until cheese is melted. Serve on buns with lettuce and tomato slices. **Yield:** 6 servings.

## Twinkle Twinkle Little Stars

*After one taste, folks will wonder why you didn't make these crunchy garlic-and-herb snacks sooner. The baked chips get their appeal from a star-shaped cookie cutter.*

**6 flour tortillas (10 inches)**
**3 tablespoons butter, melted**
**1/2 teaspoon dried basil**
**1/2 teaspoon dried thyme**
**1/4 teaspoon seasoned salt**
**1/4 teaspoon garlic powder**
**1/8 teaspoon pepper**

Brush both sides of each tortilla with butter. Combine remaining ingredients; sprinkle over one side of tortillas. With a 2-1/2-in. star-shaped cookie cutter, cut out several stars from each tortilla; discard scraps. Place stars on ungreased baking sheets. Bake at 400° for 7-9 minutes or until crisp. **Yield:** 6 servings.

## Itsy Bitsy Spider Cakes

*You'll want to catch these cute critters before they climb up the waterspout one more time. The no-bake treats take advantage of coconut-covered snack cakes.*

**3 packages (3-1/2 ounces *each*) pink Sno Balls**
**1 can (16 ounces) vanilla frosting**
**2 cups flaked coconut**
**12 cinnamon Tic Tacs**
**48 pieces red shoestring licorice (3 inches *each*)**

Spread each Sno Ball with frosting. Sprinkle with coconut. Press two Tic Tacs into frosting for eyes. For spider legs, use a metal or wooden skewer to poke four holes on opposite sides of each cake. Insert a piece of licorice into each hole. **Yield:** 6 servings.

**Editor's Note:** Hostess brand Sno Balls are coconut- and marshmallow-covered chocolate cakes with creamy filling. If white Sno Balls can be purchased in your area, eliminate the steps to frost them and coat them in coconut.

### Fairy-Tale Affair

Throwing a party with a storybook theme is easy and fun, too! Start by writing the invitations in nursery-rhyme fashion.

The day of the event, greet little guests with paper crowns instead of party hats. Or, let them choose hats and name tags based on favorite fairy-tale or nursery-rhyme characters, such as Little Bo Peep, Little Boy Blue, Thumbelina, Rumplestiltskin or the like.

This is a great time for the hosts to get into the act, too. Mom can dress up as Mother Goose while Dad portrays the giant from Jack and the Beanstalk.

For a fun game, spray plastic eggs with gold paint and fill them with candy or coins. Hide them and ask the children to find the magical golden eggs.

With playful party food and whimsical activities, a happy ending is sure to be had by all.

# Garden Goodies Will Delight Green Thumbs

WHEN summertime's on the way, celebrate with this menu that would make Mother Nature proud.

## Carrot-Shaped Cheese Spread

*Cultivate compliments with this quick cracker spread coated with crushed tortilla chips. Taco seasoning, green onions and ripe olives dress up the thick cheese mixture.*

**2 packages (8 ounces *each*) cream cheese, softened**
**1 cup (4 ounces) shredded cheddar cheese**
**1 can (2-1/4 ounces) sliced ripe olives, drained**
**3 green onions, chopped**
**1 jar (2 ounces) diced pimientos, drained**
**5 teaspoons taco seasoning**
**3/4 cup finely crushed nacho tortilla chips**
**Celery leaves**
**Assorted crackers**

In a mixing bowl, beat the cream cheese and cheddar cheese until blended. Stir in the olives, onions, pimientos and taco seasoning. On a serving plate, shape mixture into a carrot shape; press crushed nacho chips onto entire surface. Place celery leaves at top of carrot. Serve with crackers. **Yield:** 10-12 servings.

## Garden Snake Sandwiches

*Frozen dough streamlines assembly of this sandwich arranged like a slithering snake. Curry, raisins and sunflower kernels flavor the chicken salad inside.*

**12 frozen bread dough dinner rolls, thawed**
**3-1/2 cups cubed cooked chicken**
**1/2 cup mayonnaise**
**1 celery rib, chopped**
**1/4 cup raisins**
**3 tablespoons sunflower kernels**
**1/2 teaspoon salt**
**1/4 teaspoon pepper**
**1/4 teaspoon curry powder**
**12 lettuce leaves**
**12 tomato slices**
**2 ripe olive slices**
**1 green onion**
**6 cherry tomatoes, halved**

Arrange rolls in an S shape 1/2 in. apart on a large greased baking sheet. Cover and let rise in a warm place for 30-35 minutes or until doubled. Bake at 350° for 12-17 minutes or until golden brown. Carefully remove to a wire rack.

In a bowl, combine the chicken, mayonnaise, celery, raisins, sunflower kernels, salt, pepper and curry powder. Split rolls in half horizontally (do not separate rolls). Layer with chicken mixture, lettuce and tomato slices; replace roll tops.

Use toothpicks to attach olive slices to first sandwich for snake's eyes. Cut green portion of onion into tongue shape; insert into sandwich. Place cherry tomato halves on remaining sandwiches; secure with toothpicks. **Yield:** 1 dozen.

## Flowering Peach Puffs

*Prepared puff pastry makes it easy to create these tempting treats layered with a creamy spread.*

**1 sheet frozen puff pastry, thawed**
**2 cups very thinly sliced fresh *or* frozen peaches**
**1 tablespoon sugar**
**1 package (3 ounces) cream cheese, softened**
**2 tablespoons confectioners' sugar**
**1/2 teaspoon vanilla extract**
**2 cups whipped topping**
**6 fresh raspberries**

On a lightly floured surface, roll pastry to 1/8-in. thickness. Cut out six circles with a floured 3-1/2-in. round cookie cutter. Place on an ungreased baking sheet. Cut leaves from the scraps, using a floured 1-1/2-in. leaf-shaped cookie cutter; place on baking sheet. Bake at 400° for 8-10 minutes or until golden brown. Remove to wire racks to cool.

In a large bowl, toss peaches with sugar; set aside. In a small mixing bowl, beat cream cheese, confectioners' sugar and vanilla until smooth. Fold in the whipped topping.

Split pastry circles in half. Spread about 2 tablespoons cream cheese mixture over the bottom half of each; replace tops. Spread about 1 tablespoon cream cheese mixture on the top of each. Arrange peach slices in an overlapping circular pattern on the cream cheese layer. Garnish each with a raspberry and puff pastry leaves. **Yield:** 6 servings.

## Dragonfly Snacks

*You won't need a net to catch these delightful dragonflies. Store-bought cookies and pretzels are dipped in candy coating and sprinkled with sugar.*

**8 ounces white candy coating, finely chopped**
**6 Pirouette cookies**
**Colored sugar**
**12 pretzel twists**
**12 large marshmallows**

Line an ungreased baking sheet with waxed paper; set aside. Place candy coating in a shallow microwave-safe dish. Microwave at 30% power for 3-4 minutes or until melted, stirring every 30 seconds. Coat cookies with candy coating. Place on prepared pan. Sprinkle with colored sugar. Freeze for 15 minutes or until firm.

If necessary, warm remaining candy coating. Dip the pretzels in the coating. Press two pretzels against each cookie, propping with the marshmallows (see photo). Immediately sprinkle with colored sugar. Let stand until set. Carefully remove dragonflies from waxed paper and marshmallows. **Yield:** 6 servings.

**Editor's Note:** This recipe was tested in a 1,100-watt microwave.

# Movie Munchies Will Receive Rave Reviews

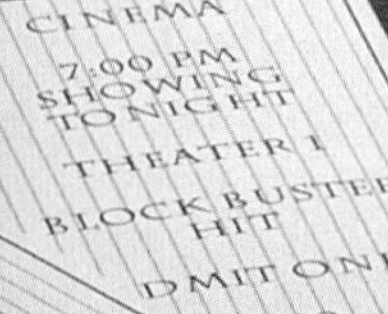

WANT to make your video nights or at-home matinees extra special? Here's the ticket! Just turn to these cinematic snacks produced by the home economists in our Test Kitchen.

Each silver-screen recipe will quickly please even the pickiest critics, thanks to homemade taste that theater fare can't match.

In a starring role, the cheesy nachos we've presented are a hearty choice for hungry film fans. Using precooked chicken makes this southwestern favorite simple to fix.

Don't forget the popcorn! Our home economists created a crunchy cinnamon-sugar version that'll keep movie buffs happily munching. And for another satisfying snack, offer soft pretzels with a sweet mustard sauce.

Before the final credits roll, serve your own "film reel" ice cream sandwiches. All in all, your motion-picture menu will be a tough act to follow.

## Cinema Chicken Nachos

*You'll have a blockbuster hit with these cheesy tortilla chips covered with popular southwestern toppings. Since the nachos call for packaged cooked chicken, they're a cinch to throw together in just 10 minutes. Plus, you can easily adjust or customize the ingredients to suit your family's taste.*

**1/2 pound Mexican process cheese (Velveeta), cubed**
**6 cups tortilla chips**
**2 packages (6 ounces *each*) ready-to-use southwestern chicken strips, chopped**
**2 medium tomatoes, chopped**
**4 green onions, chopped**
**1 can (2-1/4 ounces) sliced ripe olives, drained**

In a microwave-safe bowl, melt cheese. Divide tortilla chips among four serving plates. Top with the cheese, chicken, tomatoes, onions and olives. **Yield:** 4 servings.

## Cinnamon Popcorn

*With a sensational cinnamon-sugar coating, this recipe turns plain popcorn into a sweet treat that moviegoers are sure to reward with thumbs-up approval. Oven baking keeps the unique popcorn crisp. For extra fun, serve the snack in individual theater-style boxes.*

**2 quarts popped popcorn**
**1 egg white**
**1/2 cup sugar**
**1 teaspoon dried orange peel**
**1/2 teaspoon ground cinnamon**
**1/4 teaspoon salt**

Place popcorn in a greased 15-in. x 10-in. x 1-in. baking pan. In a small mixing bowl, beat the egg white, sugar, orange peel, cinnamon and salt until well blended. Pour over popcorn; mix well. Bake at 300° for 30-35 minutes, stirring once. Cool completely. Store in an airtight container. **Yield:** 2 quarts.

## Soft Pretzels with Mustard

*This double feature of dippers and sauce takes only a short time to prepare. The little pretzels are easily shaped using refrigerated breadstick dough. While they bake, mix together the mustard dip.*

**1 tube (11 ounces) refrigerated breadsticks**
**1 egg white, lightly beaten**
**Coarse salt**
**1/2 cup Dijon mustard**
**1/4 cup maple syrup**
**1 tablespoon brown sugar**
**1/2 teaspoon dried parsley flakes**

On an unfloured surface, roll each breadstick into a 20-in. rope; twist into a pretzel shape. Place 2 in. apart on ungreased baking sheets. Brush with egg white and sprinkle with salt.

Bake at 375° for 10-13 minutes or until lightly browned. Remove to a wire rack. For mustard dip, combine the remaining ingredients in a small bowl. Serve with pretzels. **Yield:** 1 dozen.

## Ice Cream Film Reels

*Roll 'em out, and these culinary conclusions may just steal the show! Simple homemade peanut butter cookies sandwich ice cream for a fun and frosty finale. A piece of fruit roll is wrapped around each sandwich for the "film".*

**4 egg whites**
**2 cups creamy peanut butter**
**1-2/3 cups sugar**
**1 cup milk chocolate M&M's**
**7-1/2 cups vanilla ice cream**
**15 pieces (about 18 inches *each*) Fruit by the Foot fruit roll**

In a small mixing bowl, beat egg whites until stiff peaks form. In a large mixing bowl, combine peanut butter and sugar; fold in egg whites. Drop by rounded tablespoonfuls 2 in. apart onto lightly greased baking sheets. Flatten into 3-in. circles with a fork dipped in sugar.

Arrange M&M's around the top edges of half of the cookies. Bake at 325° for 15-20 minutes or until set. Cool for 2 minutes before removing from pans to wire racks to cool completely.

To assemble reels, place 1/2 cup ice cream on the bottom of each plain cookie; top with M&M's-topped cookies. Wrap in plastic wrap. Place on a baking sheet; freeze. Just before serving, wrap a piece of fruit roll around each reel. **Yield:** 15 servings.

### Say Cheese

Don't have the Mexican process cheese called for in Cinema Chicken Nachos? There's no need to miss out on the fun. Just cube regular process cheese, set it in a microwave-safe bowl and stir in a little salsa. As the cheese melts, mix in additional salsa to taste.

# Chapter 4

# Give Me 5 or Fewer

IT'S SOMETHING cooks can count on: Recipes that call for a smaller number of ingredients often take less time to prepare.

So it's no surprise that time-conscious cooks with non-stop schedules frequently stay away from long lists of ingredients.

With just five items—or fewer—needed per recipe, each delicious dish offered in this chapter is simple to assemble.

But while these tasty entrees, side dishes, soups, salads and desserts have a short ingredient list, they're long on flavor. So you can serve homemade foods your whole family will appreciate and ask for again.

**LESS IS MORE.** Clockwise from top left: Pecan Caramel Candies, Fast Fruit Salsa, Savory Chicken Dinner and Onion Pork Tenderloins (recipes on pp. 64 and 65).

## Swiss Onion Loaf

*A packaged hot roll mix speeds along preparation of this savory golden brown bread. Let the loaf cool completely before slicing...if you can wait that long! I think it's especially good with beef stew in the winter.*
*—Lois Schneider, Madison, Wisconsin*

**1 cup (4 ounces) shredded Swiss cheese**
**2 tablespoons dried minced onion**
**1 package (16 ounces) hot roll mix**
**1 tablespoon butter, melted**

In a bowl, combine the cheese and minced onion with the dry ingredients of the hot roll mix. Prepare the mix according to the package directions. Turn onto a floured surface; knead until smooth and elastic, about 6-8 minutes. Shape into a 5-in. ball and place on a greased baking sheet.

Cover and let rise in a warm place for 30 minutes or until doubled. Bake at 375° for 25-30 minutes or until golden brown. Brush with butter. Remove to a wire rack to cool. **Yield:** 1 loaf.

## Simple Shepherd's Pie

*Our son Charlie loves to cook and often helps out with preparing meals and making snacks. Whenever we have leftover mashed potatoes, Charlie puts together this supper dish the next day. The savory and satisfying pie with frozen vegetables and ground beef is a great main course and goes well with a green salad.* *—Lera Joe Bayer*
*Wirtz, Virginia*

**1 pound ground beef**
**2 cans (10-3/4 ounces *each*) condensed cream of potato soup, undiluted**
**1-1/2 cups frozen peas, thawed**
**1-1/2 cups frozen sliced carrots, thawed**
**4 cups mashed potatoes (with added milk and butter)**

In a large skillet, cook beef over medium heat until no longer pink; drain. Add the soup, peas and carrots. Pour into a greased 11-in. x 7-in. x 2-in. baking dish. Top with potatoes. Bake, uncovered, at 350° for 30-40 minutes or until heated through. **Yield:** 4 servings.

## Peanut Butter Cream Fudge

*This crowd-pleasing candy recipe calls for everyday ingredients I almost always have in my cupboard and refrigerator. With a smooth texture and lots of nutty flavor, the fudge is sure to get smiles from peanut butter lovers of all ages. I can stir up a batch in a snap.*
*—Margaret Hammond, Logan, Ohio*

**2 cups sugar**
**1 cup (8 ounces) sour cream**
**1/8 teaspoon salt**
**1 cup peanut butter**
**1 teaspoon vanilla extract**

In a heavy saucepan, combine the sugar, sour cream and salt; bring to a boil. Cover and simmer for 5 minutes. Uncover and cook over medium heat until a candy thermometer reads 238° (soft-ball stage). Remove from the heat; stir in peanut butter and vanilla. With a wooden spoon, beat until thick and creamy, about 5 minutes. Transfer to a buttered 8-in. square dish. Cool and cut into squares. Store in the refrigerator. **Yield:** about 1-1/2 pounds.

**Editor's Note:** Reduced-fat or generic brands of peanut butter are not recommended for this recipe.

## Sausage Rolls

*When I was at a New Year's Day event, a friend gave me this delicious recipe. Refrigerated crescent dough hurries along the tasty rolls that can be served for Sunday brunch, as an after-school snack or as a party appetizer. I like that they don't require a long list of ingredients.*
*—Raylene Myers, Mesquite, Texas*

**1 pound bulk pork sausage**
**1 package (8 ounces) cream cheese, cubed**
**2 tubes (8 ounces *each*) refrigerated crescent rolls**

In a skillet, cook sausage over medium heat until no longer pink; drain. Stir in the cream cheese until melted. Separate each tube of crescent dough into four rectangles; seal the seams and perforations. Spread the rectangles with the sausage mixture. Roll up jelly-roll style, starting with a long side. Pinch the seams and ends to seal. Place with the seam side down on an ungreased baking sheet.

Bake at 350° for 20-25 minutes or until golden brown. Let stand 5 minutes before cutting each roll diagonally into fourths. **Yield:** 8 servings.

## Basil-Buttered French Bread

*(Pictured at right)*

*I prepare this warm, great-tasting bread whenever I want to round out a quick dinner. After brushing the thick slices with basil-flavored butter, I simply pop them in a hot oven for a few minutes shortly before mealtime.* *—Dixie Terry*
*Goreville, Illinois*

**2 tablespoons butter, melted**
**1/2 teaspoon dried basil**
**4 slices French bread (1 inch thick)**

In a small bowl, combine butter and basil. Brush butter mixture over one side of each bread slice. Place buttered side up on an ungreased baking sheet. Bake, uncovered, at 400° for 5 minutes or until golden brown. **Yield:** 4 servings.

## Spicy Creamed Corn

*(Pictured at right)*

*One of my family's favorite vegetables is corn, and this quick, creamy creation is so easy to put together on a hectic weeknight or busy Saturday. The simple medley that in-*

*cludes onion, green chilies and sweet red pepper tastes delicious and nicely complements chicken, turkey or most any main dish.* —*Nancy McDonald, Burns, Wyoming*

**1 package (3 ounces) cream cheese, cubed**
**1 can (15-1/4 ounces) whole kernel corn, drained**
**1 can (4 ounces) chopped green chilies**
**1/4 cup sliced green onions**
**1/4 cup chopped sweet red pepper**

In a saucepan, heat the cream cheese until melted. Add the corn, chilies, green onions and red pepper. Cook and stir until heated through. **Yield:** 4 servings.

## Italian Chicken

*(Pictured below)*

*To save time on busy weekdays, I place thawed chicken and salad dressing in a pan in the morning, cover it and refrigerate. When it's time to cook dinner, I simply add cheese and bake.* —*Anita Keppinger, Philomath, Oregon*

✓ Uses less fat, sugar or salt. Includes Nutritional Analysis and Diabetic Exchanges.

**4 boneless skinless chicken breast halves (1 pound)**
**1 cup Italian salad dressing**
**2 tablespoons grated Parmesan cheese**
**1/4 teaspoon salt, optional**
**Minced fresh parsley**

Place chicken in a greased 9-in. square baking dish. Drizzle with salad dressing; sprinkle with Parmesan cheese and salt if desired.

Bake, uncovered, at 375° for 20-25 minutes or until the chicken juices run clear. Sprinkle with the parsley. **Yield:** 4 servings.

**Nutritional Analysis:** One chicken breast half (prepared with fat-free salad dressing; calculated without salt) equals 177 calories, 3 g fat (1 g saturated fat), 70 mg cholesterol, 980 mg sodium, 7 g carbohydrate, trace fiber, 28 g protein. **Diabetic Exchanges:** 3 lean meat, 1/2 starch.

**Basil-Buttered French Bread**
**Spicy Creamed Corn**
**Italian Chicken**

**Cheesy Drop Biscuits**
**Honeydew Fruit Salad**
**Asparagus Beef Roll-Ups**
**Country Ham**

## Asparagus Beef Roll-Ups

*(Pictured above)*

*I make these easy and elegant appetizers with asparagus spears, roast beef slices and a cream cheese-horseradish spread. I serve them at all of my parties and have received many recipe requests. They're a snap to assemble.* *—Kris Krueger Plano, Texas*

**1-1/2 cups water**
**36 fresh asparagus spears, trimmed**
**1 carton (8 ounces) spreadable chive and onion cream cheese**
**3 to 5 tablespoons prepared horseradish**
**2 packages (5 ounces *each*) thinly sliced roast beef**

In a large skillet, bring water to a boil. Add asparagus; cover and boil for 2-3 minutes or until crisp-tender. Drain and immediately place asparagus in ice water. Drain and pat dry.

In a small mixing bowl, combine cream cheese and horseradish. Pat beef slices dry with paper towels. Spread each slice with a thin layer of cream cheese mixture; top with an asparagus spear. Roll up tightly. Refrigerate until serving. **Yield:** 3 dozen.

## Honeydew Fruit Salad

*(Pictured above)*

*Our Test Kitchen created this refreshing medley that's a colorful addition to Easter dinner or most any meal.*

✓ Uses less fat, sugar or salt. Includes Nutritional Analysis and Diabetic Exchanges.

**1 can (20 ounces) unsweetened pineapple chunks**
**4-1/2 teaspoons cornstarch**
**1 large honeydew, cut into balls *or* cubes**
**1 can (15 ounces) mandarin oranges, drained**
**1 tablespoon minced fresh mint**

Drain pineapple, reserving juice; set pineapple aside. In a small saucepan, combine cornstarch and pineapple juice until smooth. Bring to a boil; cook and stir for 2 minutes or until thickened. Cover and refrigerate until cool. In a large serving bowl, combine the honeydew, oranges, mint and reserved pineapple. Stir in pineapple juice mixture. Cover and refrigerate until serving. **Yield:** 8 servings.

**Nutritional Analysis:** One serving (3/4 cup) equals 117 calories, trace fat (trace saturated fat), 0 cholesterol, 22 mg sodium, 30 g carbohydrate, 2 g fiber, 1 g protein. **Diabetic Exchange:** 2 fruit.

## Country Ham

*(Pictured at left)*

*Peach preserves give this easy entree a mildly fruity flair. We like to use up the leftover ham in sandwiches, soups and omelets.* —*Pamela Proctor, Barlow, Ohio*

**1 boneless fully cooked ham (about 3 pounds)**
**3/4 cup packed brown sugar**
**2 tablespoons prepared mustard**
**1/4 cup peach preserves**

Place ham in a small foil-lined roasting pan; pierce several times with a fork. Combine brown sugar and mustard; spread over ham. Spread with peach preserves. Cover and bake at 350° for 1-1/2 hours, basting occasionally. Uncover; bake 30-45 minutes longer or until a meat thermometer reads 140°. **Yield:** 8-12 servings.

## Cheesy Drop Biscuits

*(Pictured at left)*

*It's hard to believe that these home-style biscuits require only a few items and take just 15 minutes to get in the oven. I always keep the ingredients on hand because my sons love every buttery, golden brown bite.* —*Marla Miller Englewood, Tennessee*

**2 cups self-rising flour**
**1 cup butter, melted**
**1 cup (8 ounces) sour cream**
**1 cup (4 ounces) shredded cheddar cheese**

In a large bowl, combine all ingredients until blended. Drop by rounded tablespoonfuls 2 in. apart onto lightly greased baking sheets. Bake at 350° for 20-25 minutes or until golden brown. Cool for 5 minutes before removing from pans to wire racks. Serve warm. **Yield:** 2 dozen.

**Editor's Note:** As a substitute for each cup of self-rising flour, place 1-1/2 teaspoons baking powder and 1/2 teaspoon salt in a measuring cup. Add all-purpose flour to measure 1 cup.

## Party Chicken

*After sampling this at a church dinner, I knew the entree would be well liked by my family members and friends. It features tender chicken and dried beef in a creamy sauce. If you like, serve this dish over rice.* —*Eva Snyder Widmyer Lahmansville, West Virginia*

**1 package (2-1/2 ounces) thinly sliced dried beef**
**8 boneless skinless chicken breast halves**
**1 can (10-3/4 ounces) condensed cream of celery soup, undiluted**
**1 cup (8 ounces) sour cream**
**Hot cooked rice, optional**

In a greased 13-in. x 9-in. x 2-in. baking dish, arrange beef slices to evenly cover bottom of dish. Top with chicken breasts. Combine the soup and sour cream; pour over chicken. Bake, uncovered, at 350° for 35 minutes or until the chicken juices run clear. Serve over rice if desired. **Yield:** 8 servings.

## Pizza Sticks

*I rely on refrigerated breadsticks and pizza toppings for these late-night nibbles. This is an easy snack the whole family enjoys.* —*Martha Riggs, Upton, Kentucky*

✓ Uses less fat, sugar or salt. Includes Nutritional Analysis and Diabetic Exchanges.

**1 tube (11 ounces) refrigerated breadsticks**
**1/2 cup pizza sauce**
**12 slices pepperoni, chopped**
**12 slices Canadian bacon, chopped**
**1 cup (4 ounces) shredded Italian cheese blend *or* mozzarella cheese**

Arrange breadsticks with long sides touching on a greased baking sheet. Top with pizza sauce, pepperoni, Canadian bacon and cheese. Bake at 375° for 18-22 minutes or until breadsticks are golden. Cut apart into sticks. **Yield:** 1 dozen.

**Nutritional Analysis:** One pizza stick (prepared with part-skim mozzarella) equals 172 calories, 7 g fat (2 g saturated fat), 24 mg cholesterol, 777 mg sodium, 14 g carbohydrate, 1 g fiber, 11 g protein. **Diabetic Exchanges:** 1 starch, 1 lean meat, 1 fat.

## Spinach Sausage Soup

*Chock-full of potatoes, Italian sausage and spinach, this hearty soup disappears fast. Not only is it delicious and quick, but it also freezes well.* —*Bonita Krugler Anderson, Indiana*

**1 pound bulk Italian sausage**
**4 cans (14-1/2 ounces *each*) chicken broth**
**8 red potatoes, quartered and thinly sliced**
**1 envelope Italian salad dressing mix**
**2 cups fresh *or* frozen chopped spinach**

In a large skillet, brown sausage over medium heat. Meanwhile, in a Dutch oven, combine the broth, potatoes and salad dressing mix. Bring to a boil; cover and simmer for 10 minutes or until potatoes are tender. Drain sausage; add sausage and spinach to broth mixture. Cook until heated through. **Yield:** 10 servings (2-1/2 quarts).

### Biscuit Tidbit

After I've made the dough for baking powder biscuits, I roll it into a log and slice it rather than drop it by spoonfuls onto the baking sheet. I've found that this is a quick way for me to create nice, uniform biscuits. —*Lou Wright, Rockville, Illinois*

## Orange Party Punch

*This citrusy punch was served at every birthday party I had when I was growing up. Now I prepare the refreshing beverage for my own children. To give it extra flair, float orange slices among the scoops of sherbet on top.* —*Brenda Rupert Clyde, Ohio*

**1 can (12 ounces) frozen orange juice concentrate, thawed**
**2 liters lemon-lime soda, chilled**
**1 can (46 ounces) pineapple juice, chilled**
**1 quart orange *or* pineapple sherbet**

Prepare orange juice according to package directions; pour into a punch bowl. Stir in the soda and pineapple juice. Top with scoops of sherbet. Serve immediately. **Yield:** 5-1/2 quarts.

## Spinach Rice Ham Bake

*When I was a student in college, my best friend shared this tasty casserole recipe with me. Later, when my children were toddlers, I often prepared it because it was an easy way for them to eat rice. Our family still enjoys this hearty dish full of cheese, spinach and ham.*
—*Ramona Parris, Marietta, Georgia*

**8 ounces process cheese (Velveeta), cubed**
**1/2 cup milk**
**3 cups cooked rice**
**2 cups cubed fully cooked ham**
**1 package (10 ounces) frozen chopped spinach, thawed and squeezed dry**

In a microwave-safe bowl, combine the cheese and milk. Microwave, uncovered, on high for 2 minutes or until cheese is melted; stir until smooth. Stir in the rice, ham and spinach. Transfer to a greased 1-1/2-qt. baking dish. Cover and bake at 350° for 25-30 minutes or until heated through. **Yield:** 3 servings.

**Editor's Note:** This recipe was tested in an 850-watt microwave.

## Ice Cream Sticky Buns

*A gooey caramel sauce made with ice cream coats the tender rolls in this breakfast treat. Instead of using a loaf of bread dough, thaw frozen dinner rolls and divide them in thirds for faster assembly. For a little crunch, I add some chopped pecans before serving.* —*Sharon Donat Kalispell, Montana*

**1 cup vanilla ice cream, melted**
**1/2 cup butter, melted**
**1/2 cup sugar**
**1/2 cup packed brown sugar**
**1 loaf (1 pound) frozen bread dough, thawed**

In a bowl, combine the ice cream, butter and sugars. Pour into a greased 13-in. x 9-in. x 2-in. baking dish. Cut dough into 36 pieces; arrange in dish. Cover and let rise in a warm place until doubled, about 1 hour.

Bake at 375° for 18-22 minutes or until golden brown. Cool for 2 minutes before inverting onto a serving platter. Serve warm. **Yield:** 3 dozen.

## Cherry Cheese Danish

*Here is a quick Sunday breakfast I like to whip up before going to church. I created the recipe when trying to duplicate a favorite Danish from the bakery where I worked. Sometimes I use apple pie filling instead of cherry.*
—*Melanie Schrock, Monterey, Tennessee*

**1 tube (8 ounces) refrigerated crescent rolls**
**4 tablespoons cream cheese, softened**
**1 cup cherry pie filling**
**1/2 cup vanilla frosting**

Separate crescent dough into four rectangles. Place on an ungreased baking sheet; seal perforations. Spread 1 tablespoon cream cheese onto each rectangle. Top each with 1/4 cup cherry pie filling. Bake at 375° for 10-12 minutes or until edges are golden brown. Cool for 5 minutes.

Place frosting in a small microwave-safe bowl; heat on high for 15-20 seconds. Drizzle over warm pastries. Serve warm. Refrigerate leftovers. **Yield:** 4 servings.

## Apricot Pork Chops

*(Pictured at right)*

*Convenient canned apricots nicely complement the tender pork in this sensational stovetop entree. To speed up the preparation, use a food processor or blender to quickly chop the fruit. The recipe takes only about 30 minutes to make from start to finish.* —*Ron Gardner Grand Haven, Michigan*

**1 can (15-1/4 ounces) apricot halves, undrained**
**4 bone-in pork loin chops (3/4 inch thick)**
**1 tablespoon butter**
**1 tablespoon cornstarch**
**2 tablespoons cold water**
**Salt and pepper to taste**

Place apricots in a food processor or blender; cover and process until coarsely chopped. In a large skillet, brown pork chops in butter over medium-high heat. Add apricots. Bring to a boil. Reduce heat; cover and simmer for 7-10 minutes or until meat juices run clear.

Remove the chops and keep warm. Combine cornstarch and cold water until smooth; stir into apricot mixture. Bring to a boil; cook and stir for 1 minute or until thickened. Season with salt and pepper. Serve over pork chops. **Yield:** 4 servings.

## Green Beans with Walnuts

*(Pictured at right)*

*For a simple side dish that looks and tastes nice enough for company, I perk up fresh green beans with minced garlic and chopped walnuts that I quickly toast in a skillet. Olive oil, salt and pepper are the only other ingredients I need.* —*Margaret Wilson, Hemet, California*

**1-1/2 pounds fresh green beans, cut into 2-inch pieces**
**1/2 cup coarsely chopped walnuts**
**2 tablespoons olive oil**
**1 to 2 garlic cloves, minced**
**1/2 teaspoon seasoned salt**
**1/4 teaspoon pepper**

Place beans in a large saucepan and cover with water. Bring to a boil. Cook, uncovered, for 8-10 minutes or until crisp-tender; drain. In a large skillet over medium heat, cook walnuts in oil for 1-2 minutes or until lightly browned, stirring occasionally. Add beans, garlic, seasoned salt and pepper. Cook until heated through. **Yield:** 8 servings.

## Macaroon Ice Cream Torte

*(Pictured below)*

*My family enjoys just about any frozen dessert, including this tempting torte that I often prepare for special occasions. I discovered the recipe in a ladies' club cookbook—where it was called "the girdle-buster"! It truly is a wonderful way to indulge in ice cream, macaroon cookies, toffee bits and hot fudge topping.* —*Barbara Carlucci*
*Orange Park, Florida*

**24 macaroon cookies, crumbled**
**1 quart coffee ice cream, softened**
**1 quart chocolate ice cream, softened**
**1 cup chocolate-covered English toffee bits** *or* **4 Heath candy bars (1.4 ounces** ***each*****), coarsely chopped**
**Hot fudge topping, warmed**

For crust, sprinkle a third of crumbled cookies into an ungreased 9-in. springform pan. Top with 2 cups coffee ice cream, a third of cookies, 2 cups chocolate ice cream and 1/2 cup toffee bits. Repeat layers. Cover and freeze until firm. May be frozen for up to 2 months.

Remove from the freezer 10 minutes before serving. Remove sides of pan. Cut into wedges; drizzle with hot fudge topping. **Yield:** 12-16 servings.

**Macaroon Ice Cream Torte**
**Green Beans with Walnuts**
**Apricot Pork Chops**

## Pecan Caramel Candies

*(Pictured above and on page 56)*

*With just pretzels, chocolate-caramel candies and pecans as ingredients, these tempting candies are a cinch to create but look and taste like you fussed. I often serve them alongside other desserts for guests who want only a bite of something sweet. It's easy to adjust the recipe to make as many—or as few—as you want.* —*Julie Wemhoff*
*Angola, Indiana*

**63 miniature pretzels**
**1 package (13 ounces) Rolo candies**
**63 pecan halves**

Line baking sheets with foil. Place pretzels on foil; top each pretzel with a candy. Bake at 250° for 4 minutes or until candies are softened (candies will retain their shape). Immediately place a pecan half on each candy and press down so candy fills pretzel. Cool slightly. Refrigerate for 10 minutes or until set. **Yield:** 63 candies (about 1-1/4 pounds).

## Fast Fruit Salsa

*(Pictured above and on page 57)*

*We like this refreshing and colorful salsa served with tortilla chips or spooned over grilled chicken. For a fun twist, try stirring in some diced cantaloupe or peaches when they're in season.* —*Eileen Miller*
*Woodridge, Illinois*

✓ Uses less fat, sugar or salt. Includes Nutritional Analysis and Diabetic Exchanges.

**1 can (8 ounces) unsweetened crushed pineapple, drained**
**1 can (8 ounces) mandarin oranges, drained and chopped**
**1/4 cup chopped red onion**
**1 tablespoon minced fresh cilantro**
**Tortilla chips**

In a bowl, combine the pineapple, oranges, onion and cilantro. Cover and refrigerate until serving. Serve with tortilla chips. **Yield:** 1-1/2 cups.

**Nutritional Analysis:** One 1/4-cup serving (calculated without tortilla chips) equals 31 calories, trace fat (trace saturated fat), 0 cholesterol, 1 mg sodium, 8 g carbohydrate, 1 g fiber, trace protein. **Diabetic Exchange:** 1/2 fruit.

## Savory Chicken Dinner

*(Pictured at left and on page 56)*

*No one would guess that these moist chicken breasts and tender potatoes are seasoned with herb- and garlic-flavored soup mix. —Leslie Adams, Springfield, Missouri*

**1 envelope savory herb and garlic soup mix**
**3 tablespoons water**
**4 boneless skinless chicken breast halves (6 to 8 ounces *each*)**
**2 large red potatoes, cubed**
**1 large onion, halved and cut into small wedges**

In a large resealable plastic bag, combine the soup mix and water. Add the chicken, potatoes and onion; seal bag and toss to coat. Transfer to a greased 13-in. x 9-in. x 2-in. baking dish. Bake, uncovered, at 350° for 40-45 minutes or until vegetables are tender and chicken juices run clear, stirring vegetables occasionally. **Yield:** 4 servings.

## Onion Pork Tenderloins

*(Pictured at left and on page 56)*

*I received this recipe from my mom, and it's the easiest "fancy" entree I've found. Sometimes I add sliced fresh mushrooms. —Stacie Blemings, Califon, New Jersey*

**2 pork tenderloins (1 to 1-1/4 pounds *each*)**
**2 tablespoons olive oil**
**1 envelope onion soup mix**
**1/2 cup white wine *or* chicken broth**
**1 tablespoon cornstarch**
**3/4 cup cold water**

In a large skillet over medium-high heat, brown tenderloins in oil on all sides. Sprinkle soup mix over the meat; add wine or broth to the skillet. Reduce heat. Cover and simmer for 25-30 minutes or until a meat thermometer reads 160°, adding water to the skillet if needed. Remove tenderloins and keep warm.

In a small bowl, combine the cornstarch and water until smooth; stir into pan juices. Bring to a boil; cook and stir for 2 minutes or until thickened. Serve with tenderloins. **Yield:** 8-10 servings.

## Three-Two-One Dip

*During my husband's teaching career, we did a lot of entertaining. I'd throw together this rich dip in just 15 minutes. —Evelyn Shaulis, Butler, Pennsylvania*

**3 packages (8 ounces *each*) cream cheese, cubed**
**2 cans (10-3/4 ounces *each*) condensed cream of celery soup, undiluted**
**1 pound sliced pepperoni, finely chopped**
**Assorted crackers**

In a large saucepan, combine the cream cheese, soup and pepperoni. Cook and stir over medium-low heat until cheese is melted. Serve warm with crackers. **Yield:** 6 cups.

## Fruity Punch

*I blend pineapple juice with ginger ale and top it with scoops of sherbet and ice cream. The creamy thirst-quencher makes a refreshing beverage for most any occasion. —Bernice Dufek, Running Springs, California*

**2-1/2 cups unsweetened pineapple juice**
**1 cup ginger ale, chilled**
**1 cup vanilla ice cream, softened**
**1 cup orange sherbet**

In a small punch bowl, combine the pineapple juice and ginger ale. Top with scoops of the ice cream and sherbet. Serve punch immediately. **Yield:** about 1 quart.

## Stuffing-Coated Chicken

*This recipe from an old church cookbook quickly became a favorite. I've used the microwave at work to reheat leftovers for lunch. When the aroma of garlic and Parmesan cheese grabs the attention of co-workers, they all ask for the recipe. —Patricia Inman, Litchfield, Minnesota*

**1-1/2 cups stuffing mix, finely crushed**
**2 tablespoons grated Parmesan cheese**
**1/4 cup butter, melted**
**1 garlic clove, minced**
**5 boneless skinless chicken breast halves (6 to 8 ounces *each*)**

In a shallow dish, combine the stuffing crumbs and Parmesan cheese. In another shallow dish, combine butter and garlic. Dip chicken in butter mixture, then coat with stuffing mixture. Place in a greased 13-in. x 9-in. x 2-in. baking dish.

Sprinkle with remaining stuffing mixture and drizzle with remaining butter mixture. Bake, uncovered, at 350° for 40-45 minutes or until chicken juices run clear. **Yield:** 5 servings.

### Choices for Breading Chicken

- When I'm making oven-fried chicken, I dip the chicken pieces in melted butter. Then, instead of rolling them in the coating mix, I put the mix in a screw-top jar and sprinkle the coating over both sides of the pieces. This way, I find I have less mess and waste. Leftover mix can be saved in the jar for next time. *—Marie Mills, Cincinnati, Ohio*
- Rather than dip chicken or pork chops in beaten eggs, I brush or spoon mayonnaise onto the meat and then sprinkle it with bread crumbs. This method goes quickly, and the mayonnaise keeps the meat moist. *—Ginny King, De Lancey, New York*

## Barbecued Turkey Chili

*The first time I prepared this recipe that uses convenient canned items, I entered it in a chili cook-off and ended up winning first prize. Mixing together the ingredients takes just five minutes, and my slow cooker does the rest. The flavorful chili is often requested by family and friends.*
*—Melissa Webb, Ellsworth Air Force Base, South Dakota*

**1 can (16 ounces) kidney beans, rinsed and drained**
**1 can (15-1/2 ounces) hot chili beans**
**1 can (15 ounces) turkey chili with beans**
**1 can (14-1/2 ounces) diced tomatoes, undrained**
**1/3 cup barbecue sauce**

In a 3-qt. slow cooker, combine all of the ingredients. Cover and cook on high for 4 hours or until heated through and flavors are blended. **Yield:** 4-6 servings.

## Peanut Ice Cream Pie

*Everyone in our family loves ice cream. To make that frosty treat extra special, I combine it with chopped peanut butter cups and spoon it into a store-bought chocolate crumb crust. I'll often drizzle some chocolate syrup over this overnight freezer pie before serving. —Barbara Heller Austin, Texas*

**1 quart vanilla ice cream, softened**
**6 peanut butter cups, chopped**
**1 chocolate crumb crust (8 *or* 9 inches)**
**Chocolate syrup, optional**

Place ice cream in a large bowl; fold in peanut butter cups. Spoon into the crust. Cover and freeze overnight or until set. Remove from the freezer 15 minutes before serving. Drizzle with chocolate syrup if desired. **Yield:** 6-8 servings.

## Cauliflower Cashew Salad

*Bottled ranch salad dressing provides the mild seasoning in this quick and delicious vegetable salad. Buying precut cauliflower from your supermarket's produce section helps streamline the preparation even further. For a nice crunch, I stir in plenty of cashews. —Darcy Dougherty Postville, Iowa*

✓ Uses less fat, sugar or salt. Includes Nutritional Analysis and Diabetic Exchanges.

**1 medium head cauliflower, broken into florets**
**4 medium carrots, halved and thinly sliced**
**1 cup frozen peas, thawed**
**1 bottle (8 ounces) ranch salad dressing**
**1/2 cup cashews**

In a serving bowl, combine the cauliflower, carrots and peas. Drizzle with dressing; toss to coat. Cover and refrigerate until chilled. Just before serving, stir in cashews. **Yield:** 10 servings.

**Nutritional Analysis:** One 3/4-cup serving (prepared with fat-free salad dressing) equals 109 calories, 4 g fat (1 g saturated fat), trace cholesterol, 299 mg sodium, 17 g carbohydrate, 3 g fiber, 4 g protein. **Diabetic Exchanges:** 1 starch, 1/2 fat.

## Chocolate Popcorn

*If you like milk chocolate candy bars and popcorn, you'll love this sweet snack that's ready to munch in just half an hour. —Suzanne McKinley, Lyons, Georgia*

**2 quarts unsalted popped popcorn**
**1 cup miniature marshmallows**
**1/2 cup salted peanuts**
**6 plain milk chocolate candy bars (1.55 ounces *each*)**

Place popcorn in a greased 15-in. x 10-in. x 1-in. baking pan. Sprinkle with marshmallows and peanuts. Break candy bars in half and place on top. Bake at 300° for 5 minutes. Let stand for 1 minute; toss to coat. Store in an airtight container. **Yield:** 3 quarts.

## Lemon Pound Cake

*I dress up a purchased lemon-flavored mix with a package of cream cheese to create a rich dessert that's perfect for ladies' luncheons, bridal showers and other get-togethers. Anyone who enjoys cheesecake will love it...and they'll never guess how easy the cake was to prepare.*
*—Flora Valdez, Colton, California*

✓ Uses less fat, sugar or salt. Includes Nutritional Analysis and Diabetic Exchanges.

**1 package (8 ounces) cream cheese, softened**
**3/4 cup milk**
**1 package (18-1/4 ounces) lemon cake mix**
**4 eggs**

In a mixing bowl, beat cream cheese until smooth; gradually beat in milk. Add dry cake mix and eggs; beat until combined. Beat on medium speed for 2 minutes. Pour into a greased and floured 10-in. fluted tube pan.

Bake at 350° for 40-45 minutes or until a toothpick inserted near the center comes out clean. Cool for 10 minutes before removing from pan to a wire rack to cool completely. **Yield:** 12 servings.

**Nutritional Analysis:** One slice (prepared with reduced-fat cream cheese and fat-free milk) equals 231 calories, 7 g fat (3 g saturated fat), 78 mg cholesterol, 373 mg sodium, 37 g carbohydrate, 1 g fiber, 6 g protein. **Diabetic Exchanges:** 2 starch, 1 fat, 1/2 fruit.

## Strawberry Tossed Salad

*A neighbor served this wonderful salad at a summer barbecue. I've since experimented with different ingredients, but this combination draws the most compliments. I took it to a baby shower, and not a seed was left.*
*—Lisa Lesinski-Topp, Menomonee Falls, Wisconsin*

**6 cups torn mixed salad greens**
**1 pint fresh strawberries, sliced**
**1 package (4 ounces) crumbled feta cheese**

Beef 'n' Rice Enchiladas

**1/4 cup sunflower kernels**
**Balsamic vinaigrette**

In a large salad bowl, combine the salad greens, strawberries, feta cheese and sunflower kernels. Drizzle with vinaigrette and toss to coat. Serve immediately. **Yield:** 4-6 servings.

## Cherry-Nut Chocolate Pie

*I love chocolate and cherries but couldn't find that flavor combination in any ice cream. So I came up with this rich dessert that has a nice crunch from nuts. This pie is handy to keep in the freezer for unexpected company.*
*—Diana Wilson Wing, Centerville, Utah*

**2 pints dark chocolate ice cream, softened**
**1 jar (10 ounces) maraschino cherries, drained and coarsely chopped**
**3/4 cup slivered almonds**
**1 chocolate crumb crust (8 inches)**
**Whipped topping**

In a bowl, combine the ice cream, cherries and almonds. Spoon into the crust. Cover and freeze overnight. Remove from the freezer 10 minutes before cutting. Garnish with whipped topping. **Yield:** 6-8 servings.

## Beef 'n' Rice Enchiladas

*(Pictured above)*

*With a toddler in the house, I look for dishes that are a snap to make. Loaded with beef, cheddar cheese and a flavorful rice mix, these enchiladas come together without any fuss. But they're so good that guests think I spent hours in the kitchen. —Jennifer Smith, Colona, Illinois*

**1 package (6.8 ounces) Spanish rice and vermicelli mix**
**1 pound ground beef**
**2 cans (10 ounces *each*) enchilada sauce, *divided***
**10 flour tortillas (8 inches), warmed**
**4 cups (16 ounces) shredded cheddar cheese, *divided***

Prepare rice mix according to package directions. Meanwhile, in a large skillet, cook beef over medium heat until no longer pink; drain. Stir in Spanish rice and 1-1/4 cups enchilada sauce. Spoon about 2/3 cup beef mixture down the center of each tortilla. Top each with 1/3 cup cheese; roll up.

Place in an ungreased 13-in. x 9-in. x 2-in. baking dish. Top with the remaining enchilada sauce and cheese. Bake, uncovered, at 350° for 8-10 minutes or until the cheese is melted. **Yield:** 10 enchiladas.

Candy Bar Cookie Squares
Minty Peach Halibut
Ham and Rice Medley

## Ham and Rice Medley

(Pictured above)

*Busy weeknights are easier when I prepare this simple skillet recipe that relies on left-over cooked ham and rice. I use peppers and corn to round out the tasty medley that can make either a side dish or a main course.* —Ron Gardner
Grand Haven, Michigan

**2 cups julienned fully cooked ham**
**1 medium green pepper, chopped**
**1 medium sweet red pepper, chopped**
**3 cups cooked rice**
**1 can (15-1/4 ounces) whole kernel corn, drained**

In a large skillet coated with nonstick cooking spray, saute ham and peppers until peppers are tender. Stir in the rice and corn. Cook and stir 8-10 minutes longer or until heated through. **Yield:** 4 servings.

## Candy Bar Cookie Squares

(Pictured above)

*Be prepared...these disappear fast! The sweet treats feature chunks of Snickers candy bars and use a convenient boxed yellow cake mix. If you like, try chocolate instead.* —Amy Voights, Brodhead, Wisconsin

**1 package (18-1/4 ounces) yellow cake mix**
**1/2 cup packed brown sugar**
**2 eggs**
**1/2 cup butter, melted**
**3 Snickers candy bars (2.07 ounces *each*), chopped**

In a large mixing bowl, combine the cake mix, brown sugar, eggs and butter. Beat on low speed for 2 minutes, scraping bowl occasionally. Stir in chopped candy. Spread into an ungreased 13-in. x 9-in. x 2-in. baking pan. Bake at 350° for 25-30 minutes or until a toothpick comes out clean. Cool on a wire rack. Cut into squares. **Yield:** 2 dozen.

## Minty Peach Halibut

(Pictured at left)

*I knew this golden entree was a winner when my mother-in-law—who owns every cookbook imaginable—asked for the recipe. —Dawn Mayford, Granite City, Illinois*

**1 jar (10 ounces) peach preserves**
**2 teaspoons minced fresh mint**
**4 halibut steaks (6 ounces *each*)**
**1/2 teaspoon salt**
**1/4 teaspoon pepper**

In a small saucepan, bring preserves and mint to a boil; cook and stir for 2 minutes. Remove from heat; set aside. Sprinkle fish with salt and pepper. Place on a greased broiler pan. Broil 4 in. from the heat for 5 minutes.

Spoon half of peach mixture over fish. Broil 1 minute longer; turn. Broil 3-4 minutes more or until fish flakes easily with a fork, basting once with remaining peach mixture. **Yield:** 4 servings.

## Warm Apple Slices

*Cherry soda adds fun flavor to these tender apples. I prepare the pretty red slices quickly in the microwave. —Helen Turner, Upland, Indiana*

✓ Uses less fat, sugar or salt. Includes Nutritional Analysis and Diabetic Exchanges.

**3 large tart apples, peeled and sliced**
**1 can (12 ounces) cherry soda**
**Whipped topping and ground cinnamon, optional**

Layer apple slices in an 11-in. x 7-in. x 2-in. microwave-safe dish. Pour the soda over the apples. Microwave, uncovered, on high for 5-9 minutes or until apples are tender. Serve warm with whipped topping and cinnamon if desired. **Yield:** 8 servings.

**Nutritional Analysis:** One 1/2-cup serving (calculated without whipped topping) equals 64 calories, trace fat (trace saturated fat), 0 cholesterol, 1 mg sodium, 16 g carbohydrate, 2 g fiber, trace protein. **Diabetic Exchange:** 1 fruit.

**Editor's Note:** This recipe was tested in a 1,100-watt microwave.

## Rosemary Romano Bread

*Our 8-year-old son just loves this tasty bread. It's perfect with pasta. —Lois Dykeman, Olmstead, Kentucky*

**1/2 cup butter**
**1/2 cup grated Romano cheese**
**1 garlic clove, minced**
**1 teaspoon minced fresh rosemary**
**1 loaf (1 pound) French bread, halved lengthwise**

In a microwave-safe bowl, melt the butter. Stir in the Romano cheese, garlic and rosemary. Spread over cut side of bread. Place cut side up on an ungreased baking sheet. Bake at 400° for 15 minutes or until lightly browned. Slice and serve warm. **Yield:** 14-16 servings.

## Spicy Sausage Cheese Puffs

*I've been cooking ever since I was 11 years old, and I still enjoy trying new recipes. These tasty bites boast spicy pork sausage, green chilies and cheese and make a swift appetizer or snack. —Tammy Utter, Purdy, Missouri*

**1/4 pound spicy bulk pork sausage**
**3/4 cup biscuit/baking mix**
**1 cup (4 ounces) shredded sharp cheddar cheese**
**3 tablespoons water**
**2 tablespoons canned chopped green chilies, drained**

In a small skillet, cook sausage over medium heat until no longer pink; drain and cool completely. In a bowl, combine biscuit mix and cheese. Stir in the sausage, water and chilies.

Shape into 1-in. balls. Place 2 in. apart on well-greased baking sheets. Bake at 400° for 12-15 minutes or until lightly browned. Serve warm. Refrigerate leftovers. **Yield:** 3 dozen.

## Cheesy Potato Casserole

*When my husband and I were married 12 years ago, my mother gave me a cookbook she created of my favorite recipes. This creamy dish was among them. —Paige Buckingham, Lawrence, Kansas*

**6 medium potatoes (about 2 pounds), peeled and cut into chunks**
**1 carton (8 ounces) French onion dip**
**1 cup (8 ounces) small-curd cottage cheese**
**Salt and pepper to taste**
**1/2 to 1 cup shredded cheddar cheese**

Place potatoes in a large saucepan and cover with water. Bring to a boil. Reduce heat; cover and cook for 15-20 minutes or until tender. Drain and mash potatoes. Stir in the onion dip, cottage cheese, salt and pepper.

Transfer to a greased shallow 1-1/2-qt. baking dish. Sprinkle with cheddar cheese. Bake, uncovered, at 350° for 30-40 minutes or until heated through and cheese is melted. **Yield:** 4-6 servings.

### Supermarket Savvy

- I used my computer to create a list of kitchen staples and items that I often buy at the grocery store. A printout of the list hangs on my refrigerator, and as soon as I run low on an item, I highlight it on the printout. This saves time when I'm ready to go to the store because my shopping list is largely done. *—Angela Colwell, Mechanicsville, Virginia*
- Storing a small cooler in my car trunk allows me to keep milk and other perishable items cold after shopping. That way, I can make a few stops instead of hurrying home with my groceries. If necessary, I purchase some frozen items to help keep the foods chilled. *—Margaret Stevenson, Franklin, Michigan*

## Carrot Broccoli Salad

*When I sampled this at an eatery, I was struck by the mix of sweet and salty flavors and different textures. I asked our server for the recipe, and she obliged... adding that she often makes it at home for herself.* —*Katie Watson Powell, Tennessee*

**2 cups fresh broccoli florets**
**1 cup shredded carrots**
**1/2 cup sunflower kernels**
**1/2 cup dried cranberries**
**1/2 cup coleslaw dressing**

In a small bowl, combine all ingredients. Serve or refrigerate. **Yield:** 2-3 servings.

## Italian Popcorn

*Jazz up plain popcorn using this 10-minute recipe you'll want to make time and again. Simply add butter, seasonings and Romano cheese for a fast and flavor-packed snack.* —*Nancy Reichert, Thomasville, Georgia*

**5 cups popped popcorn**
**4-1/2 teaspoons butter, melted**
**3/4 teaspoon Italian seasoning**
**1/4 teaspoon garlic salt**
**2 tablespoons grated Romano cheese**

Place the popcorn in a bowl. Combine the butter, Italian seasoning and garlic salt; pour over popcorn and toss to coat. Sprinkle with cheese; toss to coat. **Yield:** 5 cups.

## Apple Cranberry Cider

*Spiced with cinnamon sticks and cloves, this warm-you-up sipper from our Test Kitchen is sure to chase away winter's chill. Serve brimming mugs of the hot beverage with your family's favorite cookies, muffins or bread.*

**1 quart apple cider *or* juice**
**2 cups cranberry juice**
**1/3 cup packed brown sugar**
**4 whole cloves**
**2 cinnamon sticks (3 inches)**

In a large saucepan, combine the cider, cranberry juice and brown sugar. Place cloves and cinnamon sticks on a double thickness of cheesecloth; bring up the corners of the cloth and tie with kitchen string to form a bag. Add to the pan.

Bring to a boil over medium heat. Reduce heat; simmer, uncovered, for 15-20 minutes. Discard spice bag before serving. **Yield:** 6 servings.

## Creamy Chicken Crescents

*Collecting cookbooks from area churches is my hobby, and this recipe was one of my discoveries. I made changes to suit my family's tastes. The cheesy chicken dish comes together easily with a tube of refrigerated rolls.* —*Rena Laska, Bancroft, Wisconsin*

**1 tube (8 ounces) refrigerated crescent rolls**
**1 cup shredded cooked chicken**
**1/2 cup shredded cheddar cheese, *divided***
**2/3 cup condensed cream of chicken soup, undiluted**
**1/2 cup milk**

Separate crescent dough into eight triangles. Combine the chicken and 2 tablespoons cheese; place about 2 tablespoonfuls on the wide end of each triangle. Roll up and place on an ungreased baking sheet. Bake at 375° for 18-20 minutes or until golden brown.

Meanwhile, in a saucepan or microwave-safe bowl, combine soup, milk and remaining cheese. Cook until heated through and cheese is melted. Serve over crescents. **Yield:** 4 servings.

## Artichoke Olive Salmon

*After enjoying a similar Italian dish at a restaurant, I did some experimenting at home and came up with this recipe. My husband loves it and requests it often. I just top a salmon fillet with olives, artichoke hearts and diced tomatoes.* —*Michele Salazar, Plain City, Ohio*

**1 salmon fillet (20 ounces)**
**1 cup stuffed olives, chopped**
**1 can (4-1/4 ounces) chopped ripe olives**
**1 can (14 ounces) water-packed artichoke hearts, drained and chopped**
**1 can (14-1/2 ounces) diced tomatoes, drained**

Cut salmon into four pieces. Place on a piece of heavy-duty foil (about 18 in. x 15 in.). Top each piece with olives, artichokes and tomatoes. Fold foil around salmon and seal tightly. Place on a baking sheet. Bake at 350° for 35-40 minutes or until fish flakes easily with a fork. **Yield:** 4 servings.

## Holiday Wreath Cookies

*(Pictured at right)*

*Time-crunched cooks will cheer for these Christmas nibbles from our Test Kitchen staff. They used store-bought cookies, a glaze and candies to form festive wreaths.*

**1 cup plus 2 tablespoons confectioners' sugar, *divided***
**2 tablespoons light corn syrup**
**1 to 2 tablespoons water**
**Red and green gel food coloring**
**1 package (16 ounces) cutout butter cookies**
**Snowflake sprinkles and red decorating candies**

In a small bowl, combine 1 cup confectioners' sugar, corn syrup and enough water to achieve a smooth consistency. Remove 2 tablespoons glaze to another bowl; tint red. Cover and set aside. Tint remaining glaze green. Dip tops of half of the cookies in green glaze. (Save remaining cookies for another use.) Decorate with sprinkles and candies. Stir enough remaining confectioners' sugar into the red glaze to achieve piping consistency. Using a #3 round pastry tip, pipe small bows and ribbons onto cookies. Serve immediately or let stand until set. **Yield:** about 3-1/2 dozen.

**Editor's Note:** This recipe was tested with Salerno butter cookies.

## Christmas Candies

(Pictured below)

*During my childhood, my family lived in Brazil, where we relished these treats. Roll the caramel-like bites in nuts or sprinkles. —Laura Beth Dean, Christiansburg, Virginia*

**3 tablespoons baking cocoa**
**1 can (14 ounces) sweetened condensed milk**
**2 tablespoons butter**
**Finely chopped pistachios**

In a small heavy saucepan, bring the cocoa, milk and butter to a boil, stirring constantly. Reduce heat to low; cook and stir until thickened. Transfer to a small bowl. Cover and refrigerate until chilled. Roll into 1-in. balls; roll in pistachios. Store in the refrigerator. **Yield:** about 2-1/2 dozen.

## Cranberry Nut Fudge

(Pictured below)

*This fast and delicious fudge recipe is my all-time favorite. Dotted with dried cranberries, it has festive red color for the Christmas season. Chopped pecans give the sweet squares nutty flavor and crunch. In a decorative tin, they make a yummy Christmas gift. —Bobby Langley Rocky Mount, North Carolina*

**1 teaspoon butter**
**1 can (16 ounces) milk chocolate frosting**
**1 package (11-1/2 ounces) milk chocolate chips**
**1 package (6 ounces) dried cranberries**
**1/2 cup chopped pecans**

Line an 8-in. square dish with foil and grease the foil with butter; set aside. In a heavy saucepan, combine frosting and chocolate chips. Cook and stir over medium-low heat until chips are melted. Stir in cranberries and nuts. Pour into prepared pan.

Refrigerate until firm, about 2 hours. Using foil, lift fudge out of pan. Discard foil; cut the fudge into 1-in. squares. Store in the refrigerator. **Yield:** about 2 pounds.

Christmas Candies
Cranberry Nut Fudge
Holiday Wreath Cookies

# Chapter 5

# 10 Minutes to the Table

ON MANY DAYS when you're running behind, a mere 10 minutes is all the time you can find to fix delicious and satisfying food for your family.

So the next time you're hungry and truly "down to the wire" on putting a homemade meal on the table, take a deep breath and count to 10.

Then turn to this time-saving chapter to discover a speedy selection of flavorful main dishes, sandwiches, side dishes, snacks, desserts and more. Each fantastic dish takes just 10 minutes from start to finish...but tastes like you were cooking all day.

**ON-THE-RUN RECIPES.** Sweet and Sour Pork Chops and Tangy Sugar Snap Peas (both recipes on p. 79).

## Tomato Corn Salad

*(Pictured at right)*

*This flavorful side dish is both colorful and delicious. I fixed it for one of our family reunions and everyone raved about it, especially our Italian son-in-law. Since then, I've prepared the veggie salad on many occasions.* —*Rhoda McFall, Lincoln, Kansas*

Uses less fat, sugar or salt. Includes Nutritional Analysis and Diabetic Exchanges.

**1 package (16 ounces) frozen corn**
**3 medium tomatoes, diced**
**1/3 cup Italian salad dressing**
**1/4 cup minced fresh basil**
**1/2 to 1 teaspoon salt**

Place corn and a small amount of water in a microwave-safe bowl. Cover and microwave on high for 3 to 3-1/2 minutes or until corn is crisp-tender; drain. In a bowl, combine the tomatoes, salad dressing, basil and salt. Stir in corn. Serve immediately or refrigerate. Serve with a slotted spoon. **Yield:** 8 servings.

**Nutritional Analysis:** One 1/2-cup serving (prepared with fat-free salad dressing and 1/2 teaspoon salt) equals 70 calories, 1 g fat (trace saturated fat), trace cholesterol, 293 mg sodium, 16 g carbohydrate, 2 g fiber, 2 g protein. **Diabetic Exchange:** 1 starch.

**Editor's Note:** This recipe was tested in a 1,100-watt microwave.

## Open-Faced Crab Melts

*Over the years, I've seen these tasty seafood sandwiches please guests at fancy teas and last-minute suppers.* —*Florence McClelland, Fredonia, New York*

**4 English muffins, split**
**1 can (6 ounces) crabmeat, drained, flaked and cartilage removed**
**1/3 cup mayonnaise**
**1 tablespoon lemon juice**
**1/2 teaspoon pepper**
**1/4 teaspoon dried tarragon**
**1 cup (4 ounces) shredded cheddar cheese**

Broil English muffins 4-6 in. from the heat for 2-3 minutes or until golden brown. In a bowl, combine the crab, mayonnaise, lemon juice, pepper and tarragon. Spread over each muffin half; sprinkle with cheese. Broil for 2-3 minutes or until cheese is melted. **Yield:** 4 servings.

## Blushing Peaches

*I give a special treatment to canned peaches by filling them with a fluffy pink cream cheese mixture. This light and pretty dessert is a family favorite.* —*Teri Lindquist, Gurnee, Illinois*

**1 can (28 ounces) peach halves**
**8 lettuce leaves**

Tomato Corn Salad

**1 package (8 ounces) cream cheese, softened**
**2 to 3 tablespoons confectioners' sugar**
**2 tablespoons cherry juice**
**1/2 cup chopped walnuts**
**8 maraschino cherries with stems**

Drain peaches, reserving 2 tablespoons juice. Place one peach half on each lettuce leaf. In a small mixing bowl, beat the cream cheese, confectioners' sugar, cherry juice and reserved peach juice. Stir in walnuts. Spoon into peach halves; top with cherries. **Yield:** 8 servings.

## Salsa Cheese Dip

*Are you looking for a speedy dip for tortilla chips? Try this crowd-pleaser that jazzes up cream cheese with salsa and more.* —*Judy Barry, West Milford, New Jersey*

**2 packages (8 ounces *each*) cream cheese, softened**
**1 jar (16 ounces) salsa, *divided***
**1 medium green pepper, chopped**
**1 small red onion, chopped**
**1 medium tomato, seeded and chopped**
**2 cups (8 ounces) shredded Monterey Jack cheese**
**Tortilla chips**

In a small mixing bowl, beat cream cheese until smooth. Beat in 1 cup of salsa until combined. Spread onto a 12-in. serving plate. Sprinkle with green pepper, onion and tomato. Top with the remaining salsa; sprinkle with cheese. Serve with tortilla chips. **Yield:** 14-16 servings.

## Watermelon Smoothies

*This is so good in summer. The simple melon beverage is a snap to blend up.* —*Sandi Pichon, Slidell, Louisiana*

6 cups coarsely chopped seedless watermelon
1 cup lemon sherbet
12 ice cubes

Place half of the watermelon in a blender; cover and process until smooth. Add half of the sherbet and ice; cover and process until smooth. Repeat. Serve immediately in chilled glasses. **Yield:** 6 servings.

## Fruit-Topped Frozen Yogurt

*This cool refreshing dessert is easy to make for guests. I love the contrast of sweet and tart, warm and cold.*
*—Cindy Neff, Colorado Springs, Colorado*

**3 tablespoons butter**
**1 tablespoon lime juice**
**1 tablespoon honey**
**2 medium firm bananas, sliced**
**1/2 cup fresh *or* frozen sliced peaches, thawed and chopped**
**2 kiwifruit, peeled and sliced**
**1-1/2 cups halved fresh strawberries**
**4 scoops frozen vanilla yogurt**

In a skillet, melt butter over low heat. Stir in the lime juice, honey, bananas and peaches. Cook and stir gently for 1-2 minutes or until heated through. Place kiwi and strawberries in dessert dishes; top with frozen yogurt and banana mixture. **Yield:** 4 servings.

## Teriyaki Chicken Sandwiches

*I turn lemon juice, soy sauce, garlic, ginger and a little brown sugar into a lip-smacking sauce that seasons shredded cooked chicken. —Pam May, Auburn, Alabama*

**2-1/2 cups shredded cooked chicken**
**1/4 cup lemon juice**
**1/4 cup soy sauce**
**2 tablespoons sugar**
**1 tablespoon brown sugar**
**3/4 teaspoon minced garlic**
**1/2 teaspoon ground ginger**
**4 sandwich buns, split**

In a large saucepan, combine the first seven ingredients. Bring to a boil. Reduce heat; simmer, uncovered, for 3-4 minutes or until heated through. Spoon chicken mixture onto each bun. **Yield:** 4 servings.

## Tuna-Stuffed Avocados

*(Pictured at right)*

*My family loves avocados, and this delicious tuna salad is perfect on days when you don't want to spend a lot of time cooking. Served with your favorite soup and bread, it makes a tasty meal anytime. —Vicki Smith*
*Okeechobee, Florida*

**2 packages (3 ounces *each*) cream cheese, softened**
**1/4 cup mayonnaise**
**2 tablespoons finely chopped onion**
**1 tablespoon lemon juice**
**1 teaspoon celery seed**
**1/2 teaspoon pepper**
**1 can (6 ounces) tuna, drained and flaked**
**3 medium ripe avocados**

In a small mixing bowl, beat the cream cheese and mayonnaise until well blended. Add the onion, lemon juice, celery seed and pepper. Stir in the tuna. Cut avocados in half lengthwise; remove pits. Spoon tuna salad into avocado halves. Serve immediately. **Yield:** 3 servings.

### More 10-Minute Morsels

- To give plain cooked broccoli some pizzazz one night, I tried adding a few tablespoons of store-bought Alfredo sauce. It really perked up the broccoli and took only moments to do.
  *—Mary Sheldon, Brooksville, Florida*
- I create a fast-as-can-be snack, breakfast dish or dessert by putting canned or fresh fruits in a bowl and sprinkling on a bit of shredded coconut. It's yummy, refreshing and so easy. *—Jennifer Meyer Slippery Rock, Pennsylvania*
- When we'd like a quick shortcake, we cut Twinkies snack cakes in half lengthwise. For each serving, we just put two halves in a bowl and top them with strawberries and whipped cream. *—Paul Hanson Santa Maria, California*

Tuna-Stuffed Avocados

## Hot Spinach Dip

*For a different take on traditional spinach dip, I warm this rich mixture in the microwave. It's terrific with crackers, tortilla chips or fresh veggies. —Janie Obermier St. Joseph, Missouri*

- **1 package (8 ounces) cream cheese, softened**
- **1/2 cup mayonnaise**
- **1/4 cup grated Parmesan cheese**
- **1 package (10 ounces) frozen chopped spinach, thawed and squeezed dry**
- **1 cup (4 ounces) shredded mozzarella cheese**
- **Crackers *or* fresh vegetables**

In a small mixing bowl, beat the cream cheese, mayonnaise and Parmesan cheese until blended. Stir in spinach and mozzarella cheese. Spoon into an ungreased microwave-safe 9-in. pie plate. Microwave, uncovered, on high for 4-5 minutes or until bubbly, stirring twice. Serve with crackers or vegetables. **Yield:** 8-10 servings.

**Editor's Note:** This recipe was tested in a 1,100-watt microwave.

## Gingersnap Pumpkin Pudding

*(Pictured below)*

*Crushed gingersnaps give yummy crunch to this creamy dessert. I use cooked pumpkin and pie spice for the comforting fall pudding. If you like, prepare it with molasses cookies instead. —Mary Smith, Litchfield, Michigan*

- **1-3/4 cups cold milk**
- **1 package (3.4 ounces) instant cheesecake *or* vanilla pudding mix**

Gingersnap Pumpkin Pudding

- **1/2 cup canned pumpkin**
- **1/4 to 1/2 teaspoon pumpkin pie spice**
- **10 gingersnaps**
- **1 cup whipped topping**

In a bowl, whisk milk and pudding mix for 2 minutes. Stir in the pumpkin and pie spice. Let stand for 2 minutes or until soft-set. Set aside three gingersnaps; crush the rest. Fold whipped topping into pudding; spoon into dessert bowls. Sprinkle with cookie crumbs. Serve with whole gingersnaps. **Yield:** 3 servings.

## Cinnamon Apple Shakes

*Autumn flavor is abundant in this rich beverage. Just blend some applesauce, caramel topping, vanilla ice cream and a couple other ingredients for a sweet and velvety fall treat. I like that it takes only 10 minutes to make. —Natalie Carter Killeen, Texas*

- **3 cups vanilla ice cream**
- **3/4 cup milk**
- **1/2 cup cinnamon applesauce**
- **1/4 cup caramel ice cream topping**
- **1/2 teaspoon rum extract**

In a blender, combine all ingredients; cover and process until smooth. Pour into chilled glasses; serve immediately. **Yield:** 4 servings.

## Tuna-Stuffed Tomatoes

*I created these broiled tomato halves one afternoon when I wanted a warm lunch. The addition of chopped celery gives the tuna mixture a nice crunch. —Reneé McGowen Aurora, Colorado*

- **1 large tomato**
- **1 can (6 ounces) tuna, drained and flaked**
- **4 teaspoons mayonnaise**
- **1 tablespoon chopped celery**
- **1/2 teaspoon Dijon mustard**
- **1/4 teaspoon seasoned salt**

Cut the tomato in half through the stem. Scoop out pulp, leaving a 1/2-in. shell. In a bowl, combine the remaining ingredients. Fill tomato shells with tuna mixture; place on a baking sheet. Broil 3-4 in. from the heat for 4-5 minutes or until heated through. **Yield:** 2 servings.

## Grape Apple Coleslaw

*One of the reasons I like this sweet coleslaw recipe is that there are so many variations to it. It's great to just throw it all together, adding whatever fruits or nuts I feel like at the time. —Lynn Nelson, Eureka, California*

- **4 cups coleslaw mix**
- **1 cup miniature marshmallows**
- **1/2 cup raisins**
- **1 carton (6 ounces) vanilla yogurt**

1 large tart apple, chopped
1/2 cup halved green grapes
1/4 cup chopped walnuts

In a serving bowl, combine the coleslaw mix, marshmallows, raisins and yogurt. Stir in the apple, grapes and walnuts. Cover and refrigerate until serving. **Yield:** 6-8 servings.

## Almond-Turkey Cheese Spread

*I like this timely topper with crackers as a TV snack for my family. I combine cheeses and seasonings with deli turkey, almonds and sour cream. —Carolyn Hayes Marion, Illinois*

**1 package (3 ounces) cream cheese, softened**
**1/4 cup sour cream**
**1/2 teaspoon Worcestershire sauce**
**1/4 teaspoon garlic powder**
**1/2 pound smoked deli turkey, finely chopped**
**1 cup (4 ounces) shredded cheddar cheese**
**1/2 cup slivered almonds, chopped**
**Assorted crackers**

In a small mixing bowl, beat the cream cheese, sour cream, Worcestershire sauce and garlic powder until combined. Stir in the turkey, cheddar cheese and almonds. Serve with crackers. Refrigerate leftovers. **Yield:** about 1-1/2 cups.

## Beef Onion Soup

*I live alone, so I'm always looking for ways to use up leftovers like beef. This soup makes a quick lunch or dinner along with fresh veggies or a crisp green salad. —Barbara Zowada, Sheridan, Wyoming*

**1 can (10-1/2 ounces) French onion soup**
**1 cup cubed cooked beef**
**2 slices French bread (3/4 inch thick), toasted**
**1/3 cup shredded Monterey Jack cheese**
**2 teaspoons shredded Parmesan cheese, optional**

Prepare soup according to package directions; add beef. Ladle into two 2-cup ovenproof bowls. Top each with a French bread slice. Sprinkle with Monterey Jack cheese and Parmesan cheese if desired. Broil until cheese is melted. Serve immediately. **Yield:** 2 servings.

## Two-Cheese Pizzas

*(Pictured above right)*

*When time is tight, I use pita rounds to form the crust for these cute little pizzas. Cut into quarters, they make appealing appetizers when there's just a few of you. Serve wedges alone...or with pizza sauce. —Nevine Farid Overland Park, Kansas*

**1 tablespoon butter, melted**
**1/2 teaspoon garlic powder**
**2 pita breads (6 inches)**
**1 cup (4 ounces) shredded mozzarella cheese**

Two-Cheese Pizzas

**1/2 teaspoon dried basil**
**1 small tomato, diced**
**2 tablespoons grated Parmesan cheese**
**1/2 cup pizza sauce, warmed, optional**

In a small bowl, combine butter and garlic powder; brush over pitas. Sprinkle with mozzarella cheese, basil and tomato. Place on an ungreased baking sheet. Bake at 400° for 5-7 minutes or until cheese is melted. Sprinkle with Parmesan cheese. Serve with pizza sauce if desired. **Yield:** 2 servings.

### Butter Shortcut

When the recipe I'm preparing calls for butter, I remove the amount I need from the full stick. Then I take just a few moments to cut whatever is left of the stick into 1-tablespoon pats, following the measuring guide on the wrapper.

I put all of those extra butter pieces in a small glass bowl, cover it and keep it in a convenient spot in the fridge. The next time I need a tablespoon or two of butter, they're already measured out for me and ready to add to my recipe. *—Karen Cooley Pascagoula, Mississippi*

## Mozzarella Beef Sandwiches

*(Pictured at right)*

*This is a great supper when we're short on time. To make the fantastic four-ingredient sandwich, I simply jazz up slices of deli roast beef with shredded mozzarella cheese and purchased spaghetti sauce.* —*Erica Svejda Janesville, Wisconsin*

**1 loaf (20 inches) French bread**
**1-1/4 pounds thinly sliced deli roast beef**
**1 cup meatless spaghetti sauce**
**1-1/4 cups shredded mozzarella cheese**

Cut bread in half lengthwise; cut widthwise into five portions. On each bread bottom, layer beef, spaghetti sauce and cheese. Place on an ungreased baking sheet. Broil 4 in. from the heat for 1-2 minutes or until cheese is melted; replace tops. **Yield:** 5 servings.

Mozzarella Beef Sandwiches

## Creamy Floret Salad

*This medley of cauliflower, tomatoes and broccoli gets a quick kick from ranch dressing. The recipe originally called for grated Parmesan, but I prefer shredded.* —*Judy McCarthy, Derby, Kansas*

✓ Uses less fat, sugar or salt. Includes Nutritional Analysis and Diabetic Exchanges.

**2 cups cauliflowerets**
**2 cups fresh broccoli florets**
**1 cup cherry tomatoes, halved**
**1/2 cup ranch salad dressing**
**1/4 cup shredded Parmesan cheese**

In a serving bowl, combine all ingredients; toss to coat. **Yield:** 5 servings.

**Nutritional Analysis:** One 1-cup serving (prepared with fat-free ranch dressing) equals 83 calories, 2 g fat (1 g saturated fat), 2 mg cholesterol, 239 mg sodium, 13 g carbohydrate, 2 g fiber, 5 g protein. **Diabetic Exchanges:** 2 vegetable, 1/2 fat.

## Creamed Pearl Onions

*Not only is this easy side dish delicious, but it's popular with family and guests alike. Best of all, it takes about 10 minutes to prepare from start to finish. Garlic powder, nutmeg and other spices add great flavor.* —*Suzan Wiener, Spring Hill, Florida*

**1 package (16 ounces) frozen pearl onions**
**4-1/2 teaspoons butter**
**4-1/2 teaspoons all-purpose flour**
**1/4 teaspoon salt**
**1/8 to 1/4 teaspoon ground nutmeg**
**1/8 teaspoon garlic powder**
**1/8 teaspoon pepper**
**3/4 cup milk**
**Paprika**

Cook onions according to package directions. Meanwhile, in a small saucepan, melt the butter; stir in the flour, salt, nutmeg, garlic powder and pepper until smooth. Gradually stir in the milk. Bring to a boil; cook and stir for 2 minutes or until thickened. Drain onions; stir into the cream sauce. Sprinkle with paprika. **Yield:** 2-3 servings.

## Apple Spiced Oatmeal

*This thick satisfying oatmeal is wonderful when overnight guests visit for the holidays. We set up an "oatmeal bar", offering a variety of fruits and nuts to top steaming bowlsful.* —*Ericka Willea, Twin Lake, Michigan*

**1 cup quick-cooking oats**
**1-3/4 cups apple cider**
**1 tablespoon butter**
**1 teaspoon ground cinnamon**
**1/8 teaspoon salt**
**Sliced bananas and blueberries**

In a microwave-safe bowl, combine oats and cider. Microwave, uncovered, on high for 2-3 minutes or until tender. Stir in the butter, cinnamon and salt. Serve with bananas and berries. **Yield:** 2 servings.

## Ranch Coleslaw

*This is a perfect last-minute side dish. When I was a newlywed, I came up with this recipe. My husband said it was the best coleslaw he ever tasted.* —*Mellanie McCreary El Dorado, California*

**1/4 cup prepared ranch salad dressing**
**2 tablespoons mayonnaise**
**1-1/2 teaspoons sugar**
**1/4 teaspoon lemon juice**
**3-3/4 cups coleslaw mix**

In a small bowl or jar with a tight-fitting lid, combine the salad dressing, mayonnaise, sugar and lemon juice. Place the coleslaw mix in a salad bowl; add the dressing and toss to coat. **Yield:** 4 servings.

## Sweet and Sour Pork Chops

*(Pictured below and on page 72)*

*It's hard to believe that these saucy, tender pork chops require just a handful of ingredients. The tasty entree is special enough for guests but great for weeknights, too, since it's on the table in a matter of minutes.* —Deborah Anderson
*Spooner, Wisconsin*

**8 boneless pork loin chops (1/4 inch thick)**
**3 tablespoons chili sauce**
**3 tablespoons honey**
**2 tablespoons soy sauce**

Place pork chops in a greased broiler pan. In a bowl, combine the chili sauce, honey and soy sauce. Pour over pork. Broil 4 in. from the heat for 5-7 minutes or until meat juices run clear. **Yield:** 4 servings.

## Tangy Sugar Snap Peas

*(Pictured below and on page 72)*

*Our Test Kitchen staff created this mouth-watering side dish that comes together quickly in the microwave.*

✓ Uses less fat, sugar or salt. Includes Nutritional Analysis and Diabetic Exchanges.

**1 pound fresh *or* frozen sugar snap peas, thawed**
**1 small onion, halved and sliced**
**3 tablespoons water, *divided***
**4 teaspoons sugar**
**1 teaspoon cornstarch**
**1/8 teaspoon pepper**
**2 tablespoons cider vinegar**

In a large microwave-safe bowl, combine the peas, onion and 2 tablespoons water. Cover and cook on high for 5-7 minutes or until crisp-tender, stirring twice; drain. In a small microwave-safe bowl, combine the sugar, cornstarch and pepper; stir in the vinegar and remaining water until smooth. Cook, uncovered, on high for 30-45 seconds or until thickened, stirring once. Add to pea mixture; toss to coat. **Yield:** 4 servings.

**Nutritional Analysis:** One 3/4-cup serving equals 75 calories, trace fat (0 saturated fat), 0 cholesterol, 1 mg sodium, 16 g carbohydrate, 5 g fiber, 3 g protein. **Diabetic Exchange:** 3 vegetable.

**Editor's Note:** This recipe was tested in a 1,100-watt microwave.

Sweet and Sour Pork Chops
Tangy Sugar Snap Peas

# Chapter 6

# Handy Mix Tricks

SEARCHING for solutions to dinner dilemmas? A peek in the pantry may be all you need to put together a mouth-watering meal pronto!

Thanks to the wide range of convenience foods available in today's grocery stores, you can find fast answers to daily menu questions.

It can be as simple as beefing up canned goods to make a comforting casserole, jazzing up frozen potatoes for an effortless side dish or using a cake mix to create fresh-baked bars.

Or save shopping time—and money, too—by making mixes yourself. The quick creations in this chapter are easy to assemble in advance and will give you a helpful head start on meals.

**MIX MAINSTAYS.** Top to bottom: Pumpkin Dessert and Green Bean Potato Bake (both recipes on p. 89).

# Fast Fixes With Mixes

HOME-STYLE COOKING makes a meal especially satisfying. But you don't need to spend long hours in the kitchen preparing foods from scratch in order to achieve the old-fashioned taste your family craves.

Using packaged convenience foods from the supermarket, you can dish up down-home fare with little fuss on your part. So take advantage of the bottled sauces, canned pie fillings and other ready-made items available to hurry along family-pleasing meals.

## Chocolate Cookie Cake

*(Pictured below)*

*This cake is a showstopper and tastes as good as it looks. It's a quicker version of a favorite scratch cake. Using a boxed mix saves time when my schedule is hectic.*

*—Reneé Zimmer, Gig Harbor, Washington*

**1 package (18-1/4 ounces) white cake mix**
**16 cream-filled chocolate sandwich cookies, coarsely crushed**
**1 package (3 ounces) cream cheese, softened**
**2 teaspoons milk**
**2 cups heavy whipping cream**

Chocolate Cookie Cake

**3/4 cup confectioners' sugar**
**Additional cream-filled chocolate sandwich cookies**

Prepare cake batter according to package directions; stir in crushed cookies. Spoon into a greased and floured 10-in. fluted tube pan. Bake at 350° for 33-38 minutes or until a toothpick inserted near the center comes out clean. Cool for 10 minutes before removing from pan to a wire rack to cool completely.

In a small mixing bowl, beat cream cheese and milk until smooth. Beat in cream until mixture begins to thicken. Add confectioners' sugar; beat until stiff peaks form. Frost cake. Garnish with additional cookies. Refrigerate leftovers. **Yield:** 12-16 servings.

## Corn Tortilla Casserole

*I take advantage of canned ingredients, including kidney beans, cream-style corn and tomato sauce, to dress up ground beef in this great southwestern entree. Convenient corn tortillas separate each mouth-watering layer.*

*—Jane Hardy, Henderson, Texas*

**1 pound ground beef**
**1 medium onion, chopped**
**3 celery ribs, chopped**
**1 can (16 ounces) kidney beans, rinsed and drained**
**1 can (14-3/4 ounces) cream-style corn**
**1 can (8 ounces) tomato sauce**
**4-1/2 teaspoons Worcestershire sauce**
**1 teaspoon chili powder**
**1 garlic clove, minced**
**6 corn tortillas (6 inches)**
**1/2 cup shredded cheddar cheese**

In a large skillet, cook the beef, onion and celery over medium heat until meat is no longer pink and vegetables are tender; drain. Stir in the beans, corn, tomato sauce, Worcestershire sauce, chili powder and garlic; cook for 3 minutes.

Place one tortilla in a greased round 2-qt. baking dish; top with 1 cup meat mixture. Repeat layers five times. Sprinkle with cheese. Bake, uncovered, at 350° for 25-30 minutes or until bubbly. **Yield:** 6 servings.

## Pesto Chicken Pasta

*(Pictured at right)*

*Because my work shift ends at 7 p.m., I get home later in the evening and need to get dinner on the table fast. I like to double this 30-minute recipe for my family. The pasta dish is delicious served hot or cold...and can be prepared with cooked shrimp instead of chicken.*

*—Linda Sweet, Newark, Delaware*

**8 ounces uncooked ziti *or* small tube pasta**
**1 cup frozen peas and carrots**
**1 envelope pesto sauce mix**
**1 tablespoon cornstarch**
**1-1/2 cups milk**
**1 cup cubed cooked chicken**
**1/4 teaspoon salt**

**1/4 teaspoon pepper**
**1/4 cup chopped walnuts**

Cook pasta according to package directions; add peas and carrots during last 2 minutes of cooking. Meanwhile, in a small saucepan, whisk pesto mix, cornstarch and milk until smooth. Bring to a boil; cook and stir for 2 minutes or until thickened. Stir in chicken, salt and pepper.

Drain pasta mixture; place in a large serving bowl. Add the chicken mixture and toss to coat. Sprinkle with walnuts. **Yield:** 4 servings.

## Orange Refrigerator Cake

*(Pictured below)*

*This refreshing dessert is sure to disappear in a hurry at your next get-together. My mother used to prepare the recipe over 60 years ago, but she referred to it as "Icebox Cake" because we didn't have a refrigerator.* —*Marietta Martin*
*Brazil, Indiana*

**1 package (4.6 ounces) cook-and-serve vanilla pudding mix**
**1 envelope unflavored gelatin**
**1 cup orange juice**
**1 tablespoon grated orange peel**
**2 loaves (10-1/2 ounces *each*) angel food cake**
**2 cups heavy whipping cream, whipped**

Prepare pudding according to package directions; set aside. In a small saucepan, sprinkle gelatin over orange juice; let stand for 1 minute. Cook and stir over low heat until gelatin is completely dissolved. Stir into pudding. Add orange peel. Transfer to a large bowl. Cover and refrigerate for 2 hours or until cooled.

Cut one angel food cake in half widthwise. Save one half for another use. Cut remaining half into eight slices. Cut second loaf into 16 slices.

Arrange half of the cake slices in an ungreased 13-in. x 9-in. x 2-in. dish. Fold whipped cream into the pudding; spread half over the cake slices. Repeat layers. Cover and refrigerate overnight or until set. **Yield:** 12 servings.

**Orange Refrigerator Cake**
**Pesto Chicken Pasta**

## Rosy Rhubarb Dessert

*I love to bake this comforting rhubarb-and-almond delight for friends and family. Topped with yummy chopped coconut, the effortless dessert takes advantage of a packaged white cake mix and strawberry gelatin.* —*Elsie Wigdahl Ruthven, Iowa*

**4 cups chopped fresh *or* frozen rhubarb, thawed**
**1 cup sugar**
**1/4 cup strawberry gelatin powder**
**1 package (18-1/4 ounces) white cake mix**
**1 cup hot water**
**1/2 cup finely chopped flaked coconut**
**1/3 cup slivered almonds, toasted**
**6 tablespoons butter, melted**

Arrange rhubarb evenly in a greased 13-in. x 9-in. x 2-in. baking dish. Combine sugar and gelatin powder; sprinkle over rhubarb. Sprinkle dry cake mix over gelatin mixture. Pour hot water over cake mix (do not stir). Top with coconut and almonds. Drizzle with butter.

Bake at 350° for 40-45 minutes or until a toothpick inserted near the center comes out clean. Cool on a wire rack. **Yield:** 12-15 servings.

## Pineapple Upside-Down Cake

*(Pictured below)*

*Here's a traditional dessert that's been updated with purchased convenience items. Still, everyone who samples it thinks I spent all day making it from scratch. The cake actually takes only about 10 minutes to prepare before it goes in the oven.* —*Karen Ann Bland, Gove, Kansas*

Pineapple Upside-Down Cake

**1/4 cup butter, melted**
**1 can (20 ounces) sliced pineapple**
**10 pecan halves**
**1 jar (12 ounces) apricot preserves**
**1 package (18-1/4 ounces) yellow cake mix**

Pour melted butter into a well-greased 13-in. x 9-in. x 2-in. baking dish. Drain pineapple, reserving 1/4 cup juice. Arrange pineapple slices in prepared pan; place a pecan half in the center of each slice.

Combine the apricot preserves and reserved pineapple juice; spoon over the pineapple slices. Prepare the cake batter according to the package directions; pour over the pineapple.

Bake at 350° for 45-50 minutes or until a toothpick inserted near the center comes out clean. Immediately invert onto a large serving platter. Cool slightly; serve warm. **Yield:** 12-15 servings.

## Tasty Turkey Casserole

*Canned cream of chicken soup makes it easy to prepare this saucy turkey-and-broccoli bake. Swiss cheese and sour cream add richness to each hearty helping. When I need to bring something to a potluck or other get-together, I often turn to this crowd-pleasing recipe.*
—*Maureen Dongoski, Petersburg, West Virginia*

**6 cups fresh broccoli florets**
**1 cup water**
**6 cups cubed cooked turkey breast**
**1 can (10-3/4 ounces) condensed cream of chicken soup, undiluted**
**1 cup (8 ounces) sour cream**
**3/4 cup shredded Swiss cheese**

In a large saucepan, combine the broccoli and water. Bring to a boil. Reduce heat. Cover and simmer for 6-8 minutes or until crisp-tender; drain. Transfer to a 13-in. x 9-in. x 2-in. baking dish coated with nonstick cooking spray. Sprinkle with turkey.

Combine the soup and sour cream. Spoon over the turkey. Sprinkle with Swiss cheese. Bake, uncovered, at 375° for 20-25 minutes or until heated through. **Yield:** 10 servings.

## Mixed Fruit Salsa

*Ready in just 30 minutes, this delightfully different salsa can make a terrific snack—or even a dessert—served with homemade cinnamon tortilla chips. The recipe calls for fresh peaches, but you can also use frozen peaches.*
—*Laura Lancour, Milwaukee, Wisconsin*

**1 package (16 ounces) mixed frozen berries, thawed and chopped**
**2 medium peaches, diced**
**2 medium kiwifruit, peeled and diced**
**3 tablespoons sugar**
**2 tablespoons lemon juice**
**1-1/2 teaspoons grated lime peel**
**CINNAMON TORTILLA CHIPS:**
**8 flour tortillas (7 inches)**

Au Gratin Taters 'n' Chops

3 tablespoons butter, melted
3 tablespoons sugar
1-1/2 teaspoons ground cinnamon

In a large bowl, combine the first six ingredients; set aside. Brush both sides of tortillas with butter. Combine the sugar and cinnamon; sprinkle over both sides of tortillas.

Cut each into six wedges. Place on ungreased baking sheets. Bake at 400° for 6-8 minutes on each side or until crisp. Drain salsa; serve with the tortilla chips. **Yield:** 6-8 servings.

## Quick Coconut Muffins

*Whether I'm going to a family event or a church bake sale, people expect me to bring these nutty muffins. I'm always happy to oblige, since they come together quickly and are one of my favorites as well.* —*Mary Burrough Midwest City, Oklahoma*

**1 package (18-1/4 ounces) yellow cake mix**
**1/2 cup butter, softened**
**2/3 cup water**
**3 eggs**
**1 can (8 ounces) crushed pineapple, drained**
**1 cup flaked coconut**
**1 cup chopped pecans**
**1 teaspoon rum extract**
**1 teaspoon coconut extract**

In a mixing bowl, beat the cake mix and butter. Add the remaining ingredients. Fill greased or paper-lined muffin cups half full. Bake at 350° for 20-25 minutes or until a toothpick comes out clean. Cool for 5 minutes before removing from the pans to wire racks. **Yield:** 2 dozen.

## Au Gratin Taters 'n' Chops

*(Pictured above)*

*This easy entree will please adults and children alike. As a college student, I'd often prepare this recipe, only I'd decrease the number of pork chops from six to two. I'd have one right away and save the second for dinner the next day.* —*Laura Starkey, Manhattan, Kansas*

**1 package (4.9 ounces) au gratin potatoes**
**6 boneless pork loin chops (3/4 inch thick)**
**1 tablespoon vegetable oil**
**1/2 cup shredded cheddar cheese**
**4 bacon strips, cooked and crumbled**

Combine potatoes and sauce mix according to package directions. Spoon into a greased 13-in. x 9-in. x 2-in. baking dish; set aside. In a large skillet, brown pork chops in oil; arrange over potatoes.

Bake, uncovered, at 375° for 20-25 minutes or until meat juices run clear and potatoes are tender. Sprinkle cheese and bacon over chops. Bake 2-3 minutes longer or until cheese is melted. **Yield:** 6 servings.

Candy Bar Freezer Dessert
Berry-Banana Cheese Pie

## Berry-Banana Cheese Pie

*(Pictured at left)*

*I came up with this recipe one day using ingredients I had in the cupboard and refrigerator. Strawberry-banana gelatin gives fruit flavor and pretty color to the smooth cheesecake-like pie. To speed things up, I use a purchased crust.*
*—Sharon McClatchey, Muskogee, Oklahoma*

**1 package (3 ounces) strawberry-banana gelatin**
**1/4 cup sugar**
**1 cup boiling water**
**1 package (8 ounces) cream cheese, cubed**
**1 carton (8 ounces) whipped topping, thawed**
**1 extra-serving-size graham cracker crust (9 ounces)**

In a large mixing bowl, dissolve gelatin and sugar in boiling water. Beat in cream cheese until smooth. Fold in whipped topping. Pour into crust. Refrigerate for 2 hours or until set. **Yield:** 8 servings.

## Microwave Beef Casserole

*This 30-minute main dish featuring fresh mushrooms, almonds and ground beef is a lifesaver when the clock's ticking toward dinnertime. For a change of pace, I sometimes prepare the casserole using cooked wild rice. Add a vegetable and crusty rolls for a delicious dinner.*
*—Joan Hallford, North Richland Hills, Texas*

**1 pound ground beef**
**1 small onion, chopped**
**1/2 cup uncooked instant rice**
**1-1/2 cups water, *divided***
**1 can (10-3/4 ounces) condensed cream of mushroom soup, undiluted**
**1 cup slivered almonds**
**5 large fresh mushrooms, chopped**
**1 package (6 ounces) seasoned stuffing mix**
**1/4 cup butter, melted**

Crumble beef into a microwave-safe 3-qt. dish; add onion. Loosely cover and microwave on high for 5-6 minutes or until meat is no longer pink, stirring twice; drain. Stir in rice and 1/2 cup water. Cover and cook for 3 minutes. Stir in soup, almonds and mushrooms.

In a bowl, combine the stuffing mix, butter and remaining water; spoon over beef mixture. Microwave, uncovered, for 2-3 minutes or until heated through. **Yield:** 4-6 servings.

**Editor's Note:** This recipe was tested in an 850-watt microwave.

## Candy Bar Freezer Dessert

*(Pictured above)*

*I combine butter pecan ice cream and instant pudding to prepare this sweet, cool treat. But what makes it irresistible is the chopped Butterfinger candy bar that forms the crunchy topping. Since this dessert goes in the freezer, I can whip up an extra one to have on hand for especially busy days.* *—Melissa Heberer, Hoskins, Nebraska*

**2 cups crushed graham crackers (about 16 squares)**
**1 cup crushed saltines (about 30 crackers)**
**1/2 cup butter, melted**
**2 cups cold milk**
**2 packages (3.4 ounces *each*) instant vanilla pudding mix**
**1 quart butter pecan ice cream, softened**
**1 carton (8 ounces) frozen whipped topping, thawed**
**1 Butterfinger candy bar (2.1 ounces), chopped**

In a large bowl, combine the cracker crumbs and butter. Pat three-fourths of the mixture into an ungreased 13-in. x 9-in. x 2-in. dish. Refrigerate.

In a bowl, whisk the milk and pudding mixes for 2 minutes. Stir in ice cream until blended. Spread over crust. Spoon whipped topping over pudding layer; spread evenly over top.

Combine the chopped candy bar and the remaining crumb mixture; sprinkle over the whipped topping. Cover and freeze for at least 2 hours. **Yield:** 12-15 servings.

## Chicken Parmigiana

*(Pictured at right)*

*Spaghetti sauce mix is the key to the tasty breading in this elegant-looking entree. After coating and baking the chicken, I drizzle it with prepared sauce and sprinkle on mozzarella cheese. This main dish is great for both busy weeknights and weekend entertaining.* *—Trisha Lange*
*Appleton, Wisconsin*

 Uses less fat, sugar or salt. Includes Nutritional Analysis and Diabetic Exchanges.

**1/2 cup seasoned *or* plain bread crumbs**
**1/4 cup grated Parmesan cheese**
**3 tablespoons spaghetti sauce mix**
**1-1/2 teaspoons garlic powder**
**4 boneless skinless chicken breast halves (4 ounces *each*)**
**1/2 cup Italian salad dressing**
**1/2 cup meatless spaghetti sauce**
**1/4 cup shredded mozzarella cheese**

In a shallow dish, combine the first four ingredients. Dip the chicken in the salad dressing, then coat with the bread crumb mixture. Place in a greased 13-in. x 9-in. x 2-in. baking dish.

Bake, uncovered, at 350° for 35-40 minutes or until chicken juices run clear. Drizzle with spaghetti sauce and sprinkle with mozzarella cheese. Bake 5 minutes longer or until cheese is melted. **Yield:** 4 servings.

**Nutritional Analysis:** One serving (prepared with plain bread crumbs, fat-free salad dressing and part-skim mozzarella) equals 272 calories, 5 g fat (2 g saturated fat), 75 mg cholesterol, 1,128 mg sodium, 20 g carbohydrate, 1 g fiber, 34 g protein. **Diabetic Exchanges:** 3 lean meat, 1 starch, 1 vegetable.

## Herbed Potatoes

*(Pictured below)*

*No one will ever suspect that this rosemary-seasoned side dish starts with canned potatoes. Quick food ideas are a big part of my recipe collection, and these buttery potatoes are a favorite. —Jane Symens, Anchor Point, Alaska*

**1 can (15 ounces) whole potatoes, drained**
**3 tablespoons butter, melted**
**2 teaspoons minced fresh parsley**
**1/4 teaspoon dried rosemary, crushed**
**1/4 teaspoon pepper**
**Dash garlic salt**

In an ungreased 2-qt. baking dish, combine all of the ingredients. Bake, uncovered, at 350° for 15-20 minutes or until heated through, stirring occasionally. **Yield:** 3 servings.

**Herbed Potatoes**
**Chicken Parmigiana**

## Orange Fluff Salad

*My sister gave me this easy recipe that whips up in a jiffy. Unlike many gelatin recipes, this salad doesn't have to set for hours, so it's great for unexpected company.*
*—Stacey Meyer, Merced, California*

**1 cup (8 ounces) sour cream**
**1 package (3 ounces) lemon gelatin**
**2 cans (11 ounces *each*) mandarin oranges, drained**
**1 can (21 ounces) pineapple tidbits, drained**
**1 carton (8 ounces) frozen whipped topping, thawed**

Place sour cream in a bowl. Sprinkle with gelatin and stir until blended. Fold in the oranges, pineapple and whipped topping. **Yield:** 8 servings.

## Apple Dumpling Bake

*(Pictured below)*

*I received this recipe from a friend, then tweaked it a bit to fit my family's tastes. Mountain Dew soda is the "secret" ingredient in this rich apple dessert. It's a snap to make, so we enjoy it often with scoops of vanilla ice cream.*
*—Chris Shields, Monrovia, Indiana*

**2 tubes (8 ounces *each*) refrigerated crescent rolls**
**2 medium Granny Smith apples, peeled and cored**
**1 cup sugar**
**1/3 cup butter, melted**
**3/4 cup Mountain Dew soda**
**Ground cinnamon**
**Vanilla ice cream**

Unroll crescent rolls and separate dough into 16 triangles. Cut each apple into eight wedges. Wrap a crescent dough triangle around each apple wedge. Place in a greased 13-in. x 9-in. x 2-in. baking dish.

In a bowl, combine sugar and butter; sprinkle over rolls. Slowly pour the soda around the rolls (do not stir). Sprinkle with cinnamon. Bake, uncovered, at 350° for 35-40 minutes or until golden brown. Serve warm with ice cream. **Yield:** 16 dumplings.

Apple Dumpling Bake

## No-Fuss Potato Salad

*There's no need to slice potatoes for this creamy salad. I use a box of scalloped potatoes to hurry along the preparation.* *—Myra Innes, Auburn, Kansas*

**1 package (5 ounces) scalloped potatoes**
**3-2/3 cups water, *divided***
**2 tablespoons butter**
**2/3 cup mayonnaise**
**1 tablespoon prepared mustard**
**2 hard-cooked eggs, chopped**
**Paprika, optional**

Set aside the sauce packet from potato package. In a large saucepan, bring the potatoes and 3 cups water to a boil. Reduce heat; cover and simmer for 10-15 minutes or until potatoes are tender. Rinse with cold water; drain thoroughly. Transfer potatoes to a bowl. Cover and refrigerate.

In a small saucepan, melt butter. Stir in contents of reserved sauce packet. Gradually add the remaining water; stir until smooth. Bring to a boil. Remove from the heat. Cover and refrigerate for 30 minutes. Stir in mayonnaise and mustard; gently stir into potatoes. Add eggs and sprinkle with paprika if desired. Refrigerate leftovers. **Yield:** 4-6 servings.

## Sweet Onion Bread Squares

*Whether you want a savory appetizer or an accompaniment to soup, this unique specialty is sure to please. I top packaged bread dough with ham and onions, then bake it until golden.* *—Helen Lamison, Carnegie, Pennsylvania*

**1 pound sweet onions, chopped**
**1/4 cup butter, cubed**
**2 eggs**
**1/2 cup sour cream**
**1/4 teaspoon salt**
**1/4 teaspoon caraway seeds**
**2 ounces thinly sliced deli ham, chopped**
**1 loaf (1 pound) frozen bread dough, thawed**

In a large skillet, cook onions in butter over medium heat for 15-20 minutes or until golden brown, stirring frequently. In a large bowl, whisk the eggs, sour cream, salt and caraway seeds. Stir in the onions and ham.

On a lightly floured surface, roll the dough into a 16-

in. x 11-in. rectangle. Transfer to a greased 15-in. x 10-in. x 1-in. baking pan; build up edges slightly to form a crust. Spread with onion mixture. Bake at 350° for 25-30 minutes or until golden brown. Cut into squares; serve warm. **Yield:** 2 dozen.

## Au Gratin Taco Bake

*Chock-full of beef, corn, potatoes and cheese, this southwestern supper is sure to be a hit in your home. Canned ingredients help speed up the easy recipe.* —*Linda Muir*
*Big Lake, Minnesota*

- **1 pound ground beef**
- **1 package (4.9 ounces) au gratin potatoes**
- **1 can (15-1/4 ounces) whole kernel corn, undrained**
- **1 can (14-1/2 ounces) no-salt-added stewed tomatoes, undrained**
- **3/4 cup milk**
- **1/2 cup water**
- **2 tablespoons taco seasoning**
- **1 cup (4 ounces) shredded cheddar cheese**

In a large skillet, cook beef over medium heat until no longer pink; drain. Stir in the potatoes and contents of sauce mix, corn, tomatoes, milk, water and taco seasoning. Transfer to a greased 2-qt. baking dish. Cover and bake at 350° for 65-70 minutes or until potatoes are tender. Sprinkle with cheese. Bake, uncovered, 5 minutes longer or until cheese is melted. **Yield:** 4-6 servings.

## Pumpkin Dessert

*(Pictured above right and on page 80)*

*When I'm baking this cinnamon-spiced dessert, our kitchen smells wonderful. The layered pumpkin squares taste just as good and are a family favorite during the fall season. In fact, they never last very long in our house!* —*Ruth Chiarenza*
*La Vale, Maryland*

- **1 package (18-1/4 ounces) yellow cake mix**
- **1/2 cup butter, melted**
- **3 eggs**
- **1 can (30 ounces) pumpkin pie mix**
- **1 can (5 ounces) evaporated milk**
- **1/2 cup sugar**
- **1/4 cup all-purpose flour**
- **3 teaspoons ground cinnamon**

In a large mixing bowl, combine the cake mix, butter and one egg until crumbly. Set aside 2/3 cup for topping. Press the remaining crumb mixture into a greased 13-in. x 9-in. x 2-in. baking dish. In a mixing bowl, beat the remaining eggs. Add pie mix and milk; pour over crust.

Combine the sugar, flour, cinnamon and reserved crumb mixture; sprinkle over pumpkin layer. Bake at 350° for 45-50 minutes or until top is golden brown. Cool on a wire rack for 1 hour. Refrigerate for 2 hours or until chilled before cutting. **Yield:** 12-15 servings.

**Pumpkin Dessert**
**Green Bean Potato Bake**

## Green Bean Potato Bake

*(Pictured above and on page 80)*

*This colorful vegetable casserole combines packaged au gratin potatoes with just three other kitchen staples. I enjoy it most with a hearty ham dish, but it goes well with a variety of main courses.* —*Terry Hayford*
*La Mesa, California*

- **1 package (5-1/4 ounces) au gratin potatoes**
- **2 cups frozen cut green beans, thawed**
- **1 can (2-1/4 ounces) sliced ripe olives, drained**
- **2 tablespoons diced pimientos**

Prepare potatoes according to package directions. Stir in the beans, olives and pimientos. Transfer to a greased 2-qt. baking dish. Bake, uncovered, at 400° for 30-35 minutes or until potatoes are tender. Let stand for 5 minutes before serving. **Yield:** 4 servings.

### Pantry Pointers

- To me, the best-tasting mashed potatoes are made with ranch salad dressing mix. Just stir it into the potatoes when you're adding the butter and milk or cream. —*Irene Brizinski, Upland, California*
- After I've prepared my macaroni and cheese, I grab a can of crispy fried onions and sprinkle some on top for a little crunch. My kids love it this way. —*Roberta Cappon, Rochester, New York*

Valentine Brownies
Festive Spaghetti 'n' Meatballs

## Festive Spaghetti 'n' Meatballs

*(Pictured at left)*

*When I don't have enough time to make spaghetti sauce from scratch, I dress up a store-bought jar with fresh vegetables and frozen meatballs. A touch of wine makes it special. All that's left to do for a complete dinner is cook the pasta and toss together a salad.*
*—Mary Ann Kosmas, Minneapolis, Minnesota*

**1/2 pound sliced fresh mushrooms**
**1 large green pepper, julienned**
**1 large onion, halved and sliced**
**2 tablespoons olive *or* vegetable oil**
**1/4 cup red wine *or* water**
**1 jar (26 ounces) meatless spaghetti sauce**
**1 package (12 ounces) frozen cooked Italian meatballs**
**1 package (16 ounces) spaghetti**

In a large saucepan, saute the mushrooms, green pepper and onion in oil until crisp-tender; stir in wine or water. Bring to a boil; cook for 2 minutes.

Stir in the spaghetti sauce and meatballs. Return to a boil. Reduce heat; simmer, uncovered, for 10-15 minutes or until the meatballs are heated through. Meanwhile, cook the pasta according to the package directions; drain. Serve the meatballs and sauce over the spaghetti. **Yield:** 4 servings.

## Valentine Brownies

*(Pictured above)*

*I found a fun way to show loved ones how much I care. I prepare brownies from a mix, cut a heart shape out of each one and fill the center with homemade frosting. Our grandson loves to eat the little heart-shaped brownies that are left over.*
*—Susan Ohlendorf, Austin, Texas*

**1 package fudge brownie mix (13-inch x 9-inch pan size)**
**1/2 cup butter, softened**
**1-1/2 cups confectioners' sugar**
**1/4 teaspoon vanilla extract**
**1/4 cup baking cocoa**

Prepare and bake brownie mix according to package directions for fudge-like brownies. Cool completely on a wire rack.

In a small mixing bowl, cream the butter, confectioners' sugar and vanilla until smooth. Place in a heavy-duty resealable plastic bag; cut a small hole in a corner of bag; set aside.

Line a baking sheet with waxed paper. Dust with cocoa; set aside. Cut brownies into 15 rectangles. Using a 1-1/2-in. heart-shaped cookie cutter, cut out a heart from the center of each brownie. Reserve cutout centers for another use. Place brownies on prepared baking sheet. Pipe frosting into centers of brownies. **Yield:** 15 brownies.

## Desperation Chicken Dinner

*On the busiest weekdays, it's nice to know that a home-cooked meal is only 20 minutes away. To save myself a step when preparing this delicious dinner, I keep cubed cooked chicken in the freezer. Sometimes I'll substitute sliced carrots for the frozen corn.*
*—Penny Mularz, Auburn, Michigan*

**2-1/2 cups water**
**2 packages (3 ounces *each*) chicken ramen noodles**
**1-1/2 cups cubed cooked chicken**
**1/2 cup frozen peas**
**1/2 cup frozen corn**
**1 can (4 ounces) mushroom stems and pieces, drained**

In a large saucepan, bring water to a boil. Add the noodles with the contents of seasoning packets, chicken, peas and corn. Cook, uncovered, for 4-6 minutes or until vegetables and noodles are tender. Stir in the mushrooms; heat through. **Yield:** 3 servings.

## Three-in-One Banana Muffins

*With a single banana bread mix, I bake three different kinds of muffins using chocolate chips, walnuts and coconut. I came up with this idea for a brunch where I wanted a variety of treats but not lots of leftovers.*
*—Beth Kosko, Ansonia, Connecticut*

**1 package (14 ounces) banana quick bread mix**
**2/3 cup chopped walnuts, *divided***
**1/2 cup flaked coconut, *divided***
**3 tablespoons miniature semisweet chocolate chips**

Prepare banana bread batter according to package directions for muffins. Divide batter among three bowls. Fold 1/3 cup walnuts into one bowl. Fold 1/4 cup coconut into second bowl. Fold chocolate chips into third bowl.

Fill greased or paper-lined miniature muffin cups two-thirds full. Top walnut muffins with remaining walnuts; top coconut muffins with remaining coconut. Bake at 350° for 14-16 minutes or until a toothpick comes out clean. Cool for 5 minutes before removing from pans to wire racks. **Yield:** 4-1/2 dozen.

## Clam Chowder

*I tried for years to re-create a popular clam chowder from a local restaurant. When I later met the cook, I got the recipe. I couldn't believe how simple it was to prepare this rich, creamy and filling soup. It relies mostly on convenient canned ingredients but tastes like it was made from scratch. —Kathleen Buenemann, New Haven, Missouri*

**1 can (10-3/4 ounces) condensed cream of celery soup, undiluted**
**1 can (10-3/4 ounces) condensed New England clam chowder, undiluted**
**1 can (10-3/4 ounces) condensed cream of potato soup, undiluted**
**2 to 2-1/2 cups milk**
**1 teaspoon butter**
**1/4 teaspoon white pepper**
**1 can (6-1/2 ounces) chopped clams, drained**

In a large saucepan, combine the soups, milk, butter and pepper; heat through. Stir in clams; heat through. **Yield:** 6 servings.

## Cream Cheese Dessert Wedges

*(Pictured below)*

*Refrigerated buttermilk biscuits create the tender crust for these pretty slices sprinkled with cinnamon and sugar. They can be served warm or chilled, and they're extra special with fresh fruit. —Betty Claycomb, Alverton, Pennsylvania*

**1 tube (7-1/2 ounces) refrigerated buttermilk biscuits**
**1 package (8 ounces) cream cheese, softened**
**1/2 cup sugar**
**1 egg**
**1 tablespoon all-purpose flour**

**TOPPING:**
**1 tablespoon sugar**
**1/2 teaspoon ground cinnamon**

Separate biscuits into 10 pieces; place in an ungreased 9-in. round baking dish. Press onto the bottom and 1 in. up the sides, pinching edges together to seal. Bake at 350° for 5-7 minutes or until slightly puffed.

Meanwhile, in a small mixing bowl, beat cream cheese, sugar, egg and flour until smooth; pour over crust. Combine topping ingredients; sprinkle over filling. Bake for 15-20 minutes or until filling is set and crust is golden brown.

Cool on a wire rack for at least 30 minutes before cutting. Serve warm or chilled. Refrigerate leftovers. **Yield:** 8-10 servings.

Cream Cheese Dessert Wedges

Appetizer Wreath

## Appetizer Wreath

*(Pictured above)*

*I have lots of fun "decorating" this festive wreath with a savory cream cheese spread and colorful veggies. I often place a bowl of stuffed olives in the center.*
*—Shirley Privratsky, Dickinson, North Dakota*

**2 tubes (8 ounces *each*) refrigerated crescent rolls**
**1 package (8 ounces) cream cheese, softened**
**1/2 cup sour cream**
**1 teaspoon dill weed**
**1/8 teaspoon garlic powder**
**1-1/2 cups chopped fresh broccoli florets**
**1 cup finely chopped celery**
**1/2 cup finely chopped sweet red pepper**
**Celery leaves**

Remove crescent dough from packaging (do not unroll). Cut each tube into eight slices. Arrange in an 11-in. circle on an ungreased 14-in. pizza pan. Bake at 375° for 15-20 minutes or until golden brown. Cool for 5 minutes before carefully removing to a serving platter; cool completely.

In a small mixing bowl, beat the cream cheese, sour cream, dill and garlic powder until smooth. Spread over the wreath; top with the broccoli, celery and red pepper. Form a bow garnish with celery leaves. **Yield:** 16 servings.

## Apple Cider Pie

*Raised on a small farm, I've been cooking for years. I top fruit filling with a smooth cream cheese layer for a rapid and rich dessert. I serve it with our family's favorite roast pork dinner. —Elmira Trombetti, Paducah, Kentucky*

**1 can (21 ounces) apple pie filling with cinnamon**
**1 graham cracker crust (10 inches)**
**1 package (8 ounces) cream cheese, softened**
**1/4 cup sour cream**
**4 envelopes (.74 ounce *each*) instant spiced cider mix**
**1-3/4 cups whipped topping**
**1 package (1.5 ounces) crunchy granola bars without raisins, crushed**

Pour pie filling into the crust. In a small mixing bowl, beat cream cheese until smooth. Beat in the sour cream and cider mix until light and fluffy. Fold in whipped topping. Pour over pie filling. Chill until set. Just before serving, sprinkle with granola. **Yield:** 6-8 servings.

**Editor's Note:** This recipe was tested with Nature Valley Oats 'n' Honey granola bars.

## Pierogi Chicken Supper

*This easy change-of-pace dish combines chicken, cheddar cheese and onion with frozen pierogies for a complete meal. The satisfying skillet supper takes only 30 minutes to get on the table for your hungry family. —Barbara Scott*
*Walkersville, Maryland*

**1 package (16 ounces) frozen pierogies**
**1 pound boneless skinless chicken breasts, cut into 2-inch strips**
**1/2 large sweet onion, thinly sliced**
**2 tablespoons butter**
**1/4 teaspoon salt**
**1/8 teaspoon pepper**
**1/2 cup shredded cheddar cheese**

Cook pierogies according to package directions. Meanwhile, in a large nonstick skillet, saute chicken and onion in butter until chicken juices run clear; remove and keep warm.

Drain pierogies; add to skillet. Cook over medium heat until lightly browned. Return chicken mixture to the pan. Stir in salt and pepper. Sprinkle with cheese. Cover and remove from the heat. Let stand for 5 minutes or until cheese is melted. **Yield:** 4 servings.

## Rice-Stuffed Pork Chops

*Seasoned coating and rice mixes speed up these mouth-watering chops. They really impressed my husband when we were first dating. —Becky Aderman, Niagara, Wisconsin*

**2-1/4 cups water**
**1 tablespoon butter**
**1 package (5.3 ounces) instant chicken and Parmesan risotto rice and sauce mix**
**4 bone-in pork loin chops (1 inch thick)**
**1 envelope seasoned coating mix (about 1 cup)**

In a large saucepan, combine the water, butter and rice with contents of sauce mix. Bring to a boil; stir. Reduce heat; cover and simmer for 4 minutes or until the rice is almost tender. Let stand for 5 minutes.

Meanwhile, moisten pork chops with water; dip in coating mix. Cut a pocket in each chop; fill with rice mixture. Place in an ungreased 13-in. x 9-in. x 2-in. baking dish. Spoon remaining rice around chops. Bake, uncovered, at 425° for 35-40 minutes or until meat juices run clear. **Yield:** 4 servings.

**Editor's Note:** This recipe was tested with Lipton risotto mix and Shake 'n' Bake seasoned coating mix.

## Chive Biscuit Ornaments

*(Pictured below)*

*Ring in the holiday season with these tender bell-shaped bites from our Test Kitchen home economists. They used cookie cutters and whole chive "hangers" to form the warm and appetizing ornaments.*

**3-1/4 cups biscuit/baking mix**
**1/2 cup shredded cheddar cheese**
**1 tablespoon minced chives**
**1 teaspoon crushed red pepper flakes**
**1 cup heavy whipping cream**
**12 whole chives**

In a bowl, combine the biscuit mix, cheese, minced chives and pepper flakes. Stir in cream just until moistened. Turn onto a lightly floured surface; knead 8-10 times. Pat to 1/2-in. thickness. Cut with a floured 3-in. bell-shaped cookie cutter. Using a 1/2-in. round cookie cutter, cut a hole near top of each biscuit.

Place 2 in. apart on ungreased baking sheets. Bake at 450° for 8-10 minutes or until golden brown. Remove to wire racks. Thread one whole chive through each biscuit hole; tie a knot. Serve warm. **Yield:** 1 dozen.

## Tortellini Marinara

*(Pictured below)*

*My family loves this with a loaf of crusty French bread and green beans. I sometimes warm the savory supper in the slow cooker.* —*Rita Perez, Roseville, California*

**1 package (9 ounces) refrigerated cheese tortellini**
**1 pound bulk Italian sausage**
**1 package (15 ounces) refrigerated marinara sauce**
**1 can (14-1/2 ounces) diced Italian tomatoes, undrained**
**1/2 pound sliced fresh mushrooms**
**1 cup (4 ounces) shredded mozzarella cheese**

Cook tortellini according to the package directions. Meanwhile, in a large skillet, cook sausage over medium heat until no longer pink; drain. Stir in marinara sauce, tomatoes and mushrooms. Bring to a boil. Reduce heat; cover and simmer for 5 minutes or until mushrooms are tender.

Drain tortellini; stir into skillet. Sprinkle with mozzarella cheese. Remove from the heat; cover and let stand for 5 minutes or until cheese is melted. **Yield:** 8 servings.

Chive Biscuit Ornaments
Tortellini Marinara

# Homemade Mixes

ON THOSE DAYS when you have a few spare moments, consider stocking your pantry with some surefire shortcuts—these handy homemade mixes.

They're quick to whip up using ingredients you likely already have in your kitchen. Later, when you're rushing on a busy night, you'll have these ready-made creations to hurry along your cooking.

Plus, making your own mixes instead of purchasing prepared ones from the grocery store can save you some shopping time...and a little money, too.

**Editor's Note:** The contents of mixes may settle during storage. When preparing the recipe, spoon the mix into a measuring cup.

## Cobbler Mix

*(Pictured below)*

Portrait Gallery

*You can give cherries, peaches or other fruit a crunchy golden brown crust with this versatile mix. For a quick gift, put a batch of it—along with a can of pie filling and serving directions—in a decorative bag or basket.* —*Joyce Huber, Ste. Genevieve, Missouri*

Cobbler Mix

**4-1/2 cups all-purpose flour**
**2-1/2 cups sugar**
**3/4 cup buttermilk blend powder**
**3 tablespoons baking powder**
**2 teaspoons salt**
**ADDITIONAL INGREDIENTS (for each cobbler):**
**1/2 cup butter, melted**
**1 can (21 ounces) cherry pie filling *or* filling of your choice**
**1/2 cup water**

In a large bowl, combine the first five ingredients. Store in an airtight container in a cool dry place for up to 6 months. **Yield:** 4 batches (8 cups total).

**To prepare cobbler:** Pour butter into an 11-in. x 7-in. x 2-in. baking dish. Top with pie filling. In a bowl, combine 2 cups cobbler mix and water. Drop by rounded tablespoonfuls over pie filling; spread gently. Bake at 350° for 35-40 minutes or until topping is golden brown. Serve warm. **Yield:** 6-8 servings.

## Herbed Chicken Coating Mix

*Our family digs right in whenever I serve a dinner of chicken coated with this well seasoned make-ahead mix. The mouth-watering main course goes wonderfully with side dishes of mashed potatoes, fresh green beans and carrots. I put this entree on the menu especially often when those vegetables are in season.* —*Carolyn Romkes, Caledonia, Ontario*

**2 cups all-purpose flour**
**8 teaspoons dried basil**
**8 teaspoons dried thyme**
**4 teaspoons *each* salt, dried oregano, dried parsley flakes, paprika and curry powder**
**2 teaspoons pepper**
**ADDITIONAL INGREDIENTS (for each batch):**
**1 egg**
**1/3 cup butter, melted**
**1 broiler/fryer chicken (3 pounds), cut up and skin removed**

In a small bowl, combine the flour and seasonings. Store in an airtight container in a cool dry place for up to 6 months. **Yield:** 2 batches (2-1/2 cups total).

**To prepare chicken:** Place 1-1/4 cups coating mix in a large resealable plastic bag. In a shallow bowl, whisk egg and butter. Dip chicken pieces in egg mixture, then place in bag; seal and shake to coat.

Place chicken in a greased 13-in. x 9-in. x 2-in. baking dish. Bake, uncovered, at 350° for 45-50 minutes or until juices run clear. **Yield:** 4-6 servings.

## Applesauce Muffin Mix

*I adapted one of my favorite muffin recipes so I could give this homemade mix to my friends and family members for the holidays. Oats add heartiness to the golden baked bites spiced with cinnamon and nutmeg. They're yummy not only for breakfast or brunch but also as an afternoon treat or travel snack.* —*Barbara Opperwall, Wyoming, Michigan*

1/2 cup sugar
1-1/4 teaspoons baking powder
1 teaspoon ground cinnamon
1/2 teaspoon ground nutmeg
1/4 teaspoon salt
1-1/2 cups all-purpose flour, *divided*
2 tablespoons quick-cooking oats

**ADDITIONAL INGREDIENTS:**

1 egg, lightly beaten
1 cup unsweetened applesauce
1/2 cup butter, melted
1 teaspoon vanilla extract
1 tablespoon sugar

In a bowl, combine the first five ingredients. In a 1-pint glass jar, layer 3/4 cup flour, oats, sugar mixture and remaining flour. Cover and store in a cool dry place for up to 6 months. **Yield:** 1 batch (about 2 cups total).

**To prepare muffins:** In a bowl, combine the egg, applesauce, butter and vanilla. Stir in muffin mix just until moistened. Fill greased muffin cups three-fourths full. Sprinkle with sugar. Bake at 375° for 15-20 minutes or until a toothpick comes out clean. Cool for 5 minutes before removing from pan to a wire rack. **Yield:** 9 muffins.

Oatmeal Chip Cookie Mix

## Oatmeal Chip Cookie Mix

*(Pictured above right)*

*I like to give a jar of this oatmeal cookie mix along with a cookie sheet to a bride-to-be or someone who is starting out in a new home. With this gift, from-scratch treats are only a few steps away—you just add the rest of the ingredients and bake.*
*—Joan Airey, Rivers, Manitoba*

1-1/4 cups quick-cooking oats
1 cup all-purpose flour
1/2 teaspoon baking powder
1/2 teaspoon baking soda
1/4 teaspoon salt
3/4 cup milk chocolate chips
1/3 cup vanilla *or* white chips
1/2 cup slivered almonds
1/4 cup flaked coconut
1/2 cup packed brown sugar
1/2 cup sugar

**ADDITIONAL INGREDIENTS:**

1/2 cup butter, softened
1 egg
1/2 teaspoon vanilla extract

Place oats in a food processor; cover and pulse until fine; set aside. In a bowl, combine the flour, baking powder, baking soda and salt. In a 1-qt. glass jar, layer the oats, flour mixture, chips, almonds, coconut, brown sugar and sugar, packing well between each layer. Cover and store in a cool dry place for up to 6 months. **Yield:** 1 batch (about 4 cups total).

**To prepare cookies:** In a large mixing bowl, cream butter. Beat in egg and vanilla. Add cookie mix and mix well (mixture will be dry). Drop by rounded tablespoonfuls 2 in. apart onto ungreased baking sheets. Bake at 375° for 10-15 minutes or until lightly browned. Cool for 2 minutes before removing to wire racks. **Yield:** 2-1/2 dozen.

## Sesame Seed Coating Mix

*I like to use this coating on pork strips, chicken breasts and fish fillets. It also turns these stuffed pork chops into an elegant dinner. —Katie Koziolek, Hartland, Minnesota*

1-1/2 cups crushed cornflakes
1/2 cup cornmeal
1/4 cup sesame seeds, toasted
2 teaspoons lemon-pepper seasoning
1-1/2 teaspoons dried parsley flakes
1/2 teaspoon salt
1/2 teaspoon ground mustard
1/2 teaspoon paprika
1/4 teaspoon pepper

**ADDITIONAL INGREDIENTS FOR PORK CHOPS CORDON BLEU:**

4 bone-in pork loin chops (1 inch thick)
4 thin slices deli ham
1/2 cup shredded Monterey Jack cheese
2 tablespoons butter, melted

In a bowl, combine first nine ingredients. Store in an airtight container in a cool dry place for up to 6 months. **Yield:** about 4 batches (about 2 cups total).

**To prepare pork chops:** With a sharp knife, cut a pocket in the side of each chop almost to the bone. Stuff with ham and cheese. Place 1/2 cup coating mix in a shallow bowl.

Brush both sides of chops with butter, then dip into coating. Place in a greased 13-in. x 9-in. x 2-in. baking dish. Bake, uncovered, at 400° for 20 minutes. Turn chops over; bake 10-15 minutes longer or until meat juices run clear. **Yield:** 4 servings.

Cake Doughnut Mix

## Cake Doughnut Mix

(*Pictured above*)

*Thanks to this make-ahead mix recipe, I have a wonderfully quick way to prepare from-scratch doughnuts for breakfast or brunch. These nicely spiced favorites sprinkled with sugar call for everyday pantry ingredients and are truly old-fashioned treats. People enjoy them served warm with hot coffee or cold milk.* —*Diane Terry, Queensburg, New York*

**4-1/2 cups all-purpose flour**
**1 cup nonfat dry milk powder**
**1 cup sugar**
**2 tablespoons baking powder**
**1-1/2 teaspoons salt**
**1 teaspoon ground cinnamon**
**1 teaspoon ground nutmeg**
**1-1/2 cups shortening**
**ADDITIONAL INGREDIENTS (for each batch of doughnuts):**
**2 eggs**
**1/4 cup plus 1 tablespoon milk**
**2 teaspoons vanilla extract**
**Oil for deep-fat frying**
**Confectioners' sugar, optional**

In a large bowl, combine the flour, milk powder, sugar, baking powder, salt, cinnamon and nutmeg; cut in shortening until crumbly. Store in an airtight container in a cool dry place for up to 6 months. **Yield:** 2 batches (about 9 cups total).

**To prepare doughnuts:** Place 4-1/2 cups doughnut mix in a large bowl. Combine eggs, milk and vanilla; stir into doughnut mix just until moistened. Turn dough onto a floured surface; knead 15-20 times. Pat dough out to 1/2-in. thickness. Cut with a floured 3-in. doughnut cutter.

In an electric skillet or deep-fat fryer, heat oil to 375°. Fry a few doughnuts at a time until golden brown, about 1-1/2 minutes on each side. Drain on paper towels. Dust with confectioners' sugar if desired. Serve warm. **Yield:** about 1 dozen.

## Chippy Chocolate Cookie Mix

*I've had this simple recipe for a long time and got the idea of layering the mix after finding similar gift mixes in stores. I have yet to meet the person who doesn't love these yummy cookies. I sometimes use M&M's in place of the peanut butter chips.* —*Francine Wingate, New Smyrna Beach, Florida*

**1 package (18-1/4 ounces) chocolate cake mix**
**1 cup peanut butter chips**
**ADDITIONAL INGREDIENTS:**
**1/2 cup vegetable oil**
**2 eggs**

In a 1-qt. glass container, layer half of the cake mix, the peanut butter chips and remaining cake mix. Cover and store in a cool dry place up to 6 months. **Yield:** 1 batch (about 4 cups).

**To prepare cookies:** In a mixing bowl, combine cookie mix, oil and eggs; mix well. Drop by rounded tablespoonfuls 2 in. apart onto ungreased baking sheets. Bake at 350° for 14-16 minutes or until surface cracks. Remove to wire racks to cool. **Yield:** 2 dozen.

## Basic Brownie Mix

*Here's a quick answer to dessert for a busy homemaker when unexpected company comes. The simple brownie mix is so versatile, I have the option of adding different goodies to the batter if I want a change of pace. For instance, I can create a cherry or caramel-nut version.* —*Kathryn Roach, Edgemont, Arkansas*

**5 cups sugar**
**3 cups all-purpose flour**
**1 can (8 ounces) baking cocoa**
**1 teaspoon salt**
**ADDITIONAL INGREDIENTS (for each batch of brownies):**
**1/2 cup butter, melted**
**2 eggs, lightly beaten**
**1 tablespoon water**
**1/2 teaspoon vanilla extract**
**FOR CARAMEL-NUT BROWNIES:**
**1/4 cup caramel ice cream topping**
**3/4 cup chopped pecans, toasted, *divided***
**FOR CHERRY BROWNIES:**
**1/2 cup dried cherries *or* cranberries**
**1/2 cup water**
**Frosting of your choice, optional**

In a large bowl, combine the sugar, flour, cocoa and salt. Store in an airtight container in a cool dry place for up to 6 months. **Yield:** 5 batches (about 10 cups total).

**To prepare basic brownies:** In a large bowl, combine 2 cups brownie mix, butter, eggs, water and vanilla. Pour into a greased 8-in. square baking dish. Bake at 350° for

25-30 minutes or until a toothpick inserted near the center comes out clean. Cool on a wire rack. **Yield:** 9 servings.

**To prepare caramel-nut brownies:** Prepare basic brownie batter. Pour half into a greased 8-in. square baking dish. Drizzle with caramel topping and sprinkle with 1/2 cup pecans. Top with remaining batter and pecans. Bake and cool as directed. **Yield:** 9 servings.

**To prepare cherry brownies:** In a small saucepan, bring the cherries and water to a boil. Remove from the heat; let stand for 5 minutes. Drain and pat dry. Prepare basic brownie batter; stir in cherries. Pour mixture into a greased 8-in. square baking dish. Bake and cool as directed. Frost if desired. **Yield:** 9 servings.

## Ham 'n' Swiss Pie Mix

*(Pictured below right)*

*My kitchen is never without a batch of this mix. One of my favorite ways to use it is in a savory pie made with leftover cooked meat, cheese and onions. But try this creation in any recipe that calls for biscuit mix.* —*Martha Warner Lacombe, Alberta*

**4-1/2 cups all-purpose flour**
**2 tablespoons plus 1-1/2 teaspoons baking powder**
**1-1/2 teaspoons salt**
**1 cup shortening**
**ADDITIONAL INGREDIENTS (for each pie):**
**2 cups diced fully cooked ham**
**1 cup (4 ounces) shredded Swiss cheese**
**2 green onions, chopped**
**3 eggs**
**1-1/2 cups milk**
**1/4 teaspoon ground mustard**
**Dash pepper**

In a large bowl, combine flour, baking powder and salt. Cut in shortening until crumbly. Store in an airtight container in a cool dry place for up to 6 months. **Yield:** 6 batches (about 6 cups mix).

**To prepare pie:** In a bowl, combine ham, cheese and onions. Transfer to a greased 9-in. pie plate. In a mixing bowl, combine eggs, milk, mustard, pepper and 1 cup mix; beat just until blended. Pour over ham mixture. Bake at 400° for 30-35 minutes or until a knife inserted near center comes out clean. Let stand for 10 minutes before cutting. **Yield:** 6 servings.

## Wheat Pancake Mix

*(Pictured at right)*

*Spending a day making mixes like this one leaves me extra time to play with our girls or help them with homework. This simple blend of ingredients produces moist fluffy pancakes with a hearty wheat taste.*
—*Connie Fox, Tampico, Illinois*

**6 cups whole wheat flour**
**3 cups all-purpose flour**
**1-1/2 cups nonfat dry milk powder**
**1 cup sugar**
**1/2 cup toasted wheat germ**
**1/4 cup baking powder**
**1 tablespoon salt**
**2 cups shortening**
**ADDITIONAL INGREDIENTS (for each batch of pancakes):**
**1 egg**
**1-1/2 cups water**
**Maple syrup**

In a large bowl, combine the first seven ingredients. Cut in shortening until mixture resembles coarse crumbs. Store in an airtight container in a cool dry place for up to 6 months. **Yield:** 17-3/4 cups mix (about 6 batches).

**To prepare pancakes:** Place 2-3/4 cups mix in a large bowl. Combine the egg and water; stir into mix just until moistened. Pour batter by 1/4 cupfuls onto a greased hot griddle. Turn when bubbles form on top; cook until second side is golden brown. Serve with syrup. **Yield:** 11 pancakes.

**Ham 'n' Swiss Pie Mix**
**Wheat Pancake Mix**

## Cranberry Beverage Syrup

*(Pictured below)*

*This convenient recipe makes a syrup you can freeze or refrigerate, then stir into four different thirst-quenchers.*
*—Carolyn Zimmerman, Fairbury, Illinois*

**2 quarts water**
**3 pounds fresh *or* frozen cranberries**
**5 cups sugar**
**5 cinnamon sticks (3 inches *each*)**
**ADDITIONAL INGREDIENT FOR CRANBERRY COOLER:**
**1 liter ginger ale, chilled**
**ADDITIONAL INGREDIENTS FOR CRAN-APPLE DRINK:**
**2 cups apple juice, chilled**
**2 cups club soda, chilled**
**ADDITIONAL INGREDIENTS FOR CRANBERRY-LEMON SPARKLE:**
**1-1/2 quarts cold water**
**1-1/2 quarts ginger ale, chilled**
**1 can (12 ounces) frozen lemonade concentrate, thawed**
**ADDITIONAL INGREDIENTS FOR CRANBERRY TEA:**
**2 cups club soda, chilled**
**2 cups iced tea, chilled**

In a Dutch oven, bring the water, cranberries, sugar and cinnamon to a boil. Simmer, uncovered, for 10 minutes or until berries pop. Mash slightly with a potato masher; simmer 5 minutes longer.

Strain and discard pulp and cinnamon sticks. Refrigerate syrup in 2-cup portions for up to 3 days or freeze for up to 3 months. Thaw before using. **Yield:** 5 batches (about 10 cups total).

**To prepare Cranberry Cooler:** In a pitcher, combine 2 cups cranberry syrup and ginger ale. Serve over ice. **Yield:** 6 servings.

**To prepare Cran-Apple Drink:** In a pitcher, combine 2 cups cranberry syrup, apple juice and club soda. Serve over ice. **Yield:** 6 servings.

**To prepare Cranberry-Lemon Sparkle:** In a punch bowl, combine water, ginger ale, 4 cups cranberry syrup and lemonade concentrate. Serve over ice. **Yield:** 18-20 servings.

**To prepare Cranberry Tea:** In a pitcher, combine 2 cups cranberry syrup, club soda and iced tea. Serve over ice. **Yield:** 6 servings.

Cranberry Beverage Syrup
Stromboli Crust Mix

## Stromboli Crust Mix

*(Pictured below left)*

*I use this mix for stromboli crust and I get as creative as I want with the filling ingredients.*
*—Valorie Hinkle, Quakertown, Pennsylvania*

**6-3/4 cups all-purpose flour**
**1-1/4 cups nonfat dry milk powder**
**2 tablespoons plus 1-1/2 teaspoons baking powder**
**2-1/2 teaspoons salt**
**ADDITIONAL INGREDIENTS FOR STROMBOLI:**
**1/2 cup plus 1 to 3 tablespoons water**
**5 slices hard salami**
**1/2 cup shredded cheddar cheese**
**1/2 cup finely chopped fully cooked ham**
**2 medium tomatoes, chopped**
**1 cup chopped green pepper**
**1/3 cup chopped onion**
**1/2 cup shredded mozzarella cheese**
**1 tablespoon butter, melted**
**1/2 teaspoon dried oregano**
**1/4 teaspoon salt**
**1/4 teaspoon pepper**

In a large bowl, combine the first four ingredients. Store in an airtight container for up to 6 months. **Yield:** 4 batches (about 8 cups).

**To prepare stromboli:** In a large bowl, combine 2 cups crust mix and enough water to form a stiff dough. On a floured surface, roll dough into a 15-in. x 9-in. rectangle. Transfer to a greased 15-in. x 10-in. x 1-in. baking pan.

Place salami lengthwise on half of the dough to within 1/2 in. of edge. Layer with cheddar cheese, ham, tomatoes, green pepper, onion and mozzarella cheese. Fold plain side of dough over filling; seal edges well. Brush with butter; sprinkle with oregano, salt and pepper.

Bake at 400° for 30-35 minutes or until golden brown. Let stand for 10 minutes; cut with a serrated knife. **Yield:** 8 servings.

## Biscuit Baking Mix

*I need just four items for this versatile mix. I use it in recipes that call for the store-bought kind. This mix is the key to the tasty biscuits and dumplings in the following recipes.*
*—Tami Christman, Soda Springs, Idaho*

**9 cups all-purpose flour**
**1/4 cup baking powder**

Flaky Italian Biscuits
Chicken Dumpling Soup

**1 tablespoon salt**
**2 cups shortening**

In a large bowl, combine the dry ingredients. Cut in shortening until the mixture resembles coarse crumbs. Store in an airtight container in a cool dry place or in the freezer for up to 8 months. **Yield:** 12 cups.

## Chicken Dumpling Soup

*(Pictured above)*

*Featuring light dumplings made with Tami Christman's Biscuit Baking Mix (see recipe on opposite page), this old-fashioned soup always brings positive comments.*

**12 green onions, chopped**
**1/2 cup butter**
**1/2 cup all-purpose flour**
**10 cups water**
**1 package (20 ounces) frozen peas and carrots**
**2 cans (10 ounces *each*) chunk white chicken, drained, *divided***
**1/3 cup chicken bouillon granules**
**1/2 teaspoon pepper, *divided***
**5 cups Biscuit Baking Mix (recipe on page 98)**
**2 tablespoons dried parsley flakes**
**1-1/3 cups milk**

In a Dutch oven, saute onions in butter until tender. Stir in flour until blended. Gradually add water. Stir in the vegetables, one can of chicken, bouillon and 1/4 teaspoon pepper; bring to a boil.

In a bowl, combine the biscuit mix, parsley and remaining pepper. Stir in the milk just until moistened. Fold in remaining chicken. Drop by rounded tablespoonfuls onto simmering soup. Cover and simmer for 15 minutes or until a toothpick inserted in a dumpling comes out clean (do not lift cover while simmering). **Yield:** 20 servings (5 quarts).

## Flaky Italian Biscuits

*(Pictured above)*

*Keeping Biscuit Baking Mix (see recipe on opposite page) on hand makes it easy for Tami Christman to stir up a batch of these tender biscuits. Spread them with butter...or omit the Italian seasoning and serve them with honey.*

**2 cups Biscuit Baking Mix (recipe on page 98)**
**1 teaspoon Italian seasoning**
**1/2 cup milk**

Place mix and Italian seasoning in a bowl. Stir in milk just until moistened. Turn onto a floured surface; knead 10-15 times. Pat or roll out to 1/2-in. thickness; cut with a 2-1/2-in. biscuit cutter. Place 2 in. apart on an ungreased baking sheet. Bake at 425° for 15-17 minutes or until golden brown. Serve warm. **Yield:** 8 biscuits.

# Chapter 7

# Look Ahead for Lively Leftovers

MAKING MEALS out of leftovers can cut down on kitchen fuss...and also result in all-new dinners that look and taste deliciously different.

For example, transform yesterday's turkey and mashed potatoes into Sweet 'n' Sour Turkey and Peppermint Potato Candy (pictured at left).

Or, enjoy such family-pleasing fare as Ranch Turkey Pasta Dinner, Cheesy Potatoes and Ham, Corn Potato Pancakes and Turkey Potato Tetrazzini.

These sensational second-day dishes taste so good, no one will realize they're eating leftovers!

**EXTRA-SPECIAL SUPPER.** Peppermint Potato Candy and Sweet 'n' Sour Turkey (recipes on pp. 110 and 111).

## Mexican Rice with Chicken

(Pictured below)

*This skillet supper comes together in just 30 minutes when I use leftover cooked chicken and a convenient packaged rice-and-pasta mix. After I prepared this flavorful meal-in-one, I came up with the idea of serving the extras on tortillas with cheese and sour cream the next day. Both dishes were a hit with my family. —Debra Rzodkiewicz, Erie, Pennsylvania*

- **1 package (6.4 ounces) Mexican-style rice and pasta mix**
- **2 tablespoons butter**
- **1-3/4 cups water**
- **1 can (14-1/2 ounces) diced tomatoes with onions, undrained**
- **2 cups cubed cooked chicken**
- **1 jalapeno pepper, seeded and chopped**

In a large skillet, cook and stir rice and pasta mix in butter until lightly browned, about 5 minutes. Add the water, tomatoes and contents of rice seasoning packet. Bring to a boil. Reduce heat; cover and cook for 10 minutes.

Add chicken and jalapeno. Cover and cook for 8-10 minutes or until rice is tender and liquid is absorbed. **Yield:** 4 servings.

**Editor's Note:** This recipe was tested with Rice-A-Roni rice and pasta mix. When cutting or seeding hot peppers, use rubber or plastic gloves to protect your hands. Avoid touching your face.

Mexican Rice with Chicken

## Roast Beef Sandwich Spread

*Pickle relish and ketchup add a touch of sweetness to this great-tasting sandwich spread that uses up leftover beef. With a food processor, I can prepare this recipe in a snap. I often rely on it after I've made a roast. —Carolyn Zimmerman, Fairbury, Illinois*

- **4 cups cubed cooked beef**
- **1 cup sweet pickle relish**
- **1 small onion, quartered**
- **1/2 cup ketchup**
- **1/4 cup mayonnaise**
- **1 tablespoon sweet pickle juice**
- **1 teaspoon seasoned salt**
- **1/8 teaspoon pepper**
- **18 slices bread**

In a food processor, combine the beef, pickle relish and onion; cover and process until coarsely chopped.

In a large bowl, combine the ketchup, mayonnaise, pickle juice, seasoned salt and pepper. Stir in the beef mixture. Cover and refrigerate for at least 1 hour. Spread on nine slices of bread; top with remaining bread. **Yield:** 9 servings.

## Cheesy Potatoes and Ham

*I combine my leftover ham with canned mushroom soup, process cheese and just a few other ingredients to make this mashed-potato-topped casserole. My family loves it, and dinner is on the table in an hour or less. —Esther Yoder, Millersburg, Ohio*

- **1 can (10-3/4 ounces) condensed cream of mushroom soup, undiluted**
- **1 cup cubed process cheese (Velveeta)**
- **2 tablespoons butter, cubed**
- **2 cups cubed fully cooked ham**
- **1/4 cup chopped onion**
- **1-1/2 teaspoons Worcestershire sauce**
- **6 cups mashed potatoes (with added milk and butter)**

In a large saucepan, combine the soup, cheese and butter. Cook and stir over medium heat until cheese is melted. Stir in the ham, onion and Worcestershire sauce. Pour into a greased 2-qt. baking dish.

Top with the mashed potatoes. Bake, uncovered, at 350° for 30-35 minutes or until heated through. **Yield:** 4-6 servings.

## Ranch Turkey Pasta Dinner

(Pictured above right)

*This simple-but-tasty entree is a great way to finish up turkey that's left over from a holiday meal. If I happen to have extra cooked chicken on hand, I'll sometimes use that instead. Try sprinkling a little grated cheese over the top of each helping for extra flavor. —Peggy Key, Grant, Alabama*

Macaroni 'n' Cheese Soup
Ranch Turkey Pasta Dinner

**2-1/2 cups uncooked penne *or* medium tube pasta**
**6 to 8 tablespoons butter**
**1 envelope ranch salad dressing mix**
**1 cup frozen peas and carrots, thawed**
**3 cups cubed cooked turkey**

Cook pasta according to package directions. Meanwhile, in a large skillet, melt butter. Stir in salad dressing mix until smooth; heat through. Add peas and carrots; cook and stir for 2-3 minutes. Drain pasta and add to skillet. Stir in turkey and heat through. **Yield:** 4 servings.

## Macaroni 'n' Cheese Soup

*(Pictured above)*

*Chock-full of tender chicken chunks, pasta and three different kinds of vegetables, this creamy creation from the home economists in our Test Kitchen is sure to become a favorite in your household. No one will suspect that the sensational soup relies on leftover macaroni and cheese... or that the recipe takes only a half hour to prepare.*

**3-1/2 cups chicken broth**
**1-1/2 cups fresh broccoli florets**
**1 cup cauliflowerets**
**1 cup sliced carrots**
**2 cups prepared macaroni and cheese**
**1 cup heavy whipping cream**
**1 cup cubed process cheese (Velveeta)**
**1 cup cubed cooked chicken**
**Pepper to taste**

In a large saucepan, combine the broth, broccoli, cauliflower and carrots. Bring to a boil. Reduce heat; simmer, uncovered, for 10 minutes or until the vegetables are tender. Add the macaroni and cheese, whipping cream and process cheese. Cook and stir until cheese is melted. Add the chicken and pepper; heat through. **Yield:** 8 servings.

## Vegetable Shrimp Toss

(Pictured below)

*Whenever I cook too much spaghetti, I simply put it in the refrigerator. The next time I have leftover vegetables, I combine them with the extra pasta, some sauteed shrimp and shredded Parmesan cheese. The result is an easy dinner that's ready to eat in just 15 minutes.* —*Sharyn Craig*
*El Cajon, California*

**1/2 pound uncooked medium shrimp, peeled and deveined**
**1/2 teaspoon minced garlic**
**1/4 cup butter, cubed**
**2 cups cooked mixed vegetables**
**2 cups cooked spaghetti**
**2 tablespoons shredded Parmesan cheese**

In a large skillet, saute shrimp and garlic in butter until shrimp turn pink; remove and keep warm. In the same skillet, saute the vegetables until heated through.

Add the cooked spaghetti and shrimp; heat through. Sprinkle with Parmesan cheese. **Yield:** 2-3 servings.

## Coconut-Raisin Rice Pudding

*I like to warm up chilly winter evenings with this comforting oven-baked dessert. My husband even enjoys it served cold.* —*Debbie Skaggs, Shepherdsville, Kentucky*

**1/4 cup butter, melted**
**3 eggs**
**3 cups milk**
**1 cup sugar**
**2 teaspoons vanilla extract**
**3/4 teaspoon ground nutmeg**
**1/2 teaspoon salt**
**2-1/2 cups cooked rice**
**3/4 cup raisins**
**3/4 cup flaked coconut**

Place butter in a 13-in. x 9-in. x 2-in. baking dish; set aside. In a large bowl, combine eggs, milk, sugar, vanilla, nutmeg and salt. Stir in rice and raisins. Transfer to prepared baking dish.

Bake, uncovered, at 325° for 30 minutes; sprinkle with coconut. Bake 10-15 minutes longer or until a thermometer reads 160°. Serve warm. Refrigerate leftovers. **Yield:** 8 servings.

**Vegetable Shrimp Toss**

## Chili Dog Spaghetti

*On a warm summer day when I didn't feel like heating the oven, I created this recipe. I used leftover hot dogs, convenient canned items and shredded cheddar cheese to prepare the quick main dish. Now we enjoy it year-round.*
*—Karen Fehr, Fairbury, Illinois*

**6 hot dogs, halved lengthwise and sliced**
**1-1/2 teaspoons dried minced onion**
**1/2 teaspoon garlic powder**
**1/4 teaspoon pepper**
**1 tablespoon vegetable oil**
**2 cans (one 26-1/4 ounces, one 15 ounces) spaghetti**
**1 can (10-1/2 ounces) chili without beans**
**1 cup (4 ounces) shredded cheddar cheese, *divided***

In a large skillet, saute the hot dogs, onion, garlic powder and pepper in oil. Add the spaghetti, chili and 1/2 cup cheese; heat through. Sprinkle with remaining cheese. **Yield:** 6-8 servings.

## Pork Tetrazzini

*When my mother assembled this great-tasting casserole, she always used leftover turkey or ham. But the recipe is so versatile, you could substitute cooked chicken or even canned tuna—whatever suits your family's tastes. Vegetables, seasonings and sour cream give this pleasing pasta dish plenty of additional flavor.* *—Doreen Kelly Roslyn, Pennsylvania*

**1 small onion, diced**
**1 celery rib, diced**
**1 tablespoon butter**
**5 tablespoons all-purpose flour**
**1 can (14-1/2 ounces) chicken broth**
**1 cup milk**
**1 bay leaf**
**1/2 teaspoon onion salt**
**1/4 teaspoon pepper**
**2 tablespoons sour cream**
**1 tablespoon dried parsley flakes**
**1 tablespoon lemon juice**
**2 cups cooked spaghetti**
**2 cups diced cooked pork**
**2 tablespoons seasoned bread crumbs**

In a small saucepan, saute onion and celery in butter until tender. Combine flour and broth until smooth; stir into the pan.

Add the milk, bay leaf, onion salt and pepper. Bring to a boil; cook and stir for 2 minutes or until thickened. Remove from the heat. Discard bay leaf. Whisk in the sour cream, parsley and lemon juice.

Place the spaghetti in a greased 11-in. x 7-in. x 2-in. baking dish; top with pork and white sauce. Sprinkle with bread crumbs. Bake, uncovered, at 350° for 30-35 minutes or until bubbly. Let stand for 5 minutes before serving. **Yield:** 4 servings.

**Potato Ham Skillet**

## Potato Ham Skillet

*(Pictured above)*

*I use any leftover cooked ham I may have to prepare this stovetop egg supper that combines sliced potatoes, onion, cheddar cheese and green pepper. With some fresh fruit or toast on the side, this satisfying layered skillet could also make a delicious dish for breakfast or brunch. Before serving the warm wedges, I sprinkle parsley on top.*
*—Sharon Crider, Lebanon, Missouri*

✓ Uses less fat, sugar or salt. Includes Nutritional Analysis and Diabetic Exchanges.

**4-1/2 teaspoons butter**
**3 medium potatoes, peeled and thinly sliced**
**1/2 teaspoon salt**
**1/4 teaspoon pepper**
**7 green onions, chopped**
**1/2 cup chopped green pepper**
**2 cups diced fully cooked ham**
**3 eggs, lightly beaten**
**1/2 cup shredded cheddar cheese**
**Minced fresh parsley**

In a 10-in. skillet, melt butter over medium heat. In the skillet, layer half of the potatoes, salt, pepper, onions, green pepper and ham; repeat layers. Cover and cook over medium heat for 10-15 minutes or until potatoes are tender.

Pour eggs over the top. Cover and cook for 3-5 minutes or until eggs are nearly set. Sprinkle with cheese. Cover and cook 3-5 minutes longer or until cheese is melted and eggs are completely set. Cut into wedges. Sprinkle with parsley. **Yield:** 6 servings.

**Nutritional Analysis:** One serving (prepared with egg substitute and reduced-fat cheddar cheese) equals 189 calories, 7 g fat (4 g saturated fat), 28 mg cholesterol, 821 mg sodium, 16 g carbohydrate, 2 g fiber, 18 g protein. **Diabetic Exchanges:** 2 lean meat, 1 starch.

## Steak Salad

*(Pictured below)*

*Rather than use typical treatments for leftover steak, our Test Kitchen home economists toss the chilled meat with romaine, sliced mushrooms and tomato for a fresh and filling salad. Blue cheese and french-fried onions make flavorful accents. To create a tangy-sweet dressing, just whisk together olive oil and a few other ingredients.*

**4 cups torn romaine**
**3/4 cup sliced fresh mushrooms**
**1 medium tomato, seeded and chopped**
**3 tablespoons olive oil**
**5 teaspoons red wine vinegar**
**1-1/4 teaspoons sugar**
**1/2 teaspoon Worcestershire sauce**
**1/8 teaspoon salt**
**1/8 teaspoon pepper**
**1 pound cooked boneless beef sirloin steak, thinly sliced**
**1/2 cup crumbled blue cheese**
**1/2 cup french-fried onions**

In a large bowl, toss the romaine, mushrooms and tomato. In a small bowl, whisk the oil, vinegar, sugar, Worcestershire sauce, salt and pepper.

Drizzle over salad and toss to coat. Arrange on four serving plates. Top with the steak, blue cheese and onions. **Yield:** 4 servings.

**Steak Salad**

## Corn Potato Pancakes

*I love combining different foods, including any leftovers I may have in the fridge, to see what new dishes I can come up with. Using corn, seasonings, onion and common pancake ingredients, I turned extra mashed potatoes into these slightly crispy, golden brown cakes.*
*—Carolyn Wilson, Lyndon, Kansas*

**2 cups mashed potatoes (prepared with milk and butter)**
**1/4 cup all-purpose flour**
**1/4 cup cream-style corn**
**1 egg, beaten**
**3 tablespoons finely chopped onion**
**1 teaspoon minced fresh parsley**
**1/2 teaspoon salt**
**1/2 teaspoon minced garlic**
**1/8 teaspoon pepper**
**3 tablespoons vegetable oil, *divided***

In a large bowl, combine the first nine ingredients. In a large skillet, heat 1 tablespoon oil; drop four 1/4 cupfuls of batter into skillet. Cook for 1-2 minutes on each side or until golden brown. Repeat with remaining oil and batter. **Yield:** about 1 dozen.

## Hash 'n' Eggs

*With this second-day recipe, last night's corned beef and cooked potatoes can become a hearty morning meal. Our family really goes for this dish, which is on the table in 20 minutes and gets a little kick from hot pepper sauce.*
*—Dorothy Smith, El Dorado, Arkansas*

**2 tablespoons butter**
**4 cups cubed cooked potatoes**
**1 can (10-3/4 ounces) condensed cream of celery soup, undiluted**
**1/4 cup milk**
**1 teaspoon prepared mustard**
**1/4 teaspoon hot pepper sauce**
**1-1/2 cups cubed cooked corned beef (about 8 ounces)**
**4 eggs**
**Pepper to taste**

In a skillet, melt butter over medium heat. Add potatoes and cook for 2 minutes, stirring often. Stir in the soup, milk, mustard and hot pepper sauce; cook until heated through. Stir in the corned beef. Reduce heat to low.

Make four wells in potato mixture; break an egg into each well. Cover and cook for 10-15 minutes or until eggs are completely set. Add pepper to taste. **Yield:** 4 servings.

## Hot Green Rice

*Our boys have never liked spinach, but they'll happily eat this cheesy casserole that features those greens and relies on leftover cooked rice. I think the zippy jalapeno peppers I mix in help disguise the spinach taste.*
*—Judy Brown, Rockdale, Texas*

**1/2 cup chopped onion**
**2 tablespoons butter**
**1 package (10 ounces) frozen chopped spinach, thawed and well drained**
**1 cup cooked rice**
**1 can (10-3/4 ounces) condensed cream of mushroom *or* chicken soup, undiluted**
**1/4 cup milk**
**2 jalapeno peppers, seeded and chopped**
**1/2 teaspoon salt**
**1/4 teaspoon pepper**
**4 ounces process cheese (Velveeta), cubed**

In a skillet, saute onion in butter until tender. Stir in the spinach and rice. Combine the soup, milk, jalapenos, salt and pepper; add to spinach mixture and heat through. Stir in the cheese. Pour into a greased 1-1/2-qt. baking dish. Bake, uncovered, at 350° for 25-30 minutes or until heated through. **Yield:** 6 servings.

**Editor's Note:** When cutting or seeding hot peppers, use rubber or plastic gloves to protect your hands. Avoid touching your face.

## Kielbasa Pepper Pasta

*(Pictured above)*

*Let leftover sausage help you streamline tonight's dinner with this full-flavored stovetop dish. When I serve it with a green salad and garlic bread, dinner's done in only 30 minutes. —Michele Johnson, Orange, California*

**1-1/2 cups uncooked bow tie pasta**
**1/2 cup julienned green pepper**
**1/2 cup julienned sweet red pepper**
**2 tablespoons chopped red onion**
**1-1/2 teaspoons butter**
**1/2 pound fully cooked kielbasa *or* Polish sausage, cut into 1/4-inch slices**
**1/8 teaspoon salt**
**1/8 teaspoon pepper**

Cook pasta according to package directions. Meanwhile, in a large skillet, saute the peppers and onion in butter until tender. Add the sausage, salt and pepper; cook and stir until sausage is heated through. Drain pasta and add to skillet; toss to coat. **Yield:** 2 servings.

### Using Your Noodles

Have plain noodles left over from another recipe? I add enough margarine and French onion dip so that the noodles are coated. It really gives them some zip and takes almost no time at all to do. The result is a tasty side dish or take-along lunch.
*—Joanie Wiesbrock, Leonore, Kansas*

## Salami Pork Sub

*(Pictured below)*

*Our family used to drive 22 miles to enjoy these sandwiches at a restaurant. After the place was torn down to make room for a highway, I was able to get the recipe. Now I fix them at home all the time.* —*Shirley Nordblum*
*Youngsville, Pennsylvania*

**1 loaf (1 pound) unsliced French bread**
**12 slices salami**
**16 slices cooked pork (1/8 inch thick)**
**8 slices provolone cheese**
**24 thin dill pickle slices**
**Lettuce leaves**
**1/4 cup mayonnaise**
**2 tablespoons prepared mustard**

Cut bread in half lengthwise. On the bottom half, layer the salami, pork, cheese, pickles and lettuce. Combine mayonnaise and mustard; spread over cut side of top half of loaf. Place over lettuce. Cut into fourths. **Yield:** 4 servings.

## Spaghetti Ham Toss

*(Pictured below)*

*It takes only minutes to make this time-saving pasta toss. Leftover ham, canned ripe olives, sliced mushrooms and roasted red peppers lend plenty of flavor to the colorful combination of tastes. Everyone loves it.* —*Marybeth Wright*
*Maitland, Florida*

**1 package (16 ounces) spaghetti**
**4 cups cubed fully cooked ham (about 1-1/2 pounds)**
**1/2 pound fresh mushrooms, sliced**
**1 medium green pepper, chopped**
**3 garlic cloves, minced**
**2 tablespoons olive oil**
**1 jar (7-1/4 ounces) roasted sweet red peppers, drained**
**1 can (2-1/4 ounces) sliced ripe olives, drained**
**1/4 teaspoon salt**

**Salami Pork Sub**
**Spaghetti Ham Toss**

1/4 teaspoon dried basil
1/4 teaspoon pepper
2 cups (8 ounces) shredded Parmesan cheese

Cook spaghetti according to package directions. Meanwhile, in a large skillet, saute the ham, mushrooms, green pepper and garlic in oil until vegetables are crisp-tender. Stir in the red peppers, olives, salt, basil and pepper.

Drain spaghetti; place in a large bowl. Add the ham mixture and Parmesan cheese; toss. Transfer to a greased 15-in. x 10-in. x 1-in. baking pan. Broil 4 in. from the heat for 4-6 minutes or until the top is lightly browned. **Yield:** 6-8 servings.

## Turkey Potato Tetrazzini

*(Pictured at right)*

*This casserole is not only a great family dinner, but also perfect for a potluck. The dish features layers of sliced potatoes, cooked turkey, broccoli and Swiss cheese. Convenient store-bought Alfredo sauce keeps the preparation quick.*
*—Karen Bundy, Cabot, Pennsylvania*

**1 jar (16 ounces) Alfredo sauce**
**1 cup milk**
**7 medium potatoes, peeled and thinly sliced**
**4 tablespoons grated Parmesan cheese, *divided***
**1-1/2 cups diced cooked turkey *or* chicken**
**2 cups (8 ounces) shredded Swiss cheese, *divided***
**1 package (10 ounces) frozen chopped broccoli, thawed**

In a bowl, combine Alfredo sauce and milk; spread 1/4 cup into a greased 13-in. x 9-in. x 2-in. baking dish. Top with a third of the potatoes; sprinkle with 1 tablespoon Parmesan cheese.

In a bowl, combine the turkey, 1-1/2 cups Swiss cheese and the broccoli; spoon about 2 cups over the potatoes. Top with about 2/3 cup sauce mixture. Repeat the layers twice.

Cover and bake at 400° for 45 minutes. Top with remaining cheeses (dish will be full). Bake, uncovered, 20-25 minutes longer or until potatoes are tender. Let stand for 5 minutes before serving. **Yield:** 12-15 servings.

## Artichoke Rice Salad

*I can quickly throw together this delicious, unique side dish that takes advantage of an extra cup of cooked rice and includes a hint of lemon. My friends and family always enjoy the cool refreshing combination of artichoke hearts, avocado, beans and colorful peppers.*
*—Bernice Knutson, Soldier, Iowa*

**2 tablespoons vegetable oil**
**1 teaspoon lemon juice**
**1 cup garbanzo beans *or* chickpeas, rinsed and drained**
**1 cup cold cooked rice**

Turkey Potato Tetrazzini

**1 jar (6-1/2 ounces) marinated artichoke hearts, drained and quartered**
**1 medium ripe avocado, peeled and chopped**
**1/2 cup chopped green pepper**
**1/2 cup chopped sweet red pepper**
**1 medium tomato, chopped**
**1/4 cup chopped onion**
**Salt and pepper to taste**

In a large bowl, combine oil and lemon juice. Stir in the remaining ingredients. Cover and chill until serving. **Yield:** 4-6 servings.

## Mac 'n' Cheese Salad

*This creamy cold salad is so simple to make, it takes only 10 minutes to prepare from start to finish. Leftover macaroni and cheese is the key to the mouth-watering medley that's full of vegetables and seasoned with dill. As tasty as this creation is when I first mix it together, it's even better the next day...but rarely lasts that long!*
*—Doris Moore, Augusta, Illinois*

**1-1/2 cups leftover macaroni and cheese, chilled**
**1/2 cup chopped cucumber**
**1/4 cup sliced radishes**
**1/4 cup mayonnaise**
**2 tablespoons chopped onion**
**1/2 teaspoon ground mustard**
**1/8 teaspoon dill weed**

In a serving bowl, combine all of the ingredients. Serve immediately. **Yield:** 2-3 servings.

## Chicken Corn Chowder

*This is a great dish when you need a meal in a hurry. We like to make it with mushroom soup, but you can change the ingredients to accommodate your family's tastes and whatever items you have on hand. —Sharon Gentert Wendell, Idaho*

**1 can (10-3/4 ounces) condensed cream of chicken *or* mushroom soup, undiluted**
**1-1/2 cups milk**
**1 teaspoon dried minced onion**
**1/2 teaspoon dried rosemary, crushed**
**2 cups cubed cooked chicken**
**1 can (15-1/4 ounces) whole kernel corn, drained**
**1 cup (4 ounces) shredded cheddar cheese**

In a large saucepan, combine the soup, milk, onion and rosemary. Stir in chicken and corn; heat through. Add the cheese; stir until melted. **Yield:** 4-6 servings.

## Pork Sandwich Spread

*This recipe uses up extra pork and makes a satisfying solution for brown-bag lunches. I simply add mayonnaise, onion and a few other ingredients. This spread is a favorite that I turn to whenever I have leftover pork roast. —Lorraine Kramer Norfolk, Nebraska*

✓ Uses less fat, sugar or salt. Includes Nutritional Analysis and Diabetic Exchanges.

**2 cups ground cooked pork**
**1/2 cup finely chopped celery**
**1/2 cup mayonnaise**
**2 tablespoons finely chopped onion**
**2 tablespoons sweet pickle relish**
**1 tablespoon prepared mustard**
**Pepper to taste**
**12 slices white bread**

In a bowl, combine the first seven ingredients. Spread over six slices of bread, about 1-1/3 cups on each; top with remaining bread. **Yield:** 6 servings.

**Nutritional Analysis:** One sandwich (prepared with fat-free mayonnaise) equals 284 calories, 11 g fat (4 g saturated fat), 42 mg cholesterol, 542 mg sodium, 30 g carbohydrate, 2 g fiber, 15 g protein. **Diabetic Exchanges:** 2 starch, 1-1/2 lean meat, 1 fat.

## Peppermint Potato Candy

*(Pictured at right and on page 101)*

*No one will suspect that these quick minty candies started with yesterday's mashed potatoes. My friends and family can't get enough of the chocolate-covered sweets. —Cindy Reams, Philipsburg, Pennsylvania*

**3/4 cup warm mashed potatoes (prepared without milk and butter)**
**2 teaspoons butter, softened**
**1 teaspoon peppermint extract**
**1 package (2 pounds) confectioners' sugar**
**2 cups (12 ounces) semisweet chocolate chips**
**1 tablespoon shortening**

In a large mixing bowl, beat the mashed potatoes, butter and extract. Gradually beat in confectioners' sugar. Press into a foil-lined 13-in. x 9-in. x 2-in. pan.

Melt chocolate chips and shortening; spread over potato mixture. Cover and refrigerate until set. Using foil,

## Readers Reveal More Ways to Enjoy Extras

**Popular Pizza Omelets**

For a yummy breakfast or brunch, my family enjoys pizza omelets. I simply dice leftover pizza, adding it to beaten eggs. (I usually dice one large pizza slice for every six eggs.) Cook these omelets as you would any other omelets, or make a batch of scrambled eggs instead.

The beauty of this idea is that it gets my family's favorite ingredients into their omelets without having to cook various meats and chop different vegetables.

*—Carmen Valdez, Amarillo, Texas*

**Steak Stir-Fry**

After a party, we had quite a bit of leftover grilled marinated steak and vegetables. We put some into hard rolls to make sandwiches, but we still had some left.

So I sauteed the veggies in olive oil, added slices of the steak and seasoned the mixture with garlic powder, oregano and basil. When everything was warmed through, I put the mixture over hot cooked rice. Everyone loved it and nothing went to waste.

*—Annaclaire Crocco, Waterbury, Connecticut*

**Great Garlic Toast**

I have two small children who enjoy their hot dogs sliced, which means we often have extra hot dog buns. To use them up, I open the buns flat and butter them. Next, I sprinkle the buns with garlic salt and dried parsley flakes before popping them in the toaster oven or setting them a few inches beneath the broiler. They're tasty served with pasta and other Italian entrees.

I also use leftover buns for broiled open-faced ham and cheese sandwiches. The kids enjoy these warm cheesy sandwiches for lunch with fresh fruit.

*—Kathy Marples, Chandler, Arizona*

**Tasty Change for Chili**

My favorite recipe for finishing extra food involves using leftover chili as a sauce over homemade enchiladas.

For my enchiladas, I fill flour tortillas with browned ground beef, chopped onion and canned refried beans. Then I top them with the leftover chili and shredded cheese before heating them in the microwave.

*—Cathy Globe, Silver Bay, Minnesota*

Peppermint Potato Candy
Sweet 'n' Sour Turkey

lift candy out of pan. Discard foil; cut candy into 1-in. squares. Store in an airtight container. **Yield:** about 2-3/4 pounds.

## Sweet 'n' Sour Turkey

*(Pictured above and on page 100)*

*Sweet-and-sour lovers will have a lot to look forward to when they simmer up this saucy supper. Stir-fry leftover turkey, canned pineapple tidbits and veggies for the in-a-dash dinner.* —*Shanna Webb, Provo, Utah*

✓ Uses less fat, sugar or salt. Includes Nutritional Analysis and Diabetic Exchanges.

**2 tablespoons cornstarch**
**2 tablespoons brown sugar**
**1 cup chicken broth**
**2 tablespoons soy sauce**
**1 tablespoon lemon juice**
**2 celery ribs, sliced**
**2 medium carrots, sliced**
**1 small onion, cut into thin wedges**
**3 tablespoons butter, cubed**
**2 cups julienned cooked turkey**
**1 can (14 ounces) unsweetened pineapple tidbits, undrained**
**1/4 cup slivered almonds, toasted**
**Hot cooked rice, optional**

In a small bowl, combine cornstarch and brown sugar. Stir in the broth, soy sauce and lemon juice until smooth; set aside.

In a wok or large skillet, stir-fry the celery, carrots and onion in butter for 3-4 minutes or until crisp-tender. Stir broth mixture; add to the pan. Bring to a boil; cook and stir for 2 minutes or until thickened. Add the turkey, pineapple with juice and almonds; heat through. Serve over rice if desired. **Yield:** 4 servings.

**Nutritional Analysis:** One 1-1/3-cup serving (prepared with reduced-sodium chicken broth, reduced-sodium soy sauce and reduced-fat margarine; calculated without rice) equals 327 calories, 11 g fat (2 g saturated fat), 48 mg cholesterol, 642 mg sodium, 32 g carbohydrate, 3 g fiber, 25 g protein. **Diabetic Exchanges:** 2-1/2 lean meat, 2 vegetable, 1-1/2 fruit, 1 fat.

# Chapter 8

# Freezer Pleasers

AS THE CLOCK ticks down toward dinnertime, the heat is on to get fast and flavorful fare to your family. So keep your cool with make-ahead meals from the freezer.

By doing a lot of the prep work on more leisurely days, you can have an already-assembled entree that simply goes in the oven after a long day. Soon you'll have a hot and homemade dinner on the table—all the while giving kitchen fuss the cold shoulder.

In addition to main dishes, this chapter features time-easing and crowd-pleasing recipes for appetizers, desserts and salads that you can freeze to make mealtime a breeze.

**COOL CUISINE.** Top to bottom: Fudgy Ice Cream Dessert and Chicken Manicotti (recipes on pp. 120 and 121).

## Super Sloppy Joes

*(Pictured below)*

*Five ingredients and about 30 minutes are all you need to make these hearty sandwiches. They're great for family gatherings. Onion soup mix and sweet pickle relish add tangy flavor without a lot of effort on my part.* —*Marge Napalo*
*Brunswick, Ohio*

- **3 pounds ground beef**
- **3 cups ketchup**
- **2/3 cup sweet pickle relish**
- **1 envelope onion soup mix**
- **14 hamburger buns, split**

In a Dutch oven, cook beef over medium heat until no longer pink; drain. Stir in the ketchup, relish and soup mix; heat through. Spoon about 1/2 cup onto each bun. Or, cool and freeze in freezer containers for up to 3 months. **Yield:** 14 servings.

**To use frozen sloppy joes:** Thaw in the refrigerator; place in a saucepan and heat through. Serve on buns.

## Chocolate Orange Pie

*(Pictured below)*

*I dreamed up this wonderful concoction one day when I was yearning for the creamy orange ice cream treat of my childhood. With orange sherbet and vanilla ice cream, the recipe really comes close to re-creating that unforgettable taste...and also features a rich chocolaty layer sprinkled with chopped pecans.* —*Laurie LaClair*
*North Richland Hills, Texas*

- **1 cup miniature marshmallows**
- **1 cup (6 ounces) semisweet chocolate chips**
- **1 cup evaporated milk**

**Chocolate Orange Pie**
**Super Sloppy Joes**

**1 pint vanilla ice cream, softened**
**1 pint orange sherbet, softened**
**1 graham cracker crust (9 inches)**
**1/3 cup coarsely chopped pecans**

In a saucepan, combine the marshmallows, chocolate chips and milk. Bring to a boil over medium heat; cook and stir for 2 minutes or until melted. Remove from the heat. Cool completely.

Meanwhile, alternately arrange scoops of ice cream and sherbet in crust; smooth top. Pour chocolate sauce over pie; sprinkle with pecans. Cover and freeze for at least 4 hours. May be frozen for up to 2 months. **Yield:** 6-8 servings.

## Chicken Wonton Rolls

*Guests will think you fussed over these warm golden bites. I sometimes turn the recipe into a main course by using egg roll wrappers and serving the rolls with chicken gravy instead of sweet-and-sour sauce. Either way, they're delicious.*
*—Mary Dixson, Decatur, Alabama*

**1 package (3 ounces) cream cheese, softened**
**6 tablespoons butter, softened, *divided***
**2 tablespoons minced chives**
**1/2 teaspoon lemon-pepper seasoning**
**1-1/2 cups finely chopped cooked chicken**
**1 can (4 ounces) mushroom stems and pieces, drained and chopped**
**1 package (12 ounces) wonton wrappers**
**2/3 cup crushed salad croutons**
**Sweet-and-sour sauce, optional**

In a small mixing bowl, beat cream cheese, 2 tablespoons butter, chives and lemon-pepper until blended. Stir in the chicken and mushrooms. Place a rounded teaspoonful in the center of each wonton wrapper. Fold the bottom corner over filling; fold sides toward center. Moisten remaining corner with water; roll up tightly to seal.

Melt remaining butter; brush over wontons. Coat with croutons. Place on a baking sheet; freeze. Transfer to a large resealable plastic bag. May be frozen for up to 3 months.

**To use frozen wontons:** Place wontons on greased baking sheets. Bake at 425° for 10 minutes. Turn; bake 5-10 minutes longer or until lightly browned. Serve warm with sweet-and-sour sauce if desired. **Yield:** about 4 dozen.

## Nutty Ice Cream Delight

*We fell in love with this recipe the very first time we tried it. Not only do the cookie crust and thick rich chocolate topping come together easily, but adults like the layered dessert as much as children do.*
*—Carol Gillespie*
*Chambersburg, Pennsylvania*

**1 package (15 ounces) cream-filled chocolate sandwich cookie crumbs**
**1/2 cup butter, melted**
**1/8 teaspoon ground cinnamon**
**CHOCOLATE SAUCE:**
**2 cups confectioners' sugar**
**2 tablespoons malted milk powder**
**1 can (12 ounces) evaporated milk**
**1 cup (6 ounces) semisweet chocolate chips**
**1/2 cup butter, cubed**
**1/2 teaspoon vanilla extract**
**1/2 teaspoon orange extract, optional**
**2 cups salted peanuts**
**1/2 gallon peanut butter ice cream with peanut butter cup pieces *or* peanut butter swirl ice cream, softened**

In a large bowl, combine the cookie crumbs, butter and cinnamon. Press into a greased 13-in. x 9-in. x 2-in. dish. Cover and freeze until firm.

Meanwhile, in a large saucepan, combine the confectioners' sugar, malted milk powder, milk, chocolate chips and butter. Bring to a boil; cook and stir for 7-8 minutes. Remove from the heat; stir in vanilla and orange extract if desired. Cool completely.

Sprinkle peanuts over crust; spread with ice cream. Freeze. Top with chocolate sauce. Cover and freeze until firm, about 3 hours. May be frozen for up to 3 months. **Yield:** 12-15 servings.

## Handy Freezer Hints

- I roll cookie dough into logs and seal them with my Food Saver before storing them in the freezer. (If you don't have a Food Saver, wrap them tightly in plastic wrap, then heavy-duty aluminum foil.) It's easy to slice the frozen logs or thaw the dough and pinch off teaspoon-size portions before baking.
*—Donna Lauck, Philadelphia, Pennsylvania*

- Baked potatoes topped with fresh chives are one of my favorite side dishes. Since chives don't keep very long in the refrigerator, I like to mince a bunch of them and store them in a plastic container in the freezer. Every time I want chives, I simply take out the amount I want and add them to my potato. They last for months! *—Jennifer Weyenberg*
*Pearland, Texas*

- I often double or triple the amount of meat I'm grilling. After dinner, I store the extra meat in the freezer. Then, when I want a meal that's full of "just-grilled" flavor, I simply thaw and reheat the meat in the microwave. This saves a lot of time, and grilling large quantities at once is an efficient way to use your grill's coals or gas. *—Diana Duda*
*Glenwood, Illinois*

- Ever wonder what to do with the juice that's left over from canned fruit? I like to freeze it and use it in my smoothies. Blended with fresh fruit such as bananas or berries, the frozen juice gives extra flavor to an icy pick-me-up. Not only is this an easy way to use up the fruit juice, but it's a fast and healthy snack as well. *—Elizabeth Meinhart*
*Jacksonville, North Carolina*

## Cream of Zucchini Soup

*Since zucchini plants are such plentiful producers during the summer, I stir together several batches of this recipe at that time and freeze them for the two of us to enjoy later on. The simple-but-delicious cream soup is especially good when cooler weather arrives. To round out your menu, just add bread and a tossed salad.* —*Bernice Morris Marshfield, Missouri*

**1 pound zucchini, cut into 1/2-inch slices**
**2 cups water**
**1 medium onion, chopped**
**1 teaspoon chicken bouillon granules**
**1/2 teaspoon seasoned salt**
**2 cans (one 12 ounces, one 5 ounces) evaporated milk**
**1 tablespoon butter**

In a large saucepan, combine zucchini, water, onion, bouillon and seasoned salt. Bring to a boil. Reduce heat; cover and simmer for 5 minutes or until zucchini is tender. Cool slightly.

In a blender, cover and process soup in batches until pureed. Return all to the pan. Add milk and butter; cook and stir until butter is melted. Serve immediately or transfer to a freezer container. May be frozen for up to 3 months. **Yield:** 5 servings.

**To use frozen soup:** Thaw in the refrigerator overnight. Transfer to a large saucepan. Cook and stir over medium heat until heated through.

## Spinach Cheese Appetizers

*Hosting a get-together? Whether you're planning a casual gathering or a more elegant affair, you'll appreciate having these make-ahead hors d'oeurves stashed in your freezer. I just take them out and pop them in the oven about 30 minutes before serving. Loaded with cheese and spinach, the rich warm squares keep my guests coming back for more.* —*Marian Platt, Sequim, Washington*

**1/2 cup butter, melted**
**1 cup all-purpose flour**
**1 teaspoon salt**
**1 teaspoon baking powder**
**3 eggs**
**1 cup milk**
**2 packages (10 ounces *each*) frozen chopped spinach, thawed and squeezed dry**
**4 cups (16 ounces) shredded Monterey Jack cheese**

Pour butter into a 13-in. x 9-in. x 2-in. baking dish; tilt to coat. In a bowl, combine flour, salt and baking powder. Whisk eggs and milk; stir into dry ingredients just until blended. Fold in spinach and cheese. Pour into prepared dish.

Bake, uncovered, at 350° for 30-35 minutes or until a knife inserted near the center comes out clean. Cool for 5 minutes; cut into small squares. Serve immediately or transfer to a freezer container. May be frozen for up to 3 months. **Yield:** about 6-1/2 dozen.

**To use frozen appetizers:** Thaw in the refrigerator overnight. Place on baking sheet. Bake, uncovered, at 350° for 25-30 minutes or until heated through. Let stand 5 minutes before serving.

## Ice Cream Crunchies

*Four ingredients are all I need to assemble these fun and frosty bars. The crunchy peanut-butter cereal treats are so yummy with the smooth vanilla ice cream sandwiched in between. Needless to say, children absolutely love these sweet snacks...and can even help put them together because the preparation is so simple.*
—*Sady Craig, Lapeer, Michigan*

**1/2 cup light corn syrup**
**1/2 cup peanut butter**
**3 cups crisp rice cereal**
**2-1/2 cups vanilla ice cream, softened**

In a large bowl, combine corn syrup and peanut butter; stir in cereal. With buttered hands, press the mixture into a greased 13-in. x 9-in. x 2-in. pan. Refrigerate for 15 minutes.

Cut cereal mixture into 12 rectangles; remove from the pan. Place 1/2 cup ice cream on six rectangles; top with remaining rectangles.

Wrap each in plastic wrap and freeze until firm. May be frozen for up to 2 months. Cut in half before serving. **Yield:** 1 dozen.

## Mexican Fried Ice Cream

*(Pictured at right)*

*Fried ice cream is one of my favorite desserts to order from Mexican restaurants. When my sister and I found this recipe for preparing it at home, we knew it would be an impressive way to end a meal. I like to garnish the treat with whipped topping.*
—*Mandy Wright, Springville, Utah*

**1/2 gallon French vanilla ice cream, softened**
**4 teaspoons ground cinnamon**
**3 cups crushed cornflakes**
**Oil for deep-fat frying**
**Honey and whipped topping**

Scoop ice cream into nine 3-in. scoops. Dust with cinnamon and roll in cornflakes. Place on a baking sheet; freeze overnight. Wrap each scoop in plastic wrap and place in a freezer bag. May be frozen for up to 2 months.

**To fry ice cream:** In an electric skillet or deep-fat fryer, heat oil to 375°. Unwrap ice cream; fry one scoop at a time for 8-10 seconds. Place in chilled bowls. Drizzle with honey and garnish with whipped topping. **Yield:** 9 servings.

## Cheesy Kielbasa Bake

*(Pictured above right)*

*This hearty casserole featuring flavorful sausage and three kinds of cheese takes advantage of garden-fresh vegetables and handy convenience items such as purchased spaghetti*

Cheesy Kielbasa Bake
Mexican Fried Ice Cream

*sauce. Originally, my aunt served the meaty dish at family gatherings. Now I'll fix it any night of the week. It's nice to prepare a second casserole and keep it in the freezer for days that are especially hectic.* —*Kate Beckman*
*Hemet, California*

**12 ounces uncooked elbow macaroni**
**2 pounds kielbasa *or* Polish sausage, halved lengthwise and sliced**
**1 tablespoon olive oil**
**2 medium onions, chopped**
**2 medium zucchini, quartered and sliced**
**2 medium carrots, grated**
**1 garlic clove, minced**
**1 jar (26 ounces) spaghetti sauce**
**1 can (14-1/2 ounces) stewed tomatoes, undrained**
**1 egg, lightly beaten**
**1 carton (15 ounces) ricotta cheese**
**2 cups (8 ounces) shredded cheddar cheese**
**2 cups (8 ounces) shredded mozzarella cheese**
**2 green onions, chopped**

Cook macaroni according to package directions; drain and set aside. In a large skillet, brown sausage in oil over medium heat. Add the onions, zucchini, carrots and garlic; cook and stir for 5-6 minutes or until crisp-tender. Stir in spaghetti sauce and tomatoes. Bring to a boil. Reduce heat; simmer, uncovered, for 15 minutes.

In each of two greased 13-in. x 9-in. x 2-in. baking dishes, layer a fourth of the macaroni and meat sauce. Combine the egg and ricotta cheese; spoon a fourth over the sauce. Sprinkle with a fourth of the cheddar and mozzarella cheeses. Repeat the layers and top with the green onions.

Cover and bake at 350° for 15 minutes. Uncover; bake 15 minutes longer or until the cheese is melted. Serve one casserole. Cool the second casserole; cover and freeze for up to 2 months. **Yield:** 2 casseroles (8-10 servings each).

**To use frozen casserole:** Thaw in the refrigerator for 24 hours. Remove from the refrigerator 30 minutes before baking. Cover and bake at 350° for 35-40 minutes or until heated through.

## Seasoned Hamburger Mix

*I prepare a large batch of this ground beef mixture and freeze it in small portions. The seasoned meat is the beginning of many made-in-minutes meals. Among my favorites are the two recipes that follow.* —*Dorothy Smith, El Dorado, Arkansas*

- **4 pounds ground beef**
- **2 large onions, chopped**
- **1 teaspoon salt**
- **1/2 teaspoon dried oregano**
- **1/2 teaspoon pepper**
- **1/4 teaspoon garlic salt**

In a large skillet, cook beef and onions in two batches over medium heat until meat is no longer pink; drain. In a large bowl, combine the beef mixture, salt, oregano, pepper and garlic salt. Freeze in 2-cup portions for up to 3 months. **Yield:** 5 portions (10 cups total).

## Enchilada Dip

(Pictured below)

*Dorothy Smith combines some of her hamburger mix (recipe at left) with convenient canned chili, tomato sauce and enchilada sauce to create this warm dip topped with sour cream and cheddar cheese. Served alongside a bowl of tortilla chips, the Mexican snack is an easy appetizer.*

- **2 cups Seasoned Hamburger Mix (recipe at left), thawed**
- **1 can (15 ounces) chili with beans**
- **1 can (10 ounces) enchilada sauce**
- **1 can (8 ounces) tomato sauce**
- **3/4 cup corn chips**
- **1 cup (8 ounces) sour cream**
- **1/2 cup shredded cheddar cheese**
- **Tortilla chips**

In a large bowl, combine the hamburger mix, chili, enchilada sauce, tomato sauce and corn chips. Transfer to

**Taco Bean Salad**
**Enchilada Dip**

a greased shallow 2-qt. baking dish. Bake, uncovered, at 375° for 20-25 minutes or until heated through.

Dollop with the sour cream; spread carefully. Sprinkle with cheese. Bake 3-5 minutes longer or until cheese is melted. Serve with the tortilla chips. **Yield:** 10-12 servings.

## Taco Bean Salad

*(Pictured below left)*

*Storing Seasoned Hamburger Mix (recipe on opposite page) in the freezer helps Dorothy Smith beat the clock when she is making this change-of-pace tossed salad. It's chock-full of good stuff, including fresh tomato wedges, chopped avocado and canned kidney beans.*

**3 large tomatoes**
**1 head iceberg lettuce, torn**
**6 cups coarsely crushed tortilla chips**
**2 cups (8 ounces) shredded cheddar cheese**
**1 can (16 ounces) kidney beans, rinsed and drained**
**1 large ripe avocado, peeled and chopped**
**2 cups Seasoned Hamburger Mix (recipe on page 118), thawed**
**1 bottle (7 ounces) green taco sauce**
**4 green onions, chopped**
**Ranch salad dressing *or* dressing of your choice**

Chop two tomatoes; cut remaining tomato into wedges. In a large salad bowl, toss the lettuce, tortilla chips, cheese, beans, avocado and chopped tomatoes; set aside.

In a large microwave-safe bowl, combine the hamburger mix and taco sauce. Cover and microwave on high for 2-3 minutes or until heated through. Spoon over salad; toss gently. Top with tomato wedges and onions. Serve with dressing. **Yield:** 10 servings.

**Editor's Note:** This recipe was tested in a 1,100-watt microwave.

## Cheesy Rigatoni Bake

*Combining popular ingredients like pasta, cheese and tomato sauce, this is a family favorite that brings the whole gang to the table fast. In fact, one of our four children always requests the casserole as a birthday dinner.*
*—Nancy Urbine, Lancaster, Ohio*

**1 package (16 ounces) rigatoni *or* large tube pasta**
**2 tablespoons butter**
**1/4 cup all-purpose flour**
**1/2 teaspoon salt**
**2 cups milk**
**1/4 cup water**
**4 eggs, beaten**
**2 cans (8 ounces *each*) tomato sauce**
**2 cups (8 ounces) shredded mozzarella cheese**
**1/4 cup grated Parmesan cheese**

Cook pasta according to package directions. Meanwhile, in a saucepan, melt butter. Stir in flour and salt until smooth; gradually add milk and water. Bring to a boil; cook and stir for 2 minutes or until thickened.

Drain pasta; place in a large bowl. Add eggs. Spoon into two greased 8-in. square baking dishes. Top each with one can of tomato sauce and mozzarella cheese. Spoon white sauce over top; sprinkle with Parmesan cheese.

Cover and freeze one casserole for up to 3 months. Bake second casserole, uncovered, at 375° for 30-35 minutes or until a meat thermometer reads 160°. **Yield:** 2 casseroles (6-8 servings each).

**To use frozen casserole:** Thaw in the refrigerator overnight. Cover and bake at 375° for 40 minutes. Uncover; bake 7-10 minutes longer or until a meat thermometer reads 160°.

## Cherry Cream Sensation

*I made this cake by covering store-bought ice cream sandwiches with cherry pie filling and more.*
*—Victoria Zmarzley-Hahn, Northampton, Pennsylvania*

**10 ice cream sandwiches**
**1 can (21 ounces) cherry pie filling**
**1 carton (12 ounces) frozen whipped topping, thawed**
**Chocolate sprinkles, optional**

Arrange ice cream sandwiches in a single layer in a 13-in. x 9-in. x 2-in. dish. Top with pie filling, whipped topping and chocolate sprinkles if desired. Cover and freeze for at least 4 hours or until firm. May be frozen for up to 2 months. Remove from the freezer 10 minutes before cutting. **Yield:** 12 servings.

### More Icebox Ideas

- Rather than buying cubed or ground ham, I buy bone-in hams when they're on sale. I have the store butcher slice the ham about 1/2 inch thick, then cube it myself and freeze it in individual packages. For ground ham, I put boneless slices in the food processor and freeze portions in small packages. *—MariJeanne Waterbeck, Fort Worth, Texas*
- I always make extra soup, then freeze it in 1-cup containers. When I need to pack a quick lunch, I simply grab a container. As it thaws during the day, the soup keeps the rest of my lunch chilled. By noontime, my soup is ready to reheat in the microwave. *—Betsy Larimer, Somerset, Pennsylvania*
- This tip saves time when I'm baking pies. I throw together several batches of pie filling, putting each batch in its own resealable freezer storage bag. When I want a pie, I just thaw a bag while I make the crust. Then I pour the filling into the crust and bake as usual. *—Mary Ann Mento, Arlington, Vermont*
- I cube leftover bread and put it in a storage container in my freezer. For homemade croutons, I just shake the bread cubes in a resealable storage bag with seasonings and melted butter. Then I bake the cubes for a few minutes. *—Elizabeth Clark Dunnegan, Missouri*

## Chunky Oatmeal Cookies

*After I stir together this chock-full dough, I measure it out in tablespoonfuls and store it in the freezer. Then, any time we're craving homemade cookies, fresh-baked treats are just minutes away. It's so nice to be able to take the frozen balls out and pop them in the oven. In less than half an hour, we're enjoying golden goodies loaded with oats, raisins and candy pieces.* —*Sandra Castillo*
*Sun Prairie, Wisconsin*

**3/4 cup butter, softened**
**1 cup packed brown sugar**
**1/2 cup sugar**
**2 eggs**
**1 teaspoon vanilla extract**
**3 cups quick-cooking oats**
**1-1/2 cups all-purpose flour**
**1/2 teaspoon baking soda**
**1/4 teaspoon salt**
**3/4 cup raisins**
**3/4 cup Reese's Pieces *or* M&M's**

In a mixing bowl, cream butter and sugars. Beat in eggs and vanilla. Combine the oats, flour, baking soda and salt; gradually add to creamed mixture. Stir in raisins and candy. Drop by tablespoonfuls onto ungreased baking sheets. Cover and freeze.

Transfer frozen cookie dough balls to a large resealable plastic freezer bag. May be frozen for up to 3 months. **Yield:** about 3-1/2 dozen.

**To use frozen cookie dough:** Place dough balls 2 in. apart on greased baking sheets. Bake at 350° for 18-22 minutes or until golden brown. Remove to wire racks to cool.

## Sausage Rice Casserole

*I fiddled around with this recipe for quite some time, trying to adjust it to suit my family's tastes. When I served a new version of the dish and my pickiest child cleaned her plate, I knew I'd discovered the right flavor combination. The sausage casserole full of vegetables has become a favorite we enjoy often...even on days when I have only minutes to spend in the kitchen.* —*Jennifer Trost*
*West Linn, Oregon*

**2 packages (7.2 ounces *each*) rice pilaf mix**
**2 pounds bulk pork sausage**
**6 celery ribs, chopped**
**4 medium carrots, chopped**
**1 can (10-3/4 ounces) condensed cream of chicken soup, undiluted**
**1 can (10-3/4 ounces) condensed cream of mushroom soup, undiluted**
**2 teaspoons onion powder**
**1/2 teaspoon garlic powder**
**1/4 teaspoon pepper**

Prepare the rice mixes according to package directions. Meanwhile, in a large skillet, cook the sausage, celery and carrots over medium heat until the meat is no longer pink; drain. In a large bowl, combine the sausage mixture, rice mixture and the remaining ingredients. Transfer to two greased 11-in. x 7-in. x 2-in. baking dishes.

Cover and bake one casserole at 350° for 40-45 minutes or until the vegetables are tender. Cover and freeze remaining casserole for up to 3 months. **Yield:** 2 casseroles (6-8 servings each).

**To use frozen casserole:** Thaw in the refrigerator. Let stand at room temperature for 30 minutes. Bake as directed.

## Hominy Taco Chili

*This robust chili is easy to prepare with convenient canned ingredients, taco seasoning and ranch salad dressing mix. Whenever I simmer up a pot, I can be sure it'll get rave reviews from everyone at the table. The extra batch goes in the freezer and can simply be reheated the next time I'm looking for a speedy meal. I like to serve each bowlful with a helping of corn chips.* —*Barbara Wheless*
*Sheldon, South Carolina*

**1 pound ground beef**
**1 large onion, chopped**
**2 cans (15-1/2 ounces *each*) hominy, drained**
**2 cans (14-1/2 ounces *each*) stewed tomatoes, undrained**
**1 can (15-1/4 ounces) whole kernel corn, drained**
**1 can (15 ounces) pinto beans, rinsed and drained**
**1 can (15 ounces) black beans, rinsed and drained**
**1 cup water**
**1 envelope taco seasoning**
**1 envelope ranch salad dressing mix**
**2 teaspoons ground cumin**
**1/2 teaspoon garlic salt**
**1/2 teaspoon pepper**
**Corn chips, optional**

In a large saucepan or Dutch oven, cook beef and onion over medium heat until meat is no longer pink; drain. Stir in the next 11 ingredients.

Bring to a boil. Reduce heat; cover and simmer for 30 minutes. Serve half of the chili with corn chips if desired. Freeze remaining chili in a freezer container for up to 3 months. **Yield:** 2 batches (4-5 servings each).

**To use frozen chili:** Thaw in the refrigerator. Transfer to a saucepan; heat through, adding water if desired.

## Fudgy Ice Cream Dessert

*(Pictured above right and on page 112)*

*I top a rich chocolate cookie crust with vanilla ice cream, chopped peanuts and hot fudge topping to create this can't-miss dessert. Assemble it and keep it in the freezer to please your family or guests any time of year.* —*Jenny Haen*
*Red Wing, Minnesota*

**1 package (14 ounces) cream-filled chocolate sandwich cookies, crushed**

Fudgy Ice Cream Dessert
Chicken Manicotti

**7 tablespoons butter, melted**
**1/2 gallon vanilla ice cream, softened**
**1-1/2 cups finely chopped salted peanuts**
**1 carton (8 ounces) frozen whipped topping, thawed**
**1 jar (11-3/4 ounces) hot fudge ice cream topping, warmed**

In a bowl, combine cookie crumbs and butter. Set aside 1/2 cup for topping. Press remaining crumb mixture into a greased 13-in. x 9-in. x 2-in. dish. Freeze for 30 minutes. Spread ice cream over crust. Cover and freeze for 2-1/2 hours.

Sprinkle peanuts over ice cream. Cover and freeze for 1 hour. Spread with whipped topping (pan will be very full). Sprinkle with reserved crumb mixture. Freeze for 8 hours or overnight. May be frozen for up to 2 months. Remove from the freezer 15 minutes before serving. Cut into squares. Serve with hot fudge topping. **Yield:** 12-15 servings.

## Chicken Manicotti

(Pictured above and on page 112)

*When a friend of mine came home from the hospital with her newborn, I sent over this freezer casserole to help cut down mealtime fuss. She and her family raved about the saucy manicotti stuffed with tender chicken and sprinkled with mozzarella cheese. For a tasty change of pace, try substituting your favorite olives for the fresh mushrooms or using veal in place of the chicken.* —*Jamie Valocchi*
*Mesa, Arizona*

**1 tablespoon garlic powder**
**1-1/2 pounds boneless skinless chicken breasts**
**16 uncooked manicotti shells**
**2 jars (26 ounces *each*) spaghetti sauce, *divided***
**1 pound bulk Italian sausage, cooked and drained**
**1/2 pound fresh mushrooms, sliced**
**4 cups (16 ounces) shredded mozzarella cheese**
**2/3 cup water**

Rub garlic powder over chicken; cut into 1-in. strips. Stuff chicken into manicotti shells. Spread 1 cup spaghetti sauce in each of two greased 13-in. x 9-in. x 2-in. baking dishes. Place eight stuffed manicotti shells in each dish. Sprinkle with sausage and mushrooms. Pour remaining spaghetti sauce over the top. Sprinkle with cheese.

Drizzle water around the edge of each dish. Cover and bake one casserole at 375° for 65-70 minutes or until chicken juices run clear and pasta is tender. Cover and freeze remaining casserole for up to 1 month. **Yield:** 2 casseroles (4 servings each).

**To use frozen casserole:** Thaw in the refrigerator. Let stand at room temperature for about 30 minutes. Bake as directed.

## Black Forest Freezer Pie

*(Pictured below)*

*A delightful dessert is never far off when you have this layered ice cream pie in the freezer. For variety, use strawberry pie filling and a chocolate crust.* —*Angie Helms*
*Pontotoc, Mississippi*

**1 pint chocolate *or* vanilla ice cream, softened**
**1 graham cracker crust (10 inches)**
**4 ounces cream cheese, softened**
**1 cup confectioners' sugar**
**1 carton (8 ounces) frozen whipped topping, thawed**
**1 can (21 ounces) cherry pie filling, chilled**
**3 tablespoons chocolate syrup**

Spoon ice cream into pie crust; cover and freeze for 15 minutes. In a mixing bowl, beat cream cheese and confectioners' sugar until smooth; fold in whipped topping. Spread over pie. Using the back of a spoon, make an 8-in.-diameter well in the center of the pie for the pie filling. Cover and freeze for 3-4 hours or until firm. May be frozen for up to 2 months. Just before serving, spoon pie filling into the well; drizzle with chocolate syrup. Serve immediately. **Yield:** 6-8 servings.

## Fruit Slush

*(Pictured below)*

*I mix up this sweet fruity slush using raspberries and a variety of juices. Then I keep it handy in the freezer for whenever unexpected company drops by. Simply pour a little citrus soda over scoops of the colorful frozen mixture for frosty and refreshing beverages.* —*Darlene White*
*Hobson, Montana*

**1 can (46 ounces) pineapple juice**
**8 cups water**

**Fruit Slush**
**Black Forest Freezer Pie**

1 can (12 ounces) frozen lemonade concentrate, thawed
1 can (12 ounces) frozen orange juice concentrate, thawed
4 cups sugar
2 cups fresh *or* frozen unsweetened raspberries
2 envelopes unsweetened cherry soft drink mix *or* other red flavor of your choice

**ADDITIONAL INGREDIENT:**
**Grapefruit *or* other citrus soda**

In a 6-qt. container, combine the first seven ingredients. Cover and freeze for 12 hours, stirring every 2 hours. May be frozen for up to 3 months. **Yield:** about 5 quarts.

**For each serving:** Place 1/2 cup fruit slush in a glass. Add 1/2 cup soda. **Yield:** 1 cup.

## Chicken Burritos

*This mouth-watering southwestern recipe makes enough for two family-size casseroles, so you can enjoy one for supper today and freeze the other for a weeknight when you're pressed for time. The burritos are great to have on hand for quick meals or to take to potlucks.*
*—Sonya Nightingale, Burley, Idaho*

**1 large onion, chopped**
**1/4 cup chopped green pepper**
**6 tablespoons butter**
**1/2 cup all-purpose flour**
**3 cups chicken broth**
**1 can (10 ounces) diced tomatoes and green chilies**
**2 tablespoons chopped jalapeno pepper, optional**
**1 teaspoon ground cumin**
**1 teaspoon chili powder**
**1/2 teaspoon garlic powder**
**1/2 teaspoon salt**
**1 can (15 ounces) chili with beans**
**1 package (8 ounces) cream cheese, cubed**
**8 cups cubed cooked chicken**
**24 flour tortillas (6 or 7 inches)**
**6 cups (24 ounces) shredded Colby-Monterey Jack cheese**

In a large skillet, saute onion and green pepper in butter until tender. Stir in flour until blended. Gradually stir in broth.

Bring to a boil; cook and stir for 2 minutes. Reduce heat; add the tomatoes, jalapeno pepper if desired and seasonings. Cook for 5 minutes or until heated through. Stir in chili and cream cheese until cheese is melted. Stir in chicken.

Spoon about 1/2 cupful down the center of each tortilla; sprinkle each with 1/4 cup Colby-Monterey Jack cheese. Fold ends and sides over filling. Place in two greased 13-in. x 9-in. x 2-in. baking dishes. Cover and freeze one casserole for up to 3 months. Cover and bake the remaining casserole at 350° for 35-40 minutes or until heated through. **Yield:** 2 casseroles (1 dozen burritos each).

**To use frozen burritos:** Thaw in the refrigerator overnight. Bake at 350° for 50-55 minutes or until heated through.

**Editor's Note:** When cutting or seeding hot peppers, use rubber or plastic gloves to protect your hands. Avoid touching your face.

## Make-Ahead Glazed Brownies

*Since I'm often designated as the "dessert lady" for get-togethers, I frequently rely on these moist brownies for last-minute treats. I've been sharing the chocolaty snacks for years and they're on everyone's list of favorites. —Barbara Robbins*
*Delray Beach, Florida*

**1/2 cup butter, softened**
**1 cup sugar**
**1 egg**
**1/4 cup sour cream**
**1 cup all-purpose flour**
**1/2 cup baking cocoa**
**1/2 teaspoon baking powder**
**1/4 teaspoon salt**
**1/2 cup milk**

**GLAZE:**
**1/4 cup butter, softened**
**1/2 cup confectioners' sugar**
**2 tablespoons baking cocoa**
**3 tablespoons milk**
**1/2 cup chopped pecans**
**1/2 teaspoon vanilla extract**

In a large mixing bowl, cream butter and sugar. Beat in egg and sour cream. Combine the flour, cocoa, baking powder and salt; add to creamed mixture alternately with milk. Spread into a greased 13-in. x 9-in. x 2-in. baking pan. Bake at 350° for 20-25 minutes or until a toothpick inserted near the center comes out clean.

Meanwhile, in a small mixing bowl, cream butter. Gradually beat in confectioners' sugar, cocoa and milk. Stir in pecans and vanilla. Spread over warm brownies. Cool on a wire rack. Cover and freeze for up to 1 month. Thaw and cut into bars. **Yield:** 2 dozen.

### Handling Jalapenos

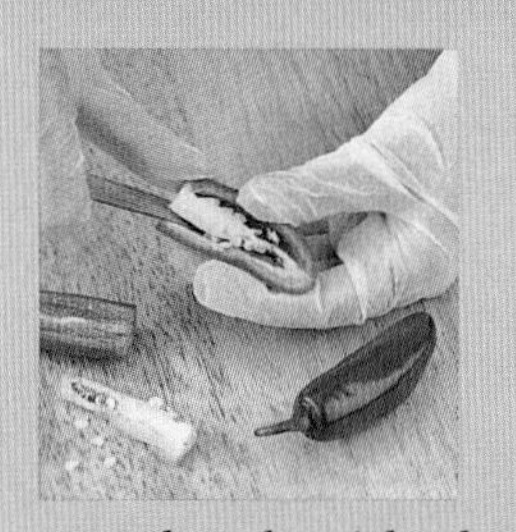

JALAPENO PEPPERS can add a tasty kick to southwestern food and other fare. If you'd like to use them in your cooking, be sure to keep the following tips in mind.

When handling jalapeno or other chili peppers, wear rubber or plastic gloves or cover your hands with plastic sandwich bags to prevent burning your skin and eyes. To reduce the heat level of the peppers, remove the seeds and membranes.

After working with peppers, wash your hands and cutting surfaces thoroughly with hot soapy water.

## Hearty Macaroni Casserole

*Give Jack Frost the cold shoulder by setting a comforting hot dish on the table. This hearty meal-in-one satisfies the biggest of appetites. Enjoy one casserole and freeze the other, or serve them both when entertaining.*

*—Joy Harris Sauers, Sioux Falls, South Dakota*

**1 package (7-1/4 ounces) macaroni and cheese dinner mix**
**1 pound ground beef**
**1 cup chopped green pepper**
**1/2 cup chopped onion**
**1 can (14-1/2 ounces) Italian diced tomatoes, undrained**
**2 cups (8 ounces) shredded cheddar cheese**
**1 cup french-fried onions**

Prepare macaroni and cheese according to package directions. Meanwhile, in a large skillet, cook the beef, green pepper and onion over medium heat until meat is no longer pink; drain. Add to prepared macaroni. Stir in tomatoes.

Spoon a quarter of the mixture into each of two greased 1-1/2-qt. baking dishes; sprinkle each with 1/2 cup cheese. Top with remaining macaroni mixture.

Sprinkle remaining cheese over one casserole. Cover and freeze for up to 3 months. Sprinkle the second casserole with french-fried onions. Bake, uncovered, at 350° for 40 minutes or until heated through. **Yield:** 2 casseroles (3-4 servings each).

**To use frozen casserole:** Completely thaw in the refrigerator. Remove from the refrigerator 30 minutes before baking. Bake as directed.

## Curry-Chutney Cheese Mold

*Featuring loads of bacon, green onions and peanuts, this exotic appetizer is a true time-saver due to its make-ahead convenience. I always make room for this spread on my cheese platter when I'm hosting a get-together.* *—Carmen Courtney Ashland, Virginia*

**3 packages (8 ounces *each*) cream cheese, softened**
**1 cup (8 ounces) sour cream**
**3/4 cup real bacon bits**
**1/2 cup finely chopped green onions**
**2 teaspoons curry powder**
**1 cup salted peanuts, finely chopped**
**1 cup raisins, finely chopped**
**ADDITIONAL INGREDIENTS (for each cheese mold):**
**1/2 cup chutney**
**1/2 cup flaked coconut, toasted**
**Assorted crackers**

In a large bowl, combine the cream cheese, sour cream, bacon, onions and curry powder. Fold in peanuts and raisins. Lightly press into two 3-cup freezer dishes coated with nonstick cooking spray.

Cover and freeze one mold for up to 1 month. Cover and freeze the second mold for at least 1 hour; unmold onto a serving plate. Top with chutney and coconut. Serve with crackers. **Yield:** 2 cheese molds (2-1/2 cups each).

**To use frozen cheese mold:** Unmold onto a serving plate; thaw in the refrigerator. Just before serving, top with chutney and coconut.

## Peppermint Whip

*This is a refreshing dessert for busy mothers. I created it to use up broken candy canes after Christmas one year. Set the whip in the refrigerator overnight to enjoy the following day, or freeze it to save time in the future.*

*—Pamela Brown, Ingersoll, Ontario*

**1 cup crushed chocolate wafers**
**1/4 cup butter, melted**
**1 cup miniature marshmallows**
**1/2 cup crushed peppermint candies**
**1/3 cup dried cranberries**
**1 cup heavy whipping cream, whipped**

In a small bowl, combine wafer crumbs and butter; set aside 1/4 cup for topping. Press remaining crumb mixture into a 9-in. square dish.

In a bowl, combine the marshmallows, candies and cranberries. Fold in the whipped cream. Spread over the crust; sprinkle with reserved crumb mixture. Freeze for up to 2 months. Remove from the freezer 5-10 minutes before serving. **Yield:** 9 servings.

## Banana Split Freeze

*(Pictured at right)*

*Cut down on hostess duties by preparing this frosty sensation ahead of time. The pretty dessert features strawberry ice cream as well as a layer of rich chocolate. My children request this for their birthday cakes.*

*—Shirley Buehler, Minnetonka, Minnesota*

**1 can (12 ounces) evaporated milk**
**1 cup (6 ounces) semisweet chocolate chips**
**1/2 cup plus 6 tablespoons butter, *divided***
**2 cups confectioners' sugar**
**1-1/2 cups graham cracker crumbs**
**3 medium ripe bananas, cut into 1/4-inch slices**
**2 quarts strawberry ice cream, softened**
**2 cups chopped pecans**
**1 carton (8 ounces) frozen whipped topping, thawed**

In a small saucepan, combine the milk, chocolate chips and 1/2 cup butter. Cook and stir over medium heat until melted and smooth. Stir in confectioners' sugar. Bring to a boil. Reduce heat; simmer, uncovered, for 12-15 minutes or until thickened, stirring frequently. Cool to room temperature.

Meanwhile, melt remaining butter; stir in cracker crumbs. Press into a greased 13-in. x 9-in. x 2-in. dish; freeze for 10 minutes. Top with bananas, ice cream and pecans. Spread cooled chocolate mixture over top. Freeze for 1 hour. Spread with whipped topping. May

Coconut Pecan Cookies
Banana Split Freeze

be frozen for up to 2 months. Remove from the freezer 15 minutes before serving. **Yield:** 15-20 servings.

## Coconut Pecan Cookies

*(Pictured above)*

*This recipe makes baking Christmas treats easier. I like to share homemade cookies with my friends every year, and these are a favorite. Freeze the dough in logs, then slice and bake the crisp buttery cookies when you need them.* —*Betty Matthews, South Haven, Michigan*

**1 cup butter, softened**
**1 cup sugar**
**1 egg**
**2-1/4 cups all-purpose flour**
**1/2 teaspoon baking soda**
**1/2 teaspoon salt**
**3 cups flaked coconut,** ***divided***
**Pecan halves**

In a large mixing bowl, cream butter and sugar. Beat in egg. Combine the flour, baking soda and salt; gradually add to creamed mixture and mix well. Stir in 2 cups coconut. Shape into six 2-in.-diameter logs. Roll in remaining coconut. Wrap in plastic wrap. Freeze for up to 3 months.

Unwrap and cut into 1/4-in. slices. Place 3 in. apart on ungreased baking sheets. Place a pecan half in the center of each. Bake at 325° for 20-25 minutes or until lightly browned. Cool for 2-3 minutes before removing to wire racks. **Yield:** about 4-1/2 dozen.

# Chapter 9

# Easy Morning Eye-Openers

A GOOD BREAKFAST can get bypassed during the early-day rush to go to work, school and other activities.

Too many times, folks either hurry to their nearest fast-food drive-thru or, worse yet, forgo a morning meal altogether.

This chapter steers you to delicious, nutritious recipes that will give your family an energizing boost to start off the day. You can even serve these tasty and quick dishes as a beautiful weekend brunch for guests.

Families on the go are sure to make time for these fast-to-fix egg dishes, beverages, pancakes, fruit salads and more.

**DAYBREAK DELIGHTS.** Clockwise from top: Blueberry Coffee Cake, Hash Brown Ham Quiche and Lime Fruit Dip (all recipes on p. 133).

Cran-Strawberry Cooler
Apricot Sausage Links
Macadamia French Toast

## Cran-Strawberry Cooler

*(Pictured at left)*

*This frothy refresher blends strawberries with cranberry juice, white grape juice and ice. It's a drink that hits the spot any time you serve it.* —*Clara Coulston*
*Washington Court House, Ohio*

**1-1/3 cups cranberry juice**
**2/3 cup white grape juice**
**9 to 10 fresh strawberries, *divided***
**4 ice cubes**
**1/2 to 1 teaspoon sugar, optional**

In a blender, combine the juices, six strawberries, ice and sugar if desired. Cover and process until smooth. Pour into glasses. Garnish with remaining strawberries. **Yield:** 3-4 servings.

## Apricot Sausage Links

*(Pictured at left)*

*This is an attractive contribution to any brunch. A nicely spiced sauce glazes hearty pork sausages, canned apricot halves and maraschino cherries to create a swift side dish that complements pancakes, waffles or French toast.* —*Joann Frazier Hensley*
*McGaheysville, Virginia*

**2 cans (15-1/4 ounces *each*) apricot halves**
**1 package (10 ounces) uncooked pork sausage links**
**1 tablespoon cornstarch**
**1 tablespoon lemon juice**
**1 teaspoon brown sugar**
**1/8 teaspoon ground cinnamon**
**8 maraschino cherries**

Drain apricots, reserving 1 cup juice. Arrange apricots in an ungreased 8-in. square baking dish; set aside. In a large skillet, cook sausages over medium heat until no longer pink; drain.

In a small saucepan, combine cornstarch and reserved apricot juice until smooth. Bring to a boil; cook and stir for 1 minute or until thickened. Stir in the lemon juice, brown sugar and cinnamon; pour over apricots. Place sausages and cherries over apricots. Bake, uncovered, at 350° for 15-20 minutes or until heated through. **Yield:** 6-8 servings.

## Macadamia French Toast

*(Pictured at left)*

*Flavored with orange juice and nutmeg, this nutty French toast bake is perfect for overnight guests because it's assembled a day ahead.* —*Beverly Ellis*
*McKenzie, Tennessee*

**1 loaf (1 pound) French bread, cut into 1-inch slices**
**4 eggs**
**2/3 cup orange juice**
**1/3 cup milk**
**1/4 cup sugar**
**1/2 teaspoon vanilla extract**
**1/4 teaspoon ground nutmeg**
**1/2 cup butter, melted**
**1/2 cup chopped macadamia nuts**
**Confectioners' sugar and maple syrup, optional**

Arrange bread slices in a greased 13-in. x 9-in. x 2-in. baking dish. In a bowl, whisk the eggs, orange juice, milk, sugar, vanilla and nutmeg until blended; pour over bread. Cover and refrigerate for 8 hours or overnight.

Pour butter into a 15-in. x 10-in. x 1-in. baking pan. Transfer bread slices to prepared pan; sprinkle with nuts. Bake, uncovered, at 400° for 20-25 minutes or until bread is golden brown. Dust with confectioners' sugar and serve with syrup if desired. **Yield:** 6-8 servings.

## Peach Waffle Syrup

*I make this sweet chunky syrup on Saturday mornings when my husband and I have extra time. Spiced with a bit of cinnamon, the 30-minute topping turns ordinary waffles into a breakfast treat we always look forward to.* —*Kristina Dalton, Coker, Alabama*

✓ Uses less fat, sugar or salt. Includes Nutritional Analysis and Diabetic Exchanges.

**1 package (20 ounces) frozen unsweetened peach slices, thawed and chopped**
**2 cups water**
**1/2 to 2/3 cup confectioners' sugar**
**1/8 teaspoon ground cinnamon**
**1 tablespoon cornstarch**
**2 tablespoons cold water**

In a large saucepan, combine the peaches, water, confectioners' sugar and cinnamon. Bring to a boil. Reduce heat; simmer, uncovered, for 20 minutes.

Combine the cornstarch and cold water until smooth; gradually add to the peach mixture. Bring to a boil; cook and stir for 2 minutes or until thickened. **Yield:** about 3-1/2 cups.

**Nutritional Analysis:** One 1/4-cup serving (prepared with 1/2 cup confectioners' sugar) equals 54 calories, trace fat (trace saturated fat), 0 cholesterol, 3 mg sodium, 14 g carbohydrate, 1 g fiber, trace protein. **Diabetic Exchange:** 1 fruit.

### Wonderful Waffles

- I use a box of banana nut bread mix to make yummy waffles. I just follow the package directions to mix the batter before cooking it on my waffle iron. —*Joanie Wiesbrock, Leonore, Illinois*
- For perfect, lump-free waffles or pancakes with a minimum of mess, I quickly mix all of the ingredients in the blender. Then I just pour the smooth batter straight onto the waffle iron or griddle. —*Ginger Ragan, Boise, Idaho*

## Banana Berry Drink

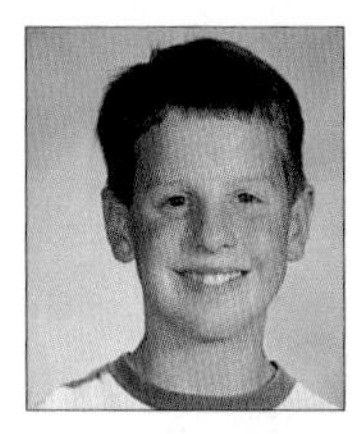

*This cold refreshing beverage is a great substitute for breakfast when you're in a hurry. Combining fruit juices, berries, a banana and yogurt, the smoothie is jam-packed with nutrition and takes just 10 minutes to whip up.* —*Eric Knoben Edgewood, Washington*

**3/4 cup orange juice, chilled**
**1/3 cup pineapple juice, chilled**
**1 cup frozen blueberries**
**1/2 cup frozen sweetened sliced strawberries**
**1/2 cup plain yogurt**
**1 small ripe banana, sliced**

Place half of each ingredient in a blender; cover and process until smooth. Pour into chilled glasses. Repeat with remaining ingredients. Serve immediately. **Yield:** 5 servings.

## Apple Waffle Grills

*(Pictured below)*

*I need only four ingredients for this handheld standby. The quick and easy sandwiches also make great lunches. My husband likes it when I add a slice of ham between the waffles.* —*Sonia Daily, Warren, Michigan*

**4 teaspoons butter**
**4 frozen waffles, thawed**
**4 slices process American cheese**
**1 medium tart apple, thinly sliced**

In a large skillet, melt butter over medium heat. Add two waffles; top each with one cheese slice, apple slices, and remaining cheese and waffles. Cook until waffles are lightly toasted on both sides and cheese is melted. **Yield:** 2 servings.

## Take-Along Raisin Squares

*Loaded with dates, chocolate chips, almonds and raisins, these moist wholesome bars are perfect when you're dashing off in the morning. They can also make a great afternoon pick-me-up, travel snack or dessert treat.* —*Shirley Glaab, Hattiesburg, Mississippi*

**1/2 cup butter, softened**
**3/4 cup packed brown sugar**
**1 egg**
**1 teaspoon vanilla extract**
**1 cup old-fashioned oats**
**1/2 cup all-purpose flour**
**1-1/4 cups raisins**
**1 cup chopped almonds**
**1 cup chopped dates**
**1/2 cup semisweet chocolate chips**
**2 tablespoons All-Bran, optional**

In a small mixing bowl, cream the butter and brown sugar until light and fluffy. Beat in the egg and vanilla. Gradually add the oats and flour. Stir in the raisins, almonds,

**Apple Waffle Grills**

dates and chocolate chips (the batter will be thick).

Spread into a greased 8-in. square baking dish. Sprinkle with bran if desired. Bake at 350° for 20-25 minutes or until a toothpick inserted near the center comes out clean. Cool completely on a wire rack. Cut into squares. **Yield:** 12 servings.

## French Toast Sandwiches

*Peanut butter and banana make this breakfast staple a kid-pleaser. I call it "Lightning Flash French Toast".*
*—Eleanor Smith, Hot Springs Village, Arkansas*

**1/4 cup peanut butter**
**4 slices whole wheat bread**
**1 small firm banana, sliced**
**2 eggs**
**1/3 cup milk**
**1/4 teaspoon ground cinnamon**
**1/4 teaspoon vanilla extract**
**1 tablespoon butter**
**Honey, optional**

Spread peanut butter on two slices of bread. Top with banana slices and remaining bread. In a shallow bowl, whisk the eggs, milk, cinnamon and vanilla. Dip both sides of sandwiches into egg mixture.

In a large skillet, melt the butter over medium heat; grill the sandwiches on both sides until golden brown. Serve with honey if desired. **Yield:** 2 servings.

## Creamed Salmon on Toast

*When our children were small and we were busy outside, we'd come in to enjoy this quick meal. We still make it when we don't feel like fussing in the kitchen.*
*—Elsie Bloom, Courtenay, British Columbia*

**3 tablespoons butter**
**3 tablespoons all-purpose flour**
**2 tablespoons chopped green onions**
**2 cups milk**
**1 can (14-3/4 ounces) salmon, drained, skin and bones removed**
**1/2 teaspoon salt, optional**
**1/8 teaspoon pepper**
**6 slices bread, toasted**

In a saucepan, melt butter over medium heat. Stir in flour until smooth; add onions. Gradually stir in milk. Bring to a boil; cook and stir for 2 minutes or until thickened. Reduce heat. Stir in salmon, salt if desired and pepper. Cook for 10-12 minutes or until heated through. Serve over toast. **Yield:** 6 servings.

## Raspberry Smoothies

*(Pictured above right)*

*This simple smoothie is a nutritious choice for kids on the go. Raspberries and banana give the not-too-sweet sipper its pleasant flavor.*
*—Heather Maté*
*Pitt Meadows, British Columbia*

**Raspberry Smoothies**
**Lemon Pineapple Smoothies**

✓ Uses less fat, sugar or salt. Includes Nutritional Analysis and Diabetic Exchanges.

**1 cup milk**
**1 cup fresh *or* frozen unsweetened raspberries**
**1 small ripe banana, cut into chunks**
**1/2 cup apple juice**
**1/2 cup raspberry yogurt**

In a blender, combine all ingredients; cover and process until blended. Pour into chilled glasses; serve immediately. **Yield:** 3 servings.

**Nutritional Analysis:** One 1-cup serving (prepared with 1% milk and reduced-fat yogurt) equals 147 calories, 2 g fat (1 g saturated fat), 8 mg cholesterol, 70 mg sodium, 29 g carbohydrate, 4 g fiber, 5 g protein. **Diabetic Exchanges:** 1 reduced-fat milk, 1 fruit.

## Lemon Pineapple Smoothies

*(Pictured above)*

*Five ingredients and a few moments are all you need to fix this citrus specialty. I originally came up with the recipe to use up leftover pineapple. It's a great dessert on a warm evening.* *—Brook Kaske, Rochester, Minnesota*

**2 cups vanilla ice cream**
**1 can (20 ounces) pineapple tidbits, drained**
**1 cup chilled lemon-lime soda**
**2 tablespoons lemonade concentrate**
**1 drop yellow food coloring, optional**

In a blender, combine all ingredients; cover and process until smooth. Pour into chilled glasses; serve immediately. **Yield:** 4 servings.

Blueberry Coffee Cake
Hash Brown Ham Quiche
Lime Fruit Dip

## Blueberry Coffee Cake

*(Pictured at left and on page 126)*

*This sweet crumb-topped cake gets its moistness from blueberries and cream cheese. When I have a few spare moments, I'll assemble the from-scratch cake and freeze it for times when I have morning guests. It's perfect with coffee and some fresh fruit.* —*Melanie Koehn*
*Colcord, Oklahoma*

**1/4 cup butter, softened**
**2/3 cup sugar**
**1 egg**
**1 cup plus 2 tablespoons all-purpose flour, *divided***
**1/2 teaspoon baking powder**
**1/4 teaspoon salt**
**1/2 cup milk**
**1 cup fresh *or* frozen blueberries**
**1 package (3 ounces) cream cheese, cubed**
**TOPPING:**
**2 tablespoons all-purpose flour**
**2 tablespoons sugar**
**1 tablespoon cold butter**

For batter, in a large mixing bowl, cream butter and sugar. Beat in egg. Combine 1 cup flour, baking powder and salt; gradually add to creamed mixture alternately with milk. Toss blueberries with remaining flour. Stir blueberries and cream cheese into creamed mixture (batter will be thick). Transfer to a greased 8-in. square baking dish.

For topping, in a small bowl, combine flour and sugar. Cut in butter until crumbly. Sprinkle over batter. Bake at 375° for 40-45 minutes or until a toothpick inserted near the center comes out clean. Cool on a wire rack. **Yield:** 6-8 servings.

**Editor's Note:** If using frozen blueberries, do not thaw before adding to batter.

## Hash Brown Ham Quiche

*(Pictured at left and on page 127)*

*Purchased hash brown potatoes form the crust for this colorful quiche that's chock-full of ham, cheddar cheese, green pepper and fresh mushrooms. The hearty dish is a family favorite for breakfast and can even make a filling supper.* —*Ella Woroniuk, Canora, Saskatchewan*

**4 cups frozen shredded hash brown potatoes**
**1/4 teaspoon salt**
**1/4 teaspoon pepper**
**3 tablespoons butter, *divided***
**1 medium onion, chopped**
**1/2 cup chopped green pepper**
**1/2 cup chopped fresh mushrooms**
**2 teaspoons all-purpose flour**
**3/4 cup diced fully cooked ham**
**3 eggs, beaten**
**1/2 cup milk**
**1/2 cup shredded cheddar cheese**

In a large skillet, saute the hash browns, salt and pepper in 2 tablespoons butter until golden brown. Press onto the bottom and up the sides of a greased 9-in. pie plate. In the same skillet, saute the onion, green pepper and mushrooms in remaining butter. Remove from the heat; sprinkle with flour. Stir in the ham, eggs and milk. Pour into hash brown crust.

Bake at 350° for 25 minutes. Sprinkle with cheese; bake 5 minutes longer or until a knife inserted near the center comes out clean. Let stand for 10 minutes before cutting. **Yield:** 6-8 servings.

## Lime Fruit Dip

*(Pictured at left and on page 126)*

*I first sampled this when one of my friends brought it to a church social. The smooth, creamy dip featuring lime custard-style yogurt is refreshing with seasonal summer fruit, and it's also wonderful during the winter with apples, oranges and bananas.* —*Mary Lou Little*
*Salt Lake City, Utah*

**1 package (8 ounces) cream cheese, softened**
**1 jar (7 ounces) marshmallow creme**
**1 carton (6 ounces) lime custard-style yogurt**
**1 drop green food coloring, optional**
**Assorted fresh fruit**

In a small mixing bowl, beat the cream cheese until smooth; beat in marshmallow creme. Fold in yogurt and food coloring if desired. Cover and refrigerate until serving. Serve with fruit. **Yield:** 2-1/2 cups.

## Oatmeal with Peach Sauce

*I warm up many crisp autumn mornings by spooning a sweet chunky fruit sauce over oatmeal. Sprinkling on slivered almonds gives it a little crunch. For variety, try replacing half of the sliced peaches with applesauce.* —*Kathy Rairigh*
*Milford, Indiana*

**2 cups diced peeled fresh *or* frozen peach slices**
**4 teaspoons maple syrup**
**3 tablespoons plus 3-1/2 cups water, *divided***
**2 teaspoons orange juice concentrate**
**1/4 teaspoon ground cinnamon**
**Dash ground ginger**
**2 cups quick-cooking oats**
**2 tablespoons raisins**
**2 tablespoons brown sugar**
**1/4 teaspoon salt**
**Milk and slivered almonds, optional**

In a large saucepan, combine peaches, syrup, 3 tablespoons water, orange juice concentrate, cinnamon and ginger. Bring to a boil. Reduce heat; simmer, uncovered, for 5 minutes.

Meanwhile, in another saucepan, bring the remaining water to a boil. Stir in the oats, raisins, brown sugar and salt. Reduce heat; simmer, uncovered, for 3 minutes, stirring occasionally. Remove from the heat; let stand for 5 minutes. Serve oatmeal with peach sauce, and milk and almonds if desired. **Yield:** 4 servings.

## Cappuccino Smoothies

*Topped with miniature marshmallows, this cool cappuccino beverage is a yummy twist on traditional fruit smoothies. My mom and I came up with the recipe together when we were trying to create an easy snack.* —*Michelle Cluney Lake Mary, Florida*

**1 cup (8 ounces) cappuccino *or* coffee yogurt**
**1/3 cup milk**
**3 tablespoons confectioners' sugar, optional**
**1 tablespoon chocolate syrup**
**1-1/2 cups ice cubes**
**1/2 cup miniature marshmallows, *divided***

In a blender, combine the yogurt, milk, sugar if desired and chocolate syrup. Add ice cubes and 1/4 cup marshmallows; cover and process until blended. Pour into chilled glasses; top with the remaining marshmallows. Serve immediately. **Yield:** 3 servings.

## Orange Crunch Yogurt

*(Pictured below)*

*It took mere minutes for the home economists in our Test Kitchen to toss together these parfaits. The crunchy granola and cashews contrast nicely with the mandarin oranges and yogurt.*

**1/3 cup granola cereal without raisins**
**1/3 cup flaked coconut**
**1/3 cup chopped cashews**
**4 cartons (6 ounces *each*) orange yogurt**
**1 can (11 ounces) mandarin oranges, drained**

In a bowl, combine the granola, coconut and cashews. In each of four parfait glasses or bowls, layer half of a container of yogurt, 2 tablespoons granola mixture, 5 or 6 orange segments, remaining yogurt and remaining granola mixture. Garnish with remaining oranges. Serve immediately. **Yield:** 4 servings.

Orange Crunch Yogurt

## Winter Warmer

*I came across this beverage recipe more than 15 years ago, when I was in high school. With cocoa mix and coffee, the hot drink truly is a warm-you-up treat on brisk days. My husband and I also enjoy it after the children go to bed.* —*Sally Seidel, Banner, Wyoming*

**2 envelopes (1 ounce *each*) instant hot cocoa mix *or* 1/2 cup instant hot cocoa mix**
**3 cups hot brewed coffee**
**1/4 cup half-and-half cream**
**3/4 teaspoon rum extract**
**1/4 cup whipped topping**
**Ground cinnamon, optional**

In a small saucepan, whisk together the cocoa mix, coffee, cream and rum extract until cocoa is dissolved. Heat through. Top each serving with whipped topping and sprinkle with cinnamon if desired. **Yield:** 2 servings.

## Hurry-Up Hoosier Sandwiches

*These simple egg sandwiches are delicious and quick to make. They're great when you're hurrying to get to work.* —*Sue Call, Beech Grove, Indiana*

**1 tablespoon butter**
**4 eggs**
**Salt and pepper to taste**
**4 slices process American cheese**
**8 slices bread, toasted**
**Mayonnaise *and/or* mustard, optional**
**4 lettuce leaves**
**4 slices fully cooked deli ham**

In a large skillet, melt butter over medium-high heat. Break each egg into the pan. Season to taste. Reduce heat to medium-low; cover and cook until yolks are nearly set. Place a cheese slice on each egg. Cook 1 minute longer. Spread each toast slice with mayonnaise and/or mustard if desired. On four toast slices, place an egg with cheese, lettuce leaf and ham slice. Top with remaining toast. **Yield:** 4 sandwiches.

## Crispy Peanut Squares

*I add peanut butter to these cereal bars that make a tasty handheld snack in the morning. You can substitute pitted dried plums for the mixed dried fruit.* —*Geraldine Stephens, Memphis, Tennessee*

Simple Shrimp Scramble

**1/4 cup packed brown sugar**
**1/4 cup light corn syrup**
**1/3 cup chunky peanut butter**
**2 cups crisp rice cereal**
**1/2 cup chopped mixed dried fruit**

In a large saucepan, combine brown sugar and corn syrup. Bring to a boil over medium heat, stirring constantly. Remove from the heat. Stir in peanut butter until blended. Stir in cereal and fruit. Press into a greased 8-in. square dish. Cool on a wire rack until firm. Cut into squares. **Yield:** 1-1/2 dozen.

## Cherry Yogurt Smoothies

*I use canned pie filling for this special smoothie. It's a favorite of mine. I think the cherries and banana are an awesome combination.* —*Katie Sloan*
*Charlotte, North Carolina*

**1 cup cranberry juice**
**1 cup (8 ounces) cherry yogurt**
**1/2 cup cherry pie filling**
**1 medium ripe banana, cut into chunks**
**1 to 1-1/2 cups ice cubes**

In a blender, combine all ingredients; cover and process until blended. Pour into chilled glasses; serve immediately. **Yield:** 4 servings.

## Simple Shrimp Scramble

*(Pictured above)*

*My husband is a big fan of breakfast. Whenever I serve this 30-minute scramble that features small shrimp and cheese, he raves over it.* —*Patty Cloninger*
*Rochester, Washington*

**1 small onion, chopped**
**1/4 cup chopped green pepper**
**1 garlic clove, minced**
**3 tablespoons butter, *divided***
**1 package (5 ounces) frozen cooked salad shrimp, thawed**
**8 eggs, lightly beaten**
**1/2 teaspoon salt**
**1/4 teaspoon pepper**
**1 cup (4 ounces) shredded cheddar *or* Colby-Monterey Jack cheese**

In a large skillet, saute the onion, green pepper and garlic in 1 tablespoon butter until tender. Stir in shrimp. Remove to a bowl and keep warm.

In the same skillet, melt the remaining butter over medium heat. Add the eggs; cook and stir until completely set. Stir in the shrimp mixture, salt and pepper. Sprinkle with cheese. Remove from the heat. Cover and let stand for 3-5 minutes or until cheese is melted. **Yield:** 4 servings.

**Mixed Fruit Salad**
**Spinach-Sausage Egg Bake**

## O'Brien Kielbasa Skillet

*When you serve this combination of breakfast favorites, be prepared to dish out second helpings—and even thirds! The satisfying skillet pairs sausage with convenient frozen O'Brien hash browns.* —*Sher Koczko*
*Winchester, California*

✓ Uses less fat, sugar or salt. Includes Nutritional Analysis and Diabetic Exchanges.

**1 pound fully cooked kielbasa *or* Polish sausage, cut into 1/2-inch slices**
**1 package (24 ounces) frozen O'Brien hash brown potatoes**
**3 tablespoons canola oil**
**Pepper to taste**

In a large skillet, brown sausage; remove with a slotted spoon and set aside. Add potatoes and oil to drippings. Cover and cook over medium heat for 10 minutes, stirring occasionally. Season with pepper. Return sausage to the pan; cover and cook until heated through. **Yield:** 6 servings.

**Nutritional Analysis:** One 1-cup serving (prepared with smoked turkey sausage) equals 261 calories, 11 g fat (2 g saturated fat), 34 mg cholesterol, 673 mg sodium, 28 g carbohydrate, 2 g fiber, 12 g protein. **Diabetic Exchanges:** 2 starch, 1 lean meat, 1 fat.

## Spinach-Sausage Egg Bake

*(Pictured at left)*

*I always cook up a storm during the holidays. Spinach and red peppers give festive Christmas color to this satisfying bake that boasts Italian sausage, lots of cheese and a short prep time.*
—*Barbara Nowakowski*
*North Tonawanda, New York*

**1 pound bulk Italian sausage**
**1/2 cup chopped onion**
**1 jar (7 ounces) roasted red peppers, drained and chopped, *divided***
**1 package (10 ounces) frozen chopped spinach, thawed and squeezed dry**
**1 cup all-purpose flour**
**1/4 cup grated Parmesan cheese**
**1 teaspoon dried basil**
**1/2 teaspoon salt**
**8 eggs**
**2 cups milk**
**1 cup (4 ounces) shredded provolone cheese**

In a large skillet, cook sausage and onion over medium heat until meat is no longer pink; drain. Transfer to a greased 3-qt. baking dish. Sprinkle with half of the red peppers; top with spinach. In a bowl, combine the flour, Parmesan cheese, basil and salt. Whisk eggs and milk; stir into flour mixture until blended. Pour over spinach.

Bake, uncovered, at 425° for 15-20 minutes or until a knife inserted near the center comes out clean. Top with provolone cheese and remaining red peppers. Bake 3-5 minutes longer or until cheese is melted. Let stand for 5 minutes before serving. **Yield:** 6 servings.

## Mixed Fruit Salad

*(Pictured at left)*

*This refreshing medley of strawberries, bananas, mandarin oranges and pineapple is accompanied by a creamy topping your guests can dollop on. I whip up the salad for family gatherings and church socials. Everyone enjoys it.* —*Gusty Crum, Dover, Ohio*

**2 medium ripe bananas, sliced**
**1 pint fresh strawberries, quartered**
**1 can (20 ounces) pineapple tidbits, drained**
**1 can (11 ounces) mandarin oranges, drained**
**1-1/2 cups whipped topping**
**1/2 cup sour cream**

In a large bowl, combine the bananas, strawberries, pineapple and oranges. In a small bowl, fold whipped topping into sour cream. Serve with fruit salad. **Yield:** 6 servings.

## Blueberry Oat Waffles

*My husband craves waffles for breakfast on weekends. This hearty berry version is one of his favorites. It's one of mine, too, since it starts with convenient buttermilk pancake mix.* —*Nancy Zimmerman*
*Cape May Court House, New Jersey*

**2 cups buttermilk pancake mix**
**1/2 cup quick-cooking oats**
**3 tablespoons sugar**
**1-1/2 cups milk**
**1 egg**
**1 tablespoon vegetable oil**
**1 cup fresh *or* frozen blueberries**

In a bowl, combine the pancake mix, oats and sugar. Whisk the milk, egg and oil; stir into dry ingredients just until combined. Fold in berries. Bake in a preheated waffle iron according to manufacturer's directions. **Yield:** 6-8 waffles.

**Editor's Note:** If using frozen blueberries, do not thaw before adding to batter.

### Creative Coffee

- To give my morning cup of coffee a little flavor, I simply stir in 1 or 2 tablespoons of hot cocoa mix. The coffee tastes just like a cafe mocha.
  —*Darlene Bantam, Lincoln, Nebraska*
- I love iced coffee. Each morning, I pour extra fresh-brewed hazelnut coffee into another glass pot and put it in the fridge. When I want iced coffee, I pour it in a mug and add cream, sugar and vanilla.
  —*Millicent Koch, Cathedral City, California*

# Chapter 10

# Casseroles and Stovetop Suppers

THE SECRET to success in the kitchen is often convenience... especially when cooks have little time on their hands.

That's why all-in-one casseroles have so much appeal. This "comfort food" is packed with a combination of meat, vegetables and more, and often goes together in mere moments before you pop it in the oven. Soon, you're serving up a satisfying main or side dish.

For even faster preparation, turn to this chapter's selection of stovetop suppers that require just minutes to make from start to finish. You'll surely file these dinners under "F" for filling, flavorful...and flat-out fast!

**SKILLET SENSATION.** Confetti Sausage 'n' Rice (recipe on p. 148).

# Catchall Casseroles

HOT from the oven, comforting casseroles blend a variety of hearty ingredients in a single dish to satisfy appetites in a hurry. Many of the following baked creations can be assembled while you wait for the oven to preheat...and most will get to the dinner table in well under an hour.

## Chicken Zucchini Casserole

*(Pictured below)*

*A co-worker of mine shared this reliable casserole recipe that was originally her grandmother's. When I make it, I use a box of refrigerated cooked chicken and some of the fresh zucchini my neighbor gives me from his garden.* —*Bev Dutro*
*Dayton, Ohio*

- **1 package (6 ounces) stuffing mix**
- **3/4 cup butter, melted**
- **3 cups diced zucchini**
- **2 cups cubed cooked chicken**
- **1 can (10-3/4 ounces) condensed cream of chicken soup, undiluted**
- **1 medium carrot, shredded**
- **1/2 cup chopped onion**
- **1/2 cup sour cream**

In a large bowl, combine stuffing mix and butter. Set aside 1/2 cup for topping. Add the zucchini, chicken, soup, carrot, onion and sour cream to the remaining stuffing mixture. Transfer to a greased 2-qt. baking dish. Sprinkle with reserved stuffing mixture. Bake, uncovered, at 350° for 40-45 minutes or until golden brown and bubbly. **Yield:** 6 servings.

Chicken Zucchini Casserole

## Salami Noodle Casserole

*If you like salami, you'll love this rich and creamy bake that also features lots of egg noodles and two cheeses. I usually prepare several casseroles at the same time—one to eat for dinner that evening and two or three to freeze for another time. It's nice to have those extras available on days when I'm especially busy.* —*Diana Duda*
*Glenwood, Illinois*

- **6-1/2 cups uncooked egg noodles**
- **1 cup chopped green pepper**
- **1/2 cup chopped onion**
- **2 tablespoons butter**
- **1 can (10-3/4 ounces) condensed cream of mushroom soup, undiluted**
- **1 cup (8 ounces) sour cream**
- **3/4 cup milk**
- **8 ounces hard salami, cubed**
- **3/4 cup shredded mozzarella cheese**
- **3/4 cup shredded provolone cheese**
- **2 tablespoons dry bread crumbs**

Cook noodles according to package directions. Meanwhile, in a large skillet, saute green pepper and onion in butter until tender. Remove from the heat; whisk in the soup, sour cream and milk until blended.

Drain noodles. Add the noodles, salami and cheeses to the soup mixture. Transfer to a greased 11-in. x 7-in. x 2-in. baking dish. Sprinkle with bread crumbs. Bake, uncovered, at 350° for 20-22 minutes or until top is lightly browned. **Yield:** 6-8 servings.

## Pepperoni Potatoes

*Whether it's a hectic weekday or a lazy Saturday afternoon, my family really enjoys this meal-in-one casserole. I rely on convenient frozen O'Brien potatoes, pepperoni, mozzarella cheese and sweet red pepper for the hearty dish. After stirring together a quick white sauce, I simply add it to the rest of the ingredients.* —*Brenda Schrag*
*Farmington, New Mexico*

- **3 tablespoons butter**
- **2 tablespoons all-purpose flour**
- **2 cups milk**
- **1 teaspoon salt**

1/2 teaspoon dried thyme
1/2 teaspoon dried parsley flakes
1/4 teaspoon dried basil
1/8 teaspoon pepper
1 package (28 ounces) frozen O'Brien hash brown potatoes, thawed
1/4 cup chopped sweet red pepper
1 cup frozen corn, thawed
1 cup (4 ounces) shredded mozzarella cheese
27 slices pepperoni, quartered

In a small saucepan, melt the butter over medium heat. Stir in flour until smooth. Gradually stir in milk. Bring to a boil; cook and stir for 2 minutes or until thickened. Remove from the heat. Stir in the seasonings.

In a greased 13-in. x 9-in. x 2-in. baking dish, layer potatoes, red pepper and corn. Top with white sauce, cheese and pepperoni. Bake, uncovered, at 375° for 25-30 minutes or until heated through. **Yield:** 12-15 servings.

## Buttery Corn Casserole

*For a sure family-pleaser, try this recipe that blends butter-flavored crackers and canned corn. The casserole is a homey side dish that my daughter likes to prepare and can whip up in less than an hour. Megan is an excellent cook and baker, and she has won several top prizes for her cooking and baking skills.* —*Lisa Whitehead*
*Caraway, Arkansas*

2 eggs, lightly beaten
1 can (5 ounces) evaporated milk
3 tablespoons butter, melted, *divided*
2 cans (15-1/4 ounces *each*) whole kernel corn, drained
2 cups (8 ounces) shredded cheddar cheese
1 cup crushed butter-flavored crackers (about 24 crackers), *divided*

In a large bowl, combine the eggs, milk, 2 tablespoons butter, corn, cheese and 1/2 cup cracker crumbs. Spoon into a greased 11-in. x 7-in. x 2-in. baking dish. Toss the remaining crumbs and butter; sprinkle over corn mixture. Bake, uncovered, at 350° for 25-30 minutes or until edges are bubbly. **Yield:** 6 servings.

## Nacho Pie

*(Pictured above right)*

*I spend a lot of time in the garden and yard, so I appreciate recipes that can be prepared in a hurry. This beefy, cheesy pie is very quick to assemble and makes a tasty main dish. I pair it with a simple lettuce salad.* —*Doris Gill*
*Sargent, Nebraska*

1 pound ground beef
1/2 cup chopped onion
1 can (8 ounces) tomato sauce
2 tablespoons taco seasoning
1 tube (8 ounces) refrigerated crescent rolls
1-1/2 cups crushed nacho tortilla chips, *divided*

Nacho Pie

1 cup (8 ounces) sour cream
1 cup (4 ounces) shredded Mexican cheese blend

In a large skillet, cook beef and onion over medium heat until meat is no longer pink; drain. Stir in tomato sauce and taco seasoning. Bring to a boil. Reduce heat; simmer, uncovered, for 5 minutes.

Meanwhile, separate crescent dough into eight triangles; place in a greased 9-in. pie plate with points toward the center. Press onto the bottom and up the sides to form a crust; seal perforations.

Sprinkle 1 cup chips over crust. Top with meat mixture. Carefully spread sour cream over meat mixture. Sprinkle with cheese and remaining chips. Bake at 350° for 20-25 minutes or until cheese is melted and crust is golden brown. Let stand for 5 minutes before cutting. **Yield:** 6-8 servings.

### Browning Ground Beef

- When I brown ground beef, I break up big pieces with a pastry blender shortly before the meat is completely cooked. The pieces are more suitable for casseroles, chili, stews and other dishes.
*—Ann Anderson, Victoria, Texas*
- To drain fat from browned ground beef, I use a spatula to push the meat to one side. I tip the pan down to let the fat drain from the meat, then I use a turkey baster to remove the fat from the pan.
*—Delores Anderson, Monticello, Minnesota*
- When I have extra time, I brown several pounds of ground beef. I spread it on a cookie sheet and freeze it solid, then transfer it to freezer bags. On busy days, I can pull out a bag to use for a casserole or any recipe that requires browned ground beef.
*—Kathy Smith, Pittsburgh, Pennsylvania*

Easy-to-Stuff Manicotti

## Easy-to-Stuff Manicotti

*(Pictured above)*

*Even children can help prepare this simplified Italian entree that's ready in under an hour. I fill each pasta shell with a piece of string cheese for a deliciously gooey center, then top the manicotti with a beefy tomato sauce. This dish is a nice alternative to the usual spaghetti and meatballs...and is just as easy to make.*
*—Suzanne Runtz, Charleston, South Carolina*

**1 package (8 ounces) manicotti shells**
**1 pound ground beef**
**1/2 cup chopped onion**
**1 jar (26 ounces) spaghetti sauce**
**14 pieces string cheese**
**1-1/2 cups (6 ounces) shredded mozzarella cheese**

Cook manicotti according to package directions. Meanwhile, in a large skillet, cook beef and onion over medium heat until meat is no longer pink; drain. Stir in the spaghetti sauce. Spread half of the meat sauce into a greased 13-in. x 9-in. x 2-in. baking dish.

Drain manicotti; stuff each shell with a piece of string cheese. Place over meat sauce; top with remaining sauce. Cover and bake at 350° for 25-30 minutes or until heated through.

Sprinkle with mozzarella cheese. Bake, uncovered, for 5-10 minutes or until the cheese is melted. **Yield:** 6-8 servings.

## Chicken Noodle Casserole

*Cayenne pepper gives a little zip to this creamy chicken bake. It's one of my most-requested dishes for potluck dinners and other get-togethers. I sometimes use spinach noodles in place of the egg noodles.* *—Cheryl Davidson*
*Fulshear, Texas*

**5 cups uncooked egg noodles**
**1/4 cup butter, cubed**
**1/2 cup all-purpose flour**
**1-1/2 cups milk**
**1 cup chicken broth**
**2 cups (16 ounces) sour cream**
**1 can (4 ounces) mushroom stems and pieces, drained**
**1 jar (4 ounces) diced pimientos, drained**
**3 teaspoons dried parsley flakes**
**2 teaspoons seasoned salt**
**1/2 teaspoon salt**
**1 teaspoon paprika**
**1/4 to 1/2 teaspoon pepper**
**1/8 to 1/4 teaspoon cayenne pepper**
**4 cups diced cooked chicken**
**1/4 cup dry bread crumbs**
**2 tablespoons shredded Parmesan cheese**

Cook noodles according to package directions. Meanwhile, in a large saucepan, melt butter; stir in flour until smooth. Gradually add milk and broth. Bring to a boil. Cook and stir for 2 minutes or until thickened. Remove from the heat. Stir in the sour cream, mushrooms, pimientos and seasonings. Drain pasta.

In a greased 3-qt. baking dish, layer half of the noodles, chicken and sauce. Repeat layers. Combine bread crumbs and Parmesan cheese. Sprinkle over top. Bake, uncovered, at 350° for 30-35 minutes or until bubbly. **Yield:** 12 servings.

## Sausage Macaroni Bake

*Because we have three active children who always keep us busy, quick casseroles are often lifesavers for me as the clock ticks down toward dinnertime. This made-in-minutes bake with plenty of spices and Italian sausage is especially popular with our family.* *—Amber Zurbrugg*
*Alliance, Ohio*

**1-1/2 cups uncooked elbow macaroni**
**3/4 pound bulk Italian sausage**
**1 small onion, chopped**
**1/4 cup chopped green pepper**
**1 can (8 ounces) tomato sauce**
**1 cup (4 ounces) shredded mozzarella cheese**
**1/2 cup grated Parmesan cheese, *divided***
**2 tablespoons minced fresh parsley**
**1 garlic clove, minced**
**1/2 teaspoon dried oregano**
**1/4 teaspoon salt**
**1/4 teaspoon dried basil**
**1/4 teaspoon pepper**

Cook macaroni according to package directions. Meanwhile, in a large skillet, cook the sausage, onion and green pepper over medium heat until meat is no longer pink; drain. Drain macaroni.

In a large bowl, combine the macaroni, sausage mixture, tomato sauce, mozzarella cheese, 1/4 cup Parmesan cheese, parsley, garlic, oregano, salt, basil and pepper. Transfer to a greased 2-qt. baking dish. Sprinkle with remaining Parmesan cheese. Bake, uncovered, at 350° for 20-25 minutes or until heated through. **Yield:** 4 servings.

## Beefy Kraut and Rice

*My husband and I are both police officers, and after a long workday, I rely on meals that come together easily. This hot dish is a snap to make and has a tangy twist that even our kids enjoy.* —*Kristi Baker, Sioux City, Iowa*

**1 pound ground beef**
**1 can (14 ounces) sauerkraut, rinsed and drained**
**1-1/2 cups water**
**1 can (10-3/4 ounces) condensed cream of mushroom soup, undiluted**
**1 cup uncooked long grain rice**
**1 envelope beefy mushroom soup mix**
**1/2 cup shredded Swiss cheese, optional**

In a large skillet, cook beef over medium heat until no longer pink; drain. In a bowl, combine the beef, sauerkraut, water, soup, rice and soup mix. Transfer to a greased 2-qt. baking dish. Cover and bake at 350° for 50-60 minutes or until rice is tender. Sprinkle with Swiss cheese if desired. Bake 5 minutes longer or until cheese is melted. **Yield:** 4-6 servings.

## Tex-Mex Lasagna

*This simple dish is one of our all-time family favorites. I like to double the recipe, making one pan for dinner that night and another to freeze. We enjoy the zippy lasagna so much, sometimes we eat the second one in the same week.* —*Cindy Osborn, Little Rock, Arkansas*

**1-1/2 pounds ground beef**
**1 can (15 ounces) tomato sauce**
**1 can (10 ounces) diced tomatoes and green chilies**
**1 envelope taco seasoning**
**1/4 teaspoon seasoned salt**
**6 corn tortillas (6 inches)**
**1 carton (16 ounces) small-curd cottage cheese**
**4 cups (16 ounces) shredded Colby-Monterey Jack cheese**

In a large skillet, cook beef over medium heat until no longer pink; drain. Add the tomato sauce, tomatoes, taco seasoning and seasoned salt. Simmer, uncovered, for 10 minutes.

Spread 1/2 cup meat sauce in a greased 13-in. x 9-in. x 2-in. baking dish. Top with two tortillas and a third of the sauce, cottage cheese and shredded cheese. Repeat layers twice. Cover; bake at 350° for 30-40 minutes or until heated through. Let stand for 5 minutes before cutting. **Yield:** 8 servings.

## Penne Salami Bake

*(Pictured below)*

*This appetizing entree is so versatile that you can add whatever vegetables you may have on hand. I've tossed in a variety of produce, including mushrooms, zucchini, peas, broccoli and pattypan squash. Just saute them with the onions and garlic, and you're well on your way toward serving a satisfying supper in about an hour.* —*Tanya Murray, Olympia, Washington*

**2 cups uncooked penne *or* medium tube pasta**
**1 small onion, diced**
**1 garlic clove, minced**
**3 tablespoons olive oil**
**2 cups canned diced tomatoes, drained**
**1 tablespoon tomato paste**
**1 medium green pepper, chopped**
**1 medium sweet red pepper, chopped**
**1/3 pound salami, cubed**
**10 pitted ripe olives, halved**
**Salt and pepper**
**1 cup (4 ounces) shredded mozzarella cheese**
**1 cup (4 ounces) shredded cheddar cheese**

Cook pasta according to package directions. Drain and set aside. In a large skillet, saute the onion and garlic in oil until tender; stir in the tomatoes, tomato paste, green and sweet red peppers, salami, olives, salt and pepper. Simmer, uncovered, for 5 minutes. Remove from the heat; stir in pasta.

Combine cheeses. Spoon half of pasta mixture into a greased 2-qt. baking dish. Sprinkle with 1-1/3 cups cheese. Top with remaining pasta and cheese. Bake, uncovered, at 350° for 15-20 minutes or until cheese is melted. **Yield:** 4-6 servings.

Penne Salami Bake

Pasta Ham Hot Dish

## Pasta Ham Hot Dish

*(Pictured above)*

*I brought this simple casserole to a potluck at work and it was a hit. You can use a pound of browned ground beef in place of the ham.* —*Judie Porath Summit, South Dakota*

**4 ounces uncooked spaghetti, broken into 2-inch pieces**
**1/4 cup chopped onion**
**1 tablespoon butter**
**2 cups cubed fully cooked ham**
**1 can (15-1/4 ounces) whole kernel corn, drained**
**1 can (14-3/4 ounces) cream-style corn**
**1 cup cubed process cheese (Velveeta)**
**1/2 teaspoon seasoned salt**

Cook spaghetti according to package directions. Meanwhile, in a small skillet, saute onion in butter until tender. Drain spaghetti; place in a large bowl.

Add the ham, corn, cheese, seasoned salt and onion mixture. Transfer to a greased 2-qt. baking dish. Cover and bake at 350° for 30-35 minutes or until cheese is melted, stirring once. **Yield:** 4-6 servings.

## Stuffed Chicken Breasts

*Baked in a creamy mushroom sauce, this easy entree is nice for a special family dinner. I serve this dish with rice, asparagus and a tossed salad.* —*Dolores Kastello Waukesha, Wisconsin*

**4 boneless skinless chicken breast halves (6 ounces *each*)**
**Salt and pepper to taste**
**1 package (6 ounces) chicken stuffing mix**
**1/2 cup chopped pecans**
**2 tablespoons butter**
**1 can (10-3/4 ounces) condensed cream of mushroom soup, undiluted**

Flatten chicken to 1/4-in. thickness; sprinkle with salt and pepper. Prepare stuffing mix according to package directions. Meanwhile, in a small skillet, saute the pecans in butter until lightly browned; add to the stuffing.

Place 1/2 cup stuffing down center of each chicken breast half; roll up and secure with a toothpick. Place seam side down in a greased shallow 1-qt. baking dish.

Spoon soup over chicken; sprinkle with remaining stuffing. Cover and bake at 400° for 25-30 minutes or until chicken juices run clear. Remove toothpicks before serving. **Yield:** 4 servings.

## Four-Vegetable Bake

*Several members of my family enjoy meatless dishes, and I'm partial to casseroles, so this tasty dish pleases everyone. It lets the goodness of the veggies come through.* —*Ruby Williams, Bogalusa, Louisiana*

**3 medium zucchini, cut into 1/4-inch slices**
**1 pound fresh mushrooms, sliced**
**1 medium onion, chopped**
**1/2 cup chopped green onions**
**8 tablespoons butter, *divided***
**1/4 cup all-purpose flour**
**1 cup milk**
**1 can (14 ounces) water-packed artichokes, drained and quartered**
**3/4 cup shredded Swiss cheese**
**1/2 teaspoon salt**
**1/4 teaspoon pepper**
**3/4 cup seasoned bread crumbs**

In a large skillet, saute the zucchini, mushrooms and onions in 3 tablespoons butter until zucchini is crisp-tender; remove and set aside. In the same skillet, melt 3 tablespoons butter. Stir in flour until smooth. Gradually stir in milk until blended. Bring to a boil; cook and stir for 2 minutes or until thickened. Stir in the zucchini mixture, artichokes, cheese, salt and pepper; mix well.

Transfer to a greased 11-in. x 7-in. x 2-in. baking dish. Melt remaining butter; toss with bread crumbs. Sprinkle over the top. Bake, uncovered, at 350° for 20-25 minutes or until bubbly and topping is lightly browned. **Yield:** 8 servings.

## Ravioli Chicken Casserole

*I threw this together once when I had to work late and my new in-laws stopped over for the first time.* —*Stacie Knackmuhs, Decatur, Illinois*

**1 package (24 ounces) frozen cheese ravioli, cooked and drained**
**3 cups cubed cooked chicken**
**6 medium fresh mushrooms, sliced**

**1/2 cup chopped green pepper**
**1/3 cup chopped onion**
**1 jar (28 ounces) meatless spaghetti sauce**
**2 cups (8 ounces) shredded mozzarella cheese**

In a greased 13-in. x 9-in. x 2-in. baking dish, layer the ravioli and chicken. Top with mushrooms, green pepper, onion and spaghetti sauce. Cover and bake at 350° for 20 minutes. Uncover; sprinkle with cheese. Bake 10-15 minutes longer or until cheese is melted. **Yield:** 10-12 servings.

## Sweet Potato Ham Bake

*Three ingredients are all you'll need for this colorful hot dish, sized perfectly for two. If I'll be having guests for dinner, I can still rely on this bake because the recipe is easy to double. It's great when I need to use up leftover holiday ham.*
*—Jennette Fourne, Detroit, Michigan*

**1 can (15 ounces) cut sweet potatoes, drained and quartered lengthwise**
**2 cups cubed fully cooked ham**
**1 cup (4 ounces) shredded cheddar cheese**

In a greased 1-qt. baking dish, layer half of the sweet potatoes, ham and cheese. Repeat layers. Cover and bake at 350° for 20 minutes. Uncover; bake 8-10 minutes longer or until cheese is melted. **Yield:** 2-3 servings.

## Creamy Turkey Casserole

*(Pictured at right)*

*This satisfying supper idea puts Thanksgiving leftovers to terrific use. I sometimes make turkey just so I have the extras for this casserole.* *—Mary Jo O'Brien Hastings, Minnesota*

**1 can (10-3/4 ounces) condensed cream of celery soup, undiluted**
**1 can (10-3/4 ounces) condensed cream of mushroom soup, undiluted**
**1 can (10-3/4 ounces) condensed cream of onion soup, undiluted**
**5 ounces process cheese (Velveeta), cubed**
**1/3 cup mayonnaise**
**4 cups cubed cooked turkey**
**1 package (16 ounces) frozen broccoli cuts, thawed**
**1-1/2 cups cooked white rice**
**1-1/2 cups cooked wild rice**
**1 can (8 ounces) sliced water chestnuts, drained**
**1 jar (4 ounces) sliced mushrooms, drained**
**1-1/2 to 2 cups salad croutons**

In a large bowl, combine the soups, cheese and mayonnaise. Stir in the turkey, broccoli, rice, water chestnuts and mushrooms. Transfer to a greased 13-in. x 9-in. x 2-in. baking dish.

Bake, uncovered, at 350° for 30 minutes; stir. Sprinkle with croutons. Bake 8-12 minutes longer or until bubbly. **Yield:** 10-12 servings.

**Editor's Note:** Reduced-fat or fat-free mayonnaise is not recommended for this recipe.

### Sweet Potatoes and Yams

Sweet potatoes and yams are similar in many ways, so they're often confused with one another. To add to the confusion, canned sweet potatoes are often labeled yams.

The sweet potato is a member of the morning glory family and native to Central America. Two varieties are readily available. One has a pale skin with a light yellow flesh and a dry mealy texture. The other has dark skin with a dark orange flesh that cooks to a moist texture. This variety is often commonly known as a yam.

True yams, though, are not readily available in this country and are seldom grown here. They are available throughout Latin America, Asia, India, West Africa, the South Pacific and the Caribbean.

Though you're not likely to find true yams at your local grocery store, yams and sweet potatoes are interchangeable in most recipes.

Creamy Turkey Casserole

# Stovetop Suppers

PLEASING your family during mealtime can be as easy as serving a delicious dish you've prepared in a saucepan or skillet. Shared by fellow busy cooks, these range-top recipes are all tried-and-true winners that are done in a dash. Most take a mere 30 minutes—or less—to make from start to finish.

## Cabbage Sausage Supper

(Pictured below)

*Everyone is surprised when they find out this flavorful combination calls for just cabbage, sausage and a few other ingredients. To complete the meal, I can whip up a no-bake fruit dessert while this dish is cooking.*

—*Ruby Williams, Bogalusa, Louisiana*

✓ Uses less fat, sugar or salt. Includes Nutritional Analysis and Diabetic Exchanges.

**2 pounds fully cooked smoked sausage, halved and cut into 3/4-inch slices**
**1 large onion, cut into eighths**
**1 medium head cabbage, chopped**
**1/2 cup water**
**1 pound carrots, cut into 1/2-inch slices**
**5 medium potatoes, peeled and cut into 3/4-inch cubes**

In a Dutch oven or soup kettle, cook sausage and onion over medium heat until sausage is lightly browned and onion is tender; drain. Add the cabbage and water. Cover and cook on low for 10 minutes. Stir in the carrots and potatoes. Cover and cook for 25-30 minutes or until the vegetables are tender. **Yield:** 12 servings.

**Nutritional Analysis:** One 1-1/4-cup serving (prepared with reduced-fat smoked sausage) equals 190 calories, 4 g fat (1 g saturated fat), 34 mg cholesterol, 675 mg sodium, 28 g carbohydrate, 4 g fiber, 13 g protein. **Diabetic Exchanges:** 2 starch, 1 lean meat.

Cabbage Sausage Supper

## Chili with Rice

*To put a different spin on chili, try this well seasoned version that has rice, ripe olives, corn and melted cheese on top. It's really quick to prepare, and you'll likely find everything you need for it in your cupboard.*

—*Margery Bryan*
*Royal City, Washington*

**1 pound ground beef**
**1 medium onion, chopped**
**1/2 cup chopped green pepper**
**1 garlic clove, minced**
**2 to 3 cups tomato juice**
**1/2 cup uncooked long grain rice**
**1 tablespoon chili powder**
**1 teaspoon salt**
**1 teaspoon dried oregano**
**1 can (16 ounces) kidney beans, rinsed and drained**
**1 cup frozen corn**
**1 can (2-1/4 ounces) sliced ripe olives, drained**
**1/2 cup shredded cheddar *or* Monterey Jack cheese**

In a large saucepan, cook the beef, onion, green pepper and garlic over medium heat until meat is no longer pink; drain. Add the tomato juice, rice, chili powder, salt and oregano. Bring to a boil. Reduce heat; cover and simmer for 20-25 minutes or until rice is tender. Stir in the beans, corn and olives. Cover and simmer for 10-15 minutes or until corn is tender.

Sprinkle with cheese; cover and cook 5 minutes longer or until cheese is melted. **Yield:** 6 servings.

## Simmered Swiss Steak

*My husband and I are beef lovers, and we truly enjoy the flavor of this tender round steak. It's simple to make, but it tastes like it took several hours.*

—*Cindy Stewart*
*Deshler, Ohio*

**1/4 cup mashed potato flakes**
**1-1/4 teaspoons garlic powder, *divided***
**1/4 teaspoon onion powder**
**1/4 teaspoon pepper**
**1 pound boneless beef round steak**

2 tablespoons vegetable oil
1 cup chopped onion
1 can (14-1/2 ounces) diced tomatoes, undrained
1/2 cup beef broth

In a bowl, combine the potato flakes, 1/4 teaspoon garlic powder, onion powder and pepper; sprinkle over steak. Pound with a mallet to tenderize.

In a large skillet over medium heat, brown steak in oil on both sides. Remove and set aside. In the same skillet, saute onion and remaining garlic powder until onion is tender. Return steak to the pan; add tomatoes and broth. Cover and simmer for 1 hour or until meat is tender. **Yield:** 4 servings.

## Tex-Mex Chicken Salad

Kapture Kids Portrait Studio

*This is a tasty alternative to traditional taco salads. If your local supermarket carries jalapeno-flavored cream cheese, try using that in place of the chopped jalapenos and plain cream cheese to save yourself a step.* —*Vicki Ann Roehrick, Kingman, Arizona*

**2 pounds boneless skinless chicken breasts, cubed**
**1/2 cup chopped seeded jalapeno peppers**
**1 green onion, sliced**
**2 tablespoons butter**
**2 cartons (8 ounces *each*) whipped cream cheese**
**1 can (14-1/2 ounces) diced tomatoes, drained**
**1/2 cup salsa**
**1/2 teaspoon salt**
**Shredded lettuce**
**1 cup (4 ounces) shredded Monterey Jack cheese**
**1 can (3.8 ounces) sliced ripe olives, drained**
**3 cups crushed tortilla chips**

In a large skillet, saute the chicken, jalapenos and onion in butter until chicken is no longer pink. Add the cream cheese, tomatoes, salsa and salt; stir until blended. Serve over lettuce; sprinkle with cheese, olives and tortilla chips. **Yield:** 6 servings.

**Editor's Note:** When cutting or seeding hot peppers, use rubber or plastic gloves to protect your hands. Avoid touching your face.

## Mushroom Pork Tenderloin

*(Pictured above right)*

*Seasoned with garlic, marjoram and a bit of lemon juice, this tender pork entree comes together easily. You can even make the mouth-watering gravy in the same skillet so you'll have less cleanup later.* —*Kathleen Mackey, Waterville, Quebec*

**1 pork tenderloin (about 1 pound)**
**1 garlic clove, peeled**

**Mushroom Pork Tenderloin**

**Paprika**
**2 tablespoons butter**
**1 cup sliced fresh mushrooms**
**2 to 3 teaspoons lemon juice**
**1/4 teaspoon dried marjoram**
**Salt and pepper to taste**
**1 tablespoon all-purpose flour**
**3/4 cup cold water**
**Hot cooked rice**

Rub pork on all sides with garlic; sprinkle with paprika. In a large skillet, brown the pork in butter. Add the mushrooms, lemon juice, marjoram, salt and pepper. Turn meat to coat with seasonings. Cover and simmer for 25-30 minutes or until a meat thermometer reads 160° and juices run clear. Remove meat and keep warm.

In a small bowl, combine the flour and cold water until smooth; stir into the pan juices. Bring to a boil; cook and stir for 2 minutes or until thickened. Slice the pork; serve with gravy and rice. **Yield:** 3 servings.

### Cleaning Fresh Mushrooms

IF THE MUSHROOMS are not too dirty, remove any sand or dirt by rubbing them with a mushroom brush or a moist paper towel. If it's necessary to wash the mushrooms, quickly rinse them (do not soak). Pat them dry immediately using a paper towel.

Confetti Sausage 'n' Rice

## Confetti Sausage 'n' Rice

*(Pictured above and on page 138)*

*Delicious and economical, this is a one-dish wonder. My husband and I came up with the hearty skillet supper when we were on a tight budget. The recipe is still a favorite of ours today. I'll even double it and bring it to potlucks, since everyone likes it.* —*Carole Magee, Canton, Ohio*

**1 pound fully cooked smoked sausage, cut into 1/2-inch slices**
**1 tablespoon butter**
**2 tablespoons chopped onion**
**1/4 cup chopped green pepper**
**1/4 cup chopped sweet red pepper**
**1/4 cup chopped celery**
**2 cups hot water**
**1 cup uncooked long grain rice**
**2/3 cup frozen peas and carrots**
**1 can (4 ounces) mushroom stems and pieces, drained**
**1/4 cup frozen corn**
**2 teaspoons chicken bouillon granules**

In a large skillet, brown the sausage in butter; remove with a slotted spoon and keep warm. In the drippings, saute the onion, peppers and celery until tender. Stir in the remaining ingredients. Bring to a boil. Reduce heat; cover and simmer for 15 minutes or until rice is tender. Return the sausage to the pan; heat through. **Yield:** 4 servings.

## Sirloin Stroganoff

*Ready in half an hour, this recipe is a super-fast way to prepare traditional beef Stroganoff without all the extra simmering that's sometimes required with other recipes. For a change of pace, I'll use boneless chicken breast strips in place of the steak. Just add a tossed green salad and dessert for a complete meal.* —*Mary Wilhelm, Sparta, Wisconsin*

**2 tablespoons plus 1 teaspoon beef stew seasoning mix**
**3/4 cup water**
**1-1/2 pounds boneless beef sirloin steak, cut into thin strips**
**1 tablespoon vegetable oil**
**1 jar (6 ounces) sliced mushrooms, drained**
**1 cup (8 ounces) sour cream**
**1 cup frozen peas, thawed**
**Hot cooked noodles**

In a small bowl, combine seasoning mix and water; set aside. In a large skillet, saute beef in oil until no longer pink; drain. Add the mushrooms and seasoning mixture. Bring to a boil. Reduce heat; cover and simmer for 5 minutes. Stir in the sour cream and peas; heat through (do not boil). Serve over noodles. **Yield:** 6 servings.

## Creamy Ham and Rice

*I have fond memories of my mother preparing this dish while we were growing up, and it was the first recipe I requested from her collection when I moved out on my own. My husband loves this hearty ham dinner and always asks me to pack the leftovers in his lunch box for work the next day.* —*Meg Fortino, Powder Springs, Georgia*

**1/2 cup chopped green pepper**
**1/4 cup butter**
**1/4 cup all-purpose flour**
**1-1/2 cups milk**
**1/2 cup mayonnaise**
**2 cups cooked rice**
**2 cups cubed fully cooked ham**
**1 can (8 ounces) sliced water chestnuts, drained**
**1/4 cup grated Parmesan cheese**
**1 jar (2 ounces) diced pimientos, drained**
**1/2 teaspoon salt**

In a large skillet, saute green pepper in butter until tender. Stir in flour until blended; gradually add the milk. Bring to a boil; cook and stir for 2 minutes or until thickened. Reduce heat to low; stir in mayonnaise until blended. Stir in remaining ingredients; heat through. **Yield:** 4 servings.

## Saucy Macaroni Skillet

*You'll take macaroni-and-cheese recipes to a whole new level with this creamy comfort food full of turkey, vegetables and crunchy almonds. I often use my oven to prepare this easy entree, but it comes together just as successfully on the stovetop. Either way, the result is a fast meal-in-one for your family.* —*Linda Stevens, Madison, Alabama*

**1-1/2 cups uncooked elbow macaroni**
**4 celery ribs, chopped**
**1/2 cup chopped green pepper**
**1/4 cup chopped onion**
**1/4 cup butter, cubed**

2 cans (10-3/4 ounces *each*) condensed cream of chicken soup, undiluted
2/3 cup milk
2 cups (8 ounces) shredded cheddar cheese
3 cups cubed cooked turkey *or* chicken
1 jar (4 ounces) diced pimientos, drained
1/2 teaspoon salt
1/4 teaspoon ground nutmeg
1/2 cup sliced almonds, toasted

Cook the macaroni according to the package directions. Meanwhile, in a large saucepan, saute the celery, green pepper and onion in butter until tender. Stir in soup and milk until blended. Add the cheese; cook and stir over medium heat until melted.

Drain macaroni. Add the macaroni, turkey, pimientos, salt and nutmeg to the soup mixture; cook and stir until heated through. Sprinkle with almonds. **Yield:** 6 servings.

## Artichoke Shrimp Linguine

*With its hint of garlic and a delicate wine sauce, this seafood sensation will have artichoke lovers asking for seconds. If you like, toss in some sliced olives, too. We often round out the menu with rolls and key lime pie.* —*Daniel Spengler, Seattle, Washington*

**4 ounces uncooked linguine**
**1/2 cup chopped sweet red pepper**
**1-1/2 teaspoons minced garlic**
**1 green onion, chopped**
**2 tablespoons olive oil**
**4-1/2 teaspoons butter**
**12 ounces uncooked medium shrimp, peeled and deveined**
**1 can (14 ounces) water-packed artichoke hearts, drained and chopped**
**1/4 cup white wine *or* chicken broth**
**1 tablespoon lemon juice**
**1/4 teaspoon salt**
**1/4 teaspoon Creole seasoning**

Cook linguine according to package directions. Meanwhile, in a large saucepan, saute the red pepper, garlic and onion in oil and butter until vegetables are crisp-tender.

Add the shrimp; saute until shrimp turn pink. Stir in the remaining ingredients; heat through. Drain the linguine; top with shrimp mixture. **Yield:** 2 servings.

## Primavera Fish Fillets

*(Pictured at right)*

*I cook tender haddock or cod fillets with celery and other vegetables in a flavorful sauce that's a cinch to create with cream of mushroom soup. Since we're watching what we eat, I usually purchase the healthier version of the soup to cut down on fat, calories and sodium. Everyone who samples this 30-minute entree enjoys it.*
—*Clara Coulston, Washington Court House, Ohio*

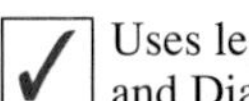
Uses less fat, sugar or salt. Includes Nutritional Analysis and Diabetic Exchanges.

**2 celery ribs, sliced**
**1 large carrot, cut into 2-inch julienne strips**
**1 small onion, chopped**
**1/4 cup water**
**2 tablespoons white wine *or* chicken broth**
**1/2 teaspoon dried thyme**
**1 can (10-3/4 ounces) condensed cream of mushroom soup, undiluted**
**1 pound frozen cod *or* haddock fillets, thawed**

In a large skillet, combine the first six ingredients. Bring to a boil. Reduce heat; cover and simmer for 5-7 minutes or until vegetables are crisp-tender. Stir in soup until blended; return to a boil. Add fillets. Reduce heat; cover and simmer for 5-7 minutes or until fish flakes easily with a fork. **Yield:** 4 servings.

**Nutritional Analysis:** One serving (prepared with reduced-fat reduced-sodium soup) equals 151 calories, 4 g fat (1 g saturated fat), 51 mg cholesterol, 415 mg sodium, 7 g carbohydrate, 1 g fiber, 21 g protein. **Diabetic Exchanges:** 2-1/2 lean meat, 1/2 starch.

**Primavera Fish Fillets**

## Bacon Chicken Alfredo

(Pictured below)

*I had a rich pasta dish similar to this at a restaurant. It was so unique that I tried to duplicate it at home a few days later. This is remarkably close, but not as fussy because it uses ready-made ingredients rather than being made from scratch. —Dana Simmons, Lancaster, Ohio*

**1 package (16 ounces) fettuccine**
**1 pound sliced bacon, diced**
**1-1/4 pounds boneless skinless chicken breasts, cubed**
**1/4 teaspoon salt**
**1/4 teaspoon pepper**
**1 jar (16 ounces) prepared Alfredo sauce**
**1 package (10 ounces) frozen chopped spinach, thawed and squeezed dry**
**1/2 teaspoon Italian seasoning**
**1/4 cup grated Parmesan cheese**

Cook fettuccine according to package directions. Meanwhile, in a large skillet, cook bacon over medium heat until crisp. Using a slotted spoon, remove to paper towels; drain, reserving 3 tablespoons drippings.

Sprinkle the chicken with salt and pepper. Cook chicken in the drippings over medium-high heat until the juices run clear.

Drain fettuccine; stir into skillet. Add the Alfredo sauce, spinach, Italian seasoning and bacon. Cook and stir until heated through. Sprinkle with Parmesan cheese. **Yield:** 6-8 servings.

Bacon Chicken Alfredo

## Skillet Enchiladas

*My family enjoys practically anything in a flour tortilla, and this is no exception. The meaty enchiladas that include onion, green chilies and cheddar cheese are so easy to fix and come together in about 30 minutes. —Regina Stock Topeka, Kansas*

**2 pounds ground beef, *divided***
**1 small onion, chopped**
**1 can (10-3/4 ounces) condensed cream of mushroom soup, undiluted**
**1 can (10 ounces) enchilada sauce**
**1/2 cup milk**
**1 can (4 ounces) chopped green chilies**
**3/4 cup water**
**1 envelope taco seasoning**
**8 flour tortillas (7 inches), warmed**
**2-1/2 cups (10 ounces) shredded cheddar cheese, *divided***

In a large skillet, cook 1 pound of beef and onion over medium heat until no longer pink; drain. Stir in the soup, enchilada sauce, milk and chilies. Bring to a boil. Reduce heat; simmer, uncovered, for 20 minutes, stirring occasionally.

Meanwhile, in another skillet, cook the remaining beef over medium heat until it is no longer pink; drain. Stir in the water and taco seasoning. Bring to a boil. Reduce the heat; simmer for 5 minutes, stirring occasionally.

Place about 1/4 cup of the taco-seasoned beef down the center of each tortilla; top with 1/4 cup cheese. Roll up and place seam side down over meat sauce in skillet. Sprinkle with the remaining cheese. Cover and cook for 1-2 minutes or until cheese is melted. **Yield:** 8 servings.

## Dutch Kielbasa

*After tasting a hearty dish at a Pennsylvania Dutch restaurant, I created my own version. I came up with this recipe that quickly became my husband's favorite. Vary the vegetables to use what you have on hand. —Jill Clark, Queensbury, New York*

**3 quarts water**
**1 cup uncooked egg noodles**
**1 cup shredded cabbage**
**1 cup frozen chopped broccoli**
**1 cup cubed fully cooked kielbasa *or* Polish sausage**
**1/2 cup chopped carrot**
**1/2 cup shredded cheddar cheese**
**1/4 cup mayonnaise**
**4-1/2 teaspoons butter**

In a Dutch oven, bring water to a boil. Add the noodles, cabbage, broccoli, sausage and carrot. Return to a boil. Cook, uncovered, for 8-10 minutes or until noodles and vegetables are tender; drain. Stir in the cheese, mayonnaise and butter. **Yield:** 2-3 servings.

## Mushroom Chicken Italiano

*My husband enjoys this easy chicken dish served with long grain and wild rice. Parsley potatoes would also be delicious with it.* —*Becky Kinnison, Celina, Ohio*

**4 boneless skinless chicken breast halves (1 pound)**
**1 tablespoon vegetable oil**
**3/4 cup creamy Italian salad dressing**
**1/4 cup white wine *or* chicken broth**
**1-1/2 cups sliced fresh mushrooms**
**Hot cooked rice**

In a large skillet, brown chicken in oil on all sides. In a bowl, combine the salad dressing, wine or broth, and mushrooms; pour over chicken. Cover and simmer for 15-20 minutes or until chicken juices run clear. Serve over rice. **Yield:** 4 servings.

## Tomato Chicken Penne

*I love how fast this creamy skillet dish is to prepare, and my whole family happily digs in when I serve it. The recipe is versatile, too. Feel free to substitute shrimp, sausage or even sliced pepperoni for the cubed chicken.* —*Cynthia Ettel Glencoe, Minnesota*

**2-1/2 cups uncooked penne *or* medium tube pasta**
**1/2 cup chopped onion**
**1 tablespoon olive oil**
**2 tablespoons white wine *or* chicken broth**
**2 cups cubed cooked chicken**
**1 can (14-1/2 ounces) diced tomatoes with roasted garlic, undrained**
**1 can (8 ounces) tomato sauce**
**1/2 cup grated Parmesan cheese**
**1/2 cup heavy whipping cream**
**1 can (4-1/4 ounces) sliced ripe olives, drained**
**1 can (4 ounces) mushroom stems and pieces, drained**

Cook pasta according to package directions. Meanwhile, in a large skillet, saute onion in oil until tender. Stir in wine or broth; cook for 1 minute. Drain pasta and add to the skillet. Add the remaining ingredients. Cook and stir over medium heat until heated through and slightly thickened. **Yield:** 8 servings.

## Chili Bean Nacho Skillet

*(Pictured above right)*

*I drive the kids to lots of activities, so this is one recipe I keep close at hand. Served with salad, it's a wholesome meal in no time.* —*Laurie Hobart Wisconsin Rapids, Wisconsin*

✓ Uses less fat, sugar or salt. Includes Nutritional Analysis and Diabetic Exchanges.

**1 pound ground beef**
**1/2 cup chopped onion**

Chili Bean Nacho Skillet

**1 can (15-1/2 ounces) chili beans, undrained**
**1 can (15 ounces) tomato sauce**
**1 can (11 ounces) Mexicorn, drained**
**1 teaspoon sugar**
**1 teaspoon chili powder**
**1/2 teaspoon dried oregano**
**1/2 to 1 cup shredded cheddar cheese**
**Tortilla chips, optional**

In a large skillet, cook beef and onion over medium heat until meat is no longer pink; drain. Stir in the beans, tomato sauce, corn, sugar, chili powder and oregano. Bring to a boil. Reduce heat; simmer, uncovered, for 10 minutes.

Sprinkle with cheese; remove from the heat. Cover; let stand for 5 minutes or until cheese is melted. Serve with tortilla chips if desired. **Yield:** 6 servings.

**Nutritional Analysis:** One 1-cup serving (prepared with lean ground beef and 1/2 cup reduced-fat cheese; calculated without chips) equals 278 calories, 8 g fat (4 g saturated fat), 44 mg cholesterol, 1,040 mg sodium, 28 g carbohydrate, 6 g fiber, 23 g protein. **Diabetic Exchanges:** 2 starch, 2 lean meat.

### Convenient Canned Beans

Some recipes call for rinsing and draining canned beans but also list water as one of the ingredients.

Canned beans are rinsed and drained in order to remove extra salt used in the canning process. If you choose to use the bean liquid for a recipe that calls for using water instead, the amount of salt and water in the recipe will need to be reduced.

# Chapter 11

# Breads in a Jiffy

BUTTERY BISCUITS...sweet coffee cakes...tender loaves... fruity muffins. Cooks agree that breads make great accompaniments to a delicious breakfast, hearty lunch or speedy supper.

You can enjoy home-baked goods such as these without spending hours in the kitchen.

The quick breads featured here promise oven-fresh flavor with less effort than traditional yeast breads require. Just mix the batter, fill the pan and pop it in the oven.

Think you don't have the time to prepare old-fashioned homemade bread from scratch? Think again! Thanks to today's bread machines, yummy yeast breads can be quick and easy to make for your family.

**BOUNTIFUL BAKING.** Top to bottom: Italian Bread Twists and Apple Coffee Cake (recipes on pp. 162 and 163).

# Oven-Fresh Quick Breads

SPICED coffee cakes...fluffy rolls...fruit-filled muffins and more. Down-home treats like these tempt with a tantalizing aroma and warm-from-the-oven goodness.

Busy cooks aren't able to spend a lot of time in the kitchen making bread. But the good news is, you don't have to take hours out of your schedule.

The following rapid recipes give you old-fashioned flavor without the work required by traditional yeast breads. The results are golden brown goodies that are sure to get smiles.

## Banana Streusel Muffins

*I'm a retired schoolteacher, and now I stay busy planning and preparing weekly meals at our church. These delightful muffins are like miniature loaves of banana bread sprinkled with a yummy crumb topping.* —*Elizabeth Viola, Rogersville, Tennessee*

**2 cups self-rising flour**
**3/4 cup sugar**
**1 egg**
**1 cup (8 ounces) plain yogurt**
**1/2 cup vegetable oil**
**1-1/3 cups mashed ripe bananas (2 to 3 medium)**
**1 cup chopped pecans *or* walnuts**
**TOPPING:**
**1/2 cup all-purpose flour**
**1/2 cup sugar**
**3 tablespoons butter, melted**
**1/2 teaspoon vanilla extract**

In a bowl, combine flour and sugar. In another bowl, beat the egg, yogurt and oil. Stir into dry ingredients just until combined. Fold in bananas and nuts. Fill greased or paper-lined muffin cups two-thirds full.

Combine topping ingredients; sprinkle over batter. Bake at 400° for 18-20 minutes or until a toothpick comes out clean. Cool for 5 minutes before removing from pans to wire racks. **Yield:** about 1-1/2 dozen.

**Editor's Note:** As a substitute for *each* cup of self-rising flour, place 1-1/2 teaspoons baking powder and 1/2 teaspoon salt in a measuring cup. Add all-purpose flour to measure 1 cup.

## Pizza Biscuits

*For fast appetizers or after-school munchies, fix a batch of these zippy bites. They're covered with onion, seasoned tomato sauce and mozzarella cheese. Add whatever pizza toppings you like.* —*Angie Marquart, Bellville, Ohio*

 Uses less fat, sugar or salt. Includes Nutritional Analysis and Diabetic Exchanges.

**1 tablespoon butter, melted**
**1/2 cup tomato sauce**
**1/4 cup chopped onion**
**1 tablespoon vegetable oil**
**1 garlic clove, minced**
**1/2 teaspoon dried basil**
**1/2 teaspoon dried oregano**
**1 tube (7-1/2 ounces) refrigerated buttermilk biscuits**
**1/3 cup shredded mozzarella cheese**

Pour butter into a 9-in. square baking dish; set aside. In a bowl, combine the tomato sauce, onion, oil, garlic, basil and oregano. Cut each biscuit into four wedges; dip into tomato mixture.

Place in prepared pan; pour any remaining tomato mixture over top. Sprinkle with mozzarella cheese. Bake at 400° for 18-22 minutes or until golden brown. Serve warm. **Yield:** 9 servings.

**Nutritional Analysis:** One serving (4 biscuit pieces, prepared with part-skim mozzarella) equals 99 calories, 4 g fat (1 g saturated fat), 6 mg cholesterol, 317 mg sodium, 13 g carbohydrate, trace fiber, 3 g protein. **Diabetic Exchanges:** 1 starch, 1/2 fat.

## Old-Fashioned Coffee Cake

*I have a large collection of buttermilk recipes, and this one brings back the flavor of old-fashioned homemade doughnuts. Sprinkled with sugar and nutmeg, pieces of the tasty cake are even more tempting when I top them with a dollop of whipped cream. It makes each slice extra special for a brunch or overnight guests.* —*Rita Reifenstein, Evans City, Pennsylvania*

**1/2 cup butter, softened**
**1-1/4 cups sugar, *divided***
**1 egg**
**2 cups all-purpose flour**
**1 teaspoon baking soda**
**1 teaspoon baking powder**
**1-1/2 teaspoons ground nutmeg, *divided***
**1 cup buttermilk**

In a small mixing bowl, cream the butter and 1 cup sugar until light and fluffy. Beat in the egg. Combine the flour, baking soda, baking powder and 1 teaspoon nutmeg; add to creamed mixture alternately with the buttermilk. Pour into a greased 9-in. square baking pan (batter will be thick).

Combine the remaining sugar and nutmeg; sprinkle over batter. Bake at 350° for 30-35 minutes or until a toothpick inserted near the center comes out clean. Cool on a wire rack. **Yield:** 9 servings.

## Parmesan Corn Muffins

*(Pictured above right)*

*I need just five ingredients to make these fragrant, tasty corn muffins that start with a handy packaged mix. I*

**Parmesan Corn Muffins**
**Cinnamon Nut Loaf**

*discovered the recipe years ago, and it's been a favorite ever since for dinner and as a snack.* —*Mary Pleasant*
*Humble, Texas*

**2 packages (10 ounces *each*) corn bread/muffin mix**
**1/3 cup grated Parmesan cheese**
**1/2 teaspoon dried rosemary, crushed**
**2 eggs, beaten**
**2/3 cup milk**

In a large bowl, combine the corn bread mix, Parmesan cheese and rosemary. Add eggs and milk; stir just until moistened. Fill greased muffin cups half full. Bake at 400° for 15-20 minutes or until a toothpick comes out clean. Cool for 5 minutes before removing from pan to a wire rack. Serve warm. **Yield:** 1 dozen.

## Cinnamon Nut Loaf

*(Pictured above)*

*This tender bread is delicious alone and even better spread with cream cheese or butter. It tastes like you spent a lot of time fussing, but it's made with convenient refrigerated biscuits.* —*Debbie Purdue, Freeland, Michigan*

**1/3 cup finely chopped pecans *or* walnuts**
**1/4 cup sugar**
**3 tablespoons butter, melted**
**2 teaspoons ground cinnamon**
**2 tubes (7-1/2 ounces *each*) refrigerated buttermilk biscuits**
**1/2 cup confectioners' sugar**
**1 tablespoon milk**

In a small bowl, combine nuts, sugar, butter and cinnamon. Separate biscuits; flatten slightly. Place about 1/2 teaspoon of nut mixture on one side of each biscuit; fold other side over filling. Press edges with a fork to seal. Forming five rows, arrange biscuits folded side down in a greased 8-in. x 4-in. x 2-in. loaf pan. Spoon remaining nut mixture over top.

Bake at 350° for 25-30 minutes or until golden brown. Cool for 10 minutes before removing from pan to a wire rack. Meanwhile, in a small bowl, combine confectioners' sugar and milk; drizzle over warm bread. Cut into slices or pull apart. **Yield:** 8-10 servings.

Peanut Butter Oat Muffins
Cherry-Pineapple Sweet Rolls

## Peanut Butter Oat Muffins

(Pictured above)

*While teaching a home economics class, I asked students to personalize a basic muffin recipe. Two students created these peanut-packed snacks. The entire class agreed that the recipe was a winner.* —Elaine Searer
McVeytown, Pennsylvania

**1-1/4 cups all-purpose flour**
**3/4 cup quick-cooking oats**
**3/4 cup packed brown sugar**
**3 teaspoons baking powder**
**1/2 teaspoon salt**
**Dash ground cinnamon**
**1 egg**
**1/4 cup peanut butter**
**1-1/4 cups milk**
**1/2 cup chopped peanuts**
**Whipped topping and additional peanuts, optional**

In a bowl, combine the flour, oats, brown sugar, baking powder, salt and cinnamon. In another bowl, beat the egg, peanut butter and milk until smooth. Stir into dry ingredients just until moistened. Fold in peanuts.

Fill greased or paper-lined muffin cups three-fourths full. Bake at 375° for 15-18 minutes or until a toothpick comes out clean. Cool for 5 minutes before removing from pan to a wire rack. Serve with whipped topping and peanuts if desired. **Yield:** 1 dozen.

**Editor's Note:** Reduced-fat or generic brands of peanut butter are not recommended for this recipe.

## Cherry-Pineapple Sweet Rolls

(Pictured above)

*Use pineapple tidbits, nuts and maraschino cherries to dress up a tube of orange-flavored sweet rolls. I came up with this when we became tired of plain cinnamon rolls. They're so quick and easy.* —Aline Kellogg
Allegan, Michigan

**1 cup pineapple tidbits**
**1/2 cup pineapple juice, *divided***
**1 tube (13.9 ounces) refrigerated orange sweet rolls with icing**
**1 teaspoon cornstarch**
**1/4 cup chopped walnuts**
**1/4 cup chopped maraschino cherries**

In a small saucepan, combine pineapple, 1/4 cup pineapple juice and 2 tablespoons of icing from sweet rolls. Cook and stir over medium heat until icing is dissolved. Combine cornstarch and remaining pineapple juice until smooth; stir into saucepan. Bring to a boil; cook and stir for 1 minute or until thickened. Remove from heat.

Sprinkle walnuts and cherries into a greased 9-in. round baking pan. Top with pineapple mixture. Arrange sweet rolls on top. Bake at 375° for 20-25 minutes or until golden brown. Immediately invert onto a serving platter. Drizzle with the remaining icing if desired. Serve warm. **Yield:** 8 servings.

## Walnut-Coconut Coffee Cake

*I bake this moist morning treat for my friends and family. My grocer likes me to bring him this coffee cake when I stop by.* —*Doris Jones, Livingston, Texas*

**1 cup vegetable oil**
**1 cup sugar**
**1 cup packed brown sugar**
**2 eggs**
**1 teaspoon vanilla extract**
**2-1/2 cups all-purpose flour**
**1 teaspoon baking soda**
**1 teaspoon salt**
**1 teaspoon ground cinnamon**
**1 cup buttermilk**
**1 cup flaked coconut**
**1 cup chopped walnuts**
**Confectioners' sugar, optional**

In a large mixing bowl, combine the oil, sugars, eggs and vanilla; mix well. Combine the flour, baking soda, salt and cinnamon; add to the egg mixture alternately with buttermilk. Stir just until moistened. Stir in coconut and walnuts just until combined.

Pour into a greased 13-in. x 9-in. x 2-in. baking pan. Bake at 350° for 45-55 minutes or until toothpick inserted near the center comes out clean. Cool on a wire rack. Dust with confectioners' sugar if desired. **Yield:** 12-15 servings.

## Chocolate Zucchini Bread

*This is a wonderful version of a traditional favorite. When my family craves something chocolaty, I treat them to this luscious zucchini loaf. Feel free to try the recipe in your bread machine if it has a quick bread setting.* —*Adriene Lujbli Gilboa, New York*

**1/2 cup butter, softened**
**1 cup sugar**
**2 eggs**
**1 teaspoon vanilla extract**
**1-1/2 cups all-purpose flour**
**3 tablespoons baking cocoa**
**1/2 teaspoon salt**
**1/2 teaspoon baking soda**
**1/2 teaspoon ground cinnamon**
**1 cup grated unpeeled zucchini**
**1/2 cup semisweet chocolate chips**

In a large mixing bowl, cream the butter and sugar. Beat in eggs and vanilla. Combine the flour, cocoa, salt, baking soda and cinnamon; gradually add to creamed mixture. Stir in the zucchini and chocolate chips.

Spoon into a greased 8-in. x 4-in. x 2-in. loaf pan. Bake at 350° for 60-70 minutes or until a toothpick inserted near the center comes out clean. Cool for 10 minutes before removing from pan to a wire rack. **Yield:** 1 loaf.

## Bacon Cheese Muffins

*Full of savory flavor, these from-scratch muffins are on the table in no time. We enjoy them alongside scrambled eggs for breakfast, and any leftovers are great later on.*
—*Jeanne Alexander, Qualicum Beach, British Columbia*

**1-1/2 cups all-purpose flour**
**1/2 cup cornmeal**
**3 teaspoons baking powder**
**1/4 teaspoon salt**
**1/4 teaspoon cayenne pepper**
**2-1/3 cups shredded cheddar cheese, *divided***
**8 bacon strips, cooked and crumbled**
**1 egg**
**1 cup milk**
**1/4 cup butter, melted**

In a bowl, combine the flour, cornmeal, baking powder, salt and cayenne. Stir in 2 cups cheese and bacon. In another bowl, combine the egg, milk and butter. Stir into the dry ingredients just until combined.

Fill greased muffin cups three-fourths full. Sprinkle with remaining cheese. Bake at 425° for 12-15 minutes or until a toothpick comes out clean. Cool for 5 minutes before removing from pan to a wire rack. Serve warm. Refrigerate leftovers. **Yield:** 1 dozen.

## Sour Cream Biscuits

*These light fluffy biscuits are some of the best you'll ever eat. I serve them with a sweet citrus butter that's also great on pancakes.* —*LaDonna Reed, Ponca City, Oklahoma*

**4 cups biscuit/baking mix**
**1 cup (8 ounces) sour cream**
**1 cup lemon-lime soda**
**ORANGE HONEY BUTTER:**
**1/2 cup butter, softened**
**1/3 cup honey**
**2 teaspoons grated orange peel**

Place the biscuit mix in a large bowl. Combine the sour cream and lemon-lime soda; stir into biscuit mix just until combined. Turn onto a floured surface; knead 4-5 times. Roll to 1/2-in. thickness; cut with a 2-1/2-in. biscuit cutter. Place on greased baking sheets. Bake at 400° for 15-20 minutes or until golden brown.

In a small mixing bowl, beat the butter, honey and orange peel until fluffy. Serve with biscuits. **Yield:** 1-1/2 dozen.

## Hazelnut Maple Muffins

*We produce our own maple syrup, so I'm always looking for new recipes for it. Served with a quick-to-fix maple butter, these sweet and nutty bites go perfectly with tea. If you like, try using mini muffin tins.* —Lillian Marcotte
Hartland, Vermont

**1/4 cup maple syrup**
**1/2 cup butter (no substitutes), cubed**
**MUFFINS:**
**2 cups all-purpose flour**
**3 teaspoons baking powder**
**1/2 teaspoon salt**
**1 egg, lightly beaten**
**2/3 cup maple syrup**
**1/2 cup milk**
**1/3 cup butter, melted**
**1/2 cup chopped hazelnuts**

For maple butter, in a small saucepan, bring maple syrup to a boil. Reduce heat; simmer, uncovered, for 2-3 minutes. Remove from the heat; stir in butter until melted. Refrigerate until mixture is spreadable.

In a large bowl, combine flour, baking powder and salt. Combine egg, maple syrup, milk and butter. Stir into dry ingredients just until moistened. Fold in hazelnuts.

Fill greased or paper-lined muffin cups two-thirds full. Bake at 375° for 18-22 minutes or until a toothpick comes out clean. Cool for 5 minutes before removing from pan to a wire rack. Serve warm with maple butter. **Yield:** 1 dozen.

## Oatmeal Scones

*Toasted chopped pecans and oats take center stage in these tender wedges. They offer great variety because I can enjoy them in a number of different ways. If I'm in the mood, I'll spread the scones with my favorite marmalade or jam. Or, I'll pair them with sharp cheddar cheese or a dab of relish at supper.* —Margaret Wilson, Hemet, California

**1 cup quick-cooking oats**
**1-3/4 cups all-purpose flour**
**1/3 cup plus 1 tablespoon sugar, *divided***
**2 teaspoons baking powder**
**1/2 teaspoon baking soda**
**1/4 teaspoon salt**
**1/2 cup cold butter**
**1/2 cup chopped pecans, toasted**
**1 egg**
**2/3 cup buttermilk**
**1/4 teaspoon ground cinnamon**

Sprinkle oats onto an ungreased baking sheet. Bake at 400° for 8-10 minutes or until lightly browned and toasted; cool. In a bowl, combine the oats, flour, 1/3 cup sugar, baking powder, baking soda and salt. Cut in butter until mixture resembles coarse crumbs. Stir in pecans. Whisk together the egg and buttermilk; add to dry ingredients just until moistened. Turn onto a floured surface; knead 10 times.

Transfer dough to a greased baking sheet. Pat into an 8-in. circle. Cut into eight wedges, but do not separate. Combine cinnamon and remaining sugar; sprinkle over dough. Bake at 400° for 17-20 minutes or until golden brown. Serve warm. **Yield:** 8 scones.

## Walnut Orange Muffins

*These glazed buttermilk muffins are so moist, no jelly is needed. The nutty treats are best served warm from the oven with a mug of coffee or hot cider. Grated peel provides the refreshing orange flavor.* —Pat Habiger
Spearville, Kansas

**1 cup butter, softened**
**1 cup sugar**
**2 eggs**
**1 cup buttermilk**
**4 tablespoons grated orange peel**
**2 cups all-purpose flour**
**1 teaspoon baking soda**
**1/4 cup chopped walnuts**
**1 cup orange juice**
**1/2 cup packed brown sugar**

In a mixing bowl, cream butter and sugar. Beat in eggs, buttermilk and orange peel. Combine flour and baking soda; add to creamed mixture just until blended. Stir in walnuts. Fill greased or paper-lined muffin cups two-thirds full. Bake at 350° for 20 minutes or until a toothpick comes out clean.

In a bowl, combine orange juice and brown sugar until dissolved. Spoon over warm muffins. Cool for 5 minutes before removing from pan to a wire rack. **Yield:** about 1 dozen.

## Speedy Lemon Bread

*Lemonade concentrate makes this bread quick because I don't have to squeeze any lemons. But the citrus flavor that results is so good, it tastes like I did! To top the scrumptious slices, I spread on cream cheese.* —Gwen Mains
Wolfeboro, New Hampshire

**2 eggs**
**1/2 cup vegetable oil**
**3 tablespoons plus 1/3 cup lemonade concentrate, *divided***
**1-1/2 cups all-purpose flour**
**1 cup sugar**
**1 teaspoon baking powder**
**1/2 cup milk**

In a mixing bowl, combine eggs, oil and 3 tablespoons lemonade concentrate. Combine flour, sugar and baking powder; add to egg mixture alternately with milk.

Pour mixture into a greased 8-in. x 4-in. x 2-in. loaf pan. Bake at 350° for 55-65 minutes or until a toothpick inserted near the center comes out clean. Drizzle remaining lemonade concentrate over top of hot bread. Cool for 10 minutes before removing from pan to a wire rack. **Yield:** 1 loaf.

## Fennel Seed Wheat Bread

*(Pictured above)*

*I enjoy all kinds of breads and rolls, but this square loaf is a favorite of mine because it's so different. The bread is also great cooked on the grill. Simply cover and grill it over medium heat for about 30 minutes.*
*—Charlotte Kidd, LaGrange, Ohio*

✓ Uses less fat, sugar or salt. Includes Nutritional Analysis and Diabetic Exchanges.

**1 package (16 ounces) hot roll mix**
**1 cup whole wheat flour**
**2 teaspoons fennel seed, crushed, *divided***
**1-1/3 cups water**
**2 tablespoons butter**
**1 egg**
**3/4 cup shredded Swiss cheese**
**1 teaspoon milk**

In a large mixing bowl, combine the flour and contents of yeast packet from hot roll mix, whole wheat flour and 1-1/2 teaspoons fennel seed. In a saucepan, heat the water and butter to 120°-130°. Add to dry ingredients; beat just until moistened. Add egg; beat until blended.

Turn onto a floured surface. Knead in the cheese until the dough is smooth and elastic, about 4-6 minutes. Pat the dough into a greased 9-in. square baking dish. Cover and let rise in a warm place until doubled, about 25 minutes.

Brush with milk and sprinkle with remaining fennel seed. Bake at 350° for 30-35 minutes or until golden brown.

Cool for 15 minutes before removing from pan to a wire rack. Cut bread into four squares; cut each into three wedges. **Yield:** 1 loaf (12 slices).

**Nutritional Analysis:** One slice (prepared with reduced-fat cheese) equals 212 calories, 4 g fat (2 g saturated fat), 26 mg cholesterol, 294 mg sodium, 34 g carbohydrate, 2 g fiber, 8 g protein. **Diabetic Exchanges:** 2 starch, 1/2 milk.

## Ham Cheddar Biscuits

*(Pictured above)*

*My husband often skipped breakfast until I created these savory biscuits. I keep a batch in the freezer, and he reheats a few in the microwave on busy mornings.*
*—Sarah Marshall, Broken Arrow, Oklahoma*

**2-1/4 cups biscuit/baking mix**
**3/4 cup milk**
**3/4 cup shredded cheddar cheese**
**1/2 cup chopped fully cooked ham**

In a bowl, combine the biscuit mix and milk just until moistened. Stir in the cheese and ham. Drop by rounded tablespoonfuls onto greased baking sheets. Bake at 450° for 8-10 minutes or until golden brown. Serve warm. **Yield:** 20 biscuits.

Parmesan Cloverleaf Rolls
Onion Cheese Bread

## Onion Cheese Bread

*(Pictured above)*

*This bread is yummy served as an appetizer or with soup. We nicknamed it Louisiana Lagniappe Bread. "Lagniappe" is Louisiana French for "extra", and this bread is extra-good. —Debbie Letzring, Pineville, Louisiana*

**1 loaf unsliced French bread (1 pound and 20 inches long)**
**8 ounces Monterey Jack cheese, cut into 1/4-inch cubes**
**1/2 cup chopped green onions *or* red onion**
**6 tablespoons butter, melted**
**4-1/2 teaspoons lemon juice**
**1-1/2 teaspoons prepared mustard**

Cut bread lengthwise down the middle to within 1/2 in. of bottom. Cut diagonally into 1-in. slices to within 1/2 in. of bottom. Repeat cuts in the opposite direction. Stuff bread with cheese and onions. Place on a double thickness of heavy-duty foil (about 24 in. x 12 in.).

Combine the butter, lemon juice and mustard; drizzle over bread. Fold foil around bread. Place on a baking sheet. Bake at 425° for 20 minutes or until cheese is melted. Unwrap; bake 5-10 minutes longer or until bread is lightly crisp. Cut into pieces; serve warm. **Yield:** 8-10 servings.

## Parmesan Cloverleaf Rolls

*(Pictured above)*

*Our Test Kitchen home economists jazzed up a convenient hot roll mix to create these pretty brown rolls that form from balls of dough. Parmesan cheese, pizza seasoning and garlic powder lend plenty of flavor when you sprinkle them over the top.*

✓ Uses less fat, sugar or salt. Includes Nutritional Analysis and Diabetic Exchanges.

**1 package (16 ounces) hot roll mix**
**2 tablespoons butter, melted**
**1/4 cup grated Parmesan cheese**
**2 teaspoons pizza seasoning**
**1/4 teaspoon garlic powder**

Prepare hot roll mix according to package directions. Divide dough into 12 portions; divide each portion into three pieces. Shape each into a ball; place three balls each in 12 well-greased muffin cups. Brush with butter.

Combine the Parmesan cheese, pizza seasoning and garlic powder; sprinkle over dough. Cover and let rise in a warm place for 10-15 minutes. Bake at 375° for 15-20 minutes or until golden brown. Remove from pan to a wire rack. Serve warm. **Yield:** 1 dozen.

**Nutritional Analysis:** One roll equals 163 calories, 4 g fat (2 g saturated fat), 6 mg cholesterol, 302 mg sodium, 27 g carbohydrate, 1 g fiber, 5 g protein. **Diabetic Exchange:** 2 starch.

## Moist Bran Muffins

*My family will eat anything with chocolate chips in it... and these muffins are no exception! If you prefer raisins, simply stir in those instead. Either way, these delightful bites are great for busy mornings.* —*Shirley Oakman, Calgary, Alberta*

**1 cup butter, softened**
**2 cups packed brown sugar**
**2 tablespoons molasses**
**2-3/4 cups all-purpose flour**
**1-1/2 cups wheat bran**
**2 teaspoons baking powder**
**1 teaspoon ground cinnamon**
**1/2 teaspoon ground nutmeg**
**1/2 teaspoon salt**
**2 eggs**
**2 cups buttermilk**
**2 cups semisweet chocolate chips *or* raisins**

In a mixing bowl, cream butter and brown sugar. Add molasses; mix well. Combine the dry ingredients. Combine eggs and buttermilk; add to creamed mixture alternately with dry ingredients. Stir in chocolate chips.

Fill greased or paper-lined muffin cups three-fourths full. Bake at 375° for 18-22 minutes or until a toothpick comes out clean. Cool 5 minutes before removing from pans to wire racks. **Yield:** 2 dozen.

**Editor's Note:** This recipe was tested with Red Mill wheat bran.

## Spice Puffs

*Four ingredients are all you need to bake up a batch of these lovely light-as-air muffins that make a sweet breakfast treat. Nicely spiced from a cake mix and cinnamon, they're my son's all-time favorite and so simple to make.* —*Sally Geipel, Franklin, Wisconsin*

**1 package (18-1/4 ounces) spice cake mix**
**1/2 cup butter, melted**
**1/2 cup sugar**
**1 teaspoon ground cinnamon**

Prepare cake batter according to package directions. Fill 24 greased or paper-lined muffin cups two-thirds full. Bake at 350° for 20-25 minutes or until a toothpick comes out clean. Remove to wire racks. Cool for 5 minutes.

Place butter in a shallow bowl. In another shallow bowl, combine sugar and cinnamon. Dip top of warm puffs in butter, then in cinnamon-sugar. Serve warm. **Yield:** 2 dozen.

## Buttery Poppy-Seed Bread

*This cake-like bread is quick, easy and very moist. The recipe makes two loaves, so I can enjoy one and share the second with a family member or friend. If you can find butter brickle or butter pecan mix, use it in place of the regular cake mix and eliminate the nuts.* —*Carol Bradley, Sun City West, Arizona*

**1 package (18-1/4 ounces) butter cake mix**
**1 package (3.4 ounces) instant coconut cream pudding mix**
**4 eggs**
**1 cup water**
**1/4 cup vegetable oil**
**2 tablespoons poppy seeds**
**1 teaspoon vanilla extract**
**1/4 cup finely chopped pecans**

In a large mixing bowl, combine the first seven ingredients. Beat on medium speed for 2 minutes. Stir in pecans. Pour into two greased 9-in. x 5-in. x 3-in. loaf pans. Bake at 350° for 35-45 minutes or until a toothpick inserted near the center comes out clean. Cool for 10 minutes before removing from pans to wire racks to cool completely. **Yield:** 2 loaves.

## Rhubarb Coffee Cake

*If you're a rhubarb lover, this cake is for you. I'm a former home economics teacher, and I received this recipe at a housewarming party during my first year of teaching. I love to cook for my family and anyone else who likes good home baking.* —*Judy Roy, Flaxcombe, Saskatchewan*

**1 cup butter, softened**
**2 cups packed brown sugar, *divided***
**1 egg**
**1 teaspoon vanilla extract**
**1 cup milk**
**2-1/2 cups all-purpose flour**
**1 teaspoon baking soda**
**1/4 teaspoon salt**
**2-1/2 cups finely chopped fresh *or* frozen rhubarb**
**1/2 teaspoon ground cinnamon**

In a mixing bowl, cream butter and 1-1/2 cups brown sugar. Add egg and vanilla, beating until light and fluffy. Add milk; beat until smooth. Combine the flour, baking soda and salt; add to creamed mixture and mix well. Fold in rhubarb. Pour into a greased 13-in. x 9-in. x 2-in. baking dish.

Combine the cinnamon and remaining brown sugar; sprinkle over batter. Bake at 325° for 30-35 minutes or until a toothpick inserted near the center comes out clean. Cool on a wire rack. **Yield:** 12-16 servings.

## Bacon Walnut Bread

*Talk about easy—this is it! The quick recipe uses a biscuit/baking mix to hurry things along, so I have time to make this bread regularly. Cheddar cheese, onion and a little hot pepper sauce add to the savory flavor.* —*Barbara Nowakowski North Tonawanda, New York*

**3 cups biscuit/baking mix**
**1 cup milk**
**2 eggs, beaten**
**2 tablespoons dried minced onion**
**Dash hot pepper sauce**
**3/4 cup shredded cheddar cheese**
**12 bacon strips, cooked and crumbled**
**1/2 cup chopped walnuts**

In a large bowl, combine the biscuit mix, milk, eggs, onion and pepper sauce just until moistened. Stir in cheese, bacon and walnuts. Spread into a greased 9-in. x 5-in. x 3-in. loaf pan.

Bake at 350° for 48-52 minutes or until a toothpick inserted near the center comes out clean. Cool for 10 minutes before removing from pan to a wire rack to cool completely. **Yield:** 1 loaf.

## Sweet Potato Biscuits

*Even people who don't care for sweet potatoes will enjoy these colorful biscuits. They taste especially good when I serve them with butter and maple syrup.*
—*Andrea Bolden, Unionville, Tennessee*

**3/4 cup mashed cooked sweet potatoes**
**2/3 cup milk**
**1/4 cup butter, melted**
**1-2/3 cups self-rising flour**
**1 tablespoon sugar**

In a bowl, combine the sweet potatoes, milk and butter. Combine the flour and sugar; stir in the sweet potato mixture just until moistened.

On a lightly floured surface, knead the dough slightly or until no longer sticky. Roll to 1/2-in. thickness; cut with a floured 2-1/2-in. biscuit cutter. Place on a lightly greased baking sheet. Bake at 425° for 10-15 minutes or until golden brown. Serve warm. **Yield:** 9 biscuits.

## Peaches 'n' Cream Muffins

*Packed with cinnamon and chunks of peaches, these muffins are always a hit. They are very easy to make, and we never have any left over.* —*Carole Fraser Toronto, Ontario*

**2 cups all-purpose flour**
**1/4 cup sugar**
**3 teaspoons baking powder**
**1 teaspoon ground cinnamon**
**1/2 teaspoon salt**
**1 can (15-1/4 ounces) sliced peaches, drained**
**4 ounces cream cheese**
**2 eggs**
**1-1/4 cups milk**
**1/3 cup honey**
**1/4 cup butter, melted**
**1 teaspoon grated lemon peel**
**1-1/2 cups bran flakes**

In a large bowl, combine the flour, sugar, baking powder, cinnamon and salt. Cut peaches and cream cheese into 1/2-in. cubes; set aside. In a bowl, beat eggs, milk, honey, butter and lemon peel until blended. Stir in the bran flakes, peaches and cream cheese. Stir into dry ingredients just until moistened.

Fill greased muffin cups three-fourths full. Bake at 400° for 18-20 minutes or until a toothpick comes out clean. Cool for 5 minutes before removing from pans to wire racks. **Yield:** 1-1/2 dozen.

## Chocolate Chip Bran Muffins

*These mouth-watering morsels are our favorite snack. The combination of chocolate and peanut butter makes them irresistible. Plus, any extras we have freeze wonderfully.*
—*Sara Meyers, Grand Rapids, Michigan*

**2-1/2 cups all-purpose flour**
**1-1/4 cups quick-cooking oats**
**1 cup sugar**
**2-1/2 teaspoons baking soda**
**1 teaspoon salt**
**1/2 cup peanut butter**
**1/3 cup vegetable oil**
**2 eggs**
**2 cups buttermilk**
**4-1/2 cups bran flakes**
**1 cup (6 ounces) semisweet chocolate chips**

In a bowl, combine the flour, oats, sugar, baking soda and salt; set aside. In a large mixing bowl, beat the peanut butter and oil until combined. Beat in the eggs and buttermilk. Stir into the dry ingredients just until moistened. Fold in the cereal and chocolate chips.

Fill greased or paper-lined muffin cups two-thirds full. Bake at 400° for 14-17 minutes or until a toothpick comes out clean. Cool for 5 minutes before removing from pans to wire racks. Serve warm. **Yield:** about 2-1/2 dozen.

## Apple Coffee Cake

*(Pictured above right and on page 152)*

*This layered coffee cake comes together easily with canned pie filling and other pantry staples. I enjoy making it for my family or even to celebrate co-workers' birthdays.*
—*Joan Kuderer, Sparta, Wisconsin*

**1/2 cup butter, softened**
**1 cup sugar**
**3 eggs**
**3 cups all-purpose flour**
**3 teaspoons baking powder**
**1 teaspoon salt**

Italian Bread Twists
Apple Coffee Cake

1-1/2 cups milk
1 can (21 ounces) apple pie filling
2 teaspoons ground cinnamon

TOPPING:
1/2 cup chopped walnuts
1/4 cup packed brown sugar
2 tablespoons butter, melted

GLAZE:
3/4 cup confectioners' sugar
1 tablespoon butter, softened
3/4 teaspoon vanilla extract
2 to 3 teaspoons water

In a large mixing bowl, cream butter and sugar. Beat in eggs. Combine the flour, baking powder and salt; add to creamed mixture alternately with milk.

Pour half into a greased 13-in. x 9-in. x 2-in. baking dish. Combine the pie filling and cinnamon; spoon over batter. Drop the remaining batter over the filling; spread gently.

Combine topping ingredients; sprinkle over batter. Bake at 350° for 40-45 minutes or until a toothpick inserted near the center comes out clean. Cool on a wire rack. Combine glaze ingredients; drizzle over warm or cooled coffee cake. **Yield:** 12-15 servings.

## Italian Bread Twists

*(Pictured above and on page 152)*

*These breadsticks and their pizza-inspired dipping sauce are irresistible. They complement most any meal.*
*—Mary Garman, Elliottsburg, Pennsylvania*

2 to 2-1/2 cups all-purpose flour
1 package (1/4 ounce) quick-rise yeast
1/2 teaspoon salt
3/4 cup water
6 teaspoons vegetable oil, *divided*
1-1/2 teaspoons honey
2 tablespoons butter, melted
4-1/2 teaspoons grated Parmesan cheese
1 tablespoon dried parsley flakes
1/2 teaspoon garlic salt

PIZZA DIPPING SAUCE:
1 can (8 ounces) pizza sauce
2 tablespoons brown sugar
4-1/2 teaspoons cider vinegar

In a large mixing bowl, combine 1-1/2 cups flour, yeast and salt. In a saucepan, heat the water, 1-1/2 teaspoons oil and honey to 120°-130°. Add to dry ingredients; beat just until moistened.

Stir in enough remaining flour to form a soft dough. Turn onto a floured surface; knead until smooth and elastic, about 6-8 minutes. Cover and let rest for 10 minutes.

Roll into a 9-in. square. Cut into 1-in. strips. Twist each strip and place 2 in. apart on a greased baking sheet. Cover and let rise in a warm place until doubled, about 20 minutes. Combine butter and remaining oil; brush over dough.

Combine Parmesan cheese, parsley and garlic salt; sprinkle over dough. Bake at 350° for 15-20 minutes or until lightly browned. Remove to a wire rack.

Meanwhile, in a small saucepan, combine sauce ingredients. Bring to a boil. Serve with warm breadsticks. **Yield:** 9 breadsticks.

Poppy Seed Cheese Bread
Banana Cranberry Muffins

## Banana Cranberry Muffins

*(Pictured above)*

*Any time I get together with friends and family members, they ask me to bring some of these colorful, yummy treats. I simply use cranberries to dress up my homemade banana muffins.* —*Gretchen Zoch*
*Boiling Springs, North Carolina*

**2 cups fresh *or* frozen cranberries**
**1-2/3 cups sugar, *divided***
**1 cup water**
**1/3 cup shortening**
**2 eggs**
**1-3/4 cups all-purpose flour**
**2 teaspoons baking powder**
**1/2 teaspoon salt**
**1/4 teaspoon baking soda**
**1 cup mashed ripe bananas (2 to 3 medium)**
**1/2 cup chopped walnuts**

In a small saucepan, bring cranberries, 1 cup sugar and water to a boil. Reduce heat; simmer, uncovered, for 5-7 minutes or until berries begin to pop. Drain and set aside.

In a large mixing bowl, cream shortening and remaining sugar. Add eggs, one at a time, beating well after each addition. Combine the flour, baking powder, salt and baking soda; add to creamed mixture alternately with bananas. Fold in cranberry mixture and walnuts.

Fill greased or paper-lined muffin cups three-fourths full. Bake at 400° for 15-20 minutes or until a toothpick comes out clean. Cool for 5 minutes before removing from pans to wire racks. **Yield:** 14 muffins.

## Poppy Seed Cheese Bread

*(Pictured above)*

*I easily dress up Italian bread with cheese, Dijon mustard and a hint of lemon juice. Try it alongside your favorite soup or serve it as a crowd-pleasing appetizer.*
—*Marianne Kmiecik, Walkersville, Maryland*

**1 loaf (1 pound) unsliced Italian bread**
**1/2 cup butter, softened**
**2 tablespoons mayonnaise**
**1 tablespoon Dijon mustard**
**1 tablespoon lemon juice**
**1 tablespoon poppy seeds**
**2 teaspoons dried minced onion**
**1-1/4 cups shredded Swiss cheese**

Cut bread into 1-in. slices to within 1/4 in. of bottom. In a small bowl, combine the butter, mayonnaise, mustard, lemon juice, poppy seeds and onion. Spread over each slice of bread; sprinkle cheese between the slices.

Place the loaf in an ungreased 15-in. x 10-in. x 1-in. baking pan. Bake at 375° for 8-10 minutes or until the cheese is melted and the bread is crisp. **Yield:** 8-10 servings.

# Bread Basics

SURPRISING your family at mealtime by offering golden brown loaves, tender rolls, mouthwatering muffins and other fresh-baked breads can require just minutes in the kitchen. To brush up on some basic techniques for baking bread—or to learn nifty new methods—turn to these helpful hints from our Test Kitchen.

## Kneading Know-How

KNEADING bread dough by hand takes about 6-8 minutes. To knead by hand, start by turning the dough onto a lightly floured surface, such as a kitchen counter.

With floured hands, fold the dough toward you and push the dough away gently with the heels of your hands. After each push, turn the dough a quarter turn and fold it in toward you again. As you work, sprinkle just enough flour on the surface so that the dough doesn't stick. Continue kneading in this way until the dough is smooth and elastic.

You may also use a stand mixer with a dough hook. Begin by kneading the dough on low speed for 3 minutes or until it is smooth and cleans the sides of the bowl. Continue to knead the dough 3-4 minutes longer or until it is smooth and elastic. Checking the dough often will prevent overmixing.

Food processors can save time by kneading the dough in 2 minutes. Check the manufacturer's directions before trying this.

## More Sizes for Muffins

IF YOU'D like to bake miniature or jumbo muffins from a traditional muffin recipe, be sure to remember the following tips.

Generally, the oven temperature will not need to be adjusted when you use mini or jumbo muffin tins instead of the traditional size. However, the baking time will most likely need to be altered.

Mini muffins will take anywhere from 10 to 15 minutes to bake while jumbo muffins will take anywhere from 20 to 40 minutes. Check jumbo muffins for doneness after 20 minutes, then every 5 to 10 minutes. Muffins are done if a toothpick inserted near the center comes out clean.

Keep in mind that the baking time for muffins will vary depending on the recipe you're preparing. The variation is due to the oven temperature and the amount of batter in each muffin cup.

If your muffin recipe does not fill all the cups in the pan, fill the empty cups with water. The muffins will bake more evenly.

Unless otherwise directed, muffins should go directly in the oven as soon as the batter is mixed. Also, take care not to overmix the batter—lumpy batter will yield more tender muffins.

## Using the Right Yeast

FOR BEST RESULTS, use the type of yeast called for in a recipe. But in a pinch, active dry yeast can be used as a substitute for quick-rise yeast in equal parts. However, the methods for incorporating the yeast and proofing the dough must be changed.

Quick-rise yeast was designed to save time and eliminate steps when baking yeast breads. Quick-rise yeast is added directly to the other dry ingredients without being dissolved the way active dry yeast is. Also, the traditional first rise is replaced with a 10-minute rest. Then, after the dough is shaped, it's allowed to rise just once before baking.

When using active dry yeast, first dissolve it in warm water before adding it to other ingredients. Use 1/4 cup of warm water (110°-115°) to dissolve each 1/4-ounce package of active dry yeast. Finally, the dough will need to rise two times before baking, once after kneading and once after shaping.

## Substitutions for Leavening Agents

BAKING SODA, baking powder and cream of tartar have a number of uses, but all three are used as leavening agents in bread and other baked goods.

Baking soda requires acidic ingredients such as buttermilk, lemon juice or molasses to activate it. Because cream of tarter is acidic, it is often used with baking soda as a leavener.

As a substitute for 1 teaspoon of cream of tartar in bread and other baked goods, use 1 teaspoon of lemon juice or vinegar.

Baking powder contains baking soda and the correct amount of acid to activate it. As a substitute for each teaspoon of baking powder, use 1/4 teaspoon baking soda and 1/2 teaspoon cream of tartar.

## Baking with Bread Flour

BREAD FLOUR is made from high-gluten hard wheat flour, which gives strength and elasticity to yeast bread doughs. Bread flour can also be used for other yeast-raised doughs, strudel, puff pastry, popovers and pasta where strength and elasticity are desired.

Bread flour is not suitable for making muffins, pie crusts, quick breads, cakes or pancakes.

Use an airtight container for storing bread flour and keep it in a cool, dry place. Stored this way, it has a shelf life of 10-15 months. For longer storage, freeze the flour in an airtight container.

# Breads at The Touch Of a Button

NOTHING pleases like the old-fashioned flavor and appealing aroma of homemade yeast bread, rolls and other baked goods. And they're a cinch to whip up when you use a convenient bread machine.

Just toss in the ingredients, turn on the switch and make a simple check. This appliance does the kneading for you, giving you fresh bread with little fuss.

## Sour Cream Potato Rolls

*I use leftover mashed potatoes and mace in the dough for these easy bread-machine rolls. They've been a favorite in our family for years. I think they're especially delicious when served warm with butter and peach jam.* —*Carol Giesbrecht, Kitchener, Ontario*

**1/2 cup sour cream**
**1/2 cup water (70° to 80°)**
**1/2 cup mashed potatoes (with added butter and milk)**
**1/4 cup butter, softened**
**2 tablespoons sugar**
**1 teaspoon salt**
**1/2 teaspoon baking soda**
**1/8 teaspoon ground mace**
**3 cups bread flour**
**3 teaspoons active dry yeast**

In bread machine pan, place all ingredients in order suggested by manufacturer. Select dough setting (check dough after 5 minutes of mixing; add 1 to 2 tablespoons of water or flour if needed).

When cycle is completed, turn dough onto a lightly floured surface. Punch dough down. Divide into 18 portions; roll each into a ball. Place on greased baking sheets. Cover and let rise in a warm place until doubled, about 30 minutes. Bake at 375° for 10-15 minutes or until golden brown. Serve warm. **Yield:** 1-1/2 dozen.

## French Bread

*My husband gave me a bread machine for Christmas the year we were married, and I use it about once a week. We like slices of this bread with a spaghetti dinner and often use the leftovers for French toast.* —*Janet Vink, Geneseo, Illinois*

**1-1/4 cups water (70° to 80°)**
**2 teaspoons sugar**
**1 teaspoon salt**
**3-1/2 cups bread flour**
**1-1/2 teaspoons active dry yeast**
**1 tablespoon cornmeal**

**GLAZE:**

**1 egg**
**1 tablespoon water**
**2 teaspoons sesame seeds, toasted, optional**

In bread machine pan, place the first five ingredients in the order suggested by the manufacturer. Select dough setting (check dough after 5 minutes of mixing; add 1 to 2 tablespoons of water or flour if needed).

When cycle is completed, turn dough onto a lightly floured surface. Divide in half. Roll each portion into a 10-in. x 8-in. rectangle. Roll up jelly-roll style, starting with a long side; pinch seams to seal.

Sprinkle a greased baking sheet with cornmeal; place loaves seam side down on prepared pan. Cover and let rise in a warm place until doubled, about 20 minutes.

Whisk egg and water; brush over loaves. With a sharp knife, make four shallow slashes across the top of each loaf. Sprinkle with sesame seeds if desired. Bake at 375° for 20-25 minutes or until golden brown. Cool on wire racks. **Yield:** 2 loaves.

## Pepper Asiago Loaf

*With its golden crust and tender interior, this high, rustic-looking white bread is a great addition to any main course. Green onions and coarsely ground pepper give it a little bite.* —*Lois Kinneberg, Phoenix, Arizona*

**1 cup water (70° to 80°)**
**1 egg**
**1 tablespoon butter, melted**
**1/2 cup nonfat dry milk powder**
**1/2 cup shredded Asiago cheese**
**4-1/2 teaspoons chopped green onions**
**1 tablespoon sugar**
**1-1/4 teaspoons salt**
**1/2 teaspoon coarsely ground pepper**
**3 cups bread flour**
**2-1/4 teaspoons active dry yeast**

In bread machine pan, place all ingredients in order suggested by manufacturer. Select basic bread setting. Choose crust color and loaf size if available.

Bake according to bread machine directions (check the dough after 5 minutes of mixing; add 1 to 2 tablespoons of water or flour if needed). **Yield:** 1 loaf (1-1/2 pounds).

**Editor's Note:** If your bread machine has a time-delay feature, we recommend you do not use it for this recipe.

## Soft Pumpkin Yeast Bread

*This large hearty loaf is a perfect way to round out fall meals. Canned pumpkin, a little brown sugar and ground walnuts give the bread its seasonal flavor and appearance without a lot of fuss on my part.* —*Sybil Brown, Highland, California*

1/2 cup canned pumpkin
1 cup warm evaporated milk (70° to 80°)
2 tablespoons butter, softened
2 tablespoons brown sugar
1/2 teaspoon salt
1/4 cup whole wheat flour
3 cups bread flour
2 to 3 teaspoons pumpkin pie spice
1/2 cup ground walnuts
2-1/4 teaspoons active dry yeast

In bread machine pan, place all ingredients in order suggested by manufacturer. Select basic bread setting. Choose crust color and loaf size if available.

Bake according to bread machine directions (check dough after 5 minutes of mixing; add 1 to 2 tablespoons of water or flour if needed). **Yield:** 1 loaf (about 1-1/2 pounds).

**Editor's Note:** If your bread machine has a time-delay feature, we recommend you do not use it for this recipe.

## Peanut Butter Twists

*Years ago, I received a bread machine for Christmas—along with a collection of recipes I could make with it. These treats that have a peanut butter filling and sweet icing drizzled on top soon became a favorite.*

*—Renea De Kam, George, Iowa*

**3/4 cup water (70° to 80°)**
**1/3 cup butter, softened**
**1 egg**
**1/4 cup nonfat dry milk powder**
**1/3 cup sugar**
**3/4 teaspoon salt**
**3 cups bread flour**
**2-1/4 teaspoons active dry yeast**

**FILLING:**
**3/4 cup creamy peanut butter**
**1/4 cup butter, softened**
**1/3 cup confectioners' sugar**

**ICING:**
**1-1/2 cups confectioners' sugar**
**2 tablespoons creamy peanut butter**
**5 to 7 tablespoons warm water**

In bread machine pan, place the first eight ingredients in order suggested by manufacturer. Select dough setting (check dough after 5 minutes of mixing; add 1 to 2 tablespoons of water or flour if needed).

When cycle is completed, turn dough onto a lightly floured surface. Punch down; cover and let stand for 10 minutes. Combine filling ingredients; set aside. Roll dough into a 24-in. x 8-in. rectangle. Spread filling to within 1/2 in. of edges. Fold rectangle in half lengthwise; cut widthwise into 24 pieces. Pinch seams to seal. Twist each piece three times.

Place 2 in. apart on greased baking sheets; pinch ends. Bake at 350° for 15-20 minutes or until lightly browned. Remove from pans to wire racks to cool. Combine icing ingredients; drizzle over twists. **Yield:** 2 dozen.

**Editor's Note:** If your bread machine has a time-delay feature, we recommend you do not use it for this recipe. Reduced-fat or generic brands of peanut butter are not recommended for this recipe.

## Spiced Raisin Bread

*(Pictured below)*

*I have two bread machines, and one is often busy baking this soft chewy loaf. The bread's nutmeg, cloves and orange peel fill my home with a wonderful aroma. Slices are great for peanut butter sandwiches.*

*—Margaret Otley, Waverly, Nebraska*

✓ Uses less fat, sugar or salt. Includes Nutritional Analysis and Diabetic Exchanges.

**1 cup plus 2 tablespoons water (70° to 80°)**
**3/4 cup raisins**
**2 tablespoons butter, softened**
**2 tablespoons brown sugar**
**2 teaspoons ground cinnamon**
**1 teaspoon salt**
**1/4 teaspoon ground nutmeg**
**1/4 teaspoon ground cloves**
**1/4 teaspoon grated orange peel**
**3 cups bread flour**
**2-1/4 teaspoons active dry yeast**

In bread machine pan, place all ingredients in order suggested by manufacturer. Select basic bread setting. Choose crust color and loaf size if available. Bake according to bread machine directions (check dough after 5 minutes of mixing; add 1 to 2 tablespoons of water or flour if needed). **Yield:** 1 loaf (1-1/2 pounds, 24 slices).

**Nutritional Analysis:** One slice equals 80 calories, 1 g fat (1 g saturated fat), 3 mg cholesterol, 110 mg sodium, 16 g carbohydrate, 1 g fiber, 2 g protein. **Diabetic Exchange:** 1 starch.

**Editor's Note:** If your bread machine has a time-delay feature, we recommend you do not use it for this recipe.

Spiced Raisin Bread

Cranberry Walnut Bread

## Cranberry Walnut Bread

*(Pictured above)*

*This family favorite comes from a collection of Amish recipes. I gave the recipe to several friends, and everyone loves it. Loaded with cranberries, nuts and cinnamon flavor, it's perfect for fall and winter.* —*Rose Wilcox Alexandria, Minnesota*

**1 cup water (70° to 80°)**
**1/4 cup packed brown sugar**
**4-1/2 teaspoons butter, softened**
**1-1/4 teaspoons salt**
**1/2 teaspoon ground cinnamon**
**3 cups bread flour**
**2-1/4 teaspoons active dry yeast**
**1/2 cup chopped walnuts**
**1/2 cup dried cranberries**

In bread machine pan, place the first seven ingredients in order suggested by manufacturer. Select basic bread setting. Choose crust color and loaf size if available. Bake according to bread machine directions (check dough after 5 minutes of mixing; add 1 to 2 tablespoons of water or flour if needed).

Just before the final kneading (your machine may audibly signal this), add the walnuts and cranberries. **Yield:** 1 loaf (1-1/2 pounds).

**Editor's Note:** If your bread machine has a time-delay feature, we recommend you do not use it for this recipe.

## Honey Wheat Breadsticks

*Not only are these breadsticks delicious, but they come together very easily. Whole wheat flour and a little honey help give them a wholesome taste and keep them on the healthy side.* —*Ted Van Schoick, Jersey Shore, Pennsylvania*

✓ Uses less fat, sugar or salt. Includes Nutritional Analysis and Diabetic Exchanges.

**1-1/3 cups water (70° to 80°)**
**3 tablespoons honey**
**2 tablespoons vegetable oil**
**1-1/2 teaspoons salt**
**2 cups bread flour**
**2 cups whole wheat flour**
**3 teaspoons active dry yeast**

In bread machine pan, place all ingredients in order suggested by manufacturer. Select dough setting (check dough after 5 minutes of mixing; add 1 to 2 tablespoons of water or flour if needed).

When cycle is completed, turn dough onto a lightly floured surface. Divide into 16 portions; shape each into a ball. Roll each into an 8-in. rope. Place 2 in. apart on greased baking sheets.

Cover and let rise in a warm place until doubled, about 30 minutes. Bake at 375° for 10-12 minutes or until golden brown. Remove to wire racks. **Yield:** 16 breadsticks.

**Nutritional Analysis:** One breadstick equals 131 calories, 2 g fat (trace saturated fat), 0 cholesterol, 222 mg sodium, 25 g carbohydrate, 2 g fiber, 4 g protein. **Diabetic Exchange:** 1-1/2 starch.

## Corned Beef Rye Bread

*Caraway seeds spark the flavor of this rustic loaf that's flecked with chopped corned beef and Swiss cheese. Slices are great alongside soup or salad.* —*Elvera Dallman Franklin, Nebraska*

**1 cup water (70° to 80°)**
**1/4 cup molasses**
**2 tablespoons butter, softened**
**1 tablespoon sugar**
**1 teaspoon salt**
**1/2 to 1 teaspoon caraway seeds**
**2-1/4 cups bread flour**
**1-1/4 cups rye flour**
**2 teaspoons active dry yeast**
**1/2 cup shredded Swiss cheese**
**1 package (2-1/2 ounces) deli corned beef, chopped**

In bread machine pan, place the first nine ingredients in order suggested by manufacturer. Select basic bread setting. Choose crust color and loaf size if available. Bake according to bread machine directions (check dough after 5 minutes of mixing; add 1 to 2 tablespoons of water or flour if needed).

Just before the final kneading (your machine may audibly signal this), add the Swiss cheese and corned beef. Refrigerate leftovers. **Yield:** 1 loaf (1-1/2 pounds).

## Three-Cheese Bread

*My husband likes trying different recipes in our bread machine. He came up with this delicious loaf that's sure to appeal to cheese lovers.* —*Debbie McCauley Little Rock, Arkansas*

**3/4 cup water (70° to 80°)**
**2 tablespoons butter, softened**

2 tablespoons sugar
1-1/2 teaspoons salt
1/2 cup shredded Swiss cheese
1/2 cup small-curd cottage cheese
3 tablespoons grated Parmesan cheese
3 cups bread flour
2-1/4 teaspoons active dry yeast

In bread machine pan, place all ingredients in order suggested by manufacturer. Select basic bread setting. Choose crust color and loaf size if available. Bake according to bread machine directions (check dough after 5 minutes of mixing; add 1 to 2 tablespoons of water or flour if needed). **Yield:** 1 loaf (1-1/2 pounds).

**Editor's Note:** If your bread machine has a time-delay feature, we recommend you do not use it for this recipe.

## Poppy Seed Yeast Bread

*Plenty of toasted sliced almonds and poppy seeds add a pleasant crunch to this light and tender lemon bread. At our house, eating the scrumptious loaf just isn't the same without the accompanying citrus spread.*
*—Vicky Wilkinson, Hartford, Kansas*

3/4 cup water (70° to 80°)
1/2 cup warm lemon yogurt (70° to 80°)
2 tablespoons honey
4-1/2 teaspoons butter, melted
2 teaspoons lemon extract
1 teaspoon salt
3 cups bread flour
4-1/2 teaspoons nonfat dry milk powder
1/2 cup sliced almonds, toasted
2 tablespoons poppy seeds
1 tablespoon grated lemon peel
2-1/4 teaspoons active dry yeast
LEMON CHEESE SPREAD:
2 eggs, lightly beaten
1/4 cup lemon juice
3 tablespoons butter, cubed
3/4 cup sugar
Dash salt
1 teaspoon grated lemon peel
1 package (3 ounces) cream cheese, softened

In bread machine pan, place the first 12 ingredients in order suggested by manufacturer. Select basic bread setting. Choose crust color and loaf size if available. Bake according to bread machine directions (check dough after 5 minutes of mixing; add 1 to 2 tablespoons of water or flour if needed).

In a heavy saucepan, combine the first five spread ingredients. Bring to a boil. Reduce heat; cook and stir over low heat until thickened. Remove from heat; cool.

In a small mixing bowl, beat lemon peel and cream cheese. Add egg mixture; mix well. Serve with bread. Refrigerate any leftover spread. **Yield:** 1 loaf (1-1/2 pounds) and 1 cup spread.

**Editor's Note:** If your bread machine has a time-delay feature, we recommend you do not use it for this recipe.

## Cheesy Sausage Loaf

*(Pictured below)*

*My bread machine is such a time-saver, particularly where this savory entree is concerned. Stuffed with pork sausage and cheese, it's a favorite with my granddaughters.*
*—Martha Gage, Mt. Enterprise, Texas*

1 cup water (70° to 80°)
4 teaspoons butter, softened
1-1/4 teaspoons salt
1 teaspoon sugar
3 cups bread flour
2-1/4 teaspoons active dry yeast
1 pound bulk pork sausage, cooked and drained
3/4 cup shredded provolone cheese
3/4 cup shredded mozzarella cheese
1/4 teaspoon garlic powder
Pepper to taste
1 egg, beaten

In bread machine pan, place the first six ingredients in order suggested by manufacturer. Select dough setting (check dough after 5 minutes of mixing; add 1 to 2 tablespoons of water or flour if needed). When cycle is completed, turn dough onto a lightly floured surface. Roll into a 16-in. x 10-in. rectangle. Cover with plastic wrap; let rest 10 minutes.

Meanwhile, combine the sausage, cheeses, garlic powder and pepper. Spread evenly over dough to within 1/2 in. of edges. Roll up jelly-roll style, starting with a long side; pinch seam to seal and tuck ends under. Place seam side down on a greased baking sheet.

Cover and let rise in a warm place for 30 minutes. Bake at 350° for 20 minutes. Brush with egg; bake 15-20 minutes longer or until lightly browned. Remove to a wire rack. Serve warm. **Yield:** 1 loaf (about 1-1/2 pounds).

**Editor's Note:** If your bread machine has a time-delay feature, we recommend you do not use it for this recipe.

Cheesy Sausage Loaf

## Almond Crescents

(Pictured below)

*Not only does the dough for these crescents mix up in the bread machine, but you can vary the amount of almonds in the filling and do the baking a day early. The recipe is from my daughter-in-law.* —*Lucille Freeman Sumner, Iowa*

**1/2 cup warm milk (70° to 80°)**
**2 eggs**
**1/4 cup butter, softened**
**1-1/2 teaspoons almond extract**
**1/3 cup sugar**
**1/2 teaspoon salt**
**3 cups plus 2 tablespoons bread flour**
**2-1/4 teaspoons active dry yeast**
**FILLING:**
**2 tablespoons butter, melted**
**1 teaspoon almond extract**
**1/2 to 3/4 cup sliced almonds**
**2 tablespoons cornmeal**
**1 egg**
**1 tablespoon water**

In bread machine pan, place the first eight ingredients in order suggested by manufacturer. Select dough setting (check dough after 5 minutes of mixing; add 1 to 2 tablespoons of water or flour if needed).

When cycle is completed, turn dough onto a lightly floured surface. Divide in half; roll each portion into a 12-in. circle. Combine the butter and almond extract; brush over the dough. Cut each circle into 12 wedges; sprinkle with almonds. Roll up each wedge from the wide end.

Grease baking sheets and sprinkle with cornmeal. Place the rolls pointed side down 2 in. apart on prepared pans. Curve the ends to form crescents. Cover and let rise in a warm place until doubled, about 50 minutes.

In a small bowl, beat egg and water; brush over dough. Bake at 350° for 13-15 minutes or until golden brown. Remove to wire racks. **Yield:** 2 dozen.

**Editor's Note:** If your bread machine has a time-delay feature, we recommend you do not use it for this recipe.

Almond Crescents

## Grape-Nuts Bread

*I like to add tasty Grape-Nuts cereal to this hearty loaf. The moist bread is so easy that I make it at least twice a week. Once, I put it together in the middle of the night when I suddenly remembered that I didn't have any bread for breakfast.* —*Debbie Hunt, Anthony, Kansas*

✓ Uses less fat, sugar or salt. Includes Nutritional Analysis and Diabetic Exchanges.

**1-2/3 cups water (70° to 80°)**
**3 tablespoons canola oil**
**4-1/2 teaspoons sugar**
**1 teaspoon salt**
**3-3/4 cups bread flour**
**3/4 cup Grape-Nuts cereal**
**1-1/2 teaspoons active dry yeast**

In bread machine pan, place all ingredients in order suggested by manufacturer. Select basic bread setting. Choose crust color and loaf size if available.

Bake according to bread machine directions (check dough after 5 minutes of mixing; add 1 to 2 tablespoons of water or flour if needed). **Yield:** 1 loaf (2 pounds, 16 slices).

**Nutritional Analysis:** One slice equals 142 calories, 3 g fat (trace saturated fat), 0 cholesterol, 181 mg sodium, 26 g carbohydrate, 1 g fiber, 4 g protein. **Diabetic Exchanges:** 1-1/2 starch, 1/2 fat.

## Cappuccino Chip Bread

*I love to cook and bake but don't always have a lot of time, so I really appreciate recipes that take advantage of my bread machine. This mocha loaf dotted with semisweet chocolate chips is one of my favorite creations.* —*Lisa Allen, Fort Wayne, Indiana*

**3/4 cup warm milk (70° to 80°)**
**1 egg, lightly beaten**
**3 tablespoons instant coffee granules**
**2 tablespoons sugar**
**2 tablespoons water**
**1 tablespoon butter, softened**
**1 teaspoon vanilla extract**
**3/4 teaspoon salt**
**3 cups bread flour**
**2 teaspoons active dry yeast**
**1/3 cup miniature semisweet chocolate chips**

In bread machine pan, place the first 10 ingredients in order suggested by manufacturer. Select basic bread setting. Choose crust color and loaf size if available. Bake according to bread machine directions (check dough after 5 minutes of mixing; add 1 to 2 tablespoons of water or flour if needed). Just before final kneading (your machine may audibly signal this), add chocolate chips.

**Yield:** 1 loaf (1-1/2 pounds).

**Editor's Note:** If your bread machine has a time-delay feature, we recommend you do not use it for this recipe.

## Mexican Bread

*Chopped green chilies and red pepper flakes add bits of color to every slice of this large, savory loaf...and one bite proves that it tastes as good as it looks. Slightly spicy with ground cumin, the cheesy bread is a great way to jazz up your sandwiches. —Loni McCoy, Blaine, Minnesota*

**1 cup plus 2 tablespoons water (70° to 80°)**
**1/2 cup shredded Monterey Jack cheese**
**1 can (4 ounces) chopped green chilies**
**1 tablespoon butter, softened**
**2 tablespoons sugar**
**1 to 2 tablespoons crushed red pepper flakes**
**1 tablespoon nonfat dry milk powder**
**1 tablespoon ground cumin**
**1-1/2 teaspoons salt**
**3-1/4 cups bread flour**
**2-1/2 teaspoons active dry yeast**

In bread machine pan, place all ingredients in order suggested by manufacturer. Select basic bread setting. Choose crust color and loaf size if available.

Bake according to bread machine directions (check dough after 5 minutes of mixing; add 1 to 2 tablespoons of water or flour if needed). **Yield:** 1 loaf (about 2 pounds).

**Editor's Note:** If your bread machine has a time-delay feature, we recommend you do not use it for this recipe.

## Herbed Dinner Rolls

*After I had my sixth child, a friend dropped off a meal that included these rolls, which start in a bread machine. They were so delicious, I went out and bought my own bread machine so I could make them myself. I've served these golden brown bites to my family countless times since. —Dana Lowry, Hickory, North Carolina*

**1 cup water (70° to 80°)**
**2 tablespoons butter, softened**
**1 egg**
**1/4 cup sugar**
**1 teaspoon salt**
**1/2 teaspoon *each* dried basil, oregano, thyme and dried rosemary, crushed**
**3-1/4 cups bread flour**
**2-1/4 teaspoons active dry yeast**
**Additional butter, melted**
**Coarse salt, optional**

In bread machine pan, place the water, softened butter, egg, sugar, salt, seasonings, flour and yeast in order suggested by manufacturer. Select dough setting (check dough after 5 minutes of mixing; add 1 to 2 tablespoons of water or flour if needed).

When cycle is completed, turn dough onto a lightly floured surface. Divide dough into 16 portions; shape each into a ball. Place 2 in. apart on greased baking sheets. Cover and let rise in a warm place until doubled, about 30 minutes.

Bake at 375° for 12-15 minutes or until golden brown. If desired, brush with butter and sprinkle with coarse salt. Remove from pans to wire racks. **Yield:** 16 rolls.

**Editor's Note:** If your bread machine has a time-delay feature, we recommend you do not use it for this recipe.

Basil Garlic Bread

## Basil Garlic Bread

*(Pictured above)*

*My family members have always been big on bread. And when I created this simple loaf, they asked for it time and again. —Christine Burger, Grafton, Wisconsin*

**2/3 cup warm milk (70° to 80°)**
**1/4 cup water (70° to 80°)**
**1/4 cup warm sour cream (70° to 80°)**
**1-1/2 teaspoons sugar**
**1 tablespoon butter, softened**
**1 tablespoon grated Parmesan cheese**
**1 teaspoon salt**
**1/2 teaspoon minced garlic**
**1/2 teaspoon dried basil**
**1/2 teaspoon garlic powder**
**3 cups bread flour**
**2-1/4 teaspoons active dry yeast**

In bread machine pan, place all ingredients in order suggested by manufacturer. Select basic bread setting. Choose crust color and loaf size if available.

Bake according to bread machine directions (check the dough after 5 minutes of mixing; add 1 to 2 tablespoons of water or flour if needed). **Yield:** 1 loaf (1-1/2 pounds).

**Editor's Note:** If your bread machine has a time-delay feature, we recommend you do not use it for this recipe.

# Chapter 12

# Snappy Soups, Salads & Sandwiches

SWIFT SUPPERS and fuss-free lunches are mere moments away when you pull together fast-to-fix soups, salads and sandwiches. For active family cooks, these mouth-watering mainstays are ideal.

Adding one or more of the rapid recipes here to your menu makes meal planning a snap.

All of these simple-yet-satisfying soups, speedy salads and shortcut sandwiches are family favorites, great-tasting and surprisingly filling.

**HEARTY HELPINGS.** Top to bottom: Robust Pepper Salad, Shortcut Minestrone and Crunchy Tuna Turnovers (all recipes on p. 182).

## Barley Waldorf Salad

*To create this tasty twist on traditional Waldorf salad, simply cook the barley as directed on the package, then combine all of the ingredients. Pop the mixture in the refrigerator until serving, and you're done! The memorable medley offers a nice change from rice and pasta salads and is delicious anytime.* —*Sara Tschetter*
*Belle Plaine, Saskatchewan*

**1 cup quick-cooking barley**
**2 large tart apples, chopped**
**1/2 cup chopped walnuts**
**1/2 cup raisins**
**1/2 cup heavy whipping cream**
**1/2 cup mayonnaise**
**4-1/2 teaspoons sugar**

Cook barley according to package directions; drain and rinse in cold water. In a small serving bowl, combine barley, apples, walnuts, raisins, cream, mayonnaise and sugar. Cover and refrigerate until serving. **Yield:** 6-8 servings.

## Butter Bean Veggie Soup

*(Pictured at right)*

*This hearty basil-seasoned soup is chock-full of five different vegetables. I like to serve big steaming bowls of it with generous helpings of corn bread fresh from the oven. On days when I'm especially tight on time, this recipe is great because it takes only about 30 minutes to make from start to finish.* —*Dorothy Bertrand, Sellersburg, Indiana*

**3 celery ribs, chopped**
**3 medium carrots, chopped**
**1 small onion, chopped**
**2 tablespoons olive oil**
**3 tablespoons all-purpose flour**
**2 cans (14-1/2 ounces *each*) chicken broth**
**2 cans (15 ounces *each*) butter beans, rinsed and drained**
**1 can (14-1/2 ounces) stewed tomatoes, cut up**
**1 teaspoon dried basil**
**1/2 teaspoon salt**
**1/2 teaspoon dried parsley flakes**
**1/4 teaspoon pepper**

In a large saucepan, saute the celery, carrots and onion in oil until tender. Stir in flour until blended. Gradually add the broth.

Stir in the remaining ingredients. Bring to a boil. Reduce heat; simmer, uncovered, for 10 minutes or until soup is heated through. **Yield:** 8 servings (about 2 quarts).

## Pepperoni Pasta Salad

*(Pictured at right)*

*Pepperoni slices and bottled Italian dressing add zip to the spiral pasta, cubed cheddar cheese and vegetables in this colorful combination. Serve it right away or assemble it ahead of time and keep it in the refrigerator. I think the longer this salad chills, the better it tastes.*
—*Shannon Lommen, Kaysville, Utah*

**2 cups uncooked tricolor spiral pasta**
**1 cup cubed cheddar cheese**
**1 cup coarsely chopped cucumber**
**1 small tomato, chopped**
**2 green onions, chopped**
**28 pepperoni slices**
**1/2 cup zesty Italian salad dressing**

Cook pasta according to package directions; drain and rinse in cold water. In a large bowl, combine the pasta, cheese, cucumber, tomato, onions and pepperoni. Add salad dressing and toss to coat. Cover and refrigerate until serving. **Yield:** 4-6 servings.

## Bacon Egg Salad Croissants

*(Pictured at right)*

*This swift sandwich idea is a great way to jazz up an old favorite for lunchtime. The creamy filling gets a taste boost from bacon and is extra special served on split croissants. For a nice crunch, I mix in plenty of diced celery.* —*Julee Wallberg*
*Reno, Nevada*

**6 hard-cooked eggs, chopped**
**1/3 cup diced celery**
**1/3 cup mayonnaise**
**1 teaspoon prepared mustard**
**1/4 teaspoon salt**
**1/8 teaspoon pepper**
**1/3 cup crumbled cooked bacon**
**4 lettuce leaves**
**4 thin tomato slices**
**4 croissants, split**

In a bowl, combine the eggs, celery, mayonnaise, mustard, salt and pepper. Fold in bacon. Place a lettuce leaf, tomato slice and 1/2 cup egg salad on each croissant. **Yield:** 4 servings.

### Eggs the Hard-Cooked Way

A green or gray layer around the yolks of hard-cooked eggs can be caused by overcooking or by a high amount of iron in the cooking water. The effect may be unsightly, but it's harmless. For best results, use the following method when hard-cooking eggs.

Place the eggs in a single layer in a saucepan and add enough water to come 1 inch above the eggs. Cover the saucepan and bring the water to a boil. Remove the pan from the heat and let it stand, covered, for 15-17 minutes. Immediately run cold water over the eggs or put them in ice water until they're completely cooled.

When you're storing uncooked eggs, it's best to keep them in their original carton in the coldest part of the refrigerator rather than on the door rack.

Butter Bean Veggie Soup
Bacon Egg Salad Croissants
Pepperoni Pasta Salad

Corny Ham Bundles
Mushroom Spinach Salad
Curried Carrot Soup

## Chili Bean Soup

*This sensational soup tastes like it simmered for hours, but it's actually easy to prepare in just 30 minutes or less. My husband enjoys his bowlful most when I serve it with cheddar cheese and tortilla chips.* —*Mary Felty*
*Kingman, Arizona*

**1 medium onion, chopped**
**3 garlic cloves, minced**
**3 tablespoons olive oil**
**4 cups vegetable broth**
**1 can (16 ounces) kidney beans, rinsed and drained**
**1 can (4 ounces) chopped green chilies**
**1/4 cup tomato paste**
**1 tablespoon soy sauce**
**1 tablespoon Worcestershire sauce**
**1-1/2 teaspoons brown sugar**
**1-1/2 teaspoons lime juice**
**1 teaspoon dried basil**
**1 teaspoon dried oregano**
**1 teaspoon ground cumin**

In a large saucepan, saute onion and garlic in oil until tender. Stir in remaining ingredients. Bring to a boil. Reduce heat; simmer, uncovered, for 15 minutes or until heated through. **Yield:** 6 servings.

## Curried Carrot Soup

*(Pictured at left)*

*Curry, ginger and garlic are the savory seasonings that give this unique, smooth soup fabulous flavor. I like to serve each helping while it's still piping hot. Try the recipe with a favorite sandwich or salad.* —*Thom Armentrout*
*Fredericksburg, Virginia*

✓ Uses less fat, sugar or salt. Includes Nutritional Analysis and Diabetic Exchanges.

**1 medium onion, finely chopped**
**3 garlic cloves, minced**
**2 tablespoons butter**
**2 teaspoons curry powder**
**1 teaspoon ground ginger**
**2 pounds carrots, thinly sliced**
**2 cans (14-1/2 ounces *each*) chicken broth**
**1 cup half-and-half cream**
**1 cup water**
**1/2 teaspoon dill weed**
**Pepper to taste**

In a large saucepan, saute onion and garlic in butter. Stir in the curry and ginger. Add the carrots and broth. Bring to a boil. Reduce heat; simmer, uncovered, for 10-15 minutes or until carrots are tender. Remove from the heat and cool slightly. In a blender or food processor, cover and process soup mixture in batches until smooth. Return to the saucepan. Add the cream, water, dill and pepper. Cook until heated through (do not boil). **Yield:** 8 servings (2 quarts).

**Nutritional Analysis:** One 1-cup serving (prepared with reduced-sodium chicken broth and fat-free half-and-half) equals 109 calories, 3 g fat (2 g saturated fat), 8 mg cholesterol, 371 mg sodium, 17 g carbohydrate, 4 g fiber, 4 g protein. **Diabetic Exchanges:** 1 starch, 1/2 fat.

## Corny Ham Bundles

*(Pictured at left)*

*These super little sandwiches are a great-tasting way to use up any leftover cooked ham I may have in the refrigerator. Plus, they come together easily with a tube of refrigerated crescent rolls.* —*Sandy DeMars*
*Crown Point, Indiana*

**1 package (3 ounces) cream cheese, softened**
**1 tablespoon mayonnaise**
**1/2 teaspoon ground mustard**
**1/4 teaspoon celery seed**
**1 cup cubed fully cooked ham**
**1/2 cup fresh *or* frozen corn**
**1/4 cup shredded Monterey Jack *or* Swiss cheese**
**2 teaspoons finely chopped onion**
**1 tube (8 ounces) refrigerated crescent rolls**
**1 tablespoon butter, melted**
**1 tablespoon finely crushed corn chips**

In a small mixing bowl, beat cream cheese, mayonnaise, mustard and celery seed until blended. Stir in ham, corn, cheese and onion. Unroll crescent roll dough and separate into four rectangles; seal seams and perforations.

Spoon about 1/2 cup ham mixture into center of each rectangle. Bring edges up to the center and pinch to seal. Brush with butter; sprinkle with corn chips. Transfer to an ungreased baking sheet. Bake at 375° for 15-20 minutes or until golden brown. **Yield:** 4 servings.

## Mushroom Spinach Salad

*(Pictured at left)*

*Spinach is one of my favorite vegetables, so my husband grows it for me every year. I always enjoy those leafy greens in this salad full of fresh mushrooms, bacon, onion and eggs. A tangy lemon-mustard dressing tops it all off.*
—*Nancy Zimmerman*
*Cape May Court House, New Jersey*

**8 cups fresh baby spinach**
**1/2 pound fresh mushrooms, sliced**
**4 green onions, chopped**
**6 bacon strips, diced**
**2 to 3 tablespoons lemon juice**
**2 tablespoons water**
**1/2 teaspoon ground mustard**
**1/4 teaspoon pepper**
**3 hard-cooked eggs, cut into wedges**

In a large salad bowl, combine the spinach, mushrooms and green onions. In a skillet, cook bacon over medium heat until crisp. Remove to paper towels to drain. Add the lemon juice, water, mustard and pepper to the drippings; cook and stir until heated through. Immediately drizzle over salad; toss gently. Top with eggs and reserved bacon. Serve immediately. **Yield:** 8 servings.

## Strawberry Romaine Salad

(Pictured below)

*I love to entertain and cook for family and friends when they drop in. When strawberries are in season, I serve this salad often. But because of its unusual combination of onion and berries, I sometimes have to encourage guests to try it. Once they do, they always come back for more.*
—*Ileen Adkins, Randle, Washington*

**8 cups torn romaine**
**1 pint fresh strawberries, sliced**
**1 small red onion, thinly sliced and separated into rings**
**POPPY SEED DRESSING:**
**1/2 cup mayonnaise**
**1/4 cup sugar**
**1/4 cup milk**
**2 tablespoons poppy seeds**
**2 tablespoons white wine vinegar**

In a large bowl, toss the romaine, strawberries and onion. In a small bowl, whisk the dressing ingredients until blended. Serve with the salad. **Yield:** 8-10 servings (1 cup dressing).

Strawberry Romaine Salad

## Shredded Carrot Salad

*I rely on just four items for this colorful crunchy salad. We love it. It's a snap to make, but if you're really looking to beat the clock, use a bag of shredded carrots.*
—*Kezia Sullivan, Sackets Harbor, New York*

**3 cups shredded carrots**
**1 cup raisins**
**1/2 cup chopped cashews**
**1/2 cup mayonnaise**

In a serving bowl, combine carrots, raisins, nuts and mayonnaise. Refrigerate the leftovers. **Yield:** 4 servings.

## Greek Chicken Sandwiches

*My wife and I enjoyed warm chicken sandwiches similar to these at a restaurant. We wanted a little more flavor, so one night I experimented and came up with this zesty version. We like it best made with Greek olives.*
—*Tom Wolf, Tigard, Oregon*

✓ Uses less fat, sugar or salt. Includes Nutritional Analysis and Diabetic Exchanges.

**1 pound boneless skinless chicken breasts, diced**
**1/4 teaspoon garlic powder**
**1 tablespoon olive oil**
**1/2 cup Caesar salad dressing**
**1/2 cup crumbled feta cheese**
**1/4 cup sliced ripe olives**
**4 French *or* Italian sandwich rolls, split**
**4 lettuce leaves**
**4 tomato slices**
**8 red onion rings**

In a large skillet, cook the chicken and garlic powder in oil over medium heat until the chicken juices run clear. Stir in the salad dressing, feta cheese and olives. Cook and stir until heated through. Serve on rolls with lettuce, tomato and red onion rings. **Yield:** 4 servings.

**Nutritional Analysis:** One sandwich (prepared with fat-free salad dressing; calculated with a standard hamburger bun) equals 393 calories, 12 g fat (4 g saturated fat), 82 mg cholesterol, 961 mg sodium, 36 g carbohydrate, 3 g fiber, 34 g protein. **Diabetic Exchanges:** 4 lean meat, 2 starch, 1 vegetable.

## Fruit 'n' Nut Tossed Salad

*With its sweet lemony dressing, this green salad comes together in only 15 minutes. Even my picky 6-year-old will eat this mix of romaine, mandarin oranges, almonds and grapes.* —*Sue Stewart, Hales Corners, Wisconsin*

**1 large bunch romaine, torn**
**1 can (11 ounces) mandarin oranges, drained**
**1 cup seedless red grapes, halved**
**1/2 cup slivered almonds, toasted**
**DRESSING:**
**1/4 cup vegetable oil**
**3 tablespoons sugar**
**3 tablespoons lemon juice**

Deli Sandwich Platter
Mozzarella Veggie Salad

**1/4 teaspoon grated lemon peel**
**Dash salt and pepper**

In a large bowl, gently toss the romaine, oranges, grapes and almonds. In a small bowl, whisk the dressing ingredients. Drizzle over salad and toss to coat. **Yield:** 10 servings.

## Mozzarella Veggie Salad

*(Pictured above)*

*Vibrant garden-fresh vegetables get fast flavor from a store-bought vinaigrette and cubed cheese in this swift lunch salad from our Test Kitchen. It's also a tasty contribution to last-minute picnics and workplace potlucks.*

**1 pint grape *or* cherry tomatoes**
**2 cups fresh broccoli florets**
**1 cup fresh cauliflowerets**
**1 cup cubed mozzarella cheese**
**3/4 cup balsamic vinaigrette**

In a large serving bowl, combine all ingredients. **Yield:** 8 servings.

## Deli Sandwich Platter

*(Pictured above)*

*The home economists in our Test Kitchen created two lip-smacking spreads to jazz up a variety of deli meats. Simply pick up some sandwich rolls, and you've got a build-your-own-sandwich bar that's sure to please at parties or other get-togethers.*

**1/3 cup mayonnaise**
**1/2 to 1 teaspoon prepared horseradish**
**1/2 teaspoon minced chives**
**1/4 to 1/2 teaspoon garlic powder**
**1/3 cup honey mustard**
**1/2 teaspoon dried tarragon**
**1/8 teaspoon ground ginger**
**Assorted deli meats and sandwich rolls**

In a small bowl, combine the mayonnaise, horseradish, chives and garlic powder. In another small bowl, combine mustard, tarragon and ginger. Arrange deli meats on a platter; serve with rolls and the mayonnaise and mustard spreads. **Yield:** about 1/3 cup of each spread.

**Sugared Walnut Fruit Salad**
**Potato Leek Soup**
**Hot Colby Ham Sandwiches**

## Hot Colby Ham Sandwiches

*(Pictured at left)*

*This yummy recipe is a favorite with friends and family. Not only are the warm sandwiches easy to assemble, but they smell so good when baking that no one can resist them. They're a staple at our get-togethers.* —*Sherry Crenshaw, Fort Worth, Texas*

- **1/2 cup butter, melted**
- **2 tablespoons prepared mustard**
- **1 tablespoon dried minced onion**
- **1 tablespoon poppy seeds**
- **2 to 3 teaspoons sugar**
- **15 dinner rolls (about 3-inch diameter), sliced**
- **15 slices Colby cheese**
- **15 thin slices deli ham (about 1 pound)**
- **2 cups (8 ounces) shredded mozzarella cheese**

In a small bowl, combine the butter, mustard, onion, poppy seeds and sugar. Place roll bottoms, cut side up, in an ungreased 15-in. x 10-in. x 1-in. baking pan. Top each with Colby cheese, ham and mozzarella cheese. Drizzle with half of the butter mixture.

Replace roll tops. Drizzle with remaining butter mixture. Bake, uncovered, at 350° for 10-15 minutes or until cheese is melted. **Yield:** 15 servings.

## Potato Leek Soup

*(Pictured at left)*

*I always like to try new and different things. So I added a package of leek soup mix to my potato soup, and my family loved it.* —*Terri Day, Rochester, Washington*

- **2 cups water**
- **2 medium potatoes, peeled and diced**
- **2 bacon strips, cooked and crumbled**
- **2 cups milk**
- **3/4 cup mashed potato flakes**
- **1 package (1.8 ounces) leek soup and dip mix**
- **Shredded cheddar cheese**

In a large saucepan, bring the water, potatoes and bacon to a boil. Reduce heat; cover and simmer for 10-15 minutes or until potatoes are tender. Reduce heat to low. Stir in the milk, potato flakes and soup mix. Cook and stir for 5 minutes or until heated through. Garnish with cheese. **Yield:** 5 servings.

## Sugared Walnut Fruit Salad

*(Pictured at left)*

*I stir sweetened walnuts into this colorful salad that includes oranges, grapes and strawberries.* —*Clara Coulston, Washington Court House, Ohio*

- **1/2 cup walnut halves**
- **1 tablespoon water**
- **1 tablespoon sugar**
- **2 medium navel oranges, peeled and sectioned**
- **2 cups seedless red grapes**
- **2 kiwifruit, peeled and chopped**
- **1 medium peach, chopped *or* 3/4 cup frozen sliced peaches, thawed and chopped**
- **1 cup sliced fresh strawberries**
- **1-1/2 teaspoons grated orange peel, optional**

In a small bowl, combine walnuts and water; drain. Toss walnuts with sugar. Spread in a single layer on a greased foil-lined baking sheet. Bake at 350° for 5-6 minutes or until golden brown. Cool on pan, stirring occasionally.

In a large salad bowl, combine the oranges, grapes, kiwi, peach and strawberries. Sprinkle with sugared walnuts; toss lightly. Sprinkle with orange peel if desired. Serve immediately. **Yield:** 4-6 servings.

## Garbanzo Bean Tomato Salad

*Garbanzo beans, sliced tomatoes and onion are chilled with a no-fuss dressing in this change-of-pace salad. Toss together the refreshing medley right before serving.* —*Barbara Carbee, Brooksville, Florida*

- **3 tablespoons vegetable oil**
- **1 tablespoon red wine vinegar**
- **1 teaspoon salt, *divided***
- **1/4 teaspoon pepper, *divided***
- **1 can (15 ounces) garbanzo beans *or* chickpeas, rinsed and drained**
- **3 medium tomatoes, thinly sliced**
- **1 medium onion, thinly sliced**
- **1 tablespoon minced fresh basil *or* 1 teaspoon dried basil**

In a bowl, combine the oil, vinegar, 1/2 teaspoon salt and 1/8 teaspoon pepper. Add beans; toss to coat. Place tomatoes in a serving bowl. Top with onion. Sprinkle with basil and remaining salt and pepper. Top with bean mixture. Cover and refrigerate for at least 1 hour. Toss just before serving. **Yield:** 4-6 servings.

### Sectioning Citrus Fruits

1. Cut a thin slice off the bottom and top of the fruit. Rest the fruit cut side down on a cutting board. Using a sharp paring knife, remove the peel and white rind.

2. Working above a bowl, slice between the membrane of a section and the fruit until the knife reaches the center. Turn the knife and follow the membrane so the fruit is released. Repeat until all the sections are removed.

## Waldorf Sandwiches

*If you like the traditional recipe for Waldorf salad, you'll enjoy the crunchy apple-and-nut filling in this sweet but satisfying sandwich. Cinnamon-raisin bread adds to the deliciously different taste. For a fancier look, trim the crust from each slice.* —*Codie Ray, Tallulah, Louisiana*

**2 cups shredded unpeeled apple**
**1 tablespoon lemon juice**
**2 celery ribs, finely chopped**
**1 cup chopped walnuts**
**1/4 cup mayonnaise**
**14 to 16 slices cinnamon-raisin bread**

In a bowl, toss apple with lemon juice. Stir in celery, walnuts and mayonnaise; mix well. Spread apple mixture on seven to eight bread slices; top with remaining bread. **Yield:** 7-8 servings.

## Crunchy Tuna Turnovers

*(Pictured at right and on page 173)*

*I used to work with a cook who considered this unique creation one of his specialties. Once I tried it, I could see why. It's a great change from an ordinary tuna sandwich. The golden brown pockets have a cheesy filling and are coated with crushed potato chips.* —*Denise Hollebeke Penhold, Alberta*

**2 cans (6 ounces *each*) tuna, drained and flaked**
**1/2 cup shredded cheddar cheese**
**1/3 cup mayonnaise**
**1/3 cup sliced ripe olives**
**1/8 to 1/4 teaspoon lemon-pepper seasoning**
**1 tube (12 ounces) refrigerated buttermilk biscuits**
**1 egg, beaten**
**1-1/4 cups crushed potato chips**

In a small bowl, combine tuna, cheese, mayonnaise, olives and lemon-pepper; set aside. On a lightly floured surface, flatten each biscuit into a 5-in. circle. Spoon 2 rounded tablespoonfuls of tuna mixture onto one side of each circle. Fold dough over filling; press edges with a fork to seal.

Place egg and potato chips in separate shallow bowls. Dip turnovers in egg, then coat with chips. Place on an ungreased baking sheet. Make a 2-1/2-in. slit in top of each turnover. Bake at 375° for 18-21 minutes or until golden brown. **Yield:** 10 turnovers.

## Robust Pepper Salad

*(Pictured at right and on page 172)*

*Bottled Italian salad dressing is the simple secret to this zesty, great-tasting dish. The recipe makes enough for about 20 people, so it's perfect when you need to take something to a potluck supper or large backyard barbecue. With a colorful mix of peppers, broccoli and onion, the salad is eye-appealing, too.* —*Gerry Weiss Oakdale, Minnesota*

**1 medium head cauliflower, broken into florets**
**1 medium bunch broccoli, broken into florets**
**1 *each* medium sweet yellow, red and orange pepper, julienned**
**1 medium red onion, halved and sliced**
**8 ounces cheddar cheese, cubed**
**1-1/2 cups zesty Italian salad dressing**

In a large bowl, combine the cauliflower, broccoli, peppers, onion and cheddar cheese. Add salad dressing; toss to coat. Cover and refrigerate for at least 4 hours. Serve with a slotted spoon. **Yield:** 20 servings.

## Shortcut Minestrone

*(Pictured at right and on page 173)*

*This soup is hearty and makes a comforting lunch or dinner on a brisk day. The spaghetti sauce provides rich flavor without a long simmering time. I further cut the prep time by using my food processor for the chopping.* —*Barbara Jellison Bellevue, Washington*

✓ Uses less fat, sugar or salt. Includes Nutritional Analysis and Diabetic Exchanges.

**4 bacon strips, diced**
**1 large onion, chopped**
**3 medium carrots, chopped**
**3 garlic cloves, minced**
**1 jar (28 ounces) spaghetti sauce**
**4 cups beef broth**
**1 can (16 ounces) kidney beans, rinsed and drained**
**1 can (15 ounces) garbanzo beans *or* chickpeas, rinsed and drained**
**2/3 cup uncooked small shell pasta**
**2 teaspoons brown sugar**
**1/2 teaspoon dried basil**
**1/2 teaspoon dried oregano**
**1 cup frozen cut green beans**
**Grated Parmesan cheese, optional**

In a Dutch oven or soup kettle, cook the bacon over medium heat until crisp. Using a slotted spoon, remove to paper towels. Drain, reserving 2 tablespoons drippings. In the drippings, saute the onion and carrots for 3-4 minutes or until tender. Add garlic; cook 2 minutes longer.

Stir in spaghetti sauce, broth and beans. Bring to a boil. Add the pasta, brown sugar, basil and oregano. Cook, uncovered, for 8-10 minutes or until pasta is tender, stirring occasionally. Add green beans; cook 5 minutes longer or until heated through. Garnish with Parmesan cheese if desired and bacon. **Yield:** 10 servings (2-1/2 quarts).

**Nutritional Analysis:** One 1-cup serving (prepared with reduced-sodium beef broth and without Parmesan cheese) equals 188 calories, 3 g fat (1 g saturated fat), 2 mg cholesterol, 560 mg sodium, 31 g carbohydrate, 7 g fiber, 10 g protein. **Diabetic Exchanges:** 2 starch, 1/2 meat.

Robust Pepper Salad
Shortcut Minestrone
Crunchy Tuna Turnovers

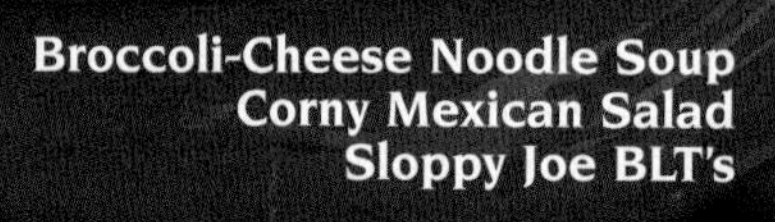

Broccoli-Cheese Noodle Soup
Corny Mexican Salad
Sloppy Joe BLT's

## Corny Mexican Salad

*(Pictured at left)*

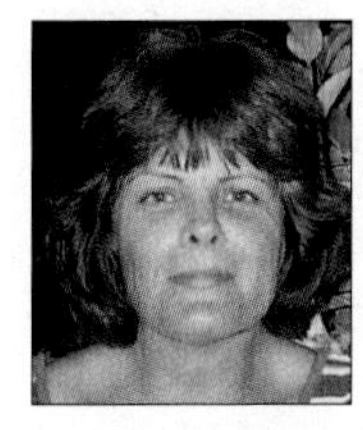

*This fresh-tasting veggie medley is tossed with a zesty oil-and-vinegar dressing. The salad is great with tortilla chips as an appetizer, but it can also be served as a side dish. Adjust the amount of hot sauce to suit your family's taste.*

*—Suzanne McKinley, Lyons, Georgia*

**2 cans (15 ounces *each*) black beans, rinsed and drained**
**1 can (11 ounces) Mexicorn, drained**
**1 medium tomato, chopped**
**1 medium ripe avocado, peeled and cubed**
**1/2 cup chopped onion**
**1/2 cup vegetable oil**
**1/4 cup red wine vinegar**
**1/2 teaspoon salt**
**1/2 teaspoon hot pepper sauce**
**Tortilla chips, optional**

In a bowl, combine the beans, corn, tomato, avocado and onion. In a small bowl, whisk the oil, vinegar, salt and hot pepper sauce; pour over bean mixture and toss to coat. Serve with tortilla chips if desired. **Yield:** 8-10 servings.

## Sloppy Joe BLT's

*(Pictured at left)*

*Not the traditional sloppy joe, this colorful sandwich combines bacon, salad greens, tomato and cheese with a mayonnaise dressing. My dad made these somewhat-messy but tasty BLT's often when we were kids.*

*—Debbie Blackburn, New Cumberland, Pennsylvania*

**4 cups hearts of romaine salad mix**
**1 large tomato, chopped**
**1 cup (4 ounces) shredded mozzarella cheese**
**1 cup (4 ounces) shredded cheddar cheese**
**1/2 cup real bacon bits**
**1/2 cup mayonnaise**
**4-1/2 teaspoons cider vinegar**
**1/4 teaspoon salt**
**1/8 teaspoon pepper**
**12 slices Italian bread (3/4 inch thick), toasted**

In a large bowl, combine the salad mix, tomato, cheeses and bacon. In a small bowl, combine the mayonnaise, vinegar, salt and pepper; spoon over salad mixture and toss to coat. Spoon about 3/4 cup over six bread slices; top with remaining bread. **Yield:** 6 servings.

## Broccoli-Cheese Noodle Soup

*(Pictured at left)*

*My husband's aunt shared the recipe for this creamy soup, which tastes like I spent all day cooking. It's very filling with a salad and bread. We often spoon the leftovers over baked potatoes.*

*—Trinity Nicholas*
*Mt. Carbon, West Virginia*

**1 package (10 ounces) frozen chopped broccoli**
**2 ounces angel hair pasta, broken into small pieces**
**1/4 cup butter**
**1 tablespoon all-purpose flour**
**1 cup water**
**3/4 cup milk**
**1/8 teaspoon pepper**
**6 ounces process cheese (Velveeta), cubed**
**1/2 cup sour cream**

Cook both the broccoli and pasta according to package directions; drain. In a large saucepan, melt butter; stir in flour until smooth. Gradually stir in the water, milk and pepper until blended. Bring to a boil; cook and stir for 2 minutes or until thickened.

Reduce heat; stir in cheese until melted. Stir in the broccoli, pasta and sour cream; heat through (do not boil). **Yield:** 4-5 servings.

## Curried Pumpkin Soup

*If you like curry, you'll love this unique soup flavored with that spice, as well as garlic, red pepper flakes and coriander. For extra flair, serve each hot bowlful with a dollop of sour cream.* *—Kathy Hill, Catlettsburg, Kentucky*

**1/3 cup chopped onion**
**1/2 teaspoon minced garlic**
**2 tablespoons butter**
**1/2 teaspoon curry powder**
**1/4 teaspoon salt**
**1/8 teaspoon ground coriander**
**Dash crushed red pepper flakes**
**1-1/2 cups chicken broth**
**1 cup half-and-half cream**
**3/4 cup canned pumpkin**

In a large saucepan, saute onion and garlic in butter until tender. Stir in the curry powder, salt, coriander and pepper flakes; cook and stir for 1 minute. Stir in broth until blended.

Bring to a boil. Reduce heat; simmer, uncovered, for 15 minutes. Whisk in the cream and pumpkin; heat through (do not boil). **Yield:** 6 servings.

### Salad Savvy

- When a pasta salad recipe calls for cubed cheese, I use individually wrapped string cheese or cheese stick snacks. I can open only the number of packages I need, and I don't end up with an open block of cheese that might spoil before it's used.
  *—Annette Marie Young, West Lafayette, Indiana*
- Making coleslaw is a breeze when I put my dressing in the food processor and add coarse chunks of cabbage. I simply pulse until the cabbage is the size I want. There's no need to stir because each morsel ends up perfectly coated with dressing.
  *—Rachel Gorski, Naples, Florida*

## Taco Po'Boys

*(Pictured at right)*

*Whenever I'm busy, I put together these southwestern chicken sandwiches that start with convenient canned refried beans and get to the table in about a half hour. Cheese, veggies and a creamy homemade spread top them off. I never have leftovers, so I know everyone really enjoys them.* —*Patricia Sanks, Camas, Washington*

**4 French sandwich rolls**
**1 can (16 ounces) refried beans, warmed**
**1 tablespoon taco seasoning**
**1/2 pound thinly sliced deli chicken**
**1 cup (4 ounces) shredded cheddar cheese**
**2 cups shredded lettuce**
**1 cup diced fresh tomatoes**
**1 can (2-1/4 ounces) sliced ripe olives, drained**
**1 medium red onion, sliced and separated into rings**
**1 can (4 ounces) chopped green chilies**
**1 cup (8 ounces) sour cream**
**1/2 medium ripe avocado, peeled and mashed**
**3 drops hot pepper sauce**

Cut rolls in half lengthwise; hollow out the bottoms, leaving 1-in. shells. Place rolls cut side up on a baking sheet. Broil 4-6 in. from the heat for 2 minutes or until toasted.

Combine the beans and taco seasoning; spread over bottom of rolls. Top with chicken, cheese, lettuce, tomatoes, olives, onion and chilies. Combine the sour cream, avocado and pepper sauce; spread over cut side of roll tops. Place over sandwiches. **Yield:** 4 servings.

## Turkey Bean Chili

*(Pictured at right)*

*Four kinds of beans and plenty of seasonings make this chunky chili a crowd-pleaser, especially when the weather's cool. Serve each bowlful with your favorite shredded cheese or a dollop of sour cream.* —*Judith Whitford East Aurora, New York*

✓ Uses less fat, sugar or salt. Includes Nutritional Analysis and Diabetic Exchanges.

**2 pounds ground turkey**
**1 cup chopped onion**
**1 cup chopped green pepper**
**4 cans (14-1/2 ounces *each*) stewed tomatoes, cut up**
**1 can (16 ounces) kidney beans, rinsed and drained**
**1 can (15-1/2 ounces) chili beans, undrained**
**1 can (15 ounces) pinto beans, rinsed and drained**
**1 can (15 ounces) black beans, rinsed and drained**
**1 jalapeno pepper, seeded and chopped**
**1 to 2 tablespoons chili powder**
**1 to 2 teaspoons ground cumin**
**1 teaspoon salt**
**1/4 teaspoon cayenne pepper**

In a Dutch oven or soup kettle, cook the turkey, onion and green pepper over medium heat until meat is no longer pink; drain. Stir in the remaining ingredients. Bring to a boil. Reduce heat; cover and simmer for 20 minutes. **Yield:** 15 servings.

**Nutritional Analysis:** One serving (1 cup) equals 230 calories, 5 g fat (2 g saturated fat), 48 mg cholesterol, 782 mg sodium, 27 g carbohydrate, 7 g fiber, 18 g protein. **Diabetic Exchanges:** 2 lean meat, 1-1/2 starch.

**Editor's Note:** When cutting and seeding hot peppers, use rubber or plastic gloves to protect your hands. Avoid touching your face.

## Blender Salad Dressing

*(Pictured at right)*

*Think from-scratch salad dressing is too time-consuming? Try this tangy creation that offers homemade taste in a hurry. I mix all the ingredients in a blender for a 10-minute topping that gives greens fabulous flavor.* —*Janice Connelley, Spring Creek, Nevada*

**1 cup vegetable oil**
**3/4 cup cider vinegar**
**1 medium onion, cut into wedges**
**1/2 cup ketchup**
**1/4 cup sugar**
**1 teaspoon salt**
**1 teaspoon ground mustard**
**1/4 teaspoon garlic powder**
**1/4 teaspoon pepper**

In a blender, combine all ingredients; cover and process until smooth. Store in the refrigerator. **Yield:** 2-3/4 cups.

## Cheesy Chicken Sandwiches

*My family and friends can't get enough of these skillet chicken sandwiches smothered with melted mozzarella cheese, green pepper and onion.* —*Jimmie Patterson Reynolds, Georgia*

**4 boneless skinless chicken breast halves**
**Salt and pepper to taste**
**1 tablespoon vegetable oil**
**1 cup chopped green pepper**
**1/2 cup chopped onion**
**4 slices mozzarella cheese**
**4 sandwich rolls, split and toasted**

Flatten chicken to 1/4-in. thickness. Season with salt and pepper. In a large skillet, cook chicken in oil for 5 minutes. Turn chicken.

Add green pepper and onion to skillet. Cook 5 minutes longer or until chicken juices run clear and vegetables are crisp-tender.

Spoon the vegetables over the chicken; top with the cheese. Remove from the heat; cover and let stand for 1 minute or until the cheese is melted. Serve on rolls. **Yield:** 4 servings.

Blender Salad Dressing
Turkey Bean Chili
Taco Po'Boys

# Chapter 13

# Timely Dishes for Two

MANY RAPID RECIPES are designed to feed a family of four...or more. But that can be too much food for newlyweds, empty nesters and others in small households.

If you cook for just a few people and don't like dealing with days of leftovers, this chapter is for you.

Enjoy flavorful entrees...delicious side dishes...tempting treats for dessert...satisfying snacks and more. No matter what fare you fix, it'll be perfectly portioned for downsized dining.

All of the following smaller-size recipes come together on the double, so they're twice as nice for time-crunched cooks.

**DOUBLY DELIGHTFUL.** Veggie-Stuffed Potatoes, Sweet 'n' Tangy Pork Chops and Seasoned Asparagus (all recipes on p. 194).

## Chocolate Mint Freeze

(Pictured below)

*This creamy five-ingredient treat is loaded with chocolate flavor and a hint of peppermint. Frosty servings are great for small get-togethers. Store any leftovers in the freezer for whenever your sweet tooth comes calling.*
*—Miriam Miller, Thorp, Wisconsin*

**1-1/2 cups cold milk**
**1 package (3.9 ounces) instant chocolate pudding mix**
**1/2 cup miniature semisweet chocolate chips**
**1 cup heavy whipping cream**
**1/4 teaspoon peppermint extract**

In a large bowl, whisk milk and pudding mix for 2 minutes; let stand for 2 minutes or until soft-set. Stir in chocolate chips. In a small mixing bowl, beat cream until it begins to thicken. Add peppermint extract; beat until soft peaks form. Fold into pudding.

Transfer to an ungreased 8-in. square dish. Cover and freeze for 2 hours or until firm. Remove from the freezer 15 minutes before cutting. **Yield:** 9 servings.

## Autumn Pork Tenderloin

(Pictured below)

*Sized right for two, this rustic and comforting entree is treated to a combination of apples, raisins and nuts. The fruit sauce adds great flavor. I serve this often, and when I double it for guests, it's always greeted with cheers.*
*—Tiffany Anderson-Taylor, Gulfport, Florida*

**1/2 teaspoon salt**
**1/4 teaspoon pepper**
**1 pork tenderloin (3/4 pound)**

**Chocolate Mint Freeze**
**Autumn Pork Tenderloin**

**1/2 cup apple juice**
**1 cup apple pie filling**
**1/4 cup raisins**
**1/4 cup chopped pecans**
**1/4 teaspoon ground cinnamon**

Rub salt and pepper over pork. Place in a large resealable plastic bag; add apple juice. Seal bag and turn to coat. Refrigerate for 30 minutes.

Drain and discard apple juice. Place pork on a rack in a roasting pan. Combine the pie filling, raisins, pecans and cinnamon; spoon over pork. Bake, uncovered, at 400° for 40-45 minutes or until a meat thermometer reads 160°. Let stand for 5 minutes before slicing. **Yield:** 2 servings.

## Smoked Salmon Pizzas

*These individual pizzas made from toasted pita breads are a tasty way to finish up extra smoked salmon for a swift snack or light lunch. Anyone who loves seafood is sure to request these cheesy rounds time and again.* —*Laura Davis, Ann Arbor, Michigan*

**2 pita breads (6 inches)**
**1/4 cup pizza sauce**
**1/4 pound smoked salmon, chopped**
**1 small red onion, halved and thinly sliced**
**1 cup (4 ounces) shredded mozzarella cheese**
**1/4 teaspoon dried oregano**

Place pitas on an ungreased baking sheet. Top with pizza sauce, salmon, onion, cheese and oregano. Bake at 425° for 7-10 minutes or until cheese is melted. **Yield:** 2 servings.

## Chicken Broccoli Supper

*This creamy, comforting meal doesn't require that you cook the chicken or macaroni first. I simply combine the ingredients, put the mixture in a baking dish and pop it in the oven.* —*Heather Oblinger, Gahanna, Ohio*

✓ Uses less fat, sugar or salt. Includes Nutritional Analysis and Diabetic Exchanges.

**1/2 pound boneless skinless chicken breasts, cubed**
**1-1/2 cups frozen broccoli florets**
**1/2 cup uncooked elbow macaroni**
**1/2 cup shredded cheddar cheese**
**1 can (10-3/4 ounces) condensed cream of chicken soup, undiluted**
**3/4 cup chicken broth**
**1/4 teaspoon garlic powder**
**1/4 teaspoon pepper**

In a large bowl, combine the chicken, broccoli, macaroni and cheese. Whisk the soup, broth, garlic powder and pepper; stir into chicken mixture. Transfer to a greased 1-1/2-qt. baking dish. Bake, uncovered, at 350° for 30 minutes.

Stir; bake 25-30 minutes longer or until chicken juices run clear and macaroni is tender. Let stand for 5 minutes before serving. **Yield:** 2 servings.

**Nutritional Analysis:** One serving (prepared with reduced-fat cheese, reduced-fat reduced-sodium soup and reduced-sodium broth) equals 403 calories, 10 g fat (6 g saturated fat), 98 mg cholesterol, 909 mg sodium, 34 g carbohydrate, 2 g fiber, 41 g protein. **Diabetic Exchanges:** 4 lean meat, 2 starch, 1 vegetable.

## Couch Potatoes

*Piled high with hearty toppings, these potatoes are always a favorite. They make an effortless meal-in-one and come together quickly in the microwave. Plus, they're a great way to use up any leftover cooked ham, chili or baked potatoes that I may have in the refrigerator.* —*Shary Geidner, Clear Lake, Iowa*

**2 large baking potatoes, baked**
**1 can (15 ounces) chili without beans**
**1/4 cup chopped green onions**
**1 jar (4 ounces) sliced mushrooms, drained**
**1 cup cubed fully cooked ham**
**1 cup (4 ounces) shredded cheddar cheese**
**Sour cream, optional**

Cut each potato in half lengthwise but not all the way through, leaving potato attached at the bottom. Push potatoes open and fluff pulp with a fork. Place on a microwave-safe plate.

Top each with the chili, onions, mushrooms, ham and cheese. Cover and microwave on high for 3 minutes or until cheese is melted. Top with sour cream if desired. **Yield:** 2 servings.

**Editor's Note:** This recipe was tested in an 850-watt microwave.

## Black Bean Soup

*I serve this simple soup with homemade bread and a green salad, and the compliments just keep pouring out of my husband. The recipe takes only about 30 minutes to prepare.* —*Cynthia Lepoutre, Spring Hill, Tennessee*

**1 large onion, chopped**
**2 garlic cloves, minced**
**1 can (14-1/2 ounces) chicken broth, *divided***
**1/2 teaspoon dried oregano**
**1/4 teaspoon dried thyme**
**1/4 teaspoon ground cumin**
**Dash cayenne pepper**
**1 can (15 ounces) black beans, rinsed and drained, *divided***

In a large saucepan, cook onion and garlic in 2 tablespoons of broth over medium heat until onion is tender. Stir in the oregano, thyme, cumin and cayenne; cook for 1 minute.

In a blender or food processor, cover and process half of the beans for 30 seconds; add to saucepan with the remaining beans and broth. Cook, uncovered, over low heat for 15 minutes or until heated through. **Yield:** 2 servings.

Double-Shell Tacos

## Double-Shell Tacos

*(Pictured above)*

*These two-shell tacos from our Test Kitchen home economists are twice the fun to eat. A warm pita spread with refried beans enfolds a crispy taco shell filled with seasoned ground beef. To top it off, simply add popular extras such as shredded cheddar cheese, sour cream and chopped veggies.*

**1/2 pound ground beef**
**2 tablespoons taco seasoning**
**1/3 cup water**
**1/2 cup refried beans**
**2 whole gyro-style pitas (6 inches)**
**2 taco shells**
**Toppings: chopped green onions, chopped tomatoes, sliced ripe olives, shredded cheddar cheese, sour cream *and/or* shredded lettuce, optional**

In a large skillet, cook beef over medium heat until no longer pink; drain. Stir in taco seasoning and water. Bring to a boil. Reduce heat; simmer, uncovered, for 3-4 minutes or until thickened.

Meanwhile, spread 1/4 cup refried beans over one side of each pita. Place on a microwave-safe plate; heat, uncovered, on high for 15-20 seconds or until warmed. Immediately wrap each pita around a taco shell. Fill with beef mixture. Serve with toppings of your choice. **Yield:** 2 servings.

## Honey Peach Cobbler

*We love peach cobbler, but we don't like the leftovers because they get soggy. This two-serving old-fashioned dessert is just the right size for my husband and me. Honey gives it an extra touch of sweetness.*
*—Diane Hixon, Niceville, Florida*

**4 canned peach halves**
**1/4 teaspoon ground cinnamon**
**4-1/2 teaspoons honey**
**1 tablespoon butter**
**1/2 cup all-purpose flour**
**1 teaspoon sugar**
**3/4 teaspoon baking powder**
**1/8 teaspoon salt**
**2 tablespoons shortening**
**3 to 4 tablespoons milk**
**Vanilla ice cream**

Place two peach halves in each of two ungreased 8-oz. custard cups. Sprinkle with cinnamon. Drizzle with honey and dot with butter. In a bowl, combine the flour, sugar, baking powder and salt. Cut in shortening until crumbly. Gradually add milk, tossing with a fork until mixture forms a ball. Drop by teaspoonfuls over peaches. Bake at 425° for 15-17 minutes or until golden brown. Serve with ice cream. **Yield:** 2 servings.

## Fried Apple Rings

*Four ingredients and a skillet are all that you'll need for these delightful apple rings. Serve them as a sweet side dish alongside pork...or top each warm helping with vanilla ice cream for a deliciously different dessert.* —*Mary Jane Ruther Trenton, New Jersey*

✓ Uses less fat, sugar or salt. Includes Nutritional Analysis and Diabetic Exchanges.

**1 tablespoon butter**
**1 tablespoon sugar**
**1-1/2 teaspoons lemon juice**
**1 medium tart apple, cored**

In a skillet, melt butter over medium heat. Stir in sugar and lemon juice. Cut the apple into four rings; add to skillet. Reduce heat. Cover and simmer for 10-15 minutes or until apple rings are tender, turning frequently. Serve warm. **Yield:** 2 servings.

**Nutritional Analysis:** One serving equals 116 calories, 6 g fat (4 g saturated fat), 15 mg cholesterol, 58 mg sodium, 17 g carbohydrate, 2 g fiber, trace protein. **Diabetic Exchanges:** 1 fruit, 1 fat.

## Beefy Chili Manicotti

*To create a sensational sauce for this manicotti stuffed with cheese and green chilies, all you have to do is jazz up a can of beef chili with sauteed onion and garlic. The zesty Italian-inspired dish tastes like you spent all afternoon in the kitchen but is actually fast and easy to make. You'll need less than 30 minutes for the prep work.*
—*Mary Vega, Fall River Mills, California*

**4 manicotti shells**
**2 tablespoons chopped onion**
**1 garlic clove, minced**
**1 tablespoon vegetable oil**
**1 can (15 ounces) chili with beans**
**1 egg, beaten**
**3/4 cup small-curd cottage cheese, drained**
**1/2 cup shredded American cheese, *divided***
**2 tablespoons chopped green chilies**

Cook the manicotti shells in boiling water for 5 minutes; drain and set aside. Meanwhile, in a skillet, saute the onion and garlic in oil until tender. Stir in the chili. Pour half of the chili mixture into a greased 1-qt. baking dish.

In a small bowl, combine egg, cottage cheese, 1/4 cup American cheese and chilies. Spoon into manicotti shells. Place over chili mixture. Top with remaining chili mixture. Cover and bake at 350° for 35 minutes. Uncover; sprinkle with remaining cheese. Bake 2-3 minutes longer or until cheese is melted. **Yield:** 2 servings.

## Cinnamon Coffee Bars

*(Pictured below)*

*I've made these bars for more than 40 years, and they're still a favorite. The recipe makes a small pan, so two people can enjoy a few and have some left to share.*
—*Marylou Crouch, Granite Falls, Washington*

**1/3 cup butter, softened**
**1 cup packed brown sugar**
**1 egg**
**1/3 cup hot strong brewed coffee**
**1-1/2 cups all-purpose flour**
**1 teaspoon baking powder**
**1 teaspoon ground cinnamon**
**1/4 teaspoon baking soda**
**1/4 teaspoon salt**
**1 cup (6 ounces) semisweet chocolate chips**
**1/2 cup chopped walnuts**
**GLAZE:**
**3/4 cup confectioners' sugar**
**1/4 teaspoon vanilla extract**
**3 to 4 teaspoons milk**

In a large mixing bowl, cream butter and brown sugar. Add egg; beat well. Beat in coffee. Combine the flour, baking powder, cinnamon, baking soda and salt; gradually add to creamed mixture.

Stir in chocolate chips and walnuts. Spread into a well-greased 8-in. square baking dish. Bake at 350° for 30-35 minutes or until a toothpick inserted near the center comes out clean.

In a small bowl, combine the confectioners' sugar, vanilla and enough milk to achieve a glaze consistency. Drizzle over warm bars. Cool completely on a wire rack before cutting. **Yield:** 1 dozen.

Cinnamon Coffee Bars

## Seasoned Asparagus

*(Pictured below and on page 188)*

*Our Test Kitchen used lemon juice and a pinch of mint to give a light fresh taste to tender asparagus.*

✓ Uses less fat, sugar or salt. Includes Nutritional Analysis and Diabetic Exchanges.

**1/2 pound fresh asparagus, trimmed**
**2 tablespoons water**
**1 tablespoon butter, melted**
**1/8 to 1/4 teaspoon dried mint**
**1/8 teaspoon salt**
**1/8 teaspoon lemon juice**
**Dash white pepper**

Place asparagus and water in a 1-qt. microwave-safe dish. Cover and microwave on high for 5 minutes or until crisp-tender; drain. Combine butter, mint, salt, lemon juice and pepper. Drizzle over asparagus; toss to coat. **Yield:** 2 servings.

**Nutritional Analysis:** One serving equals 41 calories, 3 g fat (2 g saturated fat), 8 mg cholesterol, 103 mg sodium, 2 g carbohydrate, 1 g fiber, 1 g protein. **Diabetic Exchanges:** 1 vegetable, 1/2 fat.

**Editor's Note:** This recipe was tested in a 1,100-watt microwave.

Veggie-Stuffed Potatoes
Sweet 'n' Tangy Pork Chops
Seasoned Asparagus

## Sweet 'n' Tangy Pork Chops

*(Pictured below left and on page 188)*

*I have fond memories of cooking with my mother when I was younger. In only about half an hour, she could make mouth-watering pork chops in a homemade barbecue sauce that I love. This simple yet delicious dish is still one of my all-time favorites.* —*Dennis Wolcott*
*Blossburg, Pennsylvania*

**2 bone-in pork loin chops (1 inch thick)**
**1 tablespoon vegetable oil**
**1/2 cup tomato sauce**
**1/4 cup packed brown sugar**
**1 tablespoon cider vinegar**
**3/4 teaspoon Worcestershire sauce**
**1/2 teaspoon celery salt**
**1/4 teaspoon ground nutmeg**
**1/4 teaspoon pepper**

In a large skillet, brown pork chops in oil. Combine the remaining ingredients; add to skillet. Bring to a boil. Reduce heat; simmer, uncovered, for 8-10 minutes or until pork juices run clear. Spoon sauce over pork chops. **Yield:** 2 servings.

## Veggie-Stuffed Potatoes

*(Pictured at left and on page 188)*

*Marinated artichoke hearts are an unusual but delicious addition to these impressive packed potatoes. They make a hearty side dish...or even a light meal. Bacon, broccoli, cheese and sour cream round out the savory flavor of these special potatoes.* —*Jennifer Andrzejewski*
*Grizzly Flats, California*

**2 medium baking potatoes**
**1/2 cup sour cream**
**1 cup (4 ounces) shredded cheddar cheese**
**1/2 cup frozen chopped broccoli, thawed**
**1/2 cup chopped marinated artichoke hearts**
**2 tablespoons crumbled cooked bacon**
**1/2 teaspoon garlic salt**
**1/4 teaspoon lemon-pepper seasoning**

Place potatoes on a microwave-safe plate; pierce several times with a fork. Microwave on high for 6-8 minutes or until tender. When cool enough to handle, cut a thin slice off the top of each potato and discard. Scoop out pulp of each, leaving a thin shell.

In a bowl, mash the pulp with sour cream. Stir in the cheese, broccoli, artichokes, bacon, garlic salt and lemon-pepper. Spoon into potato shells. Microwave, uncovered, on high for 1-2 minutes or until heated through. **Yield:** 2 servings.

**Editor's Note:** This recipe was tested in a 1,100-watt microwave.

Tropical Parfaits

## Tropical Parfaits

(Pictured above)

*When I'm entertaining guests, I'll often slice some bananas and include them with the mix of fruits in this layered pudding dessert. They add to the beautiful presentation and lend an extra bit of nutrition at the same time. Toasted almonds give the parfaits a pleasant crunch that contrasts nicely with the creamy ingredients.*
*—Nancy Stock, Minonk, Illinois*

**2 cups cold milk**
**1 package (3.4 ounces) instant coconut cream pudding mix**
**1 teaspoon grated lime peel, optional**
**1/2 cup pineapple tidbits**
**1/2 cup plus 1 tablespoon sliced almonds, toasted, *divided***
**1/2 cup sliced fresh strawberries**
**Whipped cream in a can**
**2 maraschino cherries**

In a bowl, whisk the milk and pudding mix for 2 minutes. Stir in lime peel if desired. In each of two 1-1/2-cup parfait glasses or dessert dishes, layer about 1/3 cup pudding mixture, 1/4 cup pineapple, 2 tablespoons almonds, 1/3 cup pudding mixture, 1/4 cup strawberries, 2 tablespoons almonds and the remaining pudding mixture. Top with whipped cream. Sprinkle with the remaining almonds. Garnish with cherries. **Yield:** 2 servings.

## Dilly Egg Salad

*I like to serve this tangy, creamy sandwich filling on bread that has been spread with Dijon mustard and topped with lettuce leaves and cheese. With a side of potato chips and a sliced apple, this egg salad sandwich is one of my favorite lunches and always satisfies my hunger when noontime rolls around.*
*—Phyllis Jarvinen*
*Webster, North Carolina*

**3 hard-cooked eggs, chopped**
**1/4 cup small-curd cottage cheese**
**1 celery rib, chopped**
**2 tablespoons dill pickle relish**
**3 tablespoons mayonnaise**
**1 teaspoon Dijon mustard**
**Salt and pepper to taste**
**4 slices bread**
**Lettuce leaves**

In a bowl, combine the eggs, cottage cheese, celery, relish, mayonnaise, mustard, salt and pepper. Spread 2/3 cup on two slices of bread; top with lettuce and remaining bread. **Yield:** 2 servings.

## Oregano Garlic Bread

*(Pictured at left)*

*When making spaghetti one night, I created this recipe to use up leftover sub rolls. It's simple to increase when you're having guests for dinner.* —*Laura Winemiller*
*Delta, Pennsylvania*

**4-1/2 teaspoons butter, softened**
**1/4 teaspoon garlic powder**
**1/8 teaspoon onion powder**
**1/8 teaspoon dried oregano**
**1/8 teaspoon paprika**
**1 submarine sandwich bun (about 6 inches), halved lengthwise**

In a small bowl, combine the butter and seasonings; spread over cut sides of bun. Place on an ungreased baking sheet. Bake at 350° for 10-15 minutes or until toasted. **Yield:** 2 servings.

## Breakfast Pitas

*My husband and I like to rely on these 15-minute pita pockets when we need a quick breakfast. For a complete meal, serve them with hash brown potatoes and fruit.*
—*Peggy Blattel, Cape Girardeau, Missouri*

**1 cup diced fully cooked ham**
**1/3 cup diced onion**
**1/3 cup diced green pepper**
**2 tablespoons butter**
**3 eggs, beaten**
**1/2 cup shredded cheddar cheese**
**1/2 teaspoon seasoned salt**
**1/4 teaspoon pepper**
**2 pita breads (6 inches), halved and warmed**

In a large skillet, saute the ham, onion and green pepper in butter until tender. Add the eggs; cook and stir over medium heat until eggs are almost set. Add the cheese, seasoned salt and pepper. Cook and stir until the eggs are completely set. Spoon into pita halves. **Yield:** 2 servings.

## Fruited Chicken Tossed Salad

*(Pictured above)*

*Almonds add crunch to this refreshing salad that comes together in just 15 minutes. A homemade citrus dressing complements chicken, peach and apricot slices tossed with lettuce and spinach.*
—*Dennis Vitale*
*New Preston, Connecticut*

**2 cups torn iceberg lettuce**
**1-1/2 cups torn spinach**
**1 cup julienned cooked chicken**
**1 medium peach, sliced**
**1 medium apricot, sliced**
**1/4 cup slivered almonds, toasted**
**CITRUS SALAD DRESSING:**
**1/4 cup orange juice**
**4-1/2 teaspoons olive oil**
**1 tablespoon cider vinegar**
**1 tablespoon honey**
**1/2 teaspoon dried tarragon**
**2 drops hot pepper sauce**
**Salt and pepper to taste**

In a large salad bowl, combine the lettuce, spinach, chicken, peach, apricot and almonds. In a jar with a tight-fitting lid, combine the dressing ingredients; shake well. Drizzle over salad and gently toss to coat. **Yield:** 2 servings.

## Pimiento Potato Salad

*If you're looking for a fuss-free way to prepare potato salad that doesn't serve a crowd, try this sure-to-please recipe. It gives you all the appeal of a favorite side dish but scales down the number of servings so you won't be stuck with leftovers.* —*Nancy Zimmerman*
*Cape May Court House, New Jersey*

**1/2 cup mayonnaise**
**1/4 cup chopped celery**
**2 tablespoons chopped onion**
**2 tablespoons chopped pimientos**
**1 tablespoon cider vinegar**
**2 teaspoons spicy brown mustard**
**1/2 teaspoon salt**
**1/4 teaspoon pepper**
**2 cups cubed cooked potatoes**
**2 tablespoons crumbled cooked bacon**

In a bowl, whisk mayonnaise, celery, onion, pimientos, vinegar, mustard, salt and pepper until smooth. Add potatoes and bacon; stir to coat. Refrigerate until serving. **Yield:** 2 servings.

## Chewy Chocolate Cookies

*Anyone who craves brownies will love these fudgy from-scratch treats for dessert or as an extra-special snack. The recipe makes fewer than a dozen large cookies that are chock-full of pecans and chocolate chunks. Ready to eat in just 30 minutes, the chewy goodies are a time-saving way to enjoy homemade sweets.* —*Miriam Miller*
*Thorp, Wisconsin*

- **8 squares (1 ounce *each*) semisweet chocolate, *divided***
- **2 tablespoons butter, softened**
- **1/3 cup packed brown sugar**
- **1 egg**
- **1/2 teaspoon vanilla extract**
- **1/4 cup all-purpose flour**
- **1/4 teaspoon baking powder**
- **1 cup chopped pecans**

In a microwave, melt four chocolate squares; cool to room temperature. Coarsely chop remaining chocolate; set aside.

In a small mixing bowl, cream butter and brown sugar. Beat in egg and vanilla. Add cooled chocolate; beat until blended.

Combine the flour and baking powder; gradually add to creamed mixture. Stir in the pecans and chopped chocolate.

Drop by 1/4 cupfuls onto an ungreased baking sheet. Bake at 350° for 10-12 minutes or until firm and tops are cracked. Let stand for 2 minutes before carefully removing to wire racks to cool completely. **Yield:** about 9 cookies.

## Cheddar Chicken Soup

*I add a few ingredients to condensed cream of chicken soup to create this rich, comforting concoction that tastes homemade. Brimming bowls of it are wonderful as a side dish, a meal starter...even a main course. Busy cooks like me also appreciate the fact that the 15-minute recipe is so simple to prepare.* —*Kathy Scott*
*Hemingford, Nebraska*

- **1/3 cup shredded carrot**
- **2 tablespoons finely chopped onion**
- **2 tablespoons butter**
- **1 can (10-3/4 ounces) condensed cream of chicken soup, undiluted**
- **1 cup water**
- **1/2 teaspoon Worcestershire sauce**
- **1/2 cup shredded cheddar cheese**

In a saucepan, saute carrot and onion in butter until tender. Stir in the soup, water and Worcestershire sauce. Bring to a boil. Reduce heat; stir in cheese until melted. **Yield:** 2 servings.

## Caramel Toffee Bombe

*(Pictured below)*

*I need only five ingredients to put together this easy, impressive and yummy dessert. Crushed gingersnap cookies form the full-flavored "shell" over vanilla ice cream that's dressed up with chopped toffee candy bars.* —*Cheryl Miller*
*Ft. Collins, Colorado*

- **3/4 cup crushed gingersnaps (about 14 cookies)**
- **3 tablespoons butter, melted**
- **1 pint vanilla ice cream, softened**
- **2 Heath candy bars (1.4 ounces *each*), chopped**
- **1/3 cup caramel ice cream topping, warmed**

Line a 3-cup bowl with plastic wrap. Combine cookie crumbs and butter; press onto the bottom and up the sides of prepared bowl.

In a large mixing bowl, beat ice cream and chopped candy bars until blended; spoon into crust. Cover and freeze until firm.

Trim edge of crust even with ice cream if necessary. Invert onto a serving platter; remove plastic wrap. Let stand 10 minutes before cutting. Drizzle with caramel topping. **Yield:** 4-6 servings.

Caramel Toffee Bombe

## Julienned Carrots 'n' Onion

*(Pictured below)*

*This slightly sweet combination of glazed carrots and sliced onion makes a tasty change of pace. It's popular every time I serve it, and no one suspects how easy the preparation is. I can make this side dish in 15 minutes.* —*Shirley Saeger Wisconsin Rapids, Wisconsin*

**1/3 cup water**
**2 medium carrots, julienned**
**1/2 medium onion, sliced**
**4 teaspoons butter**
**1 teaspoon sugar**
**1/4 teaspoon chicken bouillon granules**
**1 teaspoon cornstarch**
**1 tablespoon cold water**

In a saucepan, bring water to a boil. Add carrots, onion, butter, sugar and bouillon. Reduce heat; cover and simmer for 4-6 minutes or until vegetables are crisp-tender.

Combine cornstarch and cold water until smooth; stir into carrot mixture. Bring to a boil; cook and stir for 2 minutes or until thickened. **Yield:** 2 servings.

## Baked Salmon Fillets

*(Pictured below)*

*My aunt prepared this tender salmon one day when she invited me to stay for dinner. It was so delicious that I couldn't leave without the recipe.* —*Nella Parker Hersey, Michigan*

**Julienned Carrots 'n' Onion**
**Baked Salmon Fillets**

**1 salmon fillet (12 ounces)**
**1/4 cup butter, melted**
**1/3 cup mashed potato flakes**
**2 tablespoons dried vegetable flakes**
**1/4 teaspoon salt**
**1/4 teaspoon onion powder**
**1/4 teaspoon pepper**

Cut salmon in half. Place in a greased 11-in. x 7-in. x 2-in. baking dish. Drizzle with butter. Combine the remaining ingredients; press onto salmon. Bake, uncovered, at 350° for 30-35 minutes or until fish flakes easily with a fork. **Yield:** 2 servings.

## Chef's Salad

*I quickly toss together this smaller-size version of an all-time salad classic. Pair the fresh medley of veggies, sliced egg, deli meat and cheese with breadsticks to make a complete lunch.* —*Katie Anderson, Cheney, Washington*

**2 cups torn salad greens**
**2 green onions, chopped**
**1/4 cup chopped celery**
**4 ounces deli ham, julienned**
**4 ounces deli turkey, julienned**
**4 ounces Swiss cheese, julienned**
**1 hard-cooked egg, sliced**
**4 pitted ripe olives**
**Salad dressing of your choice**

On two serving plates, arrange the salad greens, onions, celery, ham, turkey, cheese, egg and olives. Serve with dressing. **Yield:** 2 servings.

## Warm Peach Dessert

*When you want a tempting treat that serves two, consider this peach cobbler-like delight. The warm-from-the-oven fruit is extra special with a scoop of vanilla ice cream or frozen yogurt on top.* —*Mamie Knox Punxsutawney, Pennsylvania*

✓ Uses less fat, sugar or salt. Includes Nutritional Analysis and Diabetic Exchanges.

**2 cans (one 15-1/4 ounces, one 8-1/2 ounces) sliced peaches**
**2 teaspoons cornstarch**
**2 tablespoons graham cracker crumbs**
**1/8 teaspoon ground cinnamon**
**Dash ground nutmeg**
**2 teaspoons butter, melted**

Drain peaches, reserving 1/2 cup syrup. Place peaches in a greased 1-qt. baking dish. In a small saucepan, combine cornstarch and reserved peach syrup until smooth. Bring to a boil; cook and stir for 1 minute or until thickened. Pour over peaches.

Combine graham cracker crumbs, cinnamon and nutmeg; stir in butter. Sprinkle over peaches. Bake, uncovered, at 350° for 10-15 minutes or until the topping is lightly browned. **Yield:** 2 servings.

**Nutritional Analysis:** One 1-cup serving (prepared

with reduced-sugar peaches and reduced-fat margarine) equals 212 calories, 3 g fat (trace saturated fat), 0 cholesterol, 99 mg sodium, 45 g carbohydrate, 3 g fiber, trace protein. **Diabetic Exchanges:** 1-1/2 starch, 1-1/2 fruit.

## Streusel Sweet Potatoes

*When I was visiting my husband's family in North Carolina, I got the chance to sample this wonderful Southern specialty. A sugary nut topping sweetens the comforting creation that's spiced with cinnamon and nutmeg.* —*Marilyn Hallman Mt. Prospect, Illinois*

**1-1/2 cups mashed sweet potatoes**
**1/4 cup milk**
**1 egg, lightly beaten**
**2 tablespoons sugar**
**2 tablespoons butter, melted**
**1/2 teaspoon ground cinnamon**
**1/2 teaspoon ground nutmeg**
**1/2 teaspoon vanilla extract**
**TOPPING:**
**1/4 cup chopped pecans**
**1/4 cup packed brown sugar**
**1 tablespoon all-purpose flour**
**1 tablespoon butter, melted**

In a large bowl, combine first eight ingredients. Spoon into a greased 3-cup baking dish. Combine topping ingredients; sprinkle over the potato mixture. Bake, uncovered, at 350° for 30-35 minutes or until a thermometer inserted near the center reads 160°. **Yield:** 2 servings.

## Cheesy Beef Pasta

*A satisfying supper's just 15 minutes away with this can't-miss stovetop dish. Four cheeses blend with the ground beef and tomatoes for a pasta entree that's rich and flavorful. Plus, since the recipe yields only two servings, you don't have to deal with lots of leftovers.*
—*Janalee Watkins, Vernal, Utah*

**1 cup uncooked penne *or* medium tube pasta**
**1/2 pound ground beef**
**1 can (14-1/2 ounces) diced tomatoes, undrained**
**1/2 cup chopped green onions**
**2 tablespoons cream cheese**
**1/4 cup *each* shredded Swiss, cheddar and Parmesan cheese**
**1/4 to 1/2 teaspoon salt**

Cook the pasta according to package directions. Meanwhile, in a large skillet, cook the beef over medium heat until no longer pink; drain. Stir in tomatoes. Bring to a boil.

Reduce heat; simmer, uncovered, for 3 minutes. Stir in the onions and cream cheese. Cook and stir until cream cheese is melted. Drain the pasta; add to the beef mixture. Stir in the shredded cheeses and salt. **Yield:** 2 servings.

Lemon Cheesecake

## Lemon Cheesecake

*(Pictured above)*

*A homemade chocolate crust complements the light lemon flavor of this delectable little dessert. One of my friends gave me the recipe, which is perfect for birthday dinners, anniversaries...just about any occasion.* —*Cathy Chan Calgary, Alberta*

**1/2 cup crushed chocolate wafers**
**2 tablespoons butter, melted**
**1 package (8 ounces) cream cheese, softened**
**1/2 cup sugar**
**1/2 cup sour cream**
**2 tablespoons lemon juice**
**1 tablespoon all-purpose flour**
**1 teaspoon grated lemon peel**
**1/2 teaspoon vanilla extract**
**1 egg, lightly beaten**

In a small bowl, combine the wafer crumbs and butter. Press onto the bottom of a greased 6-in. springform pan. Place pan on a baking sheet. Bake at 350° for 7-8 minutes or until set. Cool on a wire rack.

In a mixing bowl, beat the cream cheese and sugar until smooth. Beat in the sour cream, lemon juice, flour, lemon peel and vanilla. Add egg; beat on low speed just until combined. Pour over crust.

Return pan to baking sheet. Bake for 35-40 minutes or until center is almost set. Cool on a wire rack for 10 minutes. Carefully run a knife around edge of pan to loosen; cool 1 hour longer. Chill for 8 hours or overnight. Remove sides of pan before cutting. Refrigerate leftovers. **Yield:** 2-4 servings.

# Chapter 14

# Delectable Desserts

SWEETLY COMPLETE your dinners with one of these time-easing treats. Folks will think you fussed when you present these impressive—yet easy-to-make—cakes, cookies, pies and other delights.

Each irresistible dessert featured here looks and tastes special enough to serve to weekend company. Yet they're so fast to fix, you'll find yourself whipping them up for family and drop-in guests during the week.

The luscious results are sure to have them asking for more!

**TEMPTING TREATS.** Clockwise from top right: Sweetheart Coconut Cookies, Chocolate Cheesecake Pie and Strawberry Tiramisu Trifle (all recipes on p. 206).

## Berry Cookie Torte

*Our Test Kitchen bakers created this red, white and blue dessert that's perfect for patriotic and summer get-togethers. To assemble the torte, they layered large cookies with a smooth pudding mixture and berries. Then they piped star shapes at random on top using the pudding mixture and whipped topping. In between the stars, they arranged purchased cookies and more berries.*

- **1 tube (18 ounces) refrigerated sugar cookie dough**
- **1 package (8 ounces) cream cheese, softened**
- **1/2 cup confectioners' sugar**
- **1 cup cold milk**
- **1 package (3.4 ounces) instant vanilla pudding mix**
- **2 cups whipped topping, *divided***
- **1 cup fresh blueberries**
- **1 cup fresh raspberries**
- **8 miniature Milano cookies**

Divide dough into three portions. Cover and chill two portions. On a floured surface, roll remaining dough into a 9-in. circle, about 1/8 in. thick. Transfer to an ungreased baking sheet. Bake at 350° for 7-9 minutes or until lightly browned. Cool for 2 minutes; carefully remove to a wire rack to cool. Repeat twice.

In a large mixing bowl, beat cream cheese and confectioners' sugar. In a bowl, whisk milk and pudding mix for 2 minutes; beat into cream cheese mixture. Fold in 1 cup whipped topping. Cover and chill for at least 15 minutes.

Place one cookie layer on a serving plate. Top with 3/4 cup pudding mixture and 1/3 cup each blueberries and raspberries. Repeat. Top with remaining cookie layer; spread with 1/2 cup pudding mixture.

Pipe remaining whipped topping and pudding mixture over the top. Garnish with cookies and remaining berries. Serve immediately. **Yield:** 8 servings.

## Cinnamon Apple Coffee Cake

*(Pictured at right)*

*Tender apples add nice flavor to this fast-to-fix cake. It was a family favorite served warm after church on Sunday mornings. —Gertrude Hart, Oak Creek, Wisconsin*

- **1 package (9 ounces) yellow cake mix**
- **1 package (3.4 ounces) instant vanilla pudding mix**
- **2 eggs**
- **1/2 cup sour cream**
- **1/4 cup butter, melted**
- **2 medium tart apples, peeled and shredded**
- **1/2 cup sugar**
- **1/4 cup chopped walnuts**
- **1 teaspoon ground cinnamon**

In a mixing bowl, beat the cake mix, pudding mix, eggs, sour cream and butter on medium speed for 2 minutes. Pour half into a greased 8-in. square baking dish. Top with apples. Combine the sugar, nuts and cinnamon; sprinkle half over the apples. Top with remaining batter and sugar mixture. Bake at 350° for 50-55 minutes or until a toothpick inserted near the center comes out clean. Cool on a wire rack. **Yield:** 9 servings.

## Pear Gingerbread Cake

*(Pictured at right)*

*You'll need just four ingredients to stir up this sweet gingerbread treat topped with a layer of sliced pears. It's a wonderful way to dress up a packaged cake mix. If you prefer, use fresh ripe pears instead of canned. —Cindy Reams, Philipsburg, Pennsylvania*

- **1/4 cup butter, melted**
- **2 cans (15-1/4 ounces *each*) sliced pears, drained and patted dry**
- **1/3 cup sugar**
- **1 package (14-1/2 ounces) gingerbread cake mix**

Spread the butter in a 9-in. square baking dish. Arrange pear slices in rows over the butter. Sprinkle with sugar. Prepare cake mix batter according to package directions. Carefully pour over the pears. Bake at 350° for 30-35 minutes or until a toothpick inserted near the center comes out clean. Cool on a wire rack for 10 minutes before inverting onto a serving plate. **Yield:** 9 servings.

## Broiled Coconut Orange Cake

*The ingredients for this delectable dessert come right from the pantry. The little cake is great for nights when you want something sweet. —Lynda McCormick, Burkburnett, Texas*

- **1 cup sugar**
- **1 cup all-purpose flour**
- **1/4 teaspoon baking soda**
- **1/8 teaspoon salt**
- **1 can (11 ounces) mandarin oranges, drained**
- **1 egg**

**TOPPING:**

- **1/2 cup packed brown sugar**
- **2 tablespoons butter, cubed**
- **2 tablespoons milk**
- **3/4 cup flaked coconut**

In a mixing bowl, combine the sugar, flour, baking soda and salt. Add mandarin oranges and egg; beat on medium speed for 2 minutes. Pour into a greased 8-in. square baking pan. Bake at 350° for 30-40 minutes or until a toothpick inserted near the center comes out clean. Cool on a wire rack for 15 minutes.

Meanwhile, in a saucepan, combine the brown sugar, butter and milk. Bring to a boil over medium heat, stirring occasionally. Cook and stir for 2 minutes or until sugar is dissolved.

Remove from the heat; stir in coconut. Pour over warm cake. Broil 6 in. from the heat for 1-2 minutes or until the top is browned. Cool on a wire rack. **Yield:** 9 servings.

Cinnamon Apple Coffee Cake
Pear Gingerbread Cake

Festive Fruit Tart
Chocolate Cherry Cobbler
Lime Coconut Triangles

## Strawberry Pie Ice Cream

*Our home economists dressed up store-bought ice cream with whipped topping, nuts, chocolate chips and pieces of a graham cracker crust. One scoop won't be enough!*

**1 quart strawberry ice cream**
**1 cup whipped topping**
**1/3 cup coarsely chopped cashews**
**1/4 cup miniature semisweet chocolate chips**
**1 graham cracker crust (9 inches), broken into large pieces**

In a mixing bowl, beat ice cream until slightly softened. Fold in the whipped topping, cashews and chocolate chips until blended. Very gently fold in graham cracker crust pieces. Serve immediately. Store leftovers in a freezer container and freeze. **Yield:** 8-10 servings.

## Festive Fruit Tart

*(Pictured at left)*

*"Wow!" is what you'll hear when you serve this impressive dessert to company. The tart is not only pretty, it's also easy to assemble.* —*Nancy Adams, Hancock, New Hampshire*

**Pastry for single-crust pie (9 inches)**
**1 package (8 ounces) cream cheese, softened**
**3 tablespoons sugar**
**1 teaspoon vanilla extract**
**3/4 teaspoon almond extract, *divided***
**1 cup fresh blueberries**
**1 cup fresh raspberries**
**1 medium ripe peach *or* nectarine, peeled and sliced**
**2 tablespoons apricot preserves**

Press pastry onto the bottom and up the sides of an ungreased 9-in. tart pan with a removable bottom; trim edges. Generously prick the bottom with a fork. Bake at 450° for 10-12 minutes or until golden brown. Cool completely on a wire rack.

In a small mixing bowl, beat the cream cheese, sugar, vanilla and 1/2 teaspoon almond extract until smooth; spread over crust. Arrange fruit over cream cheese mixture. In a small microwave-safe bowl, combine apricot preserves and remaining almond extract. Microwave, uncovered, on high for 20-30 seconds or until warm; brush over fruit. Chill until serving. **Yield:** 10-12 servings.

## Chocolate Cherry Cobbler

*(Pictured at left)*

*This is my "dessert version" of chocolate-covered cherries. Our family loves it, and the preparation's quick using a boxed mix.* —*Marilou Robinson, Portland, Oregon*

**4 cans (15 ounces *each*) pitted dark sweet cherries, well drained**
**1 package (18-1/4 ounces) chocolate cake mix**
**1/2 cup water**
**1 egg**
**3 tablespoons vegetable oil**
**Vanilla ice cream**

Place the cherries in a greased 13-in. x 9-in. x 2-in. baking dish. In a large bowl, combine the cake mix, water, egg and oil; spread over cherries. Bake at 350° for 45-50 minutes or until a toothpick inserted near the center comes out with moist crumbs. Serve warm with ice cream. **Yield:** 12-15 servings.

## Lime Coconut Triangles

*(Pictured at left)*

*This refreshing recipe is a tempting twist on traditional lemon bars. With a nutty crust and smooth lime filling, the yummy treats are elegant dusted with sugar and cut into triangles.* —*Michele Savoldi, Delaware, Ohio*

**1 cup all-purpose flour**
**3/4 cup finely chopped flaked coconut, *divided***
**1/3 cup confectioners' sugar**
**1/4 cup finely chopped pecans**
**1/3 cup butter, melted**
**2 eggs**
**1 cup sugar**
**1/4 cup lime juice**
**1-1/2 teaspoons grated lime peel**
**1/4 teaspoon baking powder**
**Additional confectioners' sugar**

In a small bowl, combine the flour, 1/4 cup coconut, confectioners' sugar and pecans. Stir in the butter. Press into a greased 8-in. square baking dish. Bake at 350° for 15 minutes.

Meanwhile, in a large bowl, whisk the eggs. Stir in the sugar, lime juice, lime peel, baking powder and remaining coconut. Pour over crust.

Bake for 15-20 minutes or until edges are light golden brown. Cool on a wire rack. Dust with confectioners' sugar. Cut into squares; cut in half to make triangles. **Yield:** 1-1/2 dozen.

### Dusting Desserts

DECORATING bars or cakes with confectioners' sugar not only creates a pretty presentation, it adds an extra touch of sweetness to your treat.

Start by putting the sugar in a metal sieve or sifter. Then shake or sift the sugar over the baked and cooled dessert.

To make a fancy pattern, lay a purchased paper doily over the top of the dessert. Sift an even layer of sugar over the entire top, then lift the doily straight up, leaving the pattern on the dessert.

## S'more Bars

*A chewy oatmeal crust is topped with miniature marshmallows and chocolate chips to create these tasty treats. They're a great snack when we're traveling in the car and need a little pick-me-up. —Bob and Laura Frohmader Kendall, Wisconsin*

**1 cup quick-cooking oats**
**1/2 cup all-purpose flour**
**1/2 cup packed brown sugar**
**1/4 teaspoon salt**
**1/4 teaspoon baking soda**
**1/2 cup butter, melted**
**2 cups miniature marshmallows**
**1/2 cup milk chocolate chips**

In a bowl, combine the first five ingredients; stir in butter until crumbly. Press into a greased 11-in. x 7-in. x 2-in. baking dish.

Bake at 350° for 10 minutes. Sprinkle with marshmallows and chips. Bake 5-7 minutes longer or until marshmallows begin to brown. Cool on a wire rack; cut into bars. **Yield:** 1 dozen.

## Sweetheart Coconut Cookies

*(Pictured at right and on page 201)*

*Ruby-red jam and colored sugar add festive flair to these crisp sandwich cookies that are nice for Valentine's Day. My husband loves coconut, so I'm always looking for new recipes to serve on his birthday or holidays. —Jo Ellen Helmlinger, Columbus, Ohio*

**1 cup flaked coconut**
**1 cup sugar**
**3/4 cup cold butter**
**2-1/4 cups all-purpose flour**
**2 eggs, lightly beaten**
**1/2 teaspoon vanilla extract**
**GLAZE:**
**3/4 cup confectioners' sugar**
**1 tablespoon water**
**1/2 teaspoon vanilla extract**
**Red colored sugar, optional**
**1/2 cup seedless raspberry jam**

In a food processor or blender, place the coconut and sugar. Cover and process until coconut is coarsely chopped; set aside. In a large bowl, cut the butter into flour until crumbly. Stir in coconut mixture. Stir in eggs and vanilla.

On a lightly floured surface, roll out dough to 1/8-in. thickness. Cut with a 2-1/2-in. heart-shaped cookie cutter dipped in flour. Using a 1-in. heart-shaped cookie cutter, cut out the center of half of the cookies. Reroll the small cutouts if desired. Place solid and cutout cookies 1 in. apart on greased baking sheets. Bake at 375° for 7-9 minutes or until edges are lightly browned. Remove to wire racks.

Meanwhile, in a small bowl, combine the confectioners' sugar, water and vanilla; brush over the warm cookies with the cutout centers. Immediately sprinkle with colored sugar if desired. Spread 1/2 teaspoon jam over the bottom of each solid cookie; place cookies with cutout centers over jam. **Yield:** about 3-1/2 dozen.

## Strawberry Tiramisu Trifle

*(Pictured at right and on page 200)*

*We do a lot of entertaining, and I like to make this easy trifle when I want to impress people. Berries make it different from a traditional tiramisu. —Tammy Irvine Whitby, Ontario*

**1 quart fresh strawberries**
**1-1/4 cups cold milk**
**1 package (3.4 ounces) instant vanilla pudding mix**
**1 package (8 ounces) cream cheese, softened**
**4 tablespoons strong brewed coffee, room temperature, *divided***
**2 cups whipped topping**
**1 package (3 ounces) ladyfingers, split**
**6 squares (1 ounce *each*) bittersweet chocolate, grated**

Set aside three strawberries for garnish; slice the remaining strawberries. In a bowl, whisk the milk and pudding mix for 2 minutes. Let stand for 2 minutes or until soft-set.

In a large mixing bowl, beat cream cheese until smooth; gradually beat in 2 tablespoons coffee. Beat in pudding. Fold in whipped topping.

Brush the remaining coffee over ladyfingers. Line the bottom of a 3-qt. trifle or glass serving bowl with half of the ladyfingers. Top with half of the sliced berries, grated chocolate and pudding mixture; repeat layers. Cut reserved berries in half; place on trifle. Cover and refrigerate for 4 hours or overnight. **Yield:** 12 servings.

## Chocolate Cheesecake Pie

*(Pictured at right and on page 201)*

*My family and friends rave about this rich pie that starts with a ready-made graham cracker crust. The smooth slices are especially good topped with raspberry or cherry pie filling. For an elegant accent, garnish them with chocolate leaf dessert decorations. —Sandy Schwartz Brooklyn, New York*

**1 package (8 ounces) cream cheese, softened**
**1/4 cup butter, softened**
**1/3 cup sugar**
**1-1/2 teaspoons vanilla extract**
**1-1/2 cups milk chocolate chips, melted and cooled**
**1 carton (8 ounces) frozen whipped topping, thawed**
**1 graham cracker crust (9 inches)**
**Chocolate leaf dessert decorations**

In a large mixing bowl, beat the cream cheese, butter, sugar and vanilla until smooth. Beat in melted chocolate. Fold in whipped topping. Spoon into crust. Cover and chill until serving. Garnish with chocolate leaves. **Yield:** 6-8 servings.

Sweetheart Coconut Cookies
Chocolate Cheesecake Pie
Strawberry Tiramisu Trifle

Neapolitan Cake
Fluffy Lemon-Lime Pie
Sherbet Sunrise

## Neapolitan Cake

*(Pictured at left)*

*A good friend of mine gave me this surprisingly easy recipe that relies on a box mix. I like the pretty three-color cake for special events and even birthday parties. For extra flavor, add some strawberry extract to the pink portion of the batter.*
*—Marianne Waldman, Brimfield, Illinois*

**1 package (18-1/4 ounces) yellow cake mix**
**1 cup water**
**1/4 cup vegetable oil**
**3 eggs**
**8 to 10 drops red food coloring**
**1/4 cup chocolate syrup**
**1 tablespoon baking cocoa**
**Confectioners' sugar, optional**

In a large mixing bowl, combine the cake mix, water, oil and eggs. Beat on medium speed for 2 minutes. Divide batter into three equal portions.

Pour one portion into a greased 10-in. fluted tube pan. Stir red food coloring into another portion; carefully spoon into pan. Stir the chocolate syrup and cocoa into the remaining batter; carefully spoon into the pan. Do not swirl.

Bake at 350° for 40-45 minutes or until a toothpick inserted near the center comes out clean. Cool for 10 minutes before removing from the pan to a wire rack to cool completely. Dust with confectioners' sugar if desired. **Yield:** 12-16 servings.

## Sherbet Sunrise

*(Pictured at left)*

Olan Mills

*This frozen dessert is an attractive change of pace from ice cream cakes. Scoops of pineapple, raspberry and lime sherbet top a crunchy crust of rice cereal spread with whipped topping. To finish, I add extra crumbs.*
*—Barbara Thomas*
*Mankato, Kansas*

**1 cup butter, melted**
**6 cups crisp rice cereal, finely crushed**
**3/4 cup packed brown sugar**
**1 carton (8 ounces) whipped topping, thawed**
**3 tablespoons sugar**
**1 teaspoon vanilla extract**
**1 pint *each* pineapple, raspberry and lime sherbet**

In a bowl, combine the butter, cereal and brown sugar until crumbly. Set aside 3/4 cup for topping. Press remaining crumb mixture into an ungreased 13-in. x 9-in. x 2-in. dish.

In another bowl, combine whipped topping, sugar and vanilla. Carefully spread over crust. Arrange small scoops of sherbet over the top. Sprinkle with reserved crumb mixture. Cover and freeze until firm. **Yield:** 12-15 servings.

## Fluffy Lemon-Lime Pie

*(Pictured at left)*

*You can't go wrong with this refreshing treat. Simply mix together three ingredients, put the combination into a prepared crust and pop it in the refrigerator.*
*—Mrs. C.G. Rowland, Chattanooga, Tennessee*

**1 envelope (.13 ounce) unsweetened lemon-lime soft drink mix**
**1 can (14 ounces) sweetened condensed milk**
**1 carton (8 ounces) frozen whipped topping, thawed**
**1 graham cracker crust (9 inches)**

In a large bowl, dissolve soft drink mix in milk; fold in whipped topping. Spoon into crust. Cover and refrigerate for 3 hours or until set. **Yield:** 6-8 servings.

## Banana-Nut Bundt Cake

*This eye-appealing cake has a temptingly tropical twist in every slice, thanks to the chopped bananas, pineapple bits and coconut.*
*—June Yeates, Bradley, Illinois*

**3 cups all-purpose flour**
**2 cups sugar**
**1 teaspoon baking soda**
**1 teaspoon ground cinnamon**
**3 eggs, beaten**
**1 cup vegetable oil**
**2 cups finely chopped ripe bananas (about 3 medium)**
**1 can (8 ounces) crushed pineapple, undrained**
**1-1/2 teaspoons vanilla extract**
**1/2 cup flaked coconut**
**1 cup chopped nuts**

In a large bowl, combine the flour, sugar, baking soda and cinnamon. In another bowl, combine the eggs, oil, bananas, pineapple and vanilla; stir into dry ingredients just until combined. Fold in coconut and nuts. Pour into a greased 10-in. fluted tube pan.

Bake at 350° for 60-70 minutes or until a toothpick inserted near the center comes out clean. Cool for 10 minutes before removing cake from pan to a wire rack to cool completely. **Yield:** 12-16 servings.

### Picking a Tube Pan

A tube pan is a round pan with deep sides and a hollow tube in the center. Many folks call it an angel food cake pan since it is often used for baking angel food cakes. It can also be used for pound and chiffon cakes. Some tube pans have a removable bottom piece and others do not.

A fluted tube pan, which is also called a Bundt pan, has curved fluted sides and is used for baking cakes and coffee cakes.

While some recipes will work in either pan, others will not. For example, angel food cake bakes nicely in a tube pan but not a fluted tube pan.

## Raspberry Chocolate Torte

*(Pictured at right)*

*This recipe is constantly requested by family and friends. Feel free to substitute other berries.* —*Janis Murphy*
*Redondo Beach, California*

**1 package (18-1/4 ounces) devil's food cake mix**
**1 package (8 ounces) cream cheese, softened**
**1/2 cup sugar**
**1 teaspoon vanilla extract**
**1 cup finely chopped pecans**
**2 cups heavy whipping cream, whipped**
**2 pints fresh raspberries**
**1/2 cup pecan halves**

Prepare and bake the cake according to package directions, using two 9-in. round baking pans. Cool for 10 minutes before removing from pans to wire racks to cool completely.

In a large mixing bowl, beat cream cheese, sugar and vanilla until smooth; stir in chopped pecans. Fold in whipped cream. Split each cake into two horizontal layers. Place one bottom layer on a serving plate; top with a fourth of the cream cheese mixture.

Arrange 1 cup raspberries over filling; repeat layers three times. Garnish with pecan halves. Refrigerate until serving. **Yield:** 12-16 servings.

## Creamy Cappuccino Mousse

*(Pictured at right)*

*This smooth coffee mousse is simple to prepare and absolutely delicious. I also think it would be good layered with pound cake in a trifle bowl.* —*Brenda Jackson*
*Garden City, Kansas*

✓ Uses less fat, sugar or salt. Includes Nutritional Analysis and Diabetic Exchanges.

**1 package (8 ounces) cream cheese, softened**
**1/2 cup cold milk**
**1 cup strong brewed coffee, room temperature**
**1 package (3.4 ounces) instant vanilla pudding mix**
**1/4 teaspoon ground cinnamon**
**1 carton (8 ounces) frozen whipped topping, thawed, *divided***
**Additional ground cinnamon**

In a large mixing bowl, beat cream cheese until smooth. Gradually beat in milk until blended. Gradually beat in coffee. Add pudding mix and cinnamon; whisk for 2 minutes. Let stand for 5 minutes or until soft-set. Fold in 2 cups whipped topping. Spoon into six dessert dishes. Refrigerate until set. Garnish with remaining whipped topping and additional cinnamon. **Yield:** 6 servings.

**Nutritional Analysis:** One 3/4-cup serving (prepared with fat-free cream cheese, fat-free milk, sugar-free pudding mix and reduced-fat whipped topping) equals 144 calories, 5 g fat (5 g saturated fat), 3 mg cholesterol, 414 mg sodium, 15 g carbohydrate, trace fiber, 6 g protein. **Diabetic Exchanges:** 1 starch, 1 fat.

## Dutch Rhubarb Pie

*(Pictured at right)*

*I love mixing rhubarb with different fruits, combining its tart goodness with something sweet. This yummy pie begins with a convenient prepared crust and is filled with rhubarb and fresh raspberries. For an extra-special finish, I sprinkle on a streusel topping.* —*Pam Cheney*
*Onalaska, Washington*

**Pastry for single-crust pie (9 inches)**
**3 cups chopped fresh *or* frozen rhubarb**
**2 cups fresh raspberries**
**3/4 cup sugar**
**3 tablespoons all-purpose flour**
**1 teaspoon vanilla extract**
**1 egg, beaten**
**1/4 teaspoon ground nutmeg**
**TOPPING:**
**1/3 cup all-purpose flour**
**1/4 cup packed brown sugar**
**3 tablespoons butter, melted**

Line a 9-in. pie plate with pastry. Trim to 1/2 in. beyond edge of plate; flute edges. In a bowl, combine the rhubarb, raspberries, sugar, flour, vanilla and egg. Pour into crust; sprinkle with nutmeg. In a small bowl, combine the topping ingredients; sprinkle over filling.

Bake at 350° for 35-40 minutes or until filling is set and crust is golden brown (if needed, cover edges loosely with foil during the last 10 minutes to prevent overbrowning). Cool on a wire rack. **Yield:** 6-8 servings.

**Editor's Note:** If using frozen rhubarb, measure rhubarb while still frozen, then thaw completely. Drain in a colander, but do not press liquid out.

## Ladyfinger Fruit Dessert

*A rich mixture of cream cheese and marshmallow creme alternates with sliced bananas and peaches in this nut-topped treat. My daughter, Laura, and I assembled the dessert in a snap and really enjoyed it.* —*Pamela Shields*
*St. Charles, Missouri*

**1 package (8 ounces) cream cheese, softened**
**1 jar (7 ounces) marshmallow creme**
**1 package (3 ounces) ladyfingers**
**2 large firm bananas, cut into 1/4-inch slices**
**2 tablespoons flaked coconut**
**1 cup fresh *or* frozen sliced peaches**
**2 tablespoons chopped pecans, *divided***
**9 maraschino cherries, well drained**

In a small mixing bowl, beat the cream cheese and marshmallow creme until smooth. Arrange the ladyfingers in a single layer in an ungreased 8-in. square dish.

Spread with a third of the cream cheese mixture. Top with the bananas and coconut. Spread with a third of the cream cheese mixture. Top with peaches and half of the pecans. Spread with remaining cream cheese mixture; sprinkle with remaining pecans. Garnish with cherries. Refrigerate for 1 hour before cutting. **Yield:** 9 servings.

Raspberry Chocolate Torte
Creamy Cappuccino Mousse
Dutch Rhubarb Pie

Raisin Apple Tartlets
Harvest Dessert
Walnut Fudge Pie

## Pineapple Sauce for Cake

*Dressing up slices of purchased angel food or pound cake is easy with this light and fruity sauce. For a yummy variation, replace the orange marmalade with apricot preserves. You could also top each serving with ice cream or frozen yogurt as an added treat.* —*Donna Howard*
*Stoughton, Wisconsin*

**1 tablespoon sugar**
**2 teaspoons cornstarch**
**1 can (20 ounces) crushed pineapple, undrained**
**1/4 cup orange marmalade**
**1 angel food *or* pound cake, sliced**

In a small saucepan, combine the sugar, cornstarch, pineapple and orange marmalade until blended; bring to a boil. Reduce the heat; cook and stir for 2 minutes or until thickened. Cool. Serve with the cake. **Yield:** 2-1/3 cups.

## Raisin Apple Tartlets

*(Pictured at left)*

*I always get a kiss on the cheek when I make these individual pie-like treats for my husband. They're so easy to prepare, I can finish them in 15 minutes. If you like, add a dollop of whipped topping.* —*Claudia Jean Griffin*
*Beaver, Pennsylvania*

**4 cups sliced peeled tart apples**
**1/2 cup packed brown sugar**
**1/4 cup raisins**
**1/4 teaspoon ground cinnamon**
**3 tablespoons butter**
**1 tablespoon all-purpose flour**
**6 individual graham cracker shells**

In a large skillet, cook the apples, brown sugar, raisins and cinnamon in butter over medium heat until tender. Stir in the flour until blended.

Bring to a boil; cook and stir for 1 minute or until thickened. Spoon into shells. Serve warm or chilled. **Yield:** 6 servings.

## Harvest Dessert

*(Pictured at left)*

*Candy corn and tinted frosting form cute cornhusks on this dessert that's fun for harvest parties and other autumn get-togethers. If I'll be serving it on a busy day, I'll layer the pumpkin filling, whipped topping and chocolate wafers the night before.* —*Janine Freeman*
*Blaine, Washington*

**1 envelope unflavored gelatin**
**2/3 cup milk**
**1 can (15 ounces) solid-pack pumpkin**
**1 cup packed brown sugar**
**1/2 teaspoon salt**
**1/2 teaspoon *each* ground ginger, cinnamon and nutmeg**
**4 egg yolks**
**1 carton (16 ounces) frozen whipped topping, thawed, *divided***
**30 chocolate wafers**
**45 pieces candy corn**
**1/3 cup vanilla frosting**
**10 drops yellow food coloring**

In a heavy saucepan, sprinkle the gelatin over milk; let stand for 5 minutes. Cook and stir over low heat until the gelatin is dissolved. Add the pumpkin, brown sugar, salt, ginger, cinnamon and nutmeg. Cook and stir over medium-high heat until thickened and bubbly. Reduce the heat; cook and stir 2 minutes longer. Remove from the heat.

Stir a small amount of hot filling into egg yolks; return all to pan, stirring constantly. Bring to a gentle boil; cook and stir 2 minutes longer (mixture will be thick). Remove from the heat. Cover surface with waxed paper; refrigerate without stirring until cooled. Fold in half of the whipped topping.

Arrange half of the wafers in a greased 13-in. x 9-in. x 2-in. dish. Top with half of the pumpkin mixture; repeat. Spread with remaining whipped topping. Refrigerate for 3 hours or until set.

Score dessert into 15 pieces; arrange candy corn in groups of three. Combine frosting and food coloring; place in a small resealable plastic bag. Insert a #5 round pastry tip; pipe cornhusks on each piece. Cut dessert along scored lines. **Yield:** 15 servings.

## Walnut Fudge Pie

*(Pictured at left)*

*This rich recipe is wonderful for the holidays, but my family will request it any time of year. Creating the filling is a snap—I just combine the ingredients and pour the mixture into a purchased pastry shell. While the pie bakes, I have time to stir together the fudge sauce on the stovetop.* —*Jan Huntington, Painesville, Ohio*

**1/2 cup packed brown sugar**
**1/4 cup all-purpose flour**
**3 eggs, lightly beaten**
**1/4 cup butter, melted**
**1 teaspoon vanilla extract**
**2 cups (12 ounces) semisweet chocolate chips, melted**
**1-1/2 cups walnut halves**
**1 unbaked pastry shell (9 inches)**

**FUDGE SAUCE:**

**2 cups (12 ounces) semisweet chocolate chips**
**1 tablespoon butter**
**1/2 cup heavy whipping cream**
**1/4 cup strong brewed coffee**
**Coffee ice cream**

In a bowl, combine the first seven ingredients; pour into pastry shell. Bake at 375° for 25-30 minutes or until set. Cool on a wire rack.

In a saucepan, melt chocolate chips and butter. Stir in cream until smooth. Remove from the heat; stir in coffee. Serve pie with ice cream and fudge sauce. **Yield:** 8 servings.

## Saltine Toffee

*(Pictured at right)*

*Easy to prepare using pantry staples, this toffee is always a popular choice on my holiday cookie tray. The sweetly unique bites start with saltine crackers and are drizzled with white chocolate for an elegant accent.* —*Jo Ann Dalrymple Claremore, Oklahoma*

**37 saltine cracker squares**
**1 cup butter, cubed**
**3/4 cup sugar**
**2 cups (12 ounces) semisweet chocolate chips**
**1 square (1 ounce) white baking chocolate**
**1 teaspoon shortening**

Place crackers in a single layer in a foil-lined 15-in. x 10-in. x 1-in. baking pan. In a saucepan, bring butter and sugar to a boil. Reduce heat; simmer, uncovered, for 5-6 minutes or until mixture is thickened and sugar is completely dissolved. Spread over crackers.

Bake at 350° for 7-8 minutes or until bubbly. Sprinkle with chips. Bake 3-5 minutes longer or until chips begin to melt; spread chocolate evenly over top. Melt white chocolate and shortening; drizzle over toffee. Chill for 15-20 minutes or until set; break into pieces. Store in the refrigerator. **Yield:** about 1-3/4 pounds.

## Pistachio Cream Puffs

*(Pictured at right)*

*Instant pudding speeds up these delightful desserts. With a pretty green filling and a dusting of sugar, the luscious puffs are festive for the Christmas season.*
—*Helen Youngers, Kingman, Kansas*

✓ Uses less fat, sugar or salt. Includes Nutritional Analysis and Diabetic Exchanges.

**1/4 cup water**
**2 tablespoons butter**
**1/8 teaspoon salt**
**1/4 cup all-purpose flour**
**1 egg**
**2 cups cold milk**
**1 package (3.4 ounces) instant pistachio pudding mix**
**Confectioners' sugar, optional**

In a small saucepan, bring the water, butter and salt to a boil. Add the flour all at once; stir until a smooth ball forms. Remove from the heat; let stand for 5 minutes. Add the egg; beat well. Continue beating until the mixture is smooth and shiny.

Drop by rounded 1/4 cupfuls 3 in. apart onto a greased baking sheet. Bake at 400° for 25-30 minutes or until golden brown. Remove to a wire rack. Immediately split the puffs open; remove tops and set aside. Discard the soft dough from inside. Cool puffs.

In a bowl, whisk milk and pudding mix for 2 minutes. Let stand for 2 minutes or until soft-set. Just before serving, fill cream puffs and replace tops. Dust with confectioners' sugar if desired. **Yield:** 4 servings.

**Nutritional Analysis:** One cream puff (prepared with fat-free milk and sugar-free pudding; calculated without confectioners' sugar) equals 175 calories, 7 g fat (4 g saturated fat), 71 mg cholesterol, 625 mg sodium, 20 g carbohydrate, trace fiber, 7 g protein. **Diabetic Exchanges:** 1 starch, 1 fat, 1/2 fat-free milk.

## Frosty Peppermint Dessert

*(Pictured at right)*

*This creamy freeze with candy and a chocolate crust delivers make-ahead convenience. I'll often whip up two.*
—*Carolyn Satterfield, Emporia, Kansas*

**1-1/2 cups crushed chocolate wafers**
**1/4 cup sugar**
**1/4 cup butter, melted**
**1 package (8 ounces) cream cheese, softened**
**1 can (14 ounces) sweetened condensed milk**
**1 cup crushed peppermint candies**
**3 drops red food coloring, optional**
**2 cups heavy whipping cream, whipped**
**10 to 14 peppermint candies**

In a small bowl, combine the wafer crumbs, sugar and butter. Press onto the bottom and 2 in. up the sides of a greased 8-in. springform pan. Refrigerate the crust.

In a large mixing bowl, beat cream cheese. Gradually add milk, beating until smooth. Beat in crushed candies and food coloring if desired. Fold in whipped cream. Spoon into crust. Cover and freeze for 8 hours or overnight. Remove from the freezer 10 minutes before serving. Garnish with whole candies. **Yield:** 10-14 servings.

## Fruity Hazelnut Trifle

*Here's a fast and festive treat to present during the holidays. With a little help from canned pie filling, cranberry sauce and a frozen cake, it couldn't be easier.*
—*Margaret Wilson, Hemet, California*

**1-1/2 cups cold milk**
**2 tablespoons refrigerated hazelnut nondairy creamer**
**1 package (3.4 ounces) instant vanilla pudding mix**
**1 can (21 ounces) apple pie filling**
**1 can (16 ounces) whole-berry cranberry sauce**
**1 loaf (10-3/4 ounces) frozen pound cake, thawed and cubed**
**2 cups whipped topping**

In a bowl, whisk milk, creamer and pudding mix for 2 minutes. In another bowl, combine pie filling and cranberry sauce. Place a third of the cake cubes in a 3-qt. trifle bowl; layer with a fourth of the cranberry mixture and a third of the pudding mixture. Repeat layers twice.

Top with remaining cranberry mixture. Garnish with whipped topping. Cover and refrigerate until serving. **Yield:** 12-14 servings.

Frosty Peppermint Dessert
Pistachio Cream Puffs
Saltine Toffee

# Chapter 15

# Kids in the Kitchen

KIDS are eager to help prepare fun food that's easy to fix...and yummy, too! They'll be especially happy to join in when they see the fast, tasty fare in this section.

Whether you try the super main and side dishes, speedy munchies or sweet desserts, younger children can mix and measure the ingredients while older ones help you get a head start on dinner.

Your children or grandchildren are sure to appreciate the hands-on experience, and you'll enjoy the quality time spent together.

Best of all, the entire family will be pleased—and proud—to sit down to a delectable dinner they helped make.

**FUN FINGER FOOD.** Pizza Biscuit Bears (recipe on p. 224).

## Cauldron Dip

*(Pictured below)*

*This witch's cauldron doesn't hold a spooky brew—just a Halloween snack that's frightfully fun! Our Test Kitchen formed a pot by toasting a slice of rye bread, then filled it with a creamy dip that's perfect with the pretzel "logs" and sweet pepper "flames" that are placed underneath.*

- **1 cup (8 ounces) sour cream**
- **1 tablespoon dried parsley flakes**
- **1 teaspoon sugar**
- **1/2 teaspoon onion powder**
- **1/4 teaspoon garlic salt**
- **1/4 teaspoon pepper**
- **1 slice soft dark rye bread**
- **1 *each* medium sweet red, yellow and orange pepper, julienned**
- **10 pretzel rods, broken in half**

In a small bowl, combine sour cream, parsley, sugar, onion powder, garlic salt and pepper. Cover and refrigerate.

Flatten bread with a rolling pin. Press over an inverted greased 10-oz. custard cup. Top with another 10-oz. custard cup. Place on an ungreased baking sheet. Bake at 350° for 7 minutes. Carefully remove top dish. Bake 3-5 minutes longer or until bread is lightly toasted. Immediately remove the bread from the dish. Cool.

Fill bread bowl with dip. Arrange peppers and pretzels under and around bowl. **Yield:** 1 cup.

Cauldron Dip

## Peanut Butter Oat Cookies

*You won't believe how easy it is to whip up these soft chewy treats. Our kids just adore these cookies and ask for them often. —Patty Faussett, Tucson, Arizona*

- **1 cup butter, melted**
- **1 cup peanut butter**
- **3/4 cup sugar**
- **3/4 cup packed brown sugar**
- **2 eggs**
- **1 teaspoon vanilla extract**
- **1-1/4 cups whole wheat flour**
- **1 cup wheat bran**
- **3/4 cup quick-cooking oats**
- **2 teaspoons baking soda**

In a mixing bowl, cream the butter, peanut butter and sugars. Add eggs, one at a time, beating well after each addition. Stir in the vanilla. Combine the remaining ingredients; stir into creamed mixture. Drop by tablespoonfuls 2 in. apart onto ungreased baking sheets. Bake at 350° for 10-12 minutes or until golden brown. Cool for 3 minutes before removing to wire racks. **Yield:** 5 dozen.

**Editor's Note:** Reduced-fat or generic brands of peanut butter are not recommended for this recipe.

## Crunchy Caramel Snack Mix

*This irresistible finger food is a surefire hit with all ages. The sweetly coated combination of nuts, cereal and popcorn is great for packaging in sandwich bags and selling at bake sales. —Lauren Biggs, Suwanee, Georgia*

- **6 cups popped popcorn**
- **3 cups Crispix**
- **2 cups Cheerios**
- **1-1/4 cups pecan halves**
- **1-1/4 cups dry roasted peanuts**
- **1 cup packed brown sugar**
- **1/2 cup butter, cubed**
- **1/4 cup light corn syrup**
- **1 teaspoon vanilla extract**
- **1/4 teaspoon baking soda**

In a greased roasting pan, combine the popcorn, cereals and nuts. In a saucepan, bring the brown sugar, butter and corn syrup to a boil. Boil until a candy thermometer reads 250° (hard-ball stage), about 5 minutes.

Remove from heat; immediately stir in vanilla and baking soda. Drizzle over popcorn mixture; toss to coat. Transfer to a greased 15-in. x 10-in. x 1-in. baking pan. Bake, uncovered, at 250° for 1 hour, stirring every 15 minutes. **Yield:** 3 quarts.

**Editor's Note:** We recommend that you test your

candy thermometer before each use by bringing water to a boil; the thermometer should read 212°. Adjust your recipe temperature up or down based on your test.

## Mallow Pineapple Salad

*This light creamy fluff features fruit and miniature marshmallows. The salad is nice to prepare ahead of time and pop in the fridge. Just before serving, I add the bananas and chopped walnuts.* —*Kathy Robinson, Eau Claire, Wisconsin*

**1 can (20 ounces) pineapple chunks**
**1/2 cup sugar**
**2 tablespoons cornstarch**
**2 eggs, beaten**
**1 cup heavy whipping cream**
**1-1/2 cups miniature marshmallows**
**2 medium firm bananas, sliced**
**1/2 cup chopped walnuts**

Drain pineapple, reserving juice; set pineapple aside. In a saucepan, combine the sugar, cornstarch, eggs and reserved juice; mix well. Cook and stir until a thermometer reads 160°. Remove from the heat. Pour into a bowl; cool completely.

In a small mixing bowl, beat cream until stiff peaks form. Fold into cooled egg mixture. Add marshmallows and reserved pineapple. Cover and refrigerate for 4 hours. Just before serving, fold in bananas and nuts. **Yield:** 8 servings.

## Deluxe Macaroni Dinner

*This stovetop supper based on a mealtime mainstay is a real family-pleaser and rarely results in leftovers. I simply dress up a packaged macaroni-and-cheese mix by adding ground beef, onion and broccoli.* —*Michele Odstrcilek, Lemont, Illinois*

**1/2 pound ground beef**
**1 small onion, chopped**
**2 garlic cloves, minced**
**10 cups water**
**1 package (14 ounces) deluxe four-cheese macaroni and cheese dinner**
**2 cups chopped fresh broccoli**

In a large skillet, cook the beef, onion and garlic until meat is no longer pink; drain. In a large saucepan, bring the water to a boil. Add macaroni; cook for 5 minutes. Add broccoli; cook 4-5 minutes longer or until macaroni and broccoli are tender.

Drain, reserving 1/4 cup cooking liquid. Place contents of cheese sauce mix in saucepan. Stir in macaroni mixture, beef mixture and reserved liquid; heat through. **Yield:** 4-6 servings.

## Mousse-Filled Witches' Hats

*(Pictured above right)*

*These cute chocolate-covered treats will magically disappear at your house. Our Test Kitchen staff had a "spooktacular" time coming up with the rich snacks, featuring sugar cones filled with a creamy homemade mousse. Prepare them for your little goblins this Halloween.*

Mousse-Filled Witches' Hats

**1-3/4 cups heavy whipping cream, *divided***
**1 cup milk chocolate chips**
**4 squares (1 ounce *each*) semisweet chocolate, chopped**
**1/2 teaspoon shortening**
**1 package (4-3/4 ounces) chocolate sugar ice cream cones**
**Halloween sprinkles**
**12 thin chocolate wafers (2-1/4-inch diameter)**

For mousse, in a small saucepan, bring 1/2 cup cream to a boil; remove from the heat. Stir in chocolate chips until smooth. Transfer to a bowl; cool to room temperature, stirring occasionally.

In a small mixing bowl, beat the remaining cream until stiff peaks form; fold into the chocolate mixture. Cover and refrigerate.

In a microwave-safe bowl, melt semisweet chocolate and shortening; stir until smooth. Dip pointed tips of ice cream cones a third of the way into melted chocolate; roll in sprinkles. Refrigerate until set. Just before serving, spoon mousse into cones. Top each with a chocolate wafer. Invert onto a serving platter. **Yield:** 1 dozen.

Jelly Bean Bark
Bunny Cupcakes

8 drops green food coloring
12 large marshmallows
3/4 cup flaked coconut, chopped
24 miniature pink jelly beans
12 miniature red jelly beans
24 miniature white jelly beans
Red shoestring licorice
1 to 2 drops red food coloring
48 small oval sugar cookies

Prepare and bake cupcakes according to package directions. Cool on wire racks. In a bowl, combine 1 cup frosting and green food coloring; frost cupcakes. Set remaining frosting aside. Cut marshmallows in half; immediately dip cut ends into coconut. Place coconut side up on cupcakes to form heads.

Cut the pink and red jelly beans in half widthwise. Cut the white jelly beans in half lengthwise. With a toothpick, dab the reserved frosting onto the cut sides of pink jelly bean halves; attach to marshmallows for eyes. Attach red jelly beans for noses and white jelly beans for teeth.

For whiskers, cut licorice into 1-in. pieces; attach four pieces to each cupcake. Tint remaining frosting pink. Cut a small hole in corner of a resealable plastic bag; add pink frosting. For ears, pipe an oval outline toward center of each cookie; insert two ears into each cupcake. **Yield:** 2 dozen.

**Editor's Note:** This recipe was tested with Pepperidge Farm Milano cookies.

## Jelly Bean Bark

*(Pictured above)*

*Not only is this colorful candy easy to make, but it's perfect for Easter gatherings and other springtime occasions. The festive confection calls for just three ingredients and is ready to enjoy in less than an hour.* —*Mavis Diment*
*Marcus, Iowa*

**1 tablespoon butter, melted**
**1-1/4 pounds white candy coating**
**2 cups miniature jelly beans**

Line a 15-in. x 10-in. x 1-in. pan with foil. Brush with butter; set aside. Place the candy coating in a microwave-safe bowl. Microwave, uncovered, at 70% power for 3-4 minutes; stir until smooth. Spread into prepared pan. Sprinkle with jelly beans. Let stand until set before breaking into pieces. **Yield:** 2 pounds.

## Bunny Cupcakes

*(Pictured above)*

*Celebrate spring with these cute cottontails that our Test Kitchen home economists created from a packaged cake mix, prepared frosting and marshmallows. Store-bought cookies form the ears while candy gives the rapid rabbits their funny faces.*

**1 package (18-1/4 ounces) yellow cake mix**
**1 can (16 ounces) cream cheese frosting, *divided***

## Creamy Fruit Salad

*Children can't wait to eat this yummy, refreshing salad...I know ours can't! I like that it's a simple-to-make medley of wholesome apples, bananas, oranges and other fruits. The kids love the creamy coating that I create using vanilla yogurt and instant pudding.* —*Lisa Dunn*
*Red Oak, Oklahoma*

**1 can (15 ounces) fruit cocktail, drained**
**2 medium firm bananas, sliced**
**1 medium apple, diced**
**1 medium navel orange, peeled and sectioned**
**2 tablespoons instant vanilla pudding mix**
**1 carton (8 ounces) vanilla yogurt**

In a serving bowl, combine the fruit cocktail, bananas, apple and orange. Combine the pudding mix and yogurt until smooth. Add to fruit mixture; stir to coat. Refrigerate leftovers. **Yield:** 4-6 servings.

## Pear Sundaes

*Kids won't miss the ice cream in these change-of-pace sundaes from our home economists. They simply drizzled convenient canned pear halves with everyone's favorite ice cream toppings, then added whipped cream and maraschino cherries.*

**4 canned pear halves**
**Caramel ice cream topping**

Chocolate syrup
1/4 cup chopped pecans
Whipped cream in a can
4 maraschino cherries

Place each pear half in a serving dish. Drizzle with caramel topping and chocolate syrup. Sprinkle with nuts. Garnish with whipped cream and a cherry. **Yield:** 4 servings.

## Tart Cherry Crisp

*Our family first enjoyed this sweet-tart dessert after an outing to a cherry orchard. Using the fresh fruit we picked, we made not just one crisp, but several! It's especially wonderful served warm from the oven and topped with a scoop of vanilla ice cream.* —*Mrs. Grossman, Brooklyn, New York*

**4 cups pitted fresh tart cherries *or* 2 cans (14-1/2 ounces *each*) pitted tart cherries, drained**
**2 tablespoons sugar**
**1/2 cup all-purpose flour**
**1/2 cup packed brown sugar**
**1 teaspoon ground cinnamon**
**1/4 teaspoon salt**
**1/4 cup cold butter**

Place cherries in an ungreased 9-in. pie plate. Sprinkle with sugar. In a bowl, combine the flour, brown sugar, cinnamon and salt. Cut in butter until mixture resembles coarse crumbs. Sprinkle over cherries. Bake, uncovered, at 375° for 30-40 minutes or until top is bubbly. Serve warm. **Yield:** 6 servings.

## Parmesan Chicken Patties

*I have three young children, so I rely on meals that are quick and easy. These tender patties with pasta, spaghetti sauce and cheese are family-pleasers and simple enough for kids to help prepare.* —*Renee DePriest, Harrisburg, Illinois*

**4 frozen breaded chicken patties**
**1 jar (28 ounces) spaghetti sauce**
**4 slices mozzarella cheese**
**1/4 cup shredded Parmesan cheese**
**Hot cooked spaghetti**

Place chicken patties in an 11-in. x 7-in. x 2-in. microwave-safe dish. Microwave, uncovered, on high for 4 minutes. Top with spaghetti sauce and cheeses. Cover and cook 4-5 minutes longer or until heated through. Serve over spaghetti. **Yield:** 4 servings.

**Editor's Note:** This recipe was tested in an 850-watt microwave.

## Tie-Dyed Kite Cookies

*(Pictured at right)*

*Our Test Kitchen bakers had their heads happily in the clouds when they crafted these crispy sugar cookies! They "tie-dyed" refrigerated dough with food coloring and turned red licorice ropes into cute kite tails.*

**1 tube (18 ounces) refrigerated sugar cookie dough**
**2 to 4 tablespoons all-purpose flour**
**Pink, green and blue gel food coloring**
**24 to 28 pieces red shoestring licorice (9-1/2 inches *each*)**
**48 to 56 Life Savers candies**
**1/2 cup vanilla frosting**

Cut the cookie dough in half; refrigerate half of dough. On a lightly floured surface, knead 1-2 tablespoons of flour into remaining dough until dough is stiff. Press into a 5-in. circle. Top with one dot of each color food coloring; knead 5-10 times or until the color just begins to swirl.

Roll out dough to 1/8-in. thickness. Cut out with a floured 3-in. diamond-shaped cookie cutter. Place 1 in. apart on ungreased baking sheets. Bake at 350° for 10-13 minutes or until edges are lightly browned. Cool for 2 minutes before removing from pans to wire racks. Repeat with remaining dough.

Turn cookies bottom side up. For each cookie, lace one piece of licorice through one Life Saver; loop the licorice through the Life Saver again to hold the candy in place. Repeat with second Life Saver. Attach kite tails to the back of each cookie with frosting. Let stand until set (tails will be heavy). **Yield:** about 2 dozen.

**Tie-Dyed Kite Cookies**

## Bicycle Crispies

*(Pictured below)*

*Assorted colorful candies and prepared frosting turn popular crisp rice cereal bars into these two-wheel treats from our Test Kitchen home economists. Older children can help prepare the rice cereal mixtures while younger ones can decorate the sweet cycles.*

- **1 package (16 ounces) large marshmallows, *divided***
- **3 tablespoons plus 4-1/2 teaspoons butter, *divided***
- **6 cups chocolate-flavored crisp rice cereal**
- **3 cups plain crisp rice cereal**
- **1 cup vanilla frosting**
- **9 Life Savers**
- **6 pretzel sticks**
- **12 Tart 'n' Tinys candies *or* M&M's miniature baking bits**

In a large microwave-safe bowl, heat 40 marshmallows and 3 tablespoons butter, uncovered, on high for 1-2 minutes or until melted. Stir in chocolate rice cereal. With buttered hands, press into a greased 13-in. x 9-in. x 2-in. pan.

In another large microwave-safe bowl, melt 20 marshmallows with remaining butter, uncovered, on high for 1-2 minutes. Stir in plain rice cereal. With buttered hands, press into a greased 9-in. square pan.

Invert both pans onto cutting boards. Using a 2-1/2-in. round biscuit cutter, cut 12 circles from chocolate cereal mixture. Using a 2-1/2-in. triangle or Christmas tree cookie cutter, cut six triangles from plain cereal mixture.

For each bicycle, place one triangle point down on work surface; gently press two circles on either side of triangle for wheels. Using a #3 round pastry tip, pipe frosting spokes onto wheels and outline triangles.

For bicycle seat, attach a Life Saver with frosting to one side of triangle top. Insert a pretzel stick into one wheel; angle toward center of bicycle. For handlebars, cut one Life Saver in half; attach near the top of pretzel stick. Press a Tart 'n' Tiny candy into the center of each wheel. **Yield:** 6 bicycles.

Bicycle Crispies
Speedy Ice Cream

## Speedy Ice Cream

*(Pictured below left)*

*This fun "hands-on" recipe lets kids make their very own vanilla ice cream—and no special kitchen gadgets or tools are necessary. Every child I prepare this frosty treat with loves kneading the ingredients in the plastic bags and then eating the yummy results. Not only does the whole process get youngsters smiling and giggling, but it also keeps cleanup to a minimum.* —*Cindy Marshall, Bradley, California*

- **1 cup half-and-half cream**
- **1/4 cup sugar**
- **1/2 to 1 teaspoon vanilla extract**
- **4 cups coarsely crushed ice cubes**
- **3/4 cup salt**

In a small resealable plastic bag, combine the cream, sugar and vanilla. Press out air and seal. In a large resealable plastic bag, combine the ice and salt; add the sealed small bag. Seal the large bag; place in another large resealable plastic bag and seal. Shake and knead for 5-7 minutes or until cream mixture is thickened. Serve immediately or freeze. **Yield:** 1 cup.

## Sparkling Fruit Punch

*At summer events or anytime, folks enjoy cooling down with a cup or two of this icy thirst-quencher. I have had the recipe for more than 30 years and have served the punch to crowds on countless occasions. It's very good and very easy to make.* —*Edith Holliday, Flushing, Michigan*

- **4 cups cold water**
- **1 can (6 ounces) frozen orange juice concentrate, thawed**
- **3/4 cup lemonade concentrate**
- **3/4 cup grape juice concentrate**
- **2 cups ginger ale, chilled**
- **Crushed ice**

In a large bowl, combine the water and concentrates. Stir in ginger ale. Serve immediately over ice. **Yield:** 2 quarts.

Patriotic Popcorn Cake
Chippy Chocolate Cookies

## Patriotic Popcorn Cake

*(Pictured above)*

*My mother gave me this recipe, and it has been a favorite at bake sales and holiday get-togethers ever since. Children and adults love the caramel-coated treat. For faster preparation, use microwave popcorn.*
*—Teresa Lerret, Vacaville, California*

**1 package (16 ounces) miniature marshmallows**
**20 caramels**
**1/4 cup butter, cubed**
**10 cups popped popcorn**
**1-1/2 cups salted peanuts**
**1 cup red, white and blue milk chocolate M&M's**

In a microwave-safe bowl, combine the marshmallows, caramels and butter. Microwave, uncovered, on high for 3 minutes or until melted, stirring occasionally. Place popcorn in a large bowl; pour caramel mixture over popcorn and mix well.

Stir in peanuts and M&M's. Press into a well-greased 10-in. tube pan. Cool until firm. Remove from pan; cut with a serrated knife. **Yield:** 16-18 servings.

**Editor's Note:** This recipe was tested with Hershey caramels in a 1,100-watt microwave.

## Chippy Chocolate Cookies

*(Pictured above)*

*I bake a batch of these chock-full goodies any time I need to take a dessert item to a potluck supper, family gathering or other event. With a yield of about 6 dozen, the recipe creates plenty to share with a crowd of people...plus more than enough extras to fill up our cookie jar at home. They're also yummy if you substitute a white cake mix, but chocolate is my favorite.*
*—Elaine Fortner*
*Princeton, Indiana*

**2 packages (18-1/4 ounces *each*) chocolate cake mix**
**5 eggs**
**2/3 cup vegetable oil**
**1 package (10 to 12 ounces) vanilla *or* white chips**
**1 cup chopped pecans *or* walnuts**

In a large mixing bowl, beat the cake mixes, eggs and oil. Stir in the chips and nuts. Drop by rounded tablespoonfuls 2 in. apart onto ungreased baking sheets. Bake at 350° for 10-13 minutes or until set and tops are slightly cracked. Cool for 2 minutes before removing to wire racks to cool. **Yield:** about 6 dozen.

Pizza Biscuit Bears

## Pizza Biscuit Bears

*(Pictured above and on page 216)*

*Our Test Kitchen home economists set aside recipes for porridge and came up with these charming biscuits that are just right! The cute little cubs, which get their personality from pizza toppings, begin with convenient refrigerated dough and take just 30 minutes to make from start to finish. Kids love dipping the savory snack into warm pizza sauce.*

**1 tube (16.3 ounces) large refrigerated buttermilk biscuits**
**12 pepperoni slices**
**12 ripe olive slices**
**1 tablespoon chopped green pepper**
**1 jar (2 ounces) sliced pimientos, drained**
**2 tablespoons shredded mozzarella cheese**
**1 can (8 ounces) pizza sauce, warmed**

Separate biscuits; place six biscuits 3 in. apart on an ungreased baking sheet. Cut each remaining biscuit into six pieces; roll each into balls. Attach two balls to each whole biscuit for ears; pinch dough to seal. Decorate each bear with a pepperoni slice on each ear, olive slices for eyes, green pepper for nose, two pimiento strips for mouth and mozzarella cheese for furry forelock. Bake at 375° for 15-20 minutes or until golden brown. Serve with pizza sauce. **Yield:** 6 servings.

## Nutty Raisin Clusters

*Four ingredients are all you'll need to prepare these chewy chocolate bites loaded with crunchy walnuts and raisins. For a fun change of pace, try making the treats with white chocolate chips and peanuts. Or add your favorite cereal, chow mein noodles...the variations are limitless!* —*Laura Lo Russo, Riverside, Rhode Island*

**1 cup (6 ounces) semisweet chocolate chips**
**1/2 cup chopped walnuts**
**1/2 cup raisins**
**2 tablespoons honey**

In a microwave-safe bowl, melt the chocolate chips; stir until smooth. Let stand for 5 minutes. Stir in the walnuts, raisins and honey. Drop by tablespoonfuls into 15 mounds onto a waxed paper-lined baking sheet. Refrigerate until firm. **Yield:** 15 clusters.

## Cheeseburger Chowder

*This is a family favorite, especially on those cold blustery days when a steaming bowl of soup really hits the spot. Prepared with ground beef, cheddar cheese and onion, the chowder is very filling and makes a complete meal when served with corn bread or biscuits.*
—*Rebecca McCabe, Ekalaka, Montana*

**1 pound ground beef**
**1/4 cup chopped onion**
**1-1/2 cups water**
**3 teaspoons beef bouillon granules**
**1/2 teaspoon salt**
**2 cups cubed red potatoes**
**1 celery rib, thinly sliced**
**3 tablespoons all-purpose flour**
**2-1/2 cups milk, *divided***
**1 cup (4 ounces) shredded cheddar cheese**

In a large saucepan, cook beef and onion over medium heat until meat is no longer pink; drain well. Stir in the water, bouillon and salt. Add potatoes and celery. Bring to a boil. Reduce heat; cover and simmer for 15-20 minutes or until potatoes are tender.

Combine flour and 1/2 cup milk until smooth; gradually stir into beef mixture. Bring to a boil; cook and stir for 2 minutes or until thickened and bubbly. Stir in the remaining milk; heat through. Stir in cheese until melted. **Yield:** 7 servings.

## Apricot Barbecued Chicken

*A sweet glaze made with apricot preserves and barbecue sauce covers these tender chicken chunks served over rice. This is such an easy tasty recipe. Best of all, our son loves it.* —*Cindy Novak, Antioch, California*

**1 pound boneless skinless chicken breasts, cut into large chunks**
**3 garlic cloves, minced**
**1 tablespoon olive oil**
**1/2 cup apricot preserves**
**1/4 cup barbecue sauce**
**1/4 cup water**
**2 tablespoons onion soup mix**
**Hot cooked rice**

In a large skillet, cook chicken and garlic in oil until browned, about 6 minutes. Transfer to a greased 8-in. square baking dish.

In a bowl, combine apricot preserves, barbecue sauce, water and onion soup mix. Pour over chicken. Bake, uncovered, at 375° for 25-30 minutes or until chicken juices run clear. Serve with rice. **Yield:** 4 servings.

## Jelly Pancake Sandwiches

*I came up with this recipe for friends who are like me and don't care for maple syrup on their pancakes. This tasty variation is great when you're in a rush and need a good breakfast you can eat on the go. Use any jelly...or peanut butter...or both for a fun twist on traditional peanut butter and jelly sandwiches.* —*Laura Muskopf, Wooster, Ohio*

**2 cups biscuit/baking mix**
**1 teaspoon ground cinnamon**
**1/4 teaspoon salt**
**1 cup milk**
**2 eggs, beaten**
**Strawberry jelly *or* jam**

In a bowl, combine biscuit mix, cinnamon and salt. Add milk and eggs; mix well. Pour batter by 1/4 cupfuls onto a greased hot griddle. Turn when bubbles form on top of pancakes; cook until second side is golden brown. Spread half of the pancakes with jelly; top with remaining pancakes. **Yield:** 5 servings.

## Pecan Bars

*Anyone who has children will appreciate speedy bake sale recipes like this one. Made from scratch, the scrumptious cinnamon-spiced bars require only 15 minutes of preparation time before baking and call for ingredients we all keep on hand.* —*Ginny Perott, Towanda, Kansas*

**3/4 cup butter, softened**
**1 cup sugar**
**1 egg, *separated***
**2 cups all-purpose flour**
**1 teaspoon ground cinnamon**
**1/4 teaspoon salt**
**1 cup chopped pecans**

In a small mixing bowl, cream the butter and sugar. Beat in the egg yolk. Combine the flour, cinnamon and salt; gradually add to the creamed mixture and mix well. Spread into a greased 13-in. x 9-in. x 2-in. baking pan.

Beat egg white; brush over the top. Sprinkle with pecans; press down lightly. Bake at 350° for 25-30 minutes or until golden brown. Cool on a wire rack. Cut into bars. **Yield:** 6-1/2 dozen.

## Sweet Cereal Clusters

*I cover a crunchy combination of peanuts, pretzels and cereal with white candy coating for a fun snack. At bake sales, I fill small resealable storage bags with the clusters. They always disappear fast.* —*Sue Yount, McBain, Michigan*

**6 cups Corn Chex**
**3 cups miniature pretzels**
**1 jar (16 ounces) dry roasted peanuts**
**1 package (14 ounces) milk chocolate M&M's**
**1 cup raisins, optional**
**1-1/2 pounds white candy coating, melted**

In a large bowl, combine the first five ingredients. Pour candy coating over cereal mixture; stir until coated. Spread onto waxed paper-lined baking sheets. Refrigerate for 15 minutes or until set. Break into pieces. Store in an airtight container. **Yield:** about 4-1/2 pounds.

## Coconut Egg Nests

*(Pictured below)*

*Looking for an Easter activity that's a real treat for kids? Try these sweet spring goodies that children can help assemble...and then eat! The little tinted coconut nests holding jelly-bean eggs are easy to create, and you won't need a long list of ingredients.* —*Tonya Hamrick, Wallace, West Virginia*

**6 ounces white candy coating, coarsely chopped**
**6 drops green food coloring**
**1 drop yellow food coloring**
**1 cup flaked coconut**
**36 jelly beans**

In a microwave-safe bowl, melt candy coating; stir in food coloring until blended. Add coconut. Drop by tablespoonfuls onto waxed paper into 12 mounds. Make an indentation in the center of each with the end of a wooden spoon handle. Fill each with three jelly beans. Let stand until set. **Yield:** 1 dozen.

Coconut Egg Nests

## Cranberry Pecan Bars

(Pictured below)

*I mix cranberries, coconut and a little orange peel into the filling of these rich pecan bars. I happened upon the recipe while watching television. Any time I serve them, people ask for the recipe.* —*Beverly McClarren, Findlay, Ohio*

- **1 cup all-purpose flour**
- **1/2 cup finely chopped pecans**
- **1/2 cup packed brown sugar**
- **1/2 teaspoon salt**
- **6 tablespoons cold butter**

**FILLING:**

- **2 tablespoons all-purpose flour**
- **1/2 teaspoon baking powder**
- **2 eggs, beaten**
- **1 cup sugar**
- **1 tablespoon milk**
- **1 tablespoon vanilla extract**
- **1 cup fresh *or* frozen cranberries, chopped**
- **1/2 cup flaked coconut**
- **1/2 cup chopped pecans**
- **1-1/2 teaspoons grated orange peel**

In a large bowl, combine the flour, pecans, brown sugar and salt. Cut in butter until crumbly. Press into a greased 9-in. square baking dish. Bake at 350° for 15-20 minutes or until edges are lightly browned.

Meanwhile, in a large bowl, combine flour and baking powder. Combine the eggs, sugar, milk and vanilla; add to the dry ingredients. Fold in the cranberries, coconut, pecans and orange peel. Pour over crust. Bake 25-30 minutes longer or until set. Cool on a wire rack. Cut into bars. Refrigerate leftovers. **Yield:** 1 to 1-1/2 dozen.

Cranberry Pecan Bars
Cookie Turkeys

## Cookie Turkeys

(Pictured below left)

*People gobble up these sweet-tasting turkeys whenever the treats are sold at fund-raisers or featured on holiday tables. Every Thanksgiving, my cousin creates the birds out of prepared cookies and candies.* —*Sue Gronholz, Columbus, Wisconsin*

- **40 fudge-striped cookies**
- **1/4 cup chocolate frosting**
- **2 packages (5 ounces *each*) chocolate-covered cherries**
- **20 pieces candy corn**

Place 20 cookies on a flat surface, solid chocolate side down. With frosting, attach a chocolate-covered cherry to the top of each base cookie. Position another cookie perpendicular to each base cookie; attach with frosting.

With a dab of frosting, attach one piece of candy corn to the front of each cherry for the head. Let stand until set. **Yield:** 20 servings.

## Cereal Trail Mix

*All ages are sure to enjoy this easy-to-assemble snack. We spend a lot of time camping, canoeing and attending softball games. This crunchy mix is good for any of these occasions.* —*Holly Youngers, Cunningham, Kansas*

- **5 cups cookie-flavored crisp cereal**
- **5 cups Honey-Nut Cheerios**
- **5 cups miniature pretzel twists**
- **2 cups dried banana chips**
- **2 cups salted mixed nuts**

In a large bowl, combine all ingredients; mix well. Store in an airtight container. **Yield:** about 4-3/4 quarts.

## Strawberry Mousse

*This pretty pink dessert takes only minutes to prepare. Those who enjoy it rave about its smooth texture and sweet berry flavor. I like to dollop servings with whipped cream and strawberries.* —*Jody Cottle, Rigby, Idaho*

- **2 teaspoons unflavored gelatin**
- **2 tablespoons cold water**
- **1/4 cup boiling water**
- **1-1/3 cups instant strawberry drink mix**
- **2 cups heavy whipping cream**
- **2 teaspoons vanilla extract**

In a small bowl, soften gelatin in cold water; let stand for 5 minutes. Stir in boiling water until gelatin is dissolved; cool for 10 minutes.

In a mixing bowl, combine the drink mix, cream

and gelatin mixture until thickened. Beat in vanilla. Spoon into individual dishes; refrigerate for 1-2 hours or until set. **Yield:** 8 servings.

## Pasta Cheeseburger Soup

*"This tastes just like a cheeseburger" is what I always hear when I serve this satisfying soup. I combine ground beef and small shell pasta with popular burger toppings.*
*—Darlene Brenden, Salem, Oregon*

**1 pound ground beef**
**1/2 cup chopped onion**
**3 cups water**
**1 can (10-3/4 ounces) condensed cheddar cheese soup, undiluted**
**1 can (10-3/4 ounces) condensed tomato soup, undiluted**
**3 tablespoons dill pickle relish**
**1 cup uncooked small shell pasta**
**Ketchup and mustard**

In a large saucepan, cook beef and onion over medium heat until meat is no longer pink; drain. Stir in the water, soups and relish. Bring to a boil. Reduce heat; add pasta. Cook, uncovered, for 15-20 minutes or until pasta is tender, stirring occasionally. Drizzle each serving with ketchup and mustard. **Yield:** 3 servings.

## Tasty Toast Strips

*These cinnamon munchies come together in only 15 minutes for a busy-morning breakfast or fast snack. I've given the recipe to several ladies who have young children. Even adults like it.* *—Verna Eaton, Worden, Illinois*

**2 tablespoons sugar**
**2 tablespoons brown sugar**
**1 teaspoon ground cinnamon**
**1/2 teaspoon ground nutmeg**
**1/4 cup butter, melted**
**3 bread slices**

In a shallow bowl, combine the sugars, cinnamon and nutmeg. Place butter in another shallow bowl. Cut each slice of bread into four strips. Dip both sides in butter, then sprinkle with sugar mixture. Place on an ungreased baking sheet. Bake at 350° for 5-7 minutes or until golden brown. **Yield:** 1 dozen.

## Tater-Topped Dogs

*When we were raising our six children, they took turns cooking supper. Every time my oldest son's turn came around, we knew what he'd be serving—this great-tasting favorite of his. Now we make it for our grandkids.*
*—Margaret Pienta, Abilene, Texas*

**1 package (16 ounces) hot dogs**
**10 hot dog buns, split**
**2 cups mashed potatoes**
**3/4 cup shredded cheddar cheese**
**Ketchup and mustard**

**Peanut Butter Drums**

Cook hot dogs according to package directions; place in buns. Top each with small scoops of mashed potatoes; sprinkle with cheese. Place on a baking sheet; broil 4 in. from the heat for 2-4 minutes or until cheese is melted. Serve with ketchup and mustard. **Yield:** 10 servings.

## Peanut Butter Drums

*(Pictured above)*

*Little drummer boys and girls will agree—these cute musical treats can't be beat! Our home economists quickly decorated stacks of crackers and peanut butter to form the fun instruments, then joined gumdrops and pretzels for matching drumsticks.*

**1/4 cup creamy honey-nut peanut butter**
**18 butter-flavored crackers**
**4 ounces white candy coating**
**2 teaspoons shortening**
**1/2 cup vanilla frosting**
**Red and green gel food coloring**
**Miniature chocolate chips**
**12 pretzel sticks**
**12 spice gumdrops**

Spread peanut butter over 12 crackers, about 1 teaspoon on each. Stack two crackers together, peanut butter side up, to make six stacks. Top with remaining plain crackers. Melt candy coating and shortening; dip all sides of cracker stacks. Place on waxed paper-lined baking sheets; refrigerate until set.

Tint 1/4 cup frosting red and 1/4 cup frosting green. Frost tops of three stacks red and three stacks green. For drum details, pipe green frosting on red-topped stacks; pipe red frosting on green-topped stacks. Decorate with chocolate chips. Chill until serving. For drumsticks, insert pretzel sticks into gumdrops. **Yield:** 6 servings.

# Chapter 16

# Fast, Delicious...and Nutritious

IF YOU WANT fast-to-fix fare that fits today's healthier life-style, then you've turned to the right chapter. The light dishes featured here are ideal for those counting calories or trying to reduce fat, sugar or salt in their diet (and doing all this while keeping one eye on the clock).

You'll cut fat, calories, sugar and salt but not taste when you prepare these recipes. Each one includes a Nutritional Analysis and Diabetic Exchanges.

Anyone on a special diet—and even those who aren't—will enjoy these delicious and nutritious dishes.

(All the quick good-for-you foods in this book are flagged with a red checkmark in the indexes beginning on page 332.)

**LIGHTER DELIGHTS.** Top to bottom: Summer Squash Pepper Gratin and One-for-All Marinated Beef (both recipes on p. 234).

Orange-Glazed Carrots
Cantonese Beef

**All recipes in this chapter use less fat, sugar or salt and include Nutritional Analysis and Diabetic Exchanges.**

## Orange-Glazed Carrots

*(Pictured above)*

*I'm a 78-year-old who does my own cooking. This colorful side dish is nice for casual meals, and I can make it in less than 30 minutes using the microwave and five ingredients. The tender carrots get their zest from a tart yet sweet citrus glaze that relies on orange juice.*
*—Robert Wahlfeldt, Danville, Illinois*

**4 cups julienned fresh carrots**
**1/3 cup orange juice, *divided***
**2 tablespoons sugar**
**2 teaspoons cornstarch**
**1/2 teaspoon salt**

In a 1-1/2-qt. microwave-safe dish, combine carrots and 1/4 cup orange juice. Cover and microwave on high for 5-6 minutes or until carrots are crisp-tender.

Combine the sugar, cornstarch, salt and remaining orange juice until smooth; stir into carrots. Microwave, uncovered, on high for 2-3 minutes or until sauce has come to a boil and is thickened, stirring twice. Let stand for 5 minutes before serving. **Yield:** 4 servings.

**Nutritional Analysis:** One serving (3/4 cup) equals 91 calories, trace fat (trace saturated fat), 0 cholesterol, 336 mg sodium, 22 g carbohydrate, 4 g fiber, 1 g protein. **Diabetic Exchanges:** 2 vegetable, 1/2 fruit.

**Editor's Note:** This recipe was tested in a 1,100-watt microwave.

## Cantonese Beef

*(Pictured at left)*

*This delicious beef dish with flavorful vegetables, mandarin oranges and rice is always a big hit and a great meal-in-one. When I'm busy, I often cook it in the oven instead of on the stovetop. While the entree bakes, I can easily walk away and get other things done.*
*—Michelle Harvey, Noblesville, Indiana*

**1 can (11 ounces) mandarin oranges**
**2 pounds beef stew meat, cut into 1-inch cubes**
**1 small onion, sliced**
**1 tablespoon canola *or* vegetable oil**
**1-1/2 cups water**
**1/3 cup reduced-sodium soy sauce**
**1/2 teaspoon ground ginger**
**4 celery ribs, sliced**
**1 small green pepper, julienned**
**1 can (8 ounces) sliced water chestnuts, drained**
**3 tablespoons cornstarch**
**3 tablespoons cold water**
**Hot cooked rice**

Drain oranges, reserving juice; set oranges aside. In a Dutch oven, brown beef and onion in oil; drain. Stir in the water, soy sauce, ginger and reserved juice. Bring to a boil. Reduce heat; cover and simmer for 1 to 1-1/2 hours or until beef is tender.

Add celery, green pepper and water chestnuts. Cover and cook for 20-30 minutes or until vegetables are tender. Combine cornstarch and cold water until smooth; stir into beef mixture. Bring to a boil; cook and stir for 2 minutes or until thickened. Stir in reserved oranges. Serve with rice. **Yield:** 8 servings.

**Nutritional Analysis:** One 3/4-cup serving (calculated without rice) equals 233 calories, 10 g fat (3 g saturated fat), 71 mg cholesterol, 468 mg sodium, 13 g carbohydrate, 2 g fiber, 23 g protein. **Diabetic Exchanges:** 3 lean meat, 1 starch.

## Vegetable Chicken Medley

*I stir-fry this combination of tender chicken chunks, onions, broccoli, pepper and rice. Seasoned with garlic, ginger and a simple pineapple sauce, the made-in-moments main course includes crunchy chopped peanuts.*
*—Kristen Feola*
*Springfield, Missouri*

**1/2 cup coarsely chopped onion**
**1/2 cup julienned sweet red *or* green pepper**
**1/2 cup coarsely chopped fresh broccoli**
**4 green onions, chopped**
**1 tablespoon minced fresh parsley**
**2 garlic cloves, minced**
**1/2 teaspoon ground ginger**
**1/4 teaspoon pepper**
**1 tablespoon olive oil**
**2 cups chopped cooked chicken**

1-1/2 cups cooked brown rice
1 teaspoon cornstarch
1/4 cup unsweetened pineapple juice
1/4 cup reduced-sodium soy sauce
1 tablespoon chopped unsalted peanuts

In a large skillet, saute onion, red pepper, broccoli, green onions, parsley, garlic, ginger and pepper in oil until vegetables are crisp-tender. Stir in chicken and rice. In a small bowl, combine cornstarch, pineapple juice and soy sauce until smooth; stir into the skillet. Bring to a boil; cook and stir for 1 minute or until thickened. Stir in peanuts. **Yield:** 4 servings.

**Nutritional Analysis:** One serving (1 cup) equals 379 calories, 10 g fat (2 g saturated fat), 79 mg cholesterol, 889 mg sodium, 35 g carbohydrate, 4 g fiber, 35 g protein. **Diabetic Exchanges:** 3 lean meat, 2 starch, 1 vegetable, 1 fat.

## Garlic-Chive Mashed Potatoes

*Creamy and comforting, these savory spuds will complement a wide range of entrees. The potatoes get plenty of flavor from the fresh garlic and chives, as well as sour cream and chicken broth. If you prefer a slightly different texture, just stir in extra broth.* —*Leslie Cain*
*Starkville, Mississippi*

**3-1/2 pounds russet potatoes (about 5 large), peeled and quartered**
**3 garlic cloves, peeled**
**1/8 teaspoon paprika**
**1-1/2 cups (12 ounces) fat-free sour cream**
**1 cup reduced-sodium chicken broth, warmed**
**2 tablespoons minced chives**
**1 teaspoon salt**
**1/4 teaspoon pepper**

Place the potatoes, garlic and paprika in a large saucepan or Dutch oven; cover with water. Bring to a boil. Reduce heat; cover and cook for 15-20 minutes or until potatoes are tender. Drain. In a large mixing bowl, beat the potatoes and garlic. Add sour cream, broth, chives, salt and pepper; beat until smooth. **Yield:** 10 servings.

**Nutritional Analysis:** One serving (3/4 cup) equals 152 calories, trace fat (trace saturated fat), 0 cholesterol, 354 mg sodium, 33 g carbohydrate, 2 g fiber, 5 g protein. **Diabetic Exchange:** 2 starch.

## Caramel-Pecan Cheese Pie

*(Pictured at right)*

*Summers are hot here, and I try to use the oven as little as possible when the weather is warm. My family and friends love this luscious no-bake dessert that sets up in the refrigerator. No one can believe the nutty cheese pie isn't loaded with fat and calories.* —*Patsy Mullins*
*Taft, Tennessee*

**1 envelope unflavored gelatin**
**1/3 cup water**
**1/4 cup lemon juice**
**3 ounces reduced-fat cream cheese, cubed**
**1 cup nonfat dry milk powder**
**Sugar substitute equivalent to 2 tablespoons sugar**
**1 carton (8 ounces) frozen reduced-fat whipped topping, thawed**
**5 tablespoons chopped pecans, toasted,** ***divided***
**1 reduced-fat graham cracker crust (9 inches)**
**2 tablespoons fat-free caramel ice cream topping**

In a small saucepan, sprinkle gelatin over water; let stand for 1 minute. Bring to a boil, stirring until gelatin is completely dissolved. Cool slightly. In a blender or food processor, combine the lemon juice, cream cheese and gelatin mixture; cover and process until smooth. Add milk powder and sugar substitute; cover and process for 1 minute.

Transfer to a large bowl; fold in the whipped topping. Stir in 3 tablespoons of pecans. Pour into crust. Sprinkle with remaining pecans. Drizzle with caramel topping. Cover and refrigerate for 2-3 hours or until set. **Yield:** 8 servings.

**Nutritional Analysis:** One piece equals 270 calories, 12 g fat (6 g saturated fat), 6 mg cholesterol, 186 mg sodium, 31 g carbohydrate, 1 g fiber, 7 g protein. **Diabetic Exchanges:** 2 starch, 2 fat.

**Editor's Note:** This recipe was tested with Splenda No Calorie Sweetener. Look for it in the baking aisle of your grocery store.

**Caramel-Pecan Cheese Pie**

## Spicy Turkey Burgers

*(Pictured below)*

*The hot pepper sauce comes through nicely to spark the flavor of these moist turkey burgers. They're a good low-fat option without the boring taste of typical low-fat foods. No one feels deprived when these sandwiches are on the table.*
*—Mavis Diment, Marcus, Iowa*

**1/2 cup chopped onion**
**2 tablespoons reduced-fat plain yogurt**
**1 tablespoon snipped fresh dill *or* 1 teaspoon dill weed**
**1-1/2 teaspoons hot pepper sauce**
**1/2 teaspoon salt**
**1 garlic clove, minced**
**1 pound lean ground turkey**
**4 kaiser rolls, split**
**4 lettuce leaves**
**4 tomato slices**

In a large bowl, combine the onion, yogurt, dill, hot pepper sauce, salt and garlic. Crumble turkey over mixture; mix well.

Shape into four patties, each about 3/4 in. thick. Grill, uncovered, over medium-hot heat for 6-8 minutes on each side or until no longer pink. Serve on rolls with lettuce and tomato. **Yield:** 4 servings.

**Nutritional Analysis:** One serving equals 357 calories, 12 g fat (3 g saturated fat), 90 mg cholesterol, 766 mg sodium, 34 g carbohydrate, 2 g fiber, 27 g protein. **Diabetic Exchanges:** 3 lean meat, 2 starch, 1 fat.

## Creamy Dill Cucumbers

*(Pictured below)*

*My grown daughter, Jenna, and I love this quick cucumber recipe that calls for ranch dressing mix. The salad is a great side dish anytime. I always keep the ingredients on hand to fix it.*
*—Lucia Rich, St. Peters, Missouri*

**1 cup fat-free milk**
**1/2 cup reduced-fat mayonnaise**
**1/2 cup reduced-fat sour cream**
**1 envelope ranch salad dressing mix**
**2 tablespoons dill weed**
**1/8 teaspoon celery seed**
**1/8 teaspoon pepper**
**2 large cucumbers, peeled and sliced**
**2/3 cup sliced red onion, separated into rings**

In a small bowl, combine the milk, mayonnaise, sour cream, dressing mix, dill, celery seed and pepper. Stir in the cucumbers and onion. Serve with a slotted spoon. **Yield:** 8 servings.

**Nutritional Analysis:** One serving (3/4 cup) equals 108 calories, 6 g fat (2 g saturated fat), 11 mg cholesterol, 435 mg sodium, 9 g carbohydrate, 1 g fiber, 3 g protein. **Diabetic Exchanges:** 2 vegetable, 1 fat.

**Spicy Turkey Burgers**
**Creamy Dill Cucumbers**

## Fruit Cocktail Squares

*This easy frozen medley makes the most of convenient canned fruit. The frosty squares can be served as a salad or dessert.*
*—Ruth Burrus, Zionsville, Indiana*

**1 can (15 ounces) reduced-sugar fruit cocktail**
**1 package (8 ounces) fat-free cream cheese**
**1 can (15 ounces) pitted dark sweet cherries, drained**
**1 cup miniature marshmallows**

Drain fruit cocktail, reserving juice; set fruit aside. In a small mixing bowl, beat cream cheese and reserved juice until smooth. Stir in the fruit cocktail, cherries and marshmallows. Pour into an ungreased 8-in. square dish. Cover and freeze until set. Remove from the freezer 10-15 minutes before serving. Cut into squares. **Yield:** 9 servings.

**Nutritional Analysis:** One serving equals 89 calories, trace fat (trace saturated fat), 2 mg cholesterol, 144 mg sodium, 18 g carbohydrate, 1 g fiber, 4 g protein. **Diabetic Exchange:** 1 fruit.

## Pineapple Icebox Dessert

*While living in Italy, I fell in love with rich Italian tiramisu. I substituted healthier ingredients to make this pineapple version.*
*—Julie Vyska, North Las Vegas, Nevada*

**2 cups cold fat-free milk**
**1 package (1 ounce) sugar-free instant vanilla pudding mix**
**1 cup reduced-fat whipped topping**
**1 can (20 ounces) pineapple tidbits**
**2 packages (3 ounces *each*) ladyfingers**

In a bowl, whisk milk and pudding mix for 2 minutes. Fold in whipped topping; set aside. Drain pineapple, reserving 1/4 cup juice. Arrange half of the ladyfingers in an ungreased 11-in. x 7-in. x 2-in. dish.

Brush with 2 tablespoons reserved pineapple juice.

Top with half of the pudding mixture and half of the pineapple. Repeat the layers. Cover and refrigerate overnight. Cut into squares. **Yield:** 15 servings.

**Nutritional Analysis:** One serving equals 183 calories, 4 g fat (2 g saturated fat), 99 mg cholesterol, 234 mg sodium, 31 g carbohydrate, 1 g fiber, 5 g protein. **Diabetic Exchanges:** 1 starch, 1 fruit, 1/2 fat.

## Crispy Herb Bread

*I use herbs to fix this better-for-you garlic bread, which has lots of flavor but little fat. I live in garlic country, so I use it in most every dish.* —*Ruby Williams, Bogalusa, Louisiana*

- **4 teaspoons olive oil**
- **1/2 teaspoon garlic powder *or* 2 garlic cloves, minced**
- **1 loaf (8 ounces) French bread, halved lengthwise**
- **1 teaspoon dried thyme**
- **1/4 teaspoon dried marjoram**
- **3 tablespoons grated Parmesan cheese**
- **1/2 teaspoon paprika**
- **1 tablespoon minced fresh parsley**

In a small bowl, combine oil and garlic powder; brush over bread. Sprinkle with the remaining ingredients. Place on a baking sheet. Bake at 425° for 7-9 minutes or until lightly browned. Cut each half into five slices. **Yield:** 10 servings.

**Nutritional Analysis:** One slice equals 87 calories, 3 g fat (1 g saturated fat), 1 mg cholesterol, 166 mg sodium, 12 g carbohydrate, 1 g fiber, 3 g protein. **Diabetic Exchange:** 1 starch.

## Tomato Chicken Skillet

*It can be a challenge to provide quick nutritious meals our whole family likes, but this low-fat dish is an all-time favorite.* —*Tina Meekins, Port Orchard, Washington*

- **4 boneless skinless chicken breast halves (4 ounces *each*)**
- **1/2 teaspoon salt-free lemon-pepper seasoning**
- **1 tablespoon olive oil**
- **4 celery ribs *or* 1 medium green pepper, sliced**
- **1/2 cup chopped onion**
- **1 garlic clove, minced**
- **1 can (28 ounces) stewed tomatoes, undrained**
- **Hot cooked pasta *or* rice**

Sprinkle chicken with lemon-pepper. In a large skillet, brown chicken in oil over medium-high heat. Reduce heat. Add the celery, onion and garlic; saute until tender. Stir in the tomatoes. Cover and simmer for 20 minutes or until chicken juices run clear. Serve over pasta. **Yield:** 4 servings.

**Nutritional Analysis:** One serving (calculated without pasta) equals 227 calories, 5 g fat (1 g saturated fat), 66 mg cholesterol, 467 mg sodium, 18 g carbohydrate, 3 g fiber, 28 g protein. **Diabetic Exchanges:** 3 lean meat, 2 vegetable, 1/2 starch.

Onion-Garlic Bubble Bread

## Onion-Garlic Bubble Bread

*(Pictured above)*

*I've relied on this bread recipe often over the years. Frozen dough hurries along the golden pull-apart loaf. It's wonderful with Italian dishes, especially spaghetti and lasagna.* —*Charlene Bzdok, Little Falls, Minnesota*

- **1 loaf (1 pound) frozen bread dough, thawed**
- **1/2 cup finely chopped sweet onion**
- **1/2 cup butter, melted**
- **2 garlic cloves, minced**
- **1 teaspoon dried parsley flakes**
- **1/4 teaspoon salt**

Divide dough into 24 pieces. In a small bowl, combine the remaining ingredients. Dip each piece of dough into butter mixture; place in a 10-in. fluted tube pan coated with nonstick cooking spray. Cover and let rise in a warm place until doubled, about 1 hour. Bake at 375° for 20-25 minutes or until golden brown. Serve warm. **Yield:** 1 loaf (24 pieces).

**Nutritional Analysis:** One piece equals 87 calories, 5 g fat (2 g saturated fat), 10 mg cholesterol, 169 mg sodium, 10 g carbohydrate, 1 g fiber, 2 g protein. **Diabetic Exchange:** 1 starch.

### Healthy Choice for Chicken

I like to make homemade chicken soup the day before. To cut down the fat, I lay a circle of two-ply paper towels on top of the soup as it cools. I cover it and put it in the fridge. As the soup sits overnight, most of the fat rises and sticks to the towels, which I can easily remove and toss out. —*Terry Lyons, East Meadow, New York*

Summer Squash Pepper Gratin
One-for-All Marinated Beef

## Summer Squash Pepper Gratin

*(Pictured above and on page 228)*

*With layers of sliced potatoes, peppers, yellow squash and zucchini, this satisfying side dish is one of our family's all-time favorites. Plenty of cheddar cheese and oregano enhance the fresh summer flavors in this comforting creation. The colorful gratin is eye-catching and looks beautiful on a buffet table, too. —Barbara Nowakowski North Tonawanda, New York*

**1 large unpeeled potato (12 ounces)**
**3/4 cup thinly sliced green pepper**
**3/4 cup thinly sliced sweet red pepper**
**1 teaspoon olive oil**
**2 small yellow summer squash, thinly sliced**
**2 small zucchini, thinly sliced**
**1 teaspoon dried oregano**
**1/2 teaspoon salt**
**1/8 teaspoon pepper**
**1/2 cup shredded reduced-fat sharp cheddar cheese**
**1 tablespoon butter**

Pierce potato with a fork; place on a microwave-safe plate. Microwave, uncovered, on high for 2-3 minutes or until potato is tender but firm. Cool slightly; cut into thin slices.

In a microwave-safe bowl, combine the green and red peppers; drizzle with oil. Cover and microwave on high for 2 to 3-1/2 minutes or until crisp-tender.

In a 1-1/2-qt. baking dish coated with nonstick cooking spray, layer half of the potato, yellow squash, zucchini, pepper mixture, oregano, salt, pepper and cheese. Repeat layers. Dot with butter.

Cover and bake at 375° for 20-25 minutes or until squash is crisp-tender. Uncover; bake 10 minutes longer or until heated through. **Yield:** 6 servings.

**Nutritional Analysis:** One serving (1 cup) equals 121 calories, 5 g fat (3 g saturated fat), 12 mg cholesterol, 302 mg sodium, 16 g carbohydrate, 3 g fiber, 5 g protein. **Diabetic Exchanges:** 1 vegetable, 1 fat, 1/2 starch.

**Editor's Note:** This recipe was tested in a 1,100-watt microwave.

## One-for-All Marinated Beef

*(Pictured at left and on page 229)*

*I use this flavorful marinade not just for beef, but for nearly everything I put on the grill—from pork chops to chicken. The quick-to-mix marinade with garlic and soy sauce relies mainly on orange juice, which is both low in calories and a good tenderizer. —Sue Sauer, Deer River, Minnesota*

**3/4 cup orange juice**
**1/4 cup reduced-sodium soy sauce**
**2 tablespoons brown sugar**
**2 tablespoons prepared mustard**
**1 tablespoon canola oil**
**2 garlic cloves, minced**
**1 beef flank steak (1-1/2 pounds)**

In a large resealable plastic bag, combine the first six ingredients; add flank steak. Seal bag and turn to coat; refrigerate for 4 hours or overnight.

Coat grill rack with nonstick cooking spray before starting the grill. Drain and discard marinade. Grill steak, covered, over medium heat for 6-8 minutes on each side or until meat reaches desired doneness (for rare, a meat thermometer should read 140°; medium, 160°; well-done, 170°). Let stand for 10 minutes before slicing. **Yield:** 6 servings.

**Nutritional Analysis:** One serving (3 ounces cooked beef) equals 206 calories, 10 g fat (4 g saturated fat), 56 mg cholesterol, 305 mg sodium, 4 g carbohydrate, trace fiber, 23 g protein. **Diabetic Exchanges:** 3 lean meat, 1 fat.

## Tomato Mushroom Soup

*My husband and I have never been fond of the usual tomato soup, but when we tried this jazzed-up version full of fresh mushrooms, we thought it was out of this world. A friend shared the 30-minute recipe with me a while back, and I've stirred up a batch every week since. —Chris Nelson, Alliance, Ohio*

1 cup sliced fresh mushrooms
2 tablespoons chopped onion
1 garlic clove, minced
2 tablespoons butter
3 tablespoons all-purpose flour
1 can (14-1/2 ounces) reduced-sodium chicken broth
2 cups chopped seeded peeled plum tomatoes
2 tablespoons minced fresh basil *or* 2 teaspoons dried basil
1 tablespoon sugar
1/2 teaspoon salt
1/8 teaspoon pepper

In a large saucepan, saute the mushrooms, onion and garlic in butter until tender; remove with a slotted spoon and set aside.

In the same pan, combine flour and broth until smooth. Bring to a boil; cook and stir for 1-2 minutes or until thickened.

Return mushroom mixture to saucepan. Add tomatoes, basil, sugar, salt and pepper. Cook over medium heat for 5 minutes or until heated through. **Yield:** 4 servings.

**Nutritional Analysis:** One serving (1 cup) equals 95 calories, 5 g fat (3 g saturated fat), 12 mg cholesterol, 506 mg sodium, 11 g carbohydrate, 1 g fiber, 3 g protein. **Diabetic Exchanges:** 1 fat, 1/2 starch.

## Blueberry Salsa Salad

*For this deliciously different salad, start with a convenient package of mixed greens and add a sweet-tart fruit medley seasoned with onion and cilantro. I top it all with bits of blue cheese. The flavor combination sounds strange to some people at first, but they always end up loving it. The dish was a big hit when I prepared it for our 50th wedding anniversary.* —*Priscilla Gilbert*
*Indian Harbour Beach, Florida*

2 cups fresh blueberries
1 medium red apple, diced
1 large navel orange, peeled, sectioned and chopped
1/2 cup finely chopped sweet onion
1 to 2 tablespoons minced fresh cilantro
1/4 cup red wine vinegar
3 tablespoons unsweetened apple juice
2 tablespoons sugar
2 tablespoons olive oil
1/4 teaspoon salt
1 package (5 ounces) spring mix salad greens
1/2 cup crumbled blue cheese

In a large bowl, combine the blueberries, apple, orange, onion and cilantro. In a small bowl, whisk the vinegar, apple juice, sugar, oil and salt; drizzle over fruit mixture and toss to coat. Let stand for 10 minutes.

Divide salad greens among six serving plates. Using a slotted spoon, arrange blueberry salsa over greens. Drizzle with dressing left in bowl. Sprinkle with blue cheese. **Yield:** 6 servings.

**Nutritional Analysis:** One serving equals 173 calories, 9 g fat (3 g saturated fat), 13 mg cholesterol, 301 mg sodium, 21 g carbohydrate, 3 g fiber, 4 g protein. **Diabetic Exchanges:** 1-1/2 fruit, 1-1/2 fat.

## Peach Sorbet

*(Pictured below)*

*Since moving to an area where fresh-picked peaches are plentiful, I've whipped up this frosty four-ingredient treat frequently. I think it's the perfect light dessert, especially after a summer barbecue or heavier meal. When I'm entertaining, I find that calorie-conscious guests always say "yes" to this smooth, refreshing sorbet when they might decline a piece of cake or pie.* —*Mary Dixson*
*Decatur, Alabama*

1/2 cup water
3 tablespoons sugar
2 tablespoons lemon juice
4 medium ripe peaches, peeled and sliced

In a saucepan, combine the water, sugar and lemon juice. Cook and stir over medium heat until sugar is dissolved. Cool slightly; transfer to a blender.

Add the peaches; cover and process until smooth. Fill cylinder of ice cream freezer; freeze according to manufacturer's directions. Transfer sorbet to a freezer container; cover and freeze for 4 hours or until firm. **Yield:** 3 servings.

**Nutritional Analysis:** One serving (1/2 cup) equals 104 calories, 0 fat (0 saturated fat), 0 cholesterol, trace sodium, 27 g carbohydrate, 3 g fiber, 1 g protein. **Diabetic Exchange:** 1-1/2 fruit.

**Peach Sorbet**

## Creamy Poppy Seed Dressing

(Pictured below)

*I created this citrusy dressing to give my salads a different flavor. Just mix it up and pour over your favorite tossed greens...or a medley of fresh fruit.* —Marge Werner Broken Arrow, Oklahoma

**1/2 cup orange juice**
**1/2 cup fat-free mayonnaise**
**1/2 cup reduced-fat sour cream**
**2 teaspoons sugar**
**2 teaspoons lemon juice**
**1 teaspoon poppy seeds**
**1/8 teaspoon pepper**

In a jar with a tight-fitting lid, combine all of the ingredients; shake well. Cover and refrigerate until serving. **Yield:** 1-1/2 cups.

**Nutritional Analysis:** One serving (2 tablespoons salad dressing) equals 31 calories, 1 g fat (1 g saturated fat), 4 mg cholesterol, 87 mg sodium, 4 g carbohydrate, trace fiber, 1 g protein. **Diabetic Exchange:** 1/2 starch.

## Enchilada Stuffed Shells

(Pictured below)

*I served this entree to my husband, my sister and her husband, and I received many compliments. My brother-in-law is a hard-to-please eater, so when he said he loved it, I was thrilled.* —Rebecca Stout, Conroe, Texas

**15 uncooked jumbo pasta shells**
**1 pound lean ground turkey**
**1 can (10 ounces) enchilada sauce**
**1/2 teaspoon dried minced onion**
**1/4 teaspoon dried basil**
**1/4 teaspoon dried oregano**
**1/4 teaspoon ground cumin**
**1/2 cup fat-free refried beans**
**1 cup (4 ounces) reduced-fat shredded cheddar cheese**

Cook pasta according to package directions; drain. In a nonstick skillet, cook turkey over medium heat until no longer pink; drain. Stir in enchilada sauce and seasonings; set aside.

Place a rounded teaspoonful of refried beans in each pasta shell, then fill with turkey mixture. Place in an 11-in. x 7-in. x 2-in. baking dish coated with nonstick cooking spray. Cover and bake at 350° for 25 minutes. Uncover and sprinkle with cheese. Bake 5 minutes longer or until cheese is melted. **Yield:** 5 servings.

**Nutritional Analysis:** One serving (3 stuffed shells) equals 379 calories, 15 g fat (6 g saturated fat), 89 mg cholesterol, 591 mg sodium, 33 g carbohydrate, 2 g fiber, 28 g protein. **Diabetic Exchanges:** 3 lean meat, 2 starch, 1 fat.

## Jalapeno Corn Bread

*This homemade corn bread is jazzed up with green onion, cheddar cheese and jalapeno pepper. It takes just minutes to bake.* —Angela Oelschlaeger, Tonganoxie, Kansas

**1/2 cup cornmeal**
**1/2 cup all-purpose flour**
**1 teaspoon sugar**
**1/2 teaspoon salt**
**1/4 teaspoon baking powder**
**1/4 teaspoon baking soda**
**1/4 teaspoon garlic powder**

Creamy Poppy Seed Dressing
Enchilada Stuffed Shells

**1/2 cup cream-style corn**
**1/4 cup egg substitute**
**1/4 cup reduced-fat cheddar cheese**
**1/4 cup fat-free milk**
**2 tablespoons chopped green onion**
**1 tablespoon butter, melted**
**2 teaspoons chopped seeded jalapeno pepper**

In a large bowl, combine the first seven ingredients. Combine the corn, egg substitute, cheese, milk, onion, butter and jalapeno. Stir into dry ingredients just until moistened. Pour into an 8-in. square baking dish coated with nonstick cooking spray.

Bake at 425° for 12-14 minutes or until a toothpick inserted near the center comes out clean. Cut into squares; serve warm. **Yield:** 9 servings.

**Nutritional Analysis:** One serving equals 94 calories, 2 g fat (1 g saturated fat), 5 mg cholesterol, 261 mg sodium, 15 g carbohydrate, 1 g fiber, 4 g protein. **Diabetic Exchanges:** 1 starch, 1/2 fat.

**Editor's Note:** When cutting or seeding hot peppers, use rubber or plastic gloves to protect your hands. Avoid touching your face.

## Citrus Chocolate Cupcakes

*My mom and I first sampled these moist chocolaty cupcakes at her health club's annual taste test. Not only are they light and delicious, they're a breeze to make! We feel like we're indulging when we bite into these citrusy treats.* —Sara Zignego Hartford, Wisconsin

**1-1/2 cups all-purpose flour**
**1/2 cup sugar**
**1/4 cup baking cocoa**
**1 teaspoon baking soda**
**1/2 teaspoon salt**
**1/2 cup orange juice**
**1/3 cup water**
**3 tablespoons canola *or* vegetable oil**
**1 tablespoon white vinegar**
**1 teaspoon vanilla extract**
**1/3 cup miniature semisweet chocolate chips**
**1-1/2 teaspoons confectioners' sugar**

In a bowl, combine flour, sugar, cocoa, baking soda and salt. Combine the orange juice, water, oil, vinegar and vanilla. Stir into the dry ingredients just until moistened. Fold in chocolate chips. Coat muffin cups with nonstick cooking spray or use paper liners; fill half full with batter. Bake at 375° for 13-16 minutes or until a toothpick comes out clean. Cool for 5 minutes before removing from pan to a wire rack to cool completely. Just before serving, sprinkle with confectioners' sugar. **Yield:** 1 dozen.

**Nutritional Analysis:** One cupcake equals 155 calories, 5 g fat (1 g saturated fat), 0 cholesterol, 204 mg sodium, 26 g carbohydrate, 1 g fiber, 2 g protein. **Diabetic Exchanges:** 1-1/2 starch, 1 fat.

**Editor's Note:** This recipe does not use eggs.

Double-Decker Banana Cups

## Double-Decker Banana Cups

*(Pictured above)*

*These petite parfaits layer a pudding mixture with sliced bananas and graham cracker crumbs for a speedy dessert or sweet snack.* —Patricia Kinsella, Calgary, Alberta

**1 cup cold fat-free milk**
**1 package (3.4 ounces) instant vanilla pudding mix**
**1 cup reduced-fat whipped topping**
**1 cup thinly sliced firm bananas**
**4 teaspoons graham cracker crumbs**
**4 maraschino cherries with stems**

In a bowl, whisk together milk and pudding for 2 minutes. Fold in whipped topping. Refrigerate for at least 5 minutes. Divide half of pudding mixture among four dessert dishes. Top with half of the banana slices and remaining pudding mixture. Sprinkle with crumbs. Top each with the remaining banana slices and garnish with a cherry. Serve immediately. **Yield:** 4 servings.

**Nutritional Analysis:** One serving (3/4 cup) equals 193 calories, 2 g fat (2 g saturated fat), 1 mg cholesterol, 350 mg sodium, 40 g carbohydrate, 1 g fiber, 3 g protein. **Diabetic Exchanges:** 2 starch, 1/2 fruit.

### Quick Crumbs

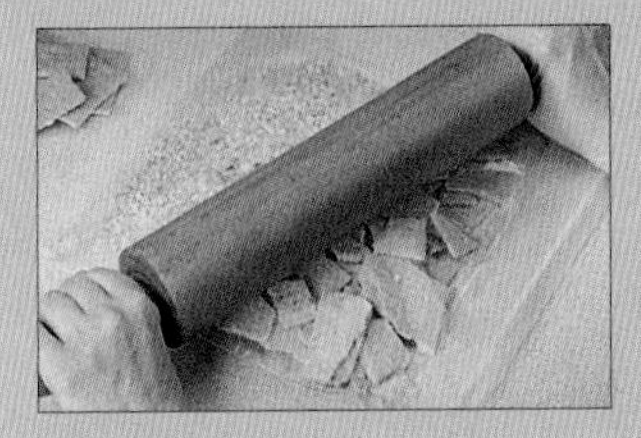

TO MAKE crumbs from graham crackers, place them in a heavy-duty resealable plastic bag and push out as much air as possible before sealing it. Then press a rolling pin over the bag, crushing the crackers to fine crumbs. You can also create crumbs using a blender or food processor following the manufacturer's directions.

Apple-Peanut Spinach Salad
Chicken Pepper Fajitas

## Chicken Pepper Fajitas

*(Pictured above)*

*This spicy skillet entree is fun to serve sizzling at the table, just like they do in restaurants. The light fajitas are full of red and green peppers, onions and chicken that's quickly marinated for a flavor boost. I can rely on this recipe when I want a main course that looks and tastes special but is on the healthier side. —Lucinda Price, Tracy, California*

**2/3 cup lime juice**
**1 tablespoon salt-free seasoning blend**
**1 tablespoon ground cumin**
**1 teaspoon chili powder**
**1 teaspoon pepper**
**1/2 teaspoon garlic powder**
**1 pound boneless skinless chicken breasts, cut into 1/4-inch strips**
**1 large onion, halved and thinly sliced**
**1 medium green pepper, julienned**
**1 medium sweet red pepper, julienned**
**6 flour tortillas (7 inches), warmed**

In a bowl, combine the first six ingredients; set aside 2 tablespoons. Pour the remaining marinade into a large resealable plastic bag; add chicken. Seal the bag and turn to coat; refrigerate for 30 minutes, turning occasionally.

In a large skillet coated with nonstick cooking spray, saute the onion and peppers until crisp-tender; remove and set aside. Drain and discard the marinade from the chicken. Add the chicken and reserved marinade to the skillet; cook for 3-5 minutes or until no longer pink. Return the vegetables to pan; heat through. Serve on tortillas. **Yield:** 6 servings.

**Nutritional Analysis:** One fajita equals 199 calories, 2 g fat (trace saturated fat), 44 mg cholesterol, 96 mg sodium, 23 g carbohydrate, 3 g fiber, 22 g protein. **Diabetic Exchanges:** 3 very lean meat, 1 starch, 1 vegetable.

## Apple-Peanut Spinach Salad

*(Pictured at left)*

*This memorable medley is not only delicious, but it also has a nutritious mix of spinach, apple chunks, peanuts and raisins. It's topped with a flavorful curry dressing that's ready in moments—I simply combine the ingredients in a jar, cover it and shake. My mom and I have been tossing together this salad for years. —Ali Lowell Winchester, Massachusetts*

**2 packages (6 ounces *each*) fresh baby spinach**
**1 medium apple, chopped**
**1/4 cup raisins**
**2 tablespoons chopped peanuts**
**2 tablespoons olive oil**
**1 tablespoon sugar**
**1 tablespoon cider vinegar**
**1 tablespoon chutney**
**3/4 teaspoon curry powder**
**1/4 teaspoon salt**

In a large bowl, combine the spinach, apple, raisins and peanuts. In a jar with a tight-fitting lid, combine the remaining ingredients; shake well. Drizzle over salad and toss to coat. **Yield:** 6 servings.

**Nutritional Analysis:** One serving (3/4 cup) equals 205 calories, 12 g fat (2 g saturated fat), 0 cholesterol, 245 mg sodium, 23 g carbohydrate, 2 g fiber, 4 g protein. **Diabetic Exchanges:** 2-1/2 fat, 1 fruit, 1 vegetable.

## Chili Mac Casserole

*With fun wagon wheel pasta and popular Tex-Mex ingredients, this beefy main dish is a sure family-pleaser and gets to the table in less than an hour. While the casserole bakes, you'll have time to assemble a mixed green salad with light dressing. Round out the menu with scoops of sherbet or frozen yogurt for dessert. —Janet Kanzler Yakima, Washington*

**1 cup uncooked wagon wheel pasta**
**1 pound lean ground beef**
**1/2 cup chopped onion**
**1/2 cup chopped green pepper**
**1 can (15 ounces) turkey chili with beans**
**1 can (14-1/2 ounces) stewed tomatoes, undrained**
**1 cup coarsely crushed baked corn chips**
**1 cup (4 ounces) reduced-fat shredded cheddar cheese, *divided***
**1/4 cup uncooked instant rice**
**1 teaspoon chili powder**
**1/4 teaspoon salt**
**1/8 teaspoon pepper**

Cook pasta according to package directions. Meanwhile, in a large nonstick skillet, cook the beef, onion and green pepper over medium heat until meat is no longer pink; drain. Stir in the chili, tomatoes, corn chips, 1/2 cup cheese, rice, chili powder, salt and pepper.

Drain pasta; add to beef mixture. Transfer to a 2-qt. baking dish coated with nonstick cooking spray. Sprinkle with remaining cheese. Bake, uncovered, at 350° for 25-30 minutes or until cheese is melted. **Yield:** 6 servings.

**Nutritional Analysis:** One serving (1 cup) equals 358 calories, 11 g fat (5 g saturated fat), 60 mg cholesterol, 847 mg sodium, 36 g carbohydrate, 4 g fiber, 28 g protein. **Diabetic Exchanges:** 3 lean meat, 2 starch, 1 vegetable.

## Crispy Potato Wedges

*French-fry fans will fall for this easy oven-baked variety and never miss the fattier kinds at fast-food restaurants. In just 10 minutes, I can have the seasoned wedges ready to pop in the oven. Try pairing them with everything from hot dogs and hamburgers to chicken strips and fish.*
*—Ruby Williams, Bogalusa, Louisiana*

**4 medium baking potatoes (about 1-1/4 pounds)**
**1 tablespoon canola oil**
**1/4 teaspoon garlic powder**
**1/4 teaspoon salt**
**1/4 teaspoon pepper**

Cut each potato into 12 wedges; place in a large bowl. Add the remaining ingredients; toss to coat. Arrange in a single layer in a 15-in. x 10-in. x 1-in. baking pan coated with nonstick cooking spray. Bake at 425° for 20 minutes. Turn; bake 25-30 minutes longer or until crisp. **Yield:** 4 servings.

**Nutritional Analysis:** One serving (12 wedges) equals 134 calories, 4 g fat (trace saturated fat), 0 cholesterol, 74 mg sodium, 27 g carbohydrate, 3 g fiber, 4 g protein. **Diabetic Exchange:** 1-1/2 starch.

## Pasta Shrimp Salad

*I prepared a similar version of this 20-minute seafood salad years ago for my daughter's graduation party. Since then, I've substituted lower-fat items for some of the ingredients, and I get many requests for the lighter recipe. The creamy dressing that coats the pasta, vegetables and shrimp tastes great.* *—Mary Ann Berquam*
*Turtle Lake, Wisconsin*

**1 package (7 ounces) small shell pasta**
**3 celery ribs, chopped**
**1 package (5 ounces) frozen small cooked shrimp, thawed**
**1 cup frozen peas, thawed**
**1/2 cup fat-free French salad dressing**
**1/2 cup reduced-fat mayonnaise**
**3 tablespoons chopped onion**
**2 teaspoons dried basil**
**2 teaspoons lemon juice**
**1/2 teaspoon garlic powder**
**1/2 teaspoon salt-free lemon-pepper seasoning**
**1/2 teaspoon salt-free seasoning blend**

Cook pasta according to package directions; drain and rinse in cold water. In a large bowl, combine pasta, celery, shrimp and peas. In a small bowl, combine remaining ingredients. Pour over pasta mixture and toss to coat. Cover and refrigerate until serving. **Yield:** 7 servings.

**Nutritional Analysis:** One serving (1 cup) equals 165 calories, 6 g fat (1 g saturated fat), 45 mg cholesterol, 392 mg sodium, 20 g carbohydrate, 2 g fiber, 7 g protein. **Diabetic Exchanges:** 1 starch, 1 lean meat, 1 vegetable.

## Cranberry Oat Cookies

*(Pictured below)*

*These yummy sweets are crunchy on the outside, chewy on the inside and dotted with dried cranberries. Whenever I'm craving a treat, I bake up a batch of these quick oat cookies. They also prove popular when I bring them to family gatherings or other events.* *—Heather Breen*
*Chicago, Illinois*

**1/2 cup plus 2 tablespoons packed brown sugar**
**1/4 cup sugar**
**1/3 cup canola oil**
**1 egg**
**1 tablespoon fat-free milk**
**3/4 teaspoon vanilla extract**
**1-1/4 cups quick-cooking oats**
**3/4 cup plus 2 tablespoons all-purpose flour**
**1/2 teaspoon baking soda**
**1/2 teaspoon salt**
**1/2 cup dried cranberries**

In a large mixing bowl, combine sugars and oil. Beat in egg, milk and vanilla. Combine oats, flour, baking soda and salt; gradually add to sugar mixture. Stir in cranberries.

Drop by tablespoonfuls onto baking sheets coated with nonstick cooking spray. Bake at 375° for 10-12 minutes or until lightly browned. Remove to wire racks. **Yield:** 2-1/2 dozen.

**Nutritional Analysis:** One cookie equals 79 calories, 3 g fat (trace saturated fat), 7 mg cholesterol, 64 mg sodium, 13 g carbohydrate, 1 g fiber, 1 g protein. **Diabetic Exchange:** 1 starch.

Cranberry Oat Cookies

## Five-Vegetable Medley

*(Pictured below)*

*To brighten up mealtime menus, simply add this colorful and delicious side dish. I cut the fresh veggies julienne-style and saute them in a little butter and white wine for a crisp-tender mix.* —*Katherine Desrosiers*
*Trail, British Columbia*

**2 medium parsnips, peeled and julienned**
**2 medium carrots, julienned**
**2 celery ribs, julienned**
**1 small turnip, peeled and julienned**
**2 tablespoons butter**
**1 medium sweet red pepper, julienned**
**1/2 cup white wine *or* chicken broth**

In a large skillet, saute the parsnips, carrots, celery and turnip in butter for 5 minutes. Add red pepper; cook and stir 1 minute longer. Add wine or broth. Bring to a boil. Reduce heat; cover and simmer for 4-6 minutes or until vegetables are tender. Serve with a slotted spoon. **Yield:** 6 servings.

**Nutritional Analysis:** One serving (1/2 cup) equals 103 calories, 4 g fat (2 g saturated fat), 10 mg cholesterol, 84 mg sodium, 13 g carbohydrate, 3 g fiber, 1 g protein. **Diabetic Exchanges:** 2 vegetable, 1 fat.

## Spinach Pork Tenderloin

*(Pictured below)*

*Stuffed with fresh spinach and artichoke hearts, these pork slices look fancy enough for guests. An easy sweet-sour sauce enhances the entree.* —*Linda Rae Lee*
*San Francisco, California*

Five-Vegetable Medley
Spinach Pork Tenderloin

**2 cups torn fresh spinach**
**1/4 cup water**
**1/2 cup frozen artichoke hearts, thawed and chopped**
**1/3 cup shredded Parmesan cheese**
**1/4 teaspoon dried rosemary, crushed**
**1 pork tenderloin (1 pound)**
**1/2 teaspoon salt, *divided***
**1/8 teaspoon pepper**

SAUCE:

**1/2 cup apple-cranberry juice concentrate**
**1/4 cup balsamic vinegar**
**1 tablespoon sugar**

In a nonstick skillet, cook the spinach in water over medium heat for 3-4 minutes or until wilted; drain well. Combine the spinach, artichokes, Parmesan cheese and rosemary; set aside.

Cut a lengthwise slit down center of tenderloin to within 1/2 in. of bottom. Open meat so it lies flat; cover with plastic wrap. Flatten to 1/4-in. thickness; remove plastic. Sprinkle meat with 1/4 teaspoon salt; top with spinach mixture.

Close meat; tie with kitchen string and secure ends with toothpicks. Sprinkle with pepper and remaining salt. Place in a shallow baking pan. Bake at 425° for 15 minutes.

Meanwhile, in a small saucepan, combine the sauce ingredients. Bring to a boil over medium heat. Reduce heat; simmer, uncovered, for 15 minutes. Pour over the meat. Bake 10 minutes longer or until a meat thermometer reads 160°. Let stand for 10 minutes before slicing. **Yield:** 4 servings.

**Nutritional Analysis:** One serving (3 ounces cooked meat with about 2 tablespoons sauce) equals 262 calories, 6 g fat (3 g saturated fat), 72 mg cholesterol, 517 mg sodium, 22 g carbohydrate, 1 g fiber, 29 g protein. **Diabetic Exchanges:** 4 very lean meat, 1 vegetable, 1 fruit, 1/2 fat.

## Breakfast Hash

*I was fixing a Western omelet for my husband while frying up potatoes in another pan. I cut up too many vegetables for the omelet and didn't want to waste them, so I added them to the potatoes. Everyone wanted a taste. Now I make this hash at least once a month.*
—*Shirley Frank, Neponset, Illinois*

**6 small potatoes, peeled and cut into 1/2-inch cubes**
**1 cup sliced fresh mushrooms**
**1 small green pepper, diced**
**1 small sweet red pepper, diced**
**1 small onion, chopped**
**1 teaspoon garlic salt**
**1 teaspoon minced fresh parsley**
**1/4 teaspoon pepper**
**2 tablespoons butter**

In a bowl, combine the first eight ingredients. In a large nonstick skillet, melt butter over medium-high heat. Add potato mixture. Cook and stir for 15-16 minutes or until potatoes are lightly browned. **Yield:** 8 servings.

**Nutritional Analysis:** One serving (1 cup) equals 111 calories, 3 g fat (2 g saturated fat), 8 mg cholesterol, 156 mg sodium, 20 g carbohydrate, 2 g fiber, 2 g protein. **Diabetic Exchanges:** 1 starch, 1 vegetable.

## Raspberry Cream Gelatin

*This pretty pink gelatin mold is bursting with raspberry flavor. If you like, garnish it with more berries and a dollop of light whipped topping.* —*Marguerite Shaeffer, Sewell, New Jersey*

- **1 package (10 ounces) frozen sweetened raspberries, thawed**
- **1 package (3 ounces) raspberry gelatin**
- **1 cup boiling water**
- **1 tablespoon lemon juice**
- **1 can (5 ounces) fat-free evaporated milk, chilled**

Drain raspberries, reserving syrup; set berries aside. In a mixing bowl, dissolve gelatin in boiling water. Stir in the lemon juice and reserved raspberry syrup. Refrigerate until partially set. Add milk. Beat on high speed until thickened, about 4 minutes. Fold in reserved raspberries. Pour into a 2-qt. bowl. Refrigerate until set. **Yield:** 10 servings.

**Nutritional Analysis:** One serving (3/4 cup) equals 72 calories, trace fat (trace saturated fat), 1 mg cholesterol, 36 mg sodium, 17 g carbohydrate, 1 g fiber, 2 g protein. **Diabetic Exchange:** 1 fruit.

## Cream Cheese Ham Omelet

*It's a cinch to whip up this rich hearty omelet filled with cream cheese, ham and onion. My husband and I are watching our cholesterol, so I use an egg substitute for this recipe. He always raves about it.* —*Michelle Revelle, Guyton, Georgia*

- **1/2 cup chopped sweet onion**
- **2 teaspoons olive oil**
- **1 cup egg substitute**
- **1/2 cup diced fully cooked lean ham**
- **1/4 teaspoon seasoned salt**
- **1/8 teaspoon pepper**
- **1/8 teaspoon paprika**
- **3 tablespoons reduced-fat cream cheese, cubed**

In a 10-in. nonstick skillet, saute onion in oil until tender. Reduce heat to medium; add egg substitute. As eggs set, lift edges, letting uncooked portion flow underneath. When the eggs are set, sprinkle ham and seasonings over one side. Top with cream cheese cubes. Fold omelet over filling. Cover and let stand for 1-2 minutes or until cream cheese is melted. **Yield:** 2 servings.

**Nutritional Analysis:** One serving equals 215 calories, 10 g fat (4 g saturated fat), 23 mg cholesterol, 905 mg sodium, 7 g carbohydrate, 1 g fiber, 22 g protein. **Diabetic Exchanges:** 2 lean meat, 1 fat, 1/2 fat-free milk.

Chocolate Angel Food Cake

## Chocolate Angel Food Cake

(Pictured above)

*When I needed a lighter dessert to serve guests who were on a restricted diet, I combined two of my favorite recipes to create this chocolate cake with raspberry sauce. I dolloped on some whipped topping, too, and everyone enjoyed it.* —*Lana Drum, Maryville, Tennessee*

- **1 package (16 ounces) angel food cake mix**
- **1-1/4 cups cold water**
- **1/2 cup baking cocoa**

**RASPBERRY SAUCE:**

- **Sugar substitute equivalent to 1/4 cup sugar**
- **2 teaspoons cornstarch**
- **1 package (12 ounces) frozen unsweetened raspberries**
- **1-1/4 cups reduced-fat whipped topping**

In a large mixing bowl, beat cake mix and water on low speed for 30 seconds. Beat on high for 45 seconds. Add cocoa; beat on high 15 seconds longer. Pour into an ungreased 10-in. tube pan. Bake at 350° for 35-40 minutes or until cake springs back when lightly touched and cracks feel dry. Immediately invert pan; cool completely.

In a saucepan, combine the sugar substitute and cornstarch; add raspberries. Cook and stir until mixture comes to a boil, about 6 minutes. Cook and stir 2 minutes longer or until the mixture is thickened. Remove saucepan from the heat; cool.

Run a knife around side and center tube of cake pan; remove cake. Strain the raspberry sauce; spoon over cake slices. Dollop with whipped topping. **Yield:** 12 servings.

**Nutritional Analysis:** One serving (1 piece of cake with 1 tablespoon raspberry sauce and 1 tablespoon whipped topping) equals 184 calories, 2 g fat (1 g saturated fat), 0 cholesterol, 329 mg sodium, 38 g carbohydrate, 2 g fiber, 4 g protein. **Diabetic Exchange:** 2-1/2 starch.

**Editor's Note:** This recipe was tested with Splenda No Calorie Sweetener. Look for it in the baking aisle of your grocery store.

# Chapter 17

# Centsible Foods—Fast and Frugal

SERVING your family a fast and satisfying meal doesn't have to cost a pretty penny.

Instead of buying convenient yet costly restaurant carryout meals or store-bought packaged dinners, turn to the speedy recipes here. These "centsible" express-eating alternatives are as easy on the family budget as they are appetizing.

Our Test Kitchen has figured the cost per serving for each delicious dish. So these fast and frugal recipes will result in prompt meals and a plumper pocketbook.

**SWIFT 'N' THRIFTY.** Breakfast Loaf (recipe on p. 249).

## Sweet-Sour Franks

*(Pictured below)*

*When I married my husband more than 30 years ago, I asked my mother-in-law for some of his favorite recipes. Knowing that we were on a tight budget, she shared this one. It's still a favorite of ours because it tastes great and comes together quickly on the stovetop.*
*—Diane Hendrixson, Wapakoneta, Ohio*

**1 can (20 ounces) pineapple tidbits**
**1 teaspoon beef bouillon granules**
**1/3 cup boiling water**
**1 tablespoon cornstarch**
**1 tablespoon brown sugar**
**2 tablespoons cider vinegar**
**1 tablespoon soy sauce**
**1 medium onion, chopped**
**1 medium green pepper, julienned**
**2 tablespoons margarine**
**5 hot dogs, halved lengthwise and cut into 1/2-inch slices**
**3 cups hot cooked rice**

Drain pineapple, reserving juice. Set aside 1 cup pineapple and 6 tablespoons juice; refrigerate remaining pineapple and juice for another use. Dissolve bouillon in water. In a small bowl, combine the cornstarch, brown sugar, vinegar, soy sauce, bouillon and reserved juice until smooth; set aside.

In a large skillet, saute the onion and green pepper in margarine. Stir cornstarch mixture; stir into skillet. Bring to a boil; cook and stir for 2 minutes or until thickened. Add the hot dogs and reserved pineapple; cook until heated through. Serve over rice. **Yield:** 3 servings (71¢ per serving).

## Oatmeal Raisin Bars

*These tender bars have a sweet raisin filling tucked between a golden oat crust and topping. They're perfect for potlucks, but the old-fashioned treats quickly disappear at family gatherings and other events, too.*
*—Rita Christianson*
*Glenburn, North Dakota*

**1 cup sugar**
**2 tablespoons plus 1-1/2 teaspoons cornstarch**
**1 teaspoon ground cinnamon**
**3 eggs, beaten**
**1-1/2 cups (12 ounces) sour cream**
**2 cups raisins**
**CRUMB MIXTURE:**
**1-3/4 cups all-purpose flour**
**1-3/4 cups quick-cooking oats**
**1 cup packed brown sugar**
**1 teaspoon baking soda**
**1/2 teaspoon salt**
**1 cup cold margarine**

In a large heavy saucepan, combine sugar, cornstarch and cinnamon. Stir in eggs, sour cream and raisins. Cook and stir over medium heat for 8-10 minutes or until a thermometer reads 160°; set aside to cool slightly.

Meanwhile, in a bowl, combine the flour, oats, brown sugar, baking soda and salt. Cut in margarine until crumbly. Firmly press 3-1/2 cups of crumb mixture into a greased 13-in. x 9-in. x 2-in. baking pan. Spread with warm raisin filling. Sprinkle with remaining crumb mixture. Bake at 350° for 25-30 minutes or until golden brown. Cool on a wire rack. Cut into bars. Refrigerate leftovers. **Yield:** about 3 dozen (20¢ per serving).

**Sweet-Sour Franks**

## Raspberry Citrus Compote

*Grapefruit is a surprising but refreshing addition to this recipe that's a wonderful twist on traditional fruit compote. With frozen raspberries and sugar, I make a sweet sauce that coats tangy citrus wedges and chopped pears. The salad is ready to serve in about an hour...and also keeps down my grocery costs.* —*Cindy Reams*
*Philipsburg, Pennsylvania*

**1/2 cup sugar**
**4-1/2 teaspoons cornstarch**
**1 cup water**
**1 package (10 ounces) frozen unsweetened raspberries, thawed**
**3 large navel oranges, peeled and sectioned**
**2 medium ripe pears, peeled and chopped**
**1 large grapefruit, peeled, sectioned and seeded**

In a saucepan, combine the sugar, cornstarch and water until smooth. Bring to a boil; cook and stir for 2 minutes or until thickened. Reduce the heat; stir in the raspberries. Simmer, uncovered, for 5 minutes or until heated through. Remove from heat. Cool to room temperature. Add the oranges, pears and grapefruit; stir gently to coat. Chill leftovers. **Yield:** 8 servings (36¢ per serving).

## Spiced Cocoa Cupcakes

*(Pictured at right)*

*To me, a good cup of hot spiced cocoa on a cool day is heavenly, and that's what these remind me of. The drizzled desserts studded with dried cranberries are a budget-friendly finish for any meal and make nice take-along treats, too.*
—*Shirley Glaab, Hattiesburg, Mississippi*

**1-1/2 cups all-purpose flour**
**3/4 cup sugar**
**1/4 cup baking cocoa**
**3/4 teaspoon baking soda**
**1/4 teaspoon salt**
**1/4 teaspoon ground cinnamon**
**1/4 teaspoon ground nutmeg**
**1 egg**
**3/4 cup applesauce**
**1/4 cup butter, melted**
**1/2 cup dried cranberries**
**1 cup confectioners' sugar**
**4-1/2 teaspoons milk**

In a bowl, combine first seven ingredients. In another bowl, whisk the egg, applesauce and butter; stir into dry ingredients just until combined. Fold in the cranberries. Fill greased or paper-lined muffin cups two-thirds full.

Bake at 350° for 18-20 minutes or until a toothpick comes out clean. Cool for 5 minutes before removing from pan to a wire rack to cool completely. In a small bowl, combine confectioners' sugar and milk until smooth. Drizzle over cupcakes. **Yield:** 1 dozen (15¢ per serving).

Spiced Cocoa Cupcakes
Turkey Noodle Soup

## Turkey Noodle Soup

*(Pictured above)*

*Homemade taste makes this chunky soup full of tender turkey, egg noodles and veggies a favorite. We enjoy it year-round, pairing it with hot bread in winter and with salad in summer. Canned chicken broth and purchased gravy mix help speed up the preparation.* —*Elaine Bickford*
*Las Vegas, Nevada*

**2 cans (14-1/2 ounces *each*) chicken broth**
**3 cups water**
**1-3/4 cups sliced carrots**
**1/2 cup chopped onion**
**2 celery ribs, sliced**
**1 package (12 ounces) frozen egg noodles**
**3 cups chopped cooked turkey**
**1 package (10 ounces) frozen peas**
**2 envelopes chicken gravy mix**
**1/2 cup cold water**

In a large saucepan, bring the broth, water, carrots, onion and celery to a boil. Reduce heat; cover and simmer for 4-6 minutes or until vegetables are crisp-tender. Add the noodles. Simmer, uncovered, for 20 minutes or until noodles are tender.

Stir in turkey and peas. Combine gravy mixes and cold water until smooth; stir into the soup. Bring to a boil; cook and stir for 2 minutes or until thickened. **Yield:** 7 servings (94¢ per serving).

Vanilla Chip Cherry Cookies

## Vanilla Chip Cherry Cookies

*(Pictured above)*

*Chopped maraschino cherries and vanilla chips make a great color and flavor combination in these sweet treats. They're a nice change from traditional chocolate chip cookies, and they're just as easy to prepare. With a yield of 4-1/2 dozen, this recipe creates enough goodies to fill up the cookie jar and share.* —*Margaret Wilson Hemet, California*

**1 cup butter, softened**
**3/4 cup sugar**
**3/4 cup packed brown sugar**
**2 eggs**
**1/4 teaspoon almond extract**
**2-1/4 cups all-purpose flour**
**1 teaspoon baking soda**
**1/2 teaspoon salt**
**1 package (10 to 12 ounces) vanilla *or* white chips**
**1 jar (10 ounces) maraschino cherries, drained and chopped**

In a large mixing bowl, cream butter and sugars. Add eggs, one at a time, beating well after each addition. Beat in almond extract. Combine the flour, baking soda and salt; gradually add to the creamed mixture. Stir in chips and cherries.

Drop by rounded tablespoonfuls 2 in. apart onto ungreased baking sheets. Bake at 350° for 10-12 minutes or until lightly browned. Remove to wire racks to cool. **Yield:** 4-1/2 dozen (20¢ per serving).

## Three-Cheese Macaroni

*This creamy homemade macaroni and cheese is quick to fix. You can add tuna or leftover ham and vegetables to make this into a main dish.* —*Melonie Corbin South St. Paul, Minnesota*

**1 package (7 ounces) elbow macaroni**
**1 can (10-3/4 ounces) condensed cheddar cheese soup, undiluted**
**2 slices process American cheese**
**1/4 cup shredded Parmesan cheese**
**1/4 cup milk**
**1 tablespoon butter**

Cook macaroni according to package directions. Meanwhile, in a large saucepan, combine the soup, cheeses, milk and butter. Cook and stir until cheese is melted. Drain macaroni; stir into cheese sauce. **Yield:** 4 servings (58¢ per serving).

## Sweet-and-Sour Kraut

*Folks who aren't fond of the "sour" in sauerkraut are sure to enjoy this deliciously different version sweetened with plenty of brown sugar. This side dish might sound a little strange, but one taste proves that it's really very good—even when served cold.* —*Margery Bryan Moses Lake, Washington*

**4 bacon strips, diced**
**1 medium onion, chopped**
**1 can (27 ounces) sauerkraut, rinsed and drained**
**1 can (14-1/2 ounces) diced tomatoes, drained**
**1 cup packed brown sugar**

In a large skillet, cook bacon over medium heat until crisp. Remove with a slotted spoon to paper towels; drain, reserving 1 tablespoon drippings. Saute onion in the drippings until tender.

Stir in sauerkraut, tomatoes, brown sugar and bacon. Bring to a boil. Transfer to a greased 1-1/2-qt. baking dish. Bake, uncovered, at 350° for 30-35 minutes or until bubbly. **Yield:** 10 servings (29¢ per serving).

## Veggie Beef Bundles

*These individual foil packets of ground beef and vegetables were a favorite meal choice when my husband and I were building a log home. We still enjoy this satisfying supper that takes advantage of onion soup mix and frozen cut green beans.* —*Carolyn Dixon, Wilmar, Arkansas*

**2 cups julienned uncooked potatoes**
**1 pound lean ground beef**
**1 envelope onion soup mix**
**1/4 cup water**
**1 cup sliced fresh mushrooms**
**1 package (9 ounces) frozen cut green beans, thawed**

Coat four pieces of heavy-duty foil (about 12 in. square) with nonstick cooking spray. Place 1/2 cup potatoes on each square. Shape beef into four patties; place over potatoes. Combine soup mix and water; spoon half over patties. Top with mushrooms, green beans and remaining soup mixture.

Fold foil around meat and vegetables and seal tightly. Place on a baking sheet. Bake at 375° for 25-30 minutes or until meat is no longer pink and potatoes are tender. **Yield:** 4 servings (78¢ per serving).

## Brown Rice Bake

*I need just four ingredients and a few minutes to assemble this cheesy side dish. Then I simply pop it in the oven, and in about half an hour, I have a tasty accompaniment to chicken dishes or other entrees.*

*—Nancy Foust, Stoneboro, Pennsylvania*

**2-1/4 cups cooked brown rice**
**1 package (10 ounces) frozen peas, thawed**
**1/2 pound process cheese (Velveeta), cubed**
**1 jar (4-1/2 ounces) sliced mushrooms, drained**

In a large bowl, combine all ingredients. Transfer to a greased 1-1/2-qt. baking dish. Cover and bake at 350° for 25-30 minutes or until heated through. **Yield:** 6 servings (55¢ per serving).

## Corn Fritter Patties

*These five-ingredient fritters are a thrifty way to enjoy a Southern staple without having to leave the comfort of home. After stirring together the batter that relies on purchased pancake mix and canned corn, I fry the patties in my electric skillet until they're golden brown.*

*—Megan Hamilton, Pineville, Missouri*

**1 cup pancake mix**
**1 egg, beaten**
**1/4 cup plus 2 tablespoons milk**
**1 can (7 ounces) whole kernel corn, drained**
**2 cups vegetable oil**

In a small bowl, combine the pancake mix, egg and milk just until moistened. Stir in the corn. In an electric skillet, heat 1/4 in. of oil over medium heat. Drop batter by 1/4 cupfuls into oil; press lightly to flatten. Cook for 2 minutes on each side or until golden brown. **Yield:** 7 patties (21¢ per serving).

## Supreme Spaghetti Salad

*(Pictured below)*

*I use bottled Italian salad dressing, shredded Parmesan cheese and a seasoning blend to perk up the pasta and fresh vegetables in this swift-to-fix salad. It's a delicious addition to any meal or picnic.*

*—Wendy Byrd, Salem, Virginia*

**1 package (1 pound) spaghetti, broken into 4-inch pieces**
**1 bottle (16 ounces) zesty Italian salad dressing**
**1 large cucumber, diced**
**1 large tomato, seeded and diced**
**1-1/2 cups fresh broccoli florets**
**2 tablespoons shredded Parmesan cheese**
**2 teaspoons Salad Supreme Seasoning**

Cook spaghetti according to package directions. Drain and rinse in cold water. Place spaghetti in a large serving bowl; add the remaining ingredients and toss to coat. Cover and refrigerate for at least 45 minutes. **Yield:** 12 servings (43¢ per serving).

**Editor's Note:** This recipe was tested with McCormick's Salad Supreme Seasoning. Look for it in the spice aisle of your grocery store.

Supreme Spaghetti Salad

## Cran-Apple Cobbler

*(Pictured below)*

*I developed this easy recipe when I wanted a quick but special dessert for my hungry husband. He loves it.*
*—Joan Gocking, Moundsville, West Virginia*

**1 can (21 ounces) apple pie filling**
**1/2 cup dried cranberries**
**1 package (7-3/4 ounces) cinnamon swirl biscuit mix**
**1/2 cup water**

In an ungreased 9-in. pie plate, combine the pie filling and cranberries. In a bowl, combine biscuit mix and water; drop by tablespoonfuls over filling.

Bake at 450° for 10-12 minutes or until lightly browned. Cover and bake 10-12 minutes longer or until topping is golden brown and a toothpick inserted in a biscuit comes out clean. Serve warm. **Yield:** 6 servings (52¢ per serving).

**Editor's Note:** You may substitute a package of Bisquick Complete Buttermilk Biscuit Mix. Just before baking, combine 1 tablespoon sugar and 1/4 teaspoon ground cinnamon; sprinkle over top.

Cran-Apple Cobbler

## Brownie Meringue Pie

*Stir chocolate cookie crumbs and chopped walnuts into a meringue mixture to create this rich dessert.*
*—Julie Moyer, Union Grove, Wisconsin*

**3 egg whites**
**1/2 teaspoon vanilla extract**
**3/4 cup sugar**
**3/4 cup crushed chocolate wafers**
**1/2 cup chopped walnuts**
**1 cup heavy whipping cream**
**2 tablespoons confectioners' sugar**

In a small mixing bowl, beat the egg whites and vanilla on medium speed until soft peaks form. Gradually beat in sugar, 1 tablespoon at a time, on high until stiff glossy peaks form. Gently fold in the wafer crumbs and nuts. Spread into a greased 9-in. pie plate.

Bake at 300° for 30-40 minutes or until the top appears dry and is lightly browned. Cool on a wire rack.

In another mixing bowl, beat the whipping cream and confectioners' sugar until stiff peaks form. Spread over the pie. Refrigerate for 3-4 hours. **Yield:** 8 servings (22¢ per serving).

## Lemon Nut Balls

*I roll these sweet soft lemon bites in a crunchy coating of pecans for a fancy finish. The goodies are easy enough for young children to help prepare.* *—Pat Tubach*
*Manhattan, Kansas*

**1/2 cup butter, melted**
**1/4 cup lemon juice**
**5 cups confectioners' sugar**
**3/4 cup nonfat dry milk powder**
**1 cup finely chopped pecans**

In a large mixing bowl, combine butter and lemon juice. Combine confectioners' sugar and milk powder; gradually add to butter mixture, beating until smooth. Refrigerate for 1 hour. Shape into 1-in. balls; roll in nuts. Store in the refrigerator. **Yield:** 6-1/2 dozen (4¢ per serving).

## Hamburger Gravy

*For an old-fashioned stick-to-your-ribs meal, try this economical entree. As a newlywed, I was so grateful to my mom for sharing this fuss-free recipe. My husband enjoys this no matter how often I serve it.* *—Sandy McKenzie*
*Braham, Minnesota*

**1 pound ground beef**
**1 can (10-3/4 ounces) condensed cream of mushroom soup, undiluted**
**1/2 cup milk**
**1 can (4 ounces) mushroom stems and pieces, drained**
**1-1/2 teaspoons beef bouillon granules**
**3 cups hot cooked mashed potatoes**

In a large skillet, cook beef over medium heat until no longer pink; drain. Stir in the soup, milk, mushrooms and bouillon. Reduce heat. Simmer, uncovered, for 10-15 min-

Breakfast Loaf

utes or until heated through, stirring occasionally. Serve over mashed potatoes. **Yield:** 4 servings (89¢ per serving).

## Sausage Rye Melts

*I love assembling these simple open-face sandwiches, which are easy on the pocketbook. I serve them with a cucumber salad. —Rose Maldet, Johnstown, Pennsylvania*

- **1/2 pound bulk pork sausage**
- **2 cups (8 ounces) shredded cheddar cheese**
- **1 can (4 ounces) chopped green chilies, drained**
- **1 can (2-1/2 ounces) sliced ripe olives, drained**
- **4 green onions, sliced**
- **10 slices rye bread**

In a skillet over medium heat, cook sausage until no longer pink; drain. Stir in the cheese, chilies, olives and onions. Spread over bread. Place on an ungreased baking sheet. Bake at 350° for 10-12 minutes or until cheese is melted. **Yield:** 5 servings (96¢ per serving).

## Broccoli Au Gratin

*With only four common ingredients, this crumb-topped gratin is a snap to whip up when I need a quick side dish. —Margaret McNeil, Memphis, Tennessee*

- **1 package (16 ounces) frozen chopped broccoli**
- **1 can (10-3/4 ounces) condensed cream of chicken soup, undiluted**
- **1/2 cup shredded cheddar cheese**
- **1/3 cup crushed butter-flavored crackers**

Cook broccoli according to package directions; drain. Stir in the soup and cheese. Transfer to a greased 1-1/2-qt. baking dish; sprinkle with the cracker crumbs. Bake, uncovered, at 350° for 15-20 minutes or until heated through. **Yield:** 4 servings (75¢ per serving).

## Breakfast Loaf

*(Pictured above and on page 242)*

*I often make this hearty sandwich when we have weekend guests. I serve it with juice and fresh fruit. If you like, add sliced mushrooms and olives to the list of ingredients. —Amy McCuan, Oakley, California*

- **6 eggs, beaten**
- **1/4 teaspoon salt**
- **1/8 teaspoon pepper**
- **1 tablespoon butter**
- **1 round loaf (1 pound) French bread**
- **6 ounces thinly sliced deli ham, *divided***
- **3/4 cup shredded Monterey Jack cheese, *divided***
- **3/4 cup shredded cheddar cheese, *divided***
- **1/2 medium sweet red pepper, thinly sliced**
- **1 medium tomato, thinly sliced**

In a small bowl, combine eggs, salt and pepper. Melt butter in a skillet; add eggs. Cook and stir until set; set aside. Cut top fourth off loaf of bread. Carefully hollow out top and bottom, leaving a 1/2-in. shell. (Discard removed bread or save for another use.) Set top aside.

In bottom of bread, place a fourth of the ham. Layer with half of Monterey Jack and cheddar cheeses, red pepper, scrambled eggs and tomato slices. Top with remaining cheeses and ham. Gently press layers together. Replace bread top and wrap tightly in foil. Bake at 350° for 25-30 minutes or until heated through. Let stand for 10 minutes before cutting. **Yield:** 6 servings (84¢ per serving).

# Chapter 18

# Timeless Recipes with Kitchen Tools

ON-THE-GO COOKS appreciate the convenience of slow cookers, microwaves, grills and pressure cookers when time is especially tight.

With just a little planning, you can easily assemble all the ingredients for flavorful food in your slow cooker. Then simply replace the lid, switch on the pot...and go!

Time-conscious cooks know the magic of a microwave. It's useful for much more than defrosting foods and reheating last night's leftovers.

When it comes to putting a meal on the table pronto, grilling is a "hot" option no matter what the season may be.

Pressure cookers are another reliable appliance that can hurry along your meals and keep the fuss to a minimum.

**SLOW-COOKED CONVENIENCE.** Clockwise from top: Pork Chop Potato Dinner, Italian Beef Sandwiches, Barbecue Sausage Bites and Butterscotch Apple Crisp (recipes on pp. 260 and 261).

# Slow-Cooked Specialties

AFTER a hectic day at work or doing other activities, there's nothing like coming home to the appetizing aroma of a just-cooked, delicious dinner you can sit down to and enjoy in minutes.

By taking a few moments to add ingredients to your slow cooker in the morning, you're well on your way toward having a satisfying supper ready for you when you walk in the door. Simply put on the lid...switch on the pot...and go!

This handy appliance slowly simmers foods to full-flavored perfection while you're gone. When you return, your family can savor a tasty homemade meal—without fussing over last-minute details.

## Creamy Swiss Steak

*When I was working, I'd put this Swiss steak in the slow cooker before I left for the day. A creamy mushroom sauce made with canned soup nicely flavors the tender round steak. It's delicious and so simple to make.*
*—Gloria Carpenter, Bancroft, Michigan*

**3/4 cup all-purpose flour**
**1 teaspoon salt**
**1/2 teaspoon pepper**
**2 pounds boneless beef round steak, cut into serving-size portions**
**2 tablespoons butter**
**1/2 cup chopped onion**
**2 cans (10-3/4 ounces *each*) condensed cream of mushroom soup, undiluted**
**1 cup water**
**Hot cooked noodles**

In a shallow bowl, combine the flour, salt and pepper; dredge beef. In a large skillet, brown beef in butter on both sides. Transfer to a 3-qt. slow cooker; top with onion. Combine soup and water; pour over onion. Cover and cook on low for 8-9 hours or until meat is tender. Serve with noodles. **Yield:** 8 servings.

## Corn Spoon Bread

*I prepare this comforting side dish with all of my holiday meals. It's moister than corn pudding made in the oven, plus the cream cheese is a rich addition. It goes great with Thanksgiving turkey or Christmas ham.*
*—Tamara Ellefson, Frederic, Wisconsin*

**1 package (8 ounces) cream cheese, softened**
**1/3 cup sugar**
**1 cup milk**
**1/2 cup egg substitute**
**2 tablespoons butter, melted**
**1 teaspoon salt**
**1/4 teaspoon ground nutmeg**
**Dash pepper**
**2-1/3 cups frozen corn, thawed**
**1 can (14-3/4 ounces) cream-style corn**
**1 package (8-1/2 ounces) corn bread/muffin mix**

In a large mixing bowl, beat cream cheese and sugar until smooth. Gradually beat in milk. Beat in the egg substitute, butter, salt, nutmeg and pepper until blended. Stir in corn and cream-style corn. Stir in corn bread mix just until moistened. Pour into a greased 3-qt. slow cooker. Cover and cook on high for 3-4 hours or until center is almost set. **Yield:** 8 servings.

## Brat Sauerkraut Supper

*This stick-to-your-ribs German dish is sure to satisfy even the biggest appetite at your house. Sliced apple and apple juice lend mellowing sweetness to tangy sauerkraut and bratwurst.*
*—Ann Christensen, Mesa, Arizona*

**1 jar (32 ounces) sauerkraut, rinsed and drained**
**2 medium red potatoes, peeled, halved and cut into thin slices**
**1 medium tart apple, peeled and cut into thick slices**
**1 small onion, chopped**
**1/2 cup apple juice**
**1/4 cup water**
**2 tablespoons brown sugar**
**1 teaspoon chicken bouillon granules**
**1 teaspoon caraway seeds**
**1 garlic clove, minced**
**1 bay leaf**
**1 pound fully cooked bratwurst links**
**6 bacon strips, cooked and crumbled**

In a 5-qt. slow cooker, combine the first 11 ingredients. Top with bratwurst. Cover and cook on high for 4-5 hours or until potatoes are tender. Discard bay leaf. Sprinkle with bacon. **Yield:** 6 servings.

## Hot Spiced Lemon Drink

*(Pictured above right)*

*I received this recipe from a lady in our church who is an excellent cook. She has shared several slow cooker recipes with us. We really enjoy the sweet-and-tangy flavor of this warm punch.*
*—Mandy Wright, Springville, Utah*

**2-1/2 quarts water**
**2 cups sugar**
**1-1/2 cups orange juice**
**1/2 cup plus 2 tablespoons lemon juice**
**1/4 cup pineapple juice**
**1 cinnamon stick (3 inches)**
**1/2 teaspoon whole cloves**

**Hot Spiced Lemon Drink**
**Chops with Fruit Stuffing**

In a 5-qt. slow cooker, combine the water, sugar and juices. Place cinnamon stick and cloves on a double thickness of cheesecloth; bring up corners of cloth and tie with kitchen string to form a bag. Place in slow cooker. Cover and cook on low for 2-3 hours or until heated through. Discard spice bag. **Yield:** about 3 quarts.

## Chops with Fruit Stuffing

*(Pictured above)*

*The aroma that fills the house as this pork dish simmers is wonderful. It combines convenient herb stuffing mix with tart apple, onion, celery and cherries. All you need to complete the meal is a green vegetable and maybe a loaf of bread.* —*Suzanne Reyes, Tustin, California*

**6 boneless pork loin chops (1/2 inch thick)**
**1 tablespoon vegetable oil**
**1 package (6 ounces) herb stuffing mix**
**2 celery ribs, chopped**
**1 medium tart apple, peeled and chopped**
**1 cup dried cherries *or* cranberries**
**1/2 cup chopped onion**
**2/3 cup chicken broth**
**1/4 cup butter, melted**

In a large skillet, brown pork chops in oil on both sides. In a large bowl, combine the remaining ingredients. Place half of the stuffing mixture in a 3-qt. slow cooker. Top with pork and remaining stuffing mixture. Cover and cook on low for 3 hours or until a meat thermometer reads 160°. **Yield:** 6 servings.

Meatball Tortellini

## Meatball Tortellini

*(Pictured above)*

*I combined some favorite staples from our freezer and pantry to come up with this easy dish. It has few ingredients and little preparation.* *—Tracie Bergeron Chauvin, Louisiana*

**1 package (16 ounces) frozen California-blend vegetables, thawed**
**1 package (14 ounces) frozen cooked Italian meatballs, thawed**
**2 cups uncooked dried cheese tortellini**
**2 cans (10-3/4 ounces *each*) condensed cream of mushroom soup, undiluted**
**2-1/4 cups water**
**1 teaspoon Creole seasoning**

In a 3-qt. slow cooker, combine the vegetables, meatballs and tortellini. In a large bowl, whisk the soup, water and Creole seasoning. Pour over vegetable-meatball mixture; stir well. Cover and cook on low for 3-4 hours or until the tortellini and vegetables are tender. **Yield:** 6-8 servings.

**Editor's Note:** The following spices may be substituted for the Creole seasoning—1/2 teaspoon *each* paprika and garlic powder, and a pinch *each* cayenne pepper, dried thyme and ground cumin.

## Chicken Bean Soup

*This surprisingly easy soup is tasty and nutritious, too. I like to top individual bowls with sprigs of fresh parsley.* *—Phyllis Shaughnessy, Livonia, New York*

✓ Uses less fat, sugar or salt. Includes Nutritional Analysis and Diabetic Exchanges.

**1 pound boneless skinless chicken breasts, cubed**
**2 cans (14-1/2 ounces *each*) chicken broth**
**2 cans (14-1/2 ounces *each*) diced Italian tomatoes, undrained**
**1 can (16 ounces) kidney beans, rinsed and drained**
**1 can (15-1/4 ounces) whole kernel corn, drained *or* 1-1/2 cups frozen corn**
**1 can (15 ounces) lima beans, rinsed and drained *or* 1-1/2 cups frozen lima beans**
**1 cup frozen peas and pearl onions**
**1 tablespoon snipped fresh dill *or* 1 teaspoon dill weed**
**1/2 teaspoon ground ginger, optional**

In a slow cooker, combine all ingredients. Cover and cook on low for 4 hours or until chicken juices run clear. **Yield:** 12 servings (3 quarts).

**Nutritional Analysis:** One 1-cup serving (prepared

with reduced-sodium chicken broth and frozen corn and lima beans) equals 257 calories, 1 g fat (trace saturated fat), 22 mg cholesterol, 635 mg sodium, 42 g carbohydrate, 10 g fiber, 21 g protein. **Diabetic Exchanges:** 2 starch, 2 lean meat, 2 vegetable.

## Rich Spinach Casserole

*I discovered this recipe while I was paging through an old slow cooker cookbook. When I took the side dish to our church sewing circle, it was a big hit.* —*Vioda Geyer, Uhrichsville, Ohio*

- **2 packages (10 ounces *each*) frozen chopped spinach, thawed and well drained**
- **2 cups (16 ounces) small-curd cottage cheese**
- **1 cup cubed process cheese (Velveeta)**
- **3/4 cup egg substitute**
- **2 tablespoons butter, cubed**
- **1/4 cup all-purpose flour**
- **1/2 teaspoon salt**

In a 3-qt. slow cooker, combine all ingredients; mix well. Cover and cook on low for 2-1/2 hours or until the cheese is melted. **Yield:** 8 servings.

## Italian Pork Chop Dinner

*My family loves this meal after church services. I just add the peas during the last half hour of cooking, and the pork chops are soon ready to enjoy. We like them most served with spaghetti, a salad and garlic bread.* —*Martina Williams, Grovetown, Georgia*

- **6 bacon strips, diced**
- **1/2 pound fresh mushrooms, sliced**
- **1 medium onion, finely chopped**
- **1 garlic clove, minced**
- **3/4 cup all-purpose flour**
- **4 teaspoons Italian seasoning, *divided***
- **1/4 teaspoon salt**
- **1/4 teaspoon garlic powder**
- **1/8 teaspoon pepper**
- **Dash cayenne pepper**
- **6 bone-in pork loin chops (1 inch thick)**
- **1 can (14-1/2 ounces) diced tomatoes, undrained**
- **1 can (14-1/2 ounces) chicken broth**
- **1 can (6 ounces) tomato paste**
- **1 package (10 ounces) frozen peas, thawed**
- **Hot cooked pasta**

In a large skillet, cook the bacon over medium heat until crisp. Using a slotted spoon, remove to paper towels. In the drippings, saute mushrooms, onion and garlic until tender. Transfer to a 5-qt. slow cooker with a slotted spoon. In a shallow bowl, combine the flour, 3 teaspoons Italian seasoning, salt, garlic powder, pepper and cayenne; coat pork chops with flour mixture.

In the same skillet, brown the pork chops; transfer to the slow cooker. Top with tomatoes and bacon. Combine the broth, tomato paste and remaining Italian seasoning; add to slow cooker.

Cover and cook on low for 4-6 hours or until pork is tender; add peas during the last 30 minutes. Serve with pasta. **Yield:** 6 servings.

## Tender Beef Brisket

*(Pictured below)*

*A touch of sugar mellows the flavorful sauce that's drizzled over this brisket. The original recipe came to me from a friend. I revised it for the slow cooker.* —*Sondra Morrow, Mesa, Arizona*

- **1 fresh beef brisket (3 to 4 pounds), trimmed and cut in half**
- **1 cup ketchup**
- **1 small onion, chopped**
- **2 tablespoons cider vinegar**
- **1 tablespoon prepared horseradish**
- **1 tablespoon prepared mustard**
- **1 teaspoon sugar**
- **1/2 teaspoon pepper**

Place the brisket in a 3-qt. slow cooker. In a bowl, combine the remaining ingredients. Pour over brisket. Cover and cook on low for 6 hours or until tender.

Remove the beef; set aside. Pour the sauce into a saucepan; cook, uncovered, over low heat for 13-15 minutes or until reduced and thickened, stirring occasionally. Slice the meat across the grain; serve with sauce. **Yield:** 6-8 servings.

**Editor's Note:** This is a fresh beef brisket, not corned beef.

Tender Beef Brisket

## Beef Vegetable Soup

*Convenient frozen vegetables, hash browns and an envelope of onion soup mix make this recipe a snap to mix up. Plus, it requires only two additional ingredients. I simply brown the ground beef, then stir everything together to simmer all day. The meaty soup is especially good served with bread or rolls.* —*Carol Calhoun*
*Sioux Falls, South Dakota*

**1 pound ground beef**
**1 can (46 ounces) tomato juice**
**1 package (16 ounces) frozen mixed vegetables, thawed**
**2 cups frozen cubed hash brown potatoes, thawed**
**1 envelope onion soup mix**

In a large skillet, cook the beef over medium heat until no longer pink; drain. Transfer to a 5-qt. slow cooker. Stir in the tomato juice, mixed vegetables, potatoes and soup mix. Cover and cook on low for 8-9 hours or until heated through. **Yield:** 10 servings.

## Herbed Slow Cooker Chicken

Olan Mills

*I use my slow cooker to prepare well-seasoned chicken breasts that cook up moist and tender. My daughter, who has two young sons to keep up with, shared this with me several years ago. I've made it repeatedly.* —*Sundra Hauck*
*Bogalusa, Louisiana*

**1 tablespoon olive oil**
**1 teaspoon paprika**
**1/2 teaspoon garlic powder**
**1/2 teaspoon seasoned salt**
**1/2 teaspoon dried thyme**
**1/2 teaspoon dried basil**
**1/2 teaspoon pepper**
**1/2 teaspoon browning sauce, optional**
**4 bone-in chicken breast halves (6 ounces *each*)**
**1/2 cup chicken broth**

In a small bowl, combine the first eight ingredients; rub over chicken. Place in a 5-qt. slow cooker; add broth. Cover and cook on low for 4-5 hours or until a meat thermometer reads 170°. **Yield:** 4 servings.

## Smoky Bean Stew

*This is an effortless meal that tastes great and pleases everyone at the table. I need just 10 minutes to get the satisfying sausage-and-bean dish started early in the day. Then I let the slow cooker do the rest of the work, and I spend the afternoon curled up with a good book. Before I know it, a hearty dinner is done and ready to enjoy.*
—*Glenda Holmes, Riley, Kansas*

**1 package (16 ounces) miniature smoked sausage links**
**1 can (16 ounces) baked beans**
**2 cups frozen cut green beans**
**2 cups frozen lima beans**
**1/2 cup packed brown sugar**
**1/2 cup thinly sliced carrot**
**1/2 cup chopped onion**
**1/2 cup ketchup**
**1 tablespoon cider vinegar**
**1 teaspoon prepared mustard**

In a 3-qt. slow cooker, combine all ingredients. Cover and cook on high for 4-5 hours or until vegetables are tender. **Yield:** 6-8 servings.

## Citrus Pork Roast

*A delicious hint of orange in the gravy makes this pork roast stand out from the crowd. Dried thyme, garlic and ginger further season each thick slice. Requiring just 15 minutes of prep work, the easy entree is an impressive main course to present to company and doesn't take up a lot of my time in the kitchen.* —*Tammy Logan*
*McComb, Ohio*

**1 boneless pork loin roast (about 3 pounds)**
**1/2 teaspoon garlic powder**
**1/2 teaspoon dried thyme**
**1/2 teaspoon ground ginger**
**1/4 teaspoon pepper**
**1 tablespoon vegetable oil**
**1 cup chicken broth**
**2 tablespoons sugar**
**2 tablespoons lemon juice**
**2 teaspoons soy sauce**
**1-1/2 teaspoons grated orange peel**
**3 tablespoons cornstarch**
**1/2 cup orange juice**

Cut roast in half. In a small bowl, combine the garlic powder, thyme, ginger and pepper; rub over roast. In a large skillet over medium heat, brown the roast on all sides in oil.

Place roast in a 5-qt. slow cooker. In a small bowl, combine the broth, sugar, lemon juice, soy sauce and orange peel; pour over roast. Cover and cook on low for 4 hours or until a meat thermometer reads 160°.

Remove roast and keep warm. In a saucepan, combine cornstarch and orange juice until smooth; stir in cooking juices. Bring to a boil; cook and stir for 2 minutes or until thickened. Serve with roast. **Yield:** 6-8 servings.

## Shredded Steak Sandwiches

*(Pictured above right)*

*I received this crowd-pleasing recipe when I was newly married over 30 years ago. Since then, it's been a family favorite that I've made countless times for large gatherings. To create fast and filling sandwiches, simply spoon the slow-cooked steak barbecue onto rolls. You could also serve the shredded meat over rice, potatoes or buttered noodles for a tasty change of pace.* —*Lee Deneau*
*Lansing, Michigan*

**3 pounds boneless beef round steak, cut into large pieces**

**2 large onions, chopped**
**3/4 cup thinly sliced celery**
**1-1/2 cups ketchup**
**1/2 to 3/4 cup water**
**1/3 cup lemon juice**
**1/3 cup Worcestershire sauce**
**3 tablespoons brown sugar**
**3 tablespoons cider vinegar**
**2 to 3 teaspoons salt**
**2 teaspoons prepared mustard**
**1-1/2 teaspoons paprika**
**1 teaspoon chili powder**
**1/2 teaspoon pepper**
**1/8 to 1/4 teaspoon hot pepper sauce**
**12 to 14 sandwich rolls, split**

Place the meat in a 5-qt. slow cooker. Add onions and celery. In a bowl, combine the ketchup, water, lemon juice, Worcestershire sauce, brown sugar, vinegar, salt, mustard, paprika, chili powder, pepper and hot pepper sauce. Pour over the meat. Cover and cook on high for 6-8 hours.

Remove the meat; cool slightly. Shred with a fork. Return to the sauce and heat through. Serve on rolls. **Yield:** 12-14 servings.

## Cheddar Spirals

*(Pictured above)*

*Our kids just love this and will sample a spoonful right from the slow cooker when they walk by. Sometimes I add cocktail sausages, Polish sausage or cubed ham to the cheesy pasta. —Heidi Ferkovich, Park Falls, Wisconsin*

**1 package (16 ounces) spiral pasta**
**2 cups half-and-half cream**
**1 can (10-3/4 ounces) condensed cheddar cheese soup, undiluted**
**1/2 cup butter, melted**
**4 cups (16 ounces) shredded cheddar cheese**

Cook pasta according to package directions; drain. In a 5-qt. slow cooker, combine the cream, soup and butter until smooth; stir in the cheese and pasta. Cover and cook on low for 2-1/2 hours or until cheese is melted. **Yield:** 12-15 servings.

## Roasted Red Pepper Sauce

*(Pictured above)*

*I often use Greek olives with the artichoke hearts to add zing to this pasta sauce. Roast the peppers yourself if you have the time. —Genie Tosh, Waynesville, Ohio*

- **4 pounds plum tomatoes (about 17), coarsely chopped**
- **1 large sweet onion, chopped**
- **1 can (29 ounces) tomato puree**
- **3 jars (7 ounces *each*) roasted sweet red peppers, drained and chopped**
- **2 jars (6-1/2 ounces *each*) marinated artichoke hearts, drained and chopped**
- **1/2 pound fresh mushrooms, quartered**
- **2 cans (2-1/4 ounces *each*) sliced ripe olives, drained**
- **1/4 cup sugar**
- **1/4 cup balsamic vinegar**
- **1/4 cup olive oil**
- **3 garlic cloves, minced**
- **1 tablespoon dried basil**
- **1 tablespoon dried oregano**
- **1 teaspoon salt**
- **Hot cooked pasta**

In a 5-qt. slow cooker, combine the first 14 ingredients. Cover and cook on high for 4 hours or until flavors are blended. Serve over pasta. **Yield:** about 15 cups.

## Potato Sausage Supper

*I fix this comforting dish at least once a month. I've taken the layered casserole to family reunions and always return with an empty slow cooker. —Patricia Ginn Delphi, Indiana*

- **4 medium potatoes, peeled and sliced**
- **1 pound fully cooked kielbasa *or* Polish sausage, cut into 1/2-inch slices**
- **2 medium onions, sliced and separated into rings**
- **1 can (10-3/4 ounces) condensed cheddar cheese soup, undiluted**
- **1 can (10-3/4 ounces) condensed cream of celery soup, undiluted**
- **1 package (10 ounces) frozen peas, thawed**

In a greased 5-qt. slow cooker, layer a third of the potatoes, sausage, onions and cheese soup. Repeat layers twice.

Pour cream of celery soup over the top. Cover and

cook on low for 5-1/2 hours or until the potatoes are tender. Add the peas and cook 30 minutes longer. **Yield:** 6-8 servings.

## Shrimp Chowder

Greg Randon

*I simmer this rich and creamy creation chock-full of shrimp, bacon, onion and corn in my slow cooker. Because the chowder is ready to serve in less than 4 hours, it can be prepared in the afternoon and enjoyed for dinner. —Will Zunino, Gretna, Louisiana*

**1/2 cup chopped onion**
**2 teaspoons butter**
**2 cans (12 ounces *each*) evaporated milk**
**2 cans (10-3/4 ounces *each*) condensed cream of potato soup, undiluted**
**2 cans (10-3/4 ounces *each*) condensed cream of chicken soup, undiluted**
**1 can (11 ounces) white *or* shoepeg corn, drained**
**1 teaspoon Creole seasoning**
**1/2 teaspoon garlic powder**
**2 pounds cooked small shrimp, peeled and deveined**
**1 package (3 ounces) cream cheese, cubed**
**4 bacon strips, cooked and crumbled**

In a small skillet, saute onion in butter until tender. In a 5-qt. slow cooker, combine the onion mixture, milk, soups, corn, Creole seasoning and garlic powder. Cover and cook on low for 3 hours. Stir in shrimp and cream cheese.

Cook 30 minutes longer or until shrimp are heated through and cheese is melted. Stir to blend. Garnish with bacon. **Yield:** 12 servings (3 quarts).

## Dilled Pot Roast

*It is hard to believe that this mouth-watering pot roast comes together so easily. I rely on dill weed, cider vinegar and a simple sour cream sauce to flavor the entree. —Amy Lingren, Jacksonville, Florida*

**2 teaspoons dill weed, *divided***
**1 teaspoon salt**
**1/4 teaspoon pepper**
**1 boneless chuck roast (2-1/2 pounds)**
**1/4 cup water**
**1 tablespoon cider vinegar**
**3 tablespoons all-purpose flour**
**1/4 cup cold water**
**1 cup (8 ounces) sour cream**
**1/2 teaspoon browning sauce, optional**
**Hot cooked rice**

In a small bowl, combine 1 teaspoon dill, salt and pepper. Sprinkle over both sides of roast. Place in a 3-qt. slow cooker. Add water and vinegar. Cover and cook on low for 7-8 hours or until the meat is tender.

Remove meat and keep warm. In a small bowl, combine flour and remaining dill; stir in cold water until smooth. Gradually stir into slow cooker. Cover and cook on high for 30 minutes or until thickened. Stir in sour cream and browning sauce if desired; heat through. Slice meat. Serve with sour cream sauce and rice. **Yield:** 6-8 servings.

## Moist 'n' Tender Wings

(Pictured below)

*These no-fuss wings are fall-off-the-bone tender. Chili sauce offers a bit of spice while molasses lends a hint of sweetness. They make a great meal with a side dish of rice. —Sharon Morcilio, Joshua Tree, California*

**25 whole chicken wings (about 5 pounds)**
**1 bottle (12 ounces) chili sauce**
**1/4 cup lemon juice**
**1/4 cup molasses**
**2 tablespoons Worcestershire sauce**
**6 garlic cloves, minced**
**1 tablespoon chili powder**
**1 tablespoon salsa**
**1 teaspoon garlic salt**
**3 drops hot pepper sauce**

Cut chicken wings into three sections; discard wing tips. Place the wings in a 5-qt. slow cooker. In a bowl, combine the remaining ingredients; pour over chicken. Stir to coat. Cover and cook on low for 8 hours or until chicken is tender. **Yield:** about 4 dozen.

**Editor's Note:** Five pounds of uncooked chicken wing sections (wingettes) may be substituted for the whole chicken wings. Omit the first step.

Moist 'n' Tender Wings

## Buffet Meatballs

*I need only five ingredients to fix these crowd-pleasing appetizers. Grape juice and apple jelly are the secrets behind the sweet yet tangy sauce that complements frozen Italian-style meatballs. Party-goers always love them.* —*Janet Anderson, Carson City, Nevada*

**1 cup grape juice**
**1 cup apple jelly**
**1 cup ketchup**
**1 can (8 ounces) tomato sauce**
**4 pounds frozen Italian-style meatballs**

In a small saucepan, combine the juice, jelly, ketchup and tomato sauce. Cook and stir over medium heat until jelly is melted; remove from the heat.

Place meatballs in a 5-qt. slow cooker. Pour sauce over the top and gently stir to coat. Cover and cook on low for 4 hours or until heated through. **Yield:** about 11 dozen.

## Cheesy Sausage Gravy

*I appreciate the make-ahead convenience of this home-style dish shared by a friend many years ago. Served over warm biscuits, the great-tasting sausage gravy that relies on cheddar cheese soup makes a hearty breakfast. I've prepared it for overnight guests, and they never fail to ask for the recipe.* —*P.J. Prusia, Raymore, Missouri*

**1 pound bulk pork sausage**
**1/4 cup butter**
**1/4 cup all-purpose flour**
**1/4 teaspoon pepper**
**2-1/2 cups milk**
**2 cans (10-3/4 ounces *each*) condensed cheddar cheese soup, undiluted**
**6 hard-cooked eggs, chopped**
**1 jar (4-1/2 ounces) sliced mushrooms, drained**
**Warm biscuits**

In a large skillet, cook sausage over medium heat until no longer pink; drain and remove sausage. In the same skillet, melt butter. Stir in flour and pepper until smooth. Gradually whisk in milk. Bring to a boil; cook and stir for 2 minutes or until thickened and bubbly.

Stir in soup until blended. Stir in eggs, mushrooms and sausage. Transfer to a slow cooker. Cover and cook on low for 7-8 hours. Stir; serve over biscuits. **Yield:** 8 servings.

## Italian Beef Sandwiches

*(Pictured above far right and on page 251)*

*My mother-in-law often served these flavorful sandwiches after church when we'd visit. Because there's little prep work, I make them on busy weeknights alongside french fries and raw veggies. Our children get excited when they smell the beef simmering in the slow cooker.* —*Jan Kent, Knoxville, Tennessee*

**1 beef tip sirloin roast (4-1/2 pounds), cut in half**
**1 can (14-1/2 ounces) beef broth**
**1 can (12 ounces) beer *or* additional beef broth**
**1 cup water**
**1/4 cup cider vinegar**
**1 envelope onion soup mix**
**1 envelope Italian salad dressing mix**
**1 garlic clove, minced**
**1-1/2 teaspoons dried oregano**
**1 teaspoon dried basil**
**10 Italian sandwich rolls (6 inches), split**

Place the roast in a 5-qt. slow cooker. Combine the broth, beer or additional broth, water, vinegar, soup mix, salad dressing mix, garlic, oregano and basil; pour over the roast. Cover and cook on low for 7-8 hours or until the meat is tender.

Remove roast. When cool enough to handle, shred meat, using two forks. Return to slow cooker and heat through. Using a slotted spoon, spoon shredded meat onto each roll. Serve juices as a dipping sauce. **Yield:** 10 servings.

## Barbecue Sausage Bites

*(Pictured at right and on page 250)*

*This sweet-and-tangy appetizer pairs pineapple chunks with three kinds of sausage. I experimented with the amounts of pineapple and barbecue sauce to suit my taste. Feel free to do the same.* —*Rebekah Randolph, Greer, South Carolina*

**1 package (1 pound) miniature smoked sausage links**
**3/4 pound fully cooked bratwurst links, cut into 1/2-inch slices**
**3/4 pound fully cooked kielbasa *or* Polish sausage, cut into 1/2-inch slices**
**1 bottle (18 ounces) barbecue sauce**
**2/3 cup orange marmalade**
**1/2 teaspoon ground mustard**
**1/8 teaspoon ground allspice**
**1 can (20 ounces) pineapple chunks, drained**

In a 3-qt. slow cooker, combine the sausages. In a small bowl, whisk the barbecue sauce, marmalade, mustard and allspice. Pour over sausage mixture; stir to coat. Cover and cook on high for 2-1/2 to 3 hours or until heated through. Stir in pineapple. Serve with toothpicks. **Yield:** 12-14 servings.

## Butterscotch Apple Crisp

*(Pictured above right and on page 250)*

*This sweet treat is a cozy way to warm up winter nights. Sliced apples are sprinkled with a tasty topping made with oats, brown sugar and butterscotch pudding mix. Served with ice cream, the saucy dessert is always well received.* —*Jolanthe Erb, Harrisonburg, Virginia*

**6 cups sliced peeled tart apples (about 5 large)**
**3/4 cup packed brown sugar**

**Pork Chop Potato Dinner**
**Italian Beef Sandwiches**
**Barbecue Sausage Bites**
**Butterscotch Apple Crisp**

- **1/2 cup all-purpose flour**
- **1/2 cup quick-cooking oats**
- **1 package (3-1/2 ounces) cook-and-serve butterscotch pudding mix**
- **1 teaspoon ground cinnamon**
- **1/2 cup cold butter**
- **Vanilla ice cream, optional**

Place apples in a 3-qt. slow cooker. In a bowl, combine the brown sugar, flour, oats, pudding mix and cinnamon. Cut in butter until mixture resembles coarse crumbs. Sprinkle over the apples.

Cover and cook on low for 5 hours or until the apples are tender. Serve with vanilla ice cream if desired. **Yield:** 6 servings.

## Pork Chop Potato Dinner

*(Pictured above and on page 250)*

*Tender chops cook on a bed of creamy potatoes in this all-in-one meal. It's a snap to assemble, thanks to frozen hash browns, canned soup, shredded cheese and french-fried onions. —Dawn Huizinga, Owatonna, Minnesota*

- **6 bone-in pork chops (1/2 inch thick)**
- **1 tablespoon vegetable oil**
- **1 package (30 ounces) frozen shredded hash brown potatoes, thawed**
- **1-1/2 cups (6 ounces) shredded cheddar cheese, *divided***
- **1 can (10-3/4 ounces) condensed cream of celery soup, undiluted**
- **1/2 cup milk**
- **1/2 cup sour cream**
- **1/2 teaspoon seasoned salt**
- **1/8 teaspoon pepper**
- **1 can (2.8 ounces) french-fried onions, *divided***

In a large skillet, brown chops in oil on both sides; set aside and keep warm. In a bowl, combine the potatoes, 1 cup cheese, soup, milk, sour cream, seasoned salt and pepper. Stir in half of the onions.

Transfer to a greased 5-qt. slow cooker; top with pork chops. Cover and cook on high for 2-1/2 to 3 hours or until meat juices run clear. Sprinkle with remaining cheese and onions. Cover and cook 10 minutes longer or until cheese is melted. **Yield:** 6 servings.

Italian Shrimp 'n' Pasta

## Italian Shrimp 'n' Pasta

*(Pictured above)*

*This dish is always a hit! The shrimp, orzo, tomatoes and cayenne pepper remind me of a Creole favorite, but the Italian seasoning adds a deliciously different twist. With strips of chicken thighs that stay nice and moist during cooking, this satisfying supper is a wonderful meal to come home to after a long day.* —*Karen Scaglione*
*Nanuet, New York*

**1 pound boneless skinless chicken thighs, cut into 2-inch x 1-inch strips**
**2 tablespoons vegetable oil**
**1 can (28 ounces) crushed tomatoes**
**2 celery ribs, chopped**
**1 medium green pepper, cut into 1-inch pieces**
**1 medium onion, coarsely chopped**
**2 garlic cloves, minced**
**1 tablespoon sugar**
**1/2 teaspoon salt**
**1/2 teaspoon Italian seasoning**
**1/8 to 1/4 teaspoon cayenne pepper**
**1 bay leaf**
**1/2 cup uncooked orzo pasta *or* other small pasta**
**1 pound cooked medium shrimp, peeled and deveined**

In a large skillet, brown chicken in oil; transfer to a 3-qt. slow cooker. Add the next 10 ingredients; mix well. Cover and cook on low for 7-8 hours or until chicken juices run clear. Discard bay leaf. Stir in the pasta; cover and cook on high for 15 minutes or until pasta is tender. Stir in shrimp; cover and cook for 2 minutes or until the shrimp are heated through. **Yield:** 6-8 servings.

## Hot Bacon Cheese Dip

*I've tried a number of appetizer recipes in the past, but this one is a surefire people-pleaser. It has lots of bacon flavor and gets my guests happily munching before dinnertime arrives. I serve the thick cheese dip with tortilla chips or slices of French bread.* —*Suzanne Whitaker*
*Knoxville, Tennessee*

**2 packages (8 ounces *each*) cream cheese, cubed**
**4 cups (16 ounces) shredded cheddar cheese**
**1 cup half-and-half cream**
**2 teaspoons Worcestershire sauce**
**1 teaspoon dried minced onion**
**1 teaspoon prepared mustard**
**16 bacon strips, cooked and crumbled**
**Tortilla chips or French bread slices**

In a 1-1/2-qt. slow cooker, combine the first six ingredients. Cover and cook for 2 hours or until the cheeses are melted, stirring occasionally. Just before serving, stir in bacon. Serve warm with tortilla chips or bread. **Yield:** 4 cups.

## Southwestern Pulled Pork

*(Pictured below)*

*The best way to describe this tender pork recipe is "yummy!" Bottled barbecue sauce, canned green chilies and a few other kitchen staples make preparation fast and easy. We like to wrap the seasoned pork in flour tortillas.*
—*Jill Hartung, Colorado Springs, Colorado*

Southwestern Pulled Pork

2 cans (4 ounces *each*) chopped green chilies
1 can (8 ounces) tomato sauce
1 cup barbecue sauce
1 large sweet onion, thinly sliced
1/4 cup chili powder
1 teaspoon ground cumin
1 teaspoon dried oregano
1 boneless pork loin roast (2 to 2-1/2 pounds)
Flour tortillas
Toppings: sour cream, shredded lettuce and chopped tomatoes, optional

In a 3-qt. slow cooker, combine the chilies, tomato sauce, barbecue sauce, onion, chili powder, cumin and oregano. Add pork. Cover and cook on low for 8-9 hours or until meat is tender.

Remove pork. When cool enough to handle, shred meat using two forks. Return to slow cooker and heat through. Serve on tortillas; top with sour cream, lettuce and tomatoes if desired. **Yield:** 6-8 servings.

## Butterscotch Dip

*If you like desserts and snacks that feature butterscotch chips, you're sure to enjoy this warm rum-flavored treat. I serve it alongside wedges of apples and pears, but feel free to try other fruits. The pecan-filled dip holds for up to two hours in the slow cooker.* —*Jeaune Hadl*
*Lexington, Kentucky*

2 packages (10 to 11 ounces *each*) butterscotch chips
2/3 cup evaporated milk
2/3 cup chopped pecans
1 tablespoon rum extract
Apple and pear wedges

In a mini slow cooker, combine the butterscotch chips and milk. Cover and cook on low for 45-50 minutes or until the chips are softened; stir until smooth. Stir in the pecans and extract. Serve warm with the fruit. **Yield:** about 3 cups.

## Chicken Soup with Beans

*(Pictured above right)*

*I put lime-flavored tortilla chips at the bottom of individual bowls before ladling in this southwestern soup. Loaded with chunks of chicken, beans, corn, tomatoes and green chilies, it's satisfying and fuss-free. I just saute the garlic and onion before combining all of the ingredients in my slow cooker.* —*Penny Peronia*
*West Memphis, Arkansas*

1 large onion, chopped
2 garlic cloves, minced
1 tablespoon vegetable oil
1-1/4 pounds boneless skinless chicken breasts, cooked and cubed
2 cans (15-1/2 ounces *each*) great northern beans, rinsed and drained
2 cans (11 ounces *each*) white *or* shoepeg corn, drained

Chicken Soup with Beans

1 can (10 ounces) diced tomatoes and green chilies, undrained
3 cups water
1 can (4 ounces) chopped green chilies
2 tablespoons lime juice
1 teaspoon lemon-pepper seasoning
1 teaspoon ground cumin
1/4 teaspoon salt
1/4 teaspoon pepper

In a skillet, saute the onion and garlic in oil until tender. Transfer to a 5-qt. slow cooker. Stir in the chicken, beans, corn, tomatoes, water, chopped green chilies, lime juice and seasonings. Cover and cook on low for 6-7 hours or until heated through. **Yield:** 12 servings (3 quarts).

### Slow-Cooking Strategy

As a busy working mom, I cook most of our meat entrees in the slow cooker. To cut down on "side dish" preparation time, I always cook whole packages of rice or noodles and freeze the leftover portions in resealable plastic bags. Later, it's easy to take them out of the bags, pop them in the microwave and have hot rice or noodles in a snap.

I do the same thing when I'm preparing potatoes. I cube and cook an entire 10-pound bag at once, then freeze some cubed and some mashed. When I need them to round out a meal, I simply "zap" them and serve up potatoes pronto. —*Jean von Bereghy*
*Oconomowoc, Wisconsin*

## Vegetable Beef Stew

(Pictured below)

*Here's a down-home dinner that slowly simmers in a flavorful gravy. I add plenty of carrots, potatoes and other vegetables to the hearty beef stew. Served with a loaf of crusty bread and a simple green salad, it makes a great meal for adults and children alike. I think it tastes even better the day after I prepare it.* —*Randee Eckstein*
*Commack, New York*

- **5 medium red potatoes, peeled and cut into 1/2-inch chunks**
- **2-1/2 cups sliced fresh mushrooms**
- **4 medium carrots, sliced**
- **2 celery ribs, thinly sliced**
- **3 bacon strips, diced**
- **1/4 cup all-purpose flour**
- **3/4 teaspoon pepper, *divided***
- **1/2 teaspoon salt, *divided***
- **2 pounds beef stew meat, cut into 3/4-inch cubes**
- **1 large onion, chopped**
- **2 garlic cloves, minced**
- **1 tablespoon vegetable oil**
- **1 can (14-1/2 ounces) beef broth**
- **1/2 cup dry red wine *or* additional beef broth**
- **1 bay leaf**
- **1/8 teaspoon dried thyme**
- **1 can (10-3/4 ounces) condensed tomato soup, undiluted**
- **1/3 cup water**
- **2 tablespoons cornstarch**
- **3 tablespoons cold water**

Place the first four ingredients in a 5-qt. slow cooker. In a large skillet, cook bacon over medium heat until crisp. Drain on paper towels. Reserve drippings.

In a large resealable plastic bag, combine the flour, 1/4 teaspoon pepper and 1/4 teaspoon salt. Add the meat; seal and shake to coat. Brown the beef, onion and garlic in the drippings and oil. Transfer to the slow cooker.

Stir in the broth, wine or additional broth, bay leaf, thyme, reserved bacon and remaining salt and pepper. Cover and cook on low for 8-9 hours or until tender. Discard bay leaf.

Combine the soup and water; add to the slow cooker. Cover and cook on high for 30 minutes. Combine the cornstarch and cold water; stir into the slow cooker. Cover and cook for 30-40 minutes or until slightly thickened. **Yield:** 7-8 servings.

**Vegetable Beef Stew**

## Mushroom Salsa Chili

*Chopped green, sweet red and yellow peppers add an extra splash of color to this chock-full chili that has two kinds of meat. I often choose this recipe when I need a meal for my hungry grandsons. Because they don't like chili that's spicy, I make it with mild salsa, but feel free to use a hotter variety if you prefer.* —*Richard Rundels*
*Waverly, Ohio*

✓ Uses less fat, sugar or salt. Includes Nutritional Analysis and Diabetic Exchanges.

- **1 pound ground beef**
- **1 pound bulk pork sausage**
- **2 cans (16 ounces *each*) kidney beans, rinsed and drained**
- **1 jar (24 ounces) chunky salsa**
- **1 can (14-1/2 ounces) diced tomatoes, undrained**
- **1 large onion, chopped**
- **1 can (8 ounces) tomato sauce**
- **1 can (4 ounces) mushroom stems and pieces, drained**
- **1/2 cup *each* chopped green pepper, sweet red and yellow pepper**
- **1/2 teaspoon dried oregano**
- **1/4 teaspoon garlic powder**
- **1/8 teaspoon dried thyme**
- **1/8 teaspoon dried marjoram**

In a large skillet, cook the beef and sausage over medium heat until meat is no longer pink; drain. Transfer meat to a 5-qt. slow cooker. Stir in the remaining ingredients. Cover and cook on low for 8-9 hours or

Burgundy Pears

until the vegetables are tender. **Yield:** 8 servings.

**Nutritional Analysis:** One 1-1/2-cup serving (prepared with lean ground beef and turkey sausage) equals 323 calories, 11 g fat (4 g saturated fat), 75 mg cholesterol, 1,019 mg sodium, 28 g carbohydrate, 8 g fiber, 27 g protein. **Diabetic Exchanges:** 3 lean meat, 2 starch.

## Burgundy Pears

*(Pictured above)*

*These warm spiced pears elevate slow cooking to a new level of elegance, yet they're incredibly easy to make. My guests can never believe how I prepare this special-looking dessert. The pears cook until tender in a sweet sauce, then I drizzle it over each serving before garnishing with whipped cream cheese.* —*Elizabeth Hanes*
*Peralta, New Mexico*

**6 medium ripe pears**
**1/3 cup sugar**
**1/3 cup Burgundy wine *or* grape juice**
**3 tablespoons orange marmalade**
**1 tablespoon lemon juice**
**1/4 teaspoon ground cinnamon**
**1/4 teaspoon ground nutmeg**
**Dash salt**
**Whipped cream cheese**

Peel pears, leaving stems intact. Core from the bottom. Stand pears upright in a 5-qt. slow cooker. In a small bowl, combine the sugar, wine or grape juice, marmalade, lemon juice, cinnamon, nutmeg and salt. Carefully pour over pears. Cover and cook on low for 3-4 hours or until tender. To serve, drizzle pears with sauce and garnish with whipped cream cheese. **Yield:** 6 servings.

## Au Gratin Garlic Potatoes

*(Pictured below)*

*With convenient cheddar cheese soup and other ingredients I usually have on hand, I turn ordinary sliced potatoes into this rich side dish. It's the perfect accompaniment to just about any main course. For extra eye-appeal, sprinkle on a little paprika.* —*Tonya Vowels*
*Vine Grove, Kentucky*

**1/2 cup milk**
**1 can (10-3/4 ounces) condensed cheddar cheese soup, undiluted**
**1 package (8 ounces) cream cheese, cubed**
**1 garlic clove, minced**
**1/4 teaspoon ground nutmeg**
**1/8 teaspoon pepper**
**2 pounds potatoes, peeled and sliced**
**1 small onion, chopped**
**Paprika, optional**

In a saucepan, heat milk over medium heat until bubbles form around side of saucepan. Remove from the heat. Add the soup, cream cheese, garlic, nutmeg and pepper; stir until smooth. Place the potatoes and onion in a 3-qt. slow cooker. Pour the milk mixture over the potato mixture; mix well. Cover and cook on low for 6-7 hours or until potatoes are tender. Sprinkle with paprika if desired. **Yield:** 6-8 servings.

Au Gratin Garlic Potatoes

## Shredded Pork with Beans

*A friend gave me this recipe, which my sons say is a keeper. For a change of pace, spoon the tasty filling into soft tortillas.* —*Sarah Johnston, Lincoln, Nebraska*

**3 pork tenderloins (about 1 pound *each*), cut into 3-inch pieces**
**2 cans (15 ounces *each*) black beans, rinsed and drained**
**1 jar (24 ounces) picante sauce**
**Hot cooked rice, optional**

In a 5-qt. slow cooker, place the pork, beans and picante sauce. Cover and cook on low for 8 hours or until pork is tender. Shred pork; return to slow cooker. Serve with rice if desired. **Yield:** 10-12 servings.

## Minestrone Soup

*(Pictured below)*

*When this hearty minestrone has about 30 minutes left to cook, I add the macaroni. That leaves me plenty of time to toss together a simple green salad and slice some bread. This dinner is so easy and delicious.* —*Kara De la vega Suisun City, California*

**6 cups chicken broth**
**1 can (15 ounces) garbanzo beans *or* chickpeas, rinsed and drained**
**1 medium potato, peeled and cubed**
**1 cup cubed deli ham**
**1/3 cup chopped onion**
**1 small carrot, chopped**
**1 celery rib, chopped**
**2 tablespoons minced fresh parsley**
**1/2 teaspoon minced garlic**
**1/2 cup uncooked elbow macaroni**
**1 can (14-1/2 ounces) diced tomatoes, undrained**
**1 package (10 ounces) frozen chopped spinach, thawed and squeezed dry**

In a 5-qt. slow cooker, combine the first nine ingredients. Cover and cook on high for 1 hour. Reduce heat to low; cook for 6-8 hours or until vegetables are almost tender.

During the last 30 minutes of cooking, stir in the macaroni. Cover and cook until macaroni is tender. Stir in the tomatoes and spinach; heat through. **Yield:** 10 servings.

Minestrone Soup

## Beef Stroganoff

*A favorite traditional dinner becomes fuss-free in the slow cooker. Tender sirloin steak in a tasty gravy is served over noodles for a home-style meal your family will request time and again.* —*Lisa VanEgmond, Annapolis, Illinois*

**3 to 4 pounds boneless beef sirloin steak, cubed**
**2 cans (14-1/2 ounces *each*) chicken broth**
**1 pound sliced fresh mushrooms**
**1 can (12 ounces) regular cola**
**1/2 cup chopped onion**
**1 envelope onion soup mix**
**2 teaspoons garlic powder**
**2 teaspoons dried parsley flakes**
**1/2 teaspoon pepper**
**2 envelopes country gravy mix**
**2 cups (16 ounces) sour cream**
**Hot cooked noodles**

In a 5-qt. slow cooker, combine the first nine ingredients. Cover and cook on low for 7-8 hours or until the beef is tender.

With a slotted spoon, remove beef and mushrooms. Place gravy mix in a large saucepan; gradually whisk in cooking liquid. Bring to a boil; cook and stir for 2 minutes or until thickened. Remove from the heat; stir in sour cream. Serve beef and mushrooms over noodles; top with gravy. **Yield:** 12-16 servings.

## Tarragon Mushroom Chicken

*To round out this saucy seasoned chicken, serve it with some rice or pasta. I often make this dish when my children and grandchildren visit. Using the slow cooker leaves me more time to enjoy their company.* —*Mary Kretschmer, Miami, Florida*

**6 boneless skinless chicken breast halves (4 ounces *each*)**
**1 can (10-3/4 ounces) condensed cream of chicken soup, undiluted**
**1 jar (4-1/2 ounces) sliced mushrooms, drained**

Wild Rice Turkey Dinner

1/2 cup sherry *or* chicken broth
2 tablespoons butter, melted
1 teaspoon dried tarragon
1 teaspoon Worcestershire sauce
1/4 teaspoon garlic powder
1/4 cup all-purpose flour

Place the chicken in a 5-qt. slow cooker. In a small bowl, combine the soup, mushrooms, sherry or broth, butter, tarragon, Worcestershire sauce and garlic powder; pour over chicken. Cover and cook on low for 4-5 hours or until chicken juices run clear.

Remove chicken and keep warm. Place the flour in a small saucepan; gradually whisk in cooking liquid until blended. Bring to a boil; cook and stir for 2 minutes or until thickened. Serve over chicken. **Yield:** 6 servings.

## Wild Rice Turkey Dinner

*(Pictured above)*

*The wild rice, squash and cranberries I use for this delicious dish are locally grown. I combine these ingredients with turkey tenderloins, onion and a few other items for a complete and satisfying supper.* —*Tabitha Dodge*
*Conover, Wisconsin*

**3/4 cup uncooked wild rice**
**1 medium butternut squash, peeled, seeded and cut into 1-inch pieces**
**1 medium onion, cut into 1-inch pieces**
**2 turkey breast tenderloins (1/2 pound *each*)**
**3 cups chicken broth**
**1/2 teaspoon salt**
**1/2 teaspoon pepper**
**1/2 teaspoon dried thyme**
**1/2 cup dried cranberries**

In a 5-qt. slow cooker, layer the rice, squash, onion and turkey. Add broth; sprinkle with salt, pepper and thyme. Cover and cook on low for 7-8 hours or until turkey juices run clear. Remove the turkey; cut into slices. Stir cranberries into rice mixture; serve with a slotted spoon. **Yield:** 4 servings.

### Spuds in the Slow Cooker

My mom came up with a great idea for beating the clock when she's serving a holiday meal or hosting another large dinner.

She cuts down on last-minute fuss by mashing the potatoes early in the day. Then, she keeps them warm in the slow cooker. She simply covers the cooker and puts it on the low setting, keeping the potatoes moist. I've tried this tip, and it really beats having to mash the potatoes immediately before the meal.

—*Kim Mlodzik, Badger, Iowa*

# Microwave Magic

TAKE your microwave to a whole new level by using it to produce these mouth-watering main courses and more. You'll discover just how helpful this common kitchen appliance can be to busy cooks.

**Editor's Note:** These recipes were tested in an 850-watt microwave.

## Sausage Scalloped Potatoes

*(Pictured below)*

*I adapted my mother's creamy entree recipe for the microwave. Now it's even easier to prepare that long-time family favorite.* —*Erlene Crusoe*
*Litchfield, Minnesota*

**1 pound fully cooked kielbasa *or* Polish sausage, cut into 1/4-inch slices**
**2 tablespoons butter**
**2 tablespoons all-purpose flour**
**1 teaspoon salt**
**1/4 teaspoon pepper**
**2 cups milk**
**4 medium red potatoes, halved and thinly sliced (3-1/2 to 4 cups)**
**1/4 cup chopped onion**
**2 tablespoons minced fresh parsley, optional**

Place sausage in a microwave-safe bowl. Microwave, uncovered, on high for 3 minutes. Drain and set aside.

Place butter in a 2-1/2-qt. microwave-safe dish. Heat on high for 45-60 seconds or until melted. Whisk in flour, salt and pepper until smooth. Gradually whisk in milk. Microwave, uncovered, on high for 8-10 minutes or until thickened and bubbly, stirring every 2 minutes.

Stir in potatoes and onion. Cover and microwave on high for 4 minutes; stir. Heat 4 minutes longer. Stir in the sausage. Cover and cook for 8-10 minutes, stirring every 4 minutes or until potatoes are tender and sausage is heated through. Stir. Let stand, covered, for 5 minutes. Sprinkle with parsley if desired. **Yield:** 4-6 servings.

## Tortilla Casserole

*This dish combines most of the food groups into a satisfying meal. With popular southwestern ingredients, the casserole pleases everyone at the table.* —*Joy Clark*
*Evansville, Wyoming*

**1 pound ground beef**
**1/2 cup chopped onion**
**1/2 cup chopped green pepper**

Sausage Scalloped Potatoes

- 1 envelope taco seasoning
- 1 can (8 ounces) tomato sauce
- 1 can (6 ounces) tomato paste
- 1/2 cup sliced ripe olives
- 1/4 cup water
- 1/2 teaspoon chili powder
- 2 eggs
- 1 cup (8 ounces) sour cream
- 1/4 teaspoon pepper
- 4 flour tortillas (7 inches)
- 2 cups crushed corn chips
- 2 cups (8 ounces) shredded Monterey Jack cheese

Crumble the meat into a 2-qt. microwave-safe dish; add the onion and green pepper. Cover and microwave on high for 5-6 minutes or until the meat is no longer pink; drain.

Stir in the taco seasoning, tomato sauce, tomato paste, olives, water and chili powder. Cover and cook at 50% power for 10 minutes or until thickened, rotating the dish once.

In a bowl, whisk the eggs, sour cream and pepper. Place two tortillas in an 11-in. x 7-in. x 2-in. microwave-safe dish. Layer with half of the sour cream mixture and meat sauce; repeat. Top with corn chips and cheese.

Microwave, uncovered, at 50% power for 10-15 minutes or until a thermometer reads 160° and cheese is melted. Let stand for 5 minutes before cutting. **Yield:** 6-8 servings.

## Chicken in Wine Sauce

*I rely on my microwave to cook this tender, full-flavored chicken. It's perfect for busy nights because it takes just 15 minutes to make from start to finish. Plus, we always have the ingredients on hand.* —*Amy Jo Cleveringa*
*Lake Havasu City, Arizona*

- 4 boneless skinless chicken breast halves (5 ounces *each*)
- 1/4 teaspoon salt
- 1/4 teaspoon pepper
- 3/4 cup dry red wine *or* chicken broth
- 1 teaspoon lemon juice
- 2 green onions, chopped
- 1/4 teaspoon dried thyme
- 3 tablespoons butter
- 2 tablespoons all-purpose flour
- 1/4 teaspoon browning sauce

Arrange chicken in a round microwave-safe dish. Sprinkle with salt and pepper. Combine wine or broth and lemon juice; pour over chicken. Sprinkle with onions and thyme.

Microwave, uncovered, on high for 5 minutes. Turn chicken; cook 2-4 minutes longer or until juices run clear. Remove chicken and keep warm, reserving juices.

In a small microwave-safe bowl, melt butter. Stir in flour until smooth. Gradually stir in 1/2 cup reserved juices. Discard remaining juices. Microwave, uncovered, on high for 1-2 minutes or until bubbly, stirring twice. Stir in browning sauce. Serve over chicken. **Yield:** 4 servings.

Shortcut Lasagna

## Shortcut Lasagna

*(Pictured above)*

*My family and friends can't get enough of this luscious home-style lasagna. It tastes like I fussed all day in the kitchen, but I can have dinner ready in an hour or less when I add some French bread and a tossed green salad. Best of all, this recipe is practically foolproof and doesn't require precooking the noodles.* —*Cindy Moore*
*Rhinelander, Wisconsin*

- 1 pound bulk Italian sausage
- 1 jar (14 ounces) meatless spaghetti sauce
- 1/2 cup chopped onion
- 1/2 cup chopped green pepper
- 1/2 cup water
- 1 can (2-1/4 ounces) sliced ripe olives, drained
- 1/4 teaspoon salt
- 6 uncooked lasagna noodles
- 1 cup ricotta cheese
- 2 cups (8 ounces) shredded mozzarella cheese, *divided*
- 1/4 to 1/2 cup grated Parmesan cheese

Crumble the sausage into a large microwave-safe bowl. Cover; microwave on high for 4-6 minutes or until the meat is no longer pink, stirring once; drain. Stir in the spaghetti sauce, onion, green pepper, water, olives and salt.

In a greased 11-in. x 7-in. x 2-in. microwave-safe dish, layer 1-1/3 cups meat sauce, three noodles, 1/2 cup ricotta cheese and 1/2 cup mozzarella cheese. Repeat layers. Top with remaining meat sauce. Sprinkle with Parmesan cheese.

Cover and microwave at 70% power for 28-32 minutes or until noodles are tender. Sprinkle with the remaining mozzarella cheese. Microwave, uncovered, on high for 1-2 minutes or until cheese is melted. Let stand for 5 minutes before cutting. **Yield:** 6 servings.

Asparagus Crab Casserole
Molasses Pretzel Snack

## Asparagus Crab Casserole

(Pictured above)

*On busy weeknights, you're sure to appreciate this creamy comfort food that seems special but can be put on the table in just 20 minutes. Add a green salad, bread and a fruit dessert for a complete dinner.* —*Diana Duda Glenwood, Illinois*

- **2 packages (8 ounces *each*) imitation crabmeat, flaked**
- **2 cups cooked rice**
- **1 package (12 ounces) frozen cut asparagus, thawed**
- **1 can (10-3/4 ounces) condensed broccoli cheese soup, undiluted**
- **1 cup milk**
- **1/3 cup chopped onion**
- **1 tablespoon lemon juice**
- **1 tablespoon butter, melted**
- **1 teaspoon dill weed**
- **1/2 teaspoon lemon-pepper seasoning**
- **1/4 cup sliced almonds, toasted, optional**

In a large bowl, combine the first 10 ingredients. Transfer to a greased 2-qt. microwave-safe dish. Cover loosely and microwave on high for 6-8 minutes or until heated through, stirring twice. Sprinkle with almonds if desired. **Yield:** 8 servings.

## Molasses Pretzel Snack

(Pictured above)

*I've given this yummy munch mix as a Christmas gift to teachers, co-workers and many others. Made with miniature pretzels, it's a nice change of pace from caramel corn.* —*Jacqueline Traffas, Medicine Lodge, Kansas*

- **1/2 cup packed brown sugar**
- **1/4 cup butter, cubed**
- **1 tablespoon corn syrup**
- **1 tablespoon molasses**
- **1/4 teaspoon salt**
- **1/4 teaspoon baking soda**
- **1/4 teaspoon almond extract**
- **5 cups miniature pretzels**
- **1 cup salted peanuts**

In a large microwave-safe bowl, combine the brown sugar, butter, corn syrup and molasses. Microwave, uncovered, on high for 45-50 seconds or until the butter is melted; stir.

Microwave 15-25 seconds longer or until mixture boils. Immediately stir in the salt, baking soda and extract (mixture will foam).

Stir in the pretzels and peanuts. Microwave on high for 20-30 seconds or until pretzels and nuts are well coated, stirring twice.

Spread into a greased 15-in. x 10-in. x 1-in. pan. Cool for 15 minutes, stirring twice. Store in an airtight container. **Yield:** about 6 cups.

## Peachy Turkey Meatballs

*These moist meatballs are so easy to make, and I don't have to worry about heating up my kitchen for dinner.* —*Brenda Thompson, Sugar Land, Texas*

✓ Uses less fat, sugar or salt. Includes Nutritional Analysis and Diabetic Exchanges.

- **1 egg**
- **1/4 cup dry bread crumbs**
- **1/4 cup sliced green onions**
- **1/4 teaspoon salt**
- **1/4 teaspoon ground ginger**
- **1 pound ground turkey**

**GINGER-PEACH SAUCE:**

- **1/4 cup peach preserves**
- **2 tablespoons golden raisins**
- **2 tablespoons soy sauce**
- **2 tablespoons ketchup**
- **1/2 teaspoon ground ginger**

**Hot cooked rice**

In a bowl, combine the first five ingredients. Crumble turkey over mixture and mix well; shape into 1-1/2-in. balls. Place in an 8-in. square microwave-safe dish.

In a bowl, combine the preserves, raisins, soy sauce, ketchup and ginger until blended. Pour over the meatballs. Cover and microwave on high for 6-8 minutes or until the meat is no longer pink. Serve over rice. **Yield:** 4 servings.

**Nutritional Analysis:** One serving (5 meatballs, prepared with reduced-sodium soy sauce and calculated without rice) equals 295 calories, 11 g fat (3 g saturated fat), 143 mg cholesterol, 721 mg sodium, 25 g carbohydrate, 1 g fiber, 23 g protein. **Diabetic Exchanges:** 3 lean meat, 1-1/2 fruit, 1 fat.

# Great Grilling

TO CUT DOWN your kitchen time, simply step outside and fire up your gas or charcoal grill. It can solve dinner dilemmas on busy days...and even hurry along a delectable dessert to top off your meal.

## Honey-Mustard Beef Kabobs

*Here's an easy entree that's sure to please mustard lovers. I rely on the tangy condiment to season these beefy skewers. A bit of the no-fuss sauce is set aside for dipping.*
*—Suzanne McKinley, Lyons, Georgia*

**1/2 cup Dijon mustard**
**1/4 cup honey**
**1 teaspoon Worcestershire sauce**
**1/4 teaspoon salt**
**1/8 teaspoon pepper**
**3/4 pound boneless beef sirloin steak, cut into 1-inch cubes**

In a bowl, combine the mustard, honey, Worcestershire sauce, salt and pepper. Pour half of the sauce into a large resealable plastic bag; add beef cubes and toss to coat. Set remaining sauce aside.

Thread beef onto metal or soaked wooden skewers. Discard marinade from beef. Grill, covered, over medium heat for 8-10 minutes or until meat reaches desired doneness, turning once. Serve with reserved sauce. **Yield:** 3 servings.

## Three-Cheese Potatoes

*With its bacon and cheese flair, this side dish makes a welcome addition to barbecues. My husband and I love these potatoes.* *—Cheryl Hille, Ashkum, Illinois*

**3 large potatoes, peeled and thinly sliced**
**1 medium onion, chopped**
**3 tablespoons grated Parmesan cheese**
**1 tablespoon minced chives**
**1/2 teaspoon seasoned salt**
**1/4 teaspoon pepper**
**2 tablespoons butter**
**1/2 cup crumbled cooked bacon**
**1/2 cup shredded mozzarella cheese**
**1/2 cup shredded cheddar cheese**

In a large bowl, combine first six ingredients. Transfer to a double thickness of greased heavy-duty foil (about 18 in. square). Dot with butter. Fold foil around potato mixture and seal tightly. Grill, covered, over medium heat for 30-35 minutes or until potatoes are tender, turning once.

Carefully open foil. Sprinkle bacon and mozzarella and cheddar cheeses over potato mixture. Grill 3-5 minutes longer or until cheese is melted. **Yield:** 4-6 servings.

## Bruschetta from the Grill

*(Pictured below)*

*Dijon mustard, mayonnaise and oregano make a sensational spread for chopped tomatoes, garlic and fresh basil in this fun twist on a favorite appetizer. It gets rave reviews whenever I serve it. Some of the prep work can be done in advance to save time later.* *—Mary Nafis*
*Chino, California*

**1 pound plum tomatoes (about 6), seeded and chopped**
**1 cup finely chopped celery *or* fennel bulb**
**1/4 cup minced fresh basil**
**3 tablespoons balsamic vinegar**
**3 tablespoons olive oil**
**3 tablespoons Dijon mustard**
**2 garlic cloves, minced**
**1/2 teaspoon salt**

MAYONNAISE SPREAD:

**1/2 cup mayonnaise**
**1/4 cup Dijon mustard**
**1 tablespoon finely chopped green onion**
**1 garlic clove, minced**
**3/4 teaspoon dried oregano**
**1 loaf (1 pound) French bread, cut into 3/4-inch slices**

In a large bowl, combine the first eight ingredients. Cover and refrigerate for at least 30 minutes. In a small bowl, combine the mayonnaise, mustard, onion, garlic and oregano; set aside.

Grill bread slices, uncovered, over medium-low heat for 1-2 minutes or until lightly toasted. Spread mayonnaise mixture over toasted side. Grill 1-2 minutes longer or until bottom of bread is toasted. Drain tomato mixture; spoon over top. **Yield:** 8-10 servings.

**Bruschetta from the Grill**

## Grilled Cake and Fruit

*Bring the convenience of outdoor cooking to dessert with toasted angel food cake "sandwiches" that hold melted chocolate and grilled fruit. They're really delicious and easy.* —*Terri Trudeau, San Gabriel, California*

**4 slices angel food cake (1 inch thick)**
**1 square (1 ounce) bittersweet chocolate, cut into fourths**
**1 medium firm banana, cut into fourths**
**8 pineapple chunks**
**1 tablespoon lemon juice**
**1/4 cup sugar**
**1/4 teaspoon ground cinnamon**
**2 kiwifruit, peeled and diced**
**8 fresh strawberries, sliced**

Cut a pocket in each slice of cake by cutting from one long side to within 1/2 in. of the opposite side. Insert a chocolate piece into each opening; set aside.

In a bowl, toss the banana, pineapple and lemon juice; drain. In a large resealable plastic bag, combine the sugar and cinnamon. Add banana and pineapple, then toss to coat; thread onto 4-in. metal or soaked wooden skewers.

Coat grill rack with nonstick cooking spray before starting the grill. Grill fruit over medium heat for 2-3 minutes on each side or until heated through. Grill cake for 1-2 minutes or until chocolate is melted, turning once. Remove fruit from skewers and place inside the cake slices. Combine kiwi and strawberries; serve over cake. **Yield:** 4 servings.

## Honey-Mustard Pork Chops

*(Pictured below)*

*I started using this recipe when my girls were little. I grilled everything because it allowed me to be outside watching the children play in the pool.* —*Angela Lott, Neshanic Station, New Jersey*

Honey-Mustard Pork Chops

**1 cup beer *or* ginger ale**
**1/2 cup prepared mustard**
**1/2 cup honey**
**1/4 cup vegetable oil**
**1 teaspoon salt**
**1 teaspoon dried rosemary, crushed**
**1/2 teaspoon dried parsley flakes**
**1/4 teaspoon pepper**
**6 boneless pork loin chops (1/2 inch thick and 4 ounces *each*)**

In a bowl, combine the first eight ingredients; mix well. Pour 1 cup marinade into a large resealable plastic bag; add the pork chops. Seal bag and turn to coat; refrigerate for at least 1 hour. Set aside 1/2 cup of the remaining marinade for basting and 3/4 cup for serving; cover and refrigerate.

Coat grill rack with nonstick cooking spray before starting the grill. Drain and discard marinade from chops. Grill, uncovered, over medium heat for 15 minutes or until juices run clear, turning and basting occasionally with 1/2 cup marinade. Serve with reserved marinade. **Yield:** 6 servings.

## Marinated Chicken Breasts

*You can bring international flair to backyard barbecues with this Indian-inspired marinade and basting sauce featuring curry and garlic. If you're not in the mood for chicken, use turkey tenderloins instead.* —*Linda Fisher, Columbus, Ohio*

✓ Uses less fat, sugar or salt. Includes Nutritional Analysis and Diabetic Exchanges.

**1 teaspoon chicken bouillon granules**
**1/2 cup warm apple juice**
**1 cup white wine *or* chicken broth**
**2 to 4 tablespoons olive oil**
**1 to 2 tablespoons curry powder**
**2 teaspoons celery salt**
**2 teaspoons soy sauce**
**1 garlic clove, peeled and sliced**
**6 bone-in chicken breast halves (about 6 ounces *each*)**

In a bowl, dissolve bouillon in apple juice. Add the wine or broth, oil, curry powder, celery salt, soy sauce and garlic; mix well. Pour 1 cup marinade into a large resealable plastic bag; add the chicken. Seal bag and turn to coat; refrigerate overnight. Cover and refrigerate remaining marinade.

Drain and discard marinade from chicken. Grill, covered, over medium heat for 35-40 minutes or until juices run clear, turning and basting occasionally with reserved marinade. **Yield:** 6 servings.

**Nutritional Analysis:** One serving (calculated with 2 tablespoons olive oil and chicken skin removed) equals 214 calories, 8 g fat (1 g saturated fat), 68 mg cholesterol, 364 mg sodium, 4 g carbohydrate, trace fiber, 25 g protein. **Diabetic Exchanges:** 3 lean meat, 1 fat.

**Editor's Note:** If using the broth instead of wine, add 2 tablespoons white wine vinegar to the marinade.

Corned Beef 'n' Cabbage

# Pressure-Cooked Possibilities

SAVE precious minutes on busy weekdays by turning to a time-easing appliance—the pressure cooker. This stovetop pot that uses pressurized steam is the convenient key to all of the following fast, flavorful fare.

## Corned Beef 'n' Cabbage

*(Pictured above)*

*I've been making this meal for more than 40 years. It is so easy and so delicious. It's especially good served with a salad of peaches and cottage cheese.* —*Ruth Warner*
*Wheat Ridge, Colorado*

- **4 cups water**
- **1 corned beef brisket with spice packet (2 pounds)**
- **1 medium head cabbage, cut into 8 wedges**
- **2 large red potatoes, cut into 2-inch chunks**
- **1 can (14-1/2 ounces) chicken broth**
- **4 large carrots, cut into 2-inch chunks**
- **1 medium onion, cut into 2-inch pieces**

In a 6-qt. pressure cooker, combine water and contents of corned beef seasoning packet; add beef. Close cover securely; place pressure regulator on vent pipe. Bring cooker to full pressure over high heat. Reduce heat to medium-high and cook for 45 minutes. (Pressure regulator should maintain a slow steady rocking motion; adjust heat if needed.)

Meanwhile, in a large saucepan, combine the cabbage, potatoes and broth. Bring to a boil. Reduce heat; cover and simmer for 10 minutes. Add carrots and onion. Cover and simmer 20-25 minutes longer or until vegetables are tender; drain.

Remove pressure cooker from the heat; allow pressure to drop on its own. Remove beef to a serving platter. Discard cooking liquid. Serve beef with cabbage, potatoes, carrots and onion. **Yield:** 4-6 servings.

**Editor's Note:** This recipe was tested at 13 pounds of pressure (psi).

## Golden Pork Loin

*A sauce made with acorn squash gives a golden look to this moist juicy pork roast.* —*Holly Ottum*
*Racine, Wisconsin*

✓ Uses less fat, sugar or salt. Includes Nutritional Analysis and Diabetic Exchanges.

- **1 teaspoon Cajun seasoning**
- **1 boneless whole pork loin roast (2 pounds)**
- **1 tablespoon vegetable oil**
- **1 medium acorn squash, peeled, seeded and cubed (about 4 cups)**
- **1 medium onion, chopped**
- **1 medium tart apple, peeled and chopped**
- **1 cup chicken broth**
- **1 to 2 garlic cloves, minced**
- **1/2 teaspoon salt**
- **1/4 teaspoon pepper**

Rub seasoning over roast. In a 6-qt. pressure cooker, brown roast in oil on all sides over medium-high heat; remove roast from the pressure cooker and drain. Add the remaining ingredients to the pressure cooker. Return roast to pressure cooker.

Close cover securely; place pressure regulator on vent pipe. Bring cooker to full pressure over high heat. Reduce heat to medium-high and cook for 27 minutes. (Pressure regulator should maintain a slow steady rocking motion; adjust heat if needed.)

Remove from the heat; allow pressure to drop on its own. Remove roast to a serving platter. Let stand for 5-10 minutes before slicing. Whisk cooked vegetable mixture until smooth. Serve with roast. **Yield:** 8 servings.

**Nutritional Analysis:** One serving (4 ounces cooked pork with 1/3 cup vegetable mixture) equals 225 calories, 10 g fat (3 g saturated fat), 64 mg cholesterol, 333 mg sodium, 11 g carbohydrate, 2 g fiber, 24 g protein. **Diabetic Exchanges:** 3 lean meat, 2 vegetable.

**Editor's Note:** This recipe was tested at 13 pounds of pressure (psi).

## Colorful Pork and Noodles

*Chopped tomato and green pepper spruce up this moist pork dish shared by our home economists.*

- **1 medium green pepper, cut into 1-inch pieces**
- **1 tablespoon vegetable oil**
- **2 pounds boneless pork, cut into 1-1/2-inch cubes**
- **1 can (10-1/2 ounces) condensed chicken broth, undiluted**
- **1 medium onion, chopped**
- **3/4 cup white wine *or* chicken broth**
- **2 garlic cloves, minced**
- **1/2 teaspoon pepper**
- **1 package (1 pound) wide egg noodles**
- **1 medium tomato, seeded and chopped**
- **6 tablespoons all-purpose flour**
- **1/2 cup cold water**
- **1/4 cup sour cream**
- **1/2 teaspoon browning sauce, optional**

In a pressure cooker, saute the green pepper in oil until crisp-tender. Remove with a slotted spoon; set aside. Brown the pork in pressure cooker over medium-high heat; drain. Stir in the broth, onion, wine or broth, garlic and pepper.

Close cover securely; place pressure regulator on vent pipe. Bring cooker to full pressure over high heat. Reduce heat to medium-high and cook for 12 minutes. (Pressure regulator should maintain a slow steady rocking motion; adjust heat if needed.)

Remove from the heat; immediately cool according to manufacturer's directions until pressure is completely reduced. Meanwhile, cook noodles according to package directions. Stir tomato and reserved green pepper into the pork mixture. Combine flour and cold water until smooth; stir into pork mixture.

Bring to a boil; cook and stir for 2 minutes or until thickened. Reduce heat to low; stir in sour cream and browning sauce if desired. Drain noodles; serve with pork mixture. **Yield:** 6-8 servings.

**Editor's Note:** This recipe was tested at 13 pounds of pressure (psi).

## Chicken with Orange Sauce

*(Pictured above right)*

*Our Test Kitchen used sliced peppers and onion to give this tender chicken dinner its attractive look. A homemade sweet-and-sour sauce delivers a hint of orange while slivered almonds offer a nice crunch.*

- **1 broiler/fryer chicken (3 to 4 pounds), cut up**
- **2 tablespoons vegetable oil**
- **1 large onion, halved and sliced**
- **1/2 medium green pepper, julienned**
- **1/2 medium sweet yellow pepper, julienned**
- **1 garlic clove, minced**
- **1/2 teaspoon grated orange peel**
- **2-1/2 cups water**

**ORANGE SAUCE:**

- **2 tablespoons cornstarch**

Chicken with Orange Sauce

- **3/4 cup orange juice**
- **1/4 cup sherry *or* chicken broth**
- **1/4 cup teriyaki sauce**
- **3 tablespoons brown sugar**
- **1 tablespoon butter**
- **1/4 teaspoon ground ginger**
- **1/2 cup slivered almonds, toasted**

In a pressure cooker, brown chicken in oil over medium-high heat; drain. Remove chicken to a 30-in. x 18-in. piece of heavy-duty foil. Top with onion, peppers, garlic and orange peel. Wrap tightly.

Place on a rack in pressure cooker; add water. Close cover securely; place pressure regulator on vent pipe. Bring cooker to full pressure over high heat. Reduce heat to medium-high; cook for 12 minutes. (Pressure regulator should maintain a slow steady rocking motion; adjust heat if needed.)

Immediately cool according to manufacturer's directions until pressure is completely reduced. In a small saucepan, combine cornstarch and orange juice until smooth. Stir in the sherry or broth, teriyaki sauce, brown sugar, butter and ginger. Bring to a boil; cook and stir for 1 minute or until thickened.

Remove chicken and vegetables to a serving platter. Top with sauce; sprinkle with almonds. **Yield:** 6 servings.

**Editor's Note:** This recipe was tested at 13 pounds of pressure (psi).

## Mashed Sweet Potatoes

*Need a swift side dish? Try these spiced sweet potatoes from our Test Kitchen. They're quick to cook and easy to mash in a food processor.*

- **3 medium sweet potatoes (2 pounds), peeled and quartered**
- **1-1/2 cups water**

**1/4 cup butter, cubed**
**3 tablespoons honey**
**1/2 teaspoon salt**
**1/4 teaspoon ground nutmeg**
**1/4 teaspoon ground cinnamon**
**1/8 teaspoon pepper**

Place sweet potatoes on rack in a 6-qt. pressure cooker; add water. Close cover securely; place pressure regulator on vent pipe. Bring cooker to full pressure over high heat. Reduce heat to medium-high and cook for 8 minutes. (Pressure regulator should maintain a slow steady rocking motion; adjust heat if needed.)

Remove from the heat; allow pressure to drop on its own. Drain. Transfer sweet potatoes to a food processor. Add the butter, honey, salt, nutmeg, cinnamon and pepper; cover and process until smooth. **Yield:** 4-6 servings.

**Editor's Note:** This recipe was tested at 13 pounds of pressure (psi).

## Parmesan Red Potatoes

*(Pictured below right)*

*Ever since I bought a pressure cooker, my busy family hasn't had to miss out on otherwise time-consuming suppers. I make cheesy potatoes that soak up flavor from chicken broth and seasonings.* —*Coleen Morrissey*
*Sweet Valley, Pennsylvania*

✓ Uses less fat, sugar or salt. Includes Nutritional Analysis and Diabetic Exchanges.

**4 unpeeled medium red potatoes, quartered**
**1/3 cup grated Parmesan cheese**
**3 teaspoons garlic powder**
**1 can (14-1/2 ounces) chicken broth**
**2 tablespoons minced fresh parsley**

Place potatoes in a 6-qt. pressure cooker. Sprinkle with Parmesan cheese and garlic powder; add broth. Close cover securely; place pressure regulator on vent pipe. Bring cooker to full pressure over high heat. Reduce heat to medium-high; cook for 6 minutes. (Pressure regulator should maintain a slow steady rocking motion; adjust heat if needed.)

Remove from the heat; immediately cool according to manufacturer's directions until pressure is completely reduced. Sprinkle with parsley. **Yield:** 4 servings.

**Nutritional Analysis:** One serving equals 137 calories, 4 g fat (2 g saturated fat), 7 mg cholesterol, 566 mg sodium, 20 g carbohydrate, 2 g fiber, 6 g protein. **Diabetic Exchanges:** 1-1/2 starch, 1/2 fat.

**Editor's Note:** This recipe was tested at 13 pounds of pressure (psi).

## Stuffed Pork Chops

*(Pictured at right)*

*Tart apple adds a delicious hint of autumn to the moist stuffing that fills these savory chops. From our home economists, the elegant entree looks like you fussed but comes together in just an hour or less.*

**1 bacon strip, diced**
**1/4 cup chopped onion**
**1/2 cup corn bread stuffing mix**
**1/2 cup chopped peeled tart apple**
**2 tablespoons chopped pecans**
**2 tablespoons raisins**
**2 tablespoons plus 1 cup chicken broth, *divided***
**1/4 teaspoon rubbed sage**
**Dash ground allspice**
**2 bone-in pork loin chops, 1 inch thick**
**1 tablespoon butter**

In a 6-qt. pressure cooker, cook the bacon and onion over medium heat until the bacon is crisp. In a small bowl, combine the bacon mixture, stuffing mix, apple, pecans, raisins, 2 tablespoons broth, sage and allspice. Cut a pocket in each pork chop by slicing almost to the bone; fill with stuffing.

In pressure cooker, brown chops in butter on both sides; add remaining broth. Close cover securely; place pressure regulator on vent pipe. Bring cooker to full pressure over high heat. Reduce heat to medium-high and cook for 15 minutes. (Pressure regulator should maintain a slow steady rocking motion; adjust heat if needed.)

Remove from the heat; immediately cool according to manufacturer's directions until pressure is completely reduced. **Yield:** 2 servings.

**Editor's Note:** This recipe was tested at 13 pounds of pressure (psi).

Stuffed Pork Chops
Parmesan Red Potatoes

# Chapter 19

# On-the-Go Odds & Ends

IF YOU like variety, just page through this quick-to-fix collection. It offers groups of theme-related recipes that taste great and save time, too.

For main courses, you'll find dishes featuring freshwater fish and ever-popular hot dogs. Or, choose from a range of crowd-pleasing pizzas.

Looking for new taste sensations? Sample couscous cuisine and recipes that include avocados. You can also perk up potatoes with tempting toppings.

Fare that boasts bananas will give your menus extra appeal. And chocolate-chip recipes are sure winners with families.

If mouth-watering munchies or unforgettable hors d'oeurves are what you're after, just turn to an array of snacks and appetizers that are swift but special.

**APPEALING EASE.** Top to bottom: Banana-Nut Green Salad and Banana Cream Dessert (both recipes on p. 280).

# Creative Couscous

ARE YOU BORED with boiling the usual pasta? Give couscous a try! These tiny pasta granules are available at most supermarkets and are fast to fix. Just consider the following recipes that take advantage of this quick-cooking alternative to other pasta and rice.

## Curried Couscous Salad

(Pictured above)

*This delightful chilled medley is nice for picnics. It can also be prepared a day early and goes well with most main dishes. —Lynn Gamache, Heriot Bay, British Columbia*

**3/4 cup water**
**1/2 cup uncooked couscous**
**1 cup frozen peas, thawed**
**3/4 cup diced cucumber**
**1 large carrot, shredded**
**1/4 cup crumbled cooked bacon**
**2 green onions, chopped**
**1 teaspoon minced fresh parsley**

**DRESSING:**

**1/4 cup olive oil**
**1 tablespoon cider vinegar**
**1 tablespoon soy sauce**
**1 teaspoon sugar**
**1 teaspoon curry powder**

In a small saucepan, bring water to a boil. Stir in couscous. Cover and remove from the heat; let stand for 5 minutes. Fluff with a fork. In a large bowl, combine the couscous, peas, cucumber, carrot, bacon, onions and parsley. Cover and refrigerate until chilled.

In a jar with a tight-fitting lid, combine the dressing ingredients; shake well. Just before serving, drizzle over salad and toss to coat. **Yield:** 4 servings.

## Couscous Chicken Supper

(Pictured at left)

*Our home economists created this meal-in-one featuring couscous. Served alongside tender strips of chicken, the pasta is topped with diced and broiled vegetables.*

**1 medium yellow summer squash, chopped**
**1 medium sweet red pepper, chopped**
**1 medium green pepper, chopped**
**1 teaspoon dried rosemary, crushed**
**1/2 teaspoon salt**
**1/4 teaspoon pepper**
**4 tablespoons olive oil, *divided***
**1 pound boneless skinless chicken breast halves**
**2 garlic cloves, minced**
**1-1/3 cups chicken broth**
**1 tablespoon dried minced onion**
**1 cup uncooked couscous**

Place the squash and peppers in an ungreased 15-in. x 10-in. x 1-in. baking pan. Sprinkle with rosemary, salt and pepper. Drizzle with 2 tablespoons oil; gently stir to coat. Broil 4 in. from the heat for 10-15 minutes or until tender, stirring every 5 minutes.

Meanwhile, in a large skillet, cook chicken and garlic in remaining oil until chicken juices run clear; remove and keep warm. Add broth and onion to the skillet; bring to a boil. Stir in couscous. Cover and remove from heat; let stand for 5 minutes. Fluff with a fork. Cut chicken into strips. Serve with couscous and vegetables. **Yield:** 4 servings.

## Pineapple Couscous Salad

*Pineapple and green chilies flavor this salad. I used to make this with rice, then decided to try couscous for something different. —Margaret Pache, Mesa, Arizona*

**3/4 cup chicken broth**
**1 cup uncooked couscous**
**1 can (20 ounces) pineapple tidbits, drained**
**1 can (4 ounces) chopped green chilies, drained**
**1/4 cup chopped pecans, toasted**
**3 green onions, chopped**
**2 tablespoons olive oil**
**1 tablespoon minced fresh mint**
**1 garlic clove, minced**
**4-1/2 cups baby spinach**

In a small saucepan, bring broth to a boil. Stir in couscous. Cover and remove from the heat; let stand for 5 minutes. Fluff with a fork. In a large bowl, combine the couscous, pineapple, chilies, pecans, onions, oil, mint and garlic; toss to coat. Refrigerate until chilled. Serve over spinach. **Yield:** 6 servings.

# Freshwater Fish

REEL IN the compliments with these rapid recipes that make the most of fresh fish—whether it's caught by an angler in your family or it's picked up at the grocery store. Each delicious dish can be prepared in a skillet on your stovetop in only 45 minutes or less.

## Trout with Mushrooms

*A mild lemon sauce accented by fresh mushrooms complements these tender trout fillets. When fish is on sale, I buy plenty to serve to my large family because we always eat it up right away.* —*Kathy Kittell, Lenexa, Kansas*

**1/2 pound fresh mushrooms, sliced**
**6 tablespoons butter, *divided***
**2 tablespoons minced fresh parsley**
**1/3 cup all-purpose flour**
**1/4 teaspoon salt**
**4 trout fillets (about 6 ounces *each*)**
**1/3 cup heavy whipping cream**
**1/2 teaspoon lemon juice**

In a large skillet, saute the mushrooms in 2 tablespoons butter until tender. Stir in the parsley. Remove the mushrooms to a serving platter; keep warm. Combine the flour and salt in a shallow dish; coat fillets with flour mixture on both sides. Add 2 tablespoons butter to the skillet. Cook trout over medium heat for 8-10 minutes on each side or until fish flakes easily with a fork; arrange over mushrooms.

For sauce, melt remaining butter in a small saucepan. Gradually stir in cream and lemon juice. Bring to a boil for 3-4 minutes or until slightly thickened, stirring constantly. Serve over trout and mushrooms. **Yield:** 4 servings.

## Crispy Cajun Panfish

*My mother is the fisherwoman in our family. Her recipe gets rave reviews, even from people who say they don't care for fish.* —*Gayle Cook, Minot, North Dakota*

**2 cups all-purpose flour**
**3 teaspoons salt**
**2 teaspoons Cajun seasoning**
**1-1/2 teaspoons pepper**
**1/8 teaspoon ground cinnamon**
**2 pounds bass, bluegill *or* crappie fillets**
**2 eggs**
**1/4 cup water**
**2 cups mashed potato flakes**
**6 tablespoons vegetable oil, *divided***

In a large resealable plastic bag, combine the first five ingredients. Add fish, one piece at a time; shake to coat. Whisk eggs and water in a shallow dish. Place potato flakes in another shallow dish. Dip each fillet in egg mixture, then coat with potato flakes. Dip fish again in egg mixture and potato flakes.

In a large skillet, heat 3 tablespoons oil over medium-high heat. Cook fish in batches for 3-4 minutes on each side or until fish flakes easily with a fork, adding oil as needed. **Yield:** 6-8 servings.

## Coconut-Crusted Perch

*(Pictured below)*

*A coconut breading lends tropical taste to tender perch served with a sweet-sour sauce for dipping. I've made this dish for my family for years. It's good with any whitefish.* —*Norma Thurber, Johnston, Rhode Island*

**1/2 cup apricot preserves**
**1/4 cup ketchup**
**1/4 cup light corn syrup**
**2 tablespoons lemon juice**
**1/4 teaspoon ground ginger**
**2 cups crushed butter-flavored crackers (about 50 crackers)**
**1 cup flaked coconut**
**2 eggs**
**2 tablespoons evaporated milk**
**1/2 teaspoon salt**
**3 pounds perch fillets**
**1 cup vegetable oil, *divided***

For sweet-sour sauce, combine the first five ingredients in a small saucepan. Bring to a boil. Reduce heat; simmer, uncovered, for 5 minutes or until slightly thickened. Remove from the heat and keep warm.

In a shallow dish, combine the cracker crumbs and coconut. In another shallow dish, whisk the eggs, milk and salt. Dip each fillet in egg mixture, then coat with crumb mixture. In a large skillet, cook fish in 3 tablespoons oil in batches over medium-high heat for 1-2 minutes on each side or until fish flakes easily with a fork, adding oil as needed. Serve with sweet-sour sauce. **Yield:** 10-12 servings.

Coconut-Crusted Perch

# Bunch of Bananas

HAS everyone gone bananas? Coast to coast, family cooks are incorporating this popular produce into more than just breads and pies. The familiar fruit is popping up in all sorts of taste-tempting recipes, including the following banana-filled fare.

## Banana-Nut Green Salad

*(Pictured below and on page 276)*

*I add sliced bananas and crunchy ginger-roasted walnuts to this tossed salad. For a change of pace, add Gorgonzola cheese.* —*Betty Jean Nichols, Eugene, Oregon*

**1 tablespoon vegetable oil**
**1 teaspoon soy sauce**
**1/4 teaspoon salt**
**1/4 teaspoon ground ginger**
**1/8 teaspoon onion powder**
**1 cup walnut halves**

**DRESSING:**

**1/3 cup orange juice**
**1/4 cup lime juice**
**1/4 cup vegetable oil**
**1/2 teaspoon salt**
**1/8 teaspoon white pepper**

**SALAD:**

**12 cups torn leaf lettuce**
**4 medium firm bananas, cut into 1/2-inch slices**
**2/3 cup crumbled blue cheese**

In a bowl, combine the oil, soy sauce, salt, ginger and onion powder. Add walnuts; toss to coat. Transfer to an ungreased baking sheet. Bake at 300° for 18-20 minutes, stirring every 5 minutes, or until nuts are lightly browned and evenly coated. Set aside.

In a small bowl, whisk dressing ingredients. In a large bowl, combine lettuce and bananas. Drizzle with dressing; toss to coat. Sprinkle with cheese and toasted walnuts. Serve immediately. **Yield:** 8-10 servings.

Banana-Nut Green Salad
Banana Cream Dessert

## Banana Cream Dessert

*(Pictured below left and on page 276)*

*No matter where I take this creamy banana dessert, I'm asked for the recipe.* —*Angel Hall, Grayville, Illinois*

**4 medium firm bananas, sliced**
**1/2 cup lemon juice**
**1-1/2 cups graham cracker crumbs (about 24 squares)**
**1/4 cup sugar**
**1/2 cup butter, melted**
**1 cup (8 ounces) sour cream**
**1 package (3.4 ounces) instant vanilla pudding mix**
**1 carton (12 ounces) frozen whipped topping, thawed**
**1/3 cup chopped pecans**

Toss bananas with lemon juice; drain well and set aside. In a bowl, combine the cracker crumbs, sugar and butter. Press into a greased 9-in. springform pan.

In a small mixing bowl, beat the sour cream and pudding mix on low speed for 2 minutes. Fold in bananas and whipped topping. Pour into prepared crust. Chill for up to 6 hours. Sprinkle with pecans. **Yield:** 8-10 servings.

## Peanut Banana Muffins

*Loaded with peanut butter chips and banana flavor, these tender muffins are my husband's favorite.*
—*Susanne Penner, Steinbach, Manitoba*

**1-1/2 cups all-purpose flour**
**1/2 cup sugar**
**1 teaspoon baking powder**
**1/2 teaspoon baking soda**
**1/2 teaspoon salt**
**1 egg**
**1/2 cup butter, melted**
**1-1/2 cups mashed ripe bananas (about 3 medium)**
**3/4 cup peanut butter chips**

In a bowl, combine flour, sugar, baking powder, baking soda and salt. In another bowl, combine the egg, butter and bananas. Stir into dry ingredients just until moistened. Fold in chips. Fill greased or paper-lined muffin cups three-fourths full. Bake at 375° for 18-22 minutes or until a toothpick comes out clean. Cool for 5 minutes before removing from pan to a wire rack. **Yield:** 1 dozen.

Glorified Hot Dogs
In-a-Hurry Hot Dog Dinner

# Hearty Hot Dogs

IF YOU'RE looking for an easy entree that will please kids as well as adults, choose hot dogs as the main ingredient. Here, fellow busy cooks share some of their most requested recipes that you can enjoy during the dog days of summer...or any time at all.

## In-a-Hurry Hot Dog Dinner

*(Pictured above)*

*This well-seasoned skillet dish combines sliced franks with plenty of green pepper, chopped celery and other vegetables. For a fuss-free meal that's ready in 30 minutes, serve this entree over noodles or rice...or pair it with dinner rolls.* —Sandra Small Niles, Ohio

**1 package (1 pound) hot dogs, halved lengthwise and sliced**
**2 tablespoons butter, *divided***
**2 medium onions, halved and sliced**
**3 celery ribs, coarsely chopped**
**1 medium green pepper, julienned**
**1 garlic clove, minced**
**1 can (14-1/2 ounces) stewed tomatoes, undrained**
**1 teaspoon dried oregano**
**1/2 teaspoon paprika**
**1/4 teaspoon pepper**
**Hot cooked noodles *or* rice**

In a large skillet, cook and stir hot dogs in 1 tablespoon butter over medium-high heat until lightly browned; remove and keep warm.

In the same skillet, saute the onions, celery, green pepper and garlic in remaining butter until tender. Add the tomatoes, oregano, paprika, pepper and hot dogs. Cook and stir until heated through. Serve over noodles or rice. **Yield:** 4-6 servings.

## Glorified Hot Dogs

*(Pictured at left)*

*My parents made these out-of-the-ordinary hot dogs every time we barbecued. They were not only a favorite in our family, but guests liked them, too. The franks are jazzed up with cheese, pickles and bacon before grilling.*
—Cheryl Gillpatrick, Loveland, Colorado

**1 large whole dill pickle (about 5 inches)**
**4 ounces cheddar *or* Colby cheese**
**8 hot dogs**
**4 teaspoons prepared mustard**
**8 bacon strips**
**8 hot dog buns**

Cut pickle lengthwise into eight thin slices. Cut cheese into eight 5-in. x 1/2-in. x 1/4-in. sticks. Cut hot dogs in half lengthwise; spread cut surfaces with mustard. On eight hot dog halves, layer a pickle slice and a cheese stick; top with remaining hot dog halves.

Place one end of a bacon strip at the end of each hot dog; push a toothpick through the bacon and both hot dog pieces. Firmly wrap the bacon around each hot dog and secure at the other end with a toothpick.

Grill, uncovered, over medium heat for 8-10 minutes or until the bacon is completely cooked, turning occasionally. Discard toothpicks. Serve in buns. **Yield:** 8 servings.

## Chili Dogs

*I make a tasty beef mixture to top plain hot dogs. Just cover the franks with any extras you like, such as mustard and onions, then ladle on this super sauce.*
—Danielle Parsons, Moscow, Idaho

**1 pound ground beef**
**2-3/4 cups warm water**
**1/3 cup barbecue sauce**
**1 to 2 teaspoons onion powder**
**3/4 teaspoon garlic salt**
**3/4 teaspoon chili powder**
**1/2 teaspoon paprika**
**1/4 to 1/2 teaspoon cayenne pepper**
**1/4 teaspoon ground mustard**
**Pepper to taste**
**5 tablespoons cornstarch**
**1/3 cup cold water**
**8 hot dogs**
**8 hot dog buns**

In a large saucepan, cook beef over medium heat until no longer pink; drain. Add the warm water, barbecue sauce and seasonings. Bring to a boil.

In a small bowl, combine cornstarch and cold water until smooth. Stir into meat sauce; cook and stir for 2 minutes or until thickened. Reduce heat; simmer, uncovered, for 10 minutes. Meanwhile, cook hot dogs according to package directions. Place in buns; top with meat sauce. **Yield:** 8 servings.

# Popular Potatoes

READY to dig into potatoes? We've presented a variety of flavorful ways to top off your plain taters—from piling them high with ham and veggies to smothering them with salsa.

**Editor's Note:** These recipes were tested in a 1,100-watt microwave.

## Loaded Potato Fans

*(Pictured below)*

*Fancy enough for company, these baked potatoes look like you fussed but are really simple to fix. Our home economists sliced each one into a fan, covering them with cheese, bacon and savory seasonings.*

**4 large baking potatoes**
**2 tablespoons butter, melted**
**3 tablespoons grated Parmesan cheese**
**1/2 teaspoon dried rosemary, crushed**
**1/4 teaspoon salt**
**1/8 teaspoon pepper**
**1/2 cup shredded cheddar cheese**
**1/4 cup real bacon bits**
**1 green onion, chopped**

Scrub potatoes. With a sharp knife, slice potatoes thinly but not all the way through, leaving slices attached at the bottom. Place on a microwave-safe plate; drizzle with butter. Combine the Parmesan cheese, rosemary, salt and pepper; sprinkle over potatoes and between slices. Microwave, uncovered, on high for 12-18 minutes or until potatoes are tender. Top with cheddar cheese, bacon and onion. Microwave for 1-2 minutes longer or until cheese is melted. **Yield:** 4 servings.

Loaded Potato Fans
Hearty Baked Potatoes

## Hearty Baked Potatoes

*(Pictured below left)*

*Adding ham to these veggie-topped spuds makes them a meal-in-one. With cheese and a tasty sauce, too, they're sure to satisfy.* —*Barbara Schindler, Napoleon, Ohio*

**4 large baking potatoes (2 pounds)**
**2-1/2 cups frozen broccoli, cauliflower and carrots**
**2 cups cubed fully cooked ham**
**1 can (10-3/4 ounces) condensed cream of broccoli soup, undiluted**
**1/2 cup shredded cheddar cheese**
**1/4 teaspoon garlic powder**
**1/4 teaspoon pepper**

Scrub and pierce potatoes; place on a microwave-safe plate. Microwave, uncovered, on high for 10-12 minutes or until tender, turning once. Meanwhile, in a small saucepan, combine the remaining ingredients. Cook and stir over medium-low heat until cheese is melted.

Cut an X in the top of each potato; fluff pulp with a fork. Top with vegetable mixture. **Yield:** 4 servings.

## Salsa Chicken Potatoes

*I serve potatoes southwestern-style with salsa and a little sour cream. My whole family likes this tasty recipe that comes together in just 20 minutes. Plus, I can prepare it using cooked chicken that's left over from another meal.*
—*Janice Torrence, Warsaw, Indiana*

**2 large baking potatoes**
**1 cup cubed cooked chicken**
**1 cup tomato sauce**
**1/2 cup salsa**
**1 tablespoon brown sugar**
**2 tablespoons sour cream**
**1 tablespoon minced fresh parsley**

Scrub and pierce potatoes; place on a microwave-safe plate. Microwave, uncovered, on high for 10-12 minutes or until tender, turning once. In a microwave-safe bowl, combine the chicken, tomato sauce, salsa and brown sugar. Cover and microwave on high for 3 minutes or until heated through. Cut an X in the top of each potato; fluff pulp with a fork. Top with chicken mixture, sour cream and parsley. **Yield:** 2 servings.

Fiesta Chopped Salad
Avocado Soup

# Avocado Ideas

WHETHER you're looking to bring a new sensation to your mealtime lineup or simply trying to add a tropical twist to a favorite family recipe, consider using appetizing avocados.

Brimming with refreshing goodness, the widely available fruit (no, it's not a vegetable) lends a subtle taste to many dishes—including these specialties.

## Fiesta Chopped Salad

(Pictured above)

*We plan on making this colorful garden feast when we find vegetables that are bursting with flavor. To enhance them, I mix together a simple homemade dressing. The fresh salad is a welcome addition to almost any entree.* —Merwyn Garbini Tucson, Arizona

✓ Uses less fat, sugar or salt. Includes Nutritional Analysis and Diabetic Exchanges.

**1 medium sweet red pepper, chopped**
**1 medium sweet yellow pepper, chopped**
**1 medium tomato, seeded and chopped**
**1 medium cucumber, seeded and chopped**
**1 small zucchini, chopped**
**2 green onions, chopped**
**2 tablespoons minced fresh parsley**
**2 tablespoons olive oil**
**1 tablespoon red wine vinegar**
**1/2 teaspoon sugar**
**1/4 teaspoon salt**
**1/4 teaspoon pepper**
**1 large ripe avocado, peeled and chopped**
**1 tablespoon lemon juice**

In a large bowl, combine the first seven ingredients. In a jar with a tight-fitting lid, combine the oil, vinegar, sugar, salt and pepper; shake well. Drizzle over vegetables and toss to coat. Toss avocado with lemon juice; sprinkle over salad. Serve with a slotted spoon. **Yield:** 8 servings.

**Nutritional Analysis:** One serving (1/2 cup) equals 91 calories, 7 g fat (1 g saturated fat), 0 cholesterol, 81 mg sodium, 7 g carbohydrate, 2 g fiber, 1 g protein. **Diabetic Exchanges:** 1-1/2 fat, 1 vegetable.

## Avocado Soup

(Pictured at left)

*Savor a deliciously different use for avocados by trying this warm, rich and comforting soup. Requiring only 20 minutes of prep time, it takes advantage of canned chicken broth and includes cubed potatoes and chopped onion.*
—Bernyce Orm, Ojai, California

**1/2 cup chopped onion**
**1 tablespoon butter**
**2 cans (14-1/2 ounces *each*) chicken broth**
**2 medium potatoes, peeled and cubed**
**1/2 teaspoon salt**
**1/4 teaspoon pepper**
**2 medium ripe avocados, peeled and quartered**
**1/2 cup sour cream**
**1/4 cup real bacon bits**

In a large saucepan, saute onion in butter until tender. Add the broth, potatoes, salt and pepper; bring to a boil. Reduce heat; cover and simmer for 15-25 minutes or until potatoes are tender. Remove from the heat; cool slightly.

Place avocados in a blender; add potato mixture. Cover and puree. Return to the pan; heat through. Garnish with sour cream and bacon. **Yield:** 6 servings.

### More Avocado Options

The California Avocado Commission offers the following ideas for using flavorful, no-fuss avocados:

- Add avocado slices to tacos or other Mexican fare for a delicious finish.
- Spread sandwich bread with pureed avocado instead of mayonnaise or other spreads.
- Enhance purchased salad greens with some chopped avocado and a little lemon juice.

# Chocolate Chips

MMMM...chocolate chips! What better way to indulge your sweet tooth than with treats featuring those rich bits? You'll discover four tempting recipes right here, thanks to chocolate-loving readers.

## Pumpkin Chip Bread

*(Pictured below)*

*I experiment with chocolate a lot in my baking. The mini semisweet chips in this bread are wonderful with the cranberries. —Shirley Glaab, Hattiesburg, Mississippi*

**2-1/4 cups all-purpose flour**
**2 cups sugar**
**2 teaspoons ground cinnamon**
**1 teaspoon baking soda**
**1/2 teaspoon *each* salt, ground ginger, nutmeg and cloves**
**2 eggs**
**1 cup canned pumpkin**
**1/2 cup vegetable oil**
**1 cup chopped fresh *or* frozen cranberries**
**3/4 cup miniature semisweet chocolate chips**

In a large bowl, combine the flour, sugar, cinnamon, baking soda, salt, ginger, nutmeg and cloves. Combine the eggs, pumpkin and oil; stir into dry ingredients just until moistened. Fold in cranberries and chocolate chips.

Transfer to two greased and floured 8-in. x 4-in. x 2-in. loaf pans. Bake at 350° for 50-55 minutes or until a toothpick inserted near the center comes out clean. Cool for 10 minutes before removing from pans to wire racks to cool completely. **Yield:** 2 loaves.

**Pumpkin Chip Bread**
**Crunchy Fudge Drops**

## Crunchy Fudge Drops

*(Pictured below left)*

*Both semisweet chocolate and butterscotch chips make these no-bake bites luscious. I take them everywhere—our church coffee hour, my card group, you name it. Nobody can eat just one. —Loraine Meyer, Bend, Oregon*

**1/2 cup semisweet chocolate chips**
**1/2 cup butterscotch chips**
**1/2 cup plus 2 tablespoons granola cereal**
**1/2 cup chopped pecans**

In a microwave-safe bowl, melt chocolate and butterscotch chips; stir until smooth. Stir in granola and pecans. Drop by rounded teaspoonfuls onto waxed paper-lined baking sheets. Refrigerate until firm. Store in an airtight container. **Yield:** 2 dozen.

## Chocolate Caramel Corn

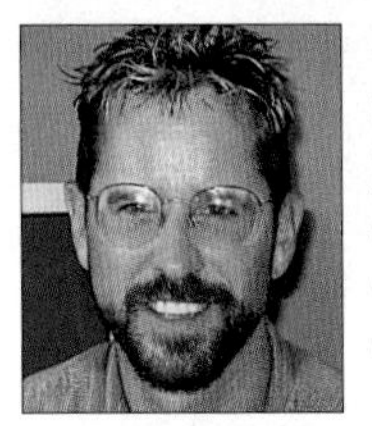

*You may want to make a double batch of this irresistible snack...it gets gobbled up fast! We purchased something similar from a local Boy Scout. We liked it so much we created our own version by coating caramel corn with rich milk chocolate. —James Claassen, Brewster, Kansas*

**1 cup milk chocolate chips**
**1 tablespoon shortening**
**6 cups caramel popcorn with peanuts**

In a microwave-safe bowl, melt chocolate chips and shortening. Place popcorn in a large bowl; drizzle with melted chocolate and stir gently. Spread on a waxed paper-lined baking sheet. Refrigerate until set. Break into pieces. Store in an airtight container. **Yield:** 6 cups.

## Chocolate Chip Pancakes

*At our house, Saturday morning always means pancakes for breakfast. To make the menu extra special, I serve up stacks of these fluffy buttermilk treats that are studded with miniature chocolate chips. —Julianne Johnson, Grove City, Minnesota*

**2 cups all-purpose flour**
**2 teaspoons sugar**
**2 teaspoons baking powder**
**1 teaspoon baking soda**
**1/4 teaspoon salt**
**2 eggs, lightly beaten**
**2 cups buttermilk**
**1/4 cup vegetable oil**
**1 cup miniature semisweet chocolate chips**

In a bowl, combine the first five ingredients. Combine the eggs, buttermilk and oil; stir into dry ingredients just until moistened. Pour the batter by 1/4 cupfuls onto a greased hot griddle.

Sprinkle each pancake with 2 teaspoons chocolate chips. Turn when bubbles form on top of pancake; cook until second side is golden brown. **Yield:** 6-8 servings.

Candy Corn Snack Mix
Apple Dip with Crisps

# Fall Finger Foods

HOSTING a Halloween party or other autumn event? Like having munchies on hand for after-school snacking? Just sample these delightful bites. From a festive candy-corn treat to onion rings and apple dippers, they'll have your family coming back for more...and most take less than 30 minutes to make.

## Candy Corn Snack Mix

*(Pictured above)*

*It's no trick—this Halloween party treat requires just three ingredients and 5 minutes to prepare. I simply mix together candy corn, M&M's and peanuts. Then I watch it all disappear! —Denise Neal, Yorba Linda, California*

**1 cup candy corn**
**1 cup milk chocolate M&M's**
**1 cup salted peanuts**

In a serving bowl, combine all ingredients. Store in an airtight container. **Yield:** 3 cups.

## Apple Dip with Crisps

*(Pictured above)*

*My sister created this recipe for a family celebration, but it's great anytime. With the tempting taste of a home-baked pie, this playful finger food pairs warm spiced apples with cute cutout shapes from a prepared crust. —Joni Karcher, Geneva, Nebraska*

**Pastry for double-crust pie (9 inches)**
**2 tablespoons plus 3/4 cup sugar, *divided***
**1-1/2 teaspoons ground cinnamon, *divided***
**6 medium tart apples, peeled and coarsely chopped**
**1/4 cup butter**
**1/4 cup all-purpose flour**
**1 cup cold water**

For the crisps, on a lightly floured surface, roll the pastry to 1/8-in. thickness. Combine 2 tablespoons sugar and 1/2 teaspoon cinnamon; sprinkle over the pastry. Cut with floured 2-1/2-in. Halloween-shaped cookie cutters. Place 1 in. apart on ungreased baking sheets. Bake at 425° for 4-6 minutes or until lightly browned. Remove to wire racks to cool.

Meanwhile, in a large skillet, saute apples and remaining sugar and cinnamon in butter until apples are tender. Combine flour and cold water until smooth; stir into skillet. Bring to a boil; cook and stir for 2 minutes or until thickened. Spoon into a serving dish. Serve warm with crisps. **Yield:** 3 cups dip and 2-3 dozen crisps.

## Hot Bean Dip

*This tasty party-starter uses prepared taco sauce and canned refried beans. Once people start dipping, they can't stop. —Michelle Sawatzky, Isle, Minnesota*

**1 pound ground beef**
**1/4 cup chopped onion**
**1 can (16 ounces) refried beans**
**1-1/4 cups shredded Monterey Jack cheese**
**1/2 cup taco sauce**
**Tortilla chips**

In a large skillet, cook beef and onion over medium heat until meat is no longer pink; drain. Reduce heat. Stir in the refried beans, Monterey Jack cheese and taco sauce; cook and stir until cheese is melted. Serve warm with tortilla chips. **Yield:** 3-1/2 cups.

## Baked Onion Rings

*Love onion rings but not the fat that comes from deep-frying them? Try these baked rings. They're great as a snack or for lunch. —Marilyn Lee, Richmond, Missouri*

**2 large sweet onions**
**2 eggs**
**1-1/2 cups crushed cornflakes**
**2 teaspoons sugar**
**1 teaspoon paprika**
**1/4 teaspoon garlic salt**
**1/4 teaspoon seasoned salt**

Cut onions into 1/2-in. slices; separate into rings. In a shallow dish, whisk eggs. In another shallow dish, combine the cornflake crumbs, sugar, paprika, garlic salt and seasoned salt. Dip onion rings into eggs, then coat with cornflake mixture. Arrange rings in a single layer on greased baking sheets. Bake at 375° for 20-25 minutes or until tender. **Yield:** 6-8 servings.

Jalapeno Sausage Pizza
Chicago-Style Pan Pizza
Buffalo Chicken Pizza

# Pleasing Pizza

ASK family members what their favorite food is, and someone is sure to answer "Pizza!" After all, who can resist a golden crust, savory sauce and toppings?

In the following section, you'll find ever-popular traditional pizzas...slices with toppings that are deliciously different...even a sweet pizza for dessert. And all of these pleasing pies get to the table pronto.

## Jalapeno Sausage Pizza

*(Pictured above)*

*This zesty pizza is a quick way to bring some spice to dinner. The biscuit mix crust gets its zip from chopped jalapenos while taco seasoning perks up the tomato sauce.*
*—Janet Choate, St. Louis, Missouri*

**2 cups biscuit/baking mix**
**1/2 cup milk**
**2 cups (8 ounces) shredded Mexican cheese blend, *divided***
**6 jalapeno peppers, seeded and chopped**
**1 envelope taco seasoning**
**1 can (8 ounces) tomato sauce**
**1 *each* medium sweet red and green pepper, chopped**
**2 green onions, chopped**
**1/4 pound bulk pork sausage, cooked and crumbled**
**1/2 cup sour cream**
**1/2 cup ranch salad dressing**
**2 cups shredded lettuce**
**1 medium tomato, chopped**
**1 can (2-1/4 ounces) sliced ripe olives, drained**

In a bowl, combine biscuit mix and milk. Stir in 1 cup cheese and jalapenos. With floured gloved hands, pat dough onto a greased 12-in. pizza pan. Bake at 400° for 10-15 minutes or until lightly browned.

Combine taco seasoning and tomato sauce; spread over crust. Top with peppers, onions, sausage and remaining cheese. Bake for 8-10 minutes or until heated through. Combine sour cream and ranch dressing; drizzle over pizza. Sprinkle with lettuce, tomato and olives. **Yield:** 6-8 slices.

**Editor's Note:** When cutting or seeding hot peppers, use rubber or plastic gloves to protect your hands. Avoid touching your face.

## Buffalo Chicken Pizza

*(Pictured above)*

*If your family likes spicy chicken wings, they'll love this pizza made with bottled buffalo wing sauce and refrigerated pizza dough. Serve blue cheese salad dressing on the side.* *—Shari DiGirolamo, Newtown, Pennsylvania*

**2 tubes (10 ounces *each*) refrigerated pizza crust**
**1 cup buffalo wing sauce, *divided***
**1-1/2 cups (6 ounces) shredded cheddar cheese**
**1-1/2 cups (6 ounces) shredded mozzarella cheese**
**2 pounds boneless skinless chicken breasts, cubed**
**1/2 teaspoon *each* garlic salt, pepper and chili powder**
**2 tablespoons butter**

**1/2 teaspoon dried oregano**
**Celery sticks and blue cheese salad dressing**

Unroll pizza crusts into a lightly greased 15-in. x 10-in. x 1-in. baking pan; flatten dough and build up edges slightly. Bake at 400° for 7 minutes. Brush dough with 3 tablespoons buffalo wing sauce. Combine cheddar and mozzarella cheeses; sprinkle a third over the crust. Set aside.

In a large skillet, cook chicken, garlic salt, pepper and chili powder in butter until chicken is browned. Add remaining wing sauce; cook and stir over medium heat until chicken juices run clear, about 5 minutes. Spoon over cheese. Sprinkle with oregano and remaining cheese.

Bake for 18-20 minutes or until crust is golden brown and cheese is melted. Serve with celery and blue cheese dressing. **Yield:** 8 slices.

**Editor's Note:** This recipe was tested with Frank's RedHot Buffalo Wing Sauce.

## Chicago-Style Pan Pizza

*(Pictured at left)*

*I developed a love for Chicago's deep-dish pizzas while attending college in the Windy City. This simple recipe relies on frozen bread dough, so I can indulge in the mouthwatering sensation without leaving home.*
*—Nikki MacDonald, Sheboygan, Wisconsin*

**1 loaf (1 pound) frozen bread dough, thawed**
**1 pound bulk Italian sausage**
**2 cups (8 ounces) shredded mozzarella cheese**
**1/2 pound sliced fresh mushrooms**
**1 small onion, chopped**
**2 teaspoons olive oil**
**1 can (28 ounces) diced tomatoes, drained**
**3/4 teaspoon dried oregano**
**1/2 teaspoon salt**
**1/2 teaspoon fennel seed, crushed**
**1/4 teaspoon garlic powder**
**1/2 cup grated Parmesan cheese**

Press dough onto bottom and up the sides of a greased 13-in. x 9-in. x 2-in. baking dish. In a large skillet, cook sausage over medium heat until no longer pink; drain. Sprinkle over dough. Top with mozzarella cheese.

In a skillet, saute mushrooms and onion in oil until onion is tender. Stir in tomatoes, oregano, salt, fennel seed and garlic powder. Spoon over mozzarella cheese. Sprinkle with Parmesan cheese. Bake at 350° for 25-35 minutes or until crust is golden brown. **Yield:** 6 slices.

## Triple Peanut Pizza

*The tasty combination of chocolate and peanut butter has been a longtime favorite of mine, and now our son, Blake, enjoys it, too. Since most 4-year-olds love pizza, I created this fun fuss-free dessert for his birthday.*
*—Tracy Houdeshell, Marion, Iowa*

**1 tube (18 ounces) refrigerated peanut butter cookie dough**
**1 cup (6 ounces) semisweet chocolate chips**
**1 package (8 ounces) cream cheese, softened**
**1/3 cup creamy peanut butter**
**1/4 cup packed brown sugar**
**1 teaspoon vanilla extract**
**2 cups chopped peanut butter cups (about 15 large)**

Press cookie dough onto a greased 14-in. pizza pan. Bake at 350° for 12-15 minutes or until golden brown. Sprinkle with chocolate chips; let stand for 4-5 minutes. Spread melted chips over crust. Freeze for 10 minutes or until set.

Meanwhile, in a small mixing bowl, beat the cream cheese, peanut butter, brown sugar and vanilla until creamy. Spread over the chocolate. Sprinkle with the peanut butter cups. Chill until serving. Refrigerate leftovers. **Yield:** 12-14 slices.

## Reuben Pizza

*(Pictured below)*

*Fridays are pizza nights at our house. We do a lot of experimenting, so we don't have the same old thing every week. This pizza is a snap to whip up with only five ingredients...and it tastes just like a Reuben sandwich.*
*—Nicole German, Hutchinson, Minnesota*

**1 prebaked Italian bread shell crust (14 ounces)**
**2/3 cup Thousand Island salad dressing**
**8 ounces thinly sliced corned beef, cut into strips**
**1 can (14 ounces) sauerkraut, rinsed and well drained**
**2 cups (8 ounces) shredded Swiss cheese**

Place the crust on a 14-in. pizza pan; spread with salad dressing. Layer with corned beef and sauerkraut; sprinkle with cheese. Bake at 400° for 12-15 minutes or until heated through and cheese is melted. **Yield:** 8 slices.

**Reuben Pizza**

Southwestern Chicken Pizza

## Southwestern Chicken Pizza

(Pictured above)

*Our family loves both Mexican food and pizza, so I decided to try combining the two. This pie smothered with southwestern toppings was the result...and we all think it's fantastic. To hurry along the recipe, I take advantage of convenient prepared salsa, packaged cooked chicken strips and a refrigerated crust.* —Robin Poust
Stevensville, Maryland

- **1 medium onion, julienned**
- **1 medium green pepper, julienned**
- **1/4 cup water**
- **1 tube (10 ounces) refrigerated pizza crust**
- **1-1/4 cups salsa**
- **2 packages (6 ounces *each*) ready-to-use southwestern chicken strips**
- **2 cups (8 ounces) shredded Mexican cheese blend**
- **1/4 teaspoon garlic powder**
- **1/4 teaspoon dried cilantro flakes**

In a microwave-safe bowl, combine the onion, green pepper and water. Cover and microwave on high for 2-4 minutes or until vegetables are crisp-tender; drain well.

Unroll pizza crust onto a greased baking sheet, stretching gently to form a 14-in. x 10-in. rectangle. Spread with salsa. Top with chicken and onion mixture. Sprinkle with cheese, garlic powder and cilantro.

Bake at 400° for 15-20 minutes or until the crust is golden and the cheese is melted. Cut into squares. **Yield:** 8 slices.

**Editor's Note:** This recipe was tested in a 1,100-watt microwave.

## Canadian Bacon Pizza Loaf

*This unique sweet-and-sour pizza bread is as much fun to assemble as it is to eat, so you may have some helpers in the kitchen. Topped with Canadian bacon, green pepper, pineapple tidbits and mozzarella cheese, the loaf was a big hit at our daughter's birthday party and tastes like a special treat on busy weeknights.* —Shirley Hartford
Baker, Louisiana

- **1 unsliced loaf (1 pound) French bread**
- **1-1/2 cups pizza sauce**
- **4 ounces Canadian bacon, chopped**
- **1 can (20 ounces) pineapple tidbits, drained**
- **1 small green pepper, sliced**
- **2 cups (8 ounces) shredded mozzarella cheese**

Cut loaf in half lengthwise; place on a baking sheet. Spread cut sides of bread with the pizza sauce. Top with the Canadian bacon, pineapple, green pepper and cheese. Broil 4-6 in. from the heat for 5-8 minutes or until cheese is melted. **Yield:** 8-10 slices.

## Seafood Pizza

(Pictured below)

*When a friend of mine shared her popular recipe for seafood enchiladas, I adapted it to create this unusual but great-tasting pie. The thick creamy cheese sauce blends wonderfully with the scallops, shrimp and imitation crabmeat. Plus, the pizza is special enough to serve company and comes together quickly.* —Sara Watters
Boscobel, Wisconsin

- **1 package (6-1/2 ounces) pizza crust mix**
- **3 tablespoons butter, *divided***
- **2 tablespoons all-purpose flour**
- **3/4 cup milk**
- **1/4 cup chicken broth**
- **1/4 cup shredded Monterey Jack cheese**
- **1/4 cup shredded Swiss cheese**
- **1/4 pound uncooked bay scallops, chopped**
- **1/4 pound cooked shrimp, peeled, deveined and chopped**

Seafood Pizza

**1/4 pound imitation crabmeat, chopped**
**2 cups (8 ounces) shredded mozzarella cheese**
**Paprika, optional**

Prepare pizza dough according to package directions. Press onto a lightly greased 12-in. pizza pan; build up edges slightly. Prick dough thoroughly with a fork. Bake at 400° for 5-6 minutes or until crust is firm and begins to brown.

Meanwhile, in a saucepan, melt 2 tablespoons butter over medium heat. Stir in flour until smooth. Gradually stir in milk and broth. Bring to a boil; cook and stir for 2 minutes or until thickened. Reduce heat. Stir in Monterey Jack and Swiss cheeses until melted. Remove from the heat.

In a skillet, melt the remaining butter over medium heat. Add scallops; cook and stir for 3-4 minutes or until firm and opaque. Stir in the shrimp, crab and 3 tablespoons cheese sauce. Remove from the heat.

Spread remaining cheese sauce over the crust. Top with the seafood mixture; sprinkle with mozzarella cheese and paprika if desired. Bake for 13-16 minutes or until golden brown. Let stand for 5-10 minutes before cutting. **Yield:** 8 slices.

## Stuffed-Crust Pizza

*There's no pizza delivery in our rural community, so I rely on this recipe instead. The edges of the no-fail homemade crust are filled with string cheese, and the hearty toppings can be varied to suit your preference. Try the dough for making breadsticks or bread bowls.*
*—Renae Jacobson, Elm Creek, Nebraska*

**1 pound ground beef**
**1 small onion, chopped**
**2-1/2 to 3 cups all-purpose flour**
**2 tablespoons Italian seasoning, *divided***
**1 package (1/4 ounce) quick-rise yeast**
**1 teaspoon sugar**
**1/2 teaspoon salt**
**1 cup water**
**3 tablespoons olive oil**
**3 tablespoons cornmeal**
**4 ounces string cheese**
**1 can (15 ounces) pizza sauce**
**1/2 cup sliced fresh mushrooms**
**1 cup (4 ounces) shredded mozzarella cheese**
**1/4 cup shredded cheddar cheese**

In a skillet, cook beef and onion until meat is no longer pink; drain and set aside. In a mixing bowl, combine 2-1/2 cups flour, 1 tablespoon Italian seasoning, yeast, sugar and salt.

In a saucepan, heat water and oil to 120°-130°. Add to the dry ingredients; beat just until moistened. Stir in enough remaining flour to form a soft dough. Let rest for 5 minutes. Sprinkle cornmeal over a greased 14-in. pizza pan.

On a lightly floured surface, roll dough into a 15-in. circle. Transfer to prepared pan, letting dough drape 1 in. over the edge. Cut string cheese in half lengthwise; place around edge of pan. Fold dough over string cheese; pinch to seal. Prick dough thoroughly with a fork. Bake at 375° for 5 minutes.

Combine pizza sauce and 2 teaspoons Italian seasoning; spread half over crust. Sprinkle with beef mixture and mushrooms; cover with remaining pizza sauce mixture. Sprinkle with shredded cheeses and remaining Italian seasoning. Bake for 18-20 minutes or until cheese is melted and crust is golden brown. **Yield:** 8 slices.

Fresh Tomato Basil Pizza

## Fresh Tomato Basil Pizza

*(Pictured above)*

*I always crave this bruschetta-like pizza in spring, when I'm planting tomatoes in our garden. The well-seasoned slices make great appetizers when the tomatoes are ripe. But you can also serve the pizza alongside a grilled entree or as a meatless main course.* *—Jennifer Headlee*
*Baxter, Iowa*

**1 tube (8 ounces) refrigerated crescent rolls**
**2 garlic cloves, minced**
**1 tablespoon olive oil**
**1/2 cup chopped fresh basil**
**8 ounces sliced provolone cheese**
**4 medium tomatoes, thinly sliced**
**1/4 cup grated Parmesan cheese**
**1/4 teaspoon pepper**

Unroll crescent dough into one long rectangle. Press into an ungreased 13-in. x 9-in. x 2-in. baking pan; seal seams and perforations. Bake at 375° for 14-16 minutes or until golden brown.

Meanwhile, in a skillet, saute the garlic in oil for 2 minutes. Reduce heat. Add basil; cook for 2 minutes or until heated through.

Arrange half of provolone cheese over crust. Layer with half of the tomatoes, basil mixture, Parmesan cheese and pepper. Repeat layers. Bake for 14-16 minutes or until cheese is melted. **Yield:** 6 slices.

## Double Sausage Pizza

*(Pictured at right)*

*This recipe has been in the family since I was a kid. It was a Sunday night ritual then, and it remains one today in my home. Dressed-up hot roll mix gives us enough dough for two flavorful crusts, so there is plenty of sausage-pepperoni pizza to serve company.* —*Emalee Satoski Union Mills, Indiana*

**1 package (16 ounces) hot roll mix**
**2 tablespoons garlic powder**
**2 tablespoons dried oregano**
**2 tablespoons Italian seasoning**
**1-1/4 cups warm water (120° to 130°)**
**2 tablespoons vegetable oil**
**1 can (15 ounces) pizza sauce**
**1/2 cup grated Parmesan cheese**
**1 pound bulk pork sausage, cooked and crumbled**
**1/2 pound sliced fresh mushrooms**
**1 package (8 ounces) sliced pepperoni**
**4 cups (28 ounces) shredded mozzarella cheese**

In a large bowl, combine the hot roll mix, contents of yeast packet, garlic powder, oregano and Italian seasoning. Stir in water and oil until dough pulls away from sides of bowl. Turn dough onto a lightly floured surface. Shape into a ball. Knead for 5 minutes or until smooth. Cover and let stand for 5 minutes.

Divide dough in half. With greased hands, press dough onto two greased 12-in. pizza pans. Prick dough thoroughly with a fork. Spread crusts with pizza sauce. Top with Parmesan cheese, sausage, mushrooms, pepperoni and mozzarella cheese. Bake at 425° for 18-20 minutes or until cheese is melted. **Yield:** 2 pizzas (8-10 slices each).

Double Sausage Pizza

BLT Pizza

## BLT Pizza

*(Pictured at left)*

*A friend shared the recipe for this cold pizza that gets its crispy crust from refrigerated crescent roll dough. My coworkers especially like it when I bring this refreshing snack in to work.* —*Dawn Thompson, Ray, North Dakota*

**1 tube (8 ounces) refrigerated crescent rolls**
**1 cup mayonnaise**
**1 tablespoon Dijon mustard**
**3 cups shredded lettuce**
**12 bacon strips, cooked and crumbled**
**1 medium tomato, seeded and chopped**
**2 green onions, thinly sliced**
**1-1/2 cups (6 ounces) shredded cheddar cheese**

Separate crescent dough into eight triangles; place on a lightly greased 14-in. pizza pan with points toward the center.

Press dough onto the bottom and up the sides of pan, forming a crust; seal perforations. Bake at 375° for 12-15 minutes or until golden brown. Cool completely. In a small bowl, combine the mayonnaise and mustard; spread over crust. Sprinkle with lettuce, bacon, tomato, onions and cheese. **Yield:** 6-8 slices.

WHEN you have guests or need munchies for your family, you don't want time-consuming recipes. So try the speedy snacks and appetizers here.

## Italian Sausage Mushrooms

*These savory bites can be made with only a handful of ingredients. —Lorie Zufall, Waynesboro, Pennsylvania*

- **1 pound bulk Italian sausage**
- **24 medium fresh mushrooms**
- **2 packages (3 ounces *each*) cream cheese, softened**
- **4 tablespoons minced fresh parsley, *divided***

In a large skillet, cook sausage over medium heat until no longer pink; drain. Remove and discard mushroom stems. Place caps on a microwave-safe plate. Microwave, uncovered, on high for 2 minutes; drain.

In a small mixing bowl, combine the cream cheese, 3 tablespoons parsley and sausage until well blended. Spoon into mushroom caps. Cover and microwave at 70% power for 5-7 minutes or until heated through; drain. Let stand for 5 minutes before serving. Sprinkle with remaining parsley. **Yield:** 2 dozen.

**Editor's Note:** This recipe was tested in a 1,100-watt microwave.

## Caramelized Onion Tartlets

*(Pictured below right)*

*I fill crunchy phyllo shells with a sweet onion mixture. I enjoy experimenting with novel flavors and ingredients. —Jerri Hansen, Council Bluffs, Iowa*

- **2 tablespoons plus 1/2 cup butter, *divided***
- **2 large sweet onions, chopped**
- **1/4 cup sugar**
- **3/4 cup hot water**
- **1 tablespoon beef bouillon granules**
- **1 cup (4 ounces) shredded Swiss cheese**
- **8 sheets phyllo dough (14 inches x 9 inches)**

In a large skillet, melt 2 tablespoons butter over medium heat. Add onions and sugar. Cook over medium heat for 15-20 minutes or until the onions are golden brown, stirring frequently. Stir in water and bouillon. Bring to a boil. Reduce heat; simmer, uncovered, for 5-7 minutes or until liquid has evaporated. Remove from the heat. Stir in cheese.

Melt remaining butter. Place one sheet of phyllo on a work surface; brush with butter. Top with second sheet; brush with butter. Cut into 12 squares. (Keep unbuttered phyllo covered with waxed paper to avoid drying out.) Repeat three times, forming 48 squares.

Press one square into a greased miniature muffin cup. Top with another square of phyllo, placing corners off-center. Spoon about 1 tablespoon onion mixture into cup. Repeat with remaining phyllo squares and onion mixture. Bake at 375° for 10-15 minutes or until golden brown. Serve warm. **Yield:** 2 dozen.

## Grilled Potato Skins

*(Pictured below)*

*Just about everyone loves these sensational appetizers. They're nice to serve outside when you invite friends over for a grilled meal. —Mitzi Sentiff, Alexandria, Virginia*

- **2 large baking potatoes**
- **2 tablespoons butter, melted**
- **2 teaspoons minced fresh rosemary *or* 1/2 teaspoon dried rosemary, crushed**
- **1/2 teaspoon salt**
- **1/2 teaspoon pepper**
- **1 cup (4 ounces) shredded cheddar cheese**
- **3 bacon strips, cooked and crumbled**
- **2 green onions, chopped**
- **Sour cream**

Cut each potato lengthwise into four wedges. Cut away the white portion, leaving 1/4 in. on the potato skins. Place skins on a microwave-safe plate. Microwave, uncovered, on high for 8-10 minutes or until tender. Combine the butter, rosemary, salt and pepper; brush over both sides of potato skins.

Grill potatoes, skin side up, uncovered, over direct medium heat for 2-3 minutes or until lightly browned. Turn potatoes and position over indirect heat; grill 2 minutes longer. Top with cheese. Cover and grill 2-3 minutes longer or until cheese is melted. Sprinkle with bacon and onions. Serve with sour cream. **Yield:** 8 appetizers.

**Editor's Note:** This recipe was tested in a 1,100-watt microwave.

Grilled Potato Skins
Carmelized Onion Tartlets

## Smoked Salmon Cucumbers

*(Pictured above)*

*This super-easy appetizer has pleased many guests at our house and is sure to be a hit at yours, too! The four-ingredient bites offer a light and refreshing taste any time of the year.* —*Cheryl Lama, Royal Oak, Michigan*

**1 large English cucumber**
**1 carton (8 ounces) spreadable chive and onion cream cheese**
**7 to 8 ounces smoked salmon, chopped**
**Minced chives**

With a fork, score cucumber peel lengthwise; cut into 1/4-in. slices. Pipe or spread cream cheese onto each slice; top with salmon. Sprinkle with chives. Refrigerate until serving. **Yield:** about 3 dozen.

## Four-Layer Cheese Spread

*When I entertain, I count on this streamlined party-starter. I invert the chilled mold onto a platter lined with baby spinach.* —*Sherry Hulsman, Louisville, Kentucky*

**1 package (8 ounces) cream cheese, softened, *divided***
**1/4 cup fresh baby spinach, chopped**
**4-1/2 teaspoons chutney**
**2 cups (8 ounces) shredded cheddar cheese**
**2/3 cup mayonnaise**
**1/2 cup chopped pecans**
**1/4 cup finely chopped onion**
**Dash hot pepper sauce**
**Additional fresh baby spinach**
**Assorted crackers and vegetables**

In a small bowl, combine 4 ounces cream cheese and chopped spinach. In another bowl, combine chutney and remaining cream cheese. In a large bowl, combine cheddar cheese, mayonnaise, pecans, onion and hot pepper sauce.

Line a 3-cup bowl with plastic wrap. Spread half of the cheddar cheese mixture in prepared bowl. Layer with the spinach and chutney mixtures. Top with remaining cheddar cheese mixture. Cover and refrigerate overnight.

Unmold onto a serving plate; garnish with additional spinach. Serve with crackers and vegetables. **Yield:** about 3 cups.

## Party Pesto Pinwheels

*(Pictured below)*

*I took a couple of my favorite recipes and combined them into these delicious hors d'oeuvres. The colorful and impressive snacks come together easily with refrigerated crescent roll dough, prepared pesto sauce and a jar of roasted red peppers.* —*Kathleen Farrell, Rochester, New York*

**1 tube (8 ounces) refrigerated crescent rolls**
**1/3 cup prepared pesto sauce**
**1/4 cup roasted sweet red peppers, drained and chopped**
**1/4 cup grated Parmesan cheese**
**1 cup pizza sauce, warmed**

Unroll crescent dough into two long rectangles; seal seams and perforations. Spread each with pesto; sprin-

kle with red peppers and Parmesan cheese. Roll each up jelly-roll style, starting with a short side.

With a sharp knife, cut each roll into 10 slices. Place cut side down 2 in. apart on two ungreased baking sheets. Bake at 400° for 8-10 minutes or until golden brown. Serve warm with pizza sauce. **Yield:** 20 servings.

## Taco Crackers

*A handful of these crispy oyster crackers is never enough. Taco seasoning and chili powder give the munchies a fun southwestern flavor. Party-goers always come back for more.* —*Diane Earnest, Newton, Illinois*

**3 packages (10 ounces *each*) oyster crackers**
**3/4 cup vegetable oil**
**1 envelope taco seasoning**
**1/2 teaspoon garlic powder**
**1/2 teaspoon dried oregano**
**1/2 teaspoon chili powder**

Place the crackers in a large roasting pan; drizzle with oil. Combine the seasonings; sprinkle over crackers and toss to coat. Bake at 350° for 15-20 minutes or until golden brown, stirring once. **Yield:** 16 cups.

## Ham Tortilla Stack

*(Pictured at right)*

*This recipe was in a cookbook my mom gave me when I got married. I've added a few of my own touches. When I take it to a potluck, I always get requests for the recipe.* —*Eileen Stegall, Omaha, Nebraska*

**3 packages (8 ounces *each*) cream cheese, softened**
**2/3 cup mayonnaise**
**1/4 cup Italian salad dressing**
**1 medium green pepper, finely chopped**
**3 green onions, finely chopped**
**1 can (2-1/4 ounces) chopped ripe olives, drained**
**1/3 cup chopped stuffed olives**
**8 flour tortillas (10 inches)**
**2-1/4 pounds shaved deli ham**

In a large mixing bowl, beat the cream cheese, mayonnaise and Italian dressing until smooth. Stir in green pepper, onions and olives. Spread about 1/2 cup over one tortilla. Top with a seventh of the ham. Repeat six times. Top with remaining tortilla. Cover and chill overnight. Cut into wedges. **Yield:** 20 servings.

## Brie with Pear Topping

*(Pictured above right)*

*I prepared this for a party, and everyone thought it was great. It is fast, easy and impressive.* —*Mary Ann Zadvorny, Stoney Creek, Ontario*

**1 round Brie cheese (8 ounces)**
**1 small ripe red pear, thinly sliced**
**2 teaspoons brown sugar**

Ham Tortilla Stack
Brie with Pear Topping

**1 tablespoon chopped pecans**
**1/4 teaspoon butter**
**Assorted crackers *or* bagel chips**

Place cheese in an ungreased ovenproof serving dish. Top with pear slices. Sprinkle with brown sugar and pecans. Dot with butter. Bake at 400° for 5-10 minutes or until cheese is softened. Serve with crackers. **Yield:** 6-8 servings.

### Making Munchies

- Extra bread can easily become a speedy snack. I lay slices on a baking pan and brush them with melted butter mixed with a seasoning, such as garlic or Italian. After baking them until they're brown, I let the slices cool and break them into pieces. —*Janet Dishong, Manheim, Pennsylvania*
- When I needed to transport 12 dozen deviled eggs to my daughter's wedding reception, I asked a local pizzeria if I could have some of their unused pizza boxes. The manager agreed, and the boxes turned out to be the perfect choice. I lined the bottom of the boxes so the eggs wouldn't slide, and the flat boxes stacked nicely in my refrigerator. —*Marquita Tuck, Columbus Indiana*
- I make an easy filling for egg rolls using leftover cooked turkey. I chop the turkey and some mushrooms, then mix them with a little gravy. Next, I center a small strip of Swiss cheese on an egg roll wrapper, top it with a tablespoon of turkey mixture and wrap the egg roll. When all of the rolls have been filled and wrapped, I carefully fry them in hot oil until golden brown. —*Kit Shaw, Boise Idaho*

## Chunky Blue Cheese Dip

*(Pictured below)*

*Every time I make this quick dip, someone asks for the recipe. It requires crumbled blue cheese and only a few other ingredients, so it's a snap to put together. I sometimes prepare the thick spread with Gorgonzola cheese and serve it with toasted pecans.* —*Sandy Schneider Naperville, Illinois*

**1 package (8 ounces) cream cheese, softened**
**1/3 cup sour cream**
**1/2 teaspoon white pepper**
**1/4 to 1/2 teaspoon salt**
**1 cup (4 ounces) crumbled blue cheese**
**1/3 cup minced chives**
**Apple and pear slices *and/or* toasted pecan halves**

In a small mixing bowl, beat the cream cheese, sour cream, pepper and salt until smooth. Fold in the blue cheese and chives. Serve with apple and pear slices and/or pecans. **Yield:** 1-3/4 cups.

## Garlic Pizza Wedges

*Our pastor made this for a get-together, and my husband and I just couldn't stay away from the hors d'oeuvres table. The cheesy slices taste great served warm, but they're still wonderful when they've cooled slightly.*
—*Krysten Johnson, Simi Valley, California*

**1 prebaked Italian bread shell crust (14 ounces)**
**1 cup grated Parmesan cheese**
**1 cup mayonnaise**
**1 small red onion, chopped**
**3-1/2 teaspoons minced garlic**
**1 tablespoon dried oregano**

Place the crust on an ungreased 14-in. pizza pan. In a small bowl, combine the Parmesan cheese, mayonnaise, onion, garlic and oregano; spread over crust. Bake at 450° for 8-10 minutes or until edges are lightly browned. Cut into wedges. **Yield:** 2 dozen.

**Editor's Note:** Reduced-fat or fat-free mayonnaise is not recommended for this recipe.

Chunky Blue Cheese Dip

Cinnamon 'n' Spice Pecans

## Cinnamon 'n' Spice Pecans

*(Pictured above)*

*Originally, these crunchy nuts were used to top a salad, but I adjusted the recipe so they could stand on their own as a snack. Cayenne pepper gives them a little kick, making the nuts a fun party-starter or hostess gift.*
*—Terry Maly, Olathe, Kansas*

**1/3 cup butter, melted**
**2 teaspoons ground cinnamon**
**3/4 teaspoon salt**
**1/2 teaspoon cayenne pepper**
**1 pound pecan halves**

In a bowl, combine the butter, cinnamon, salt and cayenne. Stir in pecans until evenly coated. Transfer to an ungreased 15-in. x 10-in. x 1-in. baking pan. Bake at 350° for 15-18 minutes or until pecans are toasted, stirring every 5 minutes. **Yield:** 4 cups.

## Cheddar Ham Cups

*When a college classmate and I threw a party for our professor, a friend contributed these savory appetizers. Everyone in the class requested the recipe before the party was done. Try the cups with chicken instead of ham if you'd like.* *—Brandi Ladner, Gulfport, Mississippi*

**2 cups (8 ounces) finely shredded cheddar cheese**
**2 packages (2-1/2 ounces *each*) thinly sliced deli ham, chopped**
**3/4 cup mayonnaise**
**1/3 cup real bacon bits**
**2 to 3 teaspoons Dijon mustard**
**1 tube (12 ounces) large refrigerated flaky biscuits**

In a bowl, combine the cheese, ham, mayonnaise, bacon and mustard. Split biscuits into thirds. Press onto the bottom and up the sides of ungreased miniature muffin cups. Fill each with about 1 tablespoon of cheese mixture.

Bake at 450° for 9-11 minutes or until golden brown and the cheese is melted. Let stand for 2 minutes before removing from the pans. Serve warm. **Yield:** 2-1/2 dozen.

## Asparagus Ham Bites

*(Pictured below)*

*Fresh asparagus, honey mustard, ham and cheese make a tasty filling for these bite-size rounds of toasted whole wheat bread. I like to assemble them ahead of time and bake them as my guests arrive.* *—Lucille Mead*
*Ilion, New York*

**6 fresh thin asparagus spears**
**6 slices whole wheat bread, crusts removed**
**1 tablespoon olive oil**
**1 tablespoon honey mustard**
**6 thin slices Monterey Jack cheese**
**6 thin slices deli ham**
**1/4 teaspoon paprika**

Trim asparagus spears to 5-1/4 in. Flatten bread with a rolling pin; brush one side of each slice with oil. Place bread, oiled side down, on an ungreased baking sheet. Spread each slice with mustard; top with cheese, ham and asparagus. Roll up tightly and place seam side down.

Bake at 350° for 12-14 minutes or until lightly crisp. Sprinkle with paprika. Cut each roll into four pieces. **Yield:** 2 dozen.

**Editor's Note:** For best results, use a firm 100% whole wheat bread.

Asparagus Ham Bites

Ham and Swiss Dip

# Beef Onion Strudel

*I collect recipes that use crescent rolls, like this one. The filling in this strudel changes depending on what's in my vegetable drawer.* —*Judy Lohse, Belvidere, Illinois*

**1-1/2 cups sliced sweet onions**
**1/4 cup butter**
**1/2 pound ground beef**
**1 teaspoon all-purpose flour**
**1 teaspoon brown sugar**
**1/2 teaspoon ground cumin**
**1/4 teaspoon salt**
**1/4 teaspoon pepper**
**1/2 cup beef broth**
**1 tube (8 ounces) refrigerated crescent rolls**
**3/4 cup shredded mozzarella cheese**
**2 tablespoons grated Parmesan cheese**

In a large skillet, saute the onions in butter until browned and caramelized; remove with a slotted spoon and keep warm. In the same skillet, cook beef over medium heat until no longer pink; drain. Stir in the flour, brown sugar, cumin, salt and pepper until blended. Gradually add the beef broth; cook for 8 minutes or until the liquid is absorbed. Stir in reserved onion.

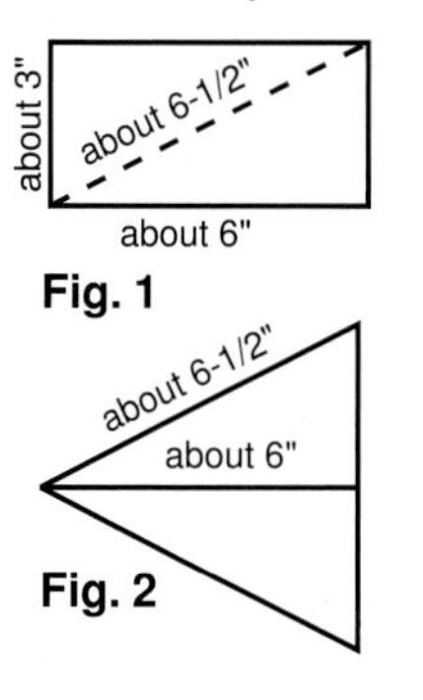


Unroll dough and separate into four rectangles. Separate each rectangle at perforation into two triangles (see Fig. 1). Pinch two 6-in. sides together to form a triangle (see Fig. 2). Repeat with remaining dough.

Place point of one triangle near the end of a greased baking sheet. Place point of second triangle in center of first triangle. Repeat with remaining triangles (see Fig. 3).

Spoon beef mixture in a 1-1/2-in.-wide strip down the center; sprinkle with the mozzarella cheese. Starting at one end, fold alternating points across filling. Pinch ends to seal. Sprinkle with Parmesan cheese. Bake at 375° for 15-20 minutes or until golden brown. Cool for 5-10 minutes before slicing. **Yield:** 8-10 servings.

# Ham and Swiss Dip

*(Pictured above)*

*I have been making this scrumptious dip for 25 years, and I can't think of a time where there haven't been multiple requests for the recipe. It's wonderful for holiday celebrations, sports parties and even brunch buffets.*
—*Laurie LaClair, North Richland Hills, Texas*

**1 package (8 ounces) cream cheese, softened**
**2/3 cup mayonnaise**
**1-1/2 cups diced fully cooked ham**
**1 cup (4 ounces) shredded Swiss cheese**
**1 tablespoon finely chopped green pepper**
**1 tablespoon spicy brown mustard**
**3/4 cup rye cracker crumbs**
**2 tablespoons butter, melted**
**Rye crackers**

In a small mixing bowl, beat cream cheese and mayonnaise until smooth. Stir in the ham, cheese, green pepper and mustard. Spread into an ungreased 9-in. pie plate.

Toss the cracker crumbs and butter; sprinkle over cream cheese mixture. Bake, uncovered, at 400° for 12-15 minutes or until heated through. Serve with crackers. **Yield:** about 3 cups.

**Editor's Note:** Reduced-fat or fat-free mayonnaise is not recommended for this recipe.

# Beer Cheese Fondue

*This thick fondue originated in my kitchen when I didn't have all of the ingredients I needed to make the recipe I initially planned to prepare. Served with bread cubes, it has since become a staple, particularly while we watch football games on television.* —*Chrystie Wear*
*Greensboro, North Carolina*

**1 loaf (20 inches) French bread, cubed**
**1/4 cup chopped onion**
**1 teaspoon minced garlic**
**1 tablespoon butter**
**1 cup beer *or* nonalcoholic beer**
**4 cups (16 ounces) shredded cheddar cheese**

1 tablespoon all-purpose flour
2 to 4 tablespoons half-and-half cream

Place bread cubes in a single layer in an ungreased 15-in. x 10-in. x 1-in. baking pan. Bake at 450° for 5-7 minutes or until lightly crisp, stirring twice.

Meanwhile, in a small saucepan, saute onion and garlic in butter until tender. Stir in beer. Bring to a boil; reduce heat to medium-low. Toss cheese and flour; stir into saucepan until melted. Stir in 2 tablespoons cream.

Transfer to a small ceramic fondue pot or slow cooker; keep warm. Add additional cream if fondue thickens. Serve with toasted bread cubes. **Yield:** about 3 cups.

## Bacon-Stuffed Mushrooms

*(Pictured below)*

*I first tried these broiled treats at my sister-in-law's house. The juicy mushroom caps and creamy filling were so fabulous that I had to get the recipe. It's hard to believe how simple, fast and easy they are. —Angela Coffman Stewartsville, Missouri*

**1 package (8 ounces) cream cheese, softened**
**1/2 cup real bacon bits**
**1 tablespoon chopped green onion**
**1/4 teaspoon garlic powder**
**1 pound whole fresh mushrooms, stems removed**

In a small mixing bowl, beat cream cheese until smooth. Stir in the bacon, onion and garlic powder. Spoon into mushroom caps. Place on an ungreased broiler pan. Broil 4-6 in. from the heat for 4-6 minutes or until heated through. Serve warm. **Yield:** about 2 dozen.

Bacon-Stuffed Mushrooms

Festive Apple Dip

## Festive Apple Dip

*(Pictured above)*

*I came up with this layered peanut butter treat when my dad gave me a big bag of apples. The dip has been one of my favorites ever since. In addition to serving it with apples, try it with graham crackers, vanilla wafers, banana chunks or animal crackers. —Theresa Tometich Coralville, Iowa*

**1 package (8 ounces) cream cheese, softened**
**1/2 cup creamy peanut butter**
**1/3 cup packed brown sugar**
**1 teaspoon vanilla extract**
**1/2 cup miniature marshmallows**
**1 jar (11-3/4 ounces) hot fudge ice cream topping**
**2 tablespoons chopped mixed nuts *or* chopped peanuts**
**3 *each* medium red and green apples, cut into wedges**
**2 tablespoons lemon juice**

In a small mixing bowl, beat the cream cheese, peanut butter, brown sugar and vanilla; stir in marshmallows. Spoon half into a 3-cup bowl; spread with half of the hot fudge topping. Repeat layers. Sprinkle with nuts. Toss the apples with lemon juice. Serve immediately with dip. **Yield:** about 2 cups.

# Chapter 20

# Company's Coming!

TOO BUSY to entertain? Not so! An impressive menu can have time-saving elements that make hosting a get-together a snap—and just as fun for the hostess as it is for the guests.

In this chapter, fellow time-crunched cooks share an assortment of favorite, fast-to-fix recipes they prepare for company.

Our Test Kitchen staff combined some of these fuss-free dishes, creating five complete meals that will keep your prep work to a minimum and delight family and friends.

Plus, you'll see how you can add special touches to your table by making easy and inexpensive favors and decorations.

**EASY ENTERTAINING.** Clockwise from top left: Mocha Truffle Cheesecake (p. 311), Appetizer Shrimp Kabobs (p. 312), Drop-In Salad (p. 313) and Garlic Chuck Roast (p. 313).

# Fresh Flavors Make Meal Memorable

TREATING your family and friends to a delicious dinner is easy when you turn to the mouth-watering menu featured here. Our Test Kitchen gathered together recipes that combine flavorful fresh ingredients with convenient purchased products, creating an impressive spread that keeps preparation time to a minimum.

## Shrimp 'n' Veggie Alfredo

*I rely on store-bought Alfredo sauce to toss together this pretty pasta dish. The 30-minute entree combines fresh shrimp and tender fettuccine with colorful peppers, peas and carrots.* —*Bonnie Jost, Manitowoc, Wisconsin*

**1 package (16 ounces) fettuccine**
**1/2 pound fresh *or* frozen sugar snap peas, thawed**
**1 medium sweet red pepper, julienned**
**2 medium carrots, julienned**
**2 garlic cloves, minced**
**3 tablespoons vegetable oil, *divided***
**1-1/2 pounds uncooked medium shrimp, peeled and deveined**
**1 jar (16 ounces) Alfredo sauce, warmed**

Cook pasta according to package directions. Meanwhile, in a large skillet, saute the peas, red pepper, carrots and garlic in 2 tablespoons oil until crisp-tender; remove and keep warm. Add remaining oil to skillet. Saute shrimp in oil until shrimp turn pink. Return vegetables to pan; mix well. Drain pasta. Place pasta on six dinner plates. Drizzle with Alfredo sauce and top with shrimp mixture. **Yield:** 6 servings.

## Onion Tomato Soup

*Fresh herbs really make the difference in the flavor of this low-fat vegetarian soup. It tastes especially delicious when it's cold out.* —*Lisa Blackwell, Henderson, North Carolina*

✓ Uses less fat, sugar or salt. Includes Nutritional Analysis and Diabetic Exchanges.

**2 cups thinly sliced onions**
**4 teaspoons olive oil**
**2-2/3 cups tomato juice**
**2 cups water**
**2 tablespoons minced fresh basil**
**2 teaspoons minced fresh oregano**
**1 teaspoon sugar**
**1 teaspoon celery salt**
**2 cups diced seeded plum tomatoes**

In a large saucepan, saute onions in oil until tender. Add the tomato juice, water, basil, oregano, sugar and celery salt. Bring to a boil. Reduce heat; simmer, uncovered, for 20 minutes, stirring occasionally. Add the tomatoes; cook 10 minutes longer. **Yield:** 6 servings.

**Nutritional Analysis:** One 1-cup serving (prepared with reduced-sodium tomato juice) equals 82 calories, 3 g fat (trace saturated fat), 0 cholesterol, 265 mg sodium, 13 g carbohydrate, 3 g fiber, 2 g protein. **Diabetic Exchange:** 1 starch.

## Garlic Cheese Quick Bread

*Whether served warm or cold, this moist loaf is a great way to round out meals. Leftovers can also make good croutons. Just cube the slices and brown them in butter in a skillet.* —*Sue Dodd, Friendsville, Tennessee*

**3 cups self-rising flour**
**1 cup (4 ounces) shredded sharp cheddar cheese**
**1/4 cup sugar**
**1 teaspoon garlic powder**
**1-1/2 cups milk**
**1/4 cup vegetable oil**
**1 egg**

In a large bowl, combine flour, cheese, sugar and garlic powder. In another bowl, whisk the milk, oil and egg. Stir into dry ingredients just until moistened. Pour into a greased 9-in. x 5-in. x 3-in. loaf pan. Bake at 350° for 55-65 minutes or until a toothpick inserted near the center comes out clean. Cool for 10 minutes before removing from pan to a wire rack. **Yield:** 1 loaf.

**Editor's Note:** As a substitute for *each* cup of self-rising flour, place 1-1/2 teaspoons baking powder and 1/2 teaspoon salt in a measuring cup. Add all-purpose flour to measure 1 cup.

## Orange Chocolate Tart

*Our Test Kitchen whipped up this delectable dessert. A fudgy filling flavored with orange extract is baked in a pastry crust, spread with whipped topping, then garnished with orange peel and chocolate hearts.*

**6 tablespoons butter**
**7 squares (1 ounce *each*) semisweet chocolate, *divided***
**1 sheet refrigerated pie pastry**
**2 eggs**
**1/2 cup sugar**
**1/4 teaspoon orange extract**
**1/2 cup all-purpose flour**
**1 cup whipped topping**
**Orange peel, optional**

In a microwave-safe dish, melt butter and five chocolate squares. Cool for 10 minutes. Meanwhile, line a 9-in. fluted tart pan with a removable bottom with pastry. Line pastry with a double thickness of heavy-duty aluminum foil. Bake at 450° for 5 minutes. Remove the foil; bake 3 minutes longer. Reduce heat to 350°.

In a small mixing bowl, beat eggs, sugar and orange extract until thickened, about 4 minutes. Stir in cooled chocolate mixture. Beat in flour; mix well. Pour into crust. Bake for 15-20 minutes or until a toothpick inserted near the center comes out clean. Cool completely on a wire rack.

Meanwhile, line a baking sheet with waxed paper; set aside. Melt remaining chocolate. Pour melted chocolate into a heavy-duty resealable plastic bag; cut a small hole in a corner of bag. Pipe eight to 10 small hearts onto the waxed paper. Refrigerate until set. Spread whipped topping on pie; garnish with chocolate hearts and orange peel if desired. Refrigerate leftovers. **Yield:** 8-10 servings.

# Dish Up Delicious Dinner on Dad's Day

SATISFY hearty appetites on Father's Day—or any time of the year—with this pleasing meal of marinated flank steak, herbed crescent rolls, savory seafood salad and sherbet dessert. Offering make-ahead convenience, the fantastic feast from readers is sure to make dinnertime extra special.

Most of these dishes can be started or completely finished the day before the event, so you won't have to fuss over lots of last-minute details.

## Gingered Flank Steak

*A simple marinade lends plenty of flavor to this flank steak. It's always my brother's birthday entree of choice.*
*—Pam Winter, St. Peters, Missouri*

**1/2 cup reduced-sodium soy sauce**
**2 tablespoons brown sugar**
**2 tablespoons Worcestershire sauce**
**1 tablespoon lemon juice**
**1/8 teaspoon minced fresh gingerroot**
**1 garlic clove, minced**
**1 beef flank steak (1 pound)**

In a bowl, combine the first six ingredients. Pour half of the marinade into a large resealable plastic bag; add steak. Seal bag and turn to coat; refrigerate for at least 8 hours or overnight. Cover and refrigerate remaining marinade.

Drain and discard marinade from steak. Grill steak, covered, over medium heat for 5-6 minutes on each side or until meat reaches desired doneness (for rare, a meat thermometer should read 140°; medium, 160°; well-done, 170°), basting occasionally with the reserved marinade. **Yield:** 4 servings.

## Basil Garlic Crescents

*I enjoy creating recipes that are effortless and impressive. Sprinkled with garlic, Parmesan cheese and flecks of basil, these buttery bite-size rolls are delicious by themselves as appetizers or served as part of a special meal. —Sharon Setzer Gig Harbor, Washington*

**1/2 cup small-curd cottage cheese**
**1/2 cup butter, softened**
**1 package (3 ounces) cream cheese, softened**
**1-1/2 cups all-purpose flour**
**2 tablespoons olive oil**
**1 cup grated Parmesan cheese**
**2 tablespoons minced fresh basil *or* 2 teaspoons dried basil**
**1 teaspoon garlic powder**

In a food processor, combine cottage cheese, butter and cream cheese; cover and process until smooth. Add flour; cover and process until mixture forms a ball.

Divide dough into two portions. On a floured surface, roll each portion into a 10-in. circle. Brush with oil. Sprinkle with Parmesan cheese, basil and garlic powder. Cut each circle into 12 wedges.

Roll up wedges from the wide end and place pointed side down 2 in. apart on greased baking sheets. Curve ends of each to form a crescent shape. Bake at 350° for 20-25 minutes or until golden brown. Remove to wire racks; serve warm. **Yield:** 2 dozen.

## Grilled Scallop Salad

*I dress up a plain green salad with scallops, asparagus, bacon and walnuts. Prepared vinaigrette dressing makes a fuss-free finish. —Dennis Reed, Henry, Illinois*

**24 asparagus spears, trimmed**
**2 tablespoons olive oil**
**1 teaspoon soy sauce**
**24 sea scallops**
**2 cups sliced fresh mushrooms**
**2 cups torn red leaf lettuce**
**2 cups torn Bibb *or* Boston lettuce**
**1/4 cup crumbled cooked bacon**
**1 cup chopped walnuts, toasted**
**2 tablespoons grated Romano cheese**
**1/2 cup balsamic vinaigrette salad dressing**

In a large saucepan, bring 6 cups water to a boil. Add asparagus; cover and boil for 3 minutes. Drain and immediately place asparagus in ice water. Drain and pat dry; set aside. In a large resealable plastic bag, combine oil and soy sauce; add scallops. Seal bag and turn to coat. Let stand for 10 minutes.

Coat grill rack with nonstick cooking spray before starting the grill. Grill scallops, uncovered, over medium heat for 7-8 minutes on each side or until the scallops are firm and opaque. Arrange mushrooms on a 9-in. square piece of heavy-duty foil coated with nonstick cooking spray. Grill mushrooms on foil, uncovered, over medium heat for 10-15 minutes or until tender, stirring often.

Arrange the lettuce on four serving plates. Top with asparagus, scallops, mushrooms, bacon, walnuts and cheese. Drizzle with dressing. **Yield:** 4 servings.

## Two-Tone Sherbet Torte

*I first prepared this beautiful dessert for a Fourth of July party. Now my mom asks me to make it for just about every event. —Kina Fink, Crown Point, Indiana*

**1-3/4 cups crushed gingersnaps (about 40 cookies)**
**1/4 cup butter, melted**
**4 cups *each* lemon and raspberry sherbet, softened**
**1 cup fresh raspberries**
**3 squares (1 ounce *each*) white chocolate**

In a bowl, combine the cookie crumbs and butter. Press into a greased 9-in. springform pan. Freeze for 15 minutes. Wrap outside of pan in foil. Carefully spread lemon sherbet over crust; freeze for 30 minutes. Top with raspberry sherbet; freeze for at least 1 hour.

Before serving, sprinkle raspberries over the top. In a small microwave-safe bowl, microwave white chocolate at 30% power for 1-2 minutes or until melted; stir until smooth. Drizzle over berries. **Yield:** 10-12 servings.

# Swift-to-Fix Fare Celebrates Summer

IF YOU enjoy outdoor entertaining, consider this seasonal spread that offers grilled recipes and complementary dishes. You'll have plenty of time for fun in the sun when you make this spiced-up chicken, corn with a savory spread, pleasing pasta and irresistible crisp.

Turn to page 317 to see how you can add festive flair to your get-together with a trimmed serving tray (pictured at left), plus other creative table toppers.

## Blackened Chicken

*This spicy chicken is basted with a peppery white sauce. Plus, there's plenty of extra sauce left over for dipping.*
*—Stephanie Kenney, Falkville, Alabama*

**1 tablespoon paprika**
**4 teaspoons sugar, *divided***
**1-1/2 teaspoons salt, *divided***
**1 teaspoon garlic powder**
**1 teaspoon dried thyme**
**1 teaspoon lemon-pepper seasoning**
**1 teaspoon cayenne pepper**
**1-1/2 to 2 teaspoons pepper, *divided***
**4 boneless skinless chicken breast halves**
**1-1/3 cups mayonnaise**
**2 tablespoons water**
**2 tablespoons cider vinegar**

In a small bowl, combine paprika, 1 teaspoon sugar, 1 teaspoon salt, garlic powder, thyme, lemon-pepper, cayenne and 1/2 to 1 teaspoon pepper; sprinkle over both sides of chicken. Set aside.

In another bowl, combine the mayonnaise, water, vinegar and remaining sugar, salt and pepper; cover and chill 1 cup for serving. Save the remaining sauce for basting.

Grill the chicken, covered, over indirect medium heat for 4-6 minutes on each side or until juices run clear, basting frequently with remaining sauce. Serve with reserved sauce. **Yield:** 4 servings.

## Savory Grilled Corn

*I love fresh corn on the cob but wanted to make it extra special, so I created this well seasoned recipe. The spread can be whipped up the night before and stored in the fridge. After that, only a few steps are left to get the corn on the grill.*
*—Darlene Markel, Salem, Oregon*

**1/2 cup mayonnaise**
**2 garlic cloves, minced**
**1/2 teaspoon dried minced onion**
**1/2 teaspoon dried parsley flakes**
**1/2 teaspoon paprika**
**1/4 teaspoon salt**
**1/4 teaspoon pepper**
**4 medium ears sweet corn, silk and husks removed**
**1/4 cup grated Parmesan cheese**

In a small bowl, combine first seven ingredients. Spread over corn; sprinkle with Parmesan cheese. Wrap each ear of corn in a double thickness of heavy-duty foil. Grill, covered, over medium heat for 30-35 minutes or until corn is tender, turning occasionally. **Yield:** 4 servings.

## Lemon-Basil Bow Ties

*Even our children enjoy this quick pasta toss. It's a delicious accompaniment to many different entrees.*
*—Michelle Harbour, Lebanon, Tennessee*

**4 cups uncooked bow tie pasta**
**1 garlic clove, minced**
**1 to 2 tablespoons olive oil**
**1 tablespoon lemon juice**
**1 teaspoon grated lemon peel**
**1/2 teaspoon salt**
**1/4 teaspoon coarsely ground pepper**
**1/2 cup loosely packed fresh basil leaves, thinly sliced**
**1/4 to 1/2 cup shredded Parmesan cheese**

Cook pasta according to package directions. Meanwhile, in a skillet, saute garlic in oil for 1 minute. Stir in the lemon juice, peel, salt and pepper. Drain pasta; add to skillet. Add basil; toss to coat. Cook and stir for 1-2 minutes or until basil is wilted. Sprinkle with Parmesan cheese. **Yield:** 4 servings.

## Raspberry Peach Crisp

*Summer fruit is put to perfect use in this comforting dessert. The juicy peaches and ripe raspberries blend beautifully together.*
*—Jennifer Eilts, Central City, Nebraska*

**5 medium ripe peaches, peeled and sliced**
**1 cup fresh raspberries**
**1 tablespoon cornstarch**
**1/2 teaspoon ground cinnamon**
**1/4 teaspoon ground ginger**
**1/3 cup apple juice concentrate**

**TOPPING:**

**1/3 cup all-purpose flour**
**1/3 cup quick-cooking oats**
**1/3 cup packed brown sugar**
**1/2 teaspoon ground cinnamon**
**1/4 cup cold butter**
**Vanilla ice cream**

Combine the peaches and raspberries in a greased 2-qt. baking dish. In a small bowl, combine the cornstarch, cinnamon, ginger and apple juice concentrate until smooth; drizzle over the fruit.

In a bowl, combine the flour, oats, brown sugar and cinnamon. Cut in the butter until crumbly. Sprinkle over the fruit.

Bake, uncovered, at 375° for 30-35 minutes or until the topping is golden brown and filling is bubbly. Serve warm with ice cream. **Yield:** 6 servings.

# Flavor Fall Occasions With Special Menu

IS AUTUMN one of your favorite seasons for welcoming dinner guests? To produce a fast feast that has a bit of fall flair, look no further than the delicious dishes offered here. From the saucy pork tenderloin to the delightfully down-home dessert, this unforgettable menu will quickly impress a crowd.

Each of the rapid reader recipes can either be prepared in advance or put together in mere moments before mealtime. When you choose this fancy fare, you'll find you need less time in the kitchen...and have more time to spend mingling with company.

## Raspberry Cheese Spread

*A party guest brought this attractive appetizer to our home, and we fell in love with it. Now I often make it myself when we entertain. I create the cheese mixture early in the day and add the berry topping when our company arrives.*
*—Jane Montgomery, Hilliard, Ohio*

**4 ounces cream cheese, softened**
**1 cup mayonnaise**
**2 cups (8 ounces) shredded mozzarella cheese**
**2 cups (8 ounces) shredded cheddar cheese**
**3 green onions, finely chopped**
**1 cup chopped pecans**
**1/4 cup seedless raspberry preserves**
**Assorted crackers**

In a small mixing bowl, beat the cream cheese and mayonnaise until blended. Beat in cheeses and onions. Stir in pecans. Spread into a plastic wrap-lined 9-in. round dish. Refrigerate until set, about 1 hour.

Invert onto a serving plate; spread with preserves. Serve with crackers. **Yield:** about 3-1/2 cups.

## Marmalade Pork Tenderloin

*This delectable pork entree is so easy to prepare. A swift ginger-marmalade sauce lends a touch of sweetness to each tender slice. —P. Buchanan, Fairfax, Virginia*

**2 pork tenderloins (about 1 pound *each*)**
**3/4 teaspoon salt, *divided***
**1/4 teaspoon pepper**
**3/4 cup orange marmalade**
**1 tablespoon water**
**1-1/2 teaspoons ground ginger**

Sprinkle pork with 1/2 teaspoon salt and pepper. Place on a rack in a shallow roasting pan. Bake, uncovered, at 425° for 15 minutes. Combine marmalade, water, ginger and remaining salt; spoon over pork. Bake 10-15 minutes longer or until a meat thermometer reads 160°. Let stand for 10 minutes before slicing. **Yield:** 6 servings.

## Basil-Sesame Green Beans

*There aren't many leftovers when I serve this to company. I mix the fresh beans with basil, chopped onion and toasted sesame seeds. —Denise Elder, Hanover, Ontario*

**4-1/2 cups cut fresh green beans**
**1 to 1-1/4 teaspoons salt**
**3 tablespoons finely chopped onion**
**3 tablespoons olive oil**
**4-1/2 teaspoons minced fresh basil *or* 1-1/4 teaspoons dried basil**
**4 teaspoons sesame seeds, toasted**

Place the beans in a saucepan and cover with water; add the salt. Bring to a boil; cover and cook for 7-10 minutes or until crisp-tender. Drain and place in a serving bowl. Add the onion, oil, basil and sesame seeds; toss to coat. **Yield:** 6 servings.

## Cranberry Molasses Cake

Stordahl Photography

*Bursting with berries, warm squares of this homemade dessert are elegant drizzled with a sweet butter sauce. Friends surprised me at my bridal shower with this wonderful cake, and it was a big hit with everyone. —Brenda Knable*
*Bagley, Minnesota*

**2-1/4 cups all-purpose flour**
**3/4 cup sugar**
**3/4 teaspoon salt**
**1/2 teaspoon baking soda**
**1/2 teaspoon baking powder**
**2 eggs**
**1 cup molasses**
**3/4 cup water**
**2-1/4 cups fresh *or* frozen cranberries, thawed**
**BUTTER SAUCE:**
**1-1/2 cups sugar**
**3/4 cup heavy whipping cream**
**3/4 cup butter, cubed**

In a large bowl, combine the flour, sugar, salt, baking soda and baking powder. In another bowl, whisk the eggs, molasses and water; stir into dry ingredients just until moistened. Fold in cranberries.

Pour into a greased 13-in. x 9-in. x 2-in. baking dish. Bake at 350° for 40-45 minutes or until a toothpick inserted near the center comes out clean.

Cool on a wire rack for 15 minutes. Meanwhile, in a saucepan, combine the sauce ingredients. Bring to a boil over medium heat, stirring constantly. Cut warm cake into squares; serve with butter sauce. **Yield:** 12-15 servings.

### Extra Pork Pleases

When I have leftover cooked pork, I turn it into a tasty dish the next day. I start by cutting it into cubes and thawing some frozen stir-fry vegetables.

I put the veggies and pork in a skillet, and it all gets quickly stir-fried with a little water and some bouillon granules for a flavorful boost. When the liquid boils, I thicken it. I like this stir-fry over noodles, so the only thing left to do is cook the pasta.
*—Bob Closson, Waterloo, Iowa*

# Holiday Feast Is Fast and Festive

HOSTING your loved ones for a sumptuous holiday spread doesn't have to mean spending endless hours in the kitchen. Here's proof!

Our home economists specially selected an elegant meal that keeps prep work to a minimum...so you'll enjoy your seasonal get-together every bit as much as your guests do.

Simply start assembling your feast the night before by baking the taste-tempting cheesecake and putting it in the refrigerator. The rest of this fast festive fare can easily be prepared on the day of the event.

## Pumpkin Pecan Cheesecake

*You're sure to draw compliments with this delectable homemade dessert. Prepare it the day before by topping a from-scratch pecan crust with luscious layers of cream cheese and spiced pumpkin. —Lorraine Darocha Mountain City, Tennessee*

**1-1/2 cups finely chopped pecans**
**2 tablespoons sugar**
**2 tablespoons butter, melted**
**CREAM CHEESE FILLING:**
**1 package (8 ounces) cream cheese, softened**
**1/4 cup sugar**
**1/2 teaspoon vanilla extract**
**1 egg, lightly beaten**
**PUMPKIN FILLING:**
**2 eggs**
**1-1/4 cups canned pumpkin**
**1 cup evaporated milk**
**1/2 cup sugar**
**1 teaspoon ground cinnamon**
**1/4 teaspoon ground ginger**
**1/4 teaspoon ground nutmeg**
**Dash salt**
**1/2 cup chopped pecans**

In a small bowl, combine the pecans, sugar and butter. Press onto the bottom and 3/4 in. up the sides of a greased 9-in. springform pan. Place pan on a baking sheet. Bake at 400° for 10 minutes.

In a small mixing bowl, beat the cream cheese, sugar and vanilla until smooth. Add egg; beat on low speed just until combined. Spread over crust. In another mixing bowl, combine the eggs, pumpkin, milk, sugar, cinnamon, ginger, nutmeg and salt; pour over the cream cheese layer.

Reduce heat to 350°. Bake for 55-60 minutes or until a knife inserted into pumpkin layer comes out clean. Cool on a wire rack for 10 minutes. Carefully run a knife around the edge of pan to loosen; cool 1 hour longer. Sprinkle with pecans. Chill overnight. Remove sides of pan before cutting. Refrigerate leftovers. **Yield:** 10-12 servings.

## Apple-Glazed Cornish Hens

*These golden brown game hens are treated to a citrusy cinnamon-apple glaze that's simple but special enough for a standout entree. It never fails to impress guests. —Donna Mussina, White Oak, Pennsylvania*

**6 Cornish game hens (22 ounces *each*)**
**1 tablespoon cornstarch**
**1 cup apple juice concentrate**
**3 lemon slices**
**1/2 teaspoon ground cinnamon**

Tie legs of each hen together; tuck wings under hens. Place on a greased rack in a roasting pan. In a small saucepan, combine the cornstarch and apple juice concentrate until smooth. Stir in the lemon slices and cinnamon. Bring to a boil; cook and stir for 1 minute or until thickened.

Spoon half of the glaze over the hens. Bake, uncovered, at 375° for 1 to 1-1/4 hours or until a meat thermometer reads 180°, basting occasionally with remaining glaze. **Yield:** 6 servings.

## Seasoned Broccoli Spears

*Dressing up broccoli is a snap with this 10-minute recipe from our Test Kitchen cooks. They flavored fresh spears with plenty of garlic salt, thyme and lemon-pepper seasoning. Easy to assemble while the main course bakes, this tasty side dish is ideal for both dinner parties and busy weeknights.*

**1-1/2 pounds fresh broccoli, cut into spears**
**1/4 cup water**
**2 tablespoons butter**
**1 teaspoon lemon-pepper seasoning**
**1/2 teaspoon garlic salt**
**1/2 teaspoon dried thyme**

Place the broccoli in a microwave-safe bowl; add water. Cover and microwave on high for 4-5 minutes or until tender; drain. Stir in the remaining ingredients. **Yield:** 6 servings.

**Editor's Note:** This recipe was tested in a 1,100-watt microwave.

## Peppered Brown Rice

*After searching through cookbooks without finding a brown rice recipe I liked, I decided to experiment and create my own. Pretty red, yellow and green peppers peek through this versatile side dish. —Orien Major Hinton, Alberta*

**1-3/4 cups water**
**1 tablespoon chicken bouillon granules**
**2 cups uncooked instant brown rice**
**1/3 cup chopped onion**
**1/3 cup *each* chopped sweet red, yellow and green pepper**
**6 to 8 fresh mushrooms, sliced**
**1 celery rib, sliced**
**2 to 3 tablespoons vegetable oil**
**1/8 teaspoon dried tarragon**

In a large saucepan, bring water and bouillon to a boil. Stir in rice. Reduce heat; cover and simmer for 10 minutes or until the water is absorbed. Meanwhile, in a large skillet, saute the vegetables in oil until tender. Stir in the tarragon and rice; heat through. **Yield:** 6 servings.

# Elegant Dishes

MIX AND MATCH any of the standout appetizers, entrees, side dishes and desserts on the following pages. No matter what fancy fare you choose for your menu, you'll put together an unforgettable meal for company...and spend only a short time in the kitchen preparing it.

## Flavorful Chicken Rolls

*(Pictured below)*

*This is a great main course for dinner guests, and they never believe how easy it is. The creamy feta-basil filling can be made early and refrigerated until I'm ready to assemble the chicken rolls. Using packaged spinach leaves and deli ham further cuts prep time. —Kandi Wysong Boiling Springs, South Carolina*

**5 large boneless skinless chicken breast halves**
**2 cups fresh baby spinach**
**4 ounces cream cheese, softened**
**4 ounces crumbled feta cheese**
**2 tablespoons chopped fresh basil *or* 2 teaspoons dried basil**
**1/4 teaspoon coarsely ground pepper**
**5 thin slices deli ham**
**1 egg**
**1 tablespoon milk**
**3/4 to 1 cup seasoned bread crumbs**

**Flavorful Chicken Rolls**

Make a lengthwise slit through the thickest portion of each chicken breast to within 1/2 in. of the opposite side. Open chicken so it lies flat; cover with plastic wrap. Flatten to 1/4-in. thickness. Discard plastic wrap. Place a single layer of spinach over chicken.

In a small bowl, combine the cream cheese, feta cheese, basil and pepper; spread over spinach. Top each chicken breast with a ham slice, trimming if necessary. Roll up and secure with toothpicks.

In a shallow bowl, beat the egg and milk. Place bread crumbs in another bowl. Dip chicken rolls in egg mixture, then coat with crumbs. Place seam side down in a greased 15-in. x 10-in. x 1-in. baking pan. Bake, uncovered, at 375° for 30-35 minutes or until chicken juices run clear. Discard toothpicks before serving. **Yield:** 5 servings.

## Marmalade Soy Wings

*Whether I use drumettes or chicken wings, these savory bites are always popular. I keep the pretty glazed appetizers warm during parties by serving them in my slow cooker. —Carole Nelson, Parkville, Missouri*

**15 whole chicken wings (about 3 pounds)**
**1 cup soy sauce**
**1 cup orange marmalade**
**3 garlic cloves, minced**
**1 teaspoon ground ginger**
**1/4 teaspoon pepper**

Cut chicken wings into three sections; discard wing tip sections. In a bowl, combine the soy sauce, marmalade, garlic, ginger and pepper. Cover and refrigerate 1/2 cup marinade for basting.

Place remaining marinade in a large resealable plastic bag. Add wing sections; seal bag and toss to coat evenly. Refrigerate for 8 hours or overnight.

Drain and discard marinade. Place chicken wings in a greased 15-in. x 10-in. x 1-in. baking pan. Bake, uncovered, at 350° for 15 minutes.

Baste with a third of reserved marinade; bake 15 minutes longer. Turn wings and baste; bake 15 minutes longer. Baste with remaining marinade. Bake 10-20 minutes more or until chicken juices run clear. **Yield:** 8 servings.

**Editor's Note:** Three pounds of uncooked chicken wing sections (wingettes) may be substituted for whole chicken wings. If using wingettes, omit the first step.

## Springtime Penne

*With ham, asparagus, onion and pasta in a creamy sauce, this stovetop supper is tasty enough for even your pickiest guests. —Cheryl Newendorp, Pella, Iowa*

✓ Uses less fat, sugar or salt. Includes Nutritional Analysis and Diabetic Exchanges.

**3 cups uncooked penne *or* medium tube pasta**
**1 pound fresh asparagus, trimmed and cut into 1-inch pieces**
**1 large onion, chopped**
**1/4 cup butter**
**1/2 pound cubed fully cooked ham**
**1/2 cup heavy whipping cream *or* whole milk**

**1/4 teaspoon pepper**
**1/8 teaspoon salt**

Cook pasta according to package directions. Meanwhile, in a large skillet, saute asparagus and onion in butter for 5-8 minutes or until asparagus is crisp-tender.

Add the ham, cream, pepper and salt; bring to a boil. Reduce heat; cook over low heat for 1 minute. Drain pasta and add to the asparagus mixture; toss to coat. Serve immediately. **Yield:** 8 servings.

**Nutritional Analysis:** One 1-cup serving (prepared with whole milk) equals 260 calories, 8 g fat (4 g saturated fat), 28 mg cholesterol, 463 mg sodium, 34 g carbohydrate, 2 g fiber, 13 g protein. **Diabetic Exchanges:** 2 starch, 1-1/2 lean meat, 1 vegetable.

## Mocha Truffle Cheesecake

*(Pictured on page 298)*

*I went through a phase when I couldn't get enough cheesecake or coffee, so I created this rich dessert. The brownie-like crust and creamy mocha layer really hit the spot.*
*—Shannon Dormady, Great Falls, Montana*

**1 package (18-1/4 ounces) devil's food cake mix**
**6 tablespoons butter, melted**
**1 egg**
**1 to 3 tablespoons instant coffee granules**

**FILLING/TOPPING:**
**2 packages (8 ounces *each*) cream cheese, softened**
**1 can (14 ounces) sweetened condensed milk**
**2 cups (12 ounces) semisweet chocolate chips, melted**
**3 to 6 tablespoons instant coffee granules**
**1/4 cup hot water**
**3 eggs, lightly beaten**
**1 cup heavy whipping cream**
**1/4 cup confectioners' sugar**
**1/2 teaspoon almond extract**

In a mixing bowl, combine cake mix, butter, egg and coffee granules. Press onto the bottom and 2 in. up the sides of a greased 10-in. springform pan.

In a mixing bowl, beat cream cheese until smooth. Beat in milk and chips. Dissolve coffee granules in water. Add coffee and eggs to cream cheese mixture; beat on low speed just until combined.

Pour into crust. Place pan on a baking sheet. Bake at 325° for 50-55 minutes or until center is almost set. Cool on a wire rack for 10 minutes. Carefully run a knife around edge of pan to loosen; cool 1 hour longer. Chill overnight.

Remove sides of pan. Just before serving, in a mixing bowl, beat cream until soft peaks form. Beat in sugar and extract until stiff peaks form. Spread over top of cheesecake. Chill leftovers. **Yield:** 12-16 servings.

## Pecan-Crusted Salmon

*These delicious salmon fillets are wonderful for company since they take only a few minutes to prepare, yet they taste like you fussed.* *—Kara Cook, Elk Ridge, Utah*

Six-Fruit Crisp

**4 salmon fillets (about 6 ounces *each*)**
**2 cups milk**
**1 cup finely chopped pecans**
**1/2 cup all-purpose flour**
**1/4 cup packed brown sugar**
**2 teaspoons seasoned salt**
**2 teaspoons pepper**
**3 tablespoons vegetable oil**

Place salmon fillets in a large resealable plastic bag; add milk. Let stand for 10 minutes; drain. In a shallow bowl, combine the pecans, flour, brown sugar, seasoned salt and pepper. Coat fillets with pecan mixture, gently pressing into the fish.

In a large skillet, brown salmon in oil over medium-high heat. Transfer to a baking sheet. Bake at 400° for 8-10 minutes or until fish flakes easily with a fork. **Yield:** 4 servings.

## Six-Fruit Crisp

*(Pictured above)*

*I combined different recipes to make up this easy dessert, and now I always keep the ingredients on hand. Serve it warm with whipped topping.* *—June Smith*
*Byron Center, Michigan*

**1 jar (25 ounces) chunky applesauce**
**1 can (20 ounces) pineapple tidbits, drained**
**1 can (15-1/4 ounces) sliced peaches, drained and chopped**
**1 can (15-1/4 ounces) sliced pears, drained and chopped**
**1 can (11 ounces) mandarin oranges, drained**
**1 can (21 ounces) cherry pie filling**

**TOPPING:**
**2 cups all-purpose flour**
**2 cups packed brown sugar**
**1 cup butter, melted**
**Whipped topping, optional**

Pour applesauce into a greased 13-in. x 9-in. x 2-in. baking dish. Layer with the pineapple, peaches, pears and mandarin oranges. Spread with pie filling.

For topping, combine the flour, brown sugar and butter. Sprinkle over pie filling. Bake at 375° for 40-45 minutes or until golden brown. Serve warm with whipped topping if desired. **Yield:** 12-15 servings.

## Teriyaki Tenderloin

*(Pictured at right)*

*This flavor-packed pork entree is so good, it's hard to believe it calls for only four ingredients and is simple to prepare. I just marinate the tenderloin overnight and then put it in the oven a short while before dinnertime. During baking, I can turn my attention to other things, such as tossing together a salad or making dessert.*
*—Tara Brouwer, Zeeland, Michigan*

**1/2 cup soy sauce**
**1/4 cup sugar**
**2 tablespoons ketchup**
**1 pork tenderloin (1 pound)**

In a large resealable plastic bag, combine soy sauce, sugar and ketchup. Add the pork tenderloin; seal bag and turn to coat. Refrigerate for 8 hours or overnight.

Drain and discard marinade. Place pork in a greased 13-in. x 9-in. x 2-in. baking dish. Bake, uncovered, at 425° for 35-40 minutes or until a meat thermometer reads 160°. Let stand for 5 minutes before slicing. **Yield:** 4 servings.

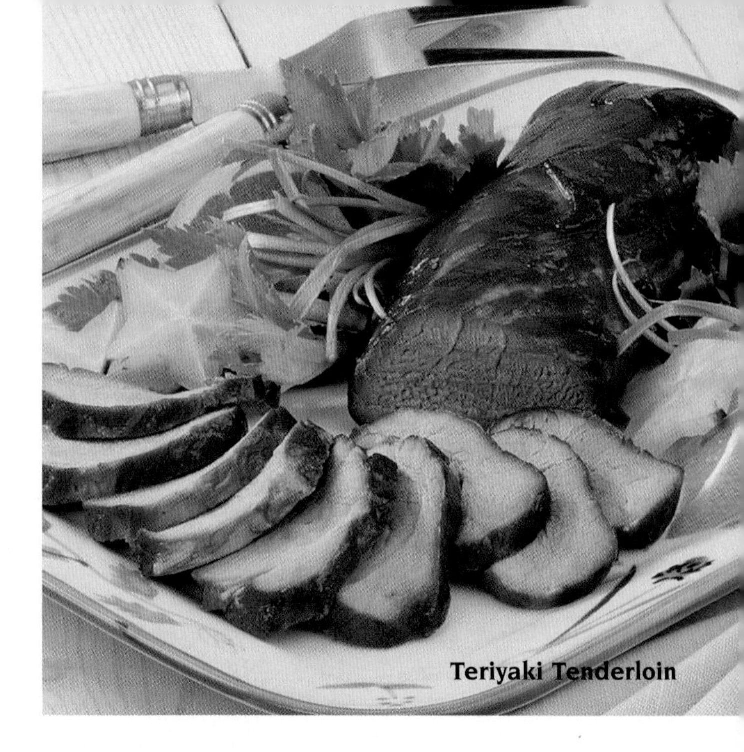
Teriyaki Tenderloin

## Elegant Scalloped Potatoes

*(Pictured below)*

*I wanted a different side dish one night, so I dressed up my usual scalloped potatoes with bacon bits, green onions and extra cheese. The result was a recipe that's special enough to make for company. Using my microwave speeds up the preparation, but I can save even more time by assembling this comforting creation a day early.*
*—Krista Wilson, Edgerton, Kansas*

**8 large baking potatoes**
**6 tablespoons butter**
**6 tablespoons all-purpose flour**
**1 to 2 teaspoons garlic powder**
**1/2 teaspoon salt**
**1/2 teaspoon pepper**
**3-1/2 cups milk**
**12 ounces process cheese (Velveeta), cubed**
**1/3 cup crumbled cooked bacon**
**1 cup (4 ounces) shredded cheddar cheese**
**1/4 cup sliced green onions**

Elegant Scalloped Potatoes

Scrub and pierce potatoes; place on a microwave-safe plate. Microwave on high for 15-20 minutes or until tender. Cool slightly.

In a saucepan, melt the butter. Stir in flour, garlic powder, salt and pepper until smooth; gradually whisk in milk. Bring to a boil; cook and stir for 2 minutes or until thickened. Add the process cheese and bacon; stir until cheese is melted. Remove from heat; set aside.

Cut the potatoes into 1/4-in. slices. Place a third of the slices in a greased 13-in. x 9-in. x 2-in. baking dish; top with a third of the cheese sauce. Repeat layers twice. Sprinkle with cheddar cheese and onions. Bake, uncovered, at 350° for 15 minutes or until cheese is melted. **Yield:** 10-12 servings.

**Editor's Note:** This recipe was tested in a 1,100-watt microwave.

## Appetizer Shrimp Kabobs

*(Pictured on page 298)*

*Talk about easy! I love this appetizer because the skewers are a breeze to put together and grill to perfection in minutes. Guests think I fussed when they see the kabobs loaded with seasoned breaded shrimp. For the finishing touch, I offer a spicy seafood sauce.* *—Dianna Knight*
*Clayton, North Carolina*

✓ Uses less fat, sugar or salt. Includes Nutritional Analysis and Diabetic Exchanges.

**3 tablespoons olive oil**
**3 garlic cloves, crushed**
**1/2 cup dry bread crumbs**
**1/2 teaspoon seafood seasoning**

**32 uncooked medium shrimp (about 1 pound), peeled and deveined**
**Seafood sauce**

...wl, combine the oil and garlic; let stand ... bowl, combine bread crumbs ... shrimp in oil mixture, then coat ...

Thread onto metal or soaked wooden skewers. Grill kabobs, covered, over medium heat for 2-3 minutes or until shrimp turn pink. Serve with seafood sauce. **Yield:** 8 servings.

**Nutritional Analysis:** One serving (4 shrimp, calculated without seafood sauce) equals 133 calories, 6 g fat (1 g saturated fat), 86 mg cholesterol, 142 mg sodium, 6 g carbohydrate, trace fiber, 12 g protein. **Diabetic Exchanges:** 1-1/2 lean meat, 1/2 starch.

## Drop-In Salad

*(Pictured on page 299)*

*When my husband and I were invited to a barbecue, I threw together this broccoli salad. I tossed in whatever I had in the fridge, and the crunchy colorful combination that resulted was a big hit. It's a nice change from lettuce salads.* —*Kimber Archuleta, Evanston, Wyoming*

**6 cups fresh broccoli florets**
**1-1/2 cups cubed cheddar cheese**
**1 large red apple, cubed**
**1 cup coarsely chopped pecans**
**1 small red onion, chopped**
**1/2 cup red wine vinaigrette *or* vinaigrette of your choice**
**1/2 teaspoon lemon juice**

In a large salad bowl, combine the first five ingredients. Combine vinaigrette and lemon juice; drizzle over salad. Toss to coat. Serve immediately. **Yield:** 8-10 servings.

## Garlic Chuck Roast

*(Pictured on page 298)*

*Having never made a roast before, I experimented with a few ingredients to come up with this hearty all-in-one meal. Not only is it easy, but the tender entree gets terrific flavor from garlic, onion and bay leaves.* —*Janet Boyer, Nemacolin, Pennsylvania*

**1 boneless beef chuck roast (3 pounds)**
**15 garlic cloves, peeled**
**1 teaspoon salt**
**1/4 teaspoon pepper**
**2 tablespoons vegetable oil**
**5 bay leaves**
**1 large onion, thinly sliced**
**2 tablespoons butter, melted**
**1-1/2 cups water**
**1 pound baby carrots**

With a sharp knife, cut 15 slits in roast; insert garlic into slits. Sprinkle meat with salt and pepper. In a Dutch oven, brown meat in oil; drain. Place bay leaves on top of roast; top with onion slices. Drizzle with butter. Add water to pan. Cover and bake at 325° for 1-1/2 hours.

Baste roast with pan juices; add carrots. Cover and bake 45-60 minutes longer or until meat and carrots are tender. Discard bay leaves. Let roast stand for 10 minutes before slicing. Thicken pan juices if desired. **Yield:** 6-8 servings.

## Black Forest Dessert

*(Pictured below)*

*This elegant treat is a cinch to make with dessert mixes, canned pie filling and whipped topping. I sometimes assemble it a few days beforehand and keep it in the freezer. I shave a chocolate bar over the top for a pretty look.* —*Connie Sibbing, Quincy, Illinois*

**1 package (11.4 ounces) no-bake chocolate lover's flavored dessert mix**
**1 package (11.1 ounces) no-bake cheesecake dessert mix**
**2 tablespoons sugar**
**2/3 cup butter, melted**
**1 carton (16 ounces) frozen whipped topping, thawed**
**1 can (21 ounces) cherry pie filling**

Set aside chocolate topping pouch from the chocolate dessert mix for garnish. In a bowl, combine contents of the crust mix packets from both mixes; add sugar and butter. Press into a 13-in. x 9-in. x 2-in. dish.

Prepare cheesecake dessert mix filling according to package directions; gently spread over crust. Prepare chocolate dessert mix filling according to package directions; carefully spread over cheesecake layer.

Spread with whipped topping. Carefully spread cherry pie filling to edges. Cover and refrigerate for at least 2 hours. Just before serving, drizzle with reserved chocolate topping. Refrigerate leftovers. **Yield:** 15 servings.

**Editor's Note:** This recipe was tested with Jell-O no-bake dessert mixes.

**Black Forest Dessert**

# Table Toppers

WHEN you're entertaining, why not take a few extra minutes to dress up your table for the occasion? It's easy when you use these inexpensive ideas from our Test Kitchen home economists. They created attractive table toppers, party favors, fancy napkin folds and more.

## Create Your Own Hot Beverage Buffet

WHETHER the gang has been sledding or building a snowman, their smiles will abound when the activity ends with steaming seasonal beverages.

The buffet shown at bottom right features thermal carafes of hot cider, hot cocoa and hot water for flavored teas.

For festive garnishing, complete the buffet with mini marshmallows, sugar cubes, whipped cream, flavored creamers or ground nutmeg. For an extra-special touch, provide colorful candy sticks or cinnamon sticks for stirring.

## Cute Cards Keep Guests in the Know

AVOID confusion when serving beverages by creating snowflake cards to identify the contents of carafes (see photo below far right). For each card, you'll need a 4-inch square of white paper and a 4-1/2-inch x 9-inch piece of colored construction paper.

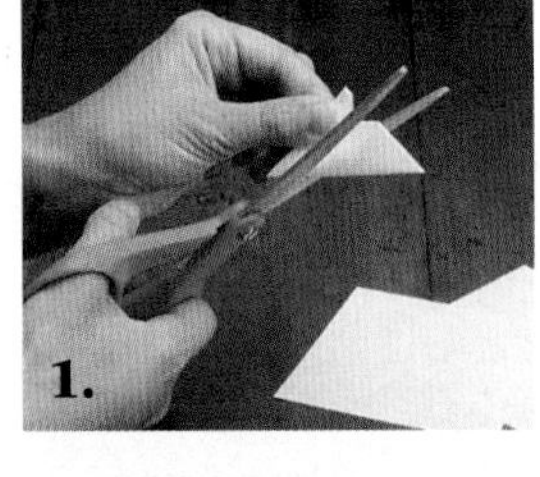
1.

To begin, fold the 4-inch square of white paper in half. Fold it in half again to create a 2-inch square. Then fold it diagonally to form a triangle.

**1.** Holding the triangle with the closed point in one hand, use a scissors to snip small shapes from two or three sides on the opposite end. (Be careful not to cut too close to the point or you won't have room for the label.) Unfold the snowflake.

2.

**2.** Fold the colored paper in half to form a square. Spread glue on the back of the snowflake and press it onto the front of the colored-paper card.

Write the name of each beverage on its own card with a pen or marker.

## No-Sew Place Mats Match Rapid Runner

IT'S EASY to brighten the table when you make this reversible runner and place mats. You can create the items shown in the photo below without using a sewing machine.

To make a table runner and four mats, we started with two 60-inch x 36-inch pieces of machine-washable polar fleece. Both pieces are visible on the fringed edges of the runner and mats, so we chose complementary colors—solid white and a snowflake print.

1.

To begin, lay one piece of fleece flat and place the other piece on top, lining up the edges. Use a sharp scissors to trim the selvage from the fabric to create straight even edges.

2.

For the runner, starting on a short side of the fabric, cut through both pieces of fleece to create a 60-inch x 13-inch rectangle.

**1.** With the pieces evenly lined up, place a ruler 4 inches from the end of a short side of the runner. Holding the ruler, start cutting through both pieces 1 inch from the right side. Cut from the end of the runner up to the ruler. Continue to cut 1-inch strips across the short side of the runner. When you are done, you should have 13 strips on both pieces.

**2.** Tie each set of upper and lower strips together with a double knot.

Repeat steps 1 and 2 for the opposite end of the table runner.

For the place mats, cut the remaining fleece into four sections, each measuring 23 x 13 inches. You should be left with a 23-inch x 8-inch piece of each fleece, which you can save for another use.

Follow steps 1 and 2 for both short ends of each place mat, and your mats will be ready to enjoy.

## Cultivate a Carrot With No-Fuss Fold

HARVEST smiles by the bushel when you "produce" these folded napkins that look like the Easter Bunny's favorite snack. They're a snap to assemble.

To create the cute carrot shown in the photo at right, you'll need a square dinner napkin. We used a bright orange cloth napkin that measured 15-1/2 inches square, but almost any size square napkin will work fine.

You'll also need some narrow ribbon. We chose orange ribbon to blend with our napkin, then cut an 18-inch piece for each napkin. Your ribbon may need to be longer or shorter, depending on the size of the napkin you use.

To begin, fold the open napkin in half and then fold it in half again to form a square. Rotate the square so it resembles a diamond with the open edges of the napkin at the top.

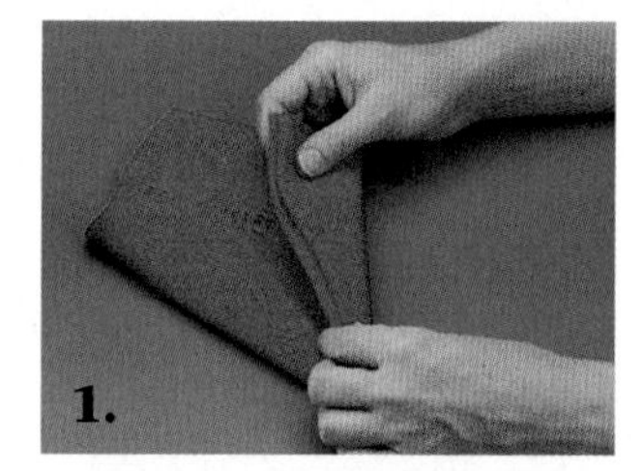
1.

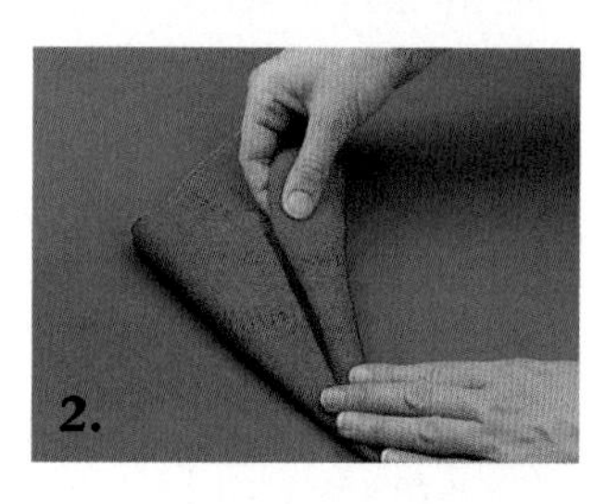
2.

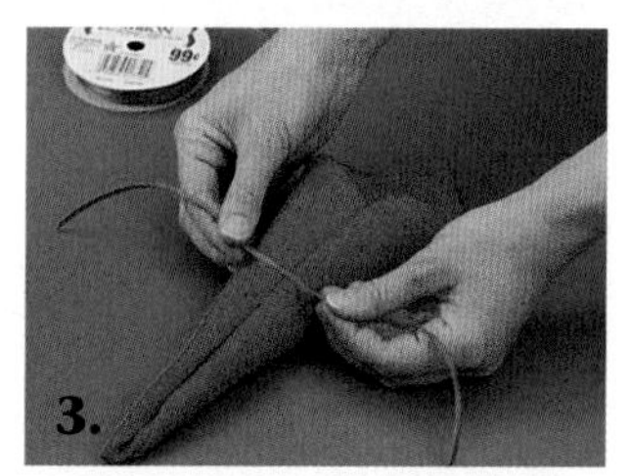
3.

4.

**1.** Fold the left side of the napkin in half, bringing the left corner of the diamond to the center. Repeat with the right side so both corners meet in the middle.

**2.** Now, fold the left side in half again. While holding the left side in place, fold the right side in half to form a carrot shape.

**3.** Tie a length of ribbon near the wider end of the napkin to hold the folds in place. Once the ribbon is tied, carefully adjust the shape of the napkin if necessary.

**4.** For the finishing touch, place a sprig or two of greenery in the open end of the napkin to produce the carrot top.

We chose leatherleaf fern because it stays fresh-looking for hours without water. You can also use fresh parsley, dill weed or whatever you have available. These greens wilt more quickly, however, so you may need to tuck them into the napkins right before calling your dinner guests to the table.

## Chocolate Bunnies Are Sweet Markers

FEW THINGS awake the child in all of us like chocolate bunnies wrapped in shiny foil. Why not surprise your guests by using these classic confections as playful place markers that they can take home?

Chocolate bunnies are available in a wide variety of shapes, sizes and prices, so you should be able to choose from plenty of options. We chose a 7-1/2-inch solid chocolate bunny wrapped in gold foil. To turn the bunny into a place marker, we simply attached a paper name tag to its neck (see photo above).

To cut out the name tag, we snipped a rectangular shape measuring 1-1/2 x 2 inches from pink construction paper. But feel free to get creative by making your tags from any material you wish and cutting them into different shapes, such as Easter eggs, tulips or carrots.

Once all of your tags are cut, use a paper punch or scissors to create a hole at the top of each one for the ribbon. Then, write a guest's name on each tag using a pen or marker.

As the next step, tie a ribbon to each tag. For each of our place markers, we used a 15-1/2-inch length of ribbon. The length of ribbon you need will depend on the size of your bunnies.

To tie an easy knot, fold your piece of ribbon in half. Next, thread the loop, or closed end, through the punched hole in the tag. Pull the ends of the ribbon over the top of the tag and then through the loop to secure the ribbon to the tag.

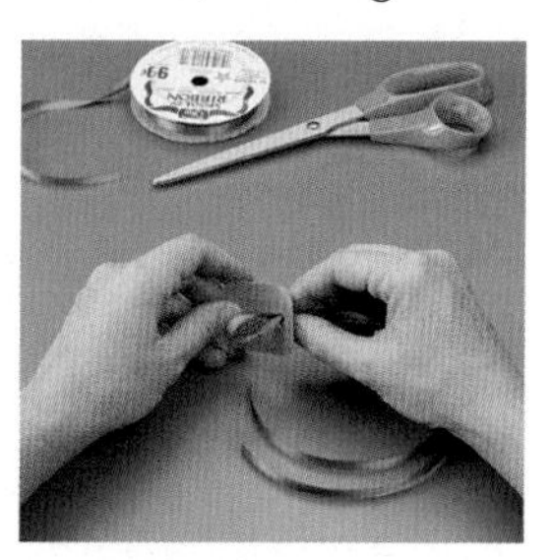

Tie the ribbon around the bunny's neck like a bow tie, making sure the name on the tag can be seen. Set the place markers around your table before your celebration begins...then let guests discover their own sweet table decoration.

## Make a Splash with Colorful Bud Vases

IT'S A SNAP to brighten your table with only a few flowers when you place them in vases of colored water. To achieve this simple look, just gather some blooms, a few clear glass bud vases and the food coloring from your pantry.

Fill each vase about two-thirds with water, then add any shade of food coloring you prefer. As little as one drop to a cup of water provides plenty of color.

Place a few flowers in each bud vase, then set a vase at each guest's place setting to make an individual bouquet (see photo at bottom far right).

Or, group a few differently shaped bud vases together, varying the flowers and the color of the water, for a sensational centerpiece (see photo above).

## Floral Napkin Rings Bloom in Minutes

DECK your dinner table with floral finery by creating these napkin rings that start with bright felt. The cheerful blooms are eye-appealing additions to tables whether you're dining indoors or out.

You'll need three differently colored sheets of felt to make three napkin rings. The felt sheets, measuring roughly 9 inches x 12 inches, cost as little as 25¢ each at a fabric or craft store.

To start, draw the three shapes needed for each napkin ring on scrap paper, using the shape diagram above right as a guide.

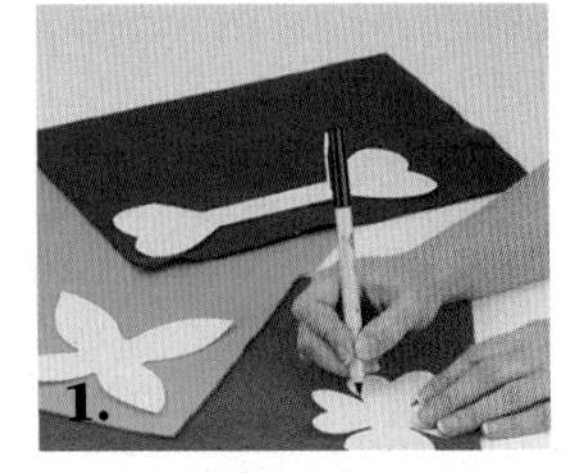

Increase the size according to your preference. We made our templates so the petal shape was about 4 inches wide, the leaf shape was about 7 inches wide and the stem/center shape was about 9 inches long. Cut out the paper shapes with scissors.

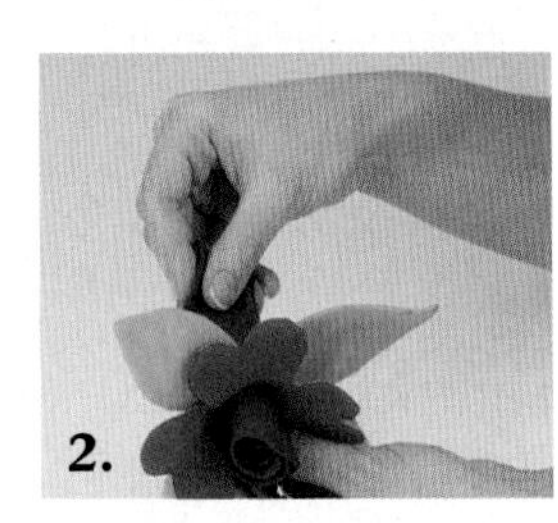

**1.** Trace each template on a different color of felt. We used green felt for the leaves, magenta for the petals and purple for the stem/center of the flower. Use a pair of scissors to cut out the shapes. Then cut a 1-inch slit in the centers of the leaf and petal shapes. Place the petal shape on top of the leaf shape, aligning the slits.

**2.** Fold the stem/center piece in half widthwise, then fold it in half lengthwise. Pull the stem's closed end partway through the slits in the center of the leaf and petal pieces.

The large ends of the stem stay above the petals to become the colorful center of the flower. Use your fingers to arrange the center as you'd like.

To use your new napkin ring, simply roll up a napkin and slide it through the ring created by the stem. Place one of these colorful blooms on each plate for a welcoming touch.

Feel free to choose a few colors of felt that coordinate with your dinnerware (see photo at bottom right), or use a variety of colors to make a mixed bouquet (see photo at bottom left).

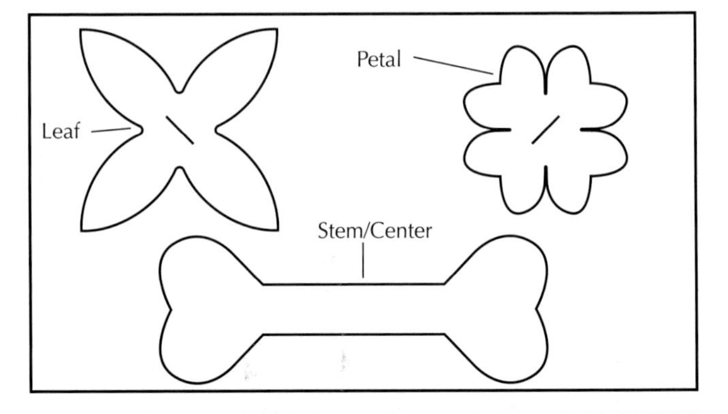


## Seed Packets Hold Silverware Settings

SAVE the pretty flower or vegetable seed packets left over from planting your garden, and you'll have a fun way to present forks, knives and spoons at a casual garden-themed dinner.

Just trim the tops of the empty seed packets, then tuck some green raffia into each one. Add one setting of silverware to each packet and place one next to each plate (see photo at bottom right).

If you're not a gardener, you can create your own seed packets. Simply fold a rectangle of thick paper into a pocket and glue or tape the edges. Then paste photos from seed catalogs on the packet fronts...or encourage your children to draw pictures of flowers or vegetables on your home-grown packets.

## Put a Patriotic Spin On Easy Centerpiece

IT'S A BREEZE to turn a few inexpensive lawn ornaments into an eye-catching arrangement for your picnic table.

Start with colorful pinwheels that cost about $1 each at garden centers or in the garden or children's toy area of discount stores.

We combined a handful of metallic-blue and silver pinwheels with one that has a patriotic design to create the simple centerpiece shown in the photo at right.

We filled a galvanized bucket with sand to hold the pinwheels, but you can use any appropriately sized container as your "vase". Then simply push the pinwheel stakes into the sand and arrange the pinwheels as desired.

With each puff of wind, your centerpiece will whirl, twirl and lend a whimsical touch to a Fourth of July barbecue or any backyard get-together.

## Decoupage a Tray To Carry the Spirit

ADD FLAIR to your outdoor dining area by decorating a carrying tray with colorful images cut from paper party napkins. Use the technique of decoupage to give the tray a patriotic theme (see photo above right). It's perfect for bringing food to the table and for removing items afterward to streamline cleanup.

**1.** First, gather your supplies. You'll need an unfinished wooden tray, sandpaper, latex paint, a foam paintbrush, decorative paper napkins, scissors, a container of decoupage finish and a small craft paintbrush. Most of these items can be found at craft and discount stores.

Wood trays, for example, are available in a variety of sizes and cost about $5 each. The decoupage finish—Mod Podge is one brand name—costs about $2 for an 8-ounce container.

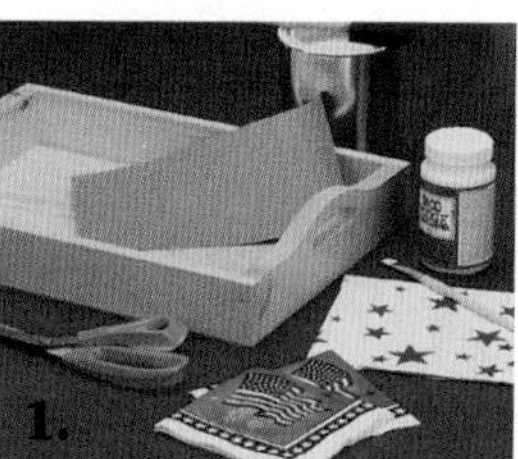
1.

Lightly sand the tray to remove any rough spots or edges, then wipe it down so it's free of dust. Use an inexpensive foam paintbrush to prime and paint the tray a solid color (we chose white). Remember to allow it to dry completely in between coats.

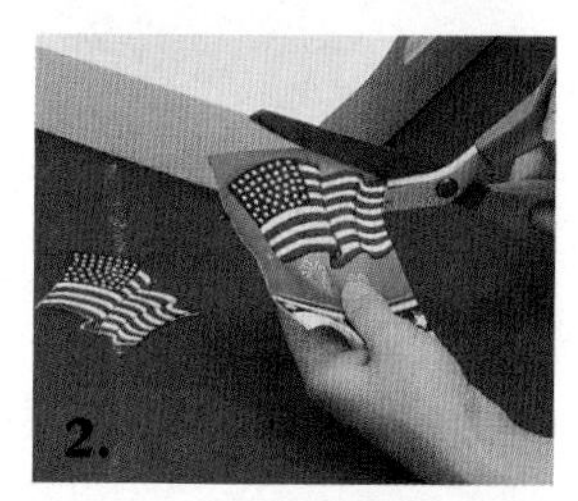
2.

**2.** Cut out the desired shapes from your paper napkins. For our patriotic theme, we cut flags and stars from beverage napkins. You could use other images from paper napkins, or from gift wrap, magazines or photos from a family album.

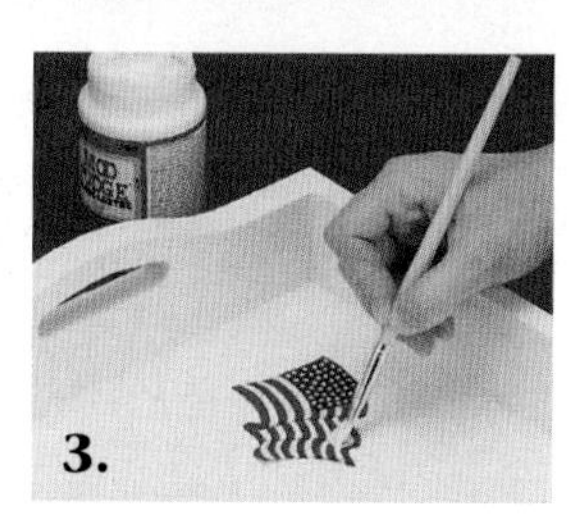
3.

**3.** Use a small craft paintbrush to apply a dab of decoupage finish to the area on the tray where you'd like to place one of the shapes. Press the shape in place, then apply the decoupage finish, starting from the middle of the shape and gently brushing toward the outer edges for a smooth look.

Continue adhering other shapes to the bottom and sides of the tray until you achieve the look you want. Then let the tray dry completely.

You may want to seal the surface with a coat of decoupage finish first. Then use the tray to carry beverages, snacks and other items to your outdoor dining area.

## Flag Candle Holder Matches Serving Tray

BRING a warm glow to an evening gathering by using the same decoupage technique to create a candle holder that coordinates with the patriotic tray.

Start with a clean glass votive holder and whatever image you'd like to use to decorate it. Use a paintbrush to dab some decoupage finish onto the candle holder and then position the image on top of it.

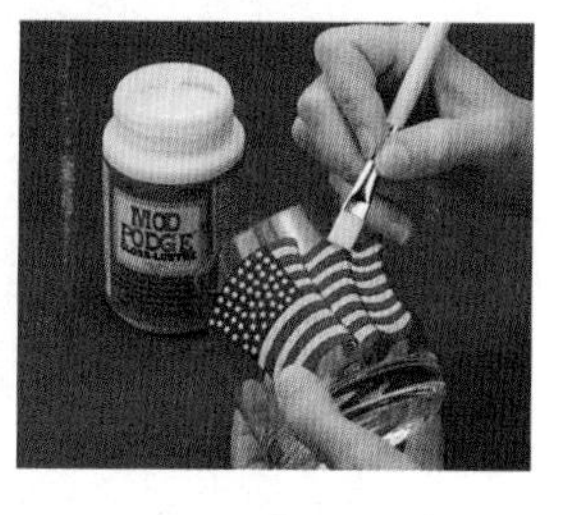

Then apply decoupage finish from the middle of the image, gently brushing toward the outer edges.

Use a cotton swab to remove any excess finish left around the edge of the image. If the excess finish has dried, remove it by gently scraping with a toothpick for a clean outline.

Then just fill the holder with a coordinating votive candle, light it and enjoy the ambience!

# Chapter 21

# Back to the Basics

MANY PEOPLE barely have a spare minute to sit and relax—much less spend time experimenting in the kitchen—during the weekday rush.

But on stress-free weekends, when you do have a few moments to spare, why not tie on an apron for a refresher course on cooking techniques...or for the chance to try recipes that are a bit more challenging?

Whether you'd like to review the basics for stirring together cool soups, fixing perfect pasta meals and making from-scratch pie crusts, or you want to learn how to spice up dinnertime, roll out extra-special egg creations or bake golden brown gingerbread, the step-by-step recipes and helpful hints here will sharpen your culinary skills.

**SWIFT AND SIMPLE.** Top to bottom: Zucchini Hamburger Pie and Blackberry Cheese Pie (recipes on p. 325).

# Summer Soups Refresh In a Jiffy

CHILLED SOUPS, such as Spain's tomato-based gazpacho, have long been prevalent in Mediterranean regions where the warm climate lends itself to this refreshing fare. But the delightful soups are gaining popularity here, finding their way to restaurant menus and dinner tables alike.

And it's no wonder. Cold soups are quick and easy to put together. For folks who are trying to increase fruits and vegetables in their diet, they're a tasty way to accomplish this goal. Plus, most chilled soups don't require any cooking, so they're especially convenient during the dog days of summer.

Best of all, these brisk blends offer busy cooks plenty of flexibility. They can be rich or light, creamy or chunky, sweet with fruit or savory with herbs and vegetables.

Since most cold soups can be made ahead of time and refrigerated until serving, they're handy for entertaining. Serve a hearty bowl alone at lunch or pair the soup with a special salad or sandwich to create a satisfying supper.

Of course, a sweet soup is great for dessert, but it also can be presented as a first course or as a between-course palate-cleanser.

If you'd like to add a refreshing chilled soup to your summer menu, the following tips will help you keep your cool:

- Because flavor diminishes somewhat when foods are chilled, it's best to taste chilled soups just before serving and adjust the seasoning if necessary. Sweet soups may require more sugar than anticipated.

Cucumber Soup

- Make the soup ahead and refrigerate it for several hours.
- Chill the serving bowls for several hours before serving.
- If you're serving a chilled soup on a buffet table, set the serving bowl in a large bowl of crushed ice and use a decorative towel or cloth to absorb the condensation.
- If you're making a chilled soup that needs to be cooked, then quickly cooled, set it in a large bowl of ice water and stir the soup until cooled.

To dress up everyday meals or elegant dinners, use your imagination when choosing serving dishes and garnishes for chilled soups.

Large coffee mugs, tall stemmed glasses and decorative custard cups are all attractive options for serving cold soups.

For a fun seasonal look, cut small cantaloupes or honeydews in half, remove the melon, then use the shells for serving sweet summer soups. In autumn, hollow out appropriately sized pumpkins, then spoon a savory soup inside for a pretty presentation of individual bowls.

Jazz up cool soups by garnishing with sour cream or yogurt. Just spoon a small amount into a resealable plastic bag, then cut a small hole in a corner of the bag. Pipe large dots of sour cream or yogurt over the soup and gently pull a toothpick through each dot to create a teardrop shape.

For a more elaborate design, pipe thin concentric circles 1/2 inch apart on top of the soup. Beginning with the central circle, gently pull a toothpick through the circles toward the outer edge. Wipe the toothpick clean and repeat to make a spiderweb pattern, working around the circles.

Be creative with soup toppings, too. For savory soups, try salad croutons, toasted nuts, fresh herbs, fried tortilla strips, shredded cheese, chow mein noodles, chopped green onions, crushed nacho cheese tortilla chips or pepper rings.

Sweet soups are terrific topped with sliced fruit, raisins, granola, toasted nuts or crushed cinnamon graham crackers.

Or set out an assortment of toppings and let your guests choose. The possibilities are endless!

## Cucumber Soup

*(Pictured at left)*

*It's easy to dress up this mild soup with a colorful selection of savory garnishes, including onions, tomatoes and minced parsley. A topping of crunchy almonds is especially nice with this smooth soup.* —*Beverly Sprague*
*Baltimore, Maryland*

✓ Uses less fat, sugar or salt. Includes Nutritional Analysis and Diabetic Exchanges.

**3 medium cucumbers**
**3 cups chicken broth**
**3 cups (24 ounces) sour cream**
**3 tablespoons cider vinegar**

**2 teaspoons salt, optional**
**1 garlic clove, minced**
**TOPPINGS:**
**2 medium tomatoes, chopped**
**3/4 cup sliced almonds, toasted**
**1/2 cup chopped green onions**
**1/2 cup minced fresh parsley**

Peel cucumbers; halve lengthwise and remove seeds. Cut into chunks. In a blender, cover and puree cucumbers and broth in small batches. Transfer to a large bowl; stir in the sour cream, vinegar, salt if desired and garlic until well blended.

Cover and refrigerate for at least 4 hours. Stir before serving. Garnish with tomatoes, almonds, onions and parsley. **Yield:** 12 servings.

**Nutritional Analysis:** One 3/4-cup serving (prepared with reduced-sodium broth and fat-free sour cream and without salt) equals 95 calories, 3 g fat (trace saturated fat), 0 cholesterol, 239 mg sodium, 11 g carbohydrate, 1 g fiber, 5 g protein. **Diabetic Exchange:** 1 reduced-fat milk.

Cold Raspberry Soup
Chilled Pea Soup

## Cold Raspberry Soup

*(Pictured at right)*

*I received this recipe about 20 years ago and made some changes until I got the flavor I wanted. The preparation takes just minutes using my blender. I serve friends this delightful soup for lunch, usually with homemade rolls and stuffed tomatoes. —Nola Rice, Miami, Arizona*

**4 cups fresh *or* frozen unsweetened raspberries, thawed**
**1/4 cup red wine *or* 1/4 cup white grape juice plus 1 teaspoon red wine vinegar**
**1/2 to 3/4 cup sugar**
**1 cup (8 ounces) sour cream**

In a blender or food processor, combine the first three ingredients; cover and process until pureed. Strain seeds if desired. Transfer to a bowl; whisk in sour cream until blended. Cover and refrigerate for at least 1 hour. **Yield:** 4-6 servings.

## Chilled Pea Soup

*(Pictured above right)*

*Take advantage of convenient frozen peas to blend together this fresh-tasting soup flecked with dill. It's wonderful as a first course or main dish for a summer meal. If you like, set aside a few peas to use for a garnish. —Anna Russell, Peterborough, Ontario*

**1 medium sweet onion, chopped**
**3 garlic cloves, minced**
**1 tablespoon olive oil**
**3 cups frozen peas, thawed**
**2 cups chicken broth**
**2 tablespoons lemon juice**
**1 tablespoon snipped fresh dill *or* 1 teaspoon dill weed**
**1/2 teaspoon salt**
**1/4 teaspoon pepper**
**1/2 cup plain yogurt**

In a large saucepan, saute onion and garlic in oil until tender. Remove from the heat. Stir in peas, broth, lemon juice, dill, salt and pepper. Place half of mixture at a time in a blender; cover and process until pureed. Return all to the blender. Add yogurt; puree until smooth. Cover and refrigerate for at least 1 hour. **Yield:** 4 servings.

## Smooth Strawberry Soup

*Each year, we wait impatiently for the strawberries to start producing so we can make this great soup. The berry flavor is complemented by a sprinkling of sweetly spiced croutons. —Janice Mitchell, Aurora, Colorado*

**1 quart strawberries, halved**
**2 cups apple juice**
**1 cup (8 ounces) sour cream**
**1/2 cup packed brown sugar**
**1/2 cup honey**
**2 tablespoons lemon juice**
**1-1/2 cups half-and-half cream**
**3 tablespoons orange juice, optional**
**CINNAMON-SUGAR CROUTONS:**
**3 slices white bread, crusts removed and cubed**
**2 tablespoons butter**
**1/2 teaspoon sugar**
**1/2 teaspoon ground cinnamon**

In a bowl, combine the first six ingredients. Place half of the mixture at a time in a blender; cover and process until pureed. Transfer to a large bowl; stir in cream and orange juice if desired. Cover and refrigerate for 2 hours.

In a skillet over medium heat, saute bread cubes in butter until golden brown. Remove from heat. Sprinkle with sugar and cinnamon; toss to coat. Cool. Stir soup before serving; garnish with croutons. **Yield:** 6 servings.

# Pleasing Pasta Is A Fast Favorite

THERE'S a world of "pastabilities" when it comes to making a quick dish that your family will crave. Staples like spaghetti with meat sauce and creamy fettuccine Alfredo satisfy everyone at the table.

However, the number of pasta options at the supermarket is enough to make even the savviest shopper's head spin.

For the most part, busy cooks rely on fast-to-cook dry pastas. See the photo below for a few of the most popular.

Spaghetti, linguine and angel hair are no-fuss noodles that suit a variety of recipes. Bow ties, wagon wheels and alphabet noodles offer a bit of fun, too.

Small shells and tubular pastas are wonderful in cold salads...and larger sizes are best suited for stuffing with fast fillings.

The convenience of dry pasta makes it a kitchen staple, but many people are discovering the quick prep times of fresh alternatives. Fresh pastas such as tortellini and ravioli are available in the dairy case and frozen food section of most grocery stores.

Another reason for the popularity of pasta, both dried and fresh, is that it's a dish anyone can toss together. Keep in mind the following tips:

- To cook pasta, surround it with plenty of water. One pound of pasta, for instance, needs 5 to 6 quarts of water.
- For additional flavor, add 1 or 2 tablespoons of salt to the water or throw in dried herbs or seasonings. Wait until the water comes to a full rolling boil before carefully adding the pasta.
- Cook only one type of pasta at a time. If you prepare two varieties together, one is likely to be done before the other.
- The best way to tell when pasta is done cooking is by tasting it. Pasta should be cooked until it is "al dente", or slightly firm when bitten. The longer pasta cooks, the spongier it becomes.
- Cooked pasta features a thin coating of starch that helps sauce adhere to it, so rinse pasta only when using it in cold salads.

There are as many pasta sauces as there are pasta types. Two of the most common are tomato and cream sauces.

The sky is the limit when it comes to the herbs and spices that can be stirred into tomato sauce. Some cooks add a bit of sugar to reduce the acidic nature of the tomatoes, while others mix in wine, broth, cooked meats or veggies.

Basic cream sauces combine the flour with a fat such as butter or oil. Whisk the mixture to prevent lumps from forming. Then, gradually add the cream and stir the sauce while bringing it to a boil.

Cream sauces should be added to pasta just before serving so the sauce won't dry out. If the cream sauce is particularly heavy, it is best suited for small pastas with lots of surface area, such as small shells.

Pesto sauce is another option. Made with basil, olive oil and nuts, it's quick to throw together, and a little goes a long way. Similarly, melted butter combined with garlic, herbs and Parmesan cheese makes a simple light sauce for long thin pasta.

## Varieties of Dried Pasta

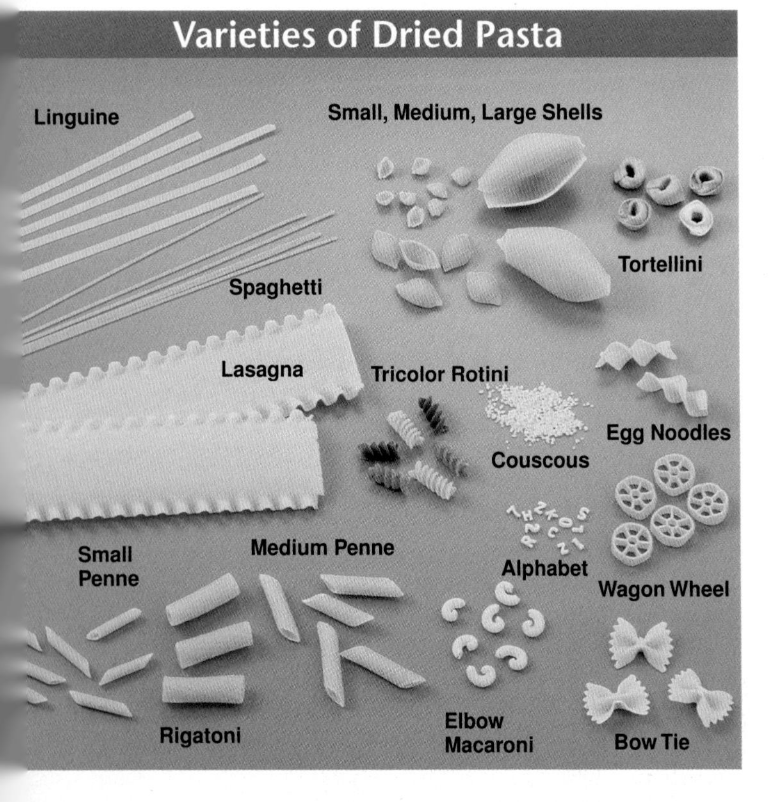


## Pesto Red Pepper Pasta

*Our Test Kitchen staff created this from-scratch pesto that comes together in minutes. Roasted sweet red peppers steal the show in the savory dish.*

**1 package (1 pound) linguine**
**2 cups loosely packed fresh basil leaves**
**1/2 cup whole blanched almonds**
**4 garlic cloves, peeled**
**1 cup olive oil**
**1/2 cup grated Parmesan cheese**
**1/4 cup grated Romano cheese**
**1/4 teaspoon salt**
**Dash pepper**
**1 cup chopped roasted sweet red peppers**

Cook linguine according to package directions. Meanwhile, for pesto, combine the basil, almonds and garlic in a blender or food processor; cover and process for 1 minute or until finely chopped. While processing, gradually add oil in a steady stream.

Add the cheeses, salt and pepper; pulse until combined. Drain linguine; toss with pesto and roasted peppers. **Yield:** 6-8 servings.

## Tomato-Feta Bow Ties

*(Pictured at right)*

*This is an easy variation on a spaghetti recipe. It can be used as a side dish or an entree when you add chicken or shrimp. —Ryan Wilcox, Rochester, Minnesota*

**1 cup uncooked bow tie pasta**
**1 teaspoon dried oregano**
**3/4 teaspoon minced garlic**
**1/4 teaspoon salt**
**1/8 teaspoon crushed red pepper flakes**
**1-1/2 teaspoons olive oil**
**1/4 cup white wine *or* chicken broth**
**1-1/2 cups chopped seeded tomatoes**
**1/2 cup crumbled feta cheese**
**2 tablespoons sunflower kernels, toasted**
**2 tablespoons minced fresh parsley**

Cook pasta according to package directions. Meanwhile, in a skillet, saute the oregano, garlic, salt and pepper flakes in oil for 1 minute. Add wine or broth; bring to a boil. Reduce heat; simmer, uncovered, for 2 minutes.

Stir in tomatoes and cheese. Cover and simmer for 10 minutes. Drain pasta; toss with tomato mixture. Sprinkle with sunflower kernels and parsley. **Yield:** 4 servings.

## Spaghetti with Meatballs

*(Pictured above right)*

*Let this hearty sauce simmer while mixing up the meatballs. I've served this pasta dish for 50 years, and people love it. —Margaret Glassic, Easton, Pennsylvania*

**1 can (29 ounces) tomato puree**
**1 can (28 ounces) diced tomatoes, undrained**
**1 cup water**
**1 can (6 ounces) tomato paste**
**1 tablespoon sugar**
**1 tablespoon dried minced onion**
**1 tablespoon dried minced garlic**
**1 tablespoon dried oregano**
**2 teaspoons salt**

**MEATBALLS:**

**1 slice bread**
**2 tablespoons milk**
**1/2 cup seasoned bread crumbs**
**1 egg, lightly beaten**
**1/2 teaspoon salt**
**1/2 teaspoon dried oregano**
**1/2 teaspoon pepper**
**1/2 pound *each* ground beef, veal and pork**
**2 tablespoons olive oil**
**3/4 pound bulk Italian sausage**
**Hot cooked spaghetti**

In a Dutch oven, combine the first nine ingredients. Bring to a boil. Reduce heat; simmer, uncovered, for 1-1/2 hours, stirring occasionally. Meanwhile, place the bread and milk in a large bowl; let stand for 5 minutes. Add the bread crumbs, egg, salt, oregano and pepper. Crumble the ground beef, veal and pork over mixture; mix well. Shape into 1-1/2-in. balls.

**Spaghetti with Meatballs**
**Tomato-Feta Bow Ties**

In a large skillet, brown meatballs in oil. Add to sauce. In the same skillet, cook sausage over medium heat until no longer pink; drain. Stir into sauce. Simmer, uncovered, for 20-30 minutes or until meatballs are no longer pink. Serve over spaghetti. **Yield:** 8 servings.

## Garlic-Shrimp Angel Hair

*This filling meal is sure to impress. I prepare a creamy sauce for broccoli, pasta and seafood. —Robbie Haferkamp, Englewood, Ohio*

**8 ounces uncooked angel hair pasta**
**3 tablespoons butter, *divided***
**4-1/2 teaspoons all-purpose flour**
**2 cups half-and-half cream**
**1/4 cup grated Parmesan cheese**
**2 tablespoons prepared pesto sauce**
**2 tablespoons minced garlic, *divided***
**1 teaspoon Worcestershire sauce**
**1 teaspoon hot pepper sauce**
**1/2 teaspoon salt**
**1/4 teaspoon pepper**
**2 cups fresh broccoli florets**
**1 pound uncooked medium shrimp, peeled and deveined**

Cook the pasta according to the package directions. Meanwhile, in a large saucepan, melt 4-1/2 teaspoons butter over medium heat. Stir in flour until smooth. Gradually add cream. Bring to a boil; cook and stir for 2 minutes or until thickened.

Stir in the grated Parmesan cheese, pesto sauce, 1 tablespoon garlic, Worcestershire sauce, hot pepper sauce, salt and pepper. Keep warm over low heat.

In a large skillet, saute broccoli in remaining butter for 5 minutes. Add shrimp and remaining garlic; cook and stir until shrimp turn pink. Stir in the cream sauce. Drain pasta; add to shrimp mixture and toss to coat. **Yield:** 4 servings.

# Preparing a Crust Is Easy as Pie

IT'S A CINCH to bake pies just like Grandma's—once you know the basics. And with these tips and recipes, you'll be blue-ribbon-bound in no time.

A golden crust made up of thin crisp layers is the hallmark of a perfect pie. Flaky crusts like that deliver so much appeal, it's hard to believe they have just three basic components—flour, fat and cold water.

Flour forms the bulk of a pastry crust, and all-purpose flour is the variety most often recommended. Most bakers add salt to the flour, and many personalize the dough by also mixing in herbs and spices.

Fat, such as shortening or butter, is responsible for the crust's flaky layers. When the flour and fat are properly combined, small pieces of fat remain solid. During baking, these bits melt, leaving spaces within the dough. As the spaces fill with steam, they expand and separate the dough into layers.

Because shortening remains firm at warmer temperatures, it is a popular choice for pie pastry. Pastry made with butter or vegetable oil is tasty but typically not as flaky as pastry made with shortening. Butter-flavored shortening is a good compromise because it offers both flakiness and flavor.

Margarine, on the other hand, is not recommended when making pie crust. Because many brands have a high water content, they can make the crust tough.

Liquid is the third ingredient required for pie pastry. It makes the dough pliable. Ice water is commonly used, but some bakers like to experiment with cold sour cream, eggs or cream cheese. Whatever the liquid, it must be very cold to help keep the fat solid for as long as possible.

The steps highlighted in the photos below show how easy it is to make a double-crust pie using the pastry recipe on the opposite page. When preparing pie pastry, remember the following:

- Do not overmix the ingredients because doing so can make the crust tough. Cut the shortening into the flour just until crumbly. When adding liquid, toss with a fork just until moistened.
- Handle the dough as little as possible. Heat from your hands can melt the shortening too soon, also causing a tough texture.
- Pastry dough that's been chilled is easier to roll out than room-temperature dough, so many bakers wrap and refrigerate their dough for 30 minutes before rolling it out. Pie dough can be wrapped and stored in the refrigerator for up to 4 days.
- Roll the dough from the center outward. Use just enough flour to keep the dough from sticking to the rolling pin and work surface. The less flour you use, the flakier the crust will be.

## Making Double-Crust Pie Pastry

**1.** Combine the flour and salt. Cut in shortening using a pastry blender just until crumbs are the size of peas.

**2.** Sprinkle a tablespoon of cold water over mixture; combine with a fork. Repeat until the dough holds together.

**3.** Divide dough in two, with one portion slightly larger than the other. Shape the halves into balls; flatten larger ball into a circle.

**4.** Roll the circle so it's 1/8 inch thick and 2 inches wider than the pie plate. Roll dough onto rolling pin and ease pastry onto the plate. Trim dough to plate's edge.

**5.** Roll second ball into a circle 1/8 inch thick. Position over filling. Cut slits in pastry. Trim to 1 inch beyond plate's edge. Fold the edge of top crust over bottom.

**6.** To flute the edges, place one thumb on the inside of the crust and your other thumb and index finger on the outside. Press dough together to seal.

• Sometimes, the bottom crust must be prebaked to prevent it from becoming soggy from the filling. In this case, you may be instructed to prick the pastry with a fork or line the crust with foil and bake it before the filling is added. If the filling is to be added to an unbaked bottom crust, don't prick the crust.

• The recipe may instruct you to cover the edges of the crust with foil. Since the edges brown the fastest, the foil prevents overbrowning.

## Pastry for Double-Crust Pie

*You need only a handful of ingredients for this classic crust from our Test Kitchen. Use it in the recipes below or add your favorite filling for a tantalizing treat.*

**2 cups all-purpose flour**
**3/4 teaspoon salt**
**2/3 cup shortening**
**6 to 7 tablespoons cold water**

In a bowl, combine flour and salt; cut in the shortening until crumbly. Gradually add water, tossing with a fork until dough forms a ball. Divide dough in half so that one ball is slightly larger than the other. Roll out larger ball to fit a 9-in. or 10-in. pie plate. Transfer pastry to pie plate. Trim pastry even with edge.

Pour desired filling into crust. Roll out second ball. Position over filling; cut slits in pastry. Trim pastry to 1 in. beyond edge of pie plate. Fold top crust over bottom crust. Flute edges. Bake according to recipe directions. **Yield:** pastry for double-crust pie (9 or 10 inches).

## Zucchini Hamburger Pie

*(Pictured above right and on page 318)*

*You'll love the crispy golden crust and hearty filling in this layered pie. It's a great way to use up homegrown zucchini. —Margery Bryan, Royal City, Washington*

**Pastry for double-crust pie (9 inches)**
**4 medium zucchini, cut into 1/4-inch slices (about 4-1/2 cups)**
**1/2 pound ground beef**
**1/2 cup finely chopped green pepper**
**1/2 cup dry bread crumbs**
**1/2 cup grated Parmesan cheese**
**1 tablespoon dried minced onion**
**1 teaspoon *each* salt, dried oregano and dried parsley flakes**
**1/2 teaspoon garlic salt**
**2 medium tomatoes, peeled and sliced**

Line a 9-in. pie plate with bottom pastry; trim even with edge of plate. Arrange half of the zucchini in pastry shell; set aside.

In a large skillet, cook beef and green pepper over medium heat until meat is no longer pink; drain. Stir in the bread crumbs, Parmesan cheese, onion, salt, oregano, parsley and garlic salt. Spoon half over the zucchini; repeat layers. Arrange tomatoes over top.

Roll out remaining pastry to fit top of pie; place over filling. Cut slits in top of pastry. Trim, flute and seal edges. Bake at 350° for 60-65 minutes or until golden brown. Let stand for 5 minutes before cutting. **Yield:** 6-8 servings.

Zucchini Hamburger Pie
Blackberry Cheese Pie

## Blackberry Cheese Pie

*(Pictured above and on page 318)*

*I serve this pie at church potlucks because everyone enjoys it. The citrus tang complements the berries and cream cheese. —Greg Curtis, Prattsville, Arkansas*

**Pastry for single-crust pie (9 inches)**
**2 packages (3 ounces *each*) cream cheese, softened**
**1/3 cup confectioners' sugar**
**1/3 cup heavy whipping cream, whipped**
**3/4 cup sugar**
**1/4 cup cornstarch**
**1 cup pineapple-orange juice**
**2 cups fresh blackberries, *divided***
**Whipped topping, optional**

Line a 9-in. pie plate with pastry; trim and flute edges. Line pastry shell with a double thickness of heavy-duty foil. Bake at 450° for 8 minutes. Remove foil; bake 5 minutes longer. Cool on a wire rack.

In a small mixing bowl, beat cream cheese and confectioners' sugar. Fold in whipped cream. Transfer to pastry shell. Refrigerate for 30 minutes.

In a saucepan, combine sugar and cornstarch. Gradually whisk in juice until smooth. Bring to a boil; cook and stir for 2 minutes or until thickened. Remove from heat.

Mash 1/2 cup blackberries; stir into juice mixture. Cool for 10 minutes, stirring several times. Fold in remaining blackberries. Spoon over cream cheese mixture. Cover and refrigerate for at least 4 hours. Garnish with whipped topping if desired. Refrigerate leftovers. **Yield:** 6-8 servings.

# Spice Up Your Meals In a Snap

SEASONED cooks know that a pinch of this herb and a dash of that spice can really perk up a dish. A well-stocked spice rack can be one of the quickest and least expensive ways to add flair to ordinary meals.

There are countless ways to make the most of the dried herbs and spices in your kitchen cabinet. Stir a pinch or two into a sauce for a change of pace. Rub a robust seasoning blend on meat or poultry before roasting or grilling. Simmer whole sprigs of herbs in a soup or stew to release their flavor.

Want to know more about stocking your spice rack? Read on to learn how to buy, use and store herbs and spices, then refer to the handy list below when you're heading to the grocery store.

## Spice List

LIKE to jazz up your meals in a hurry? Then you may want to keep these dried herbs, spices and seasoning blends on hand. Feel free to add or cross off items to suit your family's tastes.

- Allspice (ground and whole)
- Apple pie spice
- Basil
- Bay leaf
- Black pepper
- Cajun seasoning
- Caraway seeds
- Cardamom (ground and whole)
- Cayenne pepper
- Celery salt
- Celery seed
- Chili powder
- Chives (minced)
- Cloves (ground and whole)
- Cumin (ground)
- Curry powder
- Dill weed
- Garlic powder
- Garlic salt
- Ginger
- Greek seasoning
- Italian seasoning
- Lemon-pepper seasoning
- Marjoram
- Mexican seasoning
- Mint
- Mixed pickling spices
- Mustard (ground and seeds)
- Nutmeg (ground)
- Onion (minced)
- Onion powder
- Oregano
- Paprika
- Parsley flakes
- Poppy seeds
- Poultry seasoning
- Pumpkin pie spice
- Red pepper flakes (crushed)
- Rosemary
- Sage (rubbed and dried leaves)
- Salt
- Seafood seasoning
- Seasoned pepper
- Seasoned salt
- Sesame seeds
- Summer savory
- Tarragon
- Thyme

There are several things you can do to get the most flavor from herbs and spices. Their intensity depends on the oil content; the more oil, the stronger the flavor. That's why our home economists recommend rubbing dried herbs between your fingers just before using. This releases their natural oils and increases their flavor.

For stiffer herbs like rosemary that are not easily crushed between your fingers, you may want to use a mortar and pestle. But if you don't have a set, you can place the herbs in a small bowl and easily crush them with a spoon. (See box on opposite page.)

Buying herbs and spices that are already ground is a convenient time-saver for busy cooks. But if your schedule allows, you can get the most intense flavor if you buy whole spices and grind them yourself just before using.

Use a clean coffee grinder to grind whole peppercorns, cardamom, cloves and allspice. Other whole spices, like nutmeg, can be grated with a fine metal grater used to make lemon zest.

For a milder flavor in soups and warm beverages, simmer a bag of whole herbs or spices in the mixture rather than stirring ground herbs into it. Place them on a double thickness of cheesecloth; bring up the corners of the cloth and tie it with string to form a bag. Discard the spices before serving.

The flavor and aroma of herbs comes from their oils, which evaporate when exposed to air and heat. To help preserve the flavor, store them in tightly closed glass or heavy-duty plastic containers. It's best to keep them in a cool dry place, so avoid storing them in direct sunlight, over the stove or near other heat sources.

Dried whole herbs can be kept for up to 1 year before they begin to lose their flavor, while dried crushed herbs can be kept for up to 6 months.

Since herbs and spices eventually lose their flavor, buy amounts that you're likely to use in those periods of time.

To check the flavor, let your nose be your guide. Crush dried herbs with your fingers to see if they release their fragrance. If they have no aroma, they likely should be discarded.

If you'd like to make a dish that requires fresh herbs, you can use dried instead. But drying concentrates the flavor, so you'll need a smaller amount. Substitute 1 teaspoon of crumbled or dried herbs for every tablespoon of finely chopped fresh herbs called for in a recipe.

## Apple Pineapple Crisp

*Spice up this comforting crumb-topped fruit with cinnamon and nutmeg for a delightfully down-home dessert. With chopped macadamia nuts, it has a pleasant crunch that contrasts with the tender apples and pineapple. We like this treat right out of the oven.* —*Nancy Foust*
*Stoneboro, Pennsylvania*

**2/3 cup sugar**
**1 tablespoon cornstarch**
**1 teaspoon grated lemon peel**

3/4 teaspoon ground cinnamon
1/4 teaspoon ground nutmeg
4 cups sliced peeled tart apples
1 can (20 ounces) pineapple chunks, drained
3/4 cup quick-cooking oats
1/4 cup all-purpose flour
1/4 cup packed brown sugar
1/3 cup cold butter
1 jar (3-1/4 ounces) macadamia nuts, chopped

In a bowl, combine sugar, cornstarch, lemon peel, cinnamon and nutmeg. Add apples and pineapple; toss to coat. Transfer to a greased shallow 2-qt. baking dish.

In another bowl, combine oats, flour and brown sugar. Cut in butter until mixture resembles coarse crumbs. Stir in nuts; sprinkle over apple mixture. Bake, uncovered, at 375° for 30 minutes. Cover loosely with foil; bake 15 minutes longer or until apples are tender and topping is golden. **Yield:** 12-15 servings.

White Kidney Bean Salad
Grilled Halibut Steaks

## Grilled Halibut Steaks

*(Pictured at right)*

*This recipe called for salmon, but I substituted another fish with delicious results. The entree requires less time in the kitchen because all I have to do is mix up the seasoned butter, then turn it over to my husband, who does the grilling.*
*—Lisa Rowley, North East, Maryland*

**3/4 cup butter, softened**
**1 tablespoon lemon juice**
**1-1/2 teaspoons dried minced onion**
**1-1/2 teaspoons garlic salt**
**1-1/2 teaspoons dried parsley flakes**
**3/4 teaspoon dill weed**
**1/4 teaspoon sugar**
**1/4 teaspoon pepper**
**4 halibut *or* swordfish steaks, 1 inch thick**

In a small bowl, combine the first eight ingredients; let stand for 30 minutes. If grilling fish, coat grill rack with nonstick cooking spray before starting the grill. Spread 1 tablespoon herbed butter over each halibut steak.

Grill fish, buttered side down, covered, over medium heat or broil, buttered side up, 4 in. from the heat for 5-1/2 minutes. Spread 1 tablespoon herbed butter over each halibut steak; turn and spread with remaining butter. Grill or broil 5-6 minutes longer or until fish flakes easily with a fork. **Yield:** 4 servings.

## White Kidney Bean Salad

*(Pictured above right)*

*For a speedy side dish, toss together this 15-minute bean medley. It's coated with an easy homemade dressing flavored with dried basil, thyme and rosemary.*
*—Bud Mercer, Prosser, Washington*

**1 can (15 ounces) white kidney *or* cannellini beans, rinsed and drained**
**1 can (15 ounces) black beans, rinsed and drained**
**1 jar (4 ounces) diced pimientos, drained**
**1/2 cup thinly sliced red onion**
**1/4 cup olive oil**
**1/4 cup cider vinegar**
**2 tablespoons sugar**
**1/4 teaspoon *each* dried basil, thyme and rosemary, crushed**
**Dash pepper**
**1 package (10 ounces) ready-to-serve mixed salad greens**
**1 package (16 ounces) baby carrots**

In a serving bowl, combine the beans, pimientos and onion. In a jar with a tight-fitting lid, combine the oil, vinegar, sugar, herbs and pepper; shake well. Pour over bean mixture; toss to coat.

To serve, place bowl in the center of a serving platter. Arrange salad greens and carrots around the edge. **Yield:** 4-6 servings.

### Crushing Herbs

IT'S BEST to crush herbs and spices just before using them in a recipe. A mortar and pestle are the traditional tools used for crushing them. If you don't have a set, use the back of a metal spoon to crush them against the side of a small glass bowl.

# Eggs Roll Out Swift Dishes

THERE'S no need to scramble for breakfast ideas when you have eggs on hand. This versatile food can be used for an array of morning mainstays.

Eggs have three basic parts: the shell, the egg white and the yolk. While shell color can vary depending on the breed of hen that laid it, the color has no effect on egg quality, flavor or nutritional value.

Buy only refrigerated eggs that are not cracked and have not passed the carton's expiration date.

Store eggs in their original carton in your refrigerator, preferably set between 35° and 40°. Keep them on an inside shelf—not in the door. Eggs kept in the door could be exposed to temperatures greater than 40° and may become cracked if the door is slammed. Use eggs within 3 to 5 weeks of purchase.

For longer storage, consider freezing eggs. Simply crack the number of eggs that you want to freeze, beat the whites and yolks until blended and store the eggs in a labeled resealable freezer container.

Uncooked egg whites can be frozen by themselves, but yolks tend to gel when frozen alone. To slow down the gelling process, treat yolks by beating in 1-1/2 teaspoons sugar or light corn syrup into four large egg yolks.

Hard-cooked eggs become tough and watery when frozen. However, hard-cooked yolks can be frozen for use in salads or as garnishes.

Beaten eggs, egg whites, treated yolks and hard-cooked yolks can be frozen for up to 1 year. To use, simply thaw in the refrigerator overnight.

Because eggs are so versatile, many folks think past hard-cooking, scrambling and frying them. Let's review a few of the ways creative cooks use eggs.

**Omelets.** The fillings in an omelet offer a great way to customize breakfast. To make a fast omelet, beat the eggs with seasonings and milk, water or another liquid. Add the egg mixture to a buttered skillet and cook until partially set. Lift the edges, letting the uncooked egg flow underneath.

Continue to cook until the eggs are set and there is no sign of liquid. Sprinkle fillings over half of the omelet. Use a spatula or pancake turner to fold half of the omelet over the filling and continue cooking until heated through.

On occasion, an omelet recipe may direct you to combine the fillings with the eggs, then fold the omelet in half when the eggs are set.

**Frittatas.** Frittatas are unfolded omelets. For frittatas, fillings are sauteed in an ovenproof skillet before beaten eggs are added. When the eggs are thickened, the frittata is usually placed in the oven or under the broiler, where it's cooked until the eggs are set and no visible egg liquid remains.

**Stratas.** A strata is a type of casserole where a seasoned egg mixture is poured over bread, tortillas or biscuits. Stratas often need to sit overnight in the refrigerator before baking. They are tested for doneness by inserting a knife near the center. (See the "Testing Baked Egg Dishes" box, below left.)

**Quiches.** For a quiche, a seasoned egg mixture and other ingredients are baked in a pastry crust. Quiches can include anything from cooked bacon and Swiss cheese to canned seafood and vegetables. Check for doneness by using the same test used for stratas.

**Poached Eggs.** Cooked in a simmering liquid, poached eggs are sometimes served over toast or English muffins and often topped with a sauce.

To poach an egg, bring 3 inches of water to a boil in a deep skillet. Reduce heat to a gentle simmer. Crack a cold egg into a cup. Holding the cup slightly above the skillet, gently slide the egg into the water. Simmer the egg until the white is set and the yolk begins to thicken, about 3 to 5 minutes. Remove the egg with a slotted spoon.

## Testing Baked Egg Dishes

DISHES that contain beaten eggs, such as stratas and quiches, are tested for doneness by inserting a knife near the center. If the knife comes out clean, the eggs are cooked. For very cheesy egg dishes, insert a digital or instant-read thermometer near the center; it should read 160°.

## Cheddar Hash Brown Omelet

*My husband loves it when I make crescent rolls to go with this easy family favorite.* —*Betty Kleberger, Florissant, Missouri*

- **2 cups frozen shredded hash brown potatoes, thawed**
- **1/2 cup chopped onion**
- **1/2 cup chopped green pepper**
- **2 tablespoons butter**
- **1 cup diced fully cooked ham *or* Polish sausage**
- **6 eggs**
- **1/4 cup milk**
- **1/4 teaspoon pepper**
- **1/8 teaspoon salt**
- **1/2 cup shredded cheddar cheese**

In a 10-in. nonstick skillet, saute potatoes, onion and green pepper in butter until tender. Sprinkle with ham. In a bowl, beat eggs, milk, pepper and salt; add to the skillet. As the eggs set, lift edges, letting uncooked portion flow underneath. When eggs are set, remove from the heat. Sprinkle with cheddar cheese; fold omelet in half. Cover; cook for 1-2 minutes or until cheese is melted. **Yield:** 4 servings.

## Double-Cheese Eggs Benedict

*Making breakfast is my favorite part of running a bed-and-breakfast. Guests often request this egg dish that features English muffins, Canadian bacon and a simple sauce. —Megan Hakes, Wellsville, Pennsylvania*

**2 tablespoons butter**
**2 tablespoons plus 1-1/2 teaspoons all-purpose flour**
**1-1/2 cups milk**
**1/4 cup shredded cheddar cheese**
**2 tablespoons shredded Parmesan cheese**
**1/2 teaspoon Dijon mustard**
**1/8 teaspoon salt**
**1/8 teaspoon white pepper**
**POACHED EGGS:**
**1 teaspoon white vinegar**
**8 cold eggs**
**4 English muffins, split and toasted**
**8 slices Canadian bacon, warmed**
**1/2 cup bacon bits *or* cooked crumbled bacon**

For cheese sauce, in a saucepan, melt the butter. Stir in the flour until smooth; gradually add the milk. Bring to a boil; cook and stir for 2 minutes or until thickened. Stir in the cheeses, mustard, salt and pepper. Cook and stir over medium-low heat until cheese is melted. Cover and keep warm.

In a skillet with high sides, bring 2-3 in. of water and vinegar to a boil. Reduce heat; simmer gently. In two batches, break cold eggs, one at a time, into a custard cup or saucer. Holding the dish close to the water surface, slip the eggs, one at a time, into the water. Cook, uncovered, for 3-5 minutes or until the whites are completely set and the yolks begin to thicken. With a slotted spoon, remove each egg. To assemble, top each muffin half with one slice Canadian bacon, one egg, cheese sauce and bacon. **Yield:** 8 servings.

## Tex-Mex Cheese Strata

*(Pictured above right)*

*Nacho tortilla chips and green chilies add a little fun to this south-of-the-border brunch. For spicier tastes, substitute pepper Jack for the Monterey Jack cheese. —Vickie Lowrey, Fallon, Nevada*

**4 cups coarsely crushed nacho tortilla chips**
**2 cups (8 ounces) shredded Monterey Jack cheese**
**1 small onion, finely chopped**
**1 tablespoon butter**
**6 eggs**
**2-1/2 cups milk**
**1 can (4 ounces) chopped green chilies, undrained**

Tex-Mex Cheese Strata
Pepperoni Frittata

**3 tablespoons ketchup**
**1/4 teaspoon hot pepper sauce**

Arrange tortilla chips in a greased 13-in. x 9-in. x 2-in. baking dish; sprinkle with cheese and set aside. In a skillet, saute onion in butter until tender. In a bowl, whisk eggs, milk, onion, chilies, ketchup and hot pepper sauce; pour over cheese. Cover and refrigerate overnight.

Remove from the refrigerator 30 minutes before baking. Bake, uncovered, at 350° for 40-45 minutes or until a thermometer reads 160° and a knife inserted near the center comes out clean. Let stand for 5 minutes before cutting. **Yield:** 6-8 servings.

## Pepperoni Frittata

*(Pictured above)*

*We enjoy this fresh-tasting egg dish with fruit and toast. The frittata even makes a good weeknight supper. —Nancy Daly, Douglas, Wyoming*

**1-1/4 cups chopped onions**
**2 to 3 tablespoons vegetable oil**
**1 cup sliced zucchini**
**1/2 cup small cauliflowerets**
**5 eggs, beaten**
**26 slices pepperoni**
**1/3 cup grated Parmesan cheese**

In a 10-in. ovenproof skillet, saute the onions in oil until tender. Add the zucchini, cauliflower and eggs. Cover and cook over medium heat for 10-15 minutes or until eggs are nearly set.

Arrange pepperoni over eggs. Broil 6 in. from heat for 2 minutes. Sprinkle with Parmesan cheese; broil 1-2 minutes longer or until eggs are completely set and top is lightly browned. Cut into wedges. **Yield:** 6 servings.

Gingerbread Torte

# Gingerbread Is A Sweet Treat

A CHRISTMAS CLASSIC, the distinctive taste of gingerbread comes from a combination of spices and flavorings. Ground ginger steals the flavor spotlight, with molasses coming in at a close second. Other spices, including ground cinnamon, cloves and nutmeg, are sometimes also used.

If you're too busy to cut out and decorate gingerbread cookies, you can still enjoy that special gingerbread flavor. Simply stir a sprinkling of those spices into coffee, ice cream or pudding. Or, try one of the two tempting, change-of-pace recipes here.

## Gingerbread Torte

*(Pictured above)*

*This old-fashioned gingerbread cake is excellent! Lemon peel is a nice addition to the sweet cream cheese frosting.*
*—Ginger Hendricksen, Plover, Wisconsin*

**3/4 cup butter, softened**
**3/4 cup sugar**
**2 eggs**
**1 cup molasses**
**3 cups all-purpose flour**
**3 teaspoons ground ginger**
**2 teaspoons baking soda**
**1-1/2 teaspoons ground cinnamon**
**3/4 teaspoon salt**
**1 cup milk**

**CREAM CHEESE FROSTING:**
**1 package (8 ounces) cream cheese, softened**
**1/4 cup butter, softened**
**2 teaspoons grated lemon peel**
**3-3/4 cups confectioners' sugar**

Grease three 9-in. round baking pans. Line with waxed paper; grease and flour the paper. In a large mixing bowl, cream butter and sugar. Add eggs, one at a time, beating well after each addition. Beat in molasses. Combine the flour, ginger, baking soda, cinnamon and salt; add to the creamed mixture alternately with milk. Spoon into prepared pans.

Bake at 350° for 20-25 minutes or until a toothpick inserted near the center comes out clean. Cool for 10 minutes before removing from pans to wire racks to cool completely.

In a small mixing bowl, beat cream cheese and butter. Add lemon peel. Gradually beat in confectioners' sugar until smooth. Place one cake on a serving platter. Spread with about 2/3 cup frosting; repeat layers twice. Refrigerate until serving. **Yield:** 10-12 servings.

## Ginger Doughnut Twists

*Fresh doughnuts for breakfast don't get easier than this. I can make the sweet citrus glaze the night before and keep it in my refrigerator.*
*—Tiffany Anderson-Taylor*
*Gulfport, Florida*

**2 eggs**
**1/2 cup packed brown sugar**
**1/2 cup sour cream**
**1/4 cup vegetable oil**
**1/4 cup molasses**
**2-3/4 cups all-purpose flour**
**4 teaspoons ground ginger**
**2-1/2 teaspoons baking powder**
**1/2 teaspoon baking soda**
**1/2 teaspoon salt**
**1/2 teaspoon ground cinnamon**
**1/4 teaspoon ground nutmeg**
**Oil for deep-fat frying**

**LEMON GLAZE:**
**2 cups confectioners' sugar**
**3 tablespoons milk**
**1 tablespoon lemon juice**
**1 teaspoon grated lemon peel**

In a large mixing bowl, beat eggs until light and lemon-colored. Beat in the brown sugar, sour cream, oil and molasses. Combine the flour, ginger, baking powder, baking soda, salt, cinnamon and nutmeg; beat into egg mixture just until moistened.

Turn onto a floured surface; knead 10 times. Divide dough into 18 pieces. Roll each piece into a 12-in. rope. Fold in half and twist several times. Pinch ends to seal.

In an electric skillet or deep-fat fryer, heat oil to 375°. Fry twists, a few at a time, for 1 minute on each side or until golden brown. Drain on paper towels. In a shallow bowl, whisk glaze ingredients until blended. Dip warm twists in glaze to coat. Let stand until set. **Yield:** 1-1/2 dozen.

# More Hints And How-To's

COOKING can go more quickly—and be even more enjoyable—when you rely on tried-and-true techniques and fast fundamentals. These Test Kitchen tips will help you brush up on basics.

## Fast Potato Fans

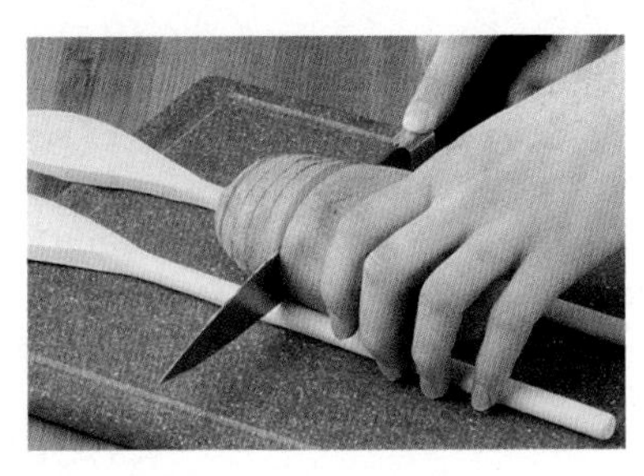

EVERYONE enjoys the flavor of baked potatoes, and dressing up the popular vegetable is a snap by slicing them into fans. To create a potato fan, set a clean uncooked potato on a cutting board. Place two wooden spoons on opposite sides of the potato, nesting its length between their handles.

With one hand holding the vegetable and the spoons in place, use a sharp knife to slice the potato widthwise. The knife should touch the handles at every slice, leaving the slices attached at the bottom.

Then, just pile on toppings and bake the potato.

## Doneness Test for Fish

THE SECRET to moist tender fish is cooking it just until it's done, because overcooking it can make it tough and dry. For best results, check for doneness at the shortest range of time directed in the recipe.

To test for doneness, insert a fork at an angle into the thickest portion of the fish and gently part it. If the fish flakes into sections, it is cooked completely. It should be opaque throughout rather than transparent, and the juices should be a milky white.

Whole fish or fish steaks are done when the fish is easily removed from the bones.

If you're still not sure if your fish is done, insert a digital or instant-read thermometer into the thickest part of the fish; it should read 140°.

## Butterflying Chicken

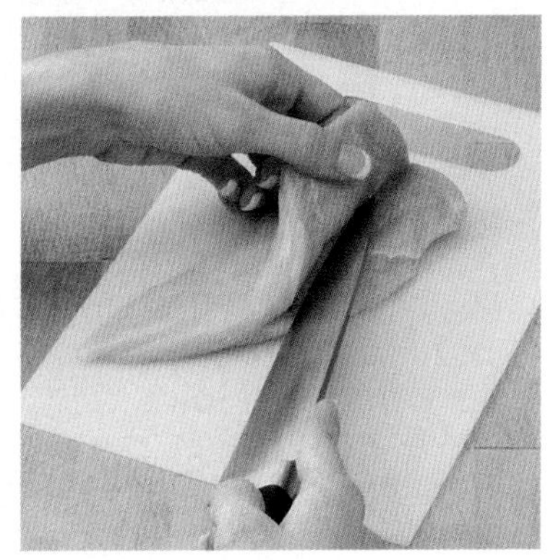

IT'S EASY to butterfly boneless skinless chicken breast halves. The result is chicken that will cook quickly and evenly because it is half of its original thickness.

Use a sharp knife to make a lengthwise slit from the thickest side of a chicken breast to within 1/2 inch of the opposite side. Open the chicken so it lies flat; cover it with plastic wrap. Use the flat side of a meat mallet to flatten it as desired.

## Smart Grilling

WHEN grilling, remember that it's not safe to reuse a platter that held uncooked meat without washing it first. To keep dishes to a minimum, follow this advice from our Test Kitchen.

Before carrying uncooked meat out to the grill, cover your platter with heavy-duty foil. After transferring the meat from the foil-covered platter to the grill, carefully remove the foil and discard it. Then use the clean platter underneath to carry the cooked meat to the table when it's done. Fewer dishes mean quicker cleanup!

## Pastry Bag Pointer

DECORATING cookies with piped frosting is a great way to give them a festive look. But holding the pastry bag with one hand while using the other hand to fill it with frosting can be tricky. That's why our home economists share this easy method.

First, secure the frosting tip and coupler on the pastry bag. Place the tip of the pastry bag in an empty tall glass. Fold the wide opening of the bag halfway over the glass.

Use a spoon to transfer frosting to the pastry bag. When it's three-fourths full, pull the sides of the pastry bag up over the frosting. Remove the bag from the glass, twist the open end to close it and apply pressure to the bag to pipe frosting on the cookies.

# General Recipe Index

*This handy index lists every recipe by food category, major ingredient and/or cooking method, so you can easily locate recipes to suit your needs.*



*✓ Recipe includes Nutritional Analysis and Diabetic Exchanges*

*✓ Recipe includes Nutritional Analysis and Diabetic Exchanges*

*✓ Recipe includes Nutritional Analysis and Diabetic Exchanges*

*✓ Recipe includes Nutritional Analysis and Diabetic Exchanges*

*✓ Recipe includes Nutritional Analysis and Diabetic Exchanges*

*✓ Recipe includes Nutritional Analysis and Diabetic Exchanges*

*✓ Recipe includes Nutritional Analysis and Diabetic Exchanges*

*✓ Recipe includes Nutritional Analysis and Diabetic Exchanges*

*✓ Recipe includes Nutritional Analysis and Diabetic Exchanges*

*✓ Recipe includes Nutritional Analysis and Diabetic Exchanges*

*✓ Recipe includes Nutritional Analysis and Diabetic Exchanges*

*✓ Recipe includes Nutritional Analysis and Diabetic Exchanges*

*✓ Recipe includes Nutritional Analysis and Diabetic Exchanges*

*✓ Recipe includes Nutritional Analysis and Diabetic Exchanges*

*✓ Recipe includes Nutritional Analysis and Diabetic Exchanges*

*✓ Recipe includes Nutritional Analysis and Diabetic Exchanges*

# Alphabetical Index

*This handy index lists every recipe in alphabetical order so you can easily find your favorite recipes.*



✓ *Recipe includes Nutritional Analysis and Diabetic Exchanges*

# D



# E



# F



*✓ Recipe includes Nutritional Analysis and Diabetic Exchanges*

# G



# H



# I



# J



# K



# L



# M



*✓ Recipe includes Nutritional Analysis and Diabetic Exchanges*

## N



## O



## P



## Q



## R



## S



✓ *Recipe includes Nutritional Analysis and Diabetic Exchanges*

## T



## V



## W



## Z



*✓ Recipe includes Nutritional Analysis and Diabetic Exchanges*